Lecture Notes in Computer Sci

T0238554

Commenced Publication in 1973
Founding and Former Series Editors:
Gerhard Goos, Juris Hartmanis, and Jan van Leeuwen

Editorial Board

Ching-Hsien Hsu   Xiaoming Li
Xuanhua Shi   Ran Zheng (Eds.)

Network and Parallel Computing

10th IFIP International Conference, NPC 2013
Guiyang, China, September 19-21, 2013
Proceedings

 Springer

Volume Editors

Ching-Hsien Hsu
Chung Hua University
Dept. of Computer Science and Information Engineering
Hsinchu, Taiwan R.O.C.
E-mail: chh@chu.edu.tw

Xiaoming Li
University of Delaware
Dept. of Electrical and Computer Engineering
Newark, DE, USA
E-mail: xli@udel.edu

Xuanhua Shi
Ran Zheng
Huazhong University of Science and Technology
School of Computer Science and Technology
Wuhan, China
E-mail: xuanhuashi@gmail.com; zhraner@hust.edu.cn

ISSN 0302-9743   e-ISSN 1611-3349
ISBN 978-3-642-40819-9   e-ISBN 978-3-642-40820-5
DOI 10.1007/978-3-642-40820-5
Springer Heidelberg New York Dordrecht London

Library of Congress Control Number: 2013947085

CR Subject Classification (1998): C.1, C.2, F.2, C.4, D.3, D.4, K.6.5

LNCS Sublibrary: SL 1 – Theoretical Computer Science and General Issues

Typesetting: Camera-ready by author, data conversion by Scientific Publishing Services, Chennai, India

Printed on acid-free paper

Springer is part of Springer Science+Business Media (www.springer.com)

Preface

On behalf of the Organizing Committee, we would like to welcome you to the 10th IFIP International Conference on Network and Parallel Computing (NPC 2013), held in the beautiful city of Guiyang, China.

As NPC enters its tenth year, it has established itself as a premiere venue for the dissemination of emerging technology and the latest advancement in the areas of network computing and parallel computing. To further improve the quality of the conference, NPC 2013 adopted a new publication model. Instead of printing regular conference proceedings, it publishes top ranked papers in a special issue of the *International Journal of Parallel Programming* (IJPP) and other accepted papers in proceedings in the *Lecture Notes in Computer Science* (LNCS) series.

We received 109 full submissions. All submissions went through a rigorous review process. We collected an average of three reviews per submission. After a detailed and intensive online discussion, the Program Committee accepted 12 papers for the IJPP special issue and 34 papers for the LNCS proceedings, representing a 42% acceptance rate.

The conference would not have been possible without the contribution of many individuals. We would like to thank all the authors, attendees, and speakers, many of whom traveled great distances to attend this conference. Our deepest gratitude goes to the Program Committee members and external reviewers for their hard work on completing the review process under a tight schedule. They put together a strong, stimulating, and informative technical program. We are very grateful for the constant support and guidance from the Steering Committee led by Kemal Ebcioglu. We must thank the local team led by Hai Jin, Yingshu Liu, and Xuanhua Shi. Their hard work made the conference a reality. We also owe thanks to the other Organizing Committee members for their enormous contribution. Finally, the conference would not succeed without the work of many dedicated volunteers.

We hope you will find the conference proceedings interesting.

September 2013

Lixin Zhang
Barbara Chapman
Ching-Hsien (Robert) Hsu
Xiaoming Li
Xuanhua Shi

Organization

Organizing Committee

General Chairs

Lixin Zhang — Institute of Computing Technology, China
Barbara Chapman — University of Houston, USA

Program Chairs

Ching-Hsien (Robert) Hsu — Chung Hua University, Taiwan
Xiaoming Li — University of Delaware, USA
Xuanhua Shi — Huazhong University of Science and Technolgy, China

Publicity Chairs

Adrien Lebre — Ecole des Mines de Nantes, France
Wenbin Jiang — Huazhong University of Science and Technology, China

Publication Chair

Ran Zheng — Huazhong University of Science and Technology, China

Finance/Registration Chair

Wei Wu — Huazhong University of Science and Technology, China

Web Chair

Junling Liang — Huazhong University of Science and Technology, China

Steering Committee

Kemal Ebcioglu — Global Supercomputing, USA (Chair)
Hai Jin — Huazhong University of Science and Technology, China
Chen Ding — University of Rochester, USA
Jack Dongarra — University of Tennessee, USA
Guangrong Gao — University of Delaware, USA
Daniel Reed — University of North Carolina, USA
Zhiwei Xu — Institute of Computing Technology, China

Yoichi Muraoka   Waseda University, Japan
Jean-Luc Gaudiot   University of California Irvine, USA
Guojie Li   The Institute of Computing Technology, China
Viktor Prasanna   University of Southern California, USA
Weisong Shi   Wayne State University, USA
Tony Hey   Microsoft, USA

Program Committee

Gagan Agrawal   Ohio State University, USA
Mehmet Balman   Lawrence Berkeley National Laboratory, USA
Michela Becchi   University of Missouri - Columbia, USA
Salima Benbernou   Université Paris Descartes, France
Surendra Byna   Lawrence Berkeley National Laboratory, USA
Hsi-Ya Chang   National Center for High-Performance
                           Computing, Taiwan
Yue-Shan Chang   National Taipei University, Taiwan
Jianwei Chen   Oracle, USA
Tzung-Shi Chen   National University of Tainan, Taiwan
Yong Chen   Texas Tech University, USA
Kenneth Chiu   SUNY Binghamton, USA
Camille Coti   University of Paris 13, France
Der-Jiunn Deng   National Changhua University of Education,
                           Taiwan
Frédéric Desprez   INRIA, France
Zhihui Du   Tsinghua University, China
Erik Elmroth   Umeå University, Sweden
Zhen Fang   AMD, USA
Gilles Fedak   INRIA, France
Binzhang Fu   Chinese Academy of Sciences, China
Cecile Germain-Renaud   Laboratoire De Recherche En Informatique
                           (LRI), France
Clemens Grelck   University of Amsterdam, The Netherlands
Ken Hawick   Massey University, New Zealand
Haiwu He   ENS Lyon, France
Yongqiang He   Facebook, USA
Jue Hong   Shenzhen Institutes of Advanced Technology,
                           Chinese Academy of Sciences, China
Rui Hou   Institutes of Advanced Technology, Chinese
                           Academy of Sciences, China
Chung-Ming Huang   National Cheng Kung University, Taiwan
Lei Huang   Prairie View A&M University, USA
Eduardo Huedo   Universidad Complutense de Madrid, Spain
Shadi Ibrahim   INRIA, France

Table of Contents

Session 3: Parallel Architectures

Session 4: Multi-core Computing and GPU

Session 5: Miscellaneous

A Virtual Network Embedding Algorithm Based on Graph Theory

Zhenxi Sun[1], Yuebin Bai[1,2,*], Songyang Wang[1], Yang Cao[3], and Shubin Xu[2]

[1] School of Computer Science and Engineering, Beihang University,
Beijing 100191, China
yuebinb@gmail.com
[2] Science and Technology on Information Transmission and Dissemination
in Communication Networks Laboratory, Shijiazhuang 050081, China
[3] School of Computer Science, Beijing University of Posts and Telecommunications,
Beijing 100876, China

Abstract. Network virtualization is becoming a promising way of removing the inherent ossification of the Internet, and has been steadily attracting more and more researchers' attention during the decades. The major challenges in this field are improving the efficiency of virtual network embedding procedure and raising the rate of virtual network requests being successfully accepted by the substrate network. This paper introduces a new virtual network embedding algorithm based on node similarity, which means the similarity between the virtual nodes and the substrate nodes. For more details, by calculating the degree of nodes both in virtual network and substrate network, which is actually the number of links associated with them, the algorithm achieves better mapping results between virtual network and the substrate network on the topology aspect.

Keywords: Virtual Network, VN Embedding, Graph Theory, Node Similarity.

1 Introduction

For recent years, Internet is not only greatly changing the ways that people communicating with each other, but also making a profound influence on the whole society. During the past four decades, the internet architecture has proven its great worth by meeting most of the requirements of distributed applications, which is improving the life of whole world. However, the remaining problems and defects of the current internet are becoming more and more prominent, such as extendibility, manageability, quality of service and power-saving, and so on. In order to solve these problems fundamentally, some researchers propose an idea of designing the architecture of future network from clean-slate so that to break the constrains of current internet. However, no matter how to change the architecture of internet, what must be kept in mind are the following three requirements:

---

* Corresponding author.

C.-H. Hsu et al. (Eds.): NPC 2013, LNCS 8147, pp. 1–12, 2013.

firstly, researchers must be able to experiment easily with new architectures on live traffic from the existing networks. Secondly, there must be a plausible deployment path for putting validated architectural ideas into practice. Thirdly, the proposed solutions should be comprehensive so that they can address the broad range of current architectural problems facing the Internet [1], instead of focusing on a single narrow problem.

To keep up with such requirements, network virtualization shows the elegant charm and powerful vitality. It allows users create virtual networks which can be viewed as the normal networks used in real life and work, then maps them to the substrate networks which can be the networks with traditional internet architectures or other already deployed networks. In this way, the users can use the virtual network to meet their demands, for example, trying the new network architecture or providing services for companies or single users. By enabling a plurality of diverse network architectures to coexist on a shared physical substrate network, virtualization mitigates the ossifying forces at work in the current internet and enables continual introduction of innovative network technologies. Such a diversified Internet would allow existing architectural deficiencies to be holistically addressed as well as enable the introduction of new architectures supporting new types of applications and services [2].

Currently, virtual network embedding algorithms mainly parted in two periods: *virtual node mapping period* and *virtual link mapping period* [3]. What's more, virtual network embedding problem, with constrains on virtual nodes and virtual links, can be reduced to the *NP*-hard *multi-way separator problem* [3], even if all the request are known in advance. Even when all the virtual nodes are already mapped, embedding the virtual links with bandwidth constraints onto substrate paths is still *NP*-hard in the *indivisible flow scenario*. As a result, there are many heuristic algorithms appears in this research area [4–7]. Although the efforts on network virtualization research view the problem in case of the fixed networks or stable networks, the efficiency on mapping virtual networks to the substrate networks still has a huge improving space. What's worse, the mobile substrate networks are paid little attentions. What will happen if the substrate network is an unstable network environment, such as MANET (Mobile Ad hoc Networks).

In order to address the network virtualization of such environments, we devise a novel mapping algorithms with forecasting techniques in this paper. Firstly, we divide the nodes in physical networks into several small groups by the state of link between nodes, then map the virtual nodes to nodes of physical networks. Secondly, after all the virtual nodes have been mapped to physical nodes, the virtual link mapping phase is finished with multi-commodity flow algorithms.

The rest of the paper is organized as follows. Section II shows the related work in network virtualization field. Section III formulates and models the virtual network embedding problem. Section IV introduces the virtual network embedding algorithms. With the experiments result of the whole algorithm analyzed in section V, the paper will draw a conclusion in section VI.

2   Related Work

Finding the optimal VN mapping solution that satisfies multiple objectives and constraints can be formulated as an *NP*-hard problem. The aspects of VN mapping algorithms appears until now include independent virtual node mapping and virtual link mapping, introduce better correlations between the two phases by facilitating the latter phase when mapping the virtual nodes to substrate networks, and simultaneously mapping virtual nodes and virtual links to the physical networks.

Being different from the embedding algorithms [4–7] that separate the virtual node mapping procedure and the virtual link mapping procedure, authors in [8, 9] introduces better correlation between the node mapping and the link mapping phases by proposing two new VN embedding algorithms D-ViNE (Deterministic VN Embedding) and R-ViNE (Randomized VN Embedding). The VN embedding problem deals with the mapping of a VN request, with constraints on virtual nodes and links, onto specific physical nodes and paths in the substrate network that has finite resources. Since multiple VNs share the underlying physical resources, efficient and effective embedding of online VN requests is of utmost importance in order to increase the utilization of substrate network resources and InP revenue [8]. Authors in [8] use mixed integer programming (MIP) formulation [10]to solve the embedding problem with binary constraints on the meta edges and linear constraints on actual substrate network links. Once all the virtual nodes have been mapped, they use the multi-commodity flow algorithm to map the virtual links onto substrate network paths between the mapped virtual nodes [4]. While the algorithms are not taking the changing topology of the substrate network into account, [11] introduces a topology-aware note ranking method. Inspired by Google's PageRank measure, authors devise a Markov random walk model, for computing topology-aware resource ranking of a node to reflect both the resource and the quality of connections of the node in the network.

The authors in [12] have proposed a distributed algorithm that simultaneously maps virtual nodes and virtual links without any centralized controller, but scalability and performance of their algorithm is still not comparable with the centralized ones. Another distributed and autonomic virtual network mapping framework is proposed in [5], where the substrate nodes integrates autonomous and intelligent agents which exchange messages and cooperate to carry out the proposed VN mapping algorithm. The paper takes nodes integration into account, but not estimate the influence from node movements brings to VN mapping efficiency. Although these algorithms have been verifying the mapping procedure in wireless network environments, physical node mobility of wireless network in the physical network environment is not taken into consideration.

3   Network Model and Problem Description

For clearly describing the VN embedding problem in MANET environments, the notation of the key elements should be defined in the very starting point. On the one hand, the notations can facilitate describing VN embedding algorithms; on the other hand, they will show what aspects the solutions have taken into consideration.

3.1   Substrate Network Description

We model substrate network an undirected and weighted graph, and note it as $G^s = (N^s, E^s)$, where G^s denotes the substrate network, N^s denotes the set of nodes in substrate network and E^s denotes the set of substrate links. Each node of substrate network $n^s \in N^s$ is associated with CPU capacity $c(n^s)$ and location information $loc(n^s)$. And each link of substrate network $e^s \in E^s$ is associated with the bandwidth $b(e^s)$, where $e^s(i, j)$ denotes the bandwidth from the node i to node j.

What the most obvious difference between MANET and traditional internet is that the influence of node mobility must be taken into consideration in the former environments. Due to the movements of substrate nodes, the substrate links would be disrupted frequently. And the topology of the substrate network finds itself in a dynamically changing state. The initial reason is the mobility of the substrate nodes, while the ultimate result is the connected and disconnected states switching in substrate links. In order to applied network virtualization into such circumstance, the link state must be taken into consideration. Thus, we define the stability of the substrate link e^s as $s(e^s) \in [0, 1]$, where the bigger value represents the more stable state of e^s.

3.2   Resources of Substrate Network

Each virtual network request should meet the following requirements. The computation requirements of virtual nodes is ultimately the computing speed of the CPU. When the virtual nodes need a 1Ghz computing speed, then the physical node should be 1GHz at least, and the higher the better. So the first requirement must be satisified is $c(n^v) \leq c(n^s)$. Similarly, the bandwidth requestment of virtual link should be smaller than the mapped physical links of substrate network. In another word, when mapping the virtual link to phsical links, the physical links bandwidth should be greater than that of the virtual link. Thus, the second requirements must be meet is $b(n^v) \leq b(n^s)$. While, the above two requirements should be applied when the physical nodes have not been mapped any virtual nodes. If not so, we should consider the remaining resources of the physical nodes and links of substrate network. The remaining computing resources (i. e. CPU capacity) is denoted by

$$\mathcal{R}_N(n^s) = c(n^s) - \sum_{\forall n^v \uparrow n^s} c(n^v)$$

which means that the substrate computing resources of the substrate node n^s is the total computing resouces subtract the resouces that already allocated to virtual nodes. In the same way, the substrate bandwidth is denoted by

$$\mathcal{R}_E(e^s) = b(e^s) - \sum_{\forall e^v \uparrow e^s} b(e^v)$$

Thus, the more widely applied constraints on mapping virtual nodes to substrate nodes is as follows

$$c(n^v) \leq c(n^s) - \mathcal{R}_N(n^s)$$

For the virtual link mapping procedure, there is a little difference from the above node mapping procedure. The fact is that one virtual link usually was mapped onto several substrate links end to end, which are called path. Thus, the remaining bandwidth of the path is decided by the smallest one.

$$\mathcal{R}_E(P) = \min_{\forall e^s \in P} (e^s)$$

Therefore, the requirements must be satisfied in virtual link mapping procedure should be

$$b(e^v) \leq \mathcal{R}_E(P), \forall P \in \{All\ the\ mapped\ substrate\ links\}$$

3.3 Network Description

A virtual network is similar as the substrate network, which is consisted of virtual nodes and virtual links. So the most fittable notations are $G^v = (N^v, E^v)$, and G^v denotes the virtual network topology, N^v denotes the set of nodes in virtual network, E^v denotes the set of virtual links of virtual network. The requirements of computation of each virtual node is described by $c(n^v)$, where $n^v \in N^v$ represents the subset of virtual nodes. In the same way, the bandwidth of each virtual link is marked by $b(e^v)$, where $e^v \in E^v$, and denotes the subset of virtual links in virtual network.

3.4 VN Embedding Problem Description

When a virtual network request arrives, the substrate network should decide whether to accept the request or not. If the request accepted, a suitable mapping solution should be proposed by the substrate network. Generally, there are two phases in the mapping procedure, which are virtual node mapping and virtual link mapping. The node mapping phase usually is followed by the virtual link mapping phase.

Figure 1 describes the process of virtual network request being mapped to the substrate network with node constraints and link constraints. The two virtual network request finally mapped to the two separate part of the substrate network. This is merely an example of virtual network mapping, the more common case is several virtual network sharing the same part of the substrate network.

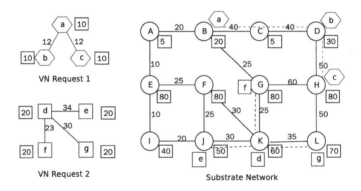

Fig. 1. Mapping virtual network request to substrate network

The leftside of figure 1 depicts the virtual network request 1 and 2, which need to be mapped onto the substrate network on the right side. The numbers in black rectangle represent the computaton capacity, in more details, that in virtual network is the VN request's requirements to the physical nodes and that in substrate network is the computation capacity the physical nodes can offer. Similarly, the number on lines shows the bandwidth of links, one for requirements, and the other one for the provided.

    Virtual network embedding problem is defined as

$$M : G^v(N^v, L^v) \rightarrow G^s(N^s, L^s)$$

from G^v to a subset of G^s, where $N^v \subset N^s$ and $L^v \subset L^s$.

Node Mapping. Virtual nodes from the same virtual network must be mapped to different substrate nodes. In the mapping $\mathcal{M}_\mathcal{N} : N^v \rightarrow N^s$, for all n^v, $m^v \in N^v$,

$$\mathcal{M}_\mathcal{N}(n^v) \in N^s$$

$$\mathcal{M}_\mathcal{N}(m^v) = \mathcal{M}_\mathcal{N}(n^v), if fm^v = n^v$$

subject to

$$c(n^v) \le c(\mathcal{M}_\mathcal{N}(n^v)) - \sum_{i^v \in N^v} c(i^v)$$

$$dis(loc(n^v), loc(\mathcal{M}_\mathcal{N}(n^v))) \le D$$

where $dis(a,b)$ is the distance of node a and node b in substrate network.

    In figure 1, the first VN request has the node map of { a → B, b → D, c → H}, and the second VN request has the node map of { d → K, e → J, f → G, g → L }. Note that in this case, there is no virtual nodes from different VN request sharing the same substrate node. But it may be appeared that virtual nodes from different VN request be mapped onto the same substrate node in the real virtual network environments.

Link Mapping. The virtual links from VN request should be mapped to one or more substrate links with path splitting and migration. It is defined by a mapping $\mathcal{M}_E : \mathcal{E}^v \to \mathcal{P}^s$ from virtual links to a subset of substrate links such that for all $e^v = (m^v, n^v) \in L^v$,

$$\mathcal{M}_E(m^v, n^v) \subseteq \mathcal{P}^s(\mathcal{M}_N(m^v), \mathcal{M}_N(n^v))$$

subject to

$$b(e^v) \le \mathcal{R}_E(\mathcal{P}), \forall \mathcal{P} \in \mathcal{M}_E(e^v)$$

3.5 Objectives

For the work in this paper, the major concentration is on improving the performance of the embedding procedure such as increasing the revenue of the virtual network and decreasing the cost of vitual network embedding which is similar to all the previous works in [4,8,9,11]. Besides, we also try our best to apply the network virtualization into wireless environments, more accurately, the Moile Ad Hoc Network environments, which is different from the works in [13–15].

Similar to previous efforts [4,8,9,11],the revenue of the virtual network request as :

$$\mathcal{R}(G^v) = \sum_{e^v \in E^v} b(e^v) + \sum_{n^v \in N^v} c(n^v)$$

While revenue gives an insight into how much an InP will gain by accepting a VN request, it is not very useful without knowing the cost the InP will incur for embedding that request. We define the cost of mapping a virtual network request as the sum of total resources allocated to virtual network.

$$\mathcal{C}(G^v) = \sum_{e^v \in E^v} \sum_{e^s \in E^s} f_{e^s}^{e^v} + \sum_{n^v \in N^v} c(n^v)$$

where $f_{e^s}^{e^v}$ denotes the total bandwidth allocated on substrate link e^s for virtual link e^v.

4   Algorithms of VN Embedding

In graph thoery [16], each node in the undirected graph has a degree noting that how many links are associated with. With the notion of node degree in mind, we divide the VN embedding into two greedy stage as most previous efforts. For the first stage, the node mapping algorithm take the effect, in which each node of the virtual network will be sorted by its degree in descending order. The reason for such processing is that the larger of the node degree means that the node will be more important in the virtual network. Further more, the node with larger degree being mapped onto the substrate network, the consequence nodes will be mapped more easily. In addition, such dealing with node mapping will increase the probability of accepting the virtual network request. The calculations of node degrees is as follows.

Algorithm 1. Calculations of node degrees

Require: The set of virtual network request $G^v = (N^v, E^v)$
Ensure: The vector of virtual nodes with descending order on node id $vNodeRank$

1: **for** each $e^v \in E^v$ **do**
2:    id← Get the first vertex id of e^v
3:    vNodeRank[id]++
4:    id← Get the second vertex id of e^v
5:    vNodeRank[id]++
6: **end for**
7: **return** $vNodeRank$;

The notion is similar with the idea in [11] on a certain extent, but the most obvious difference is that the virtual nodes with highest node ranking will be mapped onto the substrate nodes with highest node ranking in [11]. In our work, the virtual nodes with highest node ranking might not be mapped onto the substrate nodes with the same highest node ranking. We sort both the nodes in virtual network request and the substrate network by the note degree which is decided by the associated links in descending order. In order to increase the accepted ratio of VN request and improve the utilization of substrate nodes, we map the virtual nodes with highest degree and lowest cpu requirements to the substrate nodes who obtains the highest degree in substrate network environments. The virtual node mapping algorithm is as follows.

Algorithm 2. Virtual node mapping algorithm

Require: The set of virtual network request $G^v = (N^v, E^v)$
Ensure: The sequence of virtual nodes being mapped onto substrate nodes
1: Sort the virtual nodes N^v by node degree
2: Sort the substrate nodes N^s by node degree
3: **for** each $n^v \in N^v$ **do**
4:    maxdegree=degree(n^s)*1.2
5:    mindegree=degree(n^s)*0.8
6:    **for** each $n^s \in N^s$ **do**
7:      **if** $degree(n^s) \in (mindegree, maxdegree)$ **then**
8:        $potentialNodeSet \leftarrow n^s$
9:      **end if**
10:    **end for**
11:    find $n^s \in potentialNodeSet$ with least remain computing resource
12:    $n^s \leftarrow n^v$
13: **end for**

For the virtual link mapping phase, we use the greedy algorithm as follows.

Algorithm 3. Virtual link mapping algorithm

Require: The set of VN request $G^v = (N^v, E^v)$, with all the edges in Q
Ensure: The state that shows the mapping procedure succeeded or failed.
1: **while** $Q \neq \varnothing$ **do**
2:     E^v=Q. dequeue();
3:     Remove those substrate links that cannot satisfy the bandwidth requirement of
        E^v. Use the shortest path algorithm to find a link mapping solution for E^v.
4:     **if** cannot find a path for E^v **then**
5:         return FAILED
6:     **end if**
7: **end while**
8: return SUCCESS

---

5   Performance Evaluations

In this section, we first describe the performance evaluations and then present our main evaluations result with analysis. Our evaluations mainly on the ratio of accepting VN request for substrate network, the revenue of the VN and the utilization of substrate nodes and links.

5.1   Simulation Environments

Our VN embedding simulation environment is based on the simulator called ViNE-Yard. It is a discrete event simulator with about five thousand lines of code implemented by C++ language. The simulator is freely available in the address [17]. According to the previous work [8], the substrate network topology in our experiments are randomly generated with 50 nodes using the GT-ITM tool [18] (25×25) grids. Each pair of substrate nodes is randomly connected with probability 0.5. The CPU and bandwidth resources of the substrate nodes and links are real numbers uniformly distributed between 50 and 100. It's assumed that VN requests arrive in a Poisson process with an average rate of 4 VNs per 100 time units, and each one has an exponentially distributed lifetime with an average of = 1000 time units. In each VN request, the number of virtual nodes is randomly determined by a uniform distribution between 2 and 10 following similar setups to previous works [4, 6]. The average VN connectivity is fixed at 50%. The CPU requirements of the virtual nodes are real numbers uniformly distributed between 0 to 20 and the bandwidth requirements of the virtual links are uniformly distributed between 0 to 50.

5.2   Result Analysis

There are four performance metrics which are described in the former section, the accepted ratio of VN request, the revenue of VN, and utilization of substrate

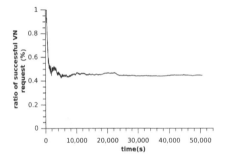
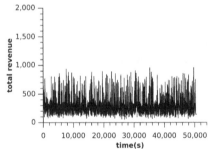

Fig. 2. VN request accepted ratio over time   **Fig. 3.** VN Revenue over time

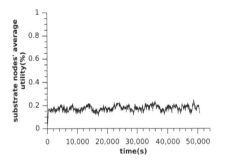
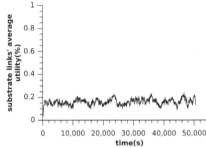

Fig. 4. Substrate nodes' average utility   **Fig. 5.** Substrate links' average utility

nodes and substrate links. The main observations we want to summarize are as follows. Firstly, figure 2 shows the changing of VN request accepted ratio over time. From the very beginning, due to the sufficient resources, both the computing resources and bandwidth in substrate network, the VN request is quickly accepted by the substrate network. While, with the passage of time, the available resources in substrate network decreases dramatically, which causes the drop down of the VN accepted ratio. After a period, the balance is established between the VN request incoming and VN cancelling. From the figures 3,4,5, it can be seen that the utilization of substrate nodes and substrate links has an obvious improving space.

6   Conclusions and Future Work

Besides the frameworks of virtual network systems, the major problems in network virtualization is the virtual network embedding problem. Improving the acceptance ratio of virtual network request is the most important aspect, not only because it can increase the revenue but also make full utilization of the resources in substrate networks. In this paper, we devised a virtual network mapping algorithm based on the similarity between the nodes in virtual networks and that in substrate networks.

The unstable link state in MANET environments is caused by the movements of nodes, we just define the link state categories without deep into the regular pattern of node movements in the paper. But the estimation against the link state is not accurate enough, we shall discover the distributions of node mobility. For example, let the node follow the random walk movement model or some other models. In other words, the link state should be estimated by finding the accurate assessment of node movement.

Current works all define the problem space by fixed CPU capacity and link bandwidth, but in the real world, they are varying all the time. So there is still spaces on improving the usage of the computing resources and bandwidth resources. What's more, the standard on selecting the appropriate nodes and links for virtual network be mapped to is various, current major works just define a fixed one on the selection standard, this is not widely applied in real environments. From the previous works, researchers propose the methods on path migration and splitting, which raise large amount of the ratio on virtual network request acceptance. While if the node migration and splitting is supported, then a virtual network request is rejected only if the total amount of bandwidth and the ability of computing required by virtual networks exceed from that of substrate networks.

Acknowledgments. We would like to thank the anonymous reviewers for their comments and suggestions. This work is supported by the project of the National Science Foundation of China under Grant No. 61073076, Ph.D. Programs Foundation of Ministry of Education of China under Grant No.20121102110018, the 2013 Open Funds of Science and Technology on Information Transmission and Dissemination in Communication Networks Laboratory, and the Postgraduate Innovation Practice Fund (YCSJ-02-02) in Beihang University.

References

[1] Anderson, T., Peterson, L., Shenker, S., Turner, J.: Overcoming the internet impasse through virtualization. Computer 38, 34–41 (2005)
[2] Turner, J., Taylor, D.: Diversifying the internet. In: IEEE Global Telecommunications Conference, GLOBECOM 2005, vol. 2 (December 2005)
[3] Chowdhury, N., Boutaba, R.: Network virtualization: state of the art and research challenges. IEEE Communications Magazine 47, 20–26 (2009)
[4] Yu, M., Yi, Y., Rexford, J., Chiang, M.: Rethinking virtual network embedding: substrate support for path splitting and migration. SIGCOMM Comput. Commun. Rev. 38, 17–29 (2008)
[5] Houidi, I., Louati, W., Zeghlache, D.: A distributed and autonomic virtual network mapping framework. In: Fourth International Conference on Autonomic and Autonomous Systems, ICAS 2008, pp. 241–247 (March 2008)
[6] Zhu, Y., Ammar, M.: Algorithms for assigning substrate network resources to virtual network components. In: Proceedings of the 25th IEEE International Conference on Computer Communications, INFOCOM 2006, pp. 1–12 (April 2006)

[7] Alkmim, G., Batista, D., Saldanha da Fonseca, N.: Optimal mapping of virtual networks. In: 2011 IEEE Global Telecommunications Conference (GLOBECOM 2011), pp. 1–6 (December 2011)

[8] Chowdhury, M., Rahman, M.R., Boutaba, R.: Vineyard: virtual network embedding algorithms with coordinated node and link mapping. IEEE/ACM Trans. Netw. 20, 206–219 (2012)

[9] Chowdhury, N., Rahman, M., Boutaba, R.: Virtual network embedding with coordinated node and link mapping. In: IEEE INFOCOM 2009, pp. 783–791 (April 2009)

[10] Schrijver, A.: Theory of linear and integer programming. Wiley, New York (1986)

[11] Cheng, X., Su, S., Zhang, Z., Wang, H., Yang, F., Luo, Y., Wang, J.: Virtual network embedding through topology-aware node ranking. SIGCOMM Comput. Commun. Rev. 41, 38–47 (2011)

[12] Houidi, I., Louati, W., Zeghlache, D.: A distributed virtual network mapping algorithm. In: IEEE International Conference on Communications, ICC 2008, pp. 5634–5640 (May 2008)

[13] Yun, D., Yi, Y.: Virtual network embedding in wireless multihop networks. In: Proceedings of the 6th International Conference on Future Internet Technologies, CFI 2011, pp. 30–33. ACM, New York (2011)

[14] Kokku, R., Mahindra, R., Zhang, H., Rangarajan, S.: Nvs: a virtualization substrate for wimax networks. In: Proceedings of the Sixteenth Annual International Conference on Mobile Computing and Networking, MobiCom 2010, pp. 233–244. ACM, New York (2010)

[15] Kokku, R., Mahindra, R., Zhang, H., Rangarajan, S.: Nvs: a substrate for virtualizing wireless resources in cellular networks. IEEE/ACM Trans. Netw. 20, 1333–1346 (2012)

[16] Graph thoery, http://en.wikipedia.org/wiki/Graph_theory

[17] Chowdhury, N.: Vine-yard simulator,
http://www.mosharaf.com/ViNE-Yard.tar.gz

[18] Zegura, E., Calvert, K., Bhattacharjee, S.: How to model an internetwork. In: Proceedings IEEE INFOCOM 1996. Fifteenth Annual Joint Conference of the IEEE Computer Societies. Networking the Next Generation, vol. 2, pp. 594–602 (March 1996)

Access Annotation for Safe Program Parallelization

Chen Ding[1] and Lei Liu[2]

[1] Department of Computer Science, University of Rochester, Rochester, USA
[2] Institute of Computing Technologies, Chinese Academy of Sciences, Beijing, P.R. China

Abstract. The safety of speculative parallelization depends on monitoring all program access to shared data. The problem is especially difficult in software-based solutions. Till now, automatic techniques use either program instrumentation, which can be costly, or virtual memory protection, which incurs false sharing. In addition, not all access requires monitoring. It is worth considering a manual approach in which programmers insert access annotations to reduce the cost and increase the precision of program monitoring.

This paper presents an interface for access annotation and two techniques to check the correctness of user annotation, i.e. whether all parallel executions are properly monitored and guaranteed to produce the sequential result. It gives a quadratic-time algorithm to check the exponential number of parallel interleavings. The paper then uses the annotation interface to parallelize several programs with uncertain parallelism. It demonstrates the efficiency of program monitoring by a performance comparison with OpenMP, which does not monitor data access or guarantee safety.

1 Introduction

With the advent of multicore processors, existing applications written in Fortran/C/C++ are increasingly adapted to parallel execution using programming interfaces such as OpenMP, Cilkplus and TBB. They are efficient but do not guarantee correctness. The correctness problem is more serious when parallelizing large program code, mainly due to several issues of uncertainty:

- *Complex code.* A task may execute low-level or dynamic code not amenable to static analysis. Example problems include exceptions in control flow, indirections in data access, dynamic memory allocation and custom memory management.
- *Partial information.* A programmer may read and understand only a part but not the whole program. The program may use separately compiled libraries.
- *Uncertain parallelism.* Parallelism may exist in most but not all iterations of a loop or in some but not all inputs of a program. Important irregular computing tasks such as mesh refinement, clustering, image segmentation, and SAT approximation cannot be fully parallelized without speculation [16].

Speculative parallelization is a technique to guard parallelism against uncertainty. To make it programmable, a number of systems provide primitives to mark a speculative task as a safe future [26], an ordered transaction [25], or a possibly parallel

C.-H. Hsu et al. (Eds.): NPC 2013, LNCS 8147, pp. 13–26, 2013.

region (*PPR*) [8]. In this paper, we call a speculative task a *PPR* task and use the support system called *BOP* for speculation on commodity multicore machines [8, 14].

Safe parallelization depends on monitoring data access, which in software is typically done in two ways. The first is program instrumentation. The cost is high if too many data accesses are instrumented. A compiler may remove unnecessary instrumentation but only for applications amenable to static analysis [21, 24]. The other solution is virtual-memory support to monitor data at page granularity, which incurs false sharing [5, 8]. While these solutions are automatic and transparent to a user, they are not most efficient or precise especially when monitoring complex code.

The monitoring problem may be better solved with programmer control. In this paper, we define an interface for access annotation and integrate it into the *BOP* system. The new interface provides two primitives for marking data writes and data reads. The user annotation may be too much or too little, causing four possible problems:

- *Insufficient annotation.* Some reads and writes should be annotated but not. Incompleteness can lead to three types of errors:
  - *Incorrect output.* Speculation does not generate sequential output.
  - *Nondeterministic output.* Speculation generates different outputs depending on *PPR* task interleaving.
  - *Partial correctness.* The annotation is sufficient for some but not all inputs.
- *Redundant annotation.* The same access may be repeatedly annotated.

To check completeness, we describe two techniques, to be applied in order:

1. *Semantic checking*, which runs the *PPR* tasks in the sequential order and checks whether the output is the same as the sequential execution. The sequential *PPR* execution is the *canonical execution*, which is different from the sequential execution as we will explain later.
2. *Determinism checking*, which uses a quadratic number of tests to check whether all parallel interleavings produce the same result as the canonical execution, which means the sequential output if applied after the first step.

Semantic checking finds missing write annotations, while determinism checking looks for missing read annotations. The time cost is linear to the number of *PPR* tasks in the former and quadratic in the latter. If both checks are passed, the annotation is sufficient for the given test input. For this input, all parallel executions are guaranteed to produce the sequential result.

For the problem of redundant annotation, we view the new interface as a solution rather than a new cause. In the program examples shown throughout the paper, we will see how the interface enables a programmer to insert minimal annotation. Still, a user may over optimize. Then the problem becomes a completeness issue, which is the same as a user being too lazy or lacking knowledge. It will require annotation checking, which is the subject of this paper.

Annotation checking is a form of debugging. It is not guaranteed to find all errors. This is a familiar limitation to the programmer. If a program runs on an untested input and produces an error, the two-step checking can be re-applied to add overlooked annotations. With the checking support, parallel coding is similar to sequential coding.

Systematic testing can be used to gain a high degree of certainty that the parallelized program has the right semantics and is safe.

The new model maintains and extends the benefits of speculative parallelization. Because of the sequential semantics, parallelized code is easier to write and understand. It can be composed with other sequential code or automatically parallelized code. There is no need for parallel debugging—the parallelized code produces the correct output if the sequential code does. A program may be fully annotated, so it no longer needs speculation. Finally, an *BOP* program can run on a cluster of machines without shared memory [12].

Next, we describe in detail the need of access annotation and the two checking techniques, before we evaluate and discuss related work.

2   Access Annotation

To properly insert access annotation, a programmer needs to understand which tasks are parallel and how they share data. Since not all tasks are parallel, not all data access requires annotation.

2.1   The Execution Model

The parallelism hint is as follows:

- bop_ppr{X}Y. The bop_ppr block suggests possible parallelism—X is likely parallel with the subsequent code Y. Y is also known as the *continuation* of X.

At run time, the *PPR* hints divide a sequential execution into a series of *PPR* tasks, numbered in an increasing order starting from 0. Any two tasks have a sequential order between them, so we can refer to them as the earlier task and the later task. We assume no nesting.[1]

A *PPR* task is dynamic. It has two parts. The *link* is the initial execution after the previous *PPR* and before the next *PPR* hint. It executes the code between two *PPR* hints. After the link, the *body* is the execution of the code inside the *PPR* hint. We call these two parts the *link* PPR and the *body* PPR. The parallelism happens between a body and all later links, and between all bodies. We call all links collectively as the *backbone*. The backbone is sequential, and the bodies are limbs hanging on the backbone. Next we show how *PPR* tasks share data and how *BOP* ensures correctness.

2.2   Data Copy and Merge

Logically, a *BOP* program is sequential, and all data is shared. In implementation, *BOP* uses a two-step strategy to share data correctly:

---

[1] In *BOP*, a bop_ppr hint is ignored if encountered inside a *PPR* task. Nested hints can be supported by assigning a linear ordering of nested tasks [17] and checking them in a way similar to checking non-nested tasks.

1. *Data copy-on-write during parallel execution. BOP* runs each task as a Unix process. For each page that the task modifies, the OS makes a private copy and hence removes all interference between *PPR* tasks.
2. *Sequential merge after parallel execution.* After a *PPR* task finishes, the changes are collected as a *PPR patch. BOP* merges the patches from multiple *PPR* tasks to ensure that the results be the same as the would-be sequential execution.

Figure 1 shows two *PPR* tasks. Although they both modify x, they do not conflict because each will do copy-on-write and then write to its private copy. After they finish, they will bundle the changes into two patches. At the merge, the x value from the later *PPR* task is kept to maintain sequential semantics.

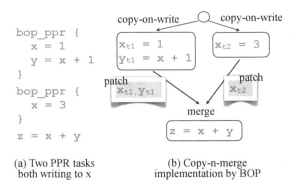

(a) Two PPR tasks
both writing to x

(b) Copy-n-merge
implementation by BOP

Fig. 1. Illustration of copy and merge: two *PPR* tasks shown in (a), data copy-on-write during and merge after the parallel execution shown in (b). After a *PPR* task, its changes are bundled into a *patch* and used by the merge step.

The two steps can be called copy-n-merge. The reason for using the strategy is compelling: copy-n-merge removes all false dependences in a parallel execution and all data races in a concurrent execution. A necessary condition for a dependence or a race is that two operations access the same memory location, and at least one is a write. By copy-on-write, no two tasks can access the same location unless it is read only. Removing this necessary condition removes any false dependence or data race, just as removing oxygen extinguishes the fire.

2.3   Access Annotation

There are two types of annotations:

- ppr_write(*addr, size*) says that the *PPR* task produces a new value for data at memory *addr* for *size* bytes.
- ppr_read(*addr, size*) says that the *PPR* task needs the latest value produced before the *PPR* task for data at *addr* for *size* bytes.

Semantically, an annotation is a requirement on the information flow. The read annotation means that the reading *PPR* task must have the up-to-date value, the value from the last write before the *PPR* task (in the sequential execution). The write annotation means that the new value should be delivered to the remaining program execution for use by later reads of the data. These two requirements are intuitive, although not entirely precise.

Operationally, the annotations are used by *BOP* to create the *PPR* patch. After a task finishes, its patch includes the set of memory locations read and modified by the task and for each modified location, the last written value, i.e. the value it has at the end of the *PPR* execution. These patches are used at the merge time for conflict checking and data commit.

An annotation may be placed anywhere and can be executed more than once during the task execution. Because *PPR* tasks do not physically share data during the execution, the annotations specify only the values coming in and going out. As a result, the same data needs at most two annotations in a *PPR* task, one for the read, and one for the write, regardless how many times the task reads or writes the data. For the writes, only the last value will be copied into the *PPR* patch. For the reads, the task must read the correct value at the *first* time.

The read annotation is needed for the reads in both the link and the body of a *PPR* task, while the write annotation is needed only for the writes in the *PPR* body. To understand this slight asymmetry, we use Table 1 to enumerate all cases of true dependences between *PPR* link and body pairs. Of the four possible (source, sink) pairings, only the last two—(body i, body j) and (body i, link j), $i < j$—are parallel. Since both types of dependences begin at a *PPR* body, it is the only place we need to be annotate for writes.

Table 1. Annotation is needed only for true dependences between body-body and body-link pairs, $i < j$

source, sink	parallel?	data sharing	annotation
link i, link j	no	direct	none
link i, body j			
body i, body j	yes	patching	ppr_write at i,
body i, link j			ppr_read at j

Access annotation is used to monitor dependences. It is indirect compared to annotating dependences explicitly. The indirect approach has several benefits. First, the number of dependence annotations may be quadratic to the length of the code, while the number of access annotations is at most linear. Second, access annotations are modular. They can be specified function by function and aggregated in larger modules without any extra effort. Finally, the source and sink locations of a dependence may be dynamic.

3   Correctness Checking

We use the following notations. *PPR* tasks are numbered from 0 to $n - 1$. Each *PPR* task, $ppr[i]$, has a link $link[i]$ and a body $body[i]$. If a program ends in a link task, for symmetry we assume there is an empty $body[n - 1]$ after $link[n - 1]$. For each task, we record two sets of memory locations, $read, write$, which are the memory locations

```
Algorithm 1: semantics checking

// 1. sequential execution
run ppr[0..n-1] in a single process
treat the data in output stmts as annotated reads
record the patches as seq_ppr[0..n-1].read/write

// 2. canonical execution
for i=1 to n-1
  run link[i]
  fork a process p to run body[i]
  wait for p to finish and get the patch
  raise error if either
     cano_ppr[i].read  != seq_ppr[i].read
     cano_ppr[i].write != seq_ppr[i].write
  copy in body[i].write
end

End Algorithm 1
```

Fig. 2. The algorithm for semantics checking

annotated by *ppr_read* and *ppr_write*. Also recorded are the values, the value at the first read for each memory location in the *read* set and the value at the last write for each location in the *write* set.

3.1 Semantics Checking

The results of a *PPR* task are communicated in a patch. If a *PPR* task writes to x, and x is not annotated by a *ppr_write*, the new value will not be included in the patch and will not be seen by computation outside the task. If the new value is only used inside the *PPR* task and not needed outside the task, the write annotation is extraneous. Omitting an extraneous annotation improves efficiency.

However, if the new value of the write is needed, directly or indirectly, to produce a program output later, then the write annotation is necessary. The absence of the annotation is an error. We call it a missing write annotation. The purpose of semantics checking is to examine the program execution for a given input and ensure that the program has no write annotation missing for this input.

The algorithm is given in Figure 2. Each *PPR* task is run twice, first in the sequential execution and second in the canonical execution. To distinguish their results, the algorithm refers to the first as *seq_ppr[i]* and the second as *cano_ppr[i]*.

A missing write annotation may cause the canonical execution to generate a different output than the sequential execution. This is detected because some of the reads will be wrong. A user can examine the canonical execution in a debugger. Debugging is conventional since there is no concurrency or non-determinism. We note that if an error is detected at $ppr[j]$, the missing write annotation may be anywhere in $ppr[0..j-1]$. Not detecting an error at $ppr[i]$ does not mean $ppr[0..i]$ has no missing annotation.

Only when the algorithm finishes, will we know whether the program has all necessary write annotations for the test input.

Correctness Proof. We prove by contradiction. Assume that semantics checking detects no error but there is an unannotated write in a *PPR* task that is actually necessary because its value is used to produce a later output. Since the write is not annotated, its value is not visible outside the *PPR*. If the value is needed to produce an output, the output in the canonical execution must be incorrect, which contradicts the assumption that the checking has succeeded.

3.2 Determinism Checking

If a task $ppr[i]$ writes x, and $ppr[j]$ reads and prints x, $i < j$, the canonical execution will be correct since the $ppr[j].write$ is merged into the backbone before $ppr[j]$ starts. $ppr[j]$ does not need a read annotation. In a real run, however, $ppr[j]$ must exhibit a true dependence to $ppr[i]$. This can be done by adding to $ppr[j]$ a read annotation for x. Parallel semantics checking is to ensure that there are enough read annotations to mark all the true dependences between *PPR* tasks.

In a parallel execution, *PPR* bodies may finish in any order. In the absence of true dependences, their patches may be merged at different times. There are two restrictions.

– *Merge time.* A patch can only be merged at the juncture between the end of a *PPR* body and the start of the next *PPR* link. Any number of patches can be merged at the same juncture.
– *Merge order.* The patches can only be added in the sequential order of the *PPR* tasks. For example, the patch for $ppr[i]$, i.e. $ppr[i].write$, can be merged only after $ppr[0..i-1].write$ have all been merged first.

Under these two restrictions, there is still much freedom in when patches are merged. For example, if $ppr[0..i-1].write$ are merged before $link[j]$, then $ppr[i].write$ may be merged before any $link[k]$ for $k \geq j$.

We can view each *PPR* body as a single unit, and the merge time as its execution time on the backbone. Then all link and body executions are serialized. The number of possible orders is the number of all legal interleavings subject to three constraints: an earlier link happens before a later link, an earlier body happens before a later body, and the link happens before the body for the same *PPR*.

The interleaving problem is similar to arranging parentheses correctly in a sequence. Let $link[i]$ and $body[i]$ be a pair of parentheses. A sequence of n open-close parentheses corresponds to the sequential execution of $2n$ link and body tasks. Any sequence of properly nested parentheses corresponds to a possible parallel interleaving. The number of different sequences is $\frac{2n!}{n!(n+1)!}$, known as the Catalan number.

A read annotation is missing in a *PPR* task if its absence can cause one or more of its annotated writes to produce a value different from the canonical execution. Determinism checking detects missing read annotations inductively for each *PPR* in sequential order.

The algorithm for determinism checking is given in Figure 3. The checking is done in a nested loop. The iterations of the outer loop are the inductive steps. At step i, $ppr[i]$

```
Algorithm 2: determinism checking

for i=1 to n-1
  run link[1..i]
  for j=1 to i-1
     run in a new process p
     copy in body[1..j].write
     run body[i] to produce the patch
     raise error if
        ppr[i].read != cano_ppr[i].read
        ppr[i].write != cano_ppr[i].write
     terminate process p
  end
end

End Algorithm 2
```

Fig. 3. The algorithm for determinism checking

is checked to have sufficient read annotations such that its patch is always the same as its patch in the canonical execution, which is the same as its patch in the sequential execution.

For the first *PPR*, there is nothing to check. For the second *PPR*, there are two cases. The *body*[0].*write* may be merged before or after *link*[1]. The checking procedure would run both cases and check whether $ppr[1]$ produces the same result as it does in the canonical execution. Suppose there is a true dependence from $ppr[0]$ to $ppr[1]$, but the absence of a read annotation in $ppr[1]$ causes this to be missed at the merge time. The checking procedure would detect an error and stop.

The inductive process checks $link[i]$ and $body[i]$ after checking all previous links and bodies. As in the canonical execution, the algorithm checks the *PPR*s sequentially in the outer loop and applies a different number of patches in each step of the inner loop. First, it runs $body[i]$ with no prior patches. Then for $j = 1, \ldots, i-1$, it includes the patches of *PPR* 0 through j.

Correctness Proof. Prove by contradiction. If the determinism checking succeeds, but in one of the speculative executions, the output is incorrect. Since all the writes are annotated, there is a read missing. The missing read at ppr[y] and the matching write is in body[x] $(x < y)$. Consider the inner loop at iteration i=y. For all iterations $j < x$, the execution of ppr[y] does not have the result of body[x]. There will be an error raised. Contradiction to the assumption that the determinism checking has succeeded.

4   Discussion

Composability of Annotations. Given the program, if we fix the hints and test for annotation correctness, we have the property that as new annotations are added for later tests, they preserve the correctness of earlier tests. New annotations do not break the correctness of previously passed tests. This property helps to bring down the cost of concurrency error testing to a level closer to sequential error testing.

Composability of Annotated Code. Multiple *BOP* tasks can be grouped to form a single task the same way sequential tasks are stringed together. In addition, *BOP* tasks may run with auto-parallelized code, since both have sequential semantics. However, when new parallelism is introduced, e.g. by adding a task or removing a barrier, old access annotations need to be checked for completeness.

Automation. Automatic techniques may be used to identify shared data accesses and annotate them using the annotation interface. Such analysis includes type inference as in Jade [22], compiler analysis as in CorD [24], and virtual memory support as in *BOP* [8]. A user may use automatic analysis in most of the program and then manually annotate critical loops or functions. The hybrid solution lets a programmer lower the monitoring cost while letting a tool perform most of the annotation work.

Shared vs. Private by Default. Most costs of speculation come from monitoring, checking, and copying shared data. *BOP* chooses to provide interface to specify shared data access because a user can minimize the monitoring cost by specifying only the data that has to be shared. Furthermore, the user can annotate data by regions rather than by elements, reducing both the number of annotation calls and the size of meta-data that the speculation system has to track and process.

Data Access vs. Data Identity. Data identity takes just one annotation per variable. Data access takes up to two annotations per datum per *PPR* (one per link task). A benefit, however, is the uniform treatment of global and heap data. A declaration-based method would have difficulties regarding dynamic data: heap data often has no static address, the access is often conditional, and the data location is often dynamically computed. Access annotation is also dynamic in that the role of data, whether shared or private, is allowed to change in different program phases. Finally, it is also more precise since the annotation can be inside arbitrary control flow to capture the condition of data access and avoid redundant annotation calls. Access annotation, however is harder to ensure completeness.

A Comparison. Table 2 compares *BOP* with other annotation schemes: annotation of private data (the rest is shared) as in OpenMP, annotation of shared data as in Treadmarks [2], annotation of shared data access as in DSTM [11], and annotation (registration) of files in distributed version control as in Mercurial.

Like DSTM, *BOP* annotation is based on data access rather than data identity. Unlike DSTM, *BOP* uses copy-n-merge (Section 2.2), which requires annotation per *PPR* not per access. In fact, the annotation can be reduced to two per task pair as shown later in an example in Section 5. Because of copy-n-merge, annotations in *BOP* are entirely local operations. Synchronization happens at the end of a task. *BOP* is similar to check-in and check-out in distributed version control, which has one copy-in and one copy-out per datum per parallel execution. Unlike check-in/check-out, not all data sharing, i.e. link-link and link-body in Table 1, requires annotation. *BOP* is also distinct in its safety guarantee and the need for correctness checking as described in this paper.

Table 2. Comparison of five annotation schemes

data sharing	annotation unit	frequency	safety
BOP copy-n-merge	access annotation	≤ 2 per datum per task	sequential
private by default	declaration, e.g. OpenMP	1 per variable	no
shared by default	allocation, e.g. Treadmarks	1 per variable	no
	access, e.g. DSTM	1 per access	transaction
version control	file, e.g. Mercurial	1 per file	no

5   Evaluation

Access annotation was used in our earlier paper, which describes the interface (including the ordered block) and the safe implementation of dependence hints [14]. As mentioned in a paragraph in Section 5.1 Experimental Setup, "*BOP* provides an annotation interface for recording data access at byte granularity." The interface described in this paper was necessary to parallel seven of the eight tests in that paper. The programs include string substitution (Section 5 of this paper), two clustering algorithms, and five SPEC benchmark programs: art, bzip2, hmmer, parser, and sjeng. The parallel speedup for these programs ranges from 5.8 to a factor of 14 when running on a 16-core machine.

Next we show performance for two of the tests. The first is string substitution, whose parallelization requires byte-granularity annotation. The second is k-means clustering, for which we compare the manual annotation with paging-based monitoring as used in the previous paper [14]. We also compare with OpenMP, which has no access annotation. OpenMP (or any other non-speculative system) cannot parallelize string substitution.

For demonstration, we test two different multi-core machines: k-means on a machine with two 2.3GHz quad-core Intel Xeon (E5520) processors with 8MB second-level cache per processor, and string substitution on a machine with four 2.5GHz quad-core AMD Opteron (8380) processors with 512KB cache per core. Both are compiled by by GCC 4.4 with "-g3". The performance is measured by the speedup over the sequential version of the program and shown in Figure 4.

String Substitution. The test program finds and replaces a pattern in 557MB of text, divided into 55,724 *PPR*s. The sequential run time is 4.4 seconds. Given the small size of each *PPR*, *BOP* uses a pool of processes rather than starting a process for each *PPR*. It uses a manager process to check correctness. When it has no checking work, the manager computes on the next *PPR*. At a conflict for safe recovery, *BOP* resumes from the last correct *PPR* and starts a new process pool.

We test the program with 5 different levels of conflicts: no conflict, 1%, 5%, 10%, and 50% conflicts. With no conflicts, the speed is improved by 94% to a factor of 5.5 with 2 to 9 processors, as shown in Figure 4. The execution time is reduced from 4.4 seconds to 0.8 second. The improvement decreases in the presence of conflicts, as the four other curves show. As expected, parallel performance is sensitive of the frequency of conflicts. The maximal speedup drops to 4.9 for 1% (551) conflicts, to 2.7 for 5% (2653) conflicts, and to 1.8 for 10% (5065) conflicts.

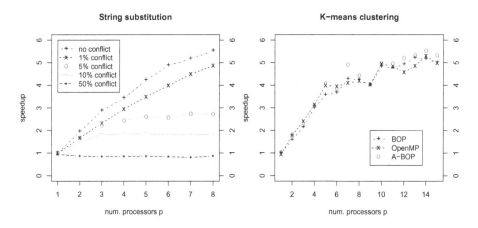

Fig. 4. Demonstration of *BOP* performance. The test of string substitution shows that *BOP* exploits speculative parallelism in the presence of unknown conflicts. The test of k-means clustering shows that *BOP*, which monitors select data, reduces the overhead of *BOP*, which monitors all data, and performs similarly to OpenMP, which does not use speculation or guarantee sequential equivalence. OpenMP cannot parallelize the string substitution.

In the case of 50% conflicts, every other *PPR* fails the correctness check and requires a rollback. The parallel execution is slower by 6% to 19%. It shows the efficiency of understudy-based error recovery in *BOP*.

K-means Clustering. The program clusters N points into k clusters iteratively. It starts with k centroids. In each step, it assigns each point to the closest centroid, and recomputes the center of each cluster as new centroids. In this test, we use 8 million points in 20 dimension space, 10 clusters, and 10 iterations. The sequential time is 110 seconds.

The original *BOP* uses page protection for all global and heap data, which includes 640MB for coordinating data, 32MB for storing cluster assignments (both old and new assignments), and 2480 bytes for the centroids. It uses padding to separate the three arrays. To avoid false sharing, it blocks the loop so each *PPR* computes on 409,600 points and use different memory pages.

The coarse granularity limits the amount of parallelism—there are 190 *PPR*s, every 19 of them are parallel. As a result, the performance does not increase linearly with the number of processors. For example, a clustering iteration takes about the same amount of time using 8 and 9 processors.

Two access annotations are used, one for the centroid array, and the other for the (new) assignment. It monitors access to 16MB data, 2.3% of total data. The speedup, shown as A-BOP in the figure, is consistently better than *BOP*, although the difference is less than 10%. The OpenMP version has a higher sequential overhead (4%). It is about the same speed as A-BOP, although at finer granularity, the OpenMP version ran faster. Overall for k-means, the needed annotation is small (2 annotations), the performance is improved over automatic monitoring and comparable to OpenMP.

6 Related Work

Software Speculative Parallelization. Software speculative parallelization was pioneered by Rauchwerger and Padua [21]. While most techniques automatically parallelized do-all loops (with limited potential on full applications [15]), several techniques provided a safe interface for expressing possible parallelism [25, 26] and likely dependence [27]. *BOP* used Unix processes to implement parallelism and dependence hints for sequential C/C++ programs [8, 12]. Process-based systems use the virtual memory protection mechanism, which transparently provides strong isolation, on-demand data replication, and complete abortability. Similar benefits can be realized for threads using the Copy-or-Discard model with compiler and run-time support [24]. Raman et al. presented a software system called SMTX that supports pipelined execution of sequential loops [19]. Recently, Feng et al. generalized the model as SpiceC (scalable parallelism via implicit copying and explicit commit) to support either speculative parallelization by default or other types of commits defined by the user [9].

The original *BOP* divides program data into three categories — shared, checked, and likely private —for complete monitoring [8]. Shared data is monitored at page granularity. Value-based checking is precise and has no false sharing. SMTX uses value-based checking for all shared data to eliminate the false sharing (at the cost of per-access monitoring and logging) [19]. Instead of automatic monitoring, this paper describes an interface for a user to control access monitoring. It shows when annotations are necessary and how to ensure their correctness. A manual interface may leverage user knowledge and enable more efficient and precise monitoring than what is possible with automatic methods alone.

The framework of task isolation and ordered commit has been used to ensure deterministic semantics and eliminate concurrency errors in multi-threaded code. Grace used processes to implement threads to eliminate deadlocks and data races [5]. Burckhardt et al. defined isolation and revision types in C# to buffer and merge concurrent data changes in r-fork/r-join threads [6]. Determinator was developed as a new operating system that buffers processes and threads in private workspaces and terminates an execution if concurrent data writes are detected [3]. CoreDet ensured determinism in threaded execution using versioned memory and a deterministic commit protocol [4]. The access annotation of *BOP* may help to make program monitoring more precise and generally applicable in these systems. The concept of executable declaration is applicable, so is the use of error recovery and speculative synchronization.

Scott and Lu gave five definitions of determinism and showed their containment relationships [23]. A language-level definition is *ExternalEvents*, which requires that the observable events in two executions be the same. An implementation level definition is *Dataflow*, which requires that two executions follow the same "reads-see-writes" relationship. *BOP* lets a programmer define external events and relies on speculation to preserve data flow. The combination enables user control over both the semantics and the cost of its enforcement.

Race Detection in Fork-Join Parallelism. On-the-fly race detection can be done efficiently for perfectly nested fork-join parallelism [17, 20]. Callahan and others showed that at the program level, the problem of post-wait race checking is co-NP hard and gave an approximate solution based on dataflow analysis [7]. They used the term *canonical execution* to mean the sequential execution of fork-join parallel constructs. The post-wait race checking can be done at run time in $O(np)$ time, where n is the number of synchronization operations and p is the number of tasks [18]. These and other results are summarized in [10]. The execution model of *BOP* is speculative, and the primitives of *PPR*s and ordered sections are hints and do not affect program semantics. The access annotation in *BOP* is used both at debugging time and at run time, so it needs the maximum efficiency. *BOP* gains efficiency from its data sharing model, which is copy-n-merge. As discussed in Section 4, *BOP* needs at most two annotations per datum per task and does not synchronize at every access. Race checkers, like DSTM mentioned in Section 4, use shared memory and have to monitor all accesses, and except for the recent Tardis system [13], update a shared data structure at each shared-data access [20].

7 Summary

We have presented a new interface for access annotation. As access monitoring becomes programmable, it becomes part of program semantics. This paper provides two techniques to check correctness: canonical execution to ensure sequential semantics and check for missing write annotations, and a quadratic-time algorithm to ensure determinism and check for missing read annotations. In addition, the paper demonstrates efficient and safe parallelization of non-trivial programs. Some of them, string substitution and time skewing, cannot be parallelized by a conventional interface like OpenMP. Others, when parallelized safely, have a similar performance as OpenMP.

The new interface gives a programmer direct control over the cost and precision of access monitoring. Much of the cost can be saved by leveraging user knowledge. It enables a user to control both the semantics and its enforcement. Finally, the interface may be used by an automatic tool, allowing the mixed use of manual and automatic parallelization.

References

1. Allen, R., Kennedy, K.: Optimizing Compilers for Modern Architectures: A Dependence-based Approach. Morgan Kaufmann Publishers (October 2001)
2. Amza, C., Cox, A.L., Dwarkadas, S., Keleher, P.J., Lu, H., Rajamony, R., Yu, W., Zwaenepoel, W.: Shared memory computing on networks of workstations. IEEE Computer 29(2), 18–28 (1996)
3. Aviram, A., Weng, S.-C., Hu, S., Ford, B.: Efficient system-enforced deterministic parallelism. In: OSDI (2010)
4. Bergan, T., Anderson, O., Devietti, J., Ceze, L., Grossman, D.: Coredet: a complier and runtime system for deterministic multithreaded execution. In: ASPLOS, pp. 53–64 (2010)
5. Berger, E.D., Yang, T., Liu, T., Novark, G.: Grace: Safe multithreaded programming for C/C++. In: OOPSLA, pp. 81–96 (2009)
6. Burckhardt, S., Baldassin, A., Leijen, D.: Concurrent programming with revisions and isolation types. In: OOPSLA, pp. 691–707 (2010)
7. Callahan, D., Kennedy, K., Subhlok, J.: Analysis of event synchronization in a parallel programming tool. In: PPoPP, pp. 21–30. ACM, New York (1990)

8. Ding, C., Shen, X., Kelsey, K., Tice, C., Huang, R., Zhang, C.: Software behavior oriented parallelization. In: PLDI, pp. 223–234 (2007)

9. Feng, M., Gupta, R., Hu, Y.: SpiceC: scalable parallelism via implicit copying and explicit commit. In: PPoPP, pp. 69–80 (2011)

10. Helmbold, D.P., McDowell, C.E.: A taxonomy of race detection algorithms. Technical Report UCSC-CRL-94-35, University of California, Santa Cruz (1994)

11. Herlihy, M., Luchangco, V., Moir, M., Scherer III, W.N.: Software transactional memory for dynamic-sized data structures. In: Proc. of the 22nd ACM Symp. on Principles of Distributed Computing, Boston, MA, pp. 92–101 (2003)

12. Jacobs, B., Bai, T., Ding, C.: Distributive program parallelization using a suggestion language. Technical Report URCS #952, Department of Computer Science, University of Rochester (2009)

13. Ji, W., Lu, L., Scott, M.L.: Tardis: Task-level access race detection by intersecting sets. In: Workshop on Determinism and Correctness in Parallel Programming (2013)

14. Ke, C., Liu, L., Zhang, C., Bai, T., Jacobs, B., Ding, C.: Safe parallel programming using dynamic dependence hints. In: OOPSLA, pp. 243–258 (2011)

15. Kejariwal, A., Tian, X., Li, W., Girkar, M., Kozhukhov, S., Saito, H., Banerjee, U., Nicolau, A., Veidenbaum, A.V., Polychronopoulos, C.D.: On the performance potential of different types of speculative thread-level parallelism. In: ICS, p. 24 (2006)

16. Kulkarni, M., Pingali, K., Walter, B., Ramanarayanan, G., Bala, K., Chew, L.P.: Optimistic parallelism requires abstractions. In: PLDI, pp. 211–222 (2007)

17. Mellor-Crummey, J.M.: On-the-fly detection of data races for programs with nested fork-join parallelism. In: SC, pp. 24–33 (1991)

18. Netzer, R.H.B., Ghosh, S.: Efficient race condition detection for shared-memory programs with post/wait synchronization. In: ICPP, pp. 242–246 (1992)

19. Raman, A., Kim, H., Mason, T.R., Jablin, T.B., August, D.I.: Speculative parallelization using software multi-threaded transactions. In: ASPLOS, pp. 65–76 (2010)

20. Raman, R., Zhao, J., Sarkar, V., Vechev, M.T., Yahav, E.: Scalable and precise dynamic datarace detection for structured parallelism. In: PLDI, pp. 531–542 (2012)

21. Rauchwerger, L., Padua, D.: The LRPD test: Speculative run-time parallelization of loops with privatization and reduction parallelization. In: PLDI, La Jolla, CA (1995)

22. Rinard, M.C., Lam, M.S.: The design, implementation, and evaluation of Jade. TOPLAS ACM 20(3), 483–545 (1998)

23. Scott, M.L., Lu, L.: Toward a formal semantic framework for deterministic parallel programming. In: The Second Workshop on Determinism and Correctness in Parallel Programming (2011)

24. Tian, C., Feng, M., Gupta, R.: Supporting speculative parallelization in the presence of dynamic data structures. In: PLDI, pp. 62–73 (2010)

25. von Praun, C., Ceze, L., Cascaval, C.: Implicit parallelism with ordered transactions. In: PPoPP, pp. 79–89 (March 2007)

26. Welc, A., Jagannathan, S., Hosking, A.L.: Safe futures for Java. In: OOPSLA, pp. 439–453 (2005)

27. Zhai, A., Steffan, J.G., Colohan, C.B., Mowry, T.C.: Compiler and hardware support for reducing the synchronization of speculative threads. ACM Trans. on Arch. and Code Opt. 5(1), 1–33 (2008)

Extracting Threaded Traces in Simulation Environments

Weixing Ji, Yi Liu, Yuanhong Huo, Yizhuo Wang, and Feng Shi

Beijing Institute of Technology, Beijing 100081, China
jwx@bit.edu.cn

Abstract. Instruction traces play an important role in analyzing and understanding the behavior of target applications; however, existing tracing tools are built on specific platforms coupled with excessive reliance on compilers and operating systems. In this paper, we propose a precise thread level instruction tracing approach for modern chip multi-processor simulators, which inserts instruction patterns into programs at the beginning of main thread and slave threads. The target threads are identified and captured in a full system simulator using the instruction patterns without any modifications to the compiler and the operating system. We implemented our approach in the GEM5 simulator and evaluations were performed to test the accuracy on x86-Linux using standard benchmarks. We compared our traces to the ones collected by a Pin-tool. Experimental results show that traces extracted by our approach exhibit high similarity to the traces collected by the Pin-tool. Our approaches of extracting traces can be easily applied to other simulators with minor modification to the instruction execution engines.

Keywords: program trace, full system simulation, multi-core processor.

1 Introduction

Instruction trace characterizes a program's dynamic behavior and is widely used for program optimization, debugging and new architecture evaluation. Particularly, memory traces, which are subsets of instruction traces, are frequently used for new memory system evaluation. Program traces are also necessary for trace driven simulators, which is a well known method for evaluating new computer architectures. Prevailing tools for collecting application execution traces include tools built based-on Pin [1] and Linux-process-tracker provided by the full system simulator Simics [2]. There are also a number of simulators and emulators available to generate traces on some platforms [3,4]. Theoretically, instruction traces can be extracted at virtually every system level, from the circuit and microcode levels to the compiler and operating-system levels [5]. However, existing trace collectors suffer from at least one of the following three limitations:

C.-H. Hsu et al. (Eds.): NPC 2013, LNCS 8147, pp. 27–38, 2013.

- Being highly dependent on operating systems and compilers and only available for one or two exiting platforms. It is difficult to add a new platform;
- Only supporting several existing ISAs, severely limiting the usage in new architecture exploration;
- Generating mixed instruction traces, which include instructions from other applications and operating system modules.

Tools built on Pin are efficient to collect traces for a single application, but it is only available for Windows and Linux running on IA-32 and x86-64. It is possible to port Pin to other platforms hosting a different operating system; and it is also possible to add a new back-end to Pin targeting a new processor family. However, this work would be time consuming and laborious. Pin-tools run as applications on existing platforms and this limits the usage when researchers are exploring new architectures. Some simulators, such as Simics features the functionality of single-process profiling only for Linux, while others, such as Solaris, are not supported at present. Besides, the techniques of instruction tracing in Simics are operating system dependent and the execution of scheduling module in the operating system triggers the tracing on and off. In case of an operating system update, the tracing functionality may lost their last straw to clutch at. The new simulator GEM5, which becomes increasingly popular in full system simulation, generates mixed instruction traces at present.

Uhlig [5] defines three aspects of metrics to evaluate the quality of traces and shows that the collected traces should be as close as possible to the actual stream of instructions made by a workload when running on a real system. In particular, the authors emphasize on the portability of trace collector. It should be easy to move the collector to other machines of the same type and to machines that are architecturally different. Finally, an ideal trace collector should be fast, inexpensive and easy to operate. In this paper, we propose a new approach to extract threaded traces in full system simulation environments that matches these criteria. This approach does not need to inspect the internal state of operating systems and does not need to change existing compilers.

In summary, this paper makes the following contributions:

- A new approach to extracting program traces in simulation environments. It generates separated traces for each target thread and filters the noisy instruction sequences out.
- An efficient implementation of our approach in simulator GEM5 on x86-Linux. Evaluations on a suite of 7 benchmarks indicate that our approach is feasible and can be easily applied to other simulators.

The rest of this paper is organized as follows: Section 2 presents our new approach to extract thread level traces for applications in simulation environments. Section 3 shows our experimental results. Section 4 discusses the related work on trace extracting, and Section 5 concludes the paper.

2   Extracting Threaded Traces in Simulation Environments

2.1   Basic Idea

The basic idea of our approach lies in that a process is composed of one or more threads, and instructions executed on processors can be separated if all the threads of one process can be identified from the view of simulators. In general, thread IDs are software concepts and they are transparent to underline hardware in most implementations. Therefore, two issues should be addressed in this approach: (1) how to identify threads for a given process, and (2) how to find instructions executed by these threads.

In state-of-art operating systems, a process is a collection of virtual memory space, code, data and system resources. Although the internal presentation of threads and processes in operating system may differ from one to another, a process always has at least one thread of execution, known as the main thread or primary thread. Additionally, one or more threads can be created by the main thread and live within the same process. These slave threads share the same resources with the main thread. The running of a single process is represented as the execution of both main thread and slave threads. Namely, the traces of a process is actually the instruction sequences that are executed in these threads. One of the key issues is how to find the main thread and salve threads without the help of the operating system and compiler. We work out a solution to this problem using the stack pointer register (SP), which is explicit or implicit defined in most processors. Usually, at the creation stage, each thread is associated to a memory region referred to as thread stack. The primary purpose of this thread stack is used to store return address, pass parameters to the callee, store function local variables and so on. On the occasion of a function invocation, a new stack frame will be allocated for the execution of that function. When function returns, the caller or the callee is responsible to deallocated this stack frame by increasing or decreasing the stack pointer. Hence, the top of the stack dynamically changes from time to time and memory locations within the stack frame are typically accessed via indirect addressing.

For most operating systems and third-party thread libraries, a large memory block is usually allocated for each thread from the virtual memory space. The virtual address of the stack is not enough to distinguish the target threads from other threads created by other applications, as all the applications have the same size of virtual spaces starting from the same virtual address. However, these stack regions are mapped to different locations in the physical memory space. In general, the allocated virtual regions are large enough and programs do not change their location and size during runtime, and therefore threads can be distinguished using their stack positions in the physical memory space. However, this does not mean that all the physical addresses allocated to the stack can be considered as the unique identifiers of the target threads. The reason for this is that the virtual-to-physical mapping may change as the stack grows back and forth. Moreover, some of the physical pages may be swapped out and in during execution. However, we find that the first page at the bottom of the stack is always in use during the whole lifetime of a thread and most of existing operating systems provide APIs to prevent that part or all of the calling process's virtual address space from being paged to the swap area. If the first page at the bottom of the stack is locked into RAM and it is not remapped during execution, then virtual-to-physical mapping will not change. It is natural that we can use the first physical pages of stacks to distinguish threads of running processes. So long as we know which thread is running on the core, instructions can be captured and directed into different output streams.

2.2 How to Obtain Traces

The following presents a step-by-step explanation of the methodology for trace extraction in a simulated full system environment.

1. An instruction pattern is defined for the target program, which is delicately designed and composed of several instructions supported by target processors;
2. A predefined small function is executed at the beginning of every target thread. This function is used to: (1) lock the first page of thread stacks in memory and (2) execute the predefined instruction pattern;
3. The source code of the program is compiled using an existing compiler and translated into machine binary;
4. At the very beginning of thread execution, the first page at the bottom of each thread stack is locked in RAM, so that the physical page will not be swapped out at runtime;
5. The simulator snoops the instruction stream of each processor core and captures the patterns that are inserted into the application;
6. When the exact instruction sequence defined in the instruction pattern is captured, the starting address $vaddrs$ and ending address $vaddre$ of current stack in the virtual space are calculated according to the content of SP and the stack size. The physical address $paddrs$ of $vaddrs$ is also obtained through virtual-to-physical translation in the execution context of the processor core. We pack $vaddrs$, $vaddre$ and $paddrs$ up in a structure and insert it into a target thread list(ttl).
7. For each instruction executed by a processor core, the simulator reads the register SP to find out the virtual address where the top of current stack is. Then we go through the ttl and test the content of SP against each virtual stack regions recorded previously. If we find that SP is pointing to one of the virtual stack regions, we translate the $vaddrs$ of the matched stack into its physical address $paddrs'$ according to current execution context. If $paddrs'$ is valid and equal to $paddrs$, which is obtained when the pattern is captured, then the instruction is included in the output trace.

   In following discussion, we assume the starting address of a stack points to the location where the bottom of the stack resides, no matter which direction the stack grows to. Therefore, the mapping from virtual address $vaddrs$ to physical address $paddrs$ does not change for a thread from the beginning to the end and this $paddrs$ can be used as the unique identifier of the target thread. Here, we need one more words for the calculation of $vaddrs$ and $vaddre$ before we proceed further. Given that the stack grows towards the lower address of the virtual space, these two addresses are calculated when the pattern is captured by:

$$vaddr_s = vaddr_{sp} - (vaddr_{sp} \bmod ps) + (k \times ps) - 1 \tag{1}$$

$$vaddr_e = vaddr_s + 1 - ss \tag{2}$$

where ps is page size and ss is stack size. k is an optional parameter and it is set to 1 in default. The reason why we can do this is that the instruction patterns are inserted at the beginning of both main and slave threads. We are certainly sure that the bottom of the stack is not far away from the address stored in the SP register when the pattern is captured. In general, there are 2 or 3 stack frames from the bottom to the frame that the pattern is capture. Hence, the distance from stack bottom to SP is no more than k pages. In most cases, the frame size of the thread function dose not exceeds the page size and k is set to 1. The starting address and the ending address of the stack can be calculated according to the size of the stack and the growing direction. The size of memory pages and the size of stacks are configurable and they can be easily figured out according to the version of the operating system and thread libraries.

To further present our idea clearly, a runtime scenario is given in Figure 1. As shown in the left part of this figure, two applications (App_1 and App_2) are started in the same operating system and run concurrently with 3 threads in total(2 for App_1 and 1 for App_2). In this case, the virtual stack of thread T_1 may overlap the virtual stack T_3 because both App_1 and App_2 have private virtual spaces, which start from the same address and spread out for the same size. However, the three virtual pages at the bottom of these stacks are mapped to different physical pages as threads do not share stacks. Given App_1 is our target application and instruction patterns will be captured by the simulator at the beginning of threads T_1 and T_2. At that moment, both SP_1 and SP_2 point to the first virtual page at the bottom of their stacks which are locked into RAM. Thus, $vaddr1_s$, $vaddr1_e$, $vaddr2_s$, and $vaddr2_e$ can be calculated using equation 1 and 2. Meanwhile, $paddr1_s$ and $paddr2_s$ are obtained by address translation using $vaddr1_s$ and $vaddr2_s$ respectively. Right now, the target thread list ttl looks like $\{\{vaddr1_s, vaddr1_e, paddr1_s\}, \{vaddr2_s, vaddr2_e, paddr2_s\}\}$. The right part of this figure shows the extracting context of an instruction. Every time when an instruction is executed by some core in the simulator, only SP_4 is read and it is used to search ttl. In the case of virtual stack overlapping, the first element $\{vaddr1_s, vaddr1_e, paddr1_s\}$ in ttl is tested and $vaddr1_s$ is translated into physical address $paddr1'_s$ in current execution context. However, it turns out that $paddr1'_s \neq paddr1_s$, which means current instruction is not belonged to any target threads. Therefore, the instruction is not included in the trace.

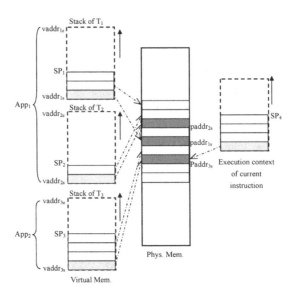

Fig. 1. Stack mapping and identification in simulation

2.3   Instruction Patterns

The instruction pattern should be delicately designed, as the same sequence of instructions may appear in the execution of both applications and operating system modules. However, if the instruction sequence in the pattern is long enough, then there will be a small possibility that the same sequence of instructions exists in the original binaries. For example, following instruction sequence in Figure 2 is an example designed for programs running on x86.

As multi-core processors are widely accepted and used now, applications running on an operating system tend to create multiple threads to fully utilize the hardware resource. It is important to have separated trace outputs for different threads, so that we get a precise instruction sequence for each thread. For this purpose, we pass the thread ID(*tid* in the last line of Figure 2) to the runtime in the pattern in a known register. This *tid* can be read from that register at the time when the pattern is captured by the simulator. Then it is stored in the *ttl* and used as an identifier for a target thread. Similarly, it is also possible to assign different thread IDs to different applications. In such a way, we can start and run multiple applications simultaneously in a system and have separated traces for all the threads created by all target applications. This feature is especially useful to analyze the dynamic execution interferences among multiple applications.

Our approach requires the user to insert instruction patterns into their source code and start the simulator with the pattern as an input. It can be implemented in most full system simulators without modifications to the compiler and the operating system, as the default size of thread stacks usually does not change. Even though the size is changed or the thread function has a very large stack frame, setting a new size in the configuration file will be able to extract correct

```
__asm__ __volatile__ ("move %0, %%eax\n\t"
                      "add $0x0, %%eax\n\t"
                      "add $0x0, %%eax\n\t"
                      :: "r"(tid)
);
```

Fig. 2. Instruction pattern for x86-Linux

traces. Our approach still work well in case of system updates, because it is not necessary to inspect the internal state operating systems.

3 Evaluation

3.1 Evaluation Method

GEM5 is a modular platform for computer system architecture research, encompassing system-level architecture as well as processor microarchitecture [3]. GEM5 provides a highly configurable simulation framework, multiple ISAs, and diverse CPU models. Our experiments were performed on x86-Linux, as it is well supported and widely used. We lock some pages of a process's virtual address space into RAM, preventing these pages from being paged to the swap area. In our implementation, *mlock* is invoked at the very beginning of each thread to lock the identification pages at the bottom of thread stacks in RAM, so that each identification page is guaranteed to be resident in RAM and mapped to a same physical page before thread termination.

We also built an instruction tracing tool based-on the framework provided by Pin. In our experiments, we compared our traces to the ones obtained by the Pin-tool on x86-Linux. To further verify the effectiveness of our approach, we run multiple benchmarks together and generate separated traces for each application in GEM5. These traces are then compared with the traces generated by the Pin-tool. Taking 4 applications (a, b, c and d) for example, we run the applications in the simulator one at a time and get four traces(a_1, b_1, c_1 and d_1), then we partition the benchmarks into 2 groups((a,b), (c,d)), and start the two benchmarks in the same group at the same time in the simulator. Then we extracted another four traces(a_2, b_2, c_2 and d_2) from the hybrid instruction streams. After that, we compared the two traces of each benchmark with their Pin-tool counterparts to see how similar they are.

Even though the simulated x86-Linux is different from the host machine in many aspects, we expect highly similar traces for a same executable binary. This is because the difference in microarchitecture dose not changes the order of instructions in the same thread; however, in effect, they are not exactly the same due to thread scheduling and synchronization. The operating system images and compilers are all provided by the GEM5 team and we didn't make any modifications to these system software. All the benchmarks are compiled with the "-static" options to make sure that no differences will be introduced into the traces by using different dynamic loaded libraries. Meanwhile, the instruction patterns are labeled by the *#pragma OPTIMIZE OFF* and *#pragma OPTIMIZE ON* pair to turn off GCC optimizations in these regions. This optimization restriction prevents the instructions in the pattern being removed or reordered, otherwise, the patterns can not be captured in the simulator while applications are running.

We use the standard multi-thread benchmarks to evaluate our approach, and all of the programs are selected from SPLASH2 [14]. For each application, only three lines of codes are inserted into the original sources: 1) including a head file defining the patterns, 2) inserting the pattern at the beginning of the main thread, and 3) inserting the same pattern at the beginning of slave threads. After that, all the benchmarks are compiled and each binary is executed on the host machine and the simulated full system in GEM5 separately. All the benchmarks we used are listed in table 1.

Table 1. Benchmarks

Benchmark	Description	Group
fft	A 1-D version of six-step FFT algorithm.	1
lu-non	Dense matrix factoring kernel.	1
radix	Integer radix sort kernel.	2
lu-con	Dense matrix factoring kernel.	2
fmm	Body interaction simulation.	3
ocean	Large-scale ocean movements simulation.	3
ocean-non	Large-scale ocean movements simulation.	3

3.2 Results

Figure 3 and 4 show the calculated similarity between two traces collected by hacked GEM5 and Pin-tool respectively. Call traces are reduced instruction traces that only contain instructions of function calls and returns. All the GEM5 traces are collected in solo-runs in the simulated full system. It shows that our traces are much similar to the ones collected by the Pin-tool. Though the the similarity of call traces is as high as up to 90% for most benchmarks, the instruction traces exhibit a relative low similarity around 85%. The reason for this is that the hacked GEM5 only starts to generate traces after instruction patterns are captured. Hence, the instructions executed at the startup phase before the main function are not included in the GEM5 traces, which add up to about 10 thousands in total. Meanwhile, we found that the difference is slightly enlarged as the number of threads increases. In order to find out the differences for the two call traces, the edit sequence for the two traces is rebuilt. From the edit sequence, we found the benchmarks with multiple threads spent much longer time at the synchronization points than their sequential versions. The threads, which run faster than others are scheduled out and in from time to time, execute a number of instructions to check the status of barriers.

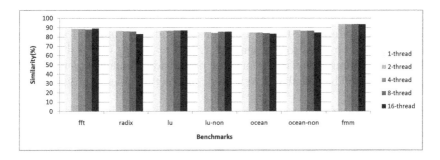

Fig. 3. Instruction trace similarity for solo-runs

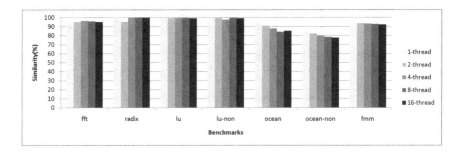

Fig. 4. Call trace similarity for for solo-runs

Even though multiple applications are started to run at the same time, our approach is capable of distinguishing one application from another with different thread IDs. We partition all the benchmarks into 3 groups. Each group has 2 or 3 benchmarks and all the benchmarks in one group are started together in the same simulated full system. The hacked simulator generated separated traces for each application. The partition of groups is given in table 1 and the calculation results for the two platforms are shown in Figure 5 and 6. Note that each instruction and call trace extracted from GEM5 in co-runs are compared with

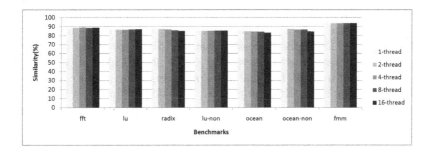

Fig. 5. Instruction trace similarity for co-runs

their counterparts collected by the Pin-tool in solo-runs. All the benchmarks in the same group were started with 1-16 threads and the simulated system was configured with 4 physical cores. Hence, target threads are swapped in and out frequently at runtime because the number of threads is much larger than that of available cores. The calculated results for instruction traces are very close to each other.

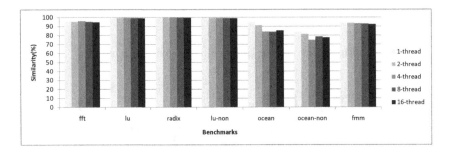

Fig. 6. Call trace similarity for co-runs

4   Related Work

Many approaches have been in use for obtaining low level instruction traces for applications, including dynamic instruction instrumentation, exploiting of hardware performance counters, utilization of the hardware monitor and instruction simulators or emulators [5].

Anita et. al. built a system for generating and analyzing traces based on link-time code modification [6], which makes the generation of a new trace easy in early days. Their system was designed for use on RISC machines and on-the-fly analysis removes most limitations on the length of traces. Binary dynamic instrumentation tools such as Pin [7], and other similar tools can collect application instruction traces by modifying the application instruction stream when running. Some tracing tools can be easily built with Pin and it widely used by researchers to obtain traces on IA-32 and x86-64.

Full system simulators and emulators, such as Simics [2], GEM5 [3], and QEMU [4], have the ability to collect instruction traces. But limitations can be found as well. The Linux-process-tracker is a Simics-provided module that allows tracking user-specified processes by either process id (pid) or file name in Linux [8], which inspects the simulated operating system and calls the callback functions when interesting things occur. The GEM5 simulator is a modular platform for computer system architecture research, encompassing system-level architecture as well as processor microarchitecture [3]. It is widely adopted in architecture research and does offer detailed instruction trace functionality mainly for debugging purpose. QEMU is a fast processor emulator using a portable dynamic instruction translator [4]. It supports many ISA(x86, ARM, MIPS,etc) both on host and guest sides and also can run in full system emulation mode. QEMU has the ability to generate memory traces.

Researchers in application profiling and performance optimization have proposed several tools and frameworks that exploit hardware devices such as hardware performance counters to collect performance data [9]; while others built hardware devices [10] [11] [12] [13] to accomplish this work. With the help of these tools, researchers can collect application traces fast and accurately. Unfortunately, these equipments are either expensive or complicated to be set up and therefore cannot be widely used.

5 Conclusion

Traces record all the information about a program's execution in the form of instruction sequences. In this paper, we propose a new approach to extract threaded traces for applications in full system simulation environments. Traces of each application are extracted from the instruction stream blended with instructions from operating system modules and other applications. Each thread in a given application is identified by an instruction pattern without inspecting the internal state of the operating system. Our approach can be applied to existing full system simulators with no changes to compilers. We implemented our instruction extraction approach in the simulator GEM5 and performed a number of experiments on the simulated full system x86-Linux. Experimental results show that traces extracted by our approach exhibit high similarity to the traces collected by a Pin-tool.

References

1. Bach, M.(M.), Charney, M., Cohn, R., Demikhovsky, E., Devor, T., Hazelwood, K., Jaleel, A., Luk, C.-K., Lyons, G., Patil, H., Tal, A.: Analyzing Parallel Programs with Pin. Computer 43(3), 34–41 (2010)
2. Virtutech. Simics User Guide for Unix 3.0, Virtutech (2007)
3. Binkert, N., Beckmann, B., Black, G., Reinhardt, S.K., Saidi, A., Basu, A., Hestness, J., Hower, D.R., Krishna, T., Sardashti, S., Sen, R., Sewell, K., Shoaib, M., Vaish, N., Hill, M.D., Wood, D.A.: The GEM5 simulator. SIGARCH Computer Architecture News 39(2), 1–7 (2011)
4. Bellard, F.: QEMU, a fast and portable dynamic translator. In: Proceedings of the Annual Conference on USENIX Annual Technical Conference, Berkeley, CA, USA, pp. 41–41 (2005)
5. Uhlig, R.A., Mudge, T.N.: Trace-driven memory simulation: a survey. ACM Computing Surveys 29(2), 128–170 (1997)
6. Borg, A., Kessler, R.E., Wall, D.W.: Generation and analysis of very long address traces. SIGARCH Computer Architecture News 18(3a), 270–279 (1990)
7. Luk, C.-K., Cohn, R., Muth, R., Patil, H., Klauser, A., Lowney, G., Wallace, S., Reddi, V.J., Hazelwood, K.: Pin: building customized program analysis tools with dynamic instrumentation. In: Proceedings of the 2005 ACM SIGPLAN Conference on Programming Language Design and Implementation, New York, NY, USA, pp. 190–200 (2005)

8. Chen, X.: SimSight: a virtual machine based dynamic call graph generator. Technical Report TR-UNL-CSE-2010-0010, University of Nebraska at Lincoln (2010)

9. Browne, S., Dongarra, J., Garner, N., London, K., Mucci, P.: A scalable cross-platform infrastructure for application performance tuning using hardware counters. In: Proceedings of the 2000 ACM/IEEE Conference on Supercomputing, Article 42, Washington, DC, USA (2000)

10. Nanda, A., Mak, K.-K., Sugarvanam, K., Sahoo, R.K., Soundarararjan, V., Smith, T.B.: MemorIES3: a programmable, real-time hardware emulation tool for multiprocessor server design. SIGARCH Computer Architecture News 28(5), 37–48 (2000)

11. Chalainanont, N., Nurvitadhi, E., Morrison, R., Su, L., Chow, K., Lu, S.L., Lai, K.: Real-time l3 cache simulations using the programmable hardware-assisted cache emulator. In: IEEE International Workshop on Workload Characterization, pp. 86–95 (2003)

12. Yoon, H.-M., Park, G.-H., Lee, K.-W., Han, T.-D., Kim, S.-D., Yang, S.-B.: Reconfigurable Address Collector and Flying Cache Simulator. In: Proceedings of the High-Performance Computing on the Information Superhighway, Washington, DC, USA, pp. 552–556 (1997)

13. Bao, Y., Chen, M., Ruan, Y., Liu, L., Fan, J., Yuan, Q., Song, B., Xu, J.: HMTT: a platform independent full-system memory trace monitoring system. In: Proceedings of the 2008 ACM SIGMETRICS International Conference on Measurement and Modeling of Computer Systems, New York, NY, USA, pp. 229–240 (2008)

14. Woo, S.C., et al.: The SPLASH-2 programs: Characterization and methodological considerations. ACM SIGARCH Computer Architecture News 23(2), 24–36 (1995)

A Fine-Grained Pipelined Implementation of LU Decomposition on SIMD Processors

Kai Zhang, ShuMing Chen*, Wei Liu, and Xi Ning

School of Computer, National University of Defense Technology
#109, Deya Road, Changsha, 410073, China
smchen@nudt.edu.cn

Abstract. The LU decomposition is a widely used method to solve the dense linear algebra in many scientific computation applications. In recent years, the single instruction multiple data (SIMD) technology has been a popular method to accelerate the LU decomposition. However, the pipeline parallelism and memory bandwidth utilization are low when the LU decomposition mapped onto SIMD processors. This paper proposes a fine-grained pipelined implementation of LU decomposition on SIMD processors. The fine-grained algorithm well utilizes data dependences of the native algorithm to explore the fine-grained parallelism among all the computation resources. By transforming the non-coalesced memory access to coalesced version, the proposed algorithm can achieve the high pipeline parallelism and the high efficient memory access. Experimental results show that the proposed technology can achieve a speedup of 1.04x to 1.82x over the native algorithm and can achieve about 89% of the peak performance on the SIMD processor.

1 Introduction

The solving of dense linear algebra with large scale is the key problem of many scientific computation applications. The famous LINPACK benchmark [1] [2], which is used to test the performance of super computers, runs the computation of a set of linear equations. There are two methods for linear algebra systems, which are direct methods and iterative methods. Usually, the direct method is very suited to dense matrices [3]. The typical direct method is solving the linear algebra with the help of LU decomposition, which makes efficient implementations, either purely in software or with hardware assistance, is therefore desirable.

Libraries for linear algebra [4] [5] with optimized subroutines have been highly tuned to run on a variety of platforms. The GPUs based system is a popular method. On the CPU/GPU hybrid architecture, the performance can be high up to 1000 GFLOPs for single precision as well as 500 GFLOPs (1 GFLOPS = 10^9 Floating Point Operations/second) for double precision. However, the memory hierarchy of GPUs is complex. Michael [6] tailored their implementation to the GPUs inverted memory hierarchy and multi-level parallelism hierarchy. They proposed a model that can accurately predict the performance of LU decomposition. Leandro [7] evaluated

---

* Corresponding author.

C.-H. Hsu et al. (Eds.): NPC 2013, LNCS 8147, pp. 39–48, 2013.

different types of memory access and their impact on the execution time of the algorithm. They showed that coalesced access to the memory leads to 15 times faster than the non-coalesced version. The task scheduling between CPUs and GPUs is also important. Optimized task scheduling can effectively reduce the computation [8-12], which is corresponding to the idea on general purpose processors [13]. Reconfigurable platforms always focus on designing high performance float-point computation units and the scalable architecture [14-16]. However, the high cost of reconfigurable hardware leads that they are not widely used.

The previous methods pay much attention on the optimization among system nodes. And the optimization on each unique node lacks of architecture transparence. The common idea of various platforms is that try to exploit sufficient parallel resources, which makes the single instruction multiple data (SIMD) technology been a popular method to accelerate the LU decomposition. This paper extends the work to optimize the LU decomposition on each node chip implemented with the modern SIMD architecture. When the LU decomposition is mapped onto SIMD processors, the native data dependences of the algorithm lead to the low pipeline parallelism and too much memory access. And the large amount of non-coalesced memory access existed in the algorithm results in much more memory access time.

To address these issues, a fine-grained pipelined implementation of LU decomposition is designed to increase the performance on SIMD processors. The proposed algorithm well utilizes data dependences to explore the fine-grained pipeline among all the computation resources. The pipeline parallelism is highly increased on the SIMD processor. The memory access operations are reduced by immediately reusing the temporary result. By using external loop unrolling method, the non-coalesced memory accesses are smartly transformed into coalesced version, which effectively reduces most of the memory access time.

The rest of the paper is organized as follows: in Section 2, we show a basic SIMD architecture which is taken as our optimization platform. Section 3 analyzes the basic LU decomposition on SIMD processors. In Section 4, we describe the proposed fine-grained pipelined algorithm. The experimental results are presented in Section 5. Finally, Section 6 concludes the paper.

2   SIMD Architecture

The SIMD technology can operate on multiple data in parallel by the control of a single instruction. Thanks to the simple control logic and the low cost hardware, it can provide high performance at low power consumption and is well applied to the design of processors, such as GPUs, AnySP [17], Cell [18] and VT [19]. Based on the above modern state-of-the-art SIMD processors, we setup a basic framework for SIMD processors. The basic SIMD processor is shown in Fig. 1 and is chosen as our platform to optimize the LU decomposition.

As is depicted in Fig. 1, a SIMD processor generally consists of a Scalar Unit (SU) and multiple Vector Processing Elements (VPEs). The SU is used to execute the communication and scalar computation. Multiple VPEs are used to accelerate the parallel computation. The number of VPEs is referred as SIMD width. Each VPE usually contains functional units such as ALU, Multiply-Accumulate (MAC) and

Load/Store (LS). The adder tree performs the reduction add operation among VPEs. The shuffle unit can rearrange the vector data among all VPEs. The LS controls the access to the on-chip vector memory (VM) which consists of multiple parallel banks. A coalesced memory access can increase the bandwidth efficiency and therefore the performance of memory-bound kernels. The shared-registers (SR) can be accessed by the SU and all VPEs.

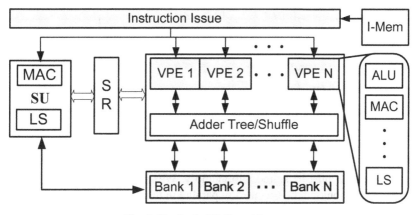

Fig. 1. The basic SIMD architecture

3   LU Decomposition

For solving a set of linear equations of the form

$$Ax = b,$$

where x and b are $n \times 1$ column vectors. The LU decomposition is used to factor a $n \times n$ matrix A into a $n \times n$ lower triangular matrix L (the diagonal entries are all 1) and a $n \times n$ triangular matrix U. Such that,

$$LUx = b.$$

Figure 2 shows the procedure of the basic LU decomposition of a matrix. The computation amount of the algorithm is $O(n^3)$. And the communication amount is $O(n^2)$. The matrix A is replaced by matrices L and U after the decomposition. The loop can be divided into two segments, which are separated by dotted lines in Fig. 2. The first segment is used to update the kth column, where the computation amount is $O(n^2)$. The second segment is used to update the right lower sub-matrix, where the computation amount of the algorithm is $O(n^3)$. As shown in Fig. 2, this algorithm has high data dependences. The updated k^{th} column of A is used to update the right lower sub-matrix. The matrix updating segment can only be executed after all the iterations of kth column updating computation. As the matrix for decomposition is always large, the updated k^{th} column cannot all reside in local registers and must be written back to memory. Although it is time cost, the updated k^{th} column must be read from memory when performing the matrix updating segment, which causes large amount of memory access operations.

```
for k = 1 to n-1
    * * * * * * * * segment 1 * * * * * * * *
    for i = k + 1 to n
        A[i,k] = A[i,k]/A[k,k];
    end for
    * * * * * * * * segment 2 * * * * * * * *
    for j = k + 1 to n
        for i = k + 1 to n
            A[i,j] = A[i,j] − A[i,k] × A[k,j];
        end for
    end for
    * * * * * * * * * * * * * * * * * * * * *
end for
```

Fig. 2. The basic LU decomposition algorithm

In the segment of updating the kth column, $A[k,k]$ is shared among all VPEs to perform the computation in parallel. The updated results cannot totally reside in registers, thus they must be stored into memory. We assume that the SIMD width is N. Totally N iterations can be executed in parallel in the segment of updating the right lower matrix, where N elements of the kth column must be loaded into registers from memory. As we can see, there are three apparent deficiencies in the above algorithm. Firstly, the high data dependences lead to the low pipeline parallelism. The two segments are totally executed in sequence. Secondly, all the temporary results, which are possible to reside in registers for reusing, are written back to the memory. Thirdly, the column data access, which causes non-coalesced access to parallel memory banks, is low efficient. To address this issue, we propose a fine-grained pipelined LU decomposition algorithm. The detail of this algorithm is explained in the next section.

4   Fine-Grained Pipelined LU Decomposition

To achieve the high pipeline parallelism and the high efficient memory access, a direct way is reducing data dependences and transforming the non-coalesced access to coalesced version. To reduce the amount of memory access, we must try to keep the temporary results, which will be reused, in local registers. Thus, we must make a detailed analysis on the program. We analyze data dependences among the two task segments of the program code. Fig. 3 shows data dependences of the basic LU decomposition algorithm.

The loop unrolling technique is a traditional method for loop accelerating. For nested loop optimization, the universal method is internal loop unrolling with software pipelining. However, this method causes the non-coalesced memory access to k^{th} and j^{th} columns of matrix A. As shown in Fig. 3, the updated $A[i,k]$ is used to update $A[i,j]$ ($j=k+1$ to n) which is the ith row of matrix A. As the updating of the ith row is executed in the external loop of the second segment, we can unroll the external loop instead of the internal loop. The unrolled loop is dispatched to all VPEs. Each

VPE execute an iteration of the external loop of segment 2. Then all VPEs access the ith row of matrix A in parallel. The non-coalesced memory access is smartly replaced by the coalesced memory access.

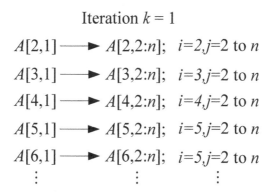

$$\text{Iteration } k = 1$$

$$A[2,1] \longrightarrow A[2,2{:}n]; \quad i{=}2,j{=}2 \text{ to } n$$

$$A[3,1] \longrightarrow A[3,2{:}n]; \quad i{=}3,j{=}2 \text{ to } n$$

$$A[4,1] \longrightarrow A[4,2{:}n]; \quad i{=}4,j{=}2 \text{ to } n$$

$$A[5,1] \longrightarrow A[5,2{:}n]; \quad i{=}5,j{=}2 \text{ to } n$$

$$A[6,1] \longrightarrow A[6,2{:}n]; \quad i{=}5,j{=}2 \text{ to } n$$

$$\vdots \qquad\qquad \vdots \qquad\qquad \vdots$$

Fig. 3. Data dependences in the LU decomposition

The SIMD execution of the ith row updating only requires the updated $A[i,k]$ but not the whole updated k^{th} column. We can start the updating of ith row as soon as the $A[i,k]$ is updated. As the $A[i,k]$ is a scalar element, we can employ the SU to compute the $A[i,k]$. The updated $A[i,k]$ is fast shared with all VPEs by using the SR without writing back to memory. The shuffle unit can broadcast $A[i,k]$ to all VPEs. Then all VPEs immediately execute the updating of ith row in SIMD way after receiving $A[i,k]$.

We can see that, the above method introduces a fine-grained pipelined algorithm for LU decomposition. The updating of sub-matrix is divided into a series updating processes for each matrix row. The updating of kth column is divided into a series updating processes for each column element. As soon as each column element is updated, it is immediately used to update the corresponding matrix row. Compared with the basic algorithm, the proposed method provides more fine-grained parallelism for the software pipeline.

The proposed software pipeline greatly corresponds to the data dependences. By software method assistance, the fine-grained pipelined LU decomposition can be easily implemented. Thus a high pipeline parallelism can be achieved. The proposed fine-grained pipelined algorithm has the following advantages: efficiently utilization of all the computation resource on the modern SIMD processor, reducing the memory access amount and transforming the non-coalesced memory access to coalesced version. The problems of low pipeline parallelism, too much memory access and low efficient memory bandwidth utilization are well solved.

Fig. 4 shows the data flow of the proposed algorithm on the SIMD architecture. As shown in Fig. 4, the kth column updating task is executed on SU. The right lower sub-matrix updating task is executed on all VPEs in SIMD way. To transform the non-coalesced memory access to coalesced version, the external loop of the sub-matrix updating segment is unrolled to be executed on all VPEs in parallel. And each VPE performs the internal loop. The SU and SIMD tasks are executed in parallel to achieve the high pipeline parallelism. The software pipelining technology is used to keep the native data dependence of the algorithm.

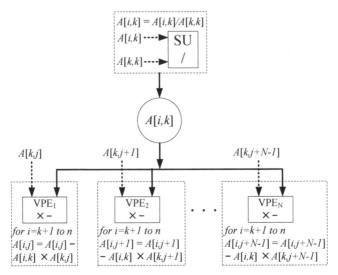

Fig. 4. The data flow of the proposed algorithm

Fig. 5 shows the code example of the proposed fine-grained pipeline algorithm. The software pipelining is not shown to simplify the description. As shown in Fig.5, the SU task and SIMD task can be executed in parallel. The SU task is executed in the scalar unit to update the kth column. As soon as each element of the kth column is updated, it is written to the SR. Then the shuffle unit broadcasts the updated element to all VPEs. Each VPE employs this element to update a matrix row. All VPEs updates the sub-matrix in parallel.

```
for k = 1 to n-1
    Initial SU task
    for i = k + 1 to n
        A[i,k] = A[i,k]/A[k,k];
    end for
    Initial SIMD task
    for j = k +1 to n
        broadcast A[i,k] to all VPEs;
        for i = k + 1 to n
            A[i,j] = A[i,j] – A[i,k] × A[k,j];
        end for
        for i = k + 1 to n
            A[i,j+1] = A[i,j+1] – A[i,k] × A[k,j+1];
        end for
            ⋮
        for i = k + 1 to n
            A[i,j+N-1] = A[i,j+N-1] – A[i,k] × A[k,j+N-1];
        end for
        j = j +N;
    end for
end for
```

Fig. 5. The proposed fine-grained pipelined LU decomposition algorithm

5   Experiment Results

We have implemented a cycle-accurate simulator FT-Matrix-Sim based on our previous single-core simulator [20] for the SIMD architecture as shown in Fig. 1. In FT-Matrix-Sim, the VM is organized as scratchpad memory and simulated with a cycle-driven system. There are 16 VPEs, each having a 32-entry register file. Each VPE contains four function units: ALU, two L/S and MAC. The MAC unit supports one float-point operation each cycle. The SU has the same units with each VPE. The VM has 16 banks. Manually optimized assemble code is used as the input of the simulator.

The architecture established by the simulator has also been implemented in Verilog hardware design language. The RTL implementation has been synthesized with Synopsys Design Complier under TSMC 65 nm technology in order to obtain the operating speeds and the cycle accurate performance simulation. The clock frequency of the synthesized circuit can be up to 500 MHz.

Fig.6 shows the performance of the proposed fine-grained pipelined LU decomposition algorithm. As can be seen, the speedup of the fine-grained algorithm over the basic algorithm can be up to 1.04x to 1.82x. The average speedup is 1.15x. The performance of the fine-grained algorithm can be up to 15.98 GFLOPS, where GFLOPS is a popular metrix for numerical computations. The peak performance of the synthesized circuit is 18 GFLOPS. Thus, we achieve 88.78% of peak performance on the SIMD processor by using the proposed fine-grained algorithm. The delectable result is that we can obtain better performance with the increasing of matrix size.

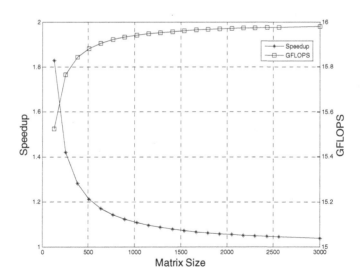

Fig. 6. The performance of proposed algorithm

The performance improvement resulting from the fine-grained algorithm is due to the following two factors: the high pipeline parallelism and the high efficient memory access. The fine-grained method greatly corresponds to the native data dependences of the algorithm. It well explores the fine-grained parallelism between the SU and multiple VPEs, which can effectively increase the pipeline parallelism and reduce the memory access amount. The external loop unrolling method of the fine-grained pipelined algorithm transforms all non-coalesced memory access to coalesced version, which is the high efficient memory access way. The coalesced method can reduce most of the memory access time. Table 1 shows the reduced memory access time of the fine-grained algorithm compared with the basic version. As can be seen, the proposed algorithm can reduce the memory access time by 90% to 96%.

The main contribution of the proposed algorithm is reducing the communication amount and hiding the computation time of updating the kth column. Both complexities of the above two tasks are $O(n^2)$. However, the total computation amount of the algorithm is $O(n^3)$. So the proportion of the performance increments brought by the proposed method goes smaller when the matrix size goes larger. But the absolute performance of the proposed algorithm is always high.

Table 1. Reduced memory access time

Size	Reduced (%)	Size	Reduced (%)	Size	Reduced (%)
128	90.15%	1024	94.85%	1920	95.85%
256	91.62%	1152	95.01%	2048	95.92%
384	92.65%	1280	95.23%	2176	95.95%
512	93.41%	1408	95.39%	2304	95.96%
640	93.81%	1536	95.53%	2432	95.97%
768	94.19%	1664	95.64%	2560	95.99%
896	94.54%	1792	95.74%	3000	95.99%

6   Conclusions

This paper proposed a fine-grained pipelined LU decomposition implementation on SIMD processors. The main performance improvement is achieved by the high pipeline parallelism and the high efficient memory access. The new algorithm well corresponds to data dependences of the native algorithm and effectively transforms the non-coalesced memory access to coalesced version, which increases the pipeline parallelism, reduces the memory access amount and increases the efficient of memory access. To illustrate our ideas, we implemented a cycle-accurate simulator and a RTL design. The RTL design was synthesized under TSMC 65 nm technology and achieved a frequency of 500 MHz. With the proposed algorithm, we can obtain a performance speedup about 1.04x to 1.82x over the basic LU decomposition algorithm. Most of the peak performance on the SIMD processor is well utilized by the proposed technology.

Acknowledgement. This work is supported by the National Natural Science Foundation of China (No.61070036) and HPC Foundation of NUDT.

References

1. Dongarra, J.J., Luszczek, P., Petitet, A.: The LINPACK benchmark: past, present and future. Concurrency and Computation: Practice and Experience 15(9), 803–820 (2003)
2. LINPACK, http://www.netlib.org/linpack
3. Michailidis, P.D., Margaritis, K.G.: Implementing parallel LU factorization with pipelining on a multicore using OpenMP. In: 2010 IEEE 13th International Conference on Computational Science and Engineering (CSE). IEEE (2010)
4. Dongarra, J.J., Walker, D.W.: Software libraries for linear algebra computations on high performance computers. SIAM Review 37(2), 151–180 (1995)
5. Whaley, R.C., Dongarra, J.J.: Automatically tuned linear algebra software. In: Proceedings of the 1998 ACM/IEEE Conference on Supercomputing (CDROM). IEEE Computer Society (1998)
6. Anderson, M.J., Sheffield, D., Keutzer, K.: A predictive model for solving small linear algebra problems in gpu registers. In: 2012 IEEE 26th International Parallel & Distributed Processing Symposium (IPDPS). IEEE (2012)
7. Cupertino, L.F., et al.: LU Decomposition on GPUs: The Impact of Memory Access. In: 2010 22nd International Symposium on Computer Architecture and High Performance Computing Workshops (SBAC-PADW). IEEE (2010)
8. Galoppo, N., et al.: LU-GPU: Efficient algorithms for solving dense linear systems on graphics hardware. In: Proceedings of the 2005 ACM/IEEE Conference on Supercomputing. IEEE Computer Society (2005)
9. Lifflander, J., et al.: Dynamic Scheduling for Work Agglomeration on Heterogeneous Clusters. In: 2012 IEEE 26th International Parallel and Distributed Processing Symposium Workshops & PhD Forum (IPDPSW). IEEE (2012)
10. Donfack, S., et al.: Hybrid static/dynamic scheduling for already optimized dense matrix factorization. In: 2012 IEEE 26th International Parallel & Distributed Processing Symposium (IPDPS). IEEE (2012)
11. Lifflander, J., et al.: Mapping dense lu factorization on multicore supercomputer nodes. In: 2012 IEEE 26th International Parallel & Distributed Processing Symposium (IPDPS). IEEE (2012)
12. Venetis, I.E., Gao, G.R.: Mapping the LU decomposition on a many-core architecture: challenges and solutions. In: Proceedings of the 6th ACM Conference on Computing Frontiers. ACM (2009)

13. Grigori, L., Demmel, J.W., Xiang, H.: Communication avoiding Gaussian elimination. In: Proceedings of the 2008 ACM/IEEE Conference on Supercomputing. IEEE Press (2008)

14. Jaiswal, M.K., Chandrachoodan, N.: Fpga-based high-performance and scalable block lu decomposition architecture. IEEE Transactions on Computers 61(1), 60–72 (2012)

15. Zhuo, L., Prasanna, V.K.: High-performance and parameterized matrix factorization on FPGAs. In: International Conference on Field Programmable Logic and Applications, FPL 2006. IEEE (2006)

16. Zhuo, L., Prasanna, V.K.: High-performance designs for linear algebra operations on reconfigurable hardware. IEEE Transactions on Computers 57(8), 1057–1071 (2008)

17. Woh, M., Seo, S., Mahlke, S., Mudge, T., Chakrabarti, C., Flautner, K.: AnySP: Anytime Anywhere Anyway Signal Processing. In: Proceedings of the 31st Annual International Symposium on Computer Architecture (ISCA 2009), Austin, Texas, June 20-24 (2009)

18. Flachs, B., Asano, S., Dhong, S.H., et al.: The Microarchitecture of the Synergistic Processor for a Cell Processor. IEEE Journal of Solid-State Circuits 41(1) (January 2006)

19. Krashinsky, R., et al.: The vector-thread architecture. In: Proceedings of the 31st Annual International Symposium on Computer Architecture. IEEE (2004)

20. Chen, S.-M., et al.: YHFT-QDSP: High-performance heterogeneous multi-core DSP. Journal of Computer Science and Technology 25(2), 214–224 (2010)

FRESA: A Frequency-Sensitive Sampling-Based Approach for Data Race Detection

Neng Huang, Zhiyuan Shao, and Hai Jin

Services Computing Technology and System Lab
Cluster and Grid Computing Lab
School of Computer Science and Technology
Huazhong University of Science and Technology, Wuhan, 430074, China
{nenghuang,zyshao,hjin}@hust.edu.cn

Abstract. Concurrent programs are difficult to debug due to the inherent concurrency and indeterminism. One of the problems is race conditions. Previous work on dynamic race detection includes fast but imprecise methods that report false alarms, and slow but precise ones that never report false alarms. Some researchers have combined these two methods. However, the overhead is still massive. This paper exploits the insight that full record on detector is unnecessary in most cases. Even prior sampling method has something to do to reduce overhead with precision guaranteed. That is, we can use a frequency-sensitive sampling approach. With our model on sampling dispatch, we can drop most unnecessary detection overhead. Experiment results on DaCapo benchmarks show that our heuristic sampling race detector is performance-faster and overhead-lower than traditional race detectors with no loss in precision, while never reporting false alarms.

Keywords: Concurrency, Data Race, Sampling, Bug Detection.

1 Introduction

Multithreading is getting more and more popular in today's software. In other words, software must become more parallel to exploit hardware trends, which are increasing the number of processors on each chip. Unfortunately, correct and scalable multithread programming is quite difficult. The instructions in different threads can be interleaved randomly. A data race occurs when two different threads access the same memory location without an ordering constraint enforced between the accesses, and at least one of the accesses is a write [18]. Data races are not necessary errors in and of themselves, but they indicate a variety of serious concurrency errors that are difficult to reproduce and debug such as atomicity violations [13], order violations [12], and sequential consistency violations [14]. As some races occur only under certain inputs, environments, or thread schedules, deploying low-overhead and precise-coverage race detection tool is necessary to achieve highly robust deployed software.

There has been much effort to develop automatic tools for detecting data races. Ultimately, the detection techniques are broadly categorized according to

C.-H. Hsu et al. (Eds.): NPC 2013, LNCS 8147, pp. 49–60, 2013.

the time they are applied to the program: static and dynamic. Static techniques [11,17,21,22,24,29] provide maximum coverage by reasoning about data races on all execution paths. However, they tend to make conservative assumptions that lead to a large number of false data races alarm. On the other hand, dynamic techniques [6, 7, 10, 20, 26, 30, 31] are more precise than static tools, but their coverage is limited to the paths and thread interleaving explored at runtime. In practice, the coverage of dynamic tools can be increased by running more tests.

Most dynamic data race detectors are not widely used due to their runtime overhead. Data race detectors like RACETRACK [30] incurs about 2x to 3x slowdown and Intel's Thread Checker [23] takes performance overhead on the order of 200x. Such large performance overhead leads to the lack of data race detectors used in practice. The main reason for this very large performance overhead is each memory operation executed by the program needs to be recorded and analyzed. LITERACE [15] uses sampling to reduce the runtime overhead of data race detector. It presents a sampling algorithm which based on the cold-region hypothesis that data races are likely to occur when a thread is executing a "cold" (infrequently accessed) region in the program. PACER [3] shows a "get what you pay for" approach that provides scalable performance and scalable odds of finding any race. It provides a qualitative improvement over prior approaches.

This paper presents a frequency-sensitive sampling-based approach called FRESA. FRESA makes a precise and coverage guarantee: no matter what sampling methods you used, it learns and updates its sampling strategy intelligently. In other words, "get what you want but pay for less".

FRESA collects and organizes historical sampling results for the next sampling. In order to make the sampler more effective, it owns a finding density table in each schedule path. Compared with previous table, FRESA computes and creates a sampling probability interval, which helps making a more appropriate proportional sampling rate.

The rest of the paper is organized as follows: section 2 introduces our motivation and section 3 describes our algorithm. In section 4, we show our experimental results and performance. We list some related work in section 5. Then we conclude our current work and future work in section 6.

2 Motivation

We motivate our work by a common program shown below.

```
public class Test{
    int test1,test2,test3;
    void func1(int x){
        test1 += x;
    }
    void func2(int x){
        test2 += x;
    }
```

```
    void func3(int x){
        test3 += x;
    }
}

public class TestTest{
    Test test = new Test();
    Thread t1 = new Thread(){      //thread t1
        public void run(){
            for(int i = 0; i < 10000; i++)
                test.func1(1);
            test.func2(1);
            test.func3(1);
        }
    }
    Thread t2 = new Thread(){      //thread t2
        public void run(){
            test.func1(1);
            for(int i = 0; i < 100; i++)
                test.func2(1);
            test.func3(1);
        }
    }
    Thread t3 = new Thread(){      //thread t3
        public void run(){
            test.func1(1);
            test.func2(1);
            test.func3(1);
        }
    }

    public static void main(){
        t1.start();
        t2.start();
        t3.start();
        t1.join();
        t2.join();
        t3.join();
    }
}
```

In the program the shared memory *test1*, *test2*, *test3* are accessed 10002, 102, 3 times respectively, which shows an asymmetrically accessed distribution by *thread1*, *thread2* and *thread3*. The asymmetry like the above program is quite common in real applications.

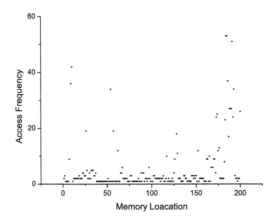

Fig. 1. A random selected 200 sequential accesses in DaCapo eclipse

We have an instrumentation in DaCapo eclipse. Figure 1 lists a random selected 200 sequential accesses frequency. Access frequency imbalance is quite obviously as shown. Previous race detection methods based on sampling never take it into account. Obviously, quite a lot overhead could be reduced through asymmetrical sampling rate.

3   FRESA Algorithm

In order to leverage the asymmetry. This section presents our FRESA algorithm. FRESA is a dynamic data race detection sampling method based on happen-before relationship, which uses a frequency statistics for the next time's sampling based on asymmetrical access information.

FRESA starts at a user-given sampling rate r_0 for every shared memory in sampling areas. It collects shared memory access frequency at run time. With the program execution, different shared memory's access frequency appears different. FRESA groups all the memories into different groups by considering their access frequencies. As more and more different memories grouped, each group can have a unique sampling rate based on user-given sampling rate. FRESA believes that the more frequently the shared memory accessed, the lower proportion the shared memory could have a data race. Since data races that occur in frequently accessed memory of well-tested programs either have already been found or fixed.

3.1   Frequency Statistics

FRESA collects the frequency of a memory location accessed, with the aim of grouping the memory of similar access frequency into the same group.

By this means, different memories can be partitioned into different groups. FRESA assigns different sampling rates to different groups.

FRESA uses a hashtable to maintain variables access frequency information. We define the memory location x in hashtable as a tuple (siteId, frequencyNum). *siteId* refers to the call site at which x is allocated and *frequencyNum* stands for the access frequency of x. We update the hashtable after every access using the algorithm below.

Algorithm 1. Hashtable Update Algorithm

1: **if** hashtable.get(siteId)!=NULL **then**
2:     frequencyNum()++
3: **else**
4:     hashtable.put(siteId,1)
5: **end if**

With the program execution, the hashtable updates at run time. Assume we get a hash map contains n different accesses x_1, x_2, x_3 ... x_n and with the relevant access frequencies f_1, f_2, f_3 ... f_n. In a general way, we first simply divide our n tuples into 5 groups. For an empirical practice, we set four group frequency threshold as $g_1 = 20$, $g_2 = 50$, $g_3=100$, $g_4 = 200$. For each (x_i, f_i), we dispatch it into a group in the following formula:

$$(x_i, f_i) \in \begin{cases} G_1 & f_i \leq g_1 \\ G_2 & g_1 < f_i \leq g_2 \\ G_3 & g_2 < f_i \leq g_3 \\ G_4 & g_3 < f_i \leq g_4 \\ G_5 & f_i > g_4 \end{cases} \tag{1}$$

We only list a simple piecewise function above. The group threshold can be different in practice due to the different frequency distribution.

3.2 Adaptive Sampling

FRESA does the same thing as PACER either in sampling periods or non-sampling periods. During sampling periods, FRESA fully tracks the happen-before relationship on all synchronization operations, and variable reads and writes, using FASTTRACK algorithm. In non-sampling periods, FRESA also reduces the space and time overheads of race detection by simplifying analysis on synchronization operations and variable reads and writes. However, FRESA adaptively changes its sampling rate using variable access frequency information. As for one access x, sampling rate r is decided by variable group classification as the following formula:

$$r_{x_i} = F(g_j | r_0) \quad x_i \in g_j \tag{2}$$

where r_{x_i} indicates the proper sampling rate for access x_i. $F\left(g_j | r_0\right)$ defines the sampling rate for group g_j.

In our experiment, we use an exponential decline equation $r_{x_i} = r_0/2^j$ $x_i \in g_j$ (j = 1, 2, 3, 4) in our example.

3.3   Theoretical Accuracy and Slowdown

Table 1 summarizes the effect of FASTTRACK, PACER and FRESA have on (1) the detection rate for any race and (2) program performance for sampling rate r and data race occurrence rate o.

Table 1. Theoretical accuracy and slowdown

	Det. race	Slowdown
FASTTRACK	o	$c_{rw} + c_{sync} n$
PACER	$o \times r$	$c_{sampling}(c_{rw} + c_{sync} n)r + c_{nonsampling}$
FRESA	$\sum_{i=1}^m o_i \times r_i$	$\sum_{i=1}^g c_{sampling}(c'_{rw} + c_{sync} n)r_i + c_{nonsampling}$

Constant c_{rw} is the slowdown due to analysis at reads and writes, and $c_{sync} n$ is the linear slowdown in the number of threads n due to analysis at synchronization operations. PACER essentially scales FASTTRACK's overhead by r, as well as a small constant factor $c_{sampling}$ due to PACER's additional complexity (e.g., indirect metadata lookups). PACER adds a slowdown $c_{non-sampling}$ during non-sampling periods, which is small and near-constant in practice. In FRESA, constant c'_{rw} is a little bigger than that in PACER as shared memory's access frequency information update.

4   Performance Evaluation

4.1   Implementation

FRESA is implemented in Jikes RVM 3.1.0[1], a high-performance Java-in-Java virtual machine [1]. FRESA is built on PACER's source code[2]. We execute all experiments on a Pentium Dual-Core CPU E5300 @2.6 GHz system with 2 GB main memory running openSUSE Linux 3.4.6-2.10. We used the multithreaded DaCapo benchmarks [2] (eclipse, hsqldb, and xalan; versions 2006-10-MR1). The range of sampling rates we use in our experiments is [0.000625, 1], and we set the minimum user given sampling rate $r_{min} = 0.01$. As data races occur infrequently and sampling decreases the probability of observing a race, we do many trials to evaluate accuracy.

---

[1] http://dacapo.anu.edu.au/regression/perf/2006-10-MR2.html
[2] http://www.jikesrvm.org/Research+Archive

4.2   Effectiveness of Data Race Detection

Figure 2(a) and 2(b) show FRESA's detection rate versus sampling rate for each benchmark. Figure 2(a) counts the average number of dynamic evaluation races per run that FRESA detects. A race's detection rate is the ratio of (1) average dynamic races per run at sampling rate r to (2) average dynamic races per run with $r = 100\%$. Each point is the average of all evaluation races' detection rates. The plot shows that FRESA reports races at a somewhat better rate than the sampling rate. However, this may have some different observations in different executions.

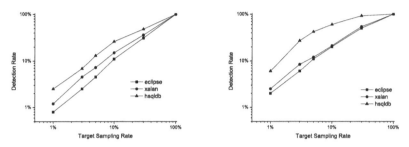

(a) FRESA's accuracy on dynamic races. (b) FRESA's accuracy on distinct races.

Fig. 2. FRESA's accuracy on dynamic and distinct races

Figure 2(b) shows the detection rate for distinct races. If a static race occurs multiple times in one trial, this plot counts it only once. The detection rate is much higher because FRESA's main concept of memory access frequency-sensitive, which means infrequent accesses have more sampling cost.

4.3   Time and Space Overheads

Time Overhead. Figures 3 shows the slowdown incurred by FRESA on each benchmark for r ranging over $[0, 100\%]$. The graphs show that FRESA has overheads that scale roughly linearly with the target sampling rate, although the slowdown factors on different benchmarks vary a lot. The slowdown factor in this experiment includes the execution time of the program, the overhead incurred by the JikesRVM platform, the overhead incurred by dynamic memory access and synchronization instrumentation and the overhead incurred by the sampling algorithms. FRESA incurs slowdowns by a factor less than 3x on three benchmarks (*eclipse, hsqldb, xalan*) at a target sampling rate of 1%, and can detect races with a relatively higher probability (80%) than PACER. When working at a target sampling rate of 100%, FRESA has no sampling effort and is functionally equivalent to FASTTRACK[21]. In this scenario, FRESA slows down the three programs by a factor of 10x on average, compared with 8x by

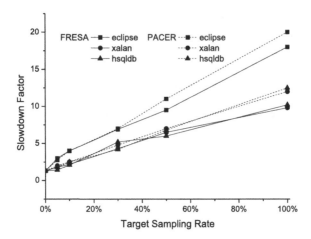

Fig. 3. Slowdown vs. sampling rates

FASTTRACK and 12x by PACER. Though FRESA uses hashtable leading to little more access time, it still incurs less time overhead than PACER due to the saving of sampling cost.

Space Overhead. Figure 4 shows the maximum live memory space overhead incurred by FRESA with various FRESA configurations. The measurement includes application, VM, PACER, and FRESA memory. For each target sampling

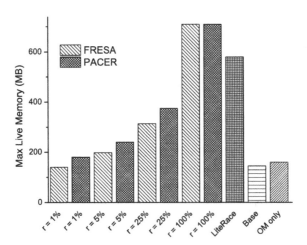

Fig. 4. Max live memory for eclipse

rate shown, we take the mean overhead over all executions. Base shows the max memory used by eclipse running on unmodified Jikes RVM. OM only adds two words per object and a few percent all-the-time overhead. The other configurations (except LITERACE) are PACER and FRESA at various sampling rates. At a sampling rate of 100%, FRESA takes no differences as PACER. At other sampling rates, FRESA uses significantly less memory than PACER. The result shows that FRESA can scale well with the sampling rate in terms of memory space used, and with a low sampling rate of $r = 1\%$, its space overhead appears to be very low.

5   Related Work

A large part of researches [4–11, 16, 17, 19–22, 24–31] focus on dynamic or static race detection. Dynamic race detection techniques are either based on lockset or on happen-before or hybrid of them. Lockset based dynamic techniques could predict data races that does not happen in a concurrent execution which leads to report many false warnings. Happen-before based techniques detect races that actually happen in an execution. Therefore, these techniques lack of good coverage though precise. On the other hand, happens-before based race detectors cannot predict races that could happen on a different schedule or they cannot create a schedule that could reveal a real race. In practice, the coverage can be increased by running more tests. Recently happens-before race detection has been successfully extended to classify harmful races with sampling. Hybrid techniques combine lockset with happens-before to make dynamic race detection both precise and predictive. But these techniques also report many false warnings. Static race detection techniques provide maximum coverage by reasoning about data races on all execution paths. However, they tend to make conservative assumptions that lead to a large number of false data races.

In general, the traditional methods using vector clocks takes $O(n)$ time and space overhead, n is the number of threads. The FASTTRACK algorithm replaces most $O(n)$ analysis with $O(1)$ analysis with precise guaranteed. However, these methods still incurs significant overhead.

A novel approach that explores the above tradeoff is sampling. LITERACE uses a sampling dispatch to decide whether to sample synchronization events only or together with all memory access of a function. On the other hand, PACER uses a more effective sampling strategy. It divides an execution into a scenario of sampling or non-sampling periods. PACER can detect race in a magic shortest data race way and with a probability of r. This significantly reduces the slowdown overheads.

A common limitation of the above techniques is that although existing precise sampling-based data race detectors such as PACER and LITERACE can effectively reduce overheads so that lightweight precise race detection can be performed efficiently in testing or post-deployment environments, they are ineffective in detecting races with much unnecessary repeated sampling cost. Our insight is that along an execution trace, a program may sample some race-infrequently variable in high sampling rate. These unnecessary sampling cost potentially indicate a saving cost degree in a sampling region. Intuitively, they may perform redundant memory access sampling, which lowers the chance of detecting rare data races and costs more unnecessary sampling overhead.

Recently, a couple of random testing techniques for concurrent programs have been proposed. These techniques randomly seed a program under test at shared memory accesses and synchronization events. Although these techniques have successfully detected bugs in many programs, they have two limitations. These techniques are not systematic or reproducible. Many researchers look for effective sampling method to solve this problem.

6   Conclusions and Future Work

Data race is a common problem in multithreaded program. It often indicates serious concurrency errors which are easy to introduce but difficult to reproduce, discover, and fix. Prior approaches reduce overhead by sampling. But they waste too many cost on repeated checking which can be omitted or reduced. In other words, frequency statistical sampling strategy could be more effective with detection precise guaranteed. This paper presents a data race detection method that provides a detection rate for each memory location that has inverse relationship with access frequency, and adds less time and a little more space overheads than PACER. FRESA achieves a qualitative improvement over prior work: its access frequency based sampling strategy suits more comfortable for performance and accuracy sensitive program, which makes it more suitable for all-the-time use in a variety of deployed environments. Our future work should simplify happen-before relationship and optimize the instrumentation with a lower cost level. In addition, we could generalize the approach to deal with different types of bugs caused by frequently access and develop new methods to further refine the approach.

Acknowledgements. Thanks to the anonymous reviewers for feedback on this work. This work is supported in part by the National High-tech R&D Program of China (863 Program) under grant No.2012AA010905.

References

1. Alpern, B., Attanasio, C.R., Cocchi, A., Lieber, D., Smith, S., Ngo, T., Barton, J.J., Hummel, S.F., Sheperd, J.C., Mergen, M.: Implementing jalapeño in java. In: Proceedings of the 14th ACM SIGPLAN Conference on Object-oriented Programming, Systems, Languages, and Applications, pp. 314–324. ACM (1999)
2. Blackburn, S.M., Garner, R., Hoffmann, C., Khang, A.M., McKinley, K.S., Bentzur, R., Diwan, A., Feinberg, D., Frampton, D., Guyer, S.Z., Hirzel, M., Hosking, A., Jump, M., Lee, H., Moss, J.E.B., Phansalkar, A., Stefanović, D., Van-Drunen, T., von Dincklage, D., Wiedermann, B.: The dacapo benchmarks: Java benchmarking development and analysis. In: Proceedings of the 21st Annual ACM SIGPLAN Conference on Object-oriented Programming Systems, Languages, and Applications, pp. 169–190. ACM (2006)

3. Bond, M.D., Coons, K.E., McKinley, K.S.: Pacer: proportional detection of data races. In: Proceedings of the 2010 ACM SIGPLAN Conference on Programming Language Design and Implementation, pp. 255–268. ACM (2010)

4. Boyapati, C., Lee, R., Rinard, M.: Ownership types for safe programming: Preventing data races and deadlocks. SIGPLAN Not. 37(11), 211–230 (2002)

5. Christiaens, M., De Bosschere, K.: Trade, a topological approach to on-the-fly race detection in java programs. In: Proceedings of the 2001 Symposium on Java TM Virtual Machine Research and Technology Symposium, vol. 1, p. 15. USENIX Association (2001)

6. Dinning, A., Schonberg, E.: Detecting access anomalies in programs with critical sections. In: Proceedings of the 1991 ACM/ONR Workshop on Parallel and Distributed Debugging, pp. 85–96. ACM (1991)

7. Elmas, T., Qadeer, S., Tasiran, S.: Goldilocks: a race and transaction-aware java runtime. In: Proceedings of the 2007 ACM SIGPLAN Conference on Programming Language Design and Implementation, pp. 245–255. ACM (2007)

8. Engler, D., Ashcraft, K.: Racerx: effective, static detection of race conditions and deadlocks. SIGOPS Oper. Syst. Rev. 37(5), 237–252 (2003)

9. Flanagan, C., Freund, S.N.: Type-based race detection for java. ACM SIGPLAN Notices 35(5), 219–232 (2000)

10. Flanagan, C., Freund, S.N.: Fasttrack: efficient and precise dynamic race detection. In: Proceedings of the 2009 ACM SIGPLAN Conference on Programming Language Design and Implementation, pp. 121–133. ACM (2009)

11. Henzinger, T.A., Jhala, R., Majumdar, R.: Race checking by context inference. In: Proceedings of the ACM SIGPLAN 2004 Conference on Programming Language Design and Implementation, pp. 1–13. ACM (2004)

12. Lu, S., Park, S., Seo, E., Zhou, Y.: Learning from mistakes: a comprehensive study on real world concurrency bug characteristics. In: Proceedings of the 13th International Conference on Architectural Support for Programming Languages and Operating Systems, pp. 329–339. ACM (2008)

13. Lu, S., Tucek, J., Qin, F., Zhou, Y.: Avio: detecting atomicity violations via access interleaving invariants. In: Proceedings of the 12th International Conference on Architectural Support for Programming Languages and Operating Systems, pp. 37–48. ACM (2006)

14. Manson, J., Pugh, W., Adve, S.V.: The java memory model. In: Proceedings of the 32nd ACM SIGPLAN-SIGACT Symposium on Principles of Programming Languages, pp. 378–391. ACM (2005)

15. Marino, D., Musuvathi, M., Narayanasamy, S.: Literace: effective sampling for lightweight data-race detection. In: Proceedings of the 2009 ACM SIGPLAN Conference on Programming Language Design and Implementation, pp. 134–143. ACM (2009)

16. Min, S.L., Choi, J.D.: An efficient cache-based access anomaly detection scheme. In: Proceedings of the Fourth International Conference on Architectural Support for Programming Languages and Operating Systems, pp. 235–244. ACM (1991)

17. Naik, M., Aiken, A., Whaley, J.: Effective static race detection for java. In: Proceedings of the Twentieth ACM Symposium on Operating Systems Principles, pp. 308–319. ACM (2006)

18. Netzer, R.H., Miller, B.P.: What are race conditions?: Some issues and formalizations. ACM Lett. Program. Lang. Syst. 1, 74–88 (1992)

19. O'Callahan, R., Choi, J.D.: Hybrid dynamic data race detection. ACM Lett. Program. Lang. Syst. 38(10), 167–178 (2003)

20. Pozniansky, E., Schuster, A.: Efficient on-the-fly data race detection in multi-threaded c++ programs. In: Proceedings of the Ninth ACM SIGPLAN Symposium on Principles and Practice of Parallel Programming, pp. 179–190. ACM (2003)

21. Pratikakis, P., Foster, J.S., Hicks, M.: Locksmith: context-sensitive correlation analysis for race detection. In: Proceedings of the 2006 ACM SIGPLAN Conference on Programming Language Design and Implementation, pp. 320–331. ACM (2006)

22. Qadeer, S., Wu, D.: Kiss: keep it simple and sequential. In: Proceedings of the ACM SIGPLAN 2004 Conference on Programming Language Design and Implementation, pp. 14–24. ACM (2004)

23. Sack, P., Bliss, B.E., Ma, Z., Petersen, P., Torrellas, J.: Accurate and efficient filtering for the intel thread checker race detector. In: Proceedings of the 1st Workshop on Architectural and System Support for Improving Software Dependability, pp. 34–41. ACM (2006)

24. Sasturkar, A., Agarwal, R., Wang, L., Stoller, S.D.: Automated type-based analysis of data races and atomicity. In: Proceedings of the Tenth ACM SIGPLAN Symposium on Principles and Practice of Parallel Programming, pp. 83–94. ACM (2005)

25. Savage, S., Burrows, M., Nelson, G., Sobalvarro, P., Anderson, T.: Eraser: A dynamic data race detector for multithreaded programs. ACM Trans. Comput. Syst. 15(4), 391–411 (1997)

26. Schonberg, E.: On-the-fly detection of access anomalies. SIGPLAN Not. 39(4) (1989)

27. Sterling, N.: Warlock: A static data race analysis tool. In: USENIX Winter, pp. 97–106 (1993)

28. Von Praun, C., Gross, T.R.: Object race detection. In: Proceedings of the 16th ACM SIGPLAN Conference on Object-oriented Programming, Systems, Languages, and Applications, vol. 36, pp. 70–82. ACM (2001)

29. Voung, J.W., Jhala, R., Lerner, S.: Relay: static race detection on millions of lines of code. In: Proceedings of the 6th Joint Meeting of the European Software Engineering Conference and the ACM SIGSOFT Symposium on the Foundations of Software Engineering, pp. 205–214. ACM (2007)

30. Yu, Y., Rodeheffer, T., Chen, W.: Racetrack: efficient detection of data race conditions via adaptive tracking. In: Proceedings of the Twentieth ACM Symposium on Operating Systems Principles, pp. 221–234. ACM (2005)

31. Zhai, K., Xu, B., Chan, W., Tse, T.: Carisma: a context-sensitive approach to race-condition sample-instance selection for multithreaded applications. In: Proceedings of the 2012 International Symposium on Software Testing and Analysis, pp. 221–231. ACM (2012)

One-to-One Disjoint Path Covers in DCell

Xi Wang, Jianxi Fan*, Baolei Cheng, Wenjun Liu, and Yan Wang

School of Computer Science and Technology, Soochow University,
Suzhou 215006, China
{20124027002,jxfan,chengbaolei,20114027003,wangyanme}@suda.edu.cn

Abstract. DCell has been proposed for one of the most important data center networks as a server centric data center network structure. DCell can support millions of servers with outstanding network capacity and provide good fault tolerance by only using commodity switches. In this paper, we prove that there exist r vertex disjoint paths $\{P_i | 1 \leq i \leq r\}$ between any two distinct vertices u and v of $DCell_k$ $(k \geq 0)$ where $r = n + k - 1$ and n is the vertex number of $DCell_0$. The result is optimal because of any vertex in $DCell_k$ has r neighbors with $r = n + k - 1$.

Keywords: DCell, Data Center Network, Disjoint Path Covers, Hamiltonian.

1 Introduction

Data centers become more and more important with the development of cloud computing. Specifically, in recent years, data centers are critical to the business of companies such as Amazon, Google, FaceBook, and Microsoft, which have already owned tremendous data centers with more than hundreds of thousands of servers. Their operations are important to offer both many on-line applications such as web search, on-line gaming, email, cloud disk and infrastructure services such as GFS [1], Map-reduce [2], and Dryad [3].

Researches showed that the traditional tree-based data center networks [4] have issues of bandwidth bottleneck, failure of single switch, etc.. In order to solve the defects of tree-based data center networks, there are many data center networks which have been proposed such as DCell [4], BCube [5], and FiConn [6, 7]. DCell has many good properties including exponential scalability, high network capacity, small diameter, and high fault tolerantly. In comparison with good capabilities of DCell, BCube is meant for container-based data center networks which only supports thousands of servers, and FiConn is not a regularly network which may raises the construction complexity.

DCells use servers as routing and forwarding infrastructure, and the multi-cast routing frequency between servers are quite high in data center networks. Multi-cast routing algorithms in DCells can be based on the Hamiltonian model as methods on [8, 9]. One-to-one disjoint path covers (also named spanning connectivity [10, 11]) are the extension of the Hamiltonian-connectivity which could

---

* Corresponding author.

C.-H. Hsu et al. (Eds.): NPC 2013, LNCS 8147, pp. 61–70, 2013.

as well as used on multi-cast routing algorithms in DCells to largely decrease deadlock and congestion, compared with tree-based multi-cast routing. However, the problem of finding disjoint path covers is NP-complete [13]. Therefore, a large amount researches on problems of disjoint path covers focused on different special networks, such as hypercubes [13–16], their variants [17–19], and others [20–22].

So far there is no work reported about the one-to-one disjoint path cover properties of DCell. In this paper, we prove that there exist r vertex disjoint paths $\{P_i | 1 \leq i \leq r\}$ between any two distinct vertices u and v of $DCell_k$ ($k \geq 0$) where n is the vertex number of $DCell_0$ and $r = n + k - 1$. The result is optimal because of any vertex in $DCell_k$ has r neighbors with $r = n + k - 1$.

This work is organized as follows. Section 2 provides the preliminary knowledge. Some basic one-to-one disjoint path covers properties are given in Section 3. We make a conclusion in Section 4.

2   Preliminaries

A data center network can be represented by a simple graph $G = (V(G), E(G))$, where $V(G)$ represents the vertex set and $E(G)$ represents the edge set, and each vertex represents a server and each edge represents a link between servers (switches can be regarded as transparent network devices [4]). The edge from vertex u to vertex v is denoted by (u, v). In this paper all graphs are simple and undirected.

We use $G_1 \cup G_2$ to denote the subgraph induced by $V(G_1) \cup V(G_2)$ of G. For $U \subseteq V(G)$, we use $G[U]$ to denote the subgraph induced by U in G, i.e., $G[U] = (U, E')$, where $E' = \{(u, v) \in E(G) | u, v \in U\}$. A path in a graph is a sequence of vertices, $P :< u_0, u_1, \ldots, u_j, \ldots u_{n-1}, u_n >$, in which no vertices are repeated and u_j, u_{j+1} are adjacent for $0 \leq j < n$. Let $V(P)$ denote the set of all vertices appearing in P. We call u_0 and u_n the terminal vertices of P. P can be denoted by $P(u_0, u_n)$, which is a path beginning with u_0 and ending at u_n. Let P_1 denote $< u_1, u_2, \ldots, u_{k-1}, u_k >$ and P_2 denote $< u_k, u_{k+1}, \ldots, u_{k+n} >$, then $P_1 + P_2$ denotes the path $< u_1, u_2, \ldots, u_k, u_{k+1}, \ldots, u_{k+n} >$. If $e = (u_k, u_{k+1})$, then $P_1 + e$ denote the path $< u_1, u_2, \ldots, u_k, u_{k+1} >$. Furthermore, if $e = (u_{k-1}, u_k)$, $P_1 - e$ denote the path $< u_1, u_2, \ldots, u_{k-1} >$.

A path in a graph G containing every vertex of G is called a Hamiltonian path (HP). $HP(u, v, G)$ can be denoted by a Hamiltonian path beginning with a vertex u and ending with another vertex v in graph G. Obviously, if $(v, u) \in E(G)$, then $HP(u, v, G) + (v, u)$ is a Hamiltonian cycle in G. A Hamiltonian graph is a graph containing a Hamiltonian cycle. G is called a Hamiltonian-connected graph if there exists a Hamiltonian path between any two different vertices of G. Obviously, if G is a Hamiltonian-connected graph, then G must be the Hamiltonian graph. Suppose that u and v are two vertices of a graph G. We say a set of r paths between u and v is an r-disjoint path cover in G if the r paths do not contain the same vertex besides u and v and their union covers all vertices of G. An r-disjoint path cover is abbreviated as an r-DPC for simplicity.

A graph G is one-to-one r-disjoint path coverable (r-DPC-able for short) if there is an r-DPC between any two vertices of G. In this paper G is r-DPC-able is not same as G is $(r+1)$-DPC-able.

For any other fundamental graph theoretical terminology, please refer to [12].

DCell uses recursively-defined structure to interconnect servers. Each server connects to different levels of DCell through multiple links. We build high-level DCell recursively form many low-level ones. Due to this structure, DCell uses only mini-switches to scale out instead of using high-end switches to scale up, and it scales doubly exponentially with server vertex degree.

We use $DCell_k$ to denote a k-dimension DCell ($k \geq 0$), $DCell_0$ is a complete graph on n vertices ($n \geq 2$). Let t_0 denote the number of vertices in a $DCell_0$, where $t_0 = n$. Let t_k denote the number of vertices in a $DCell_k$ ($k \geq 1$), where $t_k = t_{k-1} \times (t_{k-1} + 1)$. The vertex of $DCell_k$ can be labeled by $[\alpha_k, \alpha_{k-1}, \cdots, \alpha_i, \cdots, \alpha_0]$, where $\alpha_i \in \{0, 1, \cdots, t_{i-1}\}$, $i \in \{1, 2, \cdots, k\}$, and $\alpha_0 \in \{0, 1, \cdots, t_0 - 1\}$. According to the definition of $DCell_k$ [4, 23], we provide the recursive definition as Definition 1.

Definition 1. The k-dimensional DCell, $DCell_k$, is defined recursively as follows.

(1) $DCell_0$ is a complete graph consisting of n vertices labeled with $[0], [1], \cdots, [n-1]$.

(2) For any $k \geq 1$, $DCell_k$ is built from $t_{k-1} + 1$ disjoint copies $DCell_{k-1}$, according to the following steps.

(2.1) Let $DCell_{k-1}^0$ denote the graph obtained by prefixing the label of each vertex of one copy of $DCell_{k-1}$ with 0. Let $DCell_{k-1}^1$ denote the graph obtained by prefixing the label of each vertex of one copy of $DCell_{k-1}$ with 1. $\cdots$. Let $DCell_{k-1}^{t_{k-1}}$ denote the graph obtained by prefixing the label of each vertex of one copy of $DCell_{k-1}$ with t_{k-1}. Clearly, $DCell_{k-1}^0 \cong DCell_{k-1}^1 \cong \cdots \cong DCell_{k-1}^{t_{k-1}}$.

(2.2) For any $\alpha_k, \beta_k \in \{0, 1, \cdots, t_{k-1}\}$ and $\alpha_k \geq \beta_k$ (resp. $\alpha_k < \beta_k$), connecting the vertex $[\alpha_k, \alpha_{k-1}, \cdots, \alpha_i, \cdots, \alpha_1, \alpha_0]$ of $DCell_{k-1}^{\alpha_k}$ with the vertex $[\beta_k, \beta_{k-1}, \cdots, \beta_i, \cdots, \beta_1, \beta_0]$ of $DCell_{k-1}^{\beta_k}$ as follow:

$$\begin{cases} \alpha_k = \beta_0 + \sum_{j=1}^{k-1}(\beta_j \times t_{j-1}) + 1 \\ \beta_k = \alpha_0 + \sum_{j=1}^{k-1}(\alpha_j \times t_{j-1}) \end{cases} \tag{1}$$

(resp.),

$$\begin{cases} \alpha_k = \beta_0 + \sum_{j=1}^{k-1}(\beta_j \times t_{j-1}) \\ \beta_k = \alpha_0 + \sum_{j=1}^{k-1}(\alpha_j \times t_{j-1}) + 1 \end{cases} \tag{2}$$

where $\alpha_i, \beta_i \in \{0, 1, \cdots, t_{i-1}\}$, $i \in \{1, 2, \cdots, k\}$, and $\alpha_0, \beta_0 \in \{0, 1, \cdots, t_0 - 1\}$.

By Definition 1, $DCell_{k-1}^{\alpha_k}$ is a subgraph of $DCell_k$, where $\alpha_k \in \{0, 1, \cdots, t_{k-1}\}$.

Figure 1(1), 1(2), and 1(3) demonstrate $DCell_0$, $DCell_1$, and $DCell_2$ with $t_0 = 2$ respectively. 1(4) and 1(5) demonstrate $DCell_0$ and $DCell_1$ with $t_0 = 3$ respectively.

3   Main Results

In this section, we will study one-to-one disjoint path cover properties of DCell.

Theorem 1. $DCell_k$ ($k \geq 0$) is Hamiltonian-connected with $t_0 \geq 2$ except for $DCell_1$ with $t_0 = 2$. In other word, $DCell_k$ ($k \geq 0$) is 1-DPC-able with $t_0 \geq 2$ except for $DCell_1$ with $t_0 = 2$.

Proof. We omit the proof due to the page limitation.   □

Theorem 2. $DCell_k$ is a Hamiltonian graph for any $k \geq 0$. In other word, $DCell_k$ is 2-DPC-able for any $k \geq 0$.

Proof. We omit the proof due to the page limitation.   □

Lemma 1. $DCell_0$ is $(t_0 - 1)$-DPC-able with $t_0 \geq 2$.

Proof. The lemma holds for $DCell_0$ which is a complete graph [12].   □

Lemma 2. $DCell_1$ is 2-DPC-able with $t_0 = 2$.

Proof. $DCell_1$ is a cycle with 6 vertices. Therefore, $DCell_1$ is 2-DPC with $t_0 = 2$ [12].   □

Lemma 3. $DCell_2$ is 3-DPC-able with $t_0 = 2$.

Proof. For $t_0 = 2$, we use construction method to proof this lemma. We can construct an 3-DPC between u and v in $DCell_2$ for any pair of vertices $\{u, v\} \in V(DCell_2)$.

For example, the 3-DPC $\{P_1, P_2, P_3\}$ (resp. $\{R_1, R_2, R_3\}$, $\{T_1, T_2, T_3\}$, $\{S_1, S_2, S_3\}$, $\{U_1, U_2, U_3\}$) from $[0, 0, 0]$ to $[0, 0, 1]$ (resp. $[0, 1, 0]$, $[0, 1, 1]$, $[0, 2, 0]$, $[0, 2, 1]$) whose union covers $V(DCell_2)$ with $t_0 = 2$ are listed below (Similarly for the other cases).

$P_1 = < [0, 0, 0], [0, 0, 1] >$,
$P_2 = < [0, 0, 0], [0, 1, 0], [0, 1, 1], [0, 2, 1], [0, 2, 0], [0, 0, 1] >$,
$P_3 = < [0, 0, 0], [1, 0, 0], [1, 0, 1], [2, 0, 1], [2, 2, 0], [2, 2, 1], [2, 1, 1], [4, 1, 0],$
$[4, 0, 0], [4, 0, 1], [4, 2, 0], [5, 2, 0], [5, 2, 1], [6, 2, 1], [6, 1, 1], [6, 1, 0], [6, 0, 0], [6, 0, 1],$
$[6, 2, 0], [4, 2, 1], [4, 1, 1], [3, 1, 1], [3, 2, 1], [3, 2, 0], [5, 1, 1], [5, 1, 0], [5, 0, 0], [5, 0, 1],$
$[1, 2, 0], [1, 2, 1], [1, 1, 1], [1, 1, 0], [3, 0, 1], [3, 0, 0], [3, 1, 0], [2, 1, 0], [2, 0, 0], [0, 0, 1] >$.
$R_1 = < [0, 0, 0], [0, 1, 0] >$,
$R_2 = < [0, 0, 0], [0, 0, 1], [0, 2, 0], [0, 2, 1], [0, 1, 1], [0, 1, 0] >$,
$R_3 = < [0, 0, 0], [1, 0, 0], [1, 0, 1], [1, 2, 0], [1, 2, 1], [1, 1, 1], [1, 1, 0], [3, 0, 1],$

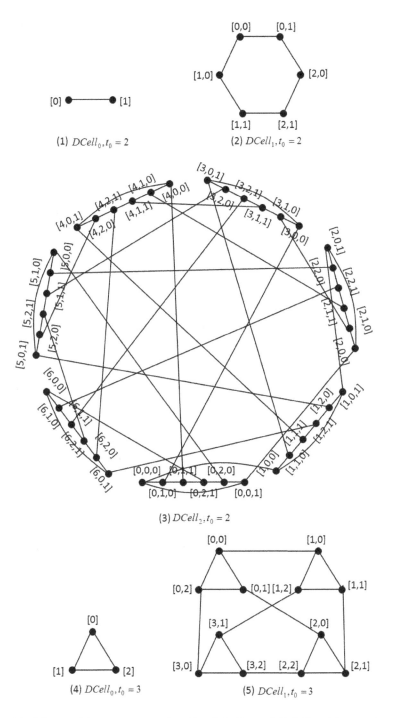

Fig. 1. (1), (2), and (3) demonstrate $DCell_0$, $DCell_1$, and $DCell_2$ with $t_0 = 2$ respectively. (4) and (5) demonstrate $DCell_0$ and $DCell_1$ with $t_0 = 3$ respectively.

$[3, 2, 0], [3, 2, 1], [3, 1, 1], [4, 1, 1], [4, 2, 1], [6, 2, 0], [6, 0, 1], [6, 0, 0], [6, 1, 0], [6, 1, 1],$
$[6, 2, 1], [5, 2, 1], [5, 1, 1], [5, 1, 0], [5, 0, 0], [5, 0, 1], [5, 2, 0], [4, 2, 0], [4, 0, 1], [4, 0, 0],$
$[4, 1, 0], [2, 1, 1], [2, 2, 1], [2, 2, 0], [2, 0, 1], [2, 0, 0], [2, 1, 0], [3, 1, 0], [3, 0, 0], [0, 1, 0] >.$

$T_1 =< [0, 0, 0], [0, 1, 0], [0, 1, 1] >,$
$T_2 =< [0, 0, 0], [0, 0, 1], [0, 2, 0], [0, 2, 1], [0, 1, 1] >,$
$T_3 =< [0, 0, 0], [1, 0, 0], [1, 0, 1], [1, 2, 0], [1, 2, 1], [1, 1, 1], [1, 1, 0], [3, 0, 1],$
$[3, 0, 0], [3, 1, 0], [2, 1, 0], [2, 0, 0], [2, 0, 1], [2, 2, 0], [2, 2, 1], [2, 1, 1], [4, 1, 0], [4, 1, 1],$
$[3, 1, 1], [3, 2, 1], [3, 2, 0], [5, 1, 1], [5, 1, 0], [5, 0, 0], [5, 0, 1], [5, 2, 0], [5, 2, 1], [6, 2, 1],$
$[6, 1, 1], [6, 1, 0], [6, 0, 0], [6, 0, 1], [6, 2, 0], [4, 2, 1], [4, 2, 0], [4, 0, 1], [4, 0, 0], [0, 1, 1] >.$

$S_1 =< [0, 0, 0], [0, 0, 1], [0, 2, 0] >,$
$S_2 =< [0, 0, 0], [0, 1, 0], [0, 1, 1], [0, 2, 1], [0, 2, 0] >,$
$S_3 =< [0, 0, 0], [1, 0, 0], [1, 0, 1], [1, 2, 0], [1, 2, 1], [1, 1, 1], [1, 1, 0], [3, 0, 1],$
$[3, 0, 0], [3, 1, 0], [3, 1, 1], [4, 1, 1], [4, 1, 0], [4, 0, 0], [4, 0, 1], [4, 2, 0], [4, 2, 1], [6, 2, 0],$
$[6, 0, 1], [6, 0, 0], [6, 1, 0], [2, 2, 1], [2, 1, 1], [2, 1, 0], [2, 0, 0], [2, 0, 1], [2, 2, 0], [5, 1, 0],$
$[5, 1, 1], [3, 2, 0], [3, 2, 1], [6, 1, 1], [6, 2, 1], [5, 2, 1], [5, 2, 0], [5, 0, 1], [5, 0, 0], [0, 2, 0] >.$

$U_1 =< [0, 0, 0], [0, 0, 1], [0, 2, 0], [0, 2, 1] >,$
$U_2 =< [0, 0, 0], [0, 1, 0], [0, 1, 1], [0, 2, 1] >,$
$U_3 =< [0, 0, 0], [1, 0, 0], [1, 0, 1], [1, 2, 0], [1, 2, 1], [1, 1, 1], [1, 1, 0], [3, 0, 1],$
$[3, 0, 0], [3, 1, 0], [2, 1, 0], [2, 0, 0], [2, 0, 1], [2, 2, 0], [5, 1, 0], [5, 0, 0], [5, 0, 1], [5, 2, 0],$
$[4, 2, 0], [4, 0, 1], [4, 0, 0], [4, 1, 0], [2, 1, 1], [2, 2, 1], [6, 1, 0], [6, 1, 1], [6, 2, 1], [5, 2, 1],$
$[5, 1, 1], [3, 2, 0], [3, 2, 1], [3, 1, 1], [4, 1, 1], [4, 2, 1], [6, 2, 0], [6, 0, 1], [6, 0, 0], [0, 2, 1] >.$ □

Lemma 4. For any $\alpha, \beta \in \{0, 1, \cdots, t_k\}$, $m \in \{1, 2, \cdots, t_k - 3\}$, and $\alpha \neq \beta$, let $x \in V(DCell_k^\alpha)$ be an arbitrary white vertex, $y \in V(DCell_k^\beta)$ be an arbitrary black vertex, and $G_0 = DCell_k^\alpha \cup DCell_k^\beta \cup (\bigcup_{\theta=0}^{m} DCell_k^{\omega_\theta})$, where $DCell_k^\alpha$, $DCell_k^\beta, DCell_k^{\omega_0}, \cdots, DCell_k^{\omega_i}, \cdots, DCell_k^{\omega_m}$ are internally vertex-independent with $i \in \{0, 1, \cdots, m\}$ and $\omega_i \in \{0, 1, \cdots, t_k\}$. Then there exists a path between x and y that containing every vertex in $DCell_k[V(G_0)]$ where $k \geq 1$ and $t_0 = 2$.

Proof. Let $G_1 = DCell_k^\alpha \cup DCell_k^\beta$. Select $z \in V(DCell_k^\alpha)$ and $u \in V(DCell_k^\gamma)$, such that $z \neq x$, $(u, z) \in E(DCell_k)$, and $DCell_k^\gamma \subseteq G_0$, where two graphs G_1 and $DCell_k^\gamma$ are internally vertex-independent. Select $\omega \in V(DCell_k^\beta)$ and $v \in V(DCell_k^\delta)$, such that $\omega \neq y$, $(\omega, v) \in E(DCell_k)$, and $DCell_k^\delta \subseteq G_0$ where three graphs G_1, $DCell_k^\gamma$, and $DCell_k^\delta$ are internally vertex-independent. According to Theorem 1, there exists a path P from x to z that containing every vertex in $DCell_k^\alpha$ and a path Q from ω to y that containing every vertex in $DCell_k^\beta$. Let $G_2 = G_0[V(\bigcup_{\theta=0}^{m} DCell_k^{\omega_\theta})]$. We can construct a path S from u to v that containing every vertex in G_2 which is similar to Theorem 1. Then there exists a path $P + (z, u) + S + (v, \omega) + Q$ between x and y that containing every vertex in $DCell_k[V(G_0)]$ where $k \geq 1$ and $t_0 = 2$.   □

Lemma 5. $DCell_k$ is $(k + 1)$-DPC-able with $k \geq 2$ and $t_0 = 2$.

Proof. We will prove this lemma by induction on the dimension k of DCell. By lemma 3, the lemma holds for $t_0 = 2$ and $k = 2$. For $t_0 = 2$, supposing that the lemma holds for $k = \tau$ ($\tau \geq 2$), we will prove that the lemma holds for $k = \tau + 1$.

For any vertex $x, y \in V(DCell_{\tau+1})$ with $x \neq y$. Let $x \in V(DCell_\tau^\alpha)$ and $y \in V(DCell_\tau^\beta)$ with $\alpha, \beta \in \{0, 1, \cdots, t_\tau\}$. We can identity α and β as follows.

Case 1. $\alpha = \beta$. There exist $(\tau + 1)$ vertex disjoint paths $\{P_i | 1 \leq i \leq \tau + 1\}$ between any two distinct vertices x and y of $DCell_\tau^\alpha$. Select $u \in V(DCell_\tau^\gamma)$ and $v \in V(DCell_\tau^\delta)$, such that $(x, u), (y, v) \in E(DCell_{\tau+1})$, where three graphs $DCell_\tau^\alpha$, $DCell_\tau^\gamma$, and $DCell_\tau^\delta$ are internally vertex-independent. According to Lemma 4, there exists a path $P_{\tau+2}$ from u to v that visits every vertex in $DCell_{\tau+1}[V(DCell_{\tau+1} - DCell_\tau^\alpha)]$. Then there exist $(\tau + 2)$ vertex disjoint paths $\{P_i | 1 \leq i \leq \tau + 2\}$ between any two distinct vertices x and y of $DCell_{\tau+1}$.

Case 2. $\alpha \neq \beta$ and $(x, y) \in E(DCell_{\tau+1})$. Let $P_1 = < x, y >$. Select $x_0 \in V(DCell_\tau^\alpha)$ (resp. $y_0 \in V(DCell_\tau^\beta)$), such that $(x, x_0) \in E(DCell_\tau^\alpha)$ (resp. $(y, y_0) \in E(DCell_\tau^\beta)$). According to the induction hypothesis, there exist $(\tau + 1)$ vertex disjoint paths $\{P_i' | 2 \leq i \leq \tau + 2\}$ (resp. $\{Q_j' | 2 \leq j \leq \tau + 2\}$) between any two distinct vertices x and x_0 (resp. y_0 and y) in $DCell_\tau^\alpha$ (resp. $DCell_\tau^\beta$). Let $P_2'' = < x, x_0 >$ (resp. $Q_2'' = < y_0, y >$), $P_i' = < x, \cdots, x_i, x_0 >$ (resp. $Q_j' = < y_0, y_j, \cdots, y >$), and $P_i'' = P_i' - (x_i, x_0)$ (resp. $Q_j'' = Q_j' - (y_0, y_j)$) with $3 \leq i \leq \tau + 2$ (resp. $3 \leq j \leq \tau + 2$). Furthermore, let $z_i \in V(DCell_\tau^{\gamma_i})$ (resp. $w_j \in V(DCell_\tau^{\delta_j})$) with $2 \leq i \leq \tau + 2$ (resp. $2 \leq j \leq \tau + 2$) and $(x_i, z_i) \in E(DCell_{\tau+1})$ (resp. $(y_i, w_j) \in E(DCell_{\tau+1})$). Let $W_0 = \bigcup_{\theta=2}^{\tau+2} DCell_\tau^{\gamma_\theta}$, $W_1 = \bigcup_{\theta=2}^{\tau+2} DCell_\tau^{\delta_\theta}$ and $W = W_0 \cup W_1 \cup DCell_\tau^\alpha \cup DCell_\tau^\beta$. For $2 \leq i \leq \tau + 2$, we can claim the following two subcases with respect to $DCell_\tau^{\gamma_i}$.

Case 2.1. $DCell_\tau^{\gamma_i} \subseteq W_1$. Select $w_j \in V(DCell_\tau^{\gamma_i})$ such that $2 \leq j \leq \tau + 2$. According to Theorem 1, there exists path a S from z_i to w_j in $DCell_\tau^{\gamma_i}$. Furthermore, let $W = W \cup DCell_\tau^{\gamma_i}$ and $P_i = P_i'' + (x_i, z_i) + S + (w_j, y_j) + Q_j''$.

Case 2.2. $DCell_\tau^{\gamma_i} \not\subseteq W_1$. Select $DCell_{\tau+1}^{\delta_j} \not\subseteq W$ such that $2 \leq j \leq \tau + 2$. Then, choose $DCell_\tau^p$ and $DCell_\tau^q$, such that three graphs $DCell_\tau^p$, $DCell_\tau^q$, and W are are internally vertex-independent with $p, q \in \{0, 1, \cdots, t_k\}$. Let $W_i' = DCell_\tau^{\gamma_i} \cup DCell_\tau^{\delta_j} \cup DCell_\tau^p \cup DCell_\tau^q$, according to Lemma 4, there exists a path S from z_i to w_j in $DCell_\tau[W_i']$. Furthermore, let $W = W \cup W_i'$ and $P_i = P_i'' + (x_i, z_i) + S + (w_j, y_j) + Q_j''$.

Furthermore, select P_i, such that $z_i \notin V(W_1)$ and $w_j \in V(W_i')$ where $2 \leq i \leq \tau + 2$ and $2 \leq j \leq \tau + 2$. According to Lemma 4, there exists path S from z_i to w_j in $DCell_{\tau+1}[V(W_i') \cup (V(DCell_{\tau+1}) - V(W))]$. Furthermore, let $P_i = P_i'' + (x_i, z_i) + S + (w_j, y_j) + Q_j''$.

According to above discussions, there exist $(\tau + 2)$ vertex disjoint paths $\{P_i | 1 \leq i \leq \tau + 2\}$ between any two distinct vertices x and y of $DCell_{\tau+1}$.

Case 3. $\alpha \neq \beta$ and $(x, y) \notin E(DCell_{\tau+1})$. Select $u \in V(DCell_{\tau+1})$ (resp. $v \in V(DCell_{\tau+1})$), such that $(x, u) \in E(DCell_{\tau+1})$ (resp. $(y, v) \in E(DCell_{\tau+1})$), $u \in DCell_\tau^\phi$ (resp. $v \in DCell_\tau^\psi$), and $\phi, \psi \in \{0, 1, \cdots, t_k\}$, where $DCell_\tau^\alpha$ and $DCell_\tau^\phi$ (resp. $DCell_\tau^\beta$ and $DCell_\tau^\psi$) are internally vertex-independent. We can claim the following three subcases with respect to u and v.

Case 3.1. $u \in V(DCell_\tau^\beta)$. Select $x_0 \in V(DCell_\tau^\alpha)$, such that $(x, x_0) \in E(DCell_\tau^\alpha)$. Let $y_0 = u$. According to the induction hypothesis, there exist $(\tau + 1)$ vertex disjoint paths $\{P_i' | 2 \le i \le \tau + 2\}$ (resp. $\{Q_j' | 1 \le j \le \tau + 1\}$) between any two distinct vertices x and x_0 (resp. y_0 and y) in $DCell_\tau^\alpha$ (resp. $DCell_\tau^\beta$). Let $P_1 = (x, y_0) + Q_1'$ and $Q_{\tau+2}'' = \emptyset$. Then, let $P_2'' = < x, x_0 >$, $P_i' = < x, \cdots, x_i, x_0 >$ (resp. $Q_j' = < y_0, y_j, \cdots, y >$), and $P_i'' = P_i' - (x_i, x_0)$ (resp. $Q_j'' = Q_j' - (y_0, y_j)$) with $3 \le i \le \tau + 2$ (resp. $2 \le j \le \tau + 1$). Furthermore, let $z_i \in V(DCell_\tau^{\gamma_i})$ (resp. $w_j \in V(DCell_\tau^{\delta_j})$), where $2 \le i \le \tau + 2$ (resp. $1 \le j \le \tau + 1$), $w_{\tau+2} = v \in V(DCell_\tau^{\delta_{\tau+2}})$, and $(x_i, z_i) \in E(DCell_{\tau+1})$ (resp. $(y_i, w_j) \in E(DCell_{\tau+1})$). The required $\{P_i | 2 \le i \le \tau + 2\}$ paths can be derived by the similar approach as the Case 2, so we skip it.

According to discussions in Case 3 and Case 3.1, there exist $(\tau + 2)$ vertex disjoint paths $\{P_i | 1 \le i \le \tau + 2\}$ between any two distinct vertices x and y of $DCell_{\tau+1}$.

Case 3.2. $v \in V(DCell_\tau^\alpha)$. The required paths can be derived by the similar approach as the Case 3.1, so we skip it.

Case 3.3. $u \notin V(DCell_\tau^\beta)$ and $v \notin V(DCell_\tau^\alpha)$. Let $P_1'' = Q_1'' = \emptyset$, $x_1 = x$, $z_1 = u$, $w_1 = v$ and $y_1 = y$. Select $x_0 \in V(DCell_\tau^\alpha)$ (resp. $y_0 \in V(DCell_\tau^\beta)$), such that $(x, x_0) \in E(DCell_\tau^\alpha)$ (resp. $(y, y_0) \in E(DCell_\tau^\beta)$). According to the induction hypothesis, there exist $(\tau + 1)$ vertex disjoint paths $\{P_i' | 2 \le i \le \tau + 2\}$ (resp. $\{Q_j' | 2 \le j \le \tau + 2\}$) between any two distinct vertices x and x_0 (resp. y_0 and y) in $DCell_\tau^\alpha$ (resp. $DCell_\tau^\beta$). Let $P_2'' = < x, x_0 >$ (resp. $Q_2'' = < y_0, y >$), $P_i' = < x, \cdots, x_i, x_0 >$ (resp. $Q_j' = < y_0, y_j, \cdots, y >$), and $P_i'' = P_i' - (x_i, x_0)$ (resp. $Q_j'' = Q_j' - (y_0, y_j)$) with $3 \le i \le \tau + 2$ (resp. $3 \le j \le \tau + 2$). Furthermore, let $z_i \in V(DCell_{\tau+1}^{\gamma_i})$ (resp. $w_j \in V(DCell_\tau^{\delta_j})$), where $2 \le i \le \tau + 2$ (resp. $2 \le j \le \tau + 2$) and $(x_i, z_i) \in E(DCell_{\tau+1})$ (resp. $(y_i, w_j) \in E(DCell_{\tau+1})$). The required $\{P_i | 1 \le i \le \tau + 2\}$ paths can be derived by the similar approach as the Case 2, so we skip it.

According to discussions in Case 3 and Case 3.3, there exist $(\tau + 2)$ vertex disjoint paths $\{P_i | 1 \le i \le \tau + 2\}$ between any two distinct vertices x and y of $DCell_{\tau+1}$.

In summary, for any two distinct vertices $x, y \in V(DCell_{\tau+1})$, there exist $(\tau + 2)$ vertex disjoint paths $\{P_i | 1 \le i \le \tau + 2\}$ between any two distinct vertices x and y of $DCell_{\tau+1}$. □

Lemma 6. For any $t_0 \ge 3$ and $k \ge 0$, $DCell_k$ is $(k + t_0 - 1)$-DPC-able.

Proof. We will prove this lemma by induction on the dimension k of DCell. For any $t_0 \ge 3$, by Lemma 1, the lemma holds for $k = 0$. For any $t_0 \ge 3$, supposing that the lemma holds for $k = \tau$, where $\tau \ge 0$, the proof that the lemma holds for $k = \tau + 1$ is similar to that of lemma 5 and thus omitted. □

Theorem 3. $DCell_k$ is $(k + t_0 - 1)$-DPC-able with $k \ge 0$.

Proof. By Lemma 1, the theorem holds for $k = 0$ and $t_0 \geq 2$. By Lemma 2, the theorem holds for $k = 1$ and $t_0 = 2$. By Lemma 5, the theorem holds for $k \geq 2$ and $t_0 = 2$. By Lemma 6, the theorem holds for $t_0 \geq 3$ and $k \geq 0$. $\square$

4   Conclusions

DCell has been proposed for one of the most important data center networks and can support millions of servers with outstanding network capacity and provide good fault tolerance by only using commodity switches. In this paper, we prove that there exist r vertex disjoint paths $\{P_i | 1 \leq i \leq r\}$ between any two distinct vertices u and v of $DCell_k$ ($k \geq 0$) where n is the vertex number of $DCell_0$ and $r = n + k - 1$. The result is optimal because of any vertex in $DCell_k$ has r neighbors with $r = n + k - 1$. According to our result, the method in [8, 9] can be used to decrease deadlock and congestion in multi-cast routing in DCell.

Acknowledgments. This work is supported by National Natural Science Foundation of China (61170021), Specialized Research Fund for the Doctoral Program of Higher Education (20103201110018), Application Foundation Research of Suzhou of China (SYG201240), and Graduate Training Excellence Program Project of Soochow University (58320235).

References

1. Ghemawat, S., Gobioff, H., Leung, S.: The Google file system. ACM SIGOPS Operating Systems Review 37(5), 29–43 (2003)
2. Dean, J., Ghemawat, S.: MapReduce: Simplified data processing on large clusters. Communications of the ACM 51(1), 107–113 (2008)
3. Isard, M., Budiu, M., Yu, Y., Birrell, A., Fetterly, D.: Dryad: distributed data-parallel programs from sequential building blocks. ACM SIGOPS Operating Systems Review 41(3), 59–72 (2007)
4. Guo, C., Wu, H., Tan, K., Shi, L., Zhang, Y., Lu, S.: Dcell: a scalable and fault-tolerant network structure for data centers. ACM SIGCOMM Computer Communication Review 38(4), 75–86 (2008)
5. Guo, C., Lu, G., Li, D., Wu, H., Zhang, X., Shi, Y., Tian, C., Zhang, Y., Lu, S.: BCube: a high performance, server-centric network architecture for modular data centers. ACM SIGCOMM Computer Communication Review 39(4), 63–74 (2009)
6. Li, D., Guo, C., Wu, H., Tan, K., Zhang, Y., Lu, S.: FiConn: Using backup port for server interconnection in data centers. In: IEEE INFOCOM, pp. 2276–2285 (2009)
7. Li, D., Guo, C., Wu, H., Tan, K., Zhang, Y., Lu, S., Wu, J.: Scalable and cost-effective interconnection of data-center servers using dual server ports. IEEE/ACM Transactions on Networking 19(1), 102–114 (2011)
8. Lin, X., Philip, P., Ni, L.: Deadlock-free multicast wormhole routing in 2-D mesh multicomputers. IEEE Transactions on Parallel and Distributed Systems 5(8), 793–804 (1994)
9. Wang, N., Yen, C., Chu, C.: Multicast communication in wormhole-routed symmetric networks with hamiltonian cycle model. Journal of Systems Architecture 51(3), 165–183 (2005)

10. Lin, C., Huang, H., Hsu, L.: On the spanning connectivity of graphs. Discrete Mathematics 307(2), 285–289 (2007)
11. Lin, C., Huang, H., Tan, J., Hsu, L.: On spanning connected graphs. Discrete Mathematics 308(7), 1330–1333 (2008)
12. West, D.B., et al.: Introduction to graph theory, p. 2. Prentice Hall, Englewood Cliffs (2001)
13. Park, J., Kim, C., Lim, S.: Many-to-many disjoint path covers in hypercube-like interconnection networks with faulty elements. IEEE Transactions on Parallel and Distributed Systems 17(3), 227–240 (2006)
14. Caha, R., Koubek, V.: Spanning multi-paths in hypercubes. Discrete Mathematics 307(16), 2053–2066 (2007)
15. Chen, X.: Many-to-many disjoint paths in faulty hypercubes. Information Sciences 179(18), 3110–3115 (2009)
16. Chen, X.: Paired many-to-many disjoint path covers of hypercubes with faulty edges. Information Processing Letters 112(3), 61–66 (2012)
17. Park, J., Kim, H., Lim, H.: Many-to-many disjoint path covers in the presence of faulty elements. IEEE Transactions on Computers 58(4), 528–540 (2009)
18. Ma, M.: The spanning connectivity of folded hypercubes. Information Sciences 180(17), 3373–3379 (2010)
19. Shih, Y., Kao, S.: One-to-one disjoint path covers on k-ary n-cubes. Theoretical Computer Science 412(35), 4513–4530 (2011)
20. Hsu, H., Lin, C., Hung, H., Hsu, L.: The spanning connectivity of the (n, k)-star graphs. International Journal of Foundations of Computer Science 17(2), 415–434 (2006)
21. Chen, X.: Unpaired many-to-many vertex-disjoint path covers of a class of bipartite graphs. Information Processing Letters 110(6), 203–205 (2010)
22. Huanga, P., Hsub, L.: The spanning connectivity of line graphs. Applied Mathematics Letters 24(9), 1614–1617 (2011)
23. Kliegl, M., Lee, J., Li, J., Zhang, X., Guo, C., Rincon, D.: Generalized DCell structure for load-balanced data center networks. In: IEEE INFOCOM Conference on Computer Communications Workshops, pp. 1–5 (2010)

A Network-Aware Virtual Machine Allocation in Cloud Datacenter

Yan Yao, Jian Cao[*], and Minglu Li

Department of Computer Science and Engineering, Shanghai Jiao Tong University, China
{yaoyan,ml-li}@sjtu.edu.cn, cao-jian@cs.sjtu.edu.cn

Abstract. In a cloud computing environment, virtual machine allocation is an important task for providing infrastructure services. Generally, the datacenters, on which a cloud computing platform runs, are distributed over a wide area network. Therefore, communication cost should be taken into consideration when allocating VMs across servers of multiple datacenters. A network-aware VM allocation algorithm for cloud is developed. It tries to minimize the communication cost and latency between servers, with the number of VMs, VM configurations and communication bandwidths are satisfied to users. Specifically, a two-dimensional knapsack algorithm is applied to solve this problem. The algorithm is evaluated and compared with other ones through experiments, which shows satisfying results.

Keywords: VM allocation; cloud datacenter; Two dimensional knapsack algorithm.

1 Introduction

Cloud computing has emerged as a new paradigm for hosting and delivering services over the Internet[1]. There are three service models in cloud computing: Infrastructure as a Service (IaaS), Platform as a Service (PaaS), and Software as a Service (SaaS) which deliver the infrastructure, platform, and software (application) as services respectively. These services are made available to consumers in an on-demand way. In order to provide users with various cloud services, many cloud providers (e.g. Amazon, Google) have built their cloud datacenters around the world.

Resource allocation is a core process in a datacenter. Recently, an increasing number of cloud providers take advantage of virtualization technologies, such as VMware [3], Xen [4], KVM [5] and OpenVZ [6], to implement a cloud datacenter. Typically, a user submit his requests, including the number of Virtual Machines (VMs for short) and their configurations through a portal of the provider. The provider will allocate the VMs in the cloud datacenters to satisfy the requirements of the user. Thus VM allocation is becoming a new problem to be solved.

There already exist many algorithms for VM allocations with different aims and assumptions [7]. Some of them try to allocate VMs in an energy efficient way[8-11].

---

[*] Corresponding author.

C.-H. Hsu et al. (Eds.): NPC 2013, LNCS 8147, pp. 71–82, 2013.

Energy consumption is a big concern for cloud providers. But other factors should be considered in VM allocation as well, such as network. Some works have been done on VMs allocation in a network-aware way [12-15]. However, there still exists several open issues to be solved. Firstly, the existing allocation algorithms considering the consumptions of network resources are designed for traditional datacenters whose network architectures are often centralized, not distribute over a wide area. In a cloud data center, the distances between different sub-datacenters greatly affect the performance of applications. In addition, the VMs requested by users have various configurations, such as different number of processors or amount of memory. Thus the issue of the heterogeneity should be considered.

In this paper, we focus on the two open issues mentioned above. As it is well known that the resource allocation problem is NP-hard, here we developed a heuristic algorithm, a Network-aware VM allocation algorithm based on Maximum Clique (MCNVMA for short), with the goal of minimizing the maximum latency in communication between the sub-datacenters. MCNVMA considers constraints on local physical resources, such as CPU and memory, as well as the network. In order to make it more practical, the VMs and the datacenters both are heterogeneous in MCNVMA.

The rest of this paper is organized as follows: Section 2 discusses related work and Section 3 introduces the problem in details. Section 4 illustrates detail steps of the MCNVMA we developed. Experimental results are illustrated in Section 5 to show performance evaluation of MCNVMA. Section 6 concludes the paper.

2   Related Work

Existing work on the allocation of VMs can be categorized into three offering models: reservation model, spot markets model and on-demand access model [17]. In the reservation model, a user purchase a bundle of resources for a period (e.g., a whole year) , during which the specified VMs can get great discount for payment in advance. Spot market model is a one-side auction market, consuming resources at a lower and flexible cost. In on-demand access model, users simply requests a specified number of the VMs, and pays for it according to a fixed schedule of fees. Here we restrict our study to on-demand access model. There are two types of VM allocation decisions to be made: initial placement [18] and optimizing (or migration) of VMs allocations over time [19]. In the current research, initial placement and VM migration as considered as separate topics, though in some cases similar algorithms may be employed. We limit our study to initial VM placement. Cluster and node are two levels considered in initial VM placement. In general, we consider physical machines are put in an unstructured resource pool so that the default is a shared cluster.

Some constraints should be satisfied when VMs are allocated to physical machines,.. Usually, the constraints are put on some specific attributes such as CPU usage, memory usage, and network usage. These constraints can be summarized into a weighted criteria used to order physical machines. If the criteria is about energy, then the algorithm tends to save energy [8-11]. If the criteria is about network, the algorithm tends to reduce the network traffic[12-15]. We briefly introduce some of them related to our work. In [12], the authors introduce a Traffic-aware VM Placement Problem (TVMPP), trying to reduce the aggregate traffic. As TVMPP is NP-hard , the authors introduce a heuristic approach to solve it. In [13], a Min Cut Ratio-aware VM Placement (MCRVMP) is proposed. It considers both constraints on local physical resources and network resources evolving from complex network topologies and dynamic routing schemas. They achieve them by exploiting the notion of network graph cuts. While both TVMPP and MCRVMP assume static and well-defined traffic demands, in [14] the authors focus on the equivalent capacity notion to consolidate VMs with uncorrelated traffic demands. Traffic demands are modeled as stochastic variables, and the optimization problem strives to place VMs while ensuring that the maximum network capacity is not violated with a particular user-defined probability. Hence, the final VM placement problem is a stochastic bin packing problem, and authors introduce a new heuristic approach to solve it. However, all the above network-aware VM allocation strategy ([12][13][14]) are designed for traditional datacenters whose network architectures are often centralized and do not distribute over a wide area. Mansoor Alicherry et. al in [15] proposed a network aware resource allocation algorithm based on distributed datacenter. They also take it make a compare with traditional datacenter and they regard the VMs as homogeny, which means all the VMs requested by users have the same number of processors and the same amount of memory. It is not applicable to real world. In this paper, we view datacenter are geographical distribution and VM requested by users are unique. The number of processors and the amount of memory of the VMs requested can be arbitrary realistic value.

3   VM Allocation Problem in Cloud Datacenters

What exactly is the VM allocation? In brief, a user requests for a service hosted in the cloud, requiring the allocation of VMs in the cloud datacenters, to meet the requested service's computational needs. The datacenter should identify the suitable physical resources for each requested VMs and allocate them.

A user's request can be specified in terms of the number of VMs, their configurations and the communication requirements. Sometimes a user may not have a priori knowledge of the communication requirements among the VMs. However we can get it by statistic analysis approach. In this paper, we assume that knowledge of the communication requirements among the VMs is already known.

We use a small dataset for ease of illustrating. In reality, it can be much larger sets of VMs and cloud datacenters. Suppose a user applies for ten VMs to run an application over a cloud infrastructure. Each VMs has fixed processor and memory (See Table 1) and the communication requirements(bandwidth) between VMs is collected (See Table 2). In Table 2, if the entry value is 0,it indicates there is no communication between two virtual machines, otherwise, it represents the necessary communication bandwidth needed. Suppose there are only five sub-datacenters to run these VMs. Each sub datacenter has some free CPU and memory capacities (see Table 3), and the distance between them are known as well(Table 4). Now, we need to find an VM allocation meeting the following requirements:

- Processor and memory requirements of VMs allocated on a sub-datacenter should not exceed its available free capacity.
- The communication requirements among VMs can be satisfied.
- The communication between VMs which belonging to different sub-datacenters (or servers) is minimized.

In this paper, each VM can be placed on arbitrary datacenters and servers. We propose a heuristic approach which consists of two consequent steps: datacenter selection and server selection. Datacenter selection is to select sub datacenters, which are geographically distributed, to place the VMs. And then assign individual VMs to the selected sub datacenters. Server selection is to determine the servers in the selected sub-datacenters and place the individual VMs to the servers. The two steps are very similar in algorithm. And here we just provide an example of selecting sub datacenters.

Table 1. VM Requirements(processor number, memory amount)

VM	Processor Requirement	Memory Requirement
VM_0	4	2
VM_1	8	8
VM_2	2	4
VM_3	8	2
VM_4	4	4
VM_5	4	6
VM_6	2	1
VM_7	9	10
VM_8	8	2
VM_9	6	4

Table 2. Communication cost between VMs（Mbps）

	VM_0	VM_1	VM_2	VM_3	VM_4	VM_5	VM_6	VM_7	VM_8	VM_9
VM_0	0	1	0.1	0.3	0	0.5	0.2	0.3	0	0.4
VM_1	1	0	0.2	0.6	0.05	0.09	0	1	0.6	0.2
VM_2	0.1	0.2	0	0.1	0.1	0.2	0.25	0	0.3	0.1
VM_3	0.3	0.6	0.1	0	0.35	0.18	0.06	0.4	0.72	0
VM_4	0	0.05	0.1	0.35	0	0.1	0.72	0.1	0.1	0.18
VM_5	0.5	0.09	0.2	0.18	0.1	0	0.35	0	0.18	0.1
VM_6	0.2	0	0.25	0.06	0.72	0.35	0	0.06	0.72	0.35
VM_7	0.3	1	0	0.4	0.1	0	0.06	0	0.4	0.5
VM_8	0	0.6	0.3	0.72	0.1	0.18	0.72	0.4	0	0.2
VM_9	0.4	0.2	0.1	0	0.18	0.1	0.35	0.5	0.2	0

Table 3. Datacenters Free Capacities

DC	Processor Capacity	Memory Capacity
DC_0	60	15
DC_1	22	18
DC_2	40	12
DC_3	20	13
DC_4	80	21

Table 4. Distance between DCs (mile)

	DC_0	DC_1	DC_2	DC_3	DC_4
DC_0	0	2	7	11	10
DC_1	2	0	5	7	1
DC_2	7	5	0	9	20
DC_3	11	7	9	0	15
DC_4	10	1	20	15	0

4   VM Allocation Algorithm

4.1   Problem Formulation

Our problem statement can be briefly described as follows:

1. m cloud datacenters are available and their resource capacities given along processor and memory dimensions. Noted as the set $DC = \{dc_1, dc_2, ..., dc_m\}$. For each $dc_i \in DC$, with the capacity $C_{dci} = (Pro_{dci}, Mem_{dci})$;
2. There are n VMs to be placed. The requirements of these VMs are given in terms of processors and memories needed, denoted as $VM = \{vm_1, vm_2, ..., vm_n\}$ and for each $vm_i \in VM$, the capacity requirement is $C_{vmi} = (Pro_{vmi}, Mem_{vmi})$;
3. The communication cost between n VMs is denoted by a matrix $Cost = (cost_{ij})_{n \times n}$;
4. The communication distance between any two sub datacenters is given, denoted as $Dis = (dis_{ij})_{m \times m}$. We regard the network resource as sufficiently enough, however in server selection phase, the constrains on communication distance is changed to the network resource (like bandwidth).
5. We need to find a mapping between VMs and sub datacenters that satisfies the VMs' resource requirements while minimizing inter-datacenter traffic and intra-datacenter traffic between VMs.

While finding such a mapping, we have to take care that the total resource requirement of the VMs placed on the same sub datacenter should not exceed the datacenter's capacity.

4.2   MCNVMA Algorithm

The basic idea of our MCNVMA algorithm is: First of all, we identify a subset of the datacenters with minimizing length of the paths between the datacenters. Additionally we need to determine the datacenter assignment for each individual VM. For this assignment, our objective is to minimize the inter datacenters traffic between the VMs.

Firstly, we select a set of datacenters to place the VMs. We view this problem as a sub-graph selection problem, which is finding a maximum sub-graph with a given diameter. For general graphs, it is an NP-hard problem and cannot be approximated within 2-ε for any ε>0[15].

Given a complete graph $G = (V, E, c, l)$. The vertices V represent the datacenters, and weights $C_{dci} = (Pro_{dci}, Mem_{dci})$ on them denote the number of processors and the amount of memory of the datacenter respectively. The edges E represent the path between the datacenters and length l on them denotes the communication distance between the sub datacenters (in server selection phase denotes bandwidth). Let s be the number of VMs requested by the user. Then we should find a sub graph of G, denoted as G', with m' vertices. G' meeting the flowing conditions<1, 2>, with minimum maximal distance.
For $\forall i \in \{1,2,...,m'\}$,

$$\sum_{j=1}^{n} Pro_{vmj}(i) \leq Pro_{dci} \tag{1}$$

$$\sum_{j=1}^{n} Mem_{vmj}(i) \leq Mem_{dci} \tag{2}$$

where $Pro_{vmj}(i)$ equals to p_j (represent the number of processors VM_j required) if VM_j is deployed on data center i, otherwise is zero; and $Mem_{vmj}(i)$ equals to m_j (represent the amount of memory VM_j required) if VM_j is deployed on datacenter ᵢ, otherwise also is zero.

Since the original graph is a complete graph, the subgraph induced by the selected vertices is also complete. And all of the complete graphs are their self-clique. Hence, our goal is to find such a clique whose length of the longest edge is minimum.

```
Algorithm: MCNVMA(G, N, W[][],Value[])
Input: G =(V, E, w, l)
    N: the amount of VMs;
    Value[]: value of VMs;
Output: min_diameter.

for each vertex v∈V
    V' ← {v}, E' ← ∅, m ← Count(V), weight ← w(v);
    AllocatedVM←TDKnapsack(weight, W, Cost);
    ToAllocateVM←W-AllocatedVM;
    Sorted the vertices of G in increasing order of length to
v, noted as u₁, u₂, u₃, ..., uₘ₋₁.
    i ← 0
```

```
while (i < m)
    weight ← w(vᵢ);
    perform two dimensional knapsack algorithm.
    diameter ← max⟨diameter, l(vⱼ, uᵢ)⟩;
    V' ← V' ∪ {uᵢ};
    E' ← E' ∪ {(v', uᵢ), v' ∈ V'};
    compute to remain to allocated VMs.
    i ← i + +
  end while
  if min_diameter >diameter
    min_diameter ←diameter
  else if min_diameter > diameter
Compare the communication cost of clique
end while
end for
return min_diameter
```

Once a datacenter is selected, we will assign individual VMs to it. This assignment is done during the process of datacenter selection. This problem can be regarded as a variant of two dimensional knapsack problem. We regard each datacenters as a knapsack and each VM as an item. The capacity of knapsack consists of available processors and memory. As mentioned in the problem statement, each item has two different kinds of cost (processors and memory). The value of each VM is the sum of the bandwidth, which is needed while communicating with others. The value is dynamic change along with the implementation of the algorithm. Our goal is to find the allocation of VMs with the maximum value under the conditions of limited capacity and minimum communication.

The algorithm finds a sub-clique satisfying the constraints that include vertex v and places VMs by invoking two dimensional knapsack algorithm which is implemented by the dynamic programming method. After completing the two dimensional knapsack algorithm, the VMs with lager communication requirement are placed on the same datacenter, then the communication cost between different datacenter is least. The algorithm finds maximum clique including vertex v by adding nodes in an increasing order of length to v, until the weight of the clique meeting the constraints. The algorithm computes the diameter of the resulting sub-clique as well. This is done by maintaining the diameter as the nodes are added. When a node is added, the diameter of the sub-graph change only if the length of the edges induced by that node is greater than the current diameter.

The algorithm finds a sub-clique meeting the constraints through the while loop for each of the vertices, and selecting the one with the smallest diameter.

4.3   Example and Analysis

Now let's illustrate how to solve the problem introduced in Section 3.2 using MCNVMA algorithm. First of all, we need to map datacenters onto the nodes of a graph(Fig. 3).

The weights of nodes correspond to the capacity of datacenters (Table 3), and the weights of edges correspond to distances between sub-datacenters (Table 4).

Firstly, we select a arbitrarily node, such as n_0 as the start node. We use two dimensional knapsack algorithm to assign VMs set on it. The sum of each row of Table 2 is the VM's value (Table 5), which changing dynamically. Now we place {VM$_3$, VM$_6$, VM$_7$, VM$_8$} on n_0. As n_1 to shortest among n_0's neighbors. Next, we select and place VMs on n_1 from the remaining VMs list ({VM$_0$, VM$_1$, VM$_2$, VM$_3$, VM$_4$, VM$_5$, VM$_9$ }). This procedure repeats until all of the VMs have been allocated.

Table 5. VM value list

VM	Value(Mbps)
VM$_0$	1.9
VM$_1$	2.1
VM$_2$	1.35
VM$_3$	2.71
VM$_4$	1.6
VM$_5$	1.7
VM$_6$	2.61
VM$_7$	2.76
VM$_8$	3.22
VM$_9$	2.03

Table 6. Result

Start node	Clique	Diameter
n_0	{ n_0, n_1, n_2}	7
n_1	{ n_1, n_4, n_0}	10
n_2	{ n_2, n_1, n_0}	7
n_3	{ n_3, n_1, n_2}	9
n_4	{ n_4, n_1, n_0}	10

We record the nodes and the diameter of the sub graph, which is induced by the nodes (Table 6). Then we select the clique with minimum diameter C={n_0, n_1, n_2}, that is datacenter DC$_0$, DC$_1$, DC$_2$.

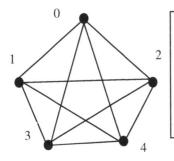

weight of vertices :
w={(60,15),(22,18),(40,12),(20,13),(80,21)}
weight of edges :
<0,1>=2,<0,2>=7,<0,3>=11,<0,4>=10
<1,2>=5,<1,3>=7,<1,4>=1
<2,3>=9,<2,4>=20
<3,4>=15

Fig. 1. Graph G=(V,E)

Analysis: In the while loop needs to sort the lengths of edges incident on a node, which takes $nlogn$ time, where n is number of datacenters. While loop in the algorithm may be executed once per node. Computing diameter takes $O(n^2)$ as there are n^2 edges. And the dynamic programming based two dimension knapsack algorithm takes $O(mn)$ time as there are m VMs and n data centers. Hence, in the worst case, the running time of *while* *loop* is $O(n^2)$. Algorithm *MCNVMA* executes *the while loop* times, one for each node so that the worst case complexity is $O(n^3)$.

5   Evaluation

5.1   Experiment Settings

We compare MCNVMA algorithm with Random algorithm and Greedy algorithm. Random algorithm selects a random datacenter and places VMs as many as possible on it randomly. If there are more VMs in the request than available in the datacenter, then the algorithm chooses the next datacenter randomly to place the remaining VMs. This process is repeated until all the VMs are placed. Greedy algorithm selects the datacenter with maximum capacity. It places as many VMs from the request as possible on that datacenter. If there are remaining VMs in the request to be placed, then the algorithm selects the next datacenter with the largest free capacity. This process continues until all the VMs are placed.

To measure the performance of the algorithms, we create random topologies and user requests, and measure the maximum distance between any two VMs in the placement output by these algorithms. The locations of datacenters are randomly selected from 500x500 grid. In each of the experiments below, we report the results as average of 100 runs.

5.2   Experiment Results

Firstly, we measure the maximum distance of the placement for a request of 100 VMs. By varying the number of datacenters, we compare the maximum distance between any two VMs, see Figures 2 and 3. MCNVMA algorithm has much smaller distance than random algorithm. The communication cost between datacenters in MCNVMA is lower than other two.

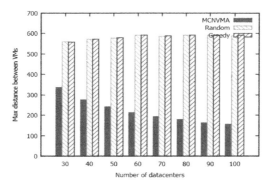

Fig. 2. Max distance for 100 VMs

Now, we set the number of datacenter to 50. We vary the number of VMs to evaluate the maximum distance and the stability of the algorithm. From figure 5 we can
see that the maximum distance computed by MCNVMA algorithm is much lower
than random algorithm and greedy algorithm. And the stability of MCNVMA is similar to the other two algorithms (Fig. 6).

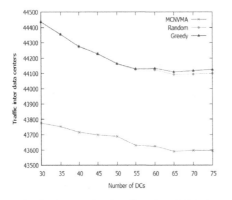

Fig. 3. Communication Cost for 100 VMs   **Fig. 4.** The number of selected datacenters for

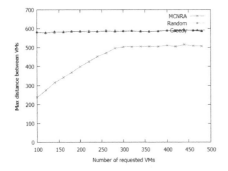
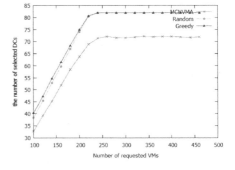

Fig. 5. Maximum distance for 50 DCs   **Fig. 6.** Algorithm Stability for 50 DCs

6   Conclusions and Future Work

In this work we provide a allocation algorithm (MCNVMA) for VMs in cloud datacenter. Each VM can has its own configuration requirements in MCNVMA. The
communication cost among VMs, which can be collected, are also defined as requirements as well. This algorithm try to find solutions with short communication
path among VMs while user's requirements can be satisfied. From experimental
results, the MNCRA algorithm reduces the communication cost between the VMs
especially in large scale datacenters.

In this paper, only network factors are considered. However, energy saving, load balancing and other factors should also be considered in real applications. We are going to explore other market models, such as spot market model as well.

Acknowledgements. This work is partially supported by China National Science Foundation (Granted Number 61073021, 61272438), Research Funds of Science and Technology Commission of Shanghai Municipality (Granted Number 11511500102, 12511502704), Cross Research Fund of Biomedical Engineering of Shanghai Jiaotong University (YG2011MS38). The work described in this paper was supported by Morgan Stanley. Morgan   Stanley and Shanghai Jiao Tong University Innovation Center of Computing in Financial Services have entered into Collaboration Agreement No. CIP-A20110324-2.

References

1. Armbrust, M., Fox, A., Griffith, R., Joseph, A.D., Katz, R., Konwinski, A., Lee, G., Patterson, D., Rabkin, A., Stoica, I., Zahari, M.: A View of Cloud Computin. Communications of the ACM 53(4), 50–58 (2010)
2. Bhardwaj, S., Jain, L., Jain, S.: Cloud computing: A study of infrastructure as a service (IAAS). International Journal of Engineering and Information Technology 2(1), 60–63 (2010)
3. Waldspurger, C.: Memory resource management in VMware ESX server. ACM SIGOPS Operating Systems Review 36(SI), 194 (2002)
4. Barham, P., Dragovic, B., Fraser, K., Hand, S., Harris, T., Ho, A., Neugebauer, R., Pratt, I., Warfield, A.: Xen and the art of virtualization. In: Proceedings of the Nineteenth ACM Symposium on Operating Systems Principles, p. 177 (2003)
5. Kivity, A., Kamay, Y., Laor, D., Lublin, U., Liguori, A.: kvm: the Linux virtual machine monitor. In: Proceedings of the Linux Symposium, vol. 1, pp. 225–230 (2007)
6. Openvz: Server virtualization open source project (2010), http://openvz.org
7. Ye, K., Huang, D., Jiang, X., et al.: Virtual machine based energy-efficient data center architecture for cloud computing: a performance perspective. In: Proceedings of the 2010 IEEE/ACM Int'l Conference on Green Computing and Communications & Int'l Conference on Cyber, Physical and Social Computing, pp. 171–178. IEEE Computer Society (2010)
8. Cao, J., Wu, Y., Li, M.: Energy efficient allocation of virtual machines in cloud computing environments based on demand forecast. In: Li, R., Cao, J., Bourgeois, J. (eds.) GPC 2012. LNCS, vol. 7296, pp. 137–151. Springer, Heidelberg (2012)
9. Beloglazov, A., Abawajy, J., Buyya, R.: Energy-aware resource allocation heuristics for efficient management of data centers for cloud computing. Future Generation Computer Systems 28(5), 755–768 (2012)
10. Buyya, R., Beloglazov, A., Abawajy, J.: Energy-efficient management of data center resources for cloud computing: a vision, architectural elements, and open challenges. In: Proceedings of the 2010 International Conference on Parallel and Distributed Processing Techniques and Applications, PDPTA 2010, Las Vegas, USA (2010)
11. Beloglazov, A., Buyya, R.: Energy efficient resource management in virtualized cloud data centers. In: Proceedings of the 2010 10th IEEE/ACM International Conference on Cluster, Cloud and Grid Computing. IEEE Computer Society (2010)

12. Meng, X., Pappas, V., Zhang, L.: Improving the scalability of data center networks with traffic-aware virtual machine placement. In: 2010 Proceedings IEEE INFOCOM, pp. 1–9. IEEE (2010)
13. Wang, M., Meng, X., Zhang, L.: Consolidating virtual machines with dynamic bandwidth demand in data centers. In: 2011 Proceedings IEEE INFOCOM, pp. 71–75. IEEE (2011)
14. Biran, O., Corradi, A., Fanelli, M., et al.: A stable network-aware vm placement for cloud systems. In: Proceedings of the 2012 12th IEEE/ACM International Symposium on Cluster, Cloud and Grid Computing (ccgrid 2012), pp. 498–506. IEEE Computer Society (2012)
15. Alicherry, M., Lakshman, T.V.: Network aware resource allocation in distributed clouds. In: 2012 Proceedings IEEE INFOCOM. IEEE (2012)
16. Liu, L., et al.: GreenCloud: a new architecture for green data center. In: Proceedings of the 6th International Conference Industry Session on Autonomic Computing and Communications Industry Session. ACM (2009)
17. Shang, S., Wu, Y., Jiang, J., Zheng, W.: An Intelligent Capacity Planning Model for Cloud Market. Journal of Internet Services and Information Security 1(1), 37–45
18. Machida, F., Kawato, M., Maeno, Y.: Redundant Virtual Machine Placement for Fault tolerant Consolidated Server Clusters. In: Proceedings of the 12th IEEE/IFIP Network Operations and Management Symposium, Osaka, Japan, pp. 32–39 (2010)
19. Lee, S., Panigrahy, R., Prabhakaran, V., Ramasubrahmanian, V., Talwar, K., Uyeda, L., Wieder, U.: Validating Heuristics for Virtual Machine Consolidation, Microsoft Research, MSR-TR-2011-9 (January 2011)

Research on the RRB+ Tree for Resource Reservation

Libing Wu[1,2,*], Ping Dang[1], Lei Nei[1,2], Jianqun Cui[3], and Bingyi Liu[1]

[1] School of Computer Science, Wuhan University, Wuhan, China
[2] State Key Laboratory of Software Engineering, Wuhan University, Wuhan, China
[3] School of Computer Science, Central China Normal University, Wuhan, China
cswlb@126.com

Abstract. The performance of the data structure has a significant impact on the overall performance of the advance resource reservation in the distributed computing. Because the query and update operations of the B+ tree are of high efficiency, so this paper proposes a B+ tree structure suitable for resource reservation - the RRB+ tree. Also, we design and implement the corresponding algorithms of query, insertion and deletion. Different with the B+ tree that insert and delete one key word at a time, the RRB+ tree insert one reservation request and delete one tree node every time. The RRB+ tree is of a higher precision of expression. With the fixed reservation admission control algorithm and the same rate of acceptance, the experimental results show that the RRB+ tree is easier to operate for the complex and changing network environment, and have a higher utilization of storage space.

Keywords: Data structure, Advance resource reservation, RRB+ tree, Loop time slot array.

1   Introduction

In high-performance distributed computing environments, some applications require access to distributed heterogeneous resources. These resources are often located in different zones and subject to different management strategies, which make it difficult to co-allocate them. In order to solve this problem, a method of resource reservation is used. It can ensure that all required resources are available at the same time in a specific period of the future time, and it can guarantee the QOS of services [1]. According to the use time of reserved resources, the resource reservation can be divided into two types - the immediate resource reservation and the advance resource reservation. The latter is more widely used because of its flexibility, and this study focus on it.

The optimization of the data structure's performance plays a pivotal role in improving the overall performance of the advance resource reservation. Data structures are mainly used to store the real-time resource reservation information, involving operations of queries, insertions, and deletions. Among the processing time of the

---

* Corresponding author.

C.-H. Hsu et al. (Eds.): NPC 2013, LNCS 8147, pp. 83–93, 2013.

resource reservation, 60% is for the processing of the data structure, 8% is for the selection of suitable resources, and the remaining 32% is for the management of the resource reservation mechanism [2]. The key problem of building a data structure suitable for resource reservation is how to speed up the query rate and reduce the data redundancy. To this end, this paper studies the B+ tree for resource reservation - the RRB+ tree. By comparison with the loop time slot array, it is of better precision of expression, and higher utilization of storage space for the complex and changing network environment.

2   Related Works

The existing data structures can be divided into two categories: slot data structures, and non-slot data structures. The time slot array [3-4] is a typical example of slot data structures. Each array element represents a time slot, and the value of it represents the amount of reserved resources. The time slot array is simple and easy for the admission control of reservation requests. However, there are also many inadequacies. First, if the duration of a request is too long, a considerable number of array elements will need to store the information, which is a waste of memory. Second, its precision of expression is very low, which means that if the unit of the array is a second, you can not describe the precise time in milliseconds. Third, the size of the array is affected by the parameters of reservation requests. The slot-based segment tree [5] is another time slot data structure. With the flexible resource reservation, Mugurel et al. improves the segment tree so that it can be better applied to actual environments [6].

In the studies of non-slot data structures, Qing Xiong et al. propose a data structure based on the single linked list [7]. The experimental results show that its memory consumption is far less than the time slot array, and greatly superior to it in time consumption when the volume of requests is not very large. Libing Wu et al. propose an improved single linked list structure - the indexed list [8]. The experiments show that its memory consumption is lower than the single linked list, and its query time is shorter than the time slot array.

The tree structures are another widely studied non-slot data structures. Tao Wang et al. propose a bandwidth reservation resource tree [9]. All leaf nodes in the tree have the same depth. Each node represents a non-empty time interval. Each leaf node occupies a time interval, and the amount of remaining resources within this interval is the same. The interval that the parent node describes is the sum of the intervals occupied by all its children. However, the experimental results [7] show that the bandwidth reservation resource tree is not as good as the slot array in both the processing ability and the memory consumption. Other tree structures include the binary search tree [10] and the resource binary tree.

3   The RRB+ Tree

The B+ tree is typically used in the database and the operating system's file system. Data in the B+ tree can be kept stable and in order. The insertion and update algorithms of the B+ tree are of logarithmic time complexity, which means that the insertion and update operations can be done efficiently. Therefore, according to the characteristics of resource reservation, we improve the B+ tree's node structure and related algorithms to obtain better performance, and that is the RRB+ tree.

The reservation requests are defined as follows:

Request = (*bw*, *ts*, *td*);

The parameter *bw* indicates the reserving bandwidth within each unit time, the parameter *ts* indicates the beginning time of the reservation, and the parameter *td* represents the reserving duration. Different from the B+ tree that insert a keyword each time, the RRB+ tree insert a reservation request, which means that the RRB+ tree consider the time values as keywords and the bandwidth of that time as a record.

3.1   Tree Node Structure

The non-leaf node of an m order RRB+ tree contains only the largest keywords of its sub trees. There are two head pointers: the pointer *root* to the root node and the pointer *first* to the leftmost leaf node. The nodes of the tree are defined as follows:

```
struct Bnode
{
        int keynum;
        int key[m+1];
        int record[m+1];
        BNode *ptr[m+1];
        BNode *parent;
        int seq;
        struct BNode *next;
};
```

The parameter *keynum* represents the number of keywords in the node, and its range is [$\lceil m/2 \rceil$, m]. (*key*, *record*, *ptr*) describes a keyword: the parameter *key* represents the value of the keyword and it used to store the time in this article; the parameter *record* shows the resource reservation information of *key*, and its initial value is 0; and the parameter *ptr* is a pointer to the sub tree associated with that keyword *key*. The parameter *parent* points to the parent node of this node, the parameter *seq* indicates that it is the *seq*-th children of the parent node, and the parameter *next* is a pointer to the next node of the same level. Each node consumes the memory of 4 * (4 + 3 * (m +1)) bytes.

Figure 1 shows a third order RRB+ tree. From the figure, we can get the current bandwidth reservation information stored in this tree: the amounts of reserved resources is 10 during the 0-14 time period, 90 during the 15-26 time period, 50 during the 27-35 time period, and so on.

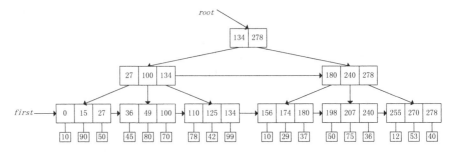

Fig. 1. Third Order RRB+ Tree

3.2 Algorithms

3.2.1 Query

After the server receives the request *Request* (*bw*, *ts*, *td*), it should find out whether the reserving start time (the keyword *ts*) is in the RRB+ tree. The query results are as follows:

(1) Empty tree;

(2) The tree is not empty, and the keyword *ts* is greater than all keywords in the current tree;

(3) The tree is not empty, *ts* is not greater than the largest keyword but it is not a keyword in the tree;

(4) The tree is not empty, and *ts* is one of the keywords.

The first two cases can be directly judged. For the first case, if the pointer *root* is null, the tree is empty. For the second case, the rightmost keyword of the node *root* is the biggest one in the tree. For the latter two cases, the query operation is similar to that of the binary sort tree. Traverse the tree from top to down since the node *root* – in every internal node, if *ts* is not bigger than a keyword of it from left to right, then enter the corresponding child node of that keyword until the traversal comes to leaf nodes. The structure of the query result is as follows:

```
struct Result
{
        BNode * ptr;
        int i;
        int tag;
};
```

The parameter *ptr* points to the leaf node where the insertion should begin for the latter two cases. For the first two cases, it will be NULL because it has to create a tree in the first case and the insertion place is clear in the second case (the rightmost leaf node). The parameter *i* indicates that the keyword *ts* should be the *i*-th keyword of the node *ptr* for the third case, and is originally the *i*-th keyword of the node *ptr* for the fourth case. For the first two cases, it will be zero. The parameter *tag* describes which one of the four cases is true for that result.

3.2.2   Insertion

On the basis of the query results above, the admission control will be done first. If it is of the first two cases, the server can directly decide the current reservation request to be admitted. For the latter two cases, the sever needs to read the resource reservation information during the time period of [*ts*, *ts* + *td*), and thus judges whether the request can be accepted. If it is able to accept the request, the corresponding insertion operation will be done.

If the tree is empty, establish a tree and insert the request. If the tree is not empty, the insertion operation will be divided into two steps: the insertion of the starting keyword *ts* and the insertion of the end keyword (*ts*+*td*). The insertion is only done in leaf nodes. When the number of keywords in the node is greater than m, it needs to be split into two nodes and their parent node should contain both biggest keywords of them, which may lead to the splits of internal nodes layers up. If the split is at the node *root*, a new one should be created. The implementation process of the internal nodes' split algorithm is as follows:

```
void Split(BNode *tmp)
while(tmp->keynum > m)
    //create a new node t as a successor to the node tmp, and the latter
    //tmp->keynum/2 keywords are moved to t
    Create(t);
    if(tmp == root)
        //create a new node as root with the node tmp and t as its children
        CreateRoot(tmp, t);
    else
        //update the node tmp's parent node so that it contains both the
        //biggest keywords of the node tmp and t
        Update(tmp->parent);
        //continue upward, to see whether the internal nodes need to split
        tmp = tmp->parent;
    end if
end while
```

For the insertion of the starting time *ts*, there will be no operation if the current tree contains the keyword *ts*(in case 4). If *ts* is greater than all the keywords in the current tree (in case 2), update the biggest keywords of each internal layer with the value of *ts* from top to down. And insert *ts* into the rightmost leaf node, setting its record value as equal as that of its previous keyword. If the tree doesn't contain the keyword *ts* and it is not greater than the largest keyword of the current tree (in case 3), insert it into the leaf node that the pointer *ptr* points to and set its record value the same as the previous keyword. Keywords' insertion may lead to leaf node's splitting and it is slightly different with the splitting algorithm of internal nodes (shown in the above algorithm) - the keyword may fall into the node *tmp* or *t* (the variables *tmp* and *t* are in the above algorithm), so the query result needs to be updated according to the real situation. The parent nodes will contain one more keyword, which may lead to the split operations upward. The insertion algorithm of *ts* is shown as follows:

```
void DealWithTs(Result r)
if(r.tag == 2)
        //update the biggest keywords of internal layers with the value of ts
top-down
        ReplaceDown(ts);
        //r.ptr is the rightmost leaf node•insert ts to r.ptr
        Update(r.ptr);
else if(r.tag == 3)
        //insert ts to r.ptr as the i-th member
        Insert(r.ptr, i);
end if
if(r.ptr->keynum > m)
        //if the leaf node splits after the insertion, update r
        SplitUpdate(r.ptr);
        if(r.ptr->parent > m)
                Split(r.ptr->parent);
        end if
end if
```

Take the 3 order RRB+ tree shown in Figure 1 as an example, insert the *request* (30, 108, 20) into it, and that leads to the calling of the insertion algorithm of *ts* at first. Insert the keyword 108 to the third leaf node on the left and set its record value equal to that of the previous keyword 100 (that is 70). Then the number of keywords in that leaf node becomes 4, greater than 3, so it must be split. After the splitting, the number of keywords in its parent node becomes 4, so it needs to split, too. The new tree is shown in Figure 2.

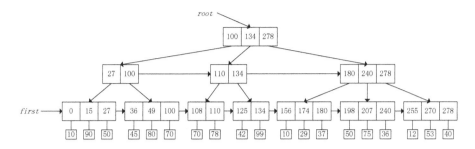

Fig. 2. After the Insertion of the *ts* (108)

To insert the *request* (30, 108, 20) completely, it needs to traverse 20 time units starting from the keyword 108. The next keyword of 108 is the keyword 110 and two units of time between them, which is less than 20, so the record value of keyword 108 updates to 100 (70 + 30 = 100). The next keyword of 110 is the keyword 125 and 15 time units between them, which is less than 18 (20 - 2 = 18), so the record value of the keyword 110 updates to 108 (78 + 30 = 108). The next keyword of 125 is the keyword 134 and 9 time units between them, which is greater than 3 (18 - 15 = 3), and then the keyword 128 (108 + 20 = 128) is inserted between the keywords 125 and 134, with its record value equal to the current record value of the keyword 125 (42), and the record value of keyword 125 becoming 72 (42 + 30 = 72). After these operations done to the tree in the Figure 2, it changes and its new state is illustrated in Figure 3.

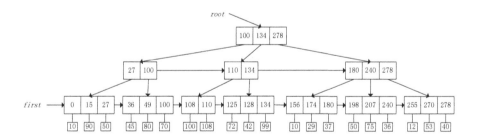

Fig. 3. After the *Request* (30, 108, 20) Inserted Completely

After the insertion of *ts*, the parameter *ptr* points to the node where the keyword *ts* has been inserted and the parameter *i* indicates the position of *ts* in the node *ptr* pointing to for all these four search results, which makes the subsequent insertion algorithm of (*ts* + *td*) transparent to the four different insertion cases and simplifies this algorithm implementation. In the (*ts* + *td*) insertion algorithm, firstly all record values of keywords during the time period [*ts*, *ts* + *td*) are updated, and then the keyword (*ts* + *td*) is inserted.

4   Comparative Experiments

4.1   The Loop Time Slot Array

As time goes on, resources that have been reserved will be used, and there are new resources available for reservation. The traditional time slot array consumes much memory, resulting in poor performance. So this paper chooses the loop time slot array as the data structure for the comparison with the RRB+ tree. As shown in Figure 4, the size of this array is represented by the parameter *MAX*, and the size of a slot is represented by the parameter *SLOT*. The initial value of the variable *time* is 0. It will point to the next slot once a slot of time has been gone, and reset the value of the prior slot zero. When it points to the slot *MAX*-1, after a slot of time it will point to the slot 0 again, i.e., the variable *time* indicates the value of the current time (Its exact value is *currentTime%MAX*). When the request *Request(bw, ts, td)* arrives, find out the starting position in the loop slot array with the values of the variables *time* and *ts*, and then the array cycle down *td* units to reserve resources.

Fig. 4. The Loop Time Slot Array

4.2   Experimental Environment

Use Visual Studio 2010 as the development platform and the programming language is C++. Characterizations of the relevant parameters are as follows:

avgI, the average interval between the time requests arrive. The moments when requests arrive follow the Poisson distribution with the parameter λ, and $avgI = \lambda$. If $\lambda == SLOT$, the server receives a request each time slot on average.

bw, the reserved bandwidth. Its value follows the uniform distribution within the range of $(b1, b2)$ and the mean value is $B = (b1 + b2) / 2$.

td, the duration. It follows the exponential distribution and the variable *E* represents its mean value.

BWMAX, the maximum bandwidth that the system can provide per unit time.

Interval, the interval between two deletions of the RRB+ tree.

4.3   Results and Analysis

The fixed reservation admission control algorithm is used to decide whether to accept a reservation request or not. In the simulation experiments, the admission control rate will be about 98% by adjusting the value of the variable *BWMAX* after the values of other parameters are set. So the performance evaluation of the two data structures will be more objective. The settings of the relevant parameters are as shown in Table 1.

Table 1. The Experimental Parameters

	m	BWMAX (KB)	SLOT (ms)	λ (ms)	$b1$ (KB/ms)	$b2$ (KB/ms)
Set 1	3	8000	1	100	100	1000
Set 2	5	8000	1	100	100	1000
Set 3	3	8000	1	100	100	1000
Set 4	3	8000	1	1000	100	1000

	B (KB/ms)	$b3$ (ms)	$b4$ (ms)	T (ms)	E (ms)	Interval (s)
Set 1	550	10	100	55	1000	1
Set 2	550	10	100	55	1000	1
Set 3	550	10	100	55	1000	60
Set 4	550	10	100	55	1000	60

The memory consumption of the RRB+ tree and the loop time slot array is shown in figure 5 below. "BD" represents the memory consumption of the RRB+ tree before deletions, "AD" represents the memory consumption of the RRB+ tree after deletions, and "Array" represents the memory consumption of the loop time slot array. In order to ensure the accuracy of experimental results, reservation requests of these four settings are the same (that means the random seed to generate the parameters of reservation requests is unchanged), and the value of the parameter *BWMAX* is also the same, so they get the same resource reservation results.

In Figure 5, the memory consumption of the loop time slot array in set 1, 2 and 3 is the same, and that in set 4 is different. That is because it takes the difference between the maximum reserved time and the current time as the actual memory consumption. And the values of λ in set 1, 2 and 3 are the same, so their resource reservation situation is the same and thus obtain the same memory consumption at the same output time. But the value of λ in set 4 is different, resulting in the different memory consumption at the same output time.

The only difference between set 1 and 2 is the different orders of trees. The orders of RRB+ trees are 3 in set 1 and 5 in set 2. And their performances of the memory consumption are almost the same. The only difference between set 1 and 3 is the frequency of deletions. The frequency is one second in set 1 and one minute in set 3, which means that the deletions will be done probably every 10 requests received in set 1 and 600 in set 3. So the memory consumption before the deletion of RRB+ tree in set 3 is much larger than that in set 1.

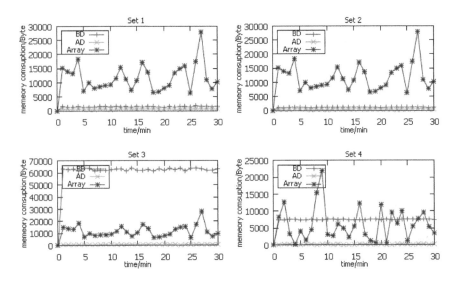

Fig. 5. Comparison of Memory Consumption

The only difference between set 3 and 4 is that the value of λ in set 4 is ten times as large as that in set 3. So it probably receives 10 reservation requests in set 3 and one in set 4 per second. And the memory consumption of the RRB+ tree in set 4 has been significantly improved compared to that in set 3.

It can be seen that the memory consumption of the RRB+ tree is far less than that of the loop time slot array, when its deletion interval is appropriate. For different kinds of reservation requests, the RRB+ tree can achieve better performance through appropriately adjusting its parameters. The memory consumption of the loop slot array only associates with the largest reserved time and the current time. And if requests reserve resources far earlier than the time they use them or the durations are too long, its memory consumption will greatly increase. Also it is hard to set the size of the loop slot array. Therefore, the storage space utilization of the RRB+ tree will be much higher than that of the loop time slot array for the complex and changing network environment.

5   Conclusions

The performance optimization of the data structure plays a pivotal role in improving the overall performance of resource reservation. Data structure is mainly used to store the real-time resource reservation information, involving the operations of query, insertion and deletion. The query and update operations of the B+ tree are of high efficiency, so this paper propose a B+ tree structure suitable for resource reservation - the RRB+ tree, and design the corresponding algorithms for it. The results of experiments compared with the loop time slot array show that the storage space utilization of the RRB+ tree will be much higher than that of the loop time slot array for the complex and changing network environments.

Acknowledgment. This work is supported by National Science Foundation of China (No. 61070010, 61170017, 61272212) and Science & Technology Plan of Wuhan city.

References

1. Zhan, G., Siwei, L.: Dynamic grid resource reservation mechanism based on resource-reservation graph. Journal of Software 22(10), 2497–2508 (2011) (in Chinese)
2. Burchard, L.-O.: Analysis of data structures for admission control of advance reservation requests. IEEE Transactions on Knowledge and Data Engineering 17(3), 413–424 (2005)
3. Burchard, L.-O., Heiss, H.-U.: Performance evaluation of data structures for admission control in bandwidth brokers. Technical Report TR-KBS-01-02, Communications and Operating Systems Group, Technical University of Berlin (May 2002)
4. Andreicaf, M.I., Ţăpuş, N.: Time slot groups - a data structure for QoS-constrained advance bandwidth reservation and admission control. In: 10th International Symposium on Symbolic and Numeric Algorithms for Scientific Computing, Timisoara, pp. 354–357 (September 2008)
5. Brodnik, A., Nilsson, A.: An efficient data structure for advance bandwidth reservations on the Internet. In: Proc. of the 3rd Conference on Computer Science and Electrical Engineering, pp. 1–5 (2002)
6. Andreicaf, M.I., Ţăpuş, N.: Efficient data structures for online QoS-constrained data transfer scheduling. In: International Symposium on Parallel and Distributed Computing, Timisoara, pp. 285–292 (July 2008)
7. Xiong, Q., Wu, C., Xing, J., Wu, L., Zhang, H.: A linked-list data structure for advance reservation admission control. In: Lu, X., Zhao, W. (eds.) ICCNMC 2005. LNCS, vol. 3619, pp. 901–910. Springer, Heidelberg (2005)
8. Wu, L., Yu, T., He, Y., Li, F.: A index linked list suited for resource reservation. Journal of WUT (Information & Management Engineering) 33(6), 904–908 (2011) (in Chinese)
9. Wang, T., Chen, J.: Bandwidth tree - a data structure for routing in networks with advance reservation. In: 21st IEEE International Performance, Computing, and Communications Conference, Phoenix, AZ, pp. 37–44 (April 2002)
10. SchelBn, O., Nilsson, A., Norrgkd, J., Pink, S.: Performance of QoS agents for provisioning network resources. In: Seventh International Workshop on Quality of Service(IWQoS 1999), London, pp. 17–26 (1999)

Totoro: A Scalable and Fault-Tolerant Data Center Network by Using Backup Port

Junjie Xie[1], Yuhui Deng[1,2], and Ke Zhou[3]

[1] Department of Computer Science, Jinan University, Guangzhou, 510632, P.R. China
xiejunjiejnu@gmail.com
[2] State Key Laboratory of Computer Architecture, Institute of Computing Technology,
Chinese Academy of Sciences, Beijing, 100190, P.R. China
tyhdeng@jnu.edu.cn
[3] School of Computer Science & Technology,
Huazhong University of Science & Technology,
Key Laboratory of Data Storage Systems, Ministry of Education of China, P.R. China

Abstract. Scalability and fault tolerance become a fundamental challenge of data center network structure due to the explosive growth of data. Both structures proposed in the area of parallel computing and structures based on tree hierarchy are not able to satisfy these two demands. In this paper, we propose Totoro, a scalable and fault-tolerant network to handle the challenges by using backup built-in Ethernet ports. We connect a bunch of servers to an intra-switch to form a basic partition. Then we utilize half of backup ports to connect those basic partitions with inter-switches to build a larger partition. Totoro is hierarchically and recursively defined and the high-level Totoro is constructed by many low-level Totoros. Totoro can scale to millions of nodes. We also design a fault-tolerant routing protocol. Its capability is very close to the performance bound. Our experiments show that Totoro is a viable interconnection structure for data centers.

Keywords: Data Center, Interconnection Network, Scalability, Fault Tolerance, Backup Port.

1   Introduction

With the development of information digitization, large amounts of data is being created exponentially every day in various fields, such as industrial manufacturing, e-commerce, and social network, etc. For example, 72 hours of video are uploaded to YouTube every minute [1]. 1 billion active Facebook users upload 250 million photos every day. If these photos are printed and piled, the height would be as tall as 80 Eiffel Towers [2]. A report from IDC even shows that 1,800EB data has been created in 2011 with a 40-60% annual increase [3]. As data increases exponentially, the scale of data centers has been increased sharply.

In recent years, governments and multinational corporations are racing to invest amounts of money to build many large data centers. For instance, Google has already

C.-H. Hsu et al. (Eds.): NPC 2013, LNCS 8147, pp. 94–105, 2013.
© IFIP International Federation for Information Processing 2013

had 19 data centers where there are more than 1 million servers. Some corporations, such as Facebook, Microsoft, Amazon, eBay and so on, have hundreds of thousands of servers in their own data centers. In this case, scalability becomes a necessary condition for data centers.

With the increasing scale of data centers, failures become quite common in the cloud environment. Failures from software, hardware, outage or even overheat will have a significant impact upon the running applications. For example, Amazon EC2 and RDS failed for several days, leading to the stoppage of some famous corporations [4]. Google also reports that 5 nodes will fail during a MapReduce job and 1 disk will fail every 6 hours in a 4,000-node cluster running MapReduce [5]. Hence, failures and their damages make fault tolerance a big challenge in the cloud environment.

In current practice, most of data centers are tree-based. At the top of its hierarchy, a tree-based data center provides the Internet services by core-routers or core-switches. However, there are three weaknesses about the top-level switches. Firstly, they can easily become the bandwidth bottleneck. Secondly, if one port fails, it will make its subtrees all isolated. In other words, they are the single points of failure. Thirdly, top-level switches are so expansive that updating will cause the steep rise in cost. In summary, tree-based structure lacks enough scalability and fault tolerance.

Fat-Tree [6] is an improved tree-based structure. It scales out with a large number of links and mini-switches. By using more redundant switches, Fat-Tree provides higher network capacity than traditional tree-based structures. But the scalability of Fat-Tree is still limited by the ports of switches fundamentally. DCell [7] is a level-based, recursively defined interconnection structure. It typically requires multiport (e.g., 3, 4 or 5) servers. DCell scales doubly exponentially with the server node degree. It is also fault tolerant and supports high network capacity. But the downside of DCell is that it trades-off the expensive core switches/routers with multiport NICs and higher wiring cost. FiConn [8] is also a new server-interconnection structure. It utilizes servers with two built-in ports and low-end commodity switches to form the structure. FiConn has a lower wiring cost than DCell. Routing in FiConn also makes a balanced use of links at different levels and is traffic-aware to better utilize the link capacities. However, the downside of FiConn is that it has lower aggregate network capacity.

Besides the structures mentioned above, there are various interconnection solutions presented in recent years, such as Portland [9], VL2 [10], CamCube [11] and so forth. These structures have their advantages in some aspects, yet they still have some deficiencies. In contrast to the existing work, we propose a new interconnection structure called Totoro. It utilizes commodity server machines with two ports as FiConn does. When constructing a high-level Totoro, the low-level Totoros use half of their available backup ports for interconnections as well. Totoro and FiConn share the similar principle to place the interconnection intelligence onto servers. In FiConn, all communication between two partitions flows through a unique link. This brings severe forwarding load to the servers at each end of this link. Unlike FiConn, there is no direct link between any two servers in Totoro. All servers communicate with each other through switches. There are multiple links connecting two partitions directly. All the data that flows from one partition to another partition can be distributed to these links. This lowers the forwarding load and makes the transmission more efficient. Totoro scales exponentially with the hierarchical level. A 3-level Totoro can hold more than 1-billion servers by using 32-port switches. Totoro is also fault tolerant, benefiting from multi-redundant links, which provides high network capacity. We also design a fault-tolerant routing mechanism, whose capacity is very close to that of shortest path algorithm (SP) with lower traffic and computation overhead.

2   Totoro Interconnection Network

2.1   Totoro Architecture

Totoro is recursively defined. It consists of a series of commodity servers with two ports and low-end switches. We connect N servers to an N-port switch to form the basic partition of Totoro, denoted by $Totoro_0$. We call this N-port switch intra-switch. Each server in $Totoro_0$ is connected to an intra-switch by using one port and the rest of ports are called available ports. If consider a $Totoro_0$ as a virtual server, we denote the number of available ports in a $Totoro_0$ as c. Obviously, there is c = N. Next, we connect each $Totoro_0$ to n-port switches by using c/2 ports. Each $Totoro_0$ is connected to c/2 switches and each switch is connected to n $Totoro_0$s. Now we get a larger partition, which is denoted by $Totoro_1$ (e.g., in Figure 1). By analogy, we connect n $Totoro_{i-1}$s to n-port switches to build a $Totoro_i$ in the similar way. Note that, we will never connect switches with switches. We call a switch connecting different partitions an inter-switch. In a $Totoro_i$, switches and links connecting different $Totoro_{i-1}$s are called level-i switches and level-i links respectively. Peculiarly, the level of intra-switch is 0.

Table 1. Useful denotations and their meanings in the following text

Denotation	Meaning
N	The number of ports on an intra-switch.
n	The number of ports on an inter-switch.
K	The top level in a Totoro.
$Totoro_i$	An ith level Totoro.
c_i	The number of available ports in a $Totoro_i$.
$[a_K, a_{K-1}, ..., a_i, ..., a_1, a_0]$	A (K+1)-tuple to denote a server, $a_i < n$ (0 < i ⩽ K) indicates which $Totoro_{i-1}$ this server is located at and $a_0 < N$ indicates the index of this server in that $Totoro_0$.
$(u - b_{K-u}, b_{K-u+1}, ..., b_i, ..., b_1, b_0)$	A combination of an integer and a (K-u+1)-tuple to denote a switch, u ⩽ K indicates that it is a level-u switch, $b_i < n$ (0 < i ⩽ K-u) indicates which $Totoro_{u+i-1}$ this switch is located at and b_0 indicates the index of this switch among level-u switches in that $Totoro_u$.

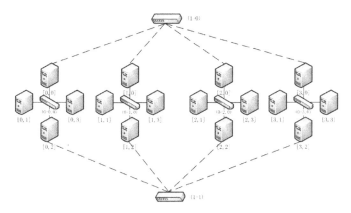

Fig. 1. A $Totoro_1$ structure with N = 4, n = 4. It is composed of 4 $Totoro_0$. Each $Totoro_0$ has 4 servers and an intra-switch with 4 ports. 4 $Totoro_0$ connect through 2 inter-switches.

If the inter-switch has n ports, we note that the number of child partitions in a parent partition is also n. If we denote the number of available ports in a $Totoro_i$ as c_i, there is $c_i = c_{i-1} * n/2$. This is because a $Totoro_i$ has n $Totoro_{i-1}$s and we connect each $Totoro_{i-1}$ to $c_i/2$ inter-switches (level-i) by using half of its available ports ($c_{i-1}/2$). It implies that the number of paths among $Totoro_i$s is n/2 times of the number of paths among $Totoro_{i-1}$s. Multiple paths make the routing protocol robust and fault tolerant. Totoro can communicate in the presence of failures with redundant links. Furthermore, the number of high-level links is n/2 times of the number of low-level links means that high-level links will not be the bottleneck of the system and Totoro has high network capacity.

At the structure of Totoro, there are several inter-switches between two partitions. Servers in a $Totoro_i$ ($0 \leq i < K$) can access servers in another $Totoro_i$ directly by multiple paths without any other $Totoro_i$. For instance, in Figure 1, server [0, 1] wants to access [1, 1]. Under normal circumstances, we can choose the path [0, 1], (0-0, 0), [0, 0], (1-0), [1, 0], (0-1, 0), [1, 1]. Assume that the link between [0, 0] and (1-0) fails, this path is unavailable now. In this case, we can choose another path [0, 1], (0-0, 0), [0, 2], (1-1), [1, 2], (0-1, 0), [1, 1]. It is still the communication between two $Totoro_0$s without any other ones. Therefore, the structure of Totoro reduces the accessing distance between servers.

Observing the structure of Totoro, we find that not all servers are connected to inter-switches. In our design philosophy, we retain a large number of available ports for expanding. Thus, our Totoro is open and convenient to be expanded. We propose expanding Totoro by increasing the hierarchical level rather than updating the switches. This helps reduce the costs of devices and management in data centers. Without high-end devices, our Totoro also scales exponentially and we will discuss about this in Section 2.2.

Algorithm 1. Totoro Building Algorithm

```
0    TotoroBuild(N, n, K) {
1      Define t_K = N * n^K
2      Define server = [a_K, a_K-1, ..., a_i, ..., a_1, a_0]
3      For tid = 0 to (t_K - 1)
4        For i = 0 to (K - 1)
5          a_i+1 = (tid / (N * n^i)) mod n
6        a_0 = tid mod N
7        Define intra-switch = (0 - a_K, a_K-1, ..., a_1, a_0)
8        Connect(server, intra-switch)
9        For i = 1 to K
10         If ((tid - 2^i-1 + 1) mod 2^i == 0)
11           Define inter-switch (u - b_K-u, ..., b_i, ..., b_0)
12           u = i
13           For j = i to (K - 1)
14             b_j = (tid / (N * n^j-1)) mod n
15           b_0 = (tid / 2^u) mod (N / n * (n/2)^u)
16           Connect(server, inter-switch)
17   }
```

Table 2. Total number of servers in Totoro$_u$ with different N, n, u

N	n	u	t_u
16	16	2	4096
24	24	2	13824
32	32	2	32768
16	16	3	65536
24	24	3	331776
32	32	3	1048576

2.2   Totoro Building Algorithm

In Totoro, we can indicate a server in two ways: Totoro tuple or Totoro ID. Totoro tuple is a (K+1)-tuple [a_K, a_{K-1}, ..., a_i, ..., a_1, a_0]. It indicates where this server is located clearly and it will help calculate the common partition of two servers. For example, servers [0, 0] and [0, 1] in Figure 1, we know that these two servers are in the same Totoro$_0$[0] due to their common prefix (i.e., [0]). Totoro ID is an unsigned integer, taking a value from t_K (t_K is the total number of servers in a Totoro$_K$). Totoro ID will be used to identify a server uniquely. Note that, the mapping between Totoro tuple and Totoro ID is a bijection. In addition, we denote a switch as a combination of an integer and a (K-u+1)-tuple, (u - b_{K-u}, b_{K-u+1}, ..., b_i,..., b_1, b_0). Algorithm 1 gives the Totoro building algorithm, which follows the principle in Section 2.1. The key in Algorithm 1 is to work out the level of the outgoing link of this server (Line 10).

Theorem 1 describes the total number of servers in Totoro$_u$:

Theorem 1:

$$t_u = N * n^u$$

Proof: A Totoro$_0$ has $t_0 = N$ servers. n Totoro$_0$s are connected to n-port inter-switches to form a Totoro$_1$. Hence, there are $t_1 = n * t_0$ servers in a Totoro$_1$. By analogy, a Totoro$_i$ ($i \leqslant u$) consists of n Totoro$_{i-1}$s and has $t_i = n * t_{i-1}$ servers. Finally, the total number of servers in a Totoro$_u$ is $t_u = N * n^u$.

3   Totoro Routing

3.1   Totoro Routing Algorithm (TRA)

Totoro routing algorithm (TRA) is simple but efficient by using Divide and Conquer algorithm. Assume that we want to work out the path from src to dst: Suppose src and

Algorithm 2. Totoro Building Algorithm

```
0  TotoroRoute(src, dst) {
1    If (src == dst)
2      Return NULL
3    Define k = lowestCommonLevel(src, dst)
4    If (k == 0)        // in the same Totoro₀
5      Return P(src, dst)
6    Else
7      Define P(m, n) = getNearestPath(src, k)
8    Return TotoroRoute(src,m)+P(m,n)+TotoroRoute (n,dst)
9  }
```

Table 3. The mean value and standard deviation of path length in TRA and Shortest Path Algorithm in Totoro$_u$ of different sizes. M_u is the maximum distance between any two servers in Totoro$_u$.

N	n	u	t_u	M_u	TRA		Shortest Path Algorithm	
					Mean	StdDev	Mean	StdDev
24	24	1	576	6	4.36	1.03	4.36	1.03
32	32	1	1024	6	4.40	1.00	4.39	1.00
48	48	1	2304	6	4.43	0.96	4.43	0.96
24	24	2	13824	10	7.61	1.56	7.39	1.32
32	32	2	32768	10	7.68	1.50	7.45	1.26

dst are in the same Totoro$_i$ but two different Totoro$_{i-1}$s. Firstly, there must be a level-i path between these two Totoro$_{i-1}$s. We denote this path as P(m, n), which implies that m and src are in the same Totoro$_{i-1}$, while n and dst are in the same Totoro$_{i-1}$. Then, we work out P(src, m) and P(n, dst) respectively with the same technique. In this process, if we find src and dst are both in the same Totoro$_0$, we just return the directed path between them. Finally, we join the P(src, m), P(m, n) and P(n, dst) for a full path. Algorithm 2 follows the whole process mentioned above. The function getNearest-Path just returns a nearest level-k path to the source host.

The SP that we use is Floyd-Warshall [13] algorithm. From Table 3, we observe that the performance of TRA is close to the SP under the conditions of different sizes. Although the SP is globally optimal, its computation complexity is as high as $O(n^3)$. It is not suitable for routing in data center. Our TRA is efficient enough and much simpler than the SP. Thus, we will build Totoro Fault-tolerant Algorithm based on TRA.

3.2   Totoro Broadcast Domain (TBD)

In order to send the packets with correct paths, servers need to detect and share the link states. Although global link states can help servers work out the optimal path, it is impossible to share the global link states in data center due to its large scale of nodes.

Therefore, we introduce the definition of Totoro Broadcast Domain (TBD) to break up the network. We define a variable called bcLevel for broadcast domain, which means that a Totoro$_{bcLevel}$ is a TBD. The server in a TBD is called inner-server, while the server connected to a TBD with an outgoing link whose level is larger than bcLevel is called outer-server. Take Figure 1 for example, assume that bcLevel = 0. Then Totoro$_0$[0] is a TBD. [1, 0], [2, 0], [3, 0], [1, 2], [2, 2], [3, 2] are the outer-servers of Totoro$_0$[0].

Servers detect the states of links connected to them and broadcast the states to its intra-switch and inter-switch (if it has) periodically. If a server receives a link state packet, it handles the packet based on the following steps: If this packet has ever been received, then just drop it. Otherwise, save the link states and determine whether the packet comes from inter-switch. If so, broadcast it to the intra-switch. If not, broadcast it to the inter-switch if this server is connected to an inter-switch with a link whose level is smaller than bcLevel.

3.3   Totoro Fault-Tolerant Routing (TFR)

In combination of TRA and TBD, we propose a distributed, fault-tolerant routing protocol for Totoro without global link states. Firstly, we give the constraint to bcLevel: bcLevel $\geqslant \log_n(2^K/N)$. It makes sure that every inner-server can find an arbitrary level link in its TBD as well as its link state.

We divide the Totoro network into several TBDs and they are connected by links with level $\geqslant$ bcLevel + 1. We use Dijkstra [12] algorithm for routing within TBD and TRA for routing between TBDs. Take Figure 1 for instance, assume that bcLevel is 0 and we want to find out the path from src[0, 2] to dst[1, 1]. Src and dst are in two different Totoro$_0$. By using TRA, we find that a level-1 link between these two

Algorithm 3. Totoro Fault-tolerant Routing Algorithm

```
0  TotoroRoute(this, pkt) {
1    If (this == pkt.dst) deliver(this, pkt) and Return
2    ElseIf (pkt.proxy == this) pkt.proxy = NULL
3    If (pkt.ttl <= 0) drop(pkt) and Return
4    pkt.ttl -= 1
5    Define next = dijkstraRouting(pkt.dst)
6    If (next == NULL)
7      If (pkt.proxy == NULL)
8        Define k = lowestCommonLevel(this, pkt.dst)
9        Define pathSet = getLocalPaths(this, k)
10       Foreach (m, n) in pathSet
11         next = dijkstraRouting(n)
12         If (next != NULL)
13           pkt.proxy = n
14           Break
15     Else
16       next = dijkstraRouting(pkt.proxy)
17   If (next != NULL) deliver(next, pkt) and Return
18   drop(pkt) and Return
19 }
```

$Totoro_0$ is required. We just get the nearest path P([0, 2], [1, 2]). In the real routing calculation, we just need to work out the next hop. Note that [1, 2] is an outer-server of this TBD. Hence, it can be simplified to work out the path from [0, 2] to [1, 2]. Then by using Dijkstra algorithm, we find that the next hop is [1, 2]. Furthermore, we add a proxy field to the packet header, which means a temporary destination. If this field is not empty, servers just need to find out the next hop to the proxy by using Dijkstra without TRA. After the packet arrives at the proxy, TRA will be used again to find out the next proxy.

If the proxy is unreachable (e.g., P([0, 2], [1, 2]) fails), we can set the proxy as [1, 0]. Then the failure will be bypassed successfully. In conclusion, TRA will be used to find out the proxy on the nearest path firstly. If it fails, TFR will reroute the packet to another proxy by using local redundant links. Moreover, if there exist several available links, TFR can choose one according to a random algorithm or the link load. Algorithm 3 shows the detailed procedure of TFR.

4   Experiment Evaluation

4.1   Evaluating Path Failure

We use simulation to evaluate the performance of Totoro under four types of failures, including link, node, switch and rack failures. In the simulation, we also use SP to compare with our TFR. The SP that we used is based on Floyd-Warshall algorithm

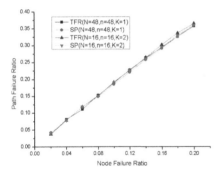

Fig. 2. Path failure ratio vs. node failure ratio

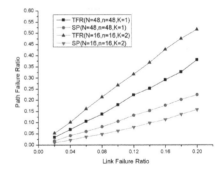

Fig. 3. Path failure ratio vs. link failure ratio

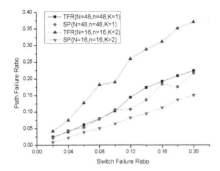

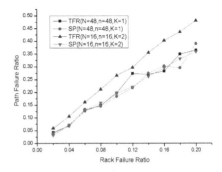

Fig. 4. Path failure ratio vs. switch failure ratio **Fig. 5.** Path failure ratio vs. rack failure ratio

and it offers a performance upper bound under the structure of Totoro. The networks where we run TFR and SP are a $Totoro_1$ (N=48, n=48, K=1, t_K=2,304) and a $Totoro_2$ (N=16, n=16, K=2, t_K=4,096). Each $Totoro_0$ is a rack. Failures are generated randomly and their ratios vary from 2% to 20%. In our simulation, each node routes packets to all the other nodes 20 times. Therefore, each simulation result is an average of 20 running results.

Figure 2 plots the path failure ratio versus the node failure ratio. It shows that the performance of TFR is almost identical to that of SP, regardless of the number of servers. The server failure is quite common as we mention in Section 1 according to [5]. The remarkable capacity of TFR benefits from the technique of rerouting, which maximizes the usage of redundant links when a node failure occurs.

Figure 3 plots the path failure ratio versus the link failure ratio. We observe that the path failure ratio of TFR increases with the link failure ratio. Our TFR performs well when the link failure ratio is small (i.e., lower than 4%). But it can not perform as well as SP when the link failure ratio increases and the performance gap between them becomes larger and larger. For instance, in the same $Totoro_2$ (N=16, n=16, K=2), the gap is about 16% (0.21 - 0.05) when the link failure ratio is 8%. It rises to 32% (0.43 - 0.11) when the link failure ratio increases to 16%. This is because link failure just result in a very few nodes' being disconnected. The SP is global optimal and it always finds out a path from the source to the destination, if it exists. Thus, SP can achieve a good performance even when the link failure ratio is high. But our TFR is not global optimal and not guaranteed to find out an existing path. We also observe that Totoro which holds more servers has a lower path failure ratio. It implies that the integrated capacity of fault tolerance will be more obvious under the condition of a large scale. This enlightens us to improve our TFR because of its huge performance improvement potential on handling link failure.

Figure 4 plots the path failure ratio versus the switch failure ratio. It shows that TFR performs almost as well as SP in $Totoro_1$ (N=48, n=48, K=1). But the performance gap between TFR and SP becomes larger and larger with the increase of switch failure ratio in the same $Totoro_2$ (N=16, n=16, K=2). We also observe that path failure ratio of SP is lower in a larger-level Totoro. It means that more redundant high-level switches help bypass the failure rather than become the single points of failure. Given this, our future work will be devoted to improving the performance of TFR under switch failure.

In our simulation, we also study the relationship between the rack failure and the path failure. We select a rack randomly and make all the nodes and links in this rack fail. Figure 5 plots the path failure ratio versus the rack failure ratio. It shows that in a low-level Totoro (e.g., $Totoro_1$), TFR achieves results very close to SP. But the capacity of TFR in a relative high-level Totoro (e.g., $Totoro_2$) could be improved. However, TFR performs still well enough when the rack failure ratio is lower than 10%.

4.2   Evaluating Network Structure

In this section, we compare Totoro with traditional Tree structure and several recent structures of Fat-Tree, DCell and FiConn to evaluate our network structure. Table 4 summarizes the topological property comparison result of different network structures. We denote the total number of servers as T.

The node degree of Totoro or FiConn approaches to 2 as k grows, but will never reach 2. They all achieve a smaller node degree than DCell, which means a lower deployment and maintenance overhead. Furthermore, Totoro and FiConn are always incomplete and highly scalable by using available backup ports.

As we all know, the smaller the diameter is, the more efficient the routing mechanism will be. The diameter of Tree is $2\log_{d-1}T$, where d is the number of switch ports. Fat-Tree has a diameter of $2\log_2T$. The upper bound of diameter of DCell is $2\log_nT-1$. And the diameter of FiConn is $O(\log T)$. They all achieve a relative small diameter. It seems that Totoro has a large diameter. But it is not accurate in practice. A low-level Totoro can hold hundreds of thousands or even millions of servers, e.g., a $Totoro_2$

Table 4. Topological property comparison of different network structures

Structure	Degree	Diameter	Bisection Width
Tree	--	$2\log_{d-1}T$	1
Fat-Tree	--	$2\log_2T$	T/2
DCell	$k + 1$	$<2\log_nT-1$	$T/4\log_nT$
FiConn	$2 - 1/2^k$	$O(\log T)$	$O(T/\log T)$
Totoro	$2 - 1/2^k$	$O(T)$	$T/2^{k+1}$

with $N = n = 48$ has 110,592 servers and a $Totoro_3$ with $N = n = 32$ has 1,048,576 servers. However, the diameters of $Totoro_2$ and $Totoro_3$ are only 10 and 18, respectively. In addition, even though the diameters of Tree and Fat-Tree are both small, they can not be comparable with Totoro since their scalability is limited by the number of switch ports.

Tree structure has a bisection width of 1 because each server or switch has only one path to the upper node. The failure of one path will make their subtrees all isolated. What's more, high-level links will become the bandwidth bottleneck. Fat-Tree overcomes these problems by using more redundant switches near the root in its hierarchy. It has a large bisection width of $T/2$. DCell has a large bisection width of $T/4long_nT$ since it has more ports on a server. And the bisection width of FiConn is $O(T/log(T))$. Totoro also has a relative large bisection width of $T/2^{k+1}$. As we have mentioned above, a low-level Totoro can hold a large number of servers. When we take a small number of k, the bisection width is large, e.g., BiW=$T/4$, $T/8$, $T/16$ when $k = 1, 2, 3$, respectively. A large bisection width means a fault-tolerant and resilient structure. Thus, we can draw a conclusion that Totoro is fault-tolerant both in the topological analysis and from the path failure evaluating above. In addition, a relative large bisection width also leads to a higher network capacity.

In a word, Totoro gains the good scalability, fault tolerance and relative high network capacity. These attractive properties all meet the current requirement of data centers. Hence, our Totoro is a viable interconnection solution for data centers.

5   Conclusion

Structures neither proposed in the area of parallel computing nor based on tree hierarchy in current practice meet the requirements of scalability and fault tolerance. This drives us to present a new structure called Totoro. Then we detail the physical structure of Totoro. It is hierarchically and recursively defined. Through topological property analysis we know that Totoro scales exponentially and it is convenient to expand Totoro by using backup built-in Ethernet ports. In addition, we elaborate a distributed and fault-tolerant routing protocol called TFR, which is designed to handle various failures. The experiments show that its capability of handling fault tolerance is very close to that of the SP, especially in the presence of server failure. Furthermore, TFR significantly reduces the network traffic of sharing link states and the computation overhead. Lastly, we compare Totoro with other interconnection structures in some aspects, including node degree, diameter, and bisection width. It shows that Totoro is able to satisfy the demands of scalability and fault tolerance. In a word, topological analysis, experiments and comparison prove that Totoro is a viable interconnection solution for data centers. One problem faced by Totoro is the failure handling under some kinds of failures. Failure handling depends largely on fault-tolerant algorithm. We have seen the huge performance improvement potential from TFR. In the future work, we will be devoted to solving this problem by using more techniques, such as multiplexing and retouring based on remote proxy.

Acknowledgments. We would like to thank the anonymous reviewers for helping us refine this paper. Their constructive comments and suggestions are very helpful. This work is supported by the National Natural Science Foundation (NSF) of China under grant (No.61272073, No. 61073064), the Scientific Research Foundation for the Returned Overseas Chinese Scholars (State Education Ministry), the Educational Commission of Guangdong Province (No. 2012KJCX0013), the Science and Technology Planning Project of Guangdong Province (No.2012A080102002), the Science and Technology Planning Project of Guangzhou (No. 2012J4100109), Open Research Fund of Key Laboratory of Computer System and Architecture, Institute of Computing Technology, Chinese Academy of Sciences (CARCH201107). The corresponding author of this paper is Yuhui Deng.

References

1. Statistics-YouTube, `http://www.youtube.com/t/press_statistics`
2. A Typical Day In the Internet, `http://www.mbaonline.com`
3. Gantz, J.F., Chute, C.: The diverse and exploding digital universe: An updated forecast of worldwide information growth through 2011. In: IDC (2008)
4. Ten worst cloud crashes in 2011, `http://www.ctocio.com/hotnews/2370.html`
5. Dean, J.: Experiences with MapReduce, an abstraction for large-scale computation. In: PACT: 15th International Conference on Parallel Architectures and Compilation Techniques, vol. 16(20), p. 1. ACM (2006)
6. Al-Fares, M., Loukissas, A., Vahdat, A.: A scalable, commodity data center network architecture. ACM SIGCOMM Computer Communication Review 38(4), 63–74 (2008)
7. Guo, C., Wu, H., Tan, K., Shi, L., Zhang, Y., Lu, S.: Dell: a scalable and fault-tolerant network structure for data centers. ACM SIGCOMM Computer Communication Review 38(4), 75–86 (2008)
8. Li, D., Guo, C., Wu, H., Tan, K., Zhang, Y., Lu, S.: FiConn: Using backup port for server interconnection in data centers. In: IEEE INFOCOM 2009, pp. 2276-2285. IEEE (2009)
9. Niranjan Mysore, R., Pamboris, A., Farrington, N., Huang, N., Miri, P., Radhakrishnan, S., Vahdat, A.: PortLand: a scalable fault-tolerant layer 2 data center network fabric. ACM SIGCOMM Computer Communication Review 39(4), 39–50 (2009)
10. Greenberg, A., Hamilton, J.R., Jain, N., Kandula, S., Kim, C., Lahiri, P., Sengupta, S.: VL2: a scalable and flexible data center network. ACM SIGCOMM Computer Communication Review 39(4), 51–62 (2009)
11. Costa, P., Donnelly, A., O'shea, G., Rowstron, A.: CamCube: a key-based data center. Technical Report MSR TR-2010-74, Microsoft Research (2010)
12. Dijkstra, E.W.: A note on two problems in connexion with graphs. Numerische Mathematik 1(1), 269–271 (1959)
13. Floyd, R.W.: Algorithm 97: shortest path. Communications of the ACM 5(6), 345 (1962)
14. Deng, Y.: RISC: A resilient interconnection network for scalable cluster storage systems. Journal of Systems Architecture 54(1), 70–80 (2008)
15. Parhami, B.: Introduction to parallel processing: algorithms and architectures. Series in Computer Science, vol. 1. Springer, Heidelberg (2006)
16. Loguinov, D., Kumar, A., Rai, V., Ganesh, S.: Graph-theoretic analysis of structured peer-to-peer systems: routing distances and fault resilience. In: Proceedings of the 2003 Conference on Applications, Technologies, Architectures, and Protocols for Computer Communications, pp. 395–406. ACM (2003)
17. Barroso, L.A., Dean, J., Holzle, U.: Web search for a planet: The Google cluster architecture. Micro IEEE 23(2), 22–28 (2003)

A Cloud Resource Allocation Mechanism Based on Mean-Variance Optimization and Double Multi-Attribution Auction

Chengxi Gao, Xingwei Wang, and Min Huang

College of Information Science and Technology, Northeastern University
Shenyang, P.R. China
gaocxresearch@gmail.com, {wangxw,mhuang}@mail.neu.edu.cn

Abstract. As a new kind of commercial model, cloud computing can integrate various kinds of resources in the network. Resource providers offer these resources to users in the form of service and receive corresponding profits. To make more rational use of the cloud resources, an effective mechanism is necessary for allocating the resources. In this paper, the price attribution and non-price attributions of both traders are analyzed. The support vector machine algorithm is utilized to predict the price, further determining the quote and bid. Then, the BP neural network algorithm is used to transfer the non-price attributions to the quality index. Finally, to maximize the total satisfaction of resource providers and resource consumers, the mean-variance optimization algorithm is adopted to obtain the optimized cloud resource allocation scheme. Simulation results have shown that the proposed mechanism is feasible and effective.

Keywords: Cloud resource, Double multi-attribution auction, BP neural network, Support vector machine, Mean-variance optimization.

1   Introduction

Cloud computing is the development of distributed computing, parallel computing, grid computing and many other technologies [1]. It can integrate various types of resources in the network, so that they can be fully utilized. Therefore, a robust resource allocation mechanism has become the focus of researches about cloud computing which can specify the billing functionalities of the system and efficiently allocate the resources while bringing the most profits.

Contemporarily, auction theory has been successfully used in solving the problem of resource allocation in many cases, which has shown good performance. Danak et al. presented a repeated auction-based allocation protocol and a utility-maximizing bidding algorithm to improve the long-term profits of the grid users [2], but they didn't consider the fraud behavior in the market mechanism. Lan et al. proposed a multi-unit Continuous Double Auction (CDA) and got a reasonable resource allocation scheme to ensure fairness between users [3], but they didn't consider the fraud behavior of the users. Tan et al. proposed a novel Stable Continuous Double Auction (SCDA) mechanism which effectively reduced the instable factors of CDA and brought good

C.-H. Hsu et al. (Eds.): NPC 2013, LNCS 8147, pp. 106–117, 2013.
© IFIP International Federation for Information Processing 2013

economic returns [4], but the mechanism was weak in the consideration of the malicious bidding behavior of users. Prodan et al. determined the resource allocation model based on the CDA mechanism [5], but they didn't predict the market price.

Besides, game theory is also practical in the area of resource allocation. Teng et al. proposed a resource pricing and allocation policy through game theory which solved the equilibrium allocation problem among different users [6], but they didn't consider the malicious bidding behavior of users. Mutz et al. designed a resource pricing mechanism based on game theory and scheduled jobs and computed payments in pseudo-polynomial time [7], but they didn't consider the Quality of Service (QoS). Wang et al. determined the transaction price through the linear pricing strategy, and used the game-theoretic algorithm to get the optimized bandwidth resource allocation scheme [8], but they didn't consider the information of historical transactions.

To sum up, the majorities of existing researches only care about the price attribution, but ignore the non-price attributions in transactions. Moreover, they lack the careful consideration about the fraud behaviors in the market mechanisms and don't forecast reasonably about the market price based on historical information.

In this paper, according to the Support Vector Machine (SVM) and Back Propagation (BP) neural network, we propose a cloud resource allocation mechanism based on Mean-Variance Optimization (MVO) algorithm and double multi-attribution auction (DMAA) mechanism. The prices of both traders are forecast based on SVM algorithm, and the non-price attributions of resource providers and resource consumers are converted into the quality indexes based on BP neural network algorithm. Combined with the DMAA mechanism, the cloud resource allocation scheme is obtained based on the MVO algorithm which aims to maximize the total satisfaction of both trades while increasing the resource utilization of providers and satisfying more consumers.

The rest of this paper is organized as follows. We introduce the system framework in Sect.2, and the auction model is discussed in Sect. 3. We talk about how to predict the price using SVM algorithm in Sect. 4 and multi-attribution processing is specified based on BP neural network algorithm in Sect. 5. We design a resource allocation scheme based on MVO algorithm in Sect. 6. The proposed mechanism is simulated and evaluated in Sect. 7 and we conclude the paper in Sect. 8.

2   System Framework

The cloud system mainly involves three roles including resource provider (*RP*), resource consumer (*RC*) and auction organizer (*AO*). The system framework is presented in Fig. 1.

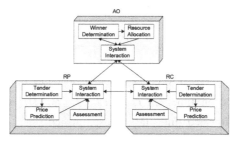

Fig. 1. System framework

As is shown in Fig. 1, the process of the system is specified as follows:

Step1: *RP* and *RC* submit their own information to *AO* to confirm the identity;

Step2: *RP* and *RC* use SVM algorithm to predict the prices and submit them to *AO* ;

Step3: If there is a matching transaction, then go to Step4.Otherwise *RP* and *RC* are notified to confirm whether or not they are willing to stay in the auction. If they are, they need to re-determine the price according to SVM algorithm and then submit the new tenders to *AO* . Otherwise they will quit the auction or wait for the next auction considering their own situation;

Step4: According to the matching results of the transaction, *AO* uses BP neural network algorithm to transfer the non-price attributions to the quality index and adopts the MVO algorithm to solve the cloud resource allocation scheme;

Step5: *AO* notifies *RP* and *RC* to update the quote and bid respectively to participate in the new round of the auction until the end;

Step6: *RC* who receives the resources pays for the service to the corresponding *RP* , and they assess each other for his performance after the transaction. *AO* updates the corresponding information.

3   Auction Model

3.1   Resource Provider

Multi-Attributions of Resource Provider. When analyzing *RP* 's trading behavior, we put forward three non-price attributions including *RP* 's quality of service (QoS_S), level of delivery (LoD_S) and level of spiteful quote ($LoSQ_S$).

Quality of Service. QoS_S is used to measure the quality of the resources that *RP* provides. $g_i \in \{1,2,3,\cdots,M\}$ represents the grade that the i-th resource consumer (RC_i) gives to *RP* where M is the total amount of *RCs* . *RP* 's quality of service in this transaction (QoS_S^{this}) is defined as in Eqn.(1) .

$$QoS_S^{this} = \frac{1}{M}\sum_{i=1}^{M} g_i \tag{1}$$

Devote *RP* 's quality of service for the last H transactions by QoS_S^{old} , so after this transaction, QoS_S is defined as in Eqn. (2).

$$QoS_S = \frac{H \cdot QoS_S^{old} + QoS_S^{this}}{H+1} \tag{2}$$

Level of Delivery. LoD_S is used to check whether or not *RP* delivers the usage rights of the resources to *RC* on time. $TEFT_B^i$, $TLFT_B^i$, TL_B^i and DT^i respectively represent RC_i 's task expected finished time, task latest finished time, task length and deal time. *RP* 's level of delivery for RC_i is devoted by LoD_i which is specified in Eqn. (3).

$$
LoD_i = \begin{cases} 0, & DT^i < TEFT_B^i - TL_B^i \ \ or \ \ DT^i > TLFT_B^i - TL_B^i \\ \dfrac{(1-\alpha)\left(DT^i - TLFT_B^i + TL_B^i\right)^2}{\left(TEFT_B^i - TLFT_B^i\right)^2} + \alpha, & TEFT_B^i - TL_B^i \le DT^i \le TLFT_B^i - TL_B^i \end{cases} \tag{3}
$$

Where $TEFT_B^i \ne TLFT_B^i$ and α is constant which is used to adjust the value of LoD_i.

So LoD_S is defined as in Eqn. (4).

$$
LoD_S = \frac{1}{M} \sum_{i=1}^{M} LoD_i \tag{4}
$$

Level of Spiteful Quote. $LoSQ_S$ is used to check whether or not *RP* has the behavior of spiteful quote or disrupting the auction market. p is the price of the resources that *RP* provides, *top* and *bottom* represent the upper and lower limits of the resource price that *AO* sets, *most* and *least* devote the highest and lowest trading price of the resources. So $LoSQ_S$ is specified in Eqn. (5).

$$
LoSQ_S = \begin{cases} 1 & , 0 < p < bottom \\ \dfrac{(p - \alpha \cdot least)^2}{(bottom - \alpha \cdot least)^2}, & bottom \le p < \alpha \cdot least \\ 0 & , \alpha \cdot least \le p \le \beta \cdot most \\ \dfrac{(p - \beta \cdot most)^2}{(top - \beta \cdot most)^2}, & \beta \cdot most < p \le top \\ 1 & , \ p > top \end{cases} \tag{5}
$$

Where α and β are constant which are used to adjust the value of $LoSQ_S$.

Satisfaction of Resource Provider. S_S^i is the satisfaction of *RP* when transacting with RC_i. X represents a kind of resources that *RP* sells. EDP_S^X and RP_S^X are the expected deal price and reserve price of this kind of resource respectively that *RP* wants to sell. $DP^{i,X}$ is the deal price and $IoQ_B^{i,X}$ represents the quality index which is calculated in Sect.5. $S_S^{i,X}$ represents the satisfaction which is specified in Eqn.(6) .

$$
S_S^{i,X} = \begin{cases} 1 & , DP^{i,X} \ge EDP_S^X \\ \beta \cdot \left(\dfrac{DP^{i,X}}{EDP_S^X} + \alpha \cdot IoQ_B^{i,X}\right), & RP_S^X \le DP^{i,X} < EDP_S^X \\ 0 & , DP^{i,X} < RP_S^X \end{cases} \tag{6}
$$

Where α and β are constant which are used to adjust the value of $S_S^{i,X}$.

As is shown in Eqn. (6),when X represents hard disk, CPU, memory or bandwidth, we can accordingly calculate $S_S^{i,harddisk}$, $S_S^{i,cpu}$, $S_S^{i,memory}$ or $S_S^{i,bandwidth}$ which respectively represents the satisfaction when transacting corresponding kind of resources. If RP and RC_i don't trade a kind of resources such as CPU, then $S_S^{i,cpu} = 0$. So S_S^i is defined as in Eqn. (7).

$$S_S^i = \frac{1}{4}\left(S_S^{i,cpu} + S_S^{i,memory} + S_S^{i,harddisk} + S_S^{i,bandwidth} \right) \tag{7}$$

S_S represents the total satisfaction of RP's transactions with $RC_1, RC_2, \cdots, RC_M$ and is defined as in Eqn.(8) .

$$S_S = \frac{1}{M}\sum_{i=1}^{M} S_S^i \tag{8}$$

3.2   Resource Consumer

Multi-Attributions of Resource Consumer. When analyzing RC's trading behavior, we put forward two non-price attributions including RC's level of payment (LoP_B) and level of spiteful bid ($LoSB_B$). LoP_B and $LoSB_B$ are quantified similarly as LoD_S and $LoSQ_S$ which have been defined previously, so we don't repeat the quantification here.

Satisfaction of Resource Consumer. S_B^i is the satisfaction of RC when transacting with RP_i (the i-th resource provider). It is similar to S_S^i ,so we don't repeat the definition here.

3.3   Auction Organizer

When the auction starts, AO submits RP's quote to the quote queue and RC's bid to the bid queue respectively. The quote queue is sorted in ascending order and *lowest_quote* represents the one at the head of the quote queue. The bid queue is sorted in descending order and *highest_bid* represents the one at the head of the bid queue.

   AO has to check whether or not there are transactions that satisfy the condition for matching which is specified as *highest_bid* $\geq$ *lowest_quote* .

4   Price Prediction

4.1   SVM Algorithm

The goal of SVM algorithm [9] is to select a function $f(\vec{x}, \vec{\alpha})$ from the regression estimation function set $\{f(\vec{x}, \alpha)\}$ which can express the mapping relationship between $\vec{x}$ and $\vec{y}$. Then we can adopt $f(\vec{x}, \vec{\alpha})$ to predict $\vec{y}$ when given $\vec{x}$.

   In this paper, we adopt symmetric overrelaxation preprocessing technology [10] to reduce the conditions of the coefficient matrix of the linear equations which can decrease the iteration time of the algorithm, thus speeding up the convergence rate and weakening the influence that rounding errors have on SVM.

4.2   Price Prediction Method Based on SVM Algorithm

In this paper, we use exponential smoothing method to predict the relationship between supply and demand. sd_j represents the j-th relationship between supply and demand in previous transactions, SA_0 represents the initial predicted value and SA_j represents the j-th predicted value which is defined in Eqn.(9).

$$SA_j = \alpha \cdot \sum_{i=0}^{j-2}(1-\alpha)^i \cdot sd_{j-1-i} + (1-\alpha)^j \cdot SA_0 \tag{9}$$

Where $1 \le j \le n+1$, α is the smoothing coefficient and $0 \le \alpha \le 1$.

The structure of RP's training samples is consisted of RP's quality index (IoQ_S), reserve price (RP_S), the relationship between supply and demand (SD), remaining sale amount (RSA_S) and predicted sale price (PSP).

The structure of RC's training samples is consisted of RC's quality index (IoQ_B), reserve price (RP_B), SD ,task urgency degree (TUD) and predicted buying price (PBP).

The process of predicting the price based on SVM algorithm is as follows:

Step1: If there is a trained SVM, then go to Step 3. Otherwise, initialize the training sample set and determine the parameters of SVM algorithm such as the error threshold and maximum iteration time;

Step2: Train SVM using the training samples and update the weights. Then save the trained SVM;

Step3: Utilize the trained SVM to predict the price and generate the sample corresponding to this price prediction as the training sample which is then added to the training sample set;

Step4: If the maximum iteration time is not reached, then go to Step 2; otherwise, output the prices and the algorithm ends.

5   Multi-Attribution Processing

5.1   BP Neural Network Algorithm

The structure of BP neural network [11] is consisted of input layer, hidden layer and output layer where input layer and output layer are single layers while hidden layer can be a single layer or multiple layers. The learning process of BP neural network [12-14] includes the forward propagation and the error back propagation of the signal. These two processes are carried out circularly until the output error of BP neural network is less than the minimum error or the preset training time is reached.

In this paper, Sigmoid function [15] is utilized as the activation function to train the samples. The weights of the BP neural network are updated after training for W times where W is constant. Variable learning rate is adopted to adjust the decline rate of errors dynamically in the process of training. Inertia factor is used to measure the impact that the weight increments of previous trainings have on the weights of current training. Chaos noise [16] is introduced into the process of weight updating so as to improve the error back-propagation process and the ability of jumping out of a local minimum point, thus enhancing the learning ability of BP neural network algorithm.

5.2   Multi-Attribution Processing Method Based on BP Neural Network Algorithm

The structure of RP 's training samples is consisted of QoS_S , LoD_S , $LoSQ_S$ and IoQ_S

The structure of RC 's training samples is consisted of LoP_B , $LoSB_B$ and IoQ_B .

The process of applying BP neural network algorithm to multi-attribution processing method is as follows:

Step1: If there is a trained BP neural network, then go to Step 3. Otherwise, initialize the training sample set and determine the parameters of BP neural network algorithm such as the error threshold and maximum iteration time;

Step2: Train the BP neural network using training samples and adjust the weights. Then save the trained BP neural network;

Step3: Utilize the trained BP neural network to transfer the non-price attributions to the quality index and generate the sample corresponding to this multi-attribution processing as the training sample which is then added to the training sample set;

Step4: If the maximum iteration time is not reached, then go to Step 2; otherwise, output the quality index and the algorithm ends.

6   Resource Allocation

In this paper, the total satisfaction of RC and RP is used as the fitness function in order to determine whether or not the allocation scheme is good.

6.1   MVO Algorithm

MVO algorithm [17] is a kind of intelligent optimization algorithms. The basic idea is to use the mean and variance of the components of the solution vectors to evolve the solution set and find the optimal solution by iteration.

6.2   Resource Allocation Based on MVO Algorithm

Step1: Determine the amount of resources of this transaction namely TA and in-itialize the related parameters of MVO algorithm such as the maximum iteration time and the dimension of variation which is devoted by c . Generate a random initial solution X according to TA ;

Step2: Calculate the fitness function value. If the termination condition is satisfied, then go to Step 5;

Step3: Create the $n-best$ population where $n-best$ population represents the set of the top n best solutions when all of the solutions are sorted in descending order according to the fitness function value. Then calculate the mean and variance of the components of the solution vectors. Choose the solution with the largest fitness function value as the father solution X_{father} ;

Step4: Randomly select c components from X_{father} and evolve and update the selected components to get the child solutions, and then go to Step2;

Step5: Output the optimal resource allocation scheme and the algorithm ends.

7   Simulation and Evaluation

The resource allocation mechanism is implemented and evaluated based on JDK and Cloudsim on the Eclipse platform. There are 200 RPs and 150 RCs participating in the auction. The parameters of the proposed algorithms are detailed in Table 1, Table 2 and Table 3. A set of cloud resource prices is selected from Amazon as is shown in Table 4, which acts as the reference of RP 's quote and RC 's bid.

Table 1. Relative Parameters to BP Neural Network Algorithm

Relative parameter	Value
Input layer node number	1
Hidden layer node number	20
Output layer node number	1
Error threshold	0.01
Number of training samples	400
Maximum iteration time	1000

Table 2. Relative Parameters to SVM Algorithm

Relative parameter	Value
Error threshold	0.01
Penalty coefficient	100
Regularization parameter	100
Maximum iteration time	1000

Table 3. Relative Parameters to MVO Algorithm

Relative parameter	Value
Scale of n-best population	10
Dimension of the solutions	4
Dimension of variation	3
Asymmetry factor	0.1
Maximum iteration time	1000

Table 4. Prices of Cloud Servers

Server Size			Linux		Windows	
RAM	Disk	Network Bandwidth	Hourly	Estimated Monthly	Hourly	Estimated Monthly
256MB	10GB	10Mbps	$0.010	$7.30	-	-
512MB	20GB	20Mbps	$0.020	$14.60	-	-
1024MB	40GB	30Mbps	$0.040	$29.20	$0.053	$37.96
2048MB	80GB	40Mbps	$0.080	$58.40	$0.106	$75.92
4096MB	160GB	50Mbps	$0.160	$116.80	$0.212	$151.84
8192MB	320GB	60Mbps	$0.320	$233.60	$0.424	$303.68
15872MB	620GB	70Mbps	$0.640	$467.20	$0.848	$607.36
30720MB	1200GB	80Mbps	$1.217	$876.00	$1.606	$1156.30

In this paper, SCDA mechanism [4] is used as the benchmark double auction mechanism which acts as the reference of the performance compared with the proposed DMAA mechanism. SCDA adds a compulsory bidding adjustment layer (CBAL) based on the traditional CDA mechanism. When RP and RC submit the prices to AO , CBAL will delete the unreasonable prices according to the historical trading prices and the supply and demand of resources. Meanwhile, SCDA sets the task queue to save the tasks to be finished and the task queue is sorted in descending order according to the bids. All of the RPs calculate the price needed to complete the first task in the task queue. If there exists RP whose quote is less than the price, then the RP with the lowest quote can transact with the RC corresponding to the first task of the task queue.

7.1   The Comparison of Resource Utilization Rate of Resource Providers

We compare the resource utilization rate of RP between the two auction mechanisms in three cases when the supply exceeds the demand, the supply equals the demand and the supply is less than the demand. The results are presented in Fig.2.

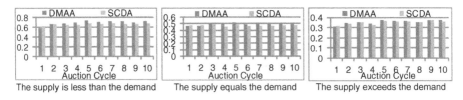

Fig. 2. The comparison of resource utilization rate

As is shown in Fig.2, at the beginning of the auction, the resource utilization rate of DMAA mechanism is slightly lower than that of SCDA mechanism. With the auction going on, the resource utilization rate of DMAA mechanism is higher than that of

SCDA mechanism. This is because that the price prediction method used in the DMAA mechanism requires a process of collecting the training samples and learning, and at the beginning of the auction, the price prediction method is still in the process of learning, so the excellent performance of the method seems vague, thus the resource utilization rate of DMAA mechanism is lower than that of SCDA mechanism. With the auction going on, the performance of the price prediction method is gradually stabilized, so the resource utilization rate of DMAA mechanism is higher than that of SCDA mechanism.

7.2   The Comparison of the Amount of Resource Consumers Whose Demands Are Satisfied

We compare the amount of resource consumers whose demands are satisfied between the two auction mechanisms in three cases when the supply exceeds the demand, the supply equals the demand and the supply is less than the demand. The results are presented in Fig.3.

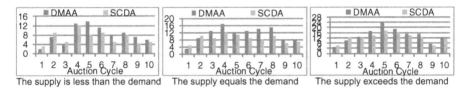

Fig. 3. The comparison of the amount of resource consumers whose demands are satisfied

As is shown in Fig.3, at the beginning of the auction, the amount calculated from DMAA mechanism is slightly lower than that from SCDA mechanism. With the auction going on, the amount calculated from DMAA mechanism is higher than that from SCDA mechanism. The reason is similar to that in the previous section.

7.3   The Comparison of the Execution Time

We compare the execution time of the two mechanisms when the amount of RCs is 30, 50, 70, 90, 110, 130 and 150 respectively, and the results are presented in Fig.4.

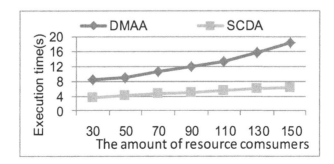

Fig. 4. The comparison of the *execution time*

As is shown in Fig.4, the execution time of the DMAA mechanism is higher than that of SCDA mechanism in all these seven conditions, and with the amount of RCs increasing, the gap of the execution time between the two mechanisms becomes larger. This is because in DMAA mechanism, the multi-attribution processing method based on BP neural network algorithm, the price prediction method based on SVM algorithm and the resource allocation scheme based on MVO algorithm will take large amounts of time for learning and iteration, but the time consumed is less than 20s in most cases. If the hardware is greatly improved, the execution time of the proposed mechanism can be reduced to within the acceptable range.

8   Conclusion

Cloud computing can integrate the distributed resources in the network and provide service to users. So a resource allocation mechanism is needed to reasonably allocate the idle resources. In this paper, MVO algorithm and DMAA mechanism are adopted to design and simulate a cloud resource allocation mechanism. In the proposed mechanism, RP and RC use SVM algorithm to predict the price and submit the tenders to AO . AO comprehensively analyzes the price attribution and non-price attributions of both traders and uses the BP neural network algorithm to transfer the non-price attributions to the quality index. To effectively allocate the resources and maximize the total satisfaction of both traders, the problem of optimal cloud resource allocation is transformed into the optimization problem of maximizing the total satisfaction. And MVO algorithm is utilized to obtain the optimized cloud resource allocation scheme. Simulation results have shown that the proposed mechanism is feasible and effective for increasing the resource utilization rate and satisfying the demands of users. It constitutes our future work to implement and test the mechanism in the actual system so as to further improve the practicality of the model and the algorithm.

Acknowledgements. This work is supported by the National Science Foundation for Distinguished Young Scholars of China under Grant No. 61225012; the National Natural Science Foundation of China under Grant No. 61070162, No. 71071028 and No. 70931001; the Specialized Research Fund of the Doctoral Program of Higher Education for the Priority Development Areas under Grant No. 20120042130003; the Specialized Research Fund for the Doctoral Program of Higher Education under Grant No. 20100042110025 and No. 20110042110024; the Specialized Development Fund for the Internet of Things from the ministry of industry and information technology of the P.R. China; the Fundamental Research Funds for the Central Universities under Grant No. N110204003 and No. N120104001.

References

1. Dikaiakos, M.D., Katsaros, D., Mehra, P., Pallis, G., Vakali, A.: Cloud Computing: Distributed Internet Computing for IT and Scientific Research. IEEE Internet Computing 13, 10–13 (2009)

2. Danak, A., Mannor, S.: Efficient bidding in dynamic grid markets. IEEE Transactions on Parallel and Distributed Systems 22, 1483–1496 (2011)
3. Lan, Y., Tong, W., Liu, Z., Hou, Y.: Multi-unit continuous double auction based resource allocation method. In: 2012 Third International Conference on Intelligent Control and Information Processing, pp. 773–777. IEEE Press, Dalian (2012)
4. Tan, Z., Gurd, J.R.: Market-based grid resource allocation using a stable continuous double auction. In: 8th IEEE/ACM International Conference on Grid Computing, pp. 283–290. IEEE Computer Society, Washington, DC (2007)
5. Prodan, R., Wieczorek, M., Frad, H.M.: Double auction-based scheduling of scientific applications in distributed grid and cloud environment. Journal of Grid Computing 9, 531–548 (2011)
6. Teng, F., Magoules, F.: Resource pricing and equilibrium allocation policy in cloud computing. In: 10th International Conference on Computer and Information Technology, pp. 195–202. IEEE Press, Bradford (2010)
7. Mutz, A., Wolski, R.: Efficient auction-based grid reservations using dynamic programming. In: 2008 ACM/IEEE conference on Supercomputing, pp. 1–8. IEEE Press, Piscataway (2008)
8. Wang, L.J., Meng, M.Q.H.: A Game Theoretical Bandwidth Allocation Mechanism for Cloud Robotics. In: 10th World Congress on Intelligent Control and Automation, pp. 3828–3833. IEEE Press, Beijing (2012)
9. Rajasegarar, S., Leckie, C., Bezdek, J.C., Palaniswami, M.: Centered hyperspherical and hyperellipsoidal one-class support vector machines for anomaly detection in sensor networks. IEEE Transactions on Information Forensics and Security 5, 518–533 (2010)
10. Xing, Y.Z.: On Issues and Applications for Least Squares Support Vector Machine. Nanjing University of Science and Technology (2009) (in Chinese)
11. Zweiri, Y.H., Seneviratne, L.D., Althoefer, K.: Stability analysis of a three-term backpropagation algorithm. Neural Networks 18, 1341–1347 (2005)
12. Suresh, S., Omkar, S.N., Mani, V.: Parallel implementation of back-propagation algorithm in networks of workstations. IEEE Transactions on Parallel and Distributed Systems 16, 24–34 (2005)
13. Zhang, F., Chang, H.Y.: Employing BP Neural Networks to Alleviate the Sparsity Issue in Collaborative Filtering Recommendation Algorithms. Journal of Computer Research and Development 43, 667–672 (2006)
14. Li, L.: The Research of Intrusion Detection Technology Based on Artificial Neural Network. National University of Defense Technology (2008) (in Chinese)
15. Richard, O.D., Peter, E.H., David, G.S.: Pattern Classification. China Machine Press, Beijing (2009) (in Chinese)
16. Azamimi, A., Uwate, Y., Nishio, Y.: Effect of chaos noise on the learning ability of back propagation algorithm in feed forward neural network. In: 6th International Colloquium on Signal Processing and Its Applications, pp. 1–4. IEEE Press, Mallaca City (2010)
17. Erlich, I., Venayagamoorthy, G.K., Worawat, N.: A Mean-Variance Optimization Algorithm. In: 2010 IEEE Congress on Evolutionary Computation, pp. 1–6. IEEE Press, Barcelona (2010)

ITC-LM: A Smart Iteration-Termination Criterion Based Live Virtual Machine Migration

Liangwei Zhu, Jianhai Chen, Qinming He, Dawei Huang, and Shuang Wu

College of Computer Science, Zhejiang Universiy,
Zheda Rd. 38, Hangzhou 310027, China
{zhulw,chenjh919,hqm,tossboyhdw,catting}@zju.edu.cn

Abstract. Live migration of virtual machines (VMs) plays an important role in grids, clouds and datacenters, and has become the cornerstone of resource management in virtualized systems. The efficiency of live migration depends on the downtime, total migration time and total transferred data. However, while migrating a memory-intensive VM, XEN/KVM often do many useless iterations of memory copy in order to reach expected downtime which can never be reached, leading to a great deal of useless data transferring and insufferable total migration time. It consumes mass of network bandwidth and CPU resource when transferring memory from one to another node. Hence, a critical task is to determine the optimal time to terminate the copy iteration for live migration. In this paper, we propose a smart iteration-termination criterion based live migration which is termed as ITC-LM, to self adaptively control when to terminate iteration. We have implemented ITC-LM into KVM/QEMU. The improvement is significant, especially when migrate a memory-intensive VM. The experimental results show that, our approach can decrease 50.33% of total transferred data on average without impairing migration downtime.

Keywords: Virtualization, Live migration, Iteration-Termination Criterion, Terminating Conditions.

1   Introduction

Virtualization technology plays an important role in cloud computing [1, 2], in which a large number of virtual machines (VMs) are dynamically allocated to multiple physical machines (PMs). Virtualization enables live migration of VMs, which provides a flexible way to relocate VMs from one physical node to another, leading to efficient resource management [3], such as load balancing and power-saving etc.

Live migration of virtual machine is the essential mechanism of virtualization, which is included in all current mainstream virtualization platforms such as KVM [4], XEN [5], VMware [6], etc. Pre-copy as default live migration method of these platforms is the most popular algorithm of live migration, which first sends VM's memory to the destination host and then resumes VM in it. In order to improve migration performance, some research employs memory compression to reduce the transferred pages during live migration.

C.-H. Hsu et al. (Eds.): NPC 2013, LNCS 8147, pp. 118–129, 2013.

However, the efficiency of current live migration methods are not always satisfying, especially in a memory-intensive scenario. Now methods keeps the iterations of copying memory until the downtime is short enough, and if the expected downtime is always too high, it stops memory copy iterations after a fixed number of memory-copy iterations. As a result, these methods usually stop memory--copy iteration too late in memory-intensive scenarios and will consume a lot of network resource of a data center, even resulting in the performance degradation of data center.

Unfortunately, the existing live migration approaches commonly ignore the problem of determination about when to terminate the iterations. In pre-copy, memory is transferred from the source node to the destination node while VM is still running on source. Modified pages which are generated in the iteration are transferred in subsequent iteration. This process based on that the VM remaining dirty pages can converge to a small value. However, there are still lots of remaining dirty pages after multiple iterations when low-bandwidth or VM with a high workload. In other words, more iterations of copy memory cannot decrease the remaining dirty pages and no more benefit to the service downtime.

In this paper, we propose a smart iteration-termination criterion (ITC) based live migration method, termed as ITC-LM. We use ITC value to determine when to terminate the iteration in live migration. Actually, ITC value changes dynamically during the live migration process. In our method, we terminate the iteration when the ITC value is less than a given threshold.

The main contributions of this paper are as follows:

First, we proposed a smart ITC-LM technique to decide when to stop iteration during live migration. To the best of our knowledge, our method is the first to consider both the iteration rounds and the convergence of remaining dirty pages.

Second, we have implemented our proposed algorithm in recent stable release of KVM/QEMU [9, 10] and show that our methods can be conveniently deployed in virtualization platform.

Eventually, we demonstrate the effectiveness of ITC-LM method in our experiments by four different kinds of workloads. The results show that ITC-LM decreases 53.35% of total migration time and 50.33% of total transferred data on average.

2   Background and Motivation

There are various algorithms of live migration. Most of these studies are mainly based on the pre-copy live migration algorithm. It basically works [21] as follows:

1) The resources of memory and VCPUs are reserved on the destination.
2) Memory of VM is sent to destination and using bitmap to log the dirty pages which rewrite during the memory copy.
3) The source continuously copies VM's memory dirty pages to the destination. A number of iterations are performed to retransfer the pages which are dirtied in previous iteration.

4) Suspend the running VM at the source, and copy remaining pages to the destination.

5) The VM is resumed on the destination.

In the best case, the approach of pre-copy can achieve an expected downtime by several iterative copy operations.

2.1 Terminating Conditions

There are some common conditions to decide the time to terminate the iterative copy operations.

Remaining Dirty Pages. Ideally, the default size of remaining dirty pages can be reached using iterative copy operations. However this is completely depending on the assumption of remaining dirty pages can converge expected size. Some application rewrite memory frequency that remaining dirty pages still very large over multiple rounds [17].

Maximum Number of Iterations. The terminative conditions of exact values for the maximum number of iteration are arguable, sometimes when the dirty rate is low compared to the transfer rate, the remaining pages will decrease quickly and down time will not have benefit from more iteration.

Hybrid Terminating Condition. Some of approaches use terminative conditions simultaneously of above two as shown in figure 1. Each iteration check the remaining pages whether below the expected remain pages, and check the number of iteration is more than the maximum number of iterations. This condition has been used in XEN, KVM/QEMU etc.

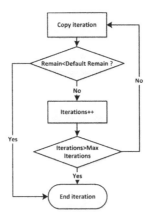

Fig. 1. A typical algorithm of use two terminative conditions simultaneously

2.2   The Problems of Common Terminating Conditions

The hybrid terminating condition can finish the live migration but the default remaining pages size and maximum number of iterations is hard to estimate. Beside, we can know that in order to minimize the size of remaining dirty pages the maximum iterations need to be set to a value that larger enough for most cases of live migration. However, a lot of useless iterations of pre-copy caused large amount of transferred data, especially when migrate a memory-intensive VM.

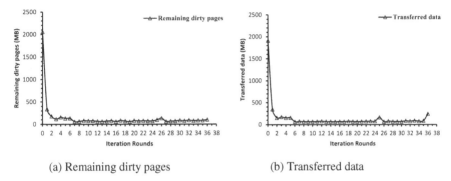

(a) Remaining dirty pages   (b) Transferred data

Fig. 2. Number of remaining dirty pages and transferred data of each migration iteration rounds when migrate a VM which running workload of RUBiS webserver workload. VM size is 2GB.

From figure 2 we observe that the remaining pages converge from the fifth iteration. But the remaining dirty pages size still bigger than the default size 30MB (some approaches use remaining pages size divide transfer rate). So iterations of copy will continuous perform until the number of iterations exceeds the maximum number which is set as thirty-seven that larger enough for most cases of live migration in our experiments.

3   Algorithm Design

Although, the live migration complete after number of iteration exceeds the maximum number, the more iteration the more network bandwidth and CPU resource it consumes and it would prolong the total migration time. Moreover, it makes applications in migrated VM suffer longer time of performance degradation.

The iterations of pre-copy are completely depending on the assumption of the remaining pages can converge to a small value. However iteration of pre-copy may never converge to a small value or even the convergence of iteration never happen when the VM's workload is high or bandwidth instability. So there should be some smart threshold to force the final iteration of a live migration which does not converge.

3.1 Terminating Condition Based on Remaining Dirty Pages

First, some notations are defined as follows:

M_{r_i} : The remaining dirty pages after ith iteration in the migrated virtual machine.

M_{t_i} : The data is transferred to destination of ith iteration.

T_i : The time of complete ith iteration used.

R_{page_i} : The average dirty pages rate of ith iteration.

R_{tran_i} : The average transferred rate of ith iteration.

The average dirty page rate of ith iteration can be calculated as

$$R_{page_i} = \frac{M_{r_i} - (M_{r_{i-1}} - M_{t_i})}{T_i} . \tag{1}$$

The average transferred rate of ith iteration can be presented as:

$$R_{tran_i} = \frac{M_{t_i}}{T_i} . \tag{2}$$

Only when R_{tran_i} is greater than R_{page_i} , the iteration can reduce the remaining pages. From formula (1) and (2) we can get:

$$M_{r_i} < M_{r_{i-1}} . \tag{3}$$

Different between two consecutive remaining pages is defined as:

$$D_i = M_i - M_{i-1} . \tag{4}$$

The above inequality indicates the remaining pages should be less than its previous round. Thus the iteration can reduce the remaining page size. Otherwise the rounds have no contribution to reach to the default value.

From formula (4), it is clear that when D_i is not less zero is a good terminative condition. However, VM's dirty page rate and transfer rate are not stable in real virtualized system, thus once we find it unreliable that the remaining dirty pages is less than its previous one.

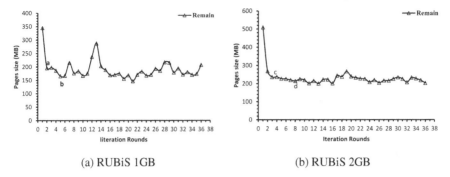

(a) RUBiS 1GB   (b) RUBiS 2GB

Fig. 3. Remain dirty pages in successive iterations. The experiments choose benchmark of RUBiS as workload for each VM memory size. In order to see clear the trend of remaining dirty pages, the first iterations are taken off from the figures. The default remaining dirty pages set as 30MB and maximum iterations is thirty-seven (a number that larger enough for most cases of live migration).

Figure 3 illustrates the remaining dirty pages fluctuate during iterations and pages will continue to reduce after a shock. In detail, if only use the condition of difference between two successive remaining dirty pages will terminate the iteration at the first shock points (see the point of a and c in Figure 3). However the remaining dirty pages will continuously decrease after these points (see the point of b and d in Figure 3).

3.2   Iteration-Termination Criterion

Based on the analysis of the iterative characteristics in the VM live migration, the key idea of the proposed method is to avoid directly terminating iterations when the remaining dirty pages do not decrease. So we give a smart iteration-termination criterion (ITC) based live migration method, termed as ITC-LM. In our method, we use ITC value to accumulative the variation tendency of remaining dirty pages and determine when to terminate the iteration in live migration. The value of ITC is relation to the difference of remaining pages between two consecutive iterations.

According to the variation of the remaining pages of iterations, if the remaining pages of current iteration are less than the previous one, then we add a trust value to ITC. The bigger ITC value means the more valuable to do iterations. On the contrary, if the remaining pages of current iteration are not less than the previous one, it means doing iterations has no benefit for reducing downtime, and then we cut down ITC value by dividing ITC value to a distrust coefficient which is used to constraint the rate of ITC descent.

We conclude ITC by formula (5) as follows.

$$ITC = \alpha(ITC + c\_trust) + (1 - \alpha)ITC / c\_distrust, \qquad (5)$$

Where α is a 0-1 constant, $\alpha = \begin{cases} 1, D_i < 0 \\ 0, D_i >= 0 \end{cases}$, c_trust is a constant value

which denotes the trust value, and $c\_distrust$ is a constant value which denotes the distrust coefficient.

According to our experiments, the value of c_trust and $c\_distrust$ is empirical and correlative. For example, when we set c_trust to 1 and set $c\_distrust$ to 2, then we obtain a good performance of live migration in our experiments and we will do more research about values of c_trust and $c\_distrust$ in our future work.

3.3   ITC-LM Algorithm

We have designed the ITC-LM Algorithm and implemented it in recent stable release of KVM/QEMU using ITC. QEMU is an open source machine emulator. KVM (for Kernel-based Virtual Machine) is a full virtualization solution for Linux on x86 hardware which containing virtualization extensions. When QEMU use KVM for its virtualization acceleration, can get a better performance. The major part of ITC-LM was implemented in QEMU. We use bitmap of memory to calculate the size of dirty pages. The pseudo code of ITC-LM algorithm is listed in follows:

Pseudo Code of ITC-LM algorithm.

```
ITC=0;c_trust=1;c_distrust=2;
pre_remain_pages_size=full_memory_size();
while(true){
   copyiteration()
   if(remain_pages_size()<pre_remain_pages_size){
         ITC=ITC+c_trust;
         pre_remain_pages_size=remain_pages_size();
      }
   else{
         ITC=ITC/c_distrust;
         if(ITC<=1)
               break;
         else
               pre_remain_pages_size=remain_pages_size();
      }
}
end_iteration();
```

4   Evaluation

In this section, we perform a series of live migration experiments with some various characteristic workloads on VM with varying working set sizes to evaluate the performance of ITC-LM algorithm by comparing with QEMU/KVM default pre-copy algorithm (Pre-default) which implemented hybrid terminating condition. In the following, we first introduce the experimental environment, and then we present the results of different benchmarks.

4.1   Experimental Environment

All live migration experiments are performed on two identical hosts as source and destination host respectively. Each host has dual Intel(R) Xeon(R) CPU E5606 @ 2.13GHZ with a total of eight cores. Each one has 16GB RAM. The host runs Ubuntu 12.04LTS with KVM module and QEMU-1.4.0. The source and destination hosts are connected via Gigabit switched Ethernet. The OS of Linux VM are all Ubuntu12.04LTS with Kernel-3.2.0 and all VM images are stored in a Network File System (NFS). We perform experiments VMs are configured with two virtual CPUs. In each experiment the nodes of source and target only run the live migration VM. Besides, we use another identical host to deployment the client emulator of RUBiS.

4.2   Overview of Workload

We perform our experiments with the following VM workloads:

1. Kernel-complication. Linux kernel compilation is a balanced workload to use the source of VM. Two parallel threads were used to run Linux 3.8.5 kernel [12] compilation.
2. Parallel Benchmarks. The NAS parallel benchmarks (NPB) [14] are a set of programs which evaluate the performance parallel performance, available in commonly-used programing models like MPI and OpenMP. In our experiments, we use Embarrassingly Parallel (EP) of NPB (NPB-EP) to simulation the parallel computing workload.
3. SPEC jbb2005 [13]. It is a SPEC'S benchmark for evaluating the performance of server side java. It provides enhanced workload with a more object-oriented manner to reflect real-world applications.
4. Dynamic web Server. Rice University Bidding System (RUBiS) [11] which is a prototype modeled after eBay.com used to evaluate patterns and application servers performance. It contains a client-browser emulator, and we implement it in a third physical host.

4.3   Experiment Results

In this section, the results from the four workloads are present. The evaluation metric of experiments primarily includes total migration time, total transferred data and downtime during live migration of virtual machine. We run live migration five times for each workload and use the arithmetic mean for each metric.

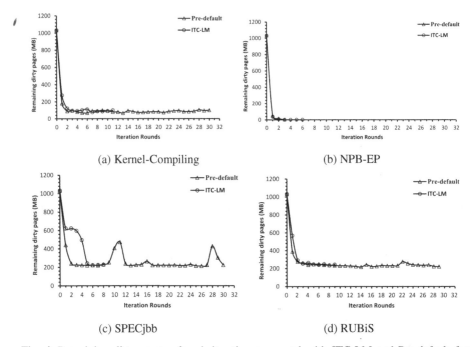

(a) Kernel-Compiling   (b) NPB-EP

(c) SPECjbb   (d) RUBiS

Fig. 4. Remaining dirty pages of each iteration compared with ITC-LM and Pre-default for each workload. (Memory 1GB)

Total Transferred Data. Figure 4 respectively shows the each iteration remaining data of during live migration of VM running. The iteration rounds of ITC-LM far less than the pre-copy default algorithm in KVM/QEMU under the workload of kernel-compile, SPECjbb and RUBiS. As figure 4 (b) shows the benchmark of NPB-EP is a compute-intensive workload and VM produce less dirty pages, and iteration ending soon. Thus two approaches both in less iteration.

Experimental results in figure 5 (a) show that compare with KMV/QEMU's default migration algorithm, ITC-LM can reduce total transferred data 50.73%, 7.74%, 69.55%,73.29% respectively in diverse workload of above, an average of 50.33%. This will lighten greatly network loads of data center.

Total Migration Time. The results in figure 5(b) show that benefit from less iteration, ITC-LM can reduce total migration time 50.54%, 17.70%, 70.03%,75.14%, an average of 53.35%. For this, the service running in live migration VM can suffer less time of the decrease of quality.

Downtime. In order to evaluate the influence of ITC-LM on downtime, experiments are performed with two memory size: 1GB and 2GB. Figure 5 (c) and (d) shows ITC-LM can get a good performance in total transferred data and total migration time while has slight influence on the downtime of live migration. This is because ITC-LM based on a smart threshold not a default remaining dirty pages or maximum iteration rounds.

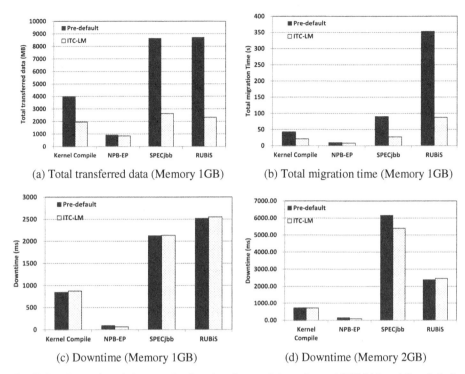

(a) Total transferred data (Memory 1GB)

(b) Total migration time (Memory 1GB)

(c) Downtime (Memory 1GB)

(d) Downtime (Memory 2GB)

Fig. 5. Total transferred data, total migration time and downtime of ITC-LM and Pre-default during live migration for four different kinds of workloads

5   Related Work

The technology of live migration is widely used in virtualization. At present, there are several types of live migration methods. The pre-copy approach is a main migration method in the mainstream virtualization platform such as KVM [4], XEN [5], VMware [6], etc.

Some research has been done to improve the performance of live migration based on pre-copy in which the widespread used method is memory compression. Zhang et al. [15] proposed a novel approach MMD to find identical and similar memory pages to redundant memory data. Delta compression technique [16] applied XOR on the current pages with kept previously sent pages in source host. Jin et al. [17] designed an adaptive memory compression based on memory page characteristics. ME2 [18] identified useful pages and then used RLE algorithm to compress data. Page rewriting frequency is related to dirty page rate. Microwiper [19] ordered dirty memory pages according their rewriting rate. Petter et al. [20] designed a page priority map on top of the dirty page bitmap and proposed dynamic page transfer reordering based on it. CR/TR-Motion [22] log execution trace on source and replay it on target host. Chiang et al. [27] proposed a bootstrapping VM introspection technique to get the information of memory pool, and skips free memory pages during migration. Jo et al. [28] first sent the memory-to-disk mapping to the host, and then fetch the contents directly from the shared storage.

Post-copy [7] resumes running VM on the target host with only its CPU state before copying the VM's memory from source host to target. Adaptive pre-paging and dynamic self-ballooning [8] can improve the post-copy performance. Hirofuchi et al. [23] through a lightweight extension implement post-copy to KVM. Besides, some researches proposed hybrid live migration [24, 25, 26] approach that use pre-copy and post-copy methods simultaneously. They do some memory copy iteration of pre-copy before the stage of post-copy method.

6   Conclusions and Future Work

In this paper, we have presented the design and implementation of a smart ITC-LM technique for live migration of virtual machines. We choose four representative server applications in modern data center to verify our algorithm. The results show that ITC-LM has a good performance in different kinds of workload. In future work, we will study trust value and distrust coefficient of ITC-LM to make our approach more effective. Furthermore, we will implement our approach to other virtualization platforms.

Acknowledgments. This work was partly supported by the National Key Technologies R&D Program under Grants No. 2011BAD21B02.

References

1. Armbrust, M., Fox, A., Griffith, R., et al.: A view of cloud computing. Communications of the ACM 53(4), 50–58 (2010)
2. Fox, A., Griffith, R., Joseph, A., et al.: Above the clouds: A Berkeley view of cloud computing. Dept. Electrical Eng. and Comput. Sciences, University of California, Berkeley, Rep. UCB/EECS, 28 (2009)
3. Wang, X., Du, Z., Chen, Y., et al.: Virtualization-based autonomic resource management for multi-tier Web applications in shared data center. Journal of Systems and Software 81(9), 1591–1608 (2008)
4. Kivity, A., Kamay, Y., Laor, D., et al.: kvm: the Linux virtual machine monitor. In: Proceedings of the Linux Symposium, vol. 1, pp. 225–230 (2007)
5. Barham, P., Dragovic, B., Fraser, K., et al.: Xen and the art of virtualization. ACM SIGOPS Operating Systems Review 37(5), 164–177 (2003)
6. Nelson, M., Lim, B.H., Hutchins, G.: Fast transparent migration for virtual machines. In: Proceedings of the Annual Conference on USENIX Annual Technical Conference, p. 25 (2005)
7. Hines, M.R., Deshpande, U., Gopalan, K.: Post-copy live migration of virtual machines. ACM SIGOPS Operating Systems Review 43(3), 14–26 (2009)
8. Hines, M.R., Gopalan, K.: Post-copy based live virtual machine migration using adaptive pre-paging and dynamic self-ballooning. In: Proceedings of the 2009 ACM SIGPLAN/ SIGOPS International Conference on Virtual Execution Environments, pp. 51–60. ACM (2009)

9. Kernel Based Virtual Machine, KVM,
   http://www.linux-kvm.org/page/Main_Page
10. QEMU, http://wiki.qemu.org/Main_Page
11. Rice University Bidding System, RUBiS, http://rubis.ow2.org/
12. Linux-kernel, https://www.kernel.org/
13. Standard Performance Evalution Corporation, SPECJbb2005,
    http://www.spec.org/jbb2005/
14. NAS Parallel Benchmarks, NPB,
    http://www.nas.nasa.gov/publications/npb.html
15. Zhang, X., Huo, Z., Ma, J., et al.: Exploiting data deduplication to accelerate live virtual machine migration. In: 2010 IEEE International Conference on Cluster Computing (CLUSTER), pp. 88–96. IEEE (2010)
16. Svärd, P., Hudzia, B., Tordsson, J., et al.: Evaluation of delta compression techniques for efficient live migration of large virtual machines. Virtual Execution Environments (VEE) 46(7), 111–120 (2011)
17. Jin, H., Deng, L., Wu, S., et al.: Live virtual machine migration with adaptive, memory compression. In: IEEE International Conference on Cluster Computing and Workshops, CLUSTER 2009, pp. 1–10. IEEE (2009)
18. Ma, Y., Wang, H., Dong, J., et al.: ME2: Efficient Live Migration of Virtual Machine with Memory Exploration and Encoding. In: 2012 IEEE International Conference on Cluster Computing (CLUSTER), pp. 610–613. IEEE (2012)
19. Du, Y., Yu, H., Shi, G., et al.: Microwiper: Efficient Memory Propagation in Live Migration of Virtual Machines. In: 2010 39th International Conference on Parallel Processing (ICPP), pp. 141–149. IEEE (2010)
20. Svard, P., Tordsson, J., Hudzia, B., et al.: High performance live migration through dynamic page transfer reordering and compression. In: 2011 IEEE Third International Conference on Cloud Computing Technology and Science (CloudCom), pp. 542–548. IEEE (2011)
21. Clark, C., Fraser, K., Hand, S., et al.: Live migration of virtual machines. In: Proceedings of the 2nd conference on Symposium on Networked Systems Design & Implementation, vol. 2, pp. 273–286. USENIX Association (2005)
22. Liu, H., Jin, H., Liao, X., et al.: Live virtual machine migration via asynchronous replication and state synchronization. IEEE Transactions on Parallel and Distributed Systems 22(12), 1986–1999 (2011)
23. Hirofuchi, T., Nakada, H., Itoh, S., et al.: Enabling instantaneous relocation of virtual machines with a lightweight vmm extension. In: 2010 10th IEEE/ACM International Conference on Cluster, Cloud and Grid Computing (CCGrid), pp. 73–83. IEEE (2010)
24. Sahni, S., Varma, V.: A Hybrid Approach to Live Migration of Virtual Machines. In: 2012 IEEE International Conference on Cloud Computing in Emerging Markets (CCEM), pp. 1–5. IEEE (2012)
25. Shribman, A., Hudzia, B.: Pre-Copy and post-copy VM live migration for memory intensive applications. In: Caragiannis, I., et al. (eds.) Euro-Par Workshops 2012. LNCS, vol. 7640, pp. 539–547. Springer, Heidelberg (2013)
26. Chen, Y., Huai, J.P., Hu, C.M.: Live migration of virtual machines based on hybrid memory copy approach. Chinese Journal of Computers 34(12), 2278–2291 (2011)
27. Chiang, J.H., Li, H.L., Chiueh, T.: Introspection-based memory de-duplication and migration. In: Proceedings of the 9th ACM SIGPLAN/SIGOPS International Conference on Virtual Execution Environments, pp. 51–62. ACM (2013)
28. Jo, C., Gustafsson, E., Son, J., et al.: Efficient live migration of virtual machines using shared storage. In: Proceedings of the 9th ACM SIGPLAN/SIGOPS International Conference on Virtual Execution Environments, pp. 41–50. ACM (2013)

A Scheduling Method for Multiple Virtual Machines Migration in Cloud

Zhenzhong Zhang[1], Limin Xiao[1], Xianchu Chen[1], and Junjie Peng[2]

[1] State Key Laboratory of Software Development Environment,
School of Computer Science and Engineering
Beihang University, Beijing, China
[2] School of Computer Engineering and Science
Shanghai University, Shanghai, China
{zzzhang,chengxc}@cse.buaa.edu.cn,
xiaolm@buaa.edu.cn, jjie.peng@shu.edu.cn

Abstract. Infrastructure as a Service(IaaS) is important in Cloud Computing, which provides on-demand virtual machines(VMs) to users. The resource management plays an important role in IaaS cloud, which deploys and relocates virtual machine on available hosts for different targets, such as load balancing, power saving and resource utilization improving. The virtual machine placement problem can be considered as a bin packing problem. Many researchers use the heuristic algorithms based approach to solve this virtual machine placement problem. However, they all focus on how to find the optimization solution for the bin packing problem of virtual machine placement. These studies did not consider the scheduling of multiple virtual machine migration that involved in the transfer process from one V-P mapping to another. Because of the large overhead produced by virtual machine migration, the optimization of multiple virtual machines migration process could reduce the overhead of resource management in IaaS cloud, and accelerate the migration process. In this paper, we analyse and formal the multiple virtual machines migration problem, and propose a scheduling method to reduce the VM migration times and accelerate the migration process. Experiments show that our method can decrease the VM migration times, reduce the traffic and accelerate the process of multiple virtual machine migration.

Keywords: Cloud Computing, Virtual Machine Schedule, Multiple Virtual Machines Migration, IaaS.

1   Introduction

Cloud computing[1] is a popular trend in current computing which attempts to provide cheap and easy access to computational resources. IaaS(Infrastructure as a Service)[2] provides infrastructure or the actual hardware to customers who are responsible to install operating systems and necessary softwares. Based on virtualization technology[3], IaaS cloud is usually provided to users in the form of Virtual

C.-H. Hsu et al. (Eds.): NPC 2013, LNCS 8147, pp. 130–142, 2013.
© IFIP International Federation for Information Processing 2013

Machines (VMs), such as Amazon EC2[4] and VMware vCloud[5]. On IaaS cloud platform, resources are provided by need as services, and it guarantees to the subscribers that it sticks to the Service Level Agreement (SLA). IaaS cloud platform needs to dynamically deploy and relocate virtual machine onto proper physical hosts in order to meet different needs, such as avoid hotspot, power saving and load balancing[5-7]. Therefore, how to dynamically and efficiently schedule virtual machines among physical hosts to meet the needs of different targets becomes a problem.

The traditional resource management methods usually schedule virtual machine or allocate resource in cloud when some certain conditions are triggered[8-10], such as threshold for load balancing. Due to the complexity and variability of a large number of virtual machines in IaaS cloud, traditional methods are difficult to carry out global resource optimization management. To address this issue, many optimization theory based virtual machine placement approaches are used to solve the resource management problem in IaaS cloud[11, 12]. In such scenario, the resource management problem is considered as a bin packing problem, which need to find the proper mapping of virtual machines to available physical machines.

Linear programming[13], genetic algorithm[14] and ant colony algorithm[15] have been used to solve the bin packing problem, and obtained good results. All these researches are focused on how to find the actual mapping of virtual machines to available physical machines(V-P mapping). However, these studies did not consider the scheduling of multiple virtual machine migration that involved in the transfer process from one V-P mapping to another. Because the virtual machine migration process needs to copy large amounts of data(memory data or even virtual disk) from the source host to the destination host, it will produce large CPU overhead and network traffic, and cost much resource. Therefore, the optimization of multiple virtual machines migration process could reduce the overhead of resource management in IaaS cloud and accelerate the migration process. The optimization includes reducing the number of virtual machine migration, and migrating small VM instead of big VM.

In this paper, we study the multiple virtual machines migration problem, and propose a scheduling method to optimize multi-virtual machine migration process. The main contributions of this paper are concluded as the followings: (1)Modeling and formalization of the multiple virtual machines migration problem; (2)A scheduling method optimizing the multiple virtual machines migration process.

2   Related Work

For resource management in cloud data center, previous work has focused on the problem of placing and replacing VMs in servers, in order to optimize resource management for different criteria, including performance, power and cost. There are some molded products and research projects on virtualized resource management, such as VMware DRS[8]. They dynamically allocate the CPU, memory and I/O resources to partitioned virtual machines according to customer's requirements, but they ignore the QoS[9]. The work in [16] minimized the number of physical machines using dynamic adaptation technique based on off-line analysis of application performance, which is seen as a function of machine utilization. The load forecasting techniques are also widely used in the management of cloud resources, such as load-balancing and resource scheduling[17]. In [18], a model-predictive controller is proposed to minimize the total power consumption of the servers in an enclosure subject to a given set of QoS constraints.

Optimization and heuristic methods are wildly used by virtual machine scheduling and placement in IaaS cloud for different targets, such as load balancing or power saving. Integer Linear Programming is used to solve an interference-aware VM placement problem(IAWMP)[13]. They first formulate this problem by an Integer Linear Programming (ILP) model to solve it optimally. They also propose a polynomial-time heuristic algorithm to efficiently solve the IAWMP problem. In [14] a general model is proposed for resources allocation of virtual machines in multi-tier distributed environments. Their model describes each virtual machine and each physical host by a multi-dimensional resource vector, allowing the coexistence of both quantitative and qualitative resources, also handling different SLAs. [15] proposes a multi-objective ant colony system algorithm for the virtual machine placement problem. Their method could efficiently obtain a set of non-dominated solutions that simultaneously minimize total resource wastage and power consumption. [19] proposes a runtime virtual machine mapping framework(GreenMap), and designs a probabilistic, heuristic algorithm to mapping VMs onto a set of physical machines under the constraint of multi-dimensional resource consumptions.

However, all above optimization and heuristic researches are focus on how to find the actual mapping of virtual machines to available physical machines(V-P mapping). Although some virtual machine migration research[20, 21] can help to accelerate virtual machine migration process, however, the scheduling of multiple virtual machine migration that involved in the transfer process from one V-P mapping to another was rarely considered. Therefore, in this paper, we will study the multiple virtual machines migration problem, and propose a scheduling method to optimize multi-virtual machine migration process.

3   Problem Analysis and Formulation

3.1   Analysis of Multiple Virtual Machines Migration Problem

In this paper, the heuristics-based resource management methods are consist of two steps, which is shown in Figure 1. Firstly, the bin packing problem of virtual machine management is solved by a heuristic based algorithm, and the global approximate optimal virtual machine groups are obtained. The VMs mapping to same physical host are in same group, called a VM-cluster. Next, For the global optimal virtual machine grouping, we also need to convert the virtual machines to physical host mapping (V-P mapping) from current state(initial VM location) to the target state(final VM location).

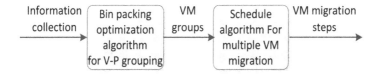

Fig. 1. The process of VM placement in IaaS cloud

The same VM group can locate on different hosts, therefore the target state is not unique. This process of V-P mapping convert involves the migration of multiple virtual machines, which could be scheduled to reduce the migration cost of VMs. Our study is focused on the optimization of the multiple virtual machines migration process. The purpose of this optimization is to minimize the overhead of CPU and network cost and avoid resource conflicts during the migration process(migration the number of virtual machines, choose the smaller virtual machine migration, adjust virtual machine migration steps to avoid conflicts). The optimization includes the choosing of VM for migration, the selecting of destination physical host, and accelerate the migration process of all VMs. For example, If several V-P mappings have same effect, we will choose the one that has minimum number of VM migration. If several V-P mapping have same VM migration steps, the one with minimal numbers of VM migration times will be chosen.

We need to develop a model to describe the scheduling problem of multiple virtual machines migration. In this model, the virtual machines which belong to same physical host are in the same group, and called a VM-cluster. At the initial moment, the VM-clusters of all virtual machines in IaaS cloud are the initial state of V-P mapping. Our schedule method is responsible for converting the V-P mapping from one type of VM-cluster to another VM-cluster. In this process, the proper physical host should be chosen for every VM-cluster, and the proper order of virtual machine migration determined, which is equivalent to create a new mapping of VM-clusters to physical hosts. Of course, this new mapping must meet the demand that the number of VM migration and the amount of traffic are as small as possible.

3.2   Formal Description of the VM Schedule Problem

We formalize the virtual machines to physical hosts mapping problem in this section. Firstly, we define some basic objects below:

- Host is denoted by $H_k(k=1,2...,N)$, and the set of hosts is $H=\{H_1,H_2,...,H_N\},(N>=1)$. V_j denotes all the virtual machines that need to be migration. The set of virtual machine is $V = \{V_1,V_2,...,V_n\}(n>=1)$. The virtual machines that locate on the same physical host form a virtual machine set. We call this set the VM-cluster which is denoted by $C_i(i=1,2...,M)$. The set of VM-cluster is $C=\{C_1,C_2,...,C_M\}$. In order to simplify this model, we require M always be no more than N, that is the number of VM-clusters should be less than or equal to the number of hosts.
- $L(V_j)$ is the amount of network traffic that generated by the migration of virtual machine V_j. Cost is the total amount of traffic generated by multiple virtual machines migration. In the initial state, each virtual machine running on a particular station host to form a set of virtual machine clusters.

- At the initial state, each virtual machine running on a particular host to form a set of VM-cluster. And it will be converted to another set of VM-cluster by our schedule method. If the virtual machine V_j belongs to a cluster C_i, it is denoted as $V_j \in C_i$. The optimal mapping of virtual machines to physical hosts will be selected by our scheduling method.

3.3   The VM Scheduling Method

After management strategy at initial state, all the virtual machines in the system are re-divided into a set of VM-clusters(shown as $V_j \in C_i$, $C_i \in C$). The establishment of mapping of virtual machines to physical hosts is equivalent to choose the suitable of physical host H_k for each VM-cluster C_i. Our multiple virtual machine migration scheduling method need to create mapping of VM-cluster set(C) to physical host set(H) as f(M→N), and select the optimal one that meet our targets(minimum migrations, etc.). Each mapping establishes a relationship between VM-clusters to hosts, and determines the target hosts that each virtual machine will migrate to. Therefore migration path of the virtual machines is also determined. Because the mapping of VM-cluster(C, the number of C is M) to physical hosts(H, the number of H is N) will generate a large number of virtual machine migration paths(A_n^m). Our scheduling algorithm needs to search for the optimal solution in all migration paths, and we will use heuristic approaches to simplify the process. After the optimal migration path is obtained, our scheduling algorithm will further determine the optimal virtual machine migration steps based on the principle of minimum system cost.

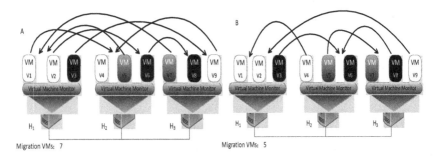

Fig. 2. The migration path of f1 and f2

We show a simple examples here, to describe our method in detail. As a case that virtual machines V1-V9 run on three hosts(H1, H2, H3). After bin packing optimization, these virtual machines are divided into three clusters(C1:V1,V2,V4,V9; C2:V3,V6,V8;C3:V5,V7). Two different mappings are available, the mapping of f1 is (C1→H2,C2→H3,C3→H1), and the mapping of f2 is (C1→H1,C2→H2,C3→H3). F1 and f2 are shown in Figure 2.A and 2.B. These two mappings correspond to two multiple virtual machine migration paths. These two migration paths choose different physical hosts for VM-clusters, resulting in a different number of VM migrations. Obviously, the path of f2 needs to migrate 5 VMs, which is less than 7 VMs of f1.

When the two mappings have the same VM migration times, the different size and load of virtual machines will also lead to a larger difference of network traffic and CPU load. For example, the migration of virtual machine with large memory and higher workload needs to copy more data and consume more CPU resources. $L(V_j)$ indicates the network traffic generated by virtual machine V_j during migration. The total transfer data of fx is Cost(fx), which is the sum of all $L(V_j)$. Like the first step, the cost of each migration paths are estimated and the one with minimum migration traffic would be chosen.

While the virtual machines starts migrate, the migrating virtual machines which have same source or destination host would migrate one by one. Because the node migration performance of host would decreased significantly due to simultaneous execution of multiple virtual machine migration. And of course, the virtual machines which their migration do not conflict with each other, could migrate at same time.

4   Design and Implementation

4.1   Host Selection Algorithm for Virtual Machine

The host selection algorithm for virtual machine is used to find the optimal mapping from all possible V-P mapping, and to obtain the proper destination hosts for the VMs. Specifically, it needs to search all A_n^m mappings of VM-cluster(C, the number is M) to physical hosts(H, the number is N), and selects the optimal mapping as the multiple virtual machine migration path. The optimal selection principle is minimum migration times of multiple migration process and minimum amount of migration network traffic(ie, the migration of VMs with smaller size will generate less network traffic). An improved genetic algorithm is be used to search the best mapping solution in this case. Due to limited space, the details of the genetic algorithm are not shown here.

1.	**Input: fs** $\in \{$fs$\mid 0 < s <= $ **MN**$\}$
2.	**for each** $f_s \in \{f_s\mid 0 < s <= M^N\}$ **do**
3.	**for each** $j\,(1<= j <= n)$ **do**
4.	**if** (The current host of V_j is not the host of V_j in fs mapping)
5.	$Y_j' = $ The host ID of V_j belong to in fs mapping;
6.	**Else**
7.	$Y_j' = Y_j$;
8.	**End for** / * We can get $<Y_1',Y_2',...,Y_n'>$ */
9.	**if** $(\sum_{j=0}^{n} Y_j \oplus Y_j' == \min\sum_{j=0}^{n} Y_j \oplus Y_j')$
10.	insert f into collection F;
11.	**End for**
12.	**for each** f in F **do**
13.	Cost(f) <= Min(F);
14.	Min(F) = Cost(f);
15.	**End for**
16.	**Output: Min(F)**

Fig. 3. The algorithm for Optimal mapping selection

The pseudo-code of our based algorithm is shown in Figure 8. The algorithm traverses all A_n^m mappings (lines 1-11) to obtain the minimum value of VM migration times and generates the set F which contains all the mappings with the minimum migration times (lines 8-9). Finally, it calculates the network traffic(Cost(f)) for each mapping in F, and select the mapping with minimum network as the return result of the algorithm (lines 12-15). In the algorithm, V_j is the virtual machine with number j, Y_j is the host where the virtual machine V_j current locates, fs is a mapping of virtual machines to hosts, Y_j' is the host that V_j will migrate to with the fs mapping, F is a set of mapping with minimum VM migration times, Cost(f) is the network traffic generate by VMs migration of mapping f and Min(F) is the mapping with minimum Cost(f) in set F.

4.2   The Migration Order and Parallelization of Multiple VMs Migration

After the selection of target hosts for multiple virtual machine hosts migration, the schedule algorithm next needs to determine the migration order of these virtual machines to be migrated. Our scheduling algorithm will generate a trituple $<V_j, H_j^s, H_j^d>$ for each virtual machine that needs to be migrated. V_j is the virtual machine need to be migrated, H_j^s and H_j^d are the source and destination hosts for migration of V_j. The order of multiple virtual machine migration could be represented by this trituple sequence. Our algorithm is mainly based on the following two principles to arrange the order of multiple virtual machine migration, and execute the migration process.

Firstly, the scheduler give priority to migrates virtual machine on high-load host to the low-load host, and give priority to migrates virtual machines with higher workload and bigger size. The migration of virtual machine will cost much CPU resource both on source and destination hosts. While priority migrate virtual machine on high-load host to low-load host, we need only consider the impact of migration on the source host(high-load host). And on the other hand, if migrate VM to a high-load host, there may be no enough resource remained for this virtual machine. Meanwhile, the scheduler priority migrate virtual machine with higher workload on source host. This is mainly because the virtual machine with higher workload is more sensitive to resource competition. A bit more workload increase will cause the performance of the application decline. But for the application on low-load virtual machine, the workload increase is tolerable. And based on the queuing theory, the VM with bigger memory size has less priority to migrate. Therefore, according to the above aspects, the scheduler can minimize the impact of VM migration on application performance.

Secondly, the parallel migration can be used for the virtual machines whose migration do not interfere with each other. For performance and stability reasons, a physical host can only deal with one virtual machine migration, either as an source host or as a destination hosts. Therefore, we can refer to the realization of processor's instruction-level parallelism to parallel processing the multiple virtual machines migration. In this case, the trituple sequence of migration VM is handled as the sequence of instructions of processor. When a VM migration is in processed, the source and destination hosts are marked busy, and reset free after VM migration. Therefore, while the source and destination hosts of the trituple being processed are not busy, the migration of this trituple could be executed immediately. Based on this strategy, our method can achieves parallel virtual machine migration, and avoid resource conflict.

5   Experiment and Evaluation

In this section, we validate and test the multiple virtual machine migration scheduling method, then analysis its performance. Using different test cases of multiple virtual machines migration to verify the effect of our schedule algorithm. The performance of our method is compared with default migration method, which migrate virtual machines one by one randomly.

For our experiment environment, we use a cluster composed by eight computer servers and one storage array. The configuration of server includes two AMD Opteron 2350 quad-core CPUs running at 2.0GHz and 12GB DDR RAM. They are all running XenServer 6.1[22]. The storage array connects four hosts through optical fiber, as a shared storage. All the servers are connected by a Gigabit LAN. The virtual machine templates are configured with one VCPU, 1GB,2GB,4GB RAM and one virtual network card. The load generator program will randomly call some of the popular applications to generate the CPU, network and disk I/O workload, such as kernel compilation, file compression, and FTP, etc.

5.1   Verify the Effectiveness of Our Algorithm

We select a test case to validate effectiveness of our scheduling algorithm. This test case uses 12 virtual machines and 8 physical hosts. The detail configuration of each virtual machine and physical host are shown in Table 1. These configurations of test case include input of algorithm, memory of VM and physical, the mapping of virtual machine to physical before and after migration, the workload of each virtual machine and physical host and the output of algorithm at stage 1 and 2.

Table 1. The configuration of test case

Input of VM-cluster	C1:v1,v2,v3,v10;C2:v4,v5,v6,v7;C3:v8,v9,v11,v12		
Information of VMs			
VM ID	Mem(MB)	Init reside host ID	Load(%)
V1	1024	H1	30%
V2	1024	H1	60%
V3	1024	H4	50%
V4	2048	H6	15%
V5	2048	H4	80%
V6	2048	H4	50%
V7	3072	H6	40%
V8	3072	H2	35%
V9	3072	H2	45%
V10	4096	H5	70%
V11	4096	H7	50%
V12	4096	H2	10%

Table 1. (*continued*)

Information of physical hosts before VMs migration			
Host ID	Mem(GB)	VMs	Load(%)
H1	12	V1,V2	15%
H2	12	V8,V9,V12	15%
H3	12	None	0%
H4	12	V3,V5,V6	30%
H5	16	V10	10%
H6	16	V4,V7	10%
H7	16	V11	10%
H8	16	None	0%
Information of physical hosts after VMs migration			
Host ID	Mem(GB)	VMs	Load(%)
H1	12	V1,V2,V3,V10	35%
H2	12	V8,V9,V11,V12	25%
H3	12	None	0%
H4	12	None	0%
H5	16	None	0%
H6	16	V4,V5,V6,V7	30%
H7	16	None	0%
H8	16	None	0%
Output of stage 1: V10-->H1, V3-->H1, V11-->H2, V5-->H6, V6-->H6			
Output of stage 2: V5,V3,V6,V10,V11			

The output of our algorithm is listed in Table 1. Because our algorithm is divided into two stages, our validation   also has two stages.

Firstly, the output of the first stage of our algorithm is a set of V-P mapping which has the minimum virtual machine migration times. For this test case, the minimum migration times is 5, and the mapping in the set is (f1: V10-->H1, V3-->H1, V11--->H2, V4-->H4, V7-->H4) and (f2: V10-->H1, V3-->H1, V11-->H2, V5-->H6, V6-->H6). Then the algorithm compares the migration traffic of each mapping, and chooses the V-P mapping with minimum migration traffic as the optimal migration path. In this test case, the Cost(f1) = L(V10)+L(V3)+L(V11)+L(V4)+L(V7) = 14GB, and Cost(f2) = L(V10)+L(V3)+L(V11)+L(V5)+ L(V6) = 13GB. Because Cost(f1) is greater than Cost(f2), our algorithm will select the f2 as the optimal migration path for multiple virtual machine migration.

Table 2. The trituple Sequence for migration step

Id	Trituple	Load(VM/Host)	Mem(MB)
1	(V10,H5->H1)	70%/10%	4096
2	(V3,H4->H1)	50%/30%	1024
3	(V11,H7->H2)	50%/10%	4096
4	(V5,H4->H6)	80%/30%	2048
5	(V6,H4->H6)	50%/30%	2048
Migration step: V5,V3,V6,V10,V11			

Table 3. The parallel migration process for multiple virtual machine migration

Time	Migrating VMs/ Mem(G)	Waiting VMs	Busy Hosts
T1	V5(2G),V10(4G),V11(4G)	V3(1G),V6(2G)	H4,H6,H5,H1,H7,H2
T2	V5(2G),V10(4G),V11(4G)	V3(1G),V6(2G)	H4,H6,H5,H1,H7,H2
T3	V10(4G),V11(4G),V6(2G)	V3(1G)	H5,H1,H7,H2,H4,H6
T4	V10(4G),V11(4G),V6(2G)	V3(1G)	H5,H1,H7,H2,H4,H6
T5	V3(1G)	None	H4,H6

The second stage of the algorithm is to generate a virtual machine migration sequence based on the optimal mapping f2 which obtained by the first stage. The migration sequence is shown as a trituple sequence in Table 2. According to our optimization strategy, the migration order output by the second stage of out algorithm is V5, V3, V6, V10, V11. This is because the virtual machine V5 has a higher workload, and the physical host V5 reside on has the highest workload in the physical hosts. The virtual machine V10 and V11 migrate at last, due to the large memory(4098MB).

The Table 3 shows the parallel migration process of multiple virtual machines based on the migration order. We divide virtual machine migration process to several periods. During each period, 1GB data could be transferred. As Table shows, the migrating VMs, waiting VMs and physical hosts which be occupied for each period during migration process. In Table 3, at T1 period, the migration of virtual machine V5 is executed. However, VM V3 and V6 are waiting due to resource confliction, and VM V10 and V11 can migrate at T1 period without interference with each other. At the beginning of T3 period, VM V5 finishes the migration. The next VM V3 could not start migration because of the destination host(H1) of V3 is busy. Thus, the VM V6 starts migration at T3 period. The VM V3 finishes migration at end of T5 period. The total time of the parallel migration are 5 periods. Compared with the 13 periods of serial migration, the parallel virtual machine migration greatly reduces migration time(160%), and avoids resource conflicts in multiple virtual machine migration.

5.2   Verify the Versatility of Our Algorithm

We choose several test cases to validate the algorithm's versatility. The detailed configuration of these test cases are shown in Table 4. 30 virtual machines are running on three physical hosts, each VM has 1GB memory. The VM-cluster inputs of five test cases are shown in Table 5.

Table 4. The distribution state of virtual machines

VM/Host	Host1	Host2	Host3
VM ID	V1~V10	V11~V20	V21~V30

Table 5. Five test cases

ID/ VM-cluster	C1	C2	C3
Case 1	1,11,12,13,14,15,16,17, 18,19	2,3,4,5,6,7,8,9,10,20,30	21,22,23,24,25,26,27,28,29
Case 2	1,2,3,5,11,12,14,17,21,2 4,25	4,13,15,16,18,19,20,22,23 ,26,28	6,7,8,9,10,27,29,30
Case 3	1,2,3,5,24,25	4,13,15,16,18,19, 26,28,11,12,14,17,21	6,7,8,9,10,27,29,30,20,22, 23
Case 4	1,14,17,21,24,25,16,18, 19,20	4,13,15, 22,23,26,28,7,8,9	6,10,27,29,30,2,3,5,11,12
Case 5	1,12,14,17,21,24,19,20, 22, 9,10,27,25	4,13,15,2,3,5,11,16,18, 23,26,28	6,7,8, 29,30

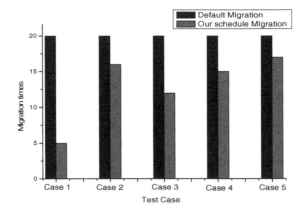

Fig. 4. Migration time of five time cases

The results of migration time for each test case are shown in Figure 4. We can see that, compared with default migration strategy, the average VM migration times of our algorithm is lower. The degree of optimization is different for each test case depending on the initial mapping state. This experiment shows that in most cases, our algorithm can optimize the process of multiple virtual machine migration.

6   Conclusion and Future Work

This paper presents a schedule method for multiple virtual machine migration. The contributions of this paper include:(1) We analyze and formal the problem of multiple virtual machine migration; (2) We propose a schedule algorithm for multiple virtual machine migration. The algorithm contains two parts. The first is finding the minimum cost VM migration path from all mapping of virtual machine to physical hosts, and the second an algorithm generating the optimization virtual machine migration sequence, and accelerating multiple virtual machine migration process based on parallelize techniques; (3) We use some experiments to verify the effectiveness and versatility of the algorithm.

In this paper, the algorithm proposed has high complexity, and it's performance is not good while dealing with large-scale multi-virtual machine migration case. Therefore, we need to improve the scalability of the our method.

Acknowledgments. This work is supported by the National Natural Science Foundation of China(61232009); the State Key Laboratory of Software Development Environment (SKLSDE-2012ZX-07); the Doctoral Fund of Ministry of Education of China (20101102110018); the Hi-Tech Research and Development Program (863) of China (2011AA01A205); the Beijing Natural Science Foundation(4122042); Shanghai Science and Technology Innovation Action Plan(11511500400)

References

1. Armbrust, M., et al.: A view of cloud computing. Communications of the ACM 53(4), 50–58 (2010)
2. Zhang, Q., Cheng, L., Boutaba, R.: Cloud computing: state-of-the-art and research challenges. Journal of Internet Services and Applications 1(1), 7–18 (2010)
3. Rosenblum, M., Garfinkel, T.: Virtual machine monitors: Current technology and future trends. Computer 38(5), 39–47 (2005)
4. Amazon Elastic Compute Cloud, http://aws.amazon.com/en/ec2/ (accessed May 2013)
5. vCloud, http://en.wikipedia.org/wiki/VCloud (accessed May 2013)
6. Ren, X., Lin, R., Zou, H.: A dynamic load balancing strategy for cloud computing platform based on exponential smoothing forecast. In: International Conference on Cloud Computing and Intelligence Systems (2011)
7. Srikantaiah, S., Kansal, A., Zhao, F.: Energy aware consolidation for cloud computing. In: USENIX Conference on Power Aware Computing and Systems (2008)
8. Vmware. Resource management with VMware DRS. VMware Whitepaper (2006)
9. Song, Y., Li, Y., Wang, H., Zhang, Y., Feng, B., Zang, H., Sun, Y.: A service-oriented priority-based resource scheduling scheme for virtualized utility computing. In: Sadayappan, P., Parashar, M., Badrinath, R., Prasanna, V.K. (eds.) HiPC 2008. LNCS, vol. 5374, pp. 220–231. Springer, Heidelberg (2008)
10. Zhang, Z., et al.: A VM-based Resource Management Method Using Statistics. In: International Conference on Parallel and Distributed Systems (2012)
11. Bobroff, N., Kochut, A., Beaty, K.: Dynamic placement of virtual machines for managing sla violations. In: International Symposium on Integrated Network Management (2007)
12. Verma, A., Ahuja, P., Neogi, A.: pMapper: power and migration cost aware application placement in virtualized systems. In: Issarny, V., Schantz, R. (eds.) Middleware 2008. LNCS, vol. 5346, pp. 243–264. Springer, Heidelberg (2008)
13. Lin, J.W., Chen, C.H.: Interference-aware virtual machine placement in cloud computing systems. In: International Conference on Computer & Information Science 2012 (2012)
14. Campegiani, P., Presti, F.L.: A general model for virtual machines resources allocation in multi-tier distributed systems. In: International Conference on Autonomic and Autonomous Systems (2009)
15. Gao, Y., et al.: A multi-objective ant colony system algorithm for virtual machine placement in cloud computing. Journal of Computer and System Sciences (2013)

16. Khanna, G., et al.: Application performance management in virtualized server environments. In: Network Operations and Management Symposium (2006)
17. Prevost, J.J., et al.: Load prediction algorithm for multi-tenant virtual machine environments. In: World Automation Congress, WAC (2012)
18. Wang, X., Wang, Y.: Coordinating power control and performance management for virtualized server clusters. Transactions on Parallel and Distributed Systems 22(2), 245–259 (2011)
19. Liao, X., Jin, H., Liu, H.: Towards a green cluster through dynamic remapping of virtual machines. Future Generation Computer Systems 28(2), 469–477 (2012)
20. Liu, H., et al.: Performance and energy modeling for live migration of virtual machines. In: International Symposium on High Performance Distributed Computing (2011)
21. Jin, H., et al.: Live virtual machine migration with adaptive, memory compression. In: International Conference on Cluster Computing and Workshops (2009)
22. Xenserver, http://www.citrix.com/products/xenserver/overview.html (accessed May 2013)

Speeding Up Galois Field Arithmetic on Intel MIC Architecture[*]

Kai Feng[1], Wentao Ma[1], Wei Huang[1], Qing Zhang[2], and Yili Gong[1,**]

[1] Computer School, Wuhan University
430072 Hubei, China
[2] Inspur (Beijing) Electronic Information Industry Co., Ltd.
100085 Beijing, China
yiligong@whu.edu.cn

Abstract. Galois Field arithmetic is the basis of LRC, RS and many other erasure coding approaches. Traditional implementations of Galois Field arithmetic use multiplication tables or discrete logarithms, which limit the speed of its computation. The Intel Many Integrated Core (MIC) Architecture provides 60 cores on chip and very wide 512-bit SIMD instructions, attractive for data intensive applications. This paper demonstrates how to leverage SIMD instructions and shared memory multiprocessing on MIC to perform Galois Field arithmetic. The experiments show that the performance of the computation is significantly enhanced.

Keywords: Galois Field Arithmetic, MIC Architecture, SIMD, OpenMP, Speedup.

1 Introduction

From disk arrays [1], cloud platforms [2] to archival systems [3] storage systems must have fault tolerance to protect themselves from data loss. Erasure codes provide the basic technology for the fault tolerance of a storage system. The classic Reed-Solomon code [4] organizes a storage system as a set of linear equations whose arithmetic is Galois Field arithmetic, termed $GF(2^w)$. W is the length of a word, the basic computing unit. Encoding and decoding of a storage system for fault tolerance are implemented by computing these linear equations by multiplying large regions of bytes by various w-bit constants in $GF(2^w)$ and combining the products using bitwise exclusive-or (XOR).

Traditional implementations of Galois Field arithmetic use multiplication tables or discrete logarithms, which limit the speed of its computation. The performance using multiplication is at least four times slower than using XOR [5]. James S. Plank et al. fast Galois Field arithmetic using 128-bit SIMD instruction [6].

---

[*] This work is supported by the National Natural Science Foundation of China under Grant No. 61100020.
[**] Corresponding author.

C.-H. Hsu et al. (Eds.): NPC 2013, LNCS 8147, pp. 143–154, 2013.

In late 2012, Intel released its commercial products based on the Many Integrated Core (MIC) architecture [7], targeting to High Performance Computing field for the PetaFLOPS era. It is based on the streamlined x86 core and similar to the architecture of the existing CPUs. Since its architectural compatibility, it can utilize existing parallelization software tools, including OpenMP [8], etc. and specialized versions of Intel's Fortran, C++ and math libraries [9]. Its SIMD instructions are further extended to very wide 512-bit and allow 512-bit numbers to be manipulated on a core simultaneously. MIC's 60 cores also greatly enhance its parallel computing capabilities.

To the best of our knowledge, how to use a computing unit as powerful as a MIC coprocessor for Galois Field arithmetic has not been discussed yet. When the operator size of SIMD instructions extends from 128 bits to 512 bits, though the number of elements keeps at 16, the size of each element changes from 8 bits to 32 bits. With smaller w, e.g. $w = 4$, the spatial utilization ratio is only $1/8$ for the multiplication table. The obvious waste needs to be avoided to save memory usage. As to larger w, e.g. $w = 32$, the existed algorithm [6] maps a word into 4 8-bit parts since the element size of 128-bit SIMD instructions is 8-bit, which in-creases complexity and decreases performance. With 32-bit elements, the over-head should be reduced.

This paper will detail how to leverage 512-bit SIMD instructions and shared memory multiprocessing to multiply regions of bytes by constants in $GF(2^w)$ for $w \in \{4, 8, 16, 32\}$. Each value of w has similar but still different implementation techniques. We will present these techniques and compare the performance of our algorithms on MIC with other approaches on other platforms.

The rest of this paper is organized as follows. The next section describes related work. Section 3 gives description about Erasure Codes and Galois Fields. Section 4 introduces 512-bit instructions used in our algorithms. Section 5 details our algorithms leveraging 512-bit SIMD instructions and OpenMP to multiply regions of bytes by constants in $GF(2^w)$ for w varying from 4 to 32. Section 6 compares and analyzes the performance of our algorithms and the others. Section 7 is the conclusion and future work.

2   Related Work

Erasure coding is an alternative to replication for fault tolerance as storage systems scale. Traditionally used in the communication field, erasure codes have gained their popularity due to lower spatial requirement under the same reliability.

Many erasure codes are based on Galois Field arithmetic, such as Pyramid codes [10], LRC codes [2], RS codes [11] and F-MSR codes [12], among which the most common one is RS codes. RS codes are used in Bigtable [13] from Google, Cassandra [14] from Facebook and Cleversafe [15]. Microsoft Azure uses LRC codes [2].

Traditional implementations of Galois Field arithmetic adopt multiplication tables or discrete logarithms. There are methods proposed to improve Galois

Field arithmetic, such as Kevin M. Greenan et al. using split multiplication tables and composite fields [16], Jianqiang Luo et al. using bit-grouping tables [17] and H. Peter Anvins approach based on fast multiplication by two [8,18] and so on.

Recently in [6] James S. Plank et al. present the algorithms of Galois Field arithmetic on CPUs using 128-bit SIMD instructions. As with [6], this paper focuses solely on multiplying regions of bytes by constants. We will exploit 512-bit SIMD instructions as well as OpenMP on MIC coprocessors.

3   Erasure Codes and Galois Fields Arithmetic

Fault tolerance of a storage system is enabled by redundancy. For Galois Field Arithmetic based erasure codes, n disks are partitioned into k disks for original data and m disks for coding information, which is calculated from the original data. When no more than m disks fail, the lost data can be recovered through the remaining disks.

For example, RAID-6 has two ($m = 2$) coding disks (C_0 and C_1), which are created from k data disks (D_i, $0{\leq}i{<}n$) as shown in Fig. 1 (a). Content of every disk is composed of w-bit words, such as d_{ih} and c_{ih} ($0{\leq}i{<}k$, $0{\leq}j{<}2$, $0{\leq}h{<}l$).

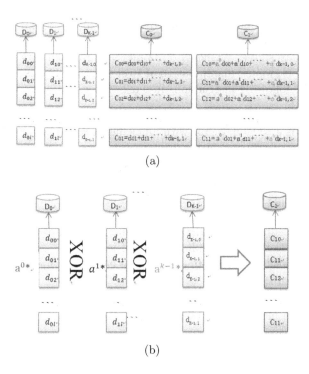

Fig. 1. The RAID-6 data disks and coding disks ($k = 4$). (a) The composition of the RAID-6. (b) How to create code disk C_1.

Here l is the number of words in a disk. The coding disks are created by a set of linear equations on the right.

The arithmetic of redundant code generation mainly includes Galois Field multiplication and addition, which correspond to multiplication and XOR operations. Taking C_1 as an example, every word d_{ih} is multiplied by a constant a^i, shown in Fig. 1 (b). The products of d_{ih} and a^i ($0 \leq i < k$) are added (XOR-ed) and the sum is c_{ih} ($0 \leq h < l$). Since the speed of XOR operations is very fast for modern computes, multiplication becomes the dominant concern with code calculating.

The selection of w decides the number of disks in the storage system for protection. For example, when using Reed-Solomon codes, $w = 4$ means the disk number cannot be larger than 16; $w = 16$ sets the limit to 65,536 disks. The value of w also greatly impacts the computation performance. Larger values of w perform much more slowly than smaller ones. Usually w is a power of 2 to match the size of machine words. Combining all the factors together, typically w is 4 or 8 for storage systems [2,15] and could be 32 and 64 for security and erasure coding purpose [17].

4   512-Bit SIMD Instructions

The Intel Many Core not only has ordinary vector floating-point units, but also uses special registers that enable packed data of up to 512 bits in length for optimal vector graphic streaming SIMD processing. These 512-bit instructions [7] can manipulate sixteen elements of 32 bits or eight elements of 64 bits at a time. In this paper, we use manipulation of 16 elements of 32 bits simultaneously. We leverage the following instructions in our implementations:

☐ _mm512_setzero_epi32(void): sets all the elements of the 512-bit vector to zero. Returns a 512-bit vector with all elements set to zero.

☐ _mm512_set1_epi32(int a): sets all 16 elements of an int32 result vector to an equal integer value specified by a. Returns an int32 vector with 16 elements each equal to integer value specified by a.

☐ _mm512_slli_epi32(_m512i v2, unsigned int count): performs an element-by-element logical left shift of int32 vector $v2$, shifting by the number of bits given by immediate count. If the shift value specified by this parameter is greater than 31 then the result of the shift is zero.

☐ _mm512_srli_epi32(_m512i v2, unsigned int count): performs an element-by-element logical right shift.

☐ _mm512_and_epi32(_m512i v2, _m512i v3): performs a bitwise AND operation between int32 vectors $v2$ and $v3$.

☐ _mm512_xor_epi32(_m512i v2, _m512i v3): performs a bitwise XOR operation between int32 vectors $v2$ and $v3$.

☐ _mm512_loadunpackhi_epi32(_m512i v1_old, void const* mt): the high 64-byte-aligned portion of the double word stream starting at the element-aligned address mt is loaded. It usually works together with the intrinsic

_mm512_loadunpacklo_epi32(__m512i v1_old, void const* mt) to load 64 bytes
in memory into a 512-bit variable.

☐ _mm512_permutevar_epi32(__m512i v2, __m512i v3): this is the real enabling
SIMD instruction for $GF(2^w)$. It permutes 32-bit blocks of int32 vector $v3$
according to indices in the int32 vector $v2$. The ith element of the result is
the jth element of $v3$, where j is the ith element of $v2$.

5   Galois Field Arithmetic on MIC

In this section, calculating yA in $GF(2^4)$, $GF(2^8)$, $GF(2^{16})$ and $GF(2^{32})$ on MIC
are presented respectively.

5.1   Calculating yA in $GF(2^4)$

When $w = 4$, each word is composed of four bits, and there are only 16 values
that a word may be. All operations are based on a 16 16 multiplication table
that is small enough to fit into main memory and can be calculated in advance.
A table lookup is needed every four bits, i.e. 2K lookups for a region of 1K bytes.

The SIMD intrinsics operates on operators composed of 16 32-bit elements
simultaneously. In the original table, each entry corresponds to the 16 4-bit
results of a number y multiplied by 16 numbers from 0 to 15. Storing only 4-bit
in a 32-bit element is obviously a waste. Thus we try to merge multiple entries
into one in the multiplication table, which is showed in Fig. 2. The products
of y and $0x0$ to $0xf$ from 8 entries are placed in 16 elements from the lowest to
highest, and in each element the product from entry 7 on the high end and the
one from entry 0 at the low end. Compressing entries 8-15, 16-23 is similar.

Since the processing element of SIMD instructions is 32-bit while $w = 4$,
every 32 bits in an element are split into 8 4-bit unit using $mask[i]$, shown in
Fig. 3 step (6). Step (7)-(9) calculated $tmp[i]$ and should be executed for $0{\leq}i{<}8$.
Finally, perform XOR operation on all tmp values and get yA. Thus 40 SIMD
instructions fulfill 128 multiplication operations.

In general the amounts of data to be computed are huge. Dividing data into
basic units of 512 bits and there are no data dependence among them. Thus it
is natural to parallelize Galois Field Arithmetic by OpenMP exploiting 60 cores
on MIC and opens up to 240 threads.

5.2   Calculating yA in $GF(2^8)$

When $w = 8$, each word is 8-bit and there are 256 values that a word may have.
In principal the method used in $GF(2^4)$ is applicable to the one in $GF(2^8)$. The
difference is that the instruction _mm512_permutevar_epi32() only works on 16-
element tables (each element is 32-bit), 256 values are too large to fit into a
16-element variable. Let a be an 8-bit word and a_h and a_l be the high-order 4
bits and low-order 4 bits of a respectively, and we have:

$$a = (a_h \ll 4) \oplus a_l. \tag{1}$$

(1) Original table entry with y = 0

00000000	00000000	00000000	00000000	00000000	00000000	00000000	00000000
00000000	00000000	00000000	00000000	00000000	00000000	00000000	00000000

Original table entry with y = 1

0000000f	0000000e	0000000d	0000000c	0000000b	0000000a	00000009	00000008
00000007	00000006	00000005	00000004	00000003	00000002	00000001	00000000

......

Original table entry with y = 7

0000000b	0000000e	00000005	00000002	00000004	00000003	0000000a	0000000d
00000006	00000001	00000008	0000000f	00000009	0000000e	00000007	00000000

(2) Compressed table entry with y ranges from 0 to 7

b4692df0	c23d1fe0	58c149d0	2e957bc0	4f1ae5b0	394ed7a0	a3b28190	d5e6b380
618f9e70	17dbac60	8d27fa50	fb73c840	9afc5630	eca86420	76543210	00000000

Fig. 2. Merge eight entries into one in the multiplication table when $w = 4$. Four entries in the original table are merged into one to fit 512-bit registers and variables on MIC. The upper line is high-order 256-bits and the lower line is low-order 256-bits. All variables are presented in hex.

(1) *table* = table entry with $y = 7$

f	e	d	c	b	a	9	8
b4692df0	c23d1fe0	58c149d0	2e957bc0	4f1ae5b0	394ed7a0	a3b28190	d5e6b380
7	**6**	**5**	**4**	**3**	**2**	**1**	**0**
618f9e70	17dbac60	8d27fa50	fb73c840	9afc5630	eca86420	76543210	00000000

(2) mask[0] = _mm512_set1_epi32(0xf)

0000000f	0000000f	0000000f	0000000f	0000000f	0000000f	0000000f	0000000f
0000000f	0000000f	0000000f	0000000f	0000000f	0000000f	0000000f	0000000f

(3) table = _mm512_srli_epi32(table, 28)
table = _mm512_and_epi32(table, mask[0])

0000000b	0000000c	00000005	00000002	00000004	00000003	0000000a	0000000d
00000006	00000001	00000008	0000000f	00000009	0000000e	00000007	00000000

(4) mask[i] = _mm512_slli_epi32(mask[0], i << 2) i: 1→7

.....f.....	.....f.....	.....f.....	.....f.....	.....f.....	.....f.....	.....f.....	.....f.....
.....f.....	.....f.....	.....f.....	.....f.....	.....f.....	.....f.....	.....f.....	.....f.....

(5) A

391d9f5a	aaab15c3	63e07e43	fb831623	391d9f6a	aaab15c4	63e07e44	fb831624
391d917b	aaab15c5	63e07e45	fb831525	391d9f8f	aaab19c6	63e07e46	fb831c26

(6) tmp[i] = _mm512_and_epi32(A, mask[i]) (0≤i<8), here i = 2

00000f00	00000500	00000c00	00000600	00000f00	00000500	00000c00	00000600
00000100	00000500	00000e00	00000500	00000f00	00000900	00000c00	00000c00

(7) tmp[i] = _mm512_srli_epi32(tmp[i], i << 2) (0≤i<8), here i = 2

0000000f	00000005	0000000c	00000006	0000000f	00000005	0000000c	00000006
00000001	00000005	0000000e	00000005	0000000f	00000009	0000000c	0000000c

(8) tmp[i] = _mm512_permutevar_epi32(tmp[i], table) (0≤i<8), here i = 2

0000000b	00000008	00000002	00000001	0000000b	00000008	00000002	00000001
00000007	00000008	0000000c	00000008	0000000b	0000000a	00000002	00000002

(9) tmp[i] = _mm512_slli_epi32(tmp[i], i << 2) (0≤i<8), here i = 2

00000b00	00000800	00000200	00000100	00000b00	00000800	00000200	00000100
00000700	00000800	00000c00	00000800	00000b00	00000a00	00000200	00000200

(10) Apply XOR operation _mm512_xor_epi32() on tmp[i] (0≤i<8) and get yA

9a75ab83	33347829	19c062f9	b4d971e9	9a75ab14	3334783f	19c062ff	b4d971ef
9a75a765	33347838	19c06cf8	b4d978e8	9a75abdb	33347a31	19c062f1	b4d972e1

Fig. 3. Multiplying a 512-bit region A by $y = 7$ in $GF(2^4)$

Thus

$$ya = y(a_h \ll 4) \oplus ya_l. \tag{2}$$

Based on the above analysis, the multiplication table is divided into two, $table_{high}$ which stores the result of $y(a_h \ll 4)$ and $table_{low}$ which storage the result of ya_l. As with $GF(2^4)$, multiplication tables are compressed and occupy

8KB memory. Fig. 4 shows the steps to extract the corresponding content from the compressed lookup tables for _mm512_permutevar_epi32() to permute. Since the lookup content for $y = 7$ is at 24-31 bit of each element in the compressed table entry, both $table_{high}$ and $table_{low}$, it is extracted by right-shifting 24 bits and masked by $0xff$.

(1) $tl = table_{low}$ entry with $y = 7$

f	e	d	c	b	a	9	8
2d22333c	2a243638	232e3934	24283c30	313a272c	363c2228	3f362d24	38302820
7	6	5	4	3	2	1	0
15121b1c	12141e18	1b1e1114	1c181410	090a0f0c	0e0c0a08	07060504	00000000

$th = table_{high}$ entry with $y = 7$

ea1a17e7	9a7a47a7	0adab767	7abae727	37874afa	47e7ea7a	d747ea7a	a727ba3a
4d3daddd	3d5dfd9d	adfd0d5d	dd9d5d1d	90a0f0c0	e0c0a080	70605040	00000000

(2) $mask =$ _mm512_set1_epi32(0xff)

000000ff	000000ff	000000ff	000000ff	000000ff	000000ff	000000ff	000000ff
000000ff	000000ff	000000ff	000000ff	000000ff	000000ff	000000ff	000000ff

(3) $tl =$ _mm512_srli_epi32(tl, 24)
$tl =$ _mm512_and_epi32(tl, mask)

0000002d	0000002a	00000023	00000024	00000031	00000036	0000003f	00000038
00000015	00000012	0000001b	0000001c	00000009	0000000e	00000007	00000000

(4) $th =$ _mm512_srli_epi32(th, 24)
$th =$ _mm512_and_epi32(th, mask)

000000ed	0000009a	0000000a	0000007a	00000037	00000047	000000d7	000000a7
0000004d	0000003d	000000ad	000000dd	00000090	000000e0	00000070	00000000

Fig. 4. Multiplying a 512-bit region A by $y = 7$ in $GF(2^8)$

After acquiring the lookup tables, the remaining steps are similar to the ones with $w = 4$ in Fig. 3, except for step (8) and (9). For $w = 8$, eight 4-bits in an element is indexed by i ($0 \leq i < 8$). When i is odd, it means that these 4 bits are high-order of a word; when it is even, these 4 bits are low-order of a word. High-order 4 bits and low-order 4 bits are subject to looking up different tables, $table_{high}$ and $table_{low}$, as well as left-shifting different bits. The revisions are as follows:

(8) for the high-order 4 bits i.e. i is odd
$tmp[i] =$ _mm512_permutevar_epi32(tmp[i], th).
for the low-order 4 bits i.e. i is even
$tmp[i] =$ _mm512_permutevar_epi32(tmp[i], tl).
(9) When i is odd: $tmp[i] =$ _mm512_slli_epi32(tmp[i], (i-1) $\ll$ 2).
When i is even: $tmp[i] =$ _mm512_slli_epi32(tmp[i], i $\ll$ 2).

5.3   Calculating yA in $GF(2^{16})$

For $GF(2^{16})$ each 16-bit word may have $2^{16} = 64K$ values. Since the instruction _mm512_permutevar_epi32() only works on 16-element tables, word a is divided into 4-bit sub-words, named a_3 through a_0:

$$a = (a_3 \ll 12) \oplus (a_2 \ll 8) \oplus (a_1 \ll 4) \oplus a_0. \qquad (3)$$

Then

$$ya = y(a_3 \ll 12) \oplus y(a_2 \ll 8) \oplus y(a_1 \ll 4) \oplus ya_0. \qquad (4)$$

Thus, we need perform 4 table lookup operations for a 16-bits word. We use compressed tables for data storage. The entries from four tables for a constant y take up 256 bytes and the total memory usage is 8 MB.

5.4   Calculating yA in $GF(2^{32})$

For $w = 32$, the processing is similar. We split each word a (32 bits) into 4-bit sub-words, named a_7 through a_0:

$$a = (a_7 \ll 28) \oplus (a_6 \ll 24) \oplus (a_5 \ll 20) \oplus (a_4 \ll 16) \oplus (a_3 \ll 12)$$
$$\oplus (a_2 \ll 8) \oplus (a_1 \ll 4) \oplus a_0. \tag{5}$$

Then

$$ya = y(a_7 \ll 28) \oplus y(a_6 \ll 24) \oplus y(a_5 \ll 20) \oplus y(a_4 \ll 16) \oplus y(a_3 \ll 12)$$
$$\oplus y(a_2 \ll 8) \oplus y(a_1 \ll 4) \oplus ya_0. \tag{6}$$

Thus we need perform 8 table lookup operations for a 32-bit word. Since the element size is 32-bit and the same as the size of Galois Field arithmetic word, w, there is no need for compression. The entries from eight tables for a constant y take up 512 bytes and the total size is 2 TB, which is too large to fit into main memory.

6   Performance Evaluation

The performance of our proposed algorithms on a MIC coprocessor is evaluated and for comparison the Multiplication Table algorithms [5] and the 128-bit SIMD algorithms from [6] are run on a CPU machine.

The MIC machine used in the experiments is Intel Xeon Phi coprocessor 5110p, 60 cores, core frequency 1.053 GHz, 8 GB GDRR5 memory, 32 KB L1 Instruction Cache, 32 KB L1 Data Cache, 512 KB unified L2 Cache. When the cores do not share data or code, the effective L2 Cache is 30 MB. The comparing machine is Intel Xeon CPU E5620 $*$ 2, 2.4 GHz, 32 KB L1 Instruction Cache, 32 KB L1 Data Cache, 256 KB L2 Cache, 12 MB L3 Cache, 32 GB memory.

The multiplication table algorithms and 128-bit SIMD algorithms are tested on CPU and MIC machines. Our proposed 512-SIMD algorithms are run on MIC with native mode. In all algorithms, regions of random values are multiplied by constants in $GF(2^w)$. For OpenMP accelerated algorithms the region size varies from 1 MB to 1 GB, while for Multiplication Table and SIMD only algorithms the size range is 1 KB to 1 GB. The results are shown in Fig. 5 - Fig. 9.

From Fig. 5 (MulTa is the abbreviation for multiplication table) it can be seen that the SIMD algorithms (128-bit SIMD on CPU and 512-bit SIMD on MIC) greatly outperform the multiplication table algorithms. When $w = 4$, the performance using SIMD on MIC is 13 times more than that of using multiplication table, and 10.6 times on CPU. We can also conclude that the performance of both algorithms on CPU is better than that on MIC, mainly because the core on CPU is more powerful than the one on MIC (2.4 GHz over 1.053 GHz). For example the multiplication table algorithm on CPU is about 1.8 times faster than on MIC and the SIMD is 1.3 times faster. With $w = 8$, 16 and 32 we have similar results and the details are omitted.

Fig. 6 presents the performance under different w values. We can see that the performance does not change much as w grows which is quite different from the conclusion from [6]. In [6] $w = 4$ and $w = 8$ perform roughly the same, $w = 16$ slightly slower and $w = 32$ slower still. This is because MIC SIMD instructions can operate on more bits (512 bits over 128 bits) simultaneously thus fewer operations needed for a word processing, which benefits larger w. For a certain w, when the region size reaches a point between 256 KB and 512 KB, the performance peaks and then drops dramatically. This is because L2 cache saturation impacts the performance greatly.

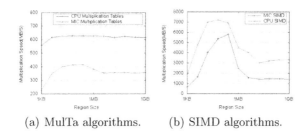

(a) MulTa algorithms.   (b) SIMD algorithms.

Fig. 5. The performance of MulTa algorithms and SIMD algorithms on CPU and MIC with $w = 4$

The results of OpenMP-based acceleration on the algorithms are shown in Fig. 7 - Fig. 9. For the multiplication table algorithm, it is always CPU-intensive thus changing the region size does little impact on performance as given in Fig. 7. For the 128-bit SIMD algorithms, before L3 cache saturates 8 threads are better than 4 threads; after the saturation they are of the same since it is I/O bound now. In the best case, the 128-bit SIMD outperforms the multiplication table by 9.5.

Fig. 8 - Fig. 9 compare the performance of the multiplication table algorithm ($w = 4$) with the 512-bit SIMD ($w = 4$, 8, 16 and 32) on MIC. Though each core on MIC is capable of 4-way hardware multi-threading, 240 threads do not have the best performance while generally speaking 180 threads are the best. The 512-bit SIMD + OpenMP algorithm is better than the multiplication table + OpenMP on MIC by 6.8 times and better than the 128-bit SIMD + OpenMP on CPU by 7.2 times.

The peak speedups for all algorithms and conditions are summarized in Table 1 with $w = 4$. Here we take the performance of the single-threaded multiplication table algorithm on CPU as the base 1.

From Fig. 9 (a) - (d) right before the combined 32 MB L2 cache saturates the computing peak can be about 220 GB/s. MIC works as a coprocessor and is connected to the host by standard PCIe x16 which has one-way bandwidth 8 GB/s theoretically. In practice, we have tested that the peak bandwidth from MIC to CPU is 7.0 GB/s and that is 6.7 GB/s from CPU to MIC. Obviously I/O is the bottleneck of Galois Field arithmetic.

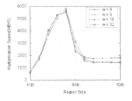 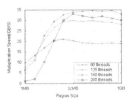

Fig. 6. The performance of SIMD algorithms on MIC with $w = 4, 8, 16$ and 32

Fig. 7. The performance of OpenMP accelerated MulTa and SIMD algorithms on CPU with 4 and 8 threads, when $w = 4$

Fig. 8. The performance of OpenMP accelerated MulTa algorithm on MIC, when $w = 4$

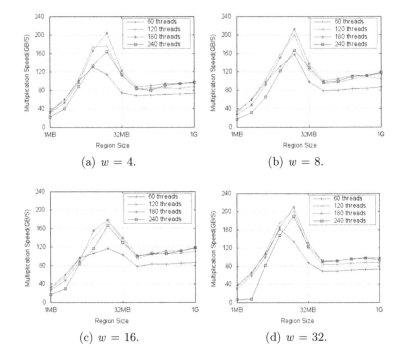

(a) $w = 4$.

(b) $w = 8$.

(c) $w = 16$.

(d) $w = 32$.

Fig. 9. The performance OpenMP accelerated 512-bit SIMD algorithms with different thread numbers on MIC

Table 1. The speedups with $w = 4$ (taking the performance of the single-threaded multiplication table on CPU as the base 1; MulTa is the abbreviation for multiplication table)

Peak Speedup	MulTa	MulTa+OpenMP	SIMD	SIMD+OpenMP
CPU(128-bit SIMD)	1	5.5	10.6	52.2
MIC(512-bit SIMD)	0.56	55.4	7.2	373.4

7   Conclusion and Future Work

In this paper, we detail how to apply 512-bit SIMD instructions with OpenMP on MIC to Galois Field arithmetic. The algorithms are evaluated with different w from 4 to 32. The performance of our algorithms is about 7.2 to 35.2 times faster than the implementations using 128-bit SIMD with OpenMP on CPU.

With 512-bit SIMD and OpenMP, cache, main memory and I/O to host become bottlenecks. In future we focus on improving the I/O performance and coordination between computation and data transfer.

Acknowledgments. We would like to thank Inspur (Beijing) Electronic Information Industry Co., Ltd offering a server with Intel Xeon Phi coprocessor for experiments.

References

1. Blaum, M., Brady, J., Bruck, J., et al.: EVENODD: An efficient scheme for tolerating double disk failures in RAID architectures. IEEE Transactions on Computers 44(2), 192–202 (1995)
2. Huang, C., Simitci, H., Xu, Y., et al.: Erasure coding in windows azure storage. In: USENIX Conference on Annual Technical Conference, USENIX ATC (2012)
3. Tansley, R., Bass, M., Smith, M.: DSpace as an open archival information system: Current status and future directions. In: Koch, T., Sølvberg, I.T. (eds.) ECDL 2003. LNCS, vol. 2769, pp. 446–460. Springer, Heidelberg (2003)
4. Plank, J.S.: A tutorial on Reed-Solomon coding for fault-tolerance in RAID-like systems. Software Practice and Experience 27(9), 995–1012 (1997)
5. Plank, J.S., Luo, J., Schuman, C.D., Xu, L., Wilcox-O'Hearn, Z.: A performance evaluation and examination of open-source erasure coding libraries for storage. In: FAST-2009: 7th Usenix Conference on File and Storage Technologies, pp. 253–265 (2009)
6. Plank, J.S., Greenan, K.M., Miller, E.L.: Screaming fast Galois Field arithmetic using Intel SIMD instructions. In: FAST-2013: 11th Usenix Conference on File and Storage Technologies, San Jose (2013)
7. Intel Corporation. Intel? C++ Compiler XE 13.1 User and Reference Guides, http://software.intel.com/sites/products/documentation/doclib/stdxe/2013/composerxe/compiler/cpp-lin/index.htm
8. OpenMP Application Program Interface, http://openmp.org/wp/

9. Intel ® Math Kernel Library for Linux* OS User's Guide, http://software.intel.com

10. Huang, C., Chen, M., Li, J.: Pyramid codes: Flexible schemes to trade space for access efficiently in reliable data storage systems. In: NCA 2007: 6th IEEE International Symposium on Network Computing Applications, Cambridge, MA (2007)

11. Kalcher, S., Lindenstruth, V.: Accelerating Galois Field arithmetic for Reed-Solomon erasure codes in storage applications. In: 2011 IEEE International Conference on Cluster Computing (CLUSTER), pp. 290–298. IEEE (2011)

12. Hu, Y., Chen, H.C.H., Lee, P.P.C., Tang, Y.: NCCloud: Applying network coding for the storage repair in a cloud-of-clouds. In: FAST-2012: 10th Usenix Conference on File and Storage Technologies, San Jose (2012)

13. Chang, F., Dean, J., Ghemawat, S., Hsieh, W.C., Wallach, D.A., Burrows, M., Chandra, T., Fikes, A., Gruber, R.E.: Bigtable: A Distributed Storage System for Structured Data. In: OSDI 2006: Seventh Symposium on Operating System Design and Implementation, Seattle, WA (2006)

14. Lakshman, A., Malik, P.: Cassandra: A Decentralized Structured Storage System. ACM SIGOPS Operating Systems Review 44(2), 35–40 (2010)

15. Resch, J.K., Plank, J.S.: AONTRS: blending security and performance in dispersed storage systems. In: FAST-2011: 9th Usenix Conference on File and Storage Technologies, San Jose, pp. 191–202 (2011)

16. Greenan, K.M., Miller, E.L., Schwarz, T.J.: Optimizing Galois Field arithmetic for diverse processor architectures and applications. In: IEEE International Symposium on Modeling, Analysis and Simulation of Computers and Telecommunication Systems, MASCOTS 2008, pp. 1–10. IEEE (2008)

17. Luo, J., Bowers, K.D., Oprea, A., Xu, L.: Efficient software implementations of large finite fields $GF(2^n)$ for secure storage applications. ACM Transactions on Storage (TOS) 8(1), 2 (2012)

18. Anvin, H.P.: The mathematics of RAID-6, http://kernel.org/pub/linux/kernel/people/hpa/raid6.pdf

Analyzing the Characteristics of Memory Subsystem on Two Different 8-Way NUMA Architectures

Qiuming Luo[1,2], Yuanyuan Zhou[1], Chang Kong[1], Guoqiang Liu[1],
Ye Cai[1,2,*], and Xiao-Hui Lin[3]

[1] National High Performance Computing Center (NHPCC), SZU, China
[2] College of Computer Science and Software Engineering, SZU, China
[3] Department of Communication Engineering, SZU, China
{lqm,caiye}@szu.edu.cn,
clarkong89@gmail.com

Abstract. Two NUMA architectures with different memory subsystems are experimentally analyzed in this paper. By applying the benchmark with various access patterns, it shows much different characteristics of memory system between Xeon E5620 with Global Queue and LS 3A with typical crossbar switch. The experiment results reveal the fact that LS 3A and Xeon E5620 have some similar features. Our study also showed some other diverse features of these two platforms: due to the different contention locations and mechanisms, the memory access model for E5620 doesn't fit for LS 3A. Through comparing, we find that one advantage of LS 3A is that it can obtain steady bandwidth on both local and remote thread, and it is more fair for local and remote access under some circumstances. Another fact is that LS 3A is not such sensitive to remote access, compared with E5620, so there will be no obvious performance degradation caused by non-local memory access.

Keywords: Memory subsystem, NUMA, Global Queue, Crossbar switch.

1   Introduction

With the increasing number of processor cores on one single machine, memory bandwidth has become the main bottleneck of computer system. Instead of using faster and bigger processor caches, NUMA has reduced the memory bandwidth issue by using asymmetric hierarchical memory model. A NUMA system contains some processors, caches, memory controllers and memory banks, using connection technologies provided by AMD's HT (HyperTransport)[1] or Intel's QPI (Quick Path Inter connect) [2] to connect with each other. Due to the NUMA factor, when a process access local memory or remote memory, they have different access delay and bandwidth. To obtain the optimal performance, previous optimization work on NUMA platform often schedule the process, move data from remote to local to maximize the

---

* Corresponding author.

C.-H. Hsu et al. (Eds.): NPC 2013, LNCS 8147, pp. 155–166, 2013.

local accesses. Some of these are based on analysis after execution [3][4][5], while others can dynamic deal with it during execution [6][7][8][9][10].

Instead of just observing local or remote memory access, the studies have made deep analyze of the inner memory controller architecture in recent two years. And they found that under some circumstance decreasing data locality may procure better performance [11][12]. This kind of study involves the detail behaviors and architecture of memory controller and it is more applicable to real application environment. After all, entirely local or remote access is not common in real applications. When we study the memory bandwidth on NUMA platform we need to consider both memory layout and the contention of local and remote memory access. We need to understand its architecture features through experiments to take full advantage of these CPU's underlying hardware power.

In this paper, we test two NUMA platforms, consisted of LS 3A processors and Intel Xeon E5620 processors, to characterize their memory performance. Then we analyze their similarities and differences, merits and shortcoming based on their difference architectures. At last, we propose a guideline to obtain best performance when using NUMA system consisted of these two processors.

2   Experimental Setup

In this section we describe the architecture details of the evaluation systems, the benchmark programs, and the experimental methodology used.

2.1   Hardware

LS 3A used in our work is an experimental CPU made by Institute of Computing Technology (Chinese Academy of Sciences). The NUMA platform made by LS 3A is consisted of dual-processors and it use HT to connect with each other. As shown in Fig.1(a), for each processor, the first level crossbar switch X1 connected with four 64-bit superscalar GS464 high performance processor cores (P0-P3)，four 1MB shared second level cache (we can also call it LLC, Last Level Cache), the two ports of HT used to connect with IO or other processors. The second level crossbar switch X2 used to connect LLC and 2 memory controllers MC0 and MC1, which also called IMC(Integrated Memory Controller). Each MC is connected with 2GB DDR2 memory, and the total memory of the system is 8GB. The frequency and width of the HT on this main board is about 200MHz and 8-bit (it can work on 800MHz and 16-bit). Two 64-bits 400MHz DDR2 controller can provide total bandwidth about 6.4GB/s. The 8 processor cores will share the L2 cache. When doing remote memory access, they go through the remote crossbar switch X1 and X2. Intel named LLC, local and remote arbitrate queue and IMC as uncore unit, and it corresponds to the part surrounded by dotted line square in Fig.1.

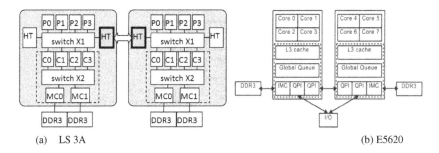

(a)   LS 3A   (b) E5620

Fig. 1. NUMA system consisted of dual-processors

In this architecture, a memory access may reach different components, such as local cache, remote LLC (L2), local memory or remote memory. And IMC also can deal with request from other nodes. So they need the support of request queuing and arbitrating mechanism. According to the official material, LS 3A use the HT port to send remote memory access request and it will contend the X1 switch network with native memory access request issued by the 4 local processor cores (include direct access to DDR and those access the LLC). And there is no detail explanation about how it arbitrates the request, so we need to figure out its inner mechanism through experiments. But from the architecture we can tell it is much different about remote memory access and local memory access path from Intel Xeon E5620. The later NUMA system is illustrated as Fig.1(b), the QPI connection, processor core and LLC layout is different from LS 3A. In E5620, the processor cores shared the L3 cache, GQ (Global Queue) is used for dealing with request from L3 cache, IMC and QPI. IMC have 4 channels and is used to connect 4 DDR3-1066 (2GB each, the total memory is 8GB). It can provide 25.6GB/s peak bandwidth. Two QPIs separately used for connecting with I/O and processors, the unidirectional peak bandwidth is 11.72GB/s and the bidirectional peak bandwidth is 23.44GB/s

The uncore unit in Intel E5620 processor is shown in Fig.2. It includes 3 components, LLC, IMC and QPI, and connected with each other with GQ. In GQ component (based on crossbar switch), there are 3 queues to deal with the miss request and update request from L2 cache and the remote access request from QPI. These queues' length is 32 items, 16 items and 12 items respectively[13]. Since every memory request goes through GQ, there are many contentions among local memory request and remote memory request on it. And GQ can reserve about 50% bandwidth for remote memory access request (This is the maximum bandwidth of remote memory access). Early version of E5500 reserves less than 50% of total bandwidth.

PMU (Performance Monitoring Unit) can used for observing and analyzing performance issues in Intel E5620 [13]. This paper used Intel E5620 for comparison, the same tests will perform on both platform.

Cache plays an important role in memory tests. In order to measure the bandwidth, we need to take advantage of cache and reduce the interference of cache. The detail information of cache on LS 3A is described in [14]. LS 3A have implement a

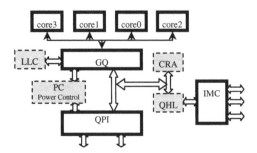

Fig. 2. Intel E5620 uncore unit

non-blocking cache technology. It can support up to 24 misses in LS 3A's cache. The Westmere (Nehalem's successor) core of Intel E5620 has private L1 and L2 cache, four Westmere cores of E5620 shared the L3 cache (LLC). Its non-blocking technology can support up to 16 caches misses. Since LS and Intel have different cache levels, capacity and pre-fetch mechanism, we need to avoid their influence about measuring the bandwidth.

2.2   Software and Benchmarks

The Linux kernel on LS 3A platform is Linux 2.6.36, the compiler version is GCC 4.4.5 and the compile parameter is gcc –fopenmp –O3. The Intel platform use Linux 2.6.32 as its kernel and the compiler version is also GCC 4.4.5, the compile parameter is gcc –fopenmp –O3 –mcmodel=medium.

This paper use STREAM [15] to test the memory access performance of each processor core, each processor and the whole system. Traid has an intensive memory access cycle. It accesses 3 arrays (a[], b[] and c[]). Their sizes all exceed the size of LLC, so they can issue enough memory access requests. The kernel cycle of Triad is showed in Fig.3.

```
for (i = 0; i < ARRAY_SIZE; i++)
{
    a[i] = b[i] + SCALAR * c[i];
}
```

Fig. 3. kernel cycle of Triad

In fact, an instance or thread is not able to saturate the maximum bandwidth of IMC, so we can't just use one Triad program to study the memory access characteristic of Intel or LS NUMA systems. Besides, we need to study the memory contention of local request and remote request. We must use at least 2 Triad instances to fulfill our work. So we made some modification on Triad and made it can produce multiple processes or threads to execute concurrently. Through using OpenMP, we can use

For direction and static schedule direction to parallelize it, the threads can share the 3 arrays and access their data set alone at the same time. The threads share the arrays, but the processes didn't share any data.

The advantage of Triad is described as below: The first one is that it is cache-starve-style[17] application and the cache will have steady missing rate, each Triad thread will not influence the cache missing of LLC[16]. The second advantage is that 94% to 99%'s read operation will reach the main memory'[12], it will not be impacted by confliction on cache line.

2.3   Measurement and Methodology

We use numactl [18] tool to control the data distribution on every node's memory and bind the threads to corresponding nodes.

To study the interference and contention on IMC and cross-process connection (HT/QPI), we defined three configurations, as fig.4 shows, about the layout of threads and data. The first configuration put threads in both L(Local, on node0) site and R(Remote, on node1) site, and put all data in L site. The second configuration put threads and data on both nodes in a cross accessing style. The third configuration put threads on L site and issue memory access to both nodes.

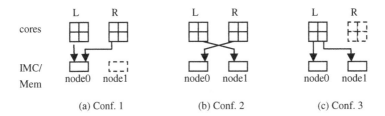

Fig. 4. Threads and data layout configurations

When measuring the memory access bandwidth, it needs to obtain the total number of memory access that arrived IMC and the time elapsed. But we can't get the total amount of memory access direct for the program or source code. The Intel's processor hardware counter can give accurate cache line size, missing rate and processor frequency [12]. But we haven't got the proper tools for LS 3A to do this, so we use the execution time of Triad as a reference. This is mainly due to Triad has a steady memory access workload, and every data only accessed once, this kind of application's execution time is decided by memory access operation[13]. In addition, both LS 3A and E5620 processor's L1 instruction cache have enough capacity to hold Triad's main cycle instructions, which means fetching instruction will not occupy the memory controller's bandwidth. So we can compute the bandwidth as below:

$$\text{Bandwidth}_{\text{total}} = \text{Bandwidth}_{\text{local}} + \text{Bandwidth}_{\text{remote}}$$
$$\text{Bandwidth}_{\text{local(or remote)}} = \frac{\text{Memory Access Size}}{\text{Exe Time}} (MB/s)$$

Due to local process and remote process need different time to finish the workload, the contention will not exist when one of them exit. We execute the processes repeatedly to keep the bandwidth contention. Therefore, the date we get is under contention.

The Intel's Nehalem micro architecture use MESIF protocol to keep cache coherent, different access states in cache line will cause different access delay. The states of LS 3A are INV、SHD and EXC, L2 cache use directory to find cache stay in which processor core. Since the modified Triad code doesn't share data, cache line will only exist M, E and I state, we don't have to take the delay variation into account.

At last, Nehalem micro architecture' SpeedStep and Turbo Burst technology [13] can change the clock frequency according to power consumption and fever situation. Therefore we close this function in BIOS to exclude its influence and provide a steady easy measure system environment.

3   Experimental Data of Memory Performance

We divide the work into several parts. The first test, using Conf.1 configuration, is to measure the local or remote bandwidth from threads on one single node, on both LS and Intel platform. The second one (still using Conf.1) then combines the local and remote access together to show the contention on one IMC. The third test is based on Conf.3 which focus on the total bandwidth of whole system based on the same configuration as previous tests. The forth test is based on Conf.2 which setup a cross accessing scenery. The last one study the confliction of local and remote access issued from same node, using Conf.3. The details are described in following sections.

3.1   Local and Remote Bandwidth for One Single IMC

In order to study the behavior of IMC serving the local and remote requests, the first test using conf. 1. In this section (xL,yR) represents the threads binding, x represents the number of local threads (on node0) and y represents the number of remote threads (on node1). There will be x+y threads executing concurrently.

The setup of (xL,0R), which means no remote access, is used to measure the local accessing. From Fig.7(a) we can see the bandwidth of serving the local access on LS platform continues to increase till it reaches the maximum thread number on signal node. And the remote memory bandwidth (with setup of 0L,yR) is about 20% less than local access bandwidth. On Intel platform, it nearly reaches the maximum bandwidth with 2 threads, and the maximum bandwidth of remote memory is 20%~30% less than local memory bandwidth.

The data show that LS can obtain increasing bandwidth with more threads, but Intel can reach the maximum bandwidth with fewer threads.

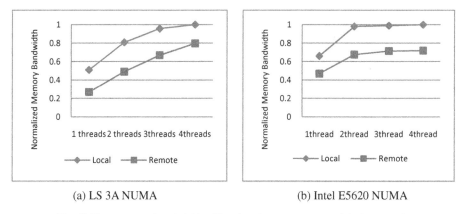

(a) LS 3A NUMA   (b) Intel E5620 NUMA

Fig. 5. The memory bandwidth of local and remote access with signal node

3.2   Local and Remote Memory Contention on One IMC

Now we test the memory contention for local and remote memory access on one node under configuration 1. In order to check out how remote access interferes with local bandwidth, we set xL from 1 to 4 with yR increased from 0 to 4 and illustrate it as Fig.6. From the figure we can see the bandwidth decreased steady with more remote access on LS 3A NUMA. But on Intel E5620 the local bandwidth decreased dramatically with 1 remote thread, and the local bandwidth decreased little when there are more than 1 remote threads. Another difference is that more local threads will obtain more local bandwidth on LS platform, while Intel platform remains the same except a little increment for 4 local threads.

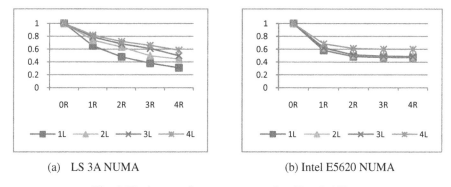

(a)   LS 3A NUMA   (b) Intel E5620 NUMA

Fig. 6. The impact of remote access to local bandwidth

We also measure the remote bandwidth impact by local threads. The details are showed in Fig.7, where remote thread number varies from 1 to 4 with local thread number varies from 0 to 4. It can say that this case is similar to previous case.

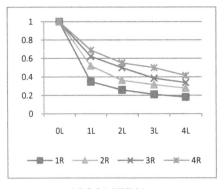
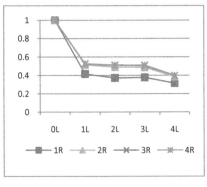

(a) LS 3A NUMA   (b) Intel E5620 NUMA

Fig. 7. Remote bandwidth impact by local memory contention

3.3   Total Memory Bandwidth

Table 1 is the total memory bandwidth with different (xL,yR) combination under configuration 1. The total memory bandwidth in this table is the normalized sum of local and remote bandwidth.

These 2 tables show that on both platform the maximum bandwidth is not at (4L,4R). The maximum for LS platform is at (4L, 3R) and the Intel platform is at (3L,2R). If there are 6 threads, the maximum bandwidth for LS is not at (4L,2R) but at (3L,3R), it is similar on both platforms. From the data we can find that on both NUMA platforms, maximizing local access can't obtain the maximum bandwidth, and when move some threads to remote node may increase the total bandwidth.

Table 1. Normalized total bandwidth with different (xL, yR) combination

(a)   LS 3A NUMA

	0R	1R	2R	3R	4R
0L	0	0.268604753	0.489641936	0.669026213	0.796305483
1L	0.510155182	0.76435979	0.93206135	1.071639386	1.167414268
2L	0.807668329	1.077136439	1.21477007	1.061157669	1.327363384
3L	0.957279374	1.221851671	1.294655035	1.428549427	1.026310918
4L	1	1.244672139	1.395384964	1.480886933	1.458042771

(b)   Intel E5620 NUMA

	0R	1R	2R	3R	4R
0L	0	0.469004798	0.675381934	0.714149411	0.718478895
1L	0.660250795	1.034590501	1.073531914	1.056589576	1.047122689
2L	0.980231839	1.205814996	1.253073808	1.245351318	1.237903597
3L	0.989410094	1.18881594	1.260403052	1.252844415	1.243145613
4L	1	1.059521274	1.057766793	1.029016999	1.021363832

3.4   Cross Pattern

We place the threads and the data they access on different nodes according to configuration2, which is defined by in Fig.4(b), to check out how the remote access of node0 and node1 interfere with each other. The detail is showed in Fig.8. On Intel's platform, when there is one opposite thread, the referenced threads' bandwidth will decrease about 30% (except for the case of 1 local threads), and there is not bandwidth lost when the remote thread number increase further. And when there is only one referenced thread, the bandwidth will decrease less than 5%. On LS Platform, the opposite thread impact is much less, with the maximum no more than 10%.   This test shows that LS's remote access's influence is much smaller than that of Intel.

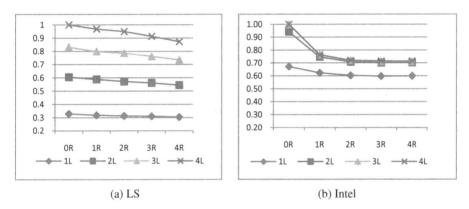

(a) LS   (b) Intel

Fig. 8. Bandwidth for cross pattern

3.5   Split Pattern

The last test setup is according to configuration 3 in Fig.4(c), and we want to check out how the local and remote access of the threads on the same node interferes with each other. We call this access pattern as split pattern. The result is showed in Fig.9.

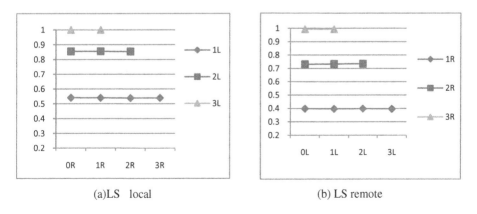

(a)LS   local   (b) LS remote

Fig. 9. Bandwidth for split pattern

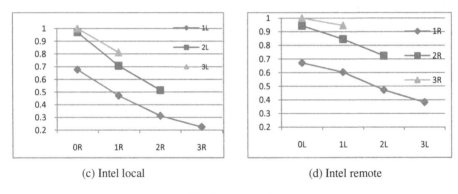

(c) Intel local   (d) Intel remote

Fig. 9. (*continued*)

The Fig.9(a) and Fig.9(b) showed that LS NUMA platform have little impact on each other. But Fig.9 (c) and Fig.9(d) shows that, on Intel NUMA platform, there is continually impact on local accesses when increasing the remote accesses. The result from split pattern apparently shows that the optimization on Intel's platform will not fit for LS platform.

4   Discussion and Conclusion

In this section, we first discuss the architectural differences between these NUMAs concerning the memory access, and then try to explain their diverse behavior.

Local threads in E5620 only need to go through GQ and IMC to access the memory, and the remote threads must go through GQ, QPI and IMC to access the memory, as illustrated in Fig.10(b). The LS 3A local access need to go through X1, X2 and IMC, and the remote access must go through X1, HT, X2 and IMC, as shown in Fig.10(a).

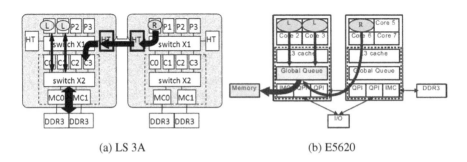

(a) LS 3A   (b) E5620

Fig. 10. Local and remote access channels (2L,1R)

When considering the rate to issue memory access, the individual LS core is not such powerful as E5620 core, because the later can saturate the IMC by only two threads/cores as Fig.5 shown. The remote access is much slower than local access, on both platforms, due to the overhead of cross-processor interconnection.

When local and remote accesses compete for the same IMC, the LS demonstrates a equally free competition and Intel demonstrates a arbitrated behavior. As Fig.6 and Fig.7 shows, the local bandwidth on LS will decrease as more remote competitive threads and vice versa, but the Intel limit the tense of competition to some degree. The arbitrative action on Intel platform will reserve 50%~60% IMC bandwidth for local accessing and 40%~50% for remote accessing, not matter how many threads/cores take part in the competition.

The total bandwidth of two IMCs demonstrates the characteristics that previous study have point out[12]. As Tab.1 shows, the best performance occurs at (3L,3R)for LS with 6 threads.

For the cross pattern case, there is little contention on LS platform because of the full duplex HT connections, but an obvious contention on GQ in Intel platform. That explain why there is a dramatic drop for Intel and a slightly decrease for LS in Fig.8.

For the last case of split pattern, there is not variation on LS platform due to the crossbar switch routing, but there is a nearly linear decrease on Intel platform due to the queuing on GQ.

Because of the different philosophies of designing, these two NUMA systems demonstrate apparently diverse behavior of memory subsystem. With GQ might make Intel platform get a better bandwidth and a little longer delay. And the GQ's arbitrative action will contain the competition between local and remote threads. With barely crossbar switch LS allow the free competition and overcome the performance degradation of unnecessary arbitrating (as the cases of cross pattern and split pattern).

When optimizing the memory performance on these platforms, the thread amount, thread binding, and memory layout should be considered with the memory subsystem's characteristics together. The best mapping of thread and data can be found according to the measured data other than barely maximizing the memory locality. Basically speaking, it needs more threads to compete for a higher bandwidth on LS architecture.

Acknowledgement. The research was jointly supported by project grant from Natural Science Foundation of China under the numbers NSFC61003272, NSFC61171071, grant from Foundation of Guangdong Province and Chinese Academy of Sciences (2011A090100037), and grants from Foundation of Shenzhen City under the numbers JCYJ20120613161137326, JCYJ2012061310222457.

References

1. Advanced Micro Devices. AMD HyperTransport Technology-based system architecture (EB/OL). AMD, Sunnyval (May 2002),
   http://www.amd.com/us/Documents/AMD_HyperTransport_Technolog
   y_based_System_Architecture_FINAL2.pdf

2. Maddox, R.A., Singh, G., Safranek, R.J.: A first look at the Intel QuickPath Interconnect (EB/OL). Intel Corporation, Hillsboto (April 28, 2009), http://www.intel.com/intelpress/articles/A_First_Look_at_the_Intelr_QuickPath_Interconnect.pdf

3. Li, H., Tandri, S., Stumm, M., Sevcik, K.C.: Locality and loop scheduling on NUMA multiprocessors. In: International Conference on Parallel Processing (ICPP). IEEE, New York (1993)

4. Marathe, J., Mueller, F.: Hardware profile-guided automatic page placement for ccNUMA systems. In: Proceedings of the Eleventh ACM SIGPLAN Symposium on Principles and Practice of Parallel Programming (PPoPP). ACM, New York (2006)

5. McCurdy, C., Vetter, J.C.: Memphis: Finding and fixing NUMA-related performance problems on multi-core platforms. In: International Symposium on Performance Analysis of Systems & Software (ISPASS). IEEE, New York (2010)

6. Ogasawara, T.: NUMA-aware memory manager with dominant-thread-based copying GC. In: Proceedings of the 24th ACM SIGPLAN Conference on Object Oriented Programming Systems Languages and Applications (OOPSLA). ACM, New York (2009)

7. Tikir, M.M., Hollingsworth, J.K.: NUMA-aware Java heaps for server applications. In: Proceedings of the 19th IEEE International Parallel and Distributed Processing Symposium (IPDPS). IEEE, Colorado (2005)

8. Tikir, M.M., Hollingsworth, J.K.: Hardware monitors for dynamic page migration. Journal of Parallel and Distributed Computing 68(9), 1186–1200 (2008)

9. Verghese, B., Devine, S., Gupta, A., et al.: Operating system support for improving data locality on CC-NUMA computer servers. In: Proceedings of the Seventh International Conference on Architectural Support for Programming Languages and Operating Systems (ASPLOS). ACM, New York (1996)

10. Wilson, K.M., Aglietti, B.B.: Dynamic page placement to improve locality in CC-NUMA multiprocessors for TPC-C. In: Proceedings of the 2001 ACM/IEEE Conference on Supercomputing (SC). ACM/IEEE, New York (2001)

11. Awasthi, M., Nellans, D.W., Sudan, K., et al.: Handling the problems and opportunities posed by multiple on-chip memory controllers. In: 19th International Conference on Parallel Architecture and Compilation Techniques (PACT). ACM, Vienna (2010)

12. Majo, Z., Gross, T.R.: Memory System Performance in a NUMA Multicore Multiprocessor. In: Proceedings of the 4th Annual International Conference on Systems and Storage (SYSTOR). ACM, New York (2011)

13. Levinthal, D.: Performance Analysis Guide for Intel Core i7 Processor and Intel Xeon 5500 Processors (EB/OL). Intel Corporation (2009), http://software.intel.com/sites/products/collateral/hpc/vtune/performance_analysis_guide.pdf

14. Wang, H., Gao, X., Chen, Y., Hu, W., et al.: Interconnection of Godson-3 Multi-Core Processor. Journal of Computer Research and Development 45(12), 2001–2010 (2008) (in Chinese)

15. McCalpin, J.D.: Memory bandwidth and machine balance in current high performance computers. IEEE Computer Society Technical Committee on Computer Architecture (TCCA) Newsletter, 19–25 (1995)

16. Intel Corporation. Intel 64 and IA-32 Architectures Optimization Reference Manual (EB/OL). Intel Corporation (April 2010), http://www.intel.com/content/dam/doc/manual/64-ia-32-architectures-optimization-manual.pdf

17. Charles, J., Jassi, P., Ananth, N.S., et al.: Evaluation of the Intel Core i7 Turbo Boost feature. In: Proceedings of the 2009 IEEE International Symposium on Workload Characterization (IISWC). IEEE, Washington (2009)

18. Kleen, A.: An NUMA API for Linux (EB/OL) (August 2004), http://www.halobates.de/numacpi3.pdf

Software/Hardware Hybrid Network-on-Chip Simulation on FPGA

Youhui Zhang[*], Peng Qu, Ziqiang Qian, Hongwei Wang, and Weimin Zheng

Department of Computer Science and Technology, Tsinghua University
100084 Beijing, China
zyh02@tsinghua.edu.cn

Abstract. In this paper, a software-and-hardware hybrid simulation method for CMP (Chip-MultiProcessor) system is designed, as well as its performance model. In detail, the NoC (Network-On-Chip) module is totally simulated by the FPGA resource; a software-and-hardware interaction interface of this module is provided so that the simulation software running on the on-chip soft core can cooperate with the NoC to complete the whole simulation. In other words, the most time-consuming and relatively-fixed part is implemented by hardware and others are implemented by software, which maintains simulation flexibility and high performance owing to the compact on-chip design. We implement this design on the Xilinx's Virtex 5 155T chip and the work frequency is 100Mhz. Compared with a typical software counterpart, the simulation speed of NoC is more than 3000 times faster; and the advantage is widened further with the increasing injection rate. Moreover, compared with another hybrid method executing the software part on the host CPU, it is still fairly faster although the host performance is much higher than the on-chip core.

Keywords: Network on chip, FPGA, Simulation.

1 Introduction

Networks-on-Chip (NoC) [1][2] is an approach to designing the communication subsystem between IP cores in a chip, which separates the on-chip communication from computing and storage to improve scalability. For multi-core architectures, NoC has been regarded as one of the crucial and common components. NoC interacts with other functions on-chip, like the cache-coherency (CC) mechanism, the cache-line distribution and so on, to affect the whole system efficiency. It means system architects and researchers must include detailed NoC simulation as part of any complete system simulation.

Detailed NoC simulation is a time-consuming process [3] [4]. Thus quite a few existing projects [5][6][7][8] have used FPGA resource to emulate NoC for high speed, and the reconfigurable feature of FPGA provides a certain degree of flexibility. Furthermore, to simulate the system rather than the NoC itself is the final destination. Thus, NoC simulation should interact with other simulation modules efficiently.

---

[*] Corresponding author.

C.-H. Hsu et al. (Eds.): NPC 2013, LNCS 8147, pp. 167–178, 2013.

This paper presents a software/hardware hybrid design for such requirements. The design principle is: the detailed and time-consuming NoC simulation is totally accomplished by the hardware resource (FPGA) and a simple but general purpose interface between the software and hardware simulations has been provided. To reduce the roundtrip transfer latency between SW and HW, we use the on-chip soft processor to execute simulation software to drive the NoC.

This paper gives the following contributions:

1. A general SW/HW hybrid simulation framework of CMP has been designed and implemented. The kernel is a configurable NoC simulator on the FPGA and some parameters such as data width, network topology, channel FIFO depth, virtual channel options, and packet length and so on can be assigned without recompiling / resynthesizing. Now in a Xilinx Virtex 5 FPGA chip, a NoC to scale to 16 nodes can be simulated with one MicroBlaze CPU on-chip and the work frequency is 100Mhz. A simple interface between SW and HW is also designed that the simulation software running on the on-chip soft core can cooperate with the NoC.
2. Performance analysis is given to show under what circumstance such a design is preferred. There are two ways to run the simulation software, on the on-chip soft CPU or on the host general-purpose CPU. The former usually works on a much lower frequency (1/10 ~ 1/30 of the latter) but its interaction speed with the hardware module is very high because they co-exist on the same chip. For the latter, the transfer trip between the FPGA and the host application is fairly long. We present a sequential and quantitative performance model for such situations
3. The running efficiency is compared with its software counterpart. Result shows that, the NoC speed is 3000 times faster than the 100% software method for the simulation of a 4X4 NoC. Moreover, two usage examples are presented: For the first, two directory-based CC protocols for the multi-core architecture design have been simulated on this framework. In this case, all parts other than the NoC are simulated on the on-chip soft core. Compared with the counterpart that executes the software part on the host CPU, its speed is much higher because the HW/SW transfer latency has been reduced remarkably. The second is a trace-driven case. Compared with the counterpart that executes all parts (including the equivalent NoC simulation implemented by software) on the host CPU, our method is much faster, too.

2   Related Work

Many NoC simulators are achieved by software. Some are standalone tools, like BookSim [3] and DARSIM [4] while others are used as the interconnection module of full-system simulators (GEMS [9], SimFlex[10], etc.). Software implementations are very easy for reconfiguration, fast to compile and deterministic. However they are quite slow, so that users often have to maintain reasonable running speed at the expenses of simulation accuracy.

Several FPGA-based NoC simulators have been designed [5], [6], [7], [8], [11] that increase simulation performance by 10 times and more. [5] presents an emulation environment implemented on an FPGA that is suitable to explore a wide range of NoC design-space. It gets a speed-up of 4 orders of magnitude with respect to a SystemC simulation of the same network. But re-generating is required when changing the configuration of the network.

DRNoC [6] solves this problem based on the re-configurability of FPGAs. Speedups of hundreds of time have been achieved in the presented use case compared with a non-reconfigurable approach (synthesis based). However, partial reconfiguration requires a special design flow and incurs area overheads; and only a few select devices are available. NoCem [7] improves emulation density over [4] and implements a 9-node mesh network on a single FPGA. Moreover, an example memory architecture exploration platform based on this tool has been provided. [8] virtualizes a single router on an FPGA, allowing the simulation of a NoC with multiple routers. An off-chip ARM processor stores N contexts for the router model and orchestrates the emulation of the N-node network. However, the off-chip ARM/FPGA communication is a performance bottleneck.

Further, DART [11] virtualizes NoC totally on the chip while no help of any off-chip CPU is needed. It provides a flexible FPGA-based NoC simulator platform by decoupling the simulator architecture from the architecture of the simulated system. This technology has been also used in some multi-core CPU simulations, like Protoflex [12], RAMPGold [13] and so on.

Our work can be regarded as an extension of the above-mentioned projects. We design a straight and efficient HW/SW interface to control and stimulate the FGPA NoC module, and give a performance model of such a hybrid design to judge in what case it is beneficial in terms of performance.

A similar hybrid work is [14]. It is focused on how to design the FPGA platform efficiently, which is used as an emulation platform for the cache and NoC designers to verify their designs in cooperation with the full-system software simulator. In contrast, our work provides a flexible NoC simulator on FPGA and all other modules, including the cache system, are implemented by software on-chip. Then, researchers can explore the design space more flexibly as less RTL (Register Transfer Level) codes are needed, and the SW/HW interaction is more efficient owing to the compact on-chip design.

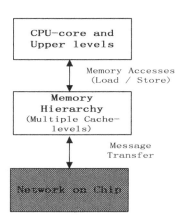

Fig. 1. Levels of the micro-architecture of CMPs

3   System Design

From the viewpoint of the system architects or researchers, a chip multi-core processor (CMP) contains the following levels (Fig.1).

- Network on Chip: Most NoCs are packet-switched. The router usually implements wormhole routing with virtual channel (VC) flow control. Each packet in the network consists of the header flit to setup a route, an arbitrary number of data flits that contain the packet's information and one tail flit that will free the router's resources. All communications, including explicit accesses issued from CPU cores or the others (like control messages used by the CC protocol), are transferred in this level.
- Memory hierarchy: It includes all of cores' local caches and / or on-chip memories. Access requests from CPU cores will be handled by this level before entering into the NoC. If CC is maintained by hardware (which is true for most CMP designs today), the corresponding components (for example, the CC directory) are also regarded as part of this level.
- CPU cores and upper-level components.

In our design, the whole NoC is emulated by FPGA and quite a few of parameters can be configured without recompiling. Detailed descriptions of parameters are listed in Table 1. Of course, the simulation scale is limited by the available on-chip resources.

Further, we wrap the hardware kernel to provide control signals for the simulation software. From the viewpoint of software, the NoC module works like a function call: when all of the upper level's architecture-states in one simulated cycle have been updated, the software simulator invokes the SW/HW interface to promote the NoC simulation a cycle. Because the HW running frequency is much higher than the software simulation[1], this sequential design does not affect the simulation speed.

Table 1. Parameters of the NoC simulator

Configurations	Valid Options
Topology	Mesh,Torus,2D-Torus
Data width	1-256 bits
Packet Length	2,4,8,16 words
Pipeline latency of the router	Arbitrary (> 3)
VC Number	0/2/4
FIFO Length	2,4,8,16

3.1   The Internal Design

From the physical view, the NoC simulator contains multiple nodes connected by a crossbar, which allows all-to-all communication mode. Because it can restrict the

---

[1] In our design, MicroBlaze and NoC both work at 100Mhz and a machine instruction on the MicroBlaze will take at least 3 cycles to complete. Therefore, during a whole NoC cycle, there is almost no progress for software.

communication pattern through this interconnect, this design is able to model the connectivity of the target topology. Then from the viewpoint of simulation, arbitrary topologies can be simulated. In the current design, we only introduce 5 entry points into one NoC node (*North, South, West, East* and *Local Access Point*), which limits the number of types that can be simulated.

Each node is a timing model, including the channel FIFOs, a router and a traffic generator: The first sends and receives data-flits to and from the node through those points; the second consists of arbitration blocks used to judge what is transmitted and when. The traffic generator connects to the *Local Access Point* to inject data flits into NoC. Each node has parameters that can be configured to match the properties of the component they simulate, without modifying the RTL codes (using VHDL generics).

- Traffic Model

Each data-flit in the NoC is described by a 32-bit value. It contains the metadata such as the source / destination addresses, the packet length, a timestamp that indicates when the flit should be forwarded, and the injection time to compute latency at the destination. The bit-width is dependent on the range of configuration parameters: For a NoC containing 16 nodes, 8 bits are used to represent the source and destination IDs, and we reserve extra 4 bits for expansion. Now the maximum of packet length is 16, so that 4 bits are used here. In addition, the timestamp occupies 6 bits and 10 bits for the latency computation.

For flow control, the credit-based mechanism is used: The upstream router keeps a count of the number of free flit buffers in each virtual channel downstream. Then, each time the upstream router forwards a flit, thus consuming a downstream buffer, it decrements the appropriate count. If the count reaches zero, no further flits can be forwarded until a buffer becomes available. Once the downstream router forwards a flit and frees the associated buffer, it sends a credit to the upstream router, causing a buffer count to be incremented. The 12-bit credit descriptor contains a timestamp (6 bits) and a virtual channel identifier.

- Timing Model

The channel FIFO models the timing information of latency of a wire link; each FIFO contains multiple virtual channels (VCs) and a RTL parameter controls the number of VCs to incorporate (up to 4 for this design). For each incoming flit, it will be queued into its VC and the internal timing logic can compute the corresponding de-queue timestamp.

The router models a four-stage wormhole VC router with credit-based flow control. Each router connects to four channel FIFOs and a traffic generator. The deterministic routing (X-Y routing) is supported because this simulator is mainly used to simulate the mesh (or mesh-like) topologies now. Router latency is modeled by incrementing the flit timestamp (it is also configurable) when it leaves. Contention in VC and switch allocation is also modeled by adjusting the timestamp appropriately.

3.2   The Configuration and Result-Collection Interface

The interface contains the following types of signals or modules:

- Packet Injection: Packet control is written to the channel FIFO for the local access point. It will contain the metadata of packet such as source / destination addresses, packet length, and so on, which will be used to route the packet.
- Statistics Export: There are three counters per traffic generator to record the number of injected and received packets and the cumulative packet latency.
- Router Metadata: These lines are used to collect running status of each router, which can be used to locate and analyze the hot spot(s). Now they mainly consist of various VC status signals (empty or full).
- Clock Signal: The clock signal of NoC is connected to a special strobe register. Once this register has been written, a clock signal of high frequency will be issued to promote the NoC simulation a cycle.
- Reset Signal: It is a synchronous signal and the configuration is lost during the reset.
- Simulation configurations: As mentioned earlier, each node has configurable parameters (packet length, VC Number, FIFO length, etc.). These parameters are chained in a 16-bit shift register. A software tool sends the configuration bits over an RS232 serial interface.

From the system point of view, the NoC is a device attached to the processor bus. Thus software can access the above-mentioned signals through the memory-address mapping mechanism.

3.3   Performance Model

A sequential simulation model is presented here. In another word, the simulation software works with the hardware NoC sequentially. It is also a common case for quite a few widely-used full-system simulators, like SIMICS+GEMS and so on. Therefore, the elapsed time for one simulated cycle, E, can be represented by Equation 1.

$$E = T_{sw} + T_{hw} + T_{interaction} \tag{1}$$

T_{sw} denotes the elapsed time of software execution and T_{hw} is the hardware time. The last one represents the roundtrip latency of HW/SW interaction.

There are two modes of sequential simulation.

- Both software and hardware simulations are completed in the same chip.

In this case, both of $T_{interaction}$ and T_{hw} are of the order of magnitude of 10 ns, while T_{sw} is much larger. For example, the test of this design shows that MicroBlaze and NoC both work at 100Mhz and a machine instruction on the MicroBlaze will take averagely 3 cycles to complete. It means the software simulation will consume tens or hundreds of instructions to finish a simulated cycle. Then, in this case E mainly depends on T_{sw}.

- The software is running on the host.

Here T_{hw} is still of the order of magnitude of 10 ns and $T_{interaction}$ is much larger. Tests show that, in our design the average roundtrip latency between the host software and the NoC is about 0.3ms (through the GB Ethernet cable). On the other hand the software execution time is smaller: for an n-core CPU to simulate m target cores (m >= n), it is about 1/(30*n) of the previous version[2] if we assume the frequency of the host CPU is 3Ghz.

In this case, E equals with (300000ns + T_{sw} / (30*n)). The conclusion is straightforward: if the operation in one simulated cycle is too complex, for example, it takes the core on-chip more than 30000 cycles (10ns per cycle) to complete, using the host CPU is preferred (just like [14] did); otherwise, the on-chip mode is better.

4   Implementation and Evaluation

4.1   Implementation

We use the open source implementation of NoC emulator [7] as the foundation, which is a body of VHDL code configurable by a top-level package file that can create a variety of Network on Chips on parameters of data-width, virtual channel implementations, topology, and in-network buffering lengths.

We wrap this emulator as described in Section 3.1 to provide the SW/HW interface. As mentioned in Section 3.2, because the NoC simulation is actually used as a timing model, the original design of in-network buffers has been simplified. In detail, the packet header is necessary to be stored and forwarded node by node; for data flits, only the corresponding arbitration and flow control behaviors should be simulated while no real data-transfer is needed.

The FPGA platform used is BEE3. One BEE3 module consists of four large Virtex-5 155T FPGA chips. In addition, up to 4 Gigabit Ethernet interfaces allow a full-duplex data communication between each BEE3 module and a host server.

This NoC simulator is created by Xilinx ISE 12.4. For a 4X4 mesh, about 60% of FPGA slices have been used and its running frequency is 100Mhz. The remaining resources are used to occupy the MicroBlaze CPU.

BEEcube Platform Studio (BPS) is employed, too, which is a system-level IDE specially designed for BEE3. We use soft registers provided by BPS to connect the software simulation to the NoC. Such a register works like a normal hardware register; the difference lies in that it is used as a bus device that software can access. In order to improve the HW/SW interaction performance, several 128-bit-wide soft registers are used to supply data as much as possible once.

---

[2] Because the detailed simulation of one core is usually implemented as a large and tightly-coupled state machine, it is difficult to be parallelized. On the other side, more than one target core can be simulated in parallel on several host CPU cores as they only interact with each other through the NoC.

Moreover, external DRAM has been mapped into the MicroBlaze's address space so that the simulation software on-chip can access enough memory space. Thus, the work flow of one simulated cycle is described as follows:

Step 1) Software reads all output signals of the hardware NoC;
Step 2) Software completes all simulated events (of the memory hierarchy and / or the above level) in the current cycle.
Step 3) Software updates all input signals of the SW/HW interface accordingly.
Step 4) Trigger the reg_clk_strobe register.

4.2   Usage Examples and Tests

• Running Performance Comparison

We use a well-known software NoC simulator, BookSim [15], as the counterpart and compare its performance with the FPGA version under different flit-injection-rates (configuration time is excluded). The flit-injection-rate defines the rate at which packets are injected into the simulator; for example, setting flit-injection-rate = 0.25 means that each node injects a new packet in one out of every four simulator cycles.

The configurations used by these two simulators are listed in Table 2.

Table 2. Configurations of the comparison

Topology	2D-Mesh
NoC Scale	4*4
FIFO length	8
Packet Length	1
Link latency per flit	1 cycle
Router pipeline latency per flit	4 cycles

One Linux server with a 3.2GHz Intel Xeon processor is used to run BookSim; multiple flit-injection-rates, from 0.05 to 0.5, are configured respectively to show the simulation performance under different loads.

The speedup (in the right part of Fig.2) is the ratio of the number of cycles simulated per second in FPGA to that in software. We observe that the software's simulation speed decreases with increasing injection rate (in the left part of Fig.4) while the hardware speed is constant. As a result, our simulator achieves greater speed-up at higher packet injection rates: The least is more than 3000 as the scale is 4X4 and the flit-injection-rate is 0.05; when the flit-injection-rate is set as 0.5, the ratio is about 6000. In addition, as the NoC scale increases, the speed gap will expand further.

• Comparison with other FPGA-based solutions

We have collected some information of existing FPGA-based NoC simulators, including the running performance, the consumed on-chip resources and the NoC scale that can be simulated, and presented them in Table 3. Because the FPGA chips used by these works are different, the comparison is for reference only.

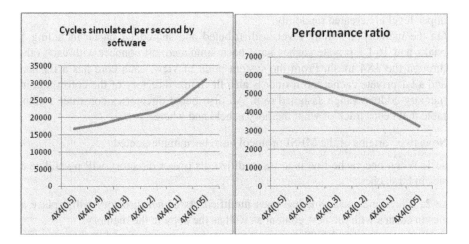

Fig. 2. Performance of the FPGA NoC simulator. In both figures, the X-axis stands for the NoC scale and flit-injection-rates. For example, 4X4(0.5) means there 16 nodes and each node injects a new packet in one out of every two simulator cycles. In the left part, the y-axis stands for the simulation speed measured in cycles per second. In the right part, the y-axis indicates the ratio of the number of cycles simulated per second in FPGA to that in software.

Table 3. Comparison with other FPGA-based simulators

	[5]	[7]	[8]	[11]	**Ours**
Running Frequency(Mhz)	50	70	6.6	50	**100**
On-chip resources (slices)	7387 (Virtex II Pro V20)	16394 (Virtex II Pro (XC2VP30))	N/A (Virtex-II 8000)	13050 (Virtex II Pro (XC2VP30))	**11005**
NoC Scale	6	9	N/A[3]	9[4]	**16**

- CC Examples

For the 4X4 mesh NoC, we simulate some directory-based CC protocols of CMP at the memory-hierarchy level to verify its function. The software is written in C and running on the soft processor on-chip. Details are presented as follows:

— The whole memory space is shared by all cores. The CC feature is kept by the distributed-directory-based hardware, which is the main simulated subject by software.

---

[3] It supports the time-division multiplexing technology, so that one physical node can simulate multiple target nodes (while the simulation speed will be degraded). For example, if a 4X4 network is simulated, the maximum simulation frequency is 206 kHz.

[4] DART supports the time-division multiplexing technology, too. Here only the number of physical nodes are given.

— No real CPU core is simulated. Instead, read / write memory accesses from the upper-level are created randomly.

— On the memory-hierarchy level, a distributed and shared L2 cache including 16 banks and 16 L1 private caches have been simulated; all connect with each other through the 4X4 mesh. From the system point of view, each core has a L2 bank and a L1 private cache; the former is also the home directory of the corresponding memory-address range assigned to it. All distributed directories construct a global table that keeps track of what memory is held and where.

Now, two variants of the MESI protocol have been implemented:

Case 1: When one cache-line is to be modified, its owner directory will invalidate all copies in L1 caches.

Case 2: When one cache-line has been modified, its owner directory will replace all copies in caches with the new content as well as the copy in the memory.

A fixed sequence of 10000 memory accesses has been simulated in these two cases; the results are presented in Table 4. We can see that the number of elapsed cycles of Case 2 is about 164.5% of that of Case 1, although its L1 cache hit-ratio is 160.9% of Case 1. The reason lies in that, for Case 2, the communication times is much larger, about 229.5% of the other; and the average transfer-latency of a message through the NoC is increased from 3.8 cycles to 4.1.

Table 4. Results of CC Examples

	Case 1	Case 2
Simulated cycles	83627	137536
Cache-hit ratio	16.31%	26.24%
Number of NoC communications	44131	101300
Average transfer-latency of a message	3.8 cycles	4.1 cycles

For Case 1, the whole simulation time is about 2.5s. According to the performance model in Section 3.2, if running the CC simulation on the host CPU that interacts with the FPGA, the time spent on the roundtrip communications will be more than 25.1s (83627 *0.3ms), which is much more than the on-chip version. Therefore, this mode is preferred for such relatively simple simulations.

In addition, if both simulations (CC and the NoC) are completed by software on the host, the estimated running-time is also longer although we take the fastest simulation speed of BookSim (about 31000 cycles per second in Fig.4).

• Trace-driven Example

This is a real usage. To compare NoC designs with different configurations, we have to simulate a few NoC architectures and use the real running trace as the input to judge the better design. The trace is collected through the following way: We use the Pin [16] to instrument the real target process; in the corresponding callback code, we simulate a 16-core CMP's memory hierarchy with the given configurations but no NoC-communication has been simulated. Till now we can get the access-trace for NoC and the collected trace contains about 3,200,000 records.

Then, we use the GB Ethernet cable to transfer records into the chip when a proxy program is running on the soft core to receive data to drive the NoC. Although the transfer latency of the Ethernet is relatively high, its throughout is enough so that the transfer is not the bottleneck.

It has consumed 29,000,000 cycles or so to complete all records, in 127s. In contrast, we use the 100% software solution and the running time is about 710s.

5   Conclusions

We have presented a method that allows multi-core system designers to simulate NoC and other layers with flexibility and fast enough speed. By providing common SW/HW interfaces, the time-consuming and relatively-fixed part, NoC, is implemented by hardware while others are implemented by software. We synthesize this design on the Xilinx's Virtex 5 155T FPGA and some example has been completed to show its availability. In addition, performance analysis is given to show under what circumstance such a design is preferred: if the operation in one simulated cycle is too complex, using the host CPU for software simulation is preferred although the slow HW/SW interaction exists; otherwise, the on-chip mode is better.

Acknowledgement. The work is supported by the High Technology Research and Development Program of China under Grant No. 2013AA01A215. The authors wish to thank Mo Tao, Li Xiaoxiao and Jiang Linhao for their tireless support of the simulation environment.

References

1. Dally, W.J., Towles, B.: Route packets, not wires: on-chip interconnection networks. In: Proceedings of Design Automation Conference (DAC 2001), Las Vegas, USA, pp. 684–689 (2001)
2. Benini, L., Micheli, G.D.: Networks on chips: a new SoC paradigm. IEEE Computer 35, 70–78 (2002)
3. Dally, W., Towles, B.: Principles and Practices of Interconnection Networks. Morgan Kaufmann Publishers Inc., San Francisco (2003)
4. Lis, M., Shim, K.S., Cho, M.H., Ren, P., Khan, O., Devadas, S.: DARSIM: a Parallel Cycle-Level NoC Simulator. In: Proceeding of 6th Annual Workshop on Modeling, Benchmarking and Simulation (June 2010)
5. Genko, N., Atienza, D., De Micheli, G., Mendias, J., Hermida, R., Catthoor, F.: A complete network-on-chip emulation framework. In: Proceeding of Design, Automation and Test in Europe, DATE (March 2005)

6. Krasteva, Y., Criado, F., de la Torre, E., Riesgo, T.: A Fast Emulation-Based NoC Proto-typing Framework. In: Proceedings of International Conference on Reconfigurable Computing and FPGAs (December 2008)
7. Schelle, G., Grunwald, D.: Onchip interconnect exploration for multicore processors utilizing FPGAs. In: Proceedings of 2nd Workshop on Architecture Research using FPGA Platforms (2006)
8. Wolkotte, P., Holzenspies, P., Smit, G.: Fast, Accurate and Detailed NoC Simulations. In: Proceedings of First International Symposium on Networks-on-Chip, NOCS 2007 (May 2007)
9. Martin, M.M.K., Sorin, D.J., Beckmann, B.M., et al.: Multifacet's general execution-driven multiprocessor simulator (GEMS) toolset. ACM SIGARCH Computer Architecture News 33, 92–99 (2005)
10. Hardavellas, N., Somogyi, S., Wenisch, T.F., Wunderlich, R.E., Chen, S., Kim, J., Falsafi, B., Hoe, J.C., Nowatzyk, A.G.: SimFlex: a fast, accurate, flexible full-system simulation framework for performance evaluation of server architecture. SIGMETRICS Perform. Eval. Rev. 31(4), 31–34 (2004)
11. Wang, D., Jerger, N.E., Steffan, Gregory Steffan, J.: DART: a programmable architecture for NoC simulation on FPGAs. In: Proceedings of the Fifth ACM/IEEE International Symposium on Networks-on-Chip (2011)
12. Chung, E.S., Papamichael, M.K., Nurvitadhi, E., Hoe, J.C., Falsafi, B., Mai, K.: ProtoFlex: Towards Scalable, Full-System Multiprocessor Simulations Using FPGAs. ACM Transactions on Reconfigurable Technology and Systems 2(2) (June 2009)
13. Asanović, K., Patterson, D., Tan, Z., Waterman, A., Avizienis, R., Lee, Y.: RAMP Gold: An FPGA-based Architecture Simulator for Multiprocessors. In: Proceedings of Design Automation Conference, DAC 2010 (2010)
14. Liu, G.X., Li, G.H., Gao, P., Qu, H., Liu, Z.Y., Wang, H.X., Xue, Y.B., Wang, D.S.: Cycle-Accurate 64+Core FPGA-Based Hybrid Simulator. In: Proceedings of 5th Annual Workshop on Architectural Research Prototyping (2010)
15. Jiang, N., Michelogiannakis, G., Becker, D., et al.: BookSim 2.0 User's Guide (2003), https://nocs.stanford.edu/cgi-bin/trac.cgi/raw-attachment/wiki/Resources/BookSim/manual.pdf
16. Berkowits, S.: Pin - A Dynamic Binary Instrumentation Tool, http://software.intel.com/en-us/articles/pin-a-dynamic-binary-instrumentation-tool

Total Exchange Routing
on Hierarchical Dual-Nets

Yamin Li[1] and Wanming Chu[2]

[1] Hosei University, Tokyo 184-8584 Japan
[2] University of Aizu, Aizu-Wakamatsu 965-8580 Japan

Abstract. The hierarchical dual-net (HDN) is a newly proposed inter-connection network for massive parallel computers. The HDN is constructed based on a symmetric product graph (base network). A k-level hierarchical dual-net, $\mathrm{HDN}(B,k,S)$, contains $n_k = (2n_0)^{2^k}/(2\prod_{i=1}^{k} s_i)$ nodes, where $S = \{G'_1, G'_2, \ldots, G'_k\}$, G'_i is a super-node and $s_i = |G'_i|$ is the number of nodes in the super-node at the level i for $1 \leq i \leq k$, and n_0 is the number of nodes in the base network B. The S is used mainly for adjusting the scale of the system. The node degree of $\mathrm{HDN}(B,k,S)$ is $d_0 + k$, where d_0 is the node degree of the base network. The HDN is node and edge symmetric and can contain huge number of nodes with small node-degree and short diameter. The total exchange is one of the most dense communication patterns and is at the heart of numerous applications and programming models in parallel computing. In this paper, we show that the total exchange routing can be done on HDN efficiently.

Keywords: interconnection network, total exchange routing.

1   Introduction

Recently, because of the advances in computer and networking technologies, supercomputers containing hundreds of thousands of nodes have been built [10]. It was predicted that the parallel systems of the next decade will contain 10 to 100 millions of nodes [2]. The interconnection network plays an important role for achieving high-performance in such ultra-scale parallel systems. The performance of an ultra-scale parallel computers depends largely on the time complexities of communication schemes, and in turn depends on the diameter of the network. An interconnection network consists of switches with multiple communication ports and cables connecting ports by following certain topologies. For an ultra-scale parallel computer, the traditional interconnection networks may no longer satisfy the requirements for the high-performance computations or efficient communications. For such an ultra-scale parallel computer, the node degree and the diameter will be the critical measures for the effectiveness of the interconnection networks. The node degree is limited by the hardware technologies and the diameter affects all kinds of communication schemes directly. The number of communication ports (node degree) in the network-on-chip (NoC) is typically 4 to 8 in current implementations. The off-chip interconnect switches can have

C.-H. Hsu et al. (Eds.): NPC 2013, LNCS 8147, pp. 179–193, 2013.

tens of ports, but the cost becomes expensive as the number of ports increases. Other important measures for the effectiveness of the interconnection networks include symmetricity, scalability, and efficient routing algorithms.

The following two categories of interconnection networks have attracted a great research attention and been used in many supercomputers' implementations. One is the hypercube-like family that has the advantage of short diameters for high-performance computing and efficient communications. The other is the 2D/3D mesh or torus family that has the advantage of small and fixed node degrees and easy implementations [1]. Traditionally, most supercomputers including those built by CRAY, IBM, SGI, and Intel use 3D tori or hypercubes. However, the node degree of the hypercube increases logarithmically as the number of nodes in the systems increases; the diameter of the 2D/3D torus becomes large in an ultra-scale parallel system. To solve these problems, the hierarchical (cluster-based) architectures are proposed in literature [3,6]. The supercomputer Roadrunner built by IBM adopts a new approach for the interconnection network [4]. It is a cluster-based architecture: the connection among clusters is fully connected, and the fat-tree is used for the connection inside a cluster.

In this paper, we first present a flexible interconnection network, called *Hierarchical Dual-Net* (HDN) [8]. The HDN is symmetric and can connect a large number of nodes with a small node degree, meanwhile keeping the diameter short. The HDN was motivated by recursive dual-net (RDN) [7]. The RDN can be viewed as a special case of HDN. The RDN has merits of low node degree and short diameter. The problem of the RDN is that it grows too fast in size, and there is no mechanism to control the rate of its growth. Different from the RDN, the scale of the HDN can be controlled by setting a set of suitable parameters while generating an expanded network through dual-construction. The HDN also adapts the cluster-based architecture. Compared to the Roadrunner, the HDN is symmetric, uses small number of links, and meanwhile keeps the diameter short. The HDN structure is also better than other popular existing networks such as hypercube and 2D/3D torus with respect to the degree and diameter. We investigate the topological properties of the HDN and show some examples of HDNs with simple base networks of small size. Then we compare them to other networks such as three-dimensional torus used in IBM Blue Gene/L [1], and hypercube. The total exchange, or all-to-all personalized communication, is one of the most dense communication patterns and is at the heart of numerous applications and programming models in parallel computing. In this paper, we present an efficient total exchange routing algorithm on a hierarchical dual-net. The time complexity $T_k(m)$ of the algorithm for an HDN(B, k, S) is $T_k(m) = (2^{k+1} - 2)(t_s + t_w m n_k/2) + 2^k T_0(m n_k/2)$, where n_k is the total number of nodes, t_s is startup latency, m is the message length in words, and t_w is the per-word transfer time.

The rest of this paper is organized as follows. Section 2 introduces the hierarchical dual-net in details. Section 3 describes the routing algorithm. Section 4 gives the total exchange routing algorithm on a hierarchical dual-net. Section 5 concludes the paper.

2   The Hierarchical Dual-Net

We begin with a brief introduction to the recursive dual-net (RDN). The RDN is constructed recursively by a dual-construction. The dual-construction is a way to expand a given symmetric graph G of size n to a new symmetric graph G^* of size $2n^2$. It generates $2n$ copies of G as subgraphs (denoted as clusters) of G^*. Half of them, n clusters, are of class 0 and the others are of class 1. The connection method is described below.

If G is symmetric then the expanded graph G^* is unique and symmetric. Therefore, the dual-construction can be applied recursively from a symmetric network (the base network). $RDN(m, k)$ denotes an RDN generated from a base network of size m by applying dual-construction k times. The problem about an RDN is that its growth rate is super-exponential $((2m)^{2^k})$. There is very little space for selection of the size of an RDN. For example, let the base network be a 3-cube, then the sizes of $RDN(8, k)$ will be 2^7, 2^{15}, and 2^{31} for $k = 1, 2$, and 3, respectively. In HDN, we provide a mechanism to control the growth rate through its expansion from a base network. This new interconnection network has a very flexible way for adjusting its size.

The *hierarchical dual-net*, $HDN(B, k, S)$, contains three sets of parameters: B is a *symmetric product graph*, we call it *base network*; k is an integer that indicates the *level* of the HDN (the number of *dual-constructions* applied); and $S = \{G'_1, G'_2, \ldots, G'_k\}$, where G'_i is a *sub-graph* of $HDN(B, k-1, S)$ and $s_i = |G'_i|$ is the number of nodes in a *super-node* at the level i for $1 \leq i \leq k$. All these terminologies will be defined in the following paragraphs.

Given r graphs $G_i = (V_i, E_i)$, $1 \leq i \leq r$, their product graph $G = G_1 \times G_2 \times \ldots \times G_r$ is defined as the graph $G = (V, E)$, where $V = \{(v_1, v_2, \ldots, v_r)|v_i \in V_i, 1 \leq i \leq r\}$ and $E = \{[(u_1, u_2, \ldots, u_r), (v_1, v_2, \ldots, v_r)]|$ for some j, $(u_j, v_j) \in E_j$ and for $i \neq j, u_i = v_i\}$.

In other words, the nodes of the product graph G are labeled with r-tuples, where the ith element of the r-tuples is chosen from the node set of the ith component graph. The edges of the product graph connect pairs of nodes whose labels are identical in all but the jth element, and the two nodes corresponding to the jth elements in the jth component graph are connected by an edge.

Meshes/tori or hypercubes are typical examples of product graphs. Given a product graph $G = G_1 \times G_2 \times \ldots \times G_r$, we define a *quotient graph* Q as $Q = G/G'$ where G' is a sub-product graph of G such that $G = G' \times Q$. A node in a product graph $G = G_1 \times \ldots \times G_i \times \ldots \times G_r$ can be represented by $(a_1, \ldots, a_i, \ldots, a_r)$ with $0 \leq a_i \leq |G_i| - 1$. We define a sub-graph G' as $G' = G''_1 \times \ldots \times G''_j \times \ldots \times G''_q$ with $G''_j = G_i$ for $1 \leq j \leq q \leq r$ and $1 \leq i \leq r$, $G''_j \neq G''_k$ if $j \neq k$ for $1 \leq j, k \leq q$. Then a node in the sub-graph G' can be represented by $(b_1, \ldots, b_i, \ldots, b_q)$ with $0 \leq b_i \leq |G''_i| - 1$. We can consider a quotient graph Q as a reduced graph of G with G' being mapped into a single node (a super-node).

A graph G is symmetric (node-symmetric) if all its nodes looks alike. A product graph is symmetric if all its component graphs are symmetric. We use the symmetric product graph as the base network for generating a hierarchical dual-net through dual-constructions. We denote the base network as $B = B_1 \times B_2 \times \ldots \times B_r$ where all the B_i, $1 \le i \le r$, are symmetric. We define a super-node of B, denoted as SN as a sub-product graph of B. That is, $SN = B_{i_1} \times B_{i_2} \times \ldots \times B_{i_q}$, where $i_j, 1 \le j \le q$, are distinct and $q \le r$.

Let $|B_i| = b_i$ be the number of nodes in B_i for $1 \le i \le r$. The HDN$(B, 0, S) = B$ is the base network. For $i > 0$, the HDN(B, i, S) is generated from HDN$(B, i - 1, S)$ by a construction to be explained below. Note that $S = \{G'_1, G'_2, \ldots, G'_k\}$, where G'_i is a sub-graph of HDN$(B, k - 1, S)$ and $s_i = |G'_i|$ is the number of nodes in a super-node at the level i for $1 \le i \le k$. First, we define a super-node of level i, denoted as SN^i, to be a sub-product graph G'_i of size s_i in B. Then, we define graph Q^i as the quotient graph HDN$(B, i - 1, S)/SN^i$. Suppose that there are N_{i-1} nodes in the HDN$(B, i-1, S)$, then the number of nodes n_i in Q^i is N_{i-1}/s_i. The s_i can be 1 or $\prod_{j=1}^{q} |B_{i_j}|$, where $1 \le i_j \le r$ and $q \le r$. That is, s_i can be a product of any number of integers in $\{b_1, b_2, \ldots, b_r\}$. For example, if $r = 3$, $b_1 = 2$, $b_2 = 3$, and $b_3 = 5$, the possible s_i can be 1, 2, 3, 5, 2×3, 2×5, 3×5, or $2 \times 3 \times 5$.

The construction of HDN(B, i, S), $1 \le i \le k$, can be defined by a two-step process: First, we perform a dual-construction on the quotient graph $Q^{i-1} =$ HDN$(B, i-1, S)/SN^i$ (HDN$(B, 0, S) = B$). Let the graph generated by the dual-construction be Q^i, and the subgraph of two nodes that is connected by a cross-edge of level i be K_2. Second, to get the HDN(B, i, S), we replace every K_2 in Q^i by a product graph $K_2 \times SN$. We call HDN$(B, i - 1, S)$ *cluster* of HDN(B, i, S).

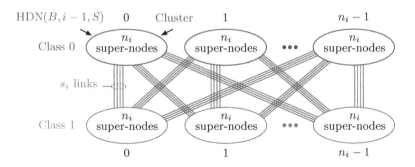

Fig. 1. Build an HDN(B, i, S) from HDN$(B, i - 1, S)$

Referring to Figure 1, an HDN(B, i, S) consists of $2n_i$ clusters which are divided into two *classes*: class 0 and class 1 with each class containing n_i clusters. That is, the number of clusters in each class is equal to the number of super-nodes in a cluster. At level i, each super-node in a cluster has s_i new links to a super-node in a distinct cluster of the other class. Because there are s_i nodes in a super-node, one node contributes a new link. The dual-construction of an RDN is a special case of the construction of an HDN with $s_i = 1$ for $1 \le i \le k$.

The indexes of the nodes in HDN(B, k, S) can be defined as follows. Let SN^k_{id} be a *super-node_id* in a cluster of HDN(B, k, S) and N^k_{id} be a *node_id* in a super-node, then a node in the HDN(B, k, S) can be represented by $(C^k, U^k_{id}, SN^k_{id}, N^k_{id})$

where C^k is the *class_id* (0 or 1) and U^k_{id} is the *cluster_id*. A cross-edge at level k connects node $(C^k, U^k_{id}, SN^k_{id}, N^k_{id})$ and node $(\overline{C^k}, SN^k_{id}, U^k_{id}, N^k_{id})$.

If we use a $2 \times 3 \times 5$ torus as the base network, Table 1 lists the number of nodes in HDN$(B, 1, S)$ and HDN$(B, 2, S)$ under the different configurations of S. The node degrees are 7 and 8 for HDN$(B, 1, S)$ and HDN$(B, 2, S)$, respectively, because the node degree of B is 6. From the table, we can see that the HDN covers the nodes range from several hundreds to several millions.

Table 1. Number of nodes in HDN(B, k, S) where B is a $2 \times 3 \times 5$ torus

$k = 1$	$s_1 = 1$	$s_1 = 2$	$s_1 = 3$	$s_1 = 5$	$s_1 = 6$	$s_1 = 10$	$s_1 = 15$	$s_1 = 30$
	1,800	900	600	360	300	180	120	60

$k = 2$	$s_2 = 1$	$s_2 = 2$	$s_2 = 3$	$s_2 = 5$	$s_2 = 6$	$s_2 = 10$	$s_2 = 15$	$s_2 = 30$
$s_1 = 1$	6,480,000	3,240,000	2,160,000	1,296,000	1,080,000	648,000	432,000	216,000
$s_1 = 2$	1,620,000	810,000	540,000	324,000	270,000	162,000	108,000	54,000
$s_1 = 3$	720,000	360,000	240,000	144,000	120,000	72,000	48,000	24,000
$s_1 = 5$	259,200	129,600	86,400	51,840	43,200	25,920	17,280	8,640
$s_1 = 6$	180,000	90,000	60,000	36,000	30,000	18,000	12,000	6,000
$s_1 = 10$	64,800	32,400	21,600	12,960	10,800	6,480	4,320	2,160
$s_1 = 15$	28,800	14,400	9,600	5,760	4,800	2,880	1,920	960
$s_1 = 30$	7,200	3,600	2,400	1,440	1,200	720	480	240

Suppose that the node degree of the base network B is d_0, the node degree of the HDN(B, k, S) is $d_0 + k$. Let N_{i-1} be the number of nodes in the HDN$(B, i - 1, S)$. There are $N_i = 2(N_{i-1}/s_i)N_{i-1} = 2N_{i-1}^2/s_i$ nodes in the HDN(B, i, S) for $1 \leq i \leq k$, where N_{i-1}/s_i is the number of clusters in each class. That is, the number of nodes in the HDN(B, k, S) is $(2n_0)^{2^k}/(2\prod_{i=1}^{k} s_i)$, where n_0 is the number of nodes in the base network.

Let the diameter of the HDN$(B, i - 1, S)$ be D_{i-1} and the diameter of the super-node (SN) be $D(SN_i)$. Then, if we map a super-node into a single node, the diameter of the quotient graph Q^{i-1} is $D(Q^{i-1}) = D_{i-1} - D(SN^i)$.

To route a node u in a cluster of class 0 (or 1) to a node v in a different cluster of the same class, we can route u along with a direct link of level i to a node u' in a cluster of class 1 (or 0). This takes one step. Then, we route u' inside the cluster to a node w' that can reach a node w in the same cluster of node v along with direct link of level i. The longest distance between nodes u' and w' is $D(Q^{i-1})$.

Similarly, we can route node w' to a node w (by one step) and then to a node v' which is in the same super-node of v (by $D(Q^{i-1})$ steps). Finally, we route v' to node v, this takes $D(SN^i)$ steps. Therefore, we have the following recurrence:

$$D_i = 2(1 + D(Q^{i-1})) + D(SN^i) = 2D_{i-1} - D(SN^i) + 2$$

Solving the above recurrence, we get the diameter D_k of HDN(B, k, S) as below:

$$D_k = 2^k D(B) - \sum_{j=0}^{k-1} 2^j D(SN^{k-j}) + 2^{k+1} - 2$$

where $D(B)$ and $D(SN^i), 1 \leq i \leq k$, are the diameters of the base network and the super-nodes, respectively. The results of the analysis in this section are summarized in the following theorem.

Theorem 1. *Assume that the base network B is a symmetric, product graph and $SN^i, 1 \leq i \leq k$, are sub-product graphs of B with $|SN^i| = s_i$. Let the number of nodes, the node-degree, and the diameter of B be n_0, d_0, and D_0, respectively. Let the diameters of $SN^i, 1 \leq i \leq k$, be $D(SN^i)$. Let $S = \{G'_1, G'_2, \ldots, G'_k\}$, where G'_i is a sub-graph of $HDN(B, k-1, S)$ and $s_i = |G'_i|$ is the number of nodes in a super-node at the level i for $1 \leq i \leq k$. Then, the number of nodes of $HDN(B, k, S)$ is $(2n_0)^{2^k}/(2\prod_{i=1}^{k} s_i)$, the node-degree is $d_0 + k$, and the diameter is $D_k = 2^k D(B) - \sum_{j=0}^{k-1} 2^j D(SN^{k-j}) + 2^{k+1} - 2$, where N is the number of nodes in $HDN(B, k, S)$.*

Table 2 lists the topological properties of the torus, n-cube, CCC [9], Dual-Cube [6], RDN, and HDN. The CCC (cube-connected cycles) is obtained by replacing a node in an n-cube with an n-node cycle. The Dual-Cube is a special case of RDN with $k = 1$ and a base network of an n-cube.

Table 2. Comparison of topological properties

Network	# of nodes	Degree	Diameter
3D Torus	$x * y * z$	6	$(x + y + z)/2$
n-cube	2^n	n	n
CCC(n)	$n * 2^n$	3	$2n + \lfloor n/2 \rfloor - 2$
Dual-Cube(n)	2^{2n-1}	n	$2n$
RDN(m,k)	$(2m)^{2^k}/2$	$d_0 + k$	$2^k * D_0 + 2^{k+1} - 2$
HDN(B,k,S)	$(2|B|)^{2^k}/(2\prod_{i=1}^{k} s_i)$	$d_0 + k$	$2^k(D(B) - \sum_{j=0}^{k-1} 2^j(D(SN^{k-j})) + 2^{k+1} - 2$

In [7], we introduced the CR (cost ratio) for measuring the combined effects of the hardware cost (node degree) and the software efficiency (diameter) of an interconnection network. Instead of CR, this paper uses a more general measure, namely *weighted cost ratio* $CR_w(G)$, for the evaluation. The $CR_w(G)$ is defined as below. Let $|(G)|$, $d(G)$, and $D(G)$ be the number of nodes, the node degree, and the diameter of G, respectively. We define $CR_w(G)$ as

$$CR_w(G) = \frac{w_1 d(G) + w_2 D(G)}{\log_2 |(G)|}$$

where w_1 and w_2 are weights for node degree and diameter, respectively. We have $w_1 + w_2 = 100\%$.

The weighted cost ratio CR_w of an n-cube is always 1 regardless of its size and weights. The CR_w for some $HDN(B, k, S)$ is shown in Table 3 where B is a $2 \times 3 \times 5$ torus and we assume $w_1 = w_2 = 50\%$. For simplicity, we use the number of nodes in super-nodes to represent S, instead of sub-graphs. From the table, we can see that the HDNs are more effective than hypercubes and tori measured by the weighted cost ratio although as the s_i increases, the CR_w becomes larger.

Table 3. CR_w with $w_1 = w_2 = 50\%$ for some HDN(B, k, S)

Network	n	d	D	CR
10-cube	1,024	10	10	1.00
3D-Tori(10)	1,000	6	15	1.05
HDN$(B, 1, (1))$	1,800	7	10	0.79
HDN$(B, 1, (2))$	900	7	9	0.82
HDN$(B, 1, (3))$	600	7	9	0.87
19-cube	524,288	19	19	1.00
3D-Tori(80)	512,000	6	120	3.32
HDN$(B, 2, (2, 2))$	810,000	8	19	0.69
HDN$(B, 2, (2, 5))$	324,000	8	18	0.71
HDN$(B, 2, (5, 2))$	129,600	8	17	0.74

The minimum CR_w shown in the list is 0.69. Unfortunately, we do not know the theoretical or experimental optimal value of CR_w up to the date we wrote this paper and it can be an open question for the future.

3   Routing on HDN

Given two nodes u and v in HDN(B, k, S), we first present a simple routing algorithm that finds a shortest path from u to v. In Section 2, we defined the product and quotient graphs. Now, we define the *difference graph* as follows. Let SN_1 and SN_2 are two super-nodes in base network B, the difference graph $SN_1 - SN_2$ is the sub-product graph of B such that $B_i, 1 \le i \le r$, is in $SN_1 - SN_2$ if and only if $B_i \subset SN_1$ and $B_i \not\subset SN_2$. For example, if $B = C_2 \times C_3 \times C_5$, $SN_1 = C_2 \times C_3$, and $SN_2 = C_3 \times C_5$ then $SN_1 - SN_2 = C_2$.

We also need a re-indexing process of nodes in the cluster, which is an HDN$(B, i - 1, S)$, for routing via cross-edges of level i since the indexes of nodes in HDN$(B, i - 1, S)$ is based on SN^{i-1} and the cross-edge of level i is defined based on SN^i. The index of a node in HDN$(B, i - 1, S)$ contains four parts $(C^{i-1}, U_{id}^{i-1}, SN_{id}^{i-1}, N_{id}^{i-1})$ as explained in the previous section.

At the construction of the ith level, HDN$(B, i - 1, S)$ becomes a cluster containing only two parts, SN_{id}^i and N_{id}^i, of the node index in HDN(B, i, S). The other two parts, C^i and U_{id}^i, are generated from the construction at the ith level. The re-indexing process that generates a 1-to-1 mapping between $(C^{i-1}, U_{id}^{i-1}, SN_{id}^{i-1}, N_{id}^{i-1})$ and (SN_{id}^i, N_{id}^i) on an HDN$(B, i - 1, S)$ is necessary for the proposed routing algorithm.

Since the number of super-nodes SN^i in HDN$(B, i - 1, S)$ equals to N_{i-1}/s_i, the range of SN_{id}^i is $2|U^{i-1}/(SN^i - SN^{i-1})| \times |(SN^{i-1} - SN^i)|$. If $s_{i-1} = s_i$ then the re-indexing is simple: 1-1 mapping between SN_{id}^i and the 3-tuple $(C_{id}^{i-1}, U_{id}^{i-1}, SN_{id}^{i-1})$. However, when $s_{i-1} \ne s_i$, the re-indexing is a little complicated and is explained below.

Let the q-tuple, $(b_{i_1}, \dots, b_{i_q})$ be the index of a node in a super-node SN, where $b_{i_1} \times \dots \times b_{i_q} = |SN|$. Then the re-indexing from $(C^{i-1}, U_{id}^{i-1}, SN_{id}^{i-1}, N_{id}^{i-1})$

to (SN_{id}^i, N_{id}^i) moves the indexes of those $B_j \subset SN^i - SN^{i-1}$ into N_{id}^i and the indexes of those $B_j \subset SN^{i-1} - SN^i$ into SN_{id}^i. For example, let $B = C_2 \times C_3 \times C_5$, $s_1 = |C_2| \times |C_3| = 6$, and $s_2 = |C_3| \times |C_5| = 15$, then, the nodes in HDN$(B, 1, S)$ can be represented by $(C^1, U_{id}^1, SN_{id}^1, N_{id}^1)$, where $C^1 = 0$ or 1, $0 \le U_{id}^1 < 5$, $0 \le SN_{id}^1 < 5$, and $0 \le N_{id}^1 < 6$. For the indexes of the nodes in HDN$(B, 2, S)$, we perform re-indexing of nodes in HDN$(B, 1, S)$, which is a cluster of HDN$(B, 2, S)$, to get (SN_{id}^2, N_{id}^2), where $0 \le SN_{id}^2 < 2 \times 5 \times 2 = 20$, and $0 \le N_{id}^2 < 3 \times 5 = 15$, obtained by swapping $|B_1|$ and $|B_3|$. That is, $|SN^2| = |C^1| \times |U^1| \times |B_1| = 2 \times 5 \times 2 = 20$, and $|N^2| = |B_2| \times |B_3| = 15$.

Table 4 shows four examples of re-indexing in detail for a cluster in the HDN$(B, 2, S)$ with $B = C_2 \times C_3 \times C_5$, $s_1 = 2 \times 3 = 6$, and $s_2 = 3 \times 5 = 15$. In the HDN$(B, 1, S)$, the node representation $(C^1, U_{id}^1, SN_{id}^1, N_{id}^1)$ can be converted to a serial number i by $i = C^1 \times (|B|/s_1)^2 \times s_1 + U_{id}^1 \times (|B|/s_1)^1 \times s_1 + SN_{id}^1 \times s_1 + N_{id}^1 = C^1 \times 150 + U_{id}^1 \times 30 + SN_{id}^1 \times 6 + N_{id}^1$. Similarly, the (SN_{id}^2, N_{id}^2) can be converted to a number $SN_{id}^2 \times s_2 + N_{id}^2 = SN_{id}^2 \times 15 + N_{id}^2$.

Table 4. Re-indexing examples

Index in HDN$(B, 1, S)$		Index in HDN$(B, 2, S)$	
$(C^1, U_{id}^1, SN_{id}^1, N_{id}^1)$	Serial number	(SN_{id}^2, N_{id}^2)	Serial number
$(0, 0, 0, 0)$	$0 \times 150 + 0 \times 30 + 0 \times 6 + 0 = \quad 0$	$(0, 0)$	$0 \times 15 + \ 0 = \quad 0$
$(1, 4, 2, 3)$	$1 \times 150 + 4 \times 30 + 2 \times 6 + 3 = 285$	$(19, 0)$	$19 \times 15 + \ 0 = 285$
$(0, 0, 2, 2)$	$0 \times 150 + 0 \times 30 + 2 \times 6 + 2 = \quad 14$	$(0, 14)$	$0 \times 15 + 14 = \quad 14$
$(1, 4, 4, 5)$	$1 \times 150 + 4 \times 30 + 4 \times 6 + 5 = 299$	$(19, 14)$	$19 \times 15 + 14 = 299$

Assume that the point-to-point routing algorithm in the base network is available. The proposed algorithm for routing node u to node v in HDN(B, k, S) works as follows. We first perform re-indexing of u and v if $k > 1$. Then, there are three cases: the two nodes are in the same cluster (Case 1), in the distinct clusters of the same class (Case 2), and in the distinct clusters of distinct classes (Case 3). Case 1 is trivial. Case 3 can be reduced to Case 2 by routing u via a cross-edge of level k. Therefore, we explain only the Case 2: The two nodes are in the distinct clusters with the same class. We first identify the super-nodes, denoted as $SN_{u'}^k$ and $SN_{v'}^k$, in the two Q^{k-1}s containing u and v, respectively, such that $SN_{u'}^k$ and $SN_{v'}^k$ are connected by a unique cross-edge of level k in Q^k from the dual-construction. Then, we route node u to node u', and node v to node v' inside the clusters of level k, respectively. Notice that, u' and v' are not unique although $SN_{u'}^k$ and $SN_{v'}^k$ are unique. The algorithm finds the u' and v' that leave u_3^k and v_3^k unchanged if possible. And then, the routing from u to v is done by routing u' to $u'' \in SN_{v'}^k$ via a cross-edge of level k in HDN(B, k, S) and routing from u'' to v' inside $SN_{v'}^k$. The algorithm is formally presented as Algorithm 1. The correctness of the algorithm and its time complexity are given in Theorem 2.

Theorem 2. *Assume that the routing algorithms in the base network B is available. In HDN(B, k, S) for $k > 0$, routing between any two nodes can be done*

Algorithm 1. HDN_ROUTING (HDN$(B, k, S), u, v$)
  input: HDN(B, k, S);
  input: node $u = (u_0^k, u_1^k, u_2^k, u_3^k)$ (the node representation of level k);
  input: node $v = (v_0^k, v_1^k, v_2^k, v_3^k)$ (the node representation of level k);
  output: a path $u \Rightarrow v$;
begin
  if $k = 0$ **then**
    Base_routing(B, u, v);
  else
    if $k > 1$ **then**   /* perform re-indexing */
      $(u_0^{k-1}, u_1^{k-1}, u_2^{k-1}, u_3^{k-1}) \leftarrow (u_2^k, u_3^k)$;
      $(v_0^{k-1}, v_1^{k-1}, v_2^{k-1}, v_3^{k-1}) \leftarrow (v_2^k, v_3^k)$;
    endif
    Case 1: $u_0^k = v_0^k$ and $u_1^k = v_1^k$ /* u, v in the same cluster */
      if $k > 1$ **then**
        HDN_ROUTING (HDN$(B, k - 1, S), u, v$);
      else
        Base_routing(B, u, v);
      endif
    Case 2: $u_0^k \neq v_0^k$ /* u, v in the clusters of distinct classes */
      $u' \leftarrow (u_0^k, u_1^k, v_1^k, u_3^k)$;
      $v' \leftarrow (v_0^k, v_1^k, u_1^k, v_3^k)$;
      if $k > 1$ **then**   /* perform re-indexing */
        $((u')_0^{k-1}, (u')_1^{k-1}, (u')_2^{k-1}, (u')_3^{k-1}) \leftarrow (v_1^k, u_3^k)$;
        $((v')_0^{k-1}, (v')_1^{k-1}, (v')_2^{k-1}, (v')_3^{k-1}) \leftarrow (u_1^k, v_3^k)$;
        HDN_ROUTING (HDN$(B, k - 1, S), u, u'$);
        HDN_ROUTING (HDN$(B, k - 1, S), v, v'$);
      else
        Base_routing(B, u, u');
        Base_routing(B, v, v');
      endif
      route u' to u'' via a cross-edge of level k;   /* $u'' = (v_0^k, v_1^k, u_1^k, u_3^k)$ */
      Base_route(B, u'', v');   /* route from u_3^k to v_3^k inside the super-node */
    Case 3: $u_0^k = v_0^k$ and $u_1^k \neq v_1^k$ /* u, v in the clusters of the same class */
      route u to w via the cross-edge of level k;
      route node w to node v as in Case 2;
  endif
end

in at most $2^k R(B) - \sum_{j=0}^{k-1} 2^j R(SN^{k-j}) + 2^{k+1} - 2$ steps, where $R(B)$ and $R(SN^i), 1 \le i \le k$, are the time complexities of the routing in B and SN^i, respectively.

Proof: We show the correctness of Algorithm 1 by induction on k. Assume that the algorithm is correct for $k - 1 \ge 0$. From the algorithm, it is clear that we need to consider only Case 2. In Case 2, nodes u' and u are in the same cluster by the definition of u'. They can be connected by the induction hypothesis. Similarly, nodes v' and v can be connected. The node u'' that is connected to u' by a cross-edge of level k and node v' are in the same super-node as can be seen from their IDs. Therefore, they can be connected by Base_routing algorithm. Next, we derive the time complexity R_k of the algorithm. In Case 2, there are two recursive calls to connect u to u' and v to v', respectively. Since the nodeIDs of u and u' are the same (so are v and v'), a recursive call takes only $R_{k-1} - R(SN^k)$ time. Since the SupernodeIDs of u'' and v' are the same, the last call to Base_route to connect u'' to v' takes only $R(SN^k)$ time. In Case 3, there is an additional routing step via a cross-edge. Therefore, the time complexity R_k of HDN_Routing(HDN$(B, k, S), u, v)$ satisfies the recurrence $R_k = 2(R_{k-1} - R(SN^k)) + R(SN^k) + 2$ for $k > 0$. Solving this recurrence, we have $R_k = 2^k R(B) - \sum_{j=0}^{k-1} 2^j R(SN^{k-j}) + 2^{k+1} - 2$ where $R(B)$ and $R(SN^i), 1 \le i \le k$, are the time complexities of the routing in B and SN^i, respectively.   □

4   Total Exchange Routing on HDN

Design of efficient routing algorithms for collective communications is the key issue in parallel computers or networks. Collective communications are required in load balancing, event synchronization, and data exchange. Based on the number of sending and receiving processors, these communications can be classified into one-to-many, one-to-all, many-to-many and all-to-all. The nature of the messages to be sent can be classified as personalized or non-personalized (multicast or broadcast). The all-to-all personalized communication (total exchange) is at the heart of numerical applications.

An important metric used to evaluate efficiency of communication is *transmission latency*, or *communication time*. The communication time depends on many factors such as contentions, switching techniques, network topologies etc. Therefore, we first define the communication model used in this paper.

We assume that the communication links are bidirectional, that is, two directly-connected processors can send messages to each other simultaneously. We also assume the processor-bounded model (one-port model) in which each node can access the network through a single input port and a single output port at a time. The port model of a network system refers to the number of internal channels at each node. In order to reduce the complexity of communication hardware, many systems support one-port communication architecture. We also assume the linear cost model in which the transfer time for a message is linearly proportional to the length of the message.

There are many switching methods. In this paper, we assume the packet switching model [5]. In this model, each packet is maintained as an entity that is passed from node to node as it moves through the network. The long message can be partitioned and transmitted as fixed-length word w. The first few bytes of a packet contains routing and control information and are referred as packet header. A packet is completely buffered at each intermediate node before it is forwarded to the next node (for this reason, the model is also called store-and-forward switching). In this paper, we allow packages that are headed for the same destination to be combined into a single message. The time to pack and unpack messages is included in the startup latency. The packet switching model is suitable for collective communication in MPP since it is safer than other switching models such as virtual cut-through switching. With packet switching model, the communication time for a message of length m (number of fixed-length words) to be sent to a node of distance d is $d(t_s + mt_w)$, where t_s is startup latency, the time required for the system to handle the message at the sending node, t_w is the per-word transfer time ($1/t_w$ is the bandwidth of the communication links). Through this paper, we will use the formula above for estimating the communication times of the proposed algorithms.

In total exchange, each node sends a distinct message of size m to every other node. The total number of messages is p^2 (a node also has a message for itself). Referring to Figures 2 and 3, the algorithm for total exchange in HDN can be

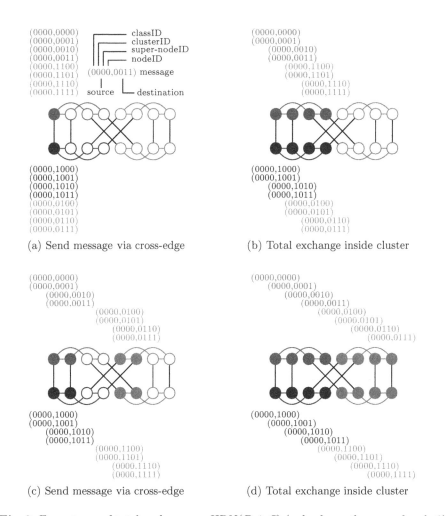

(a) Send message via cross-edge

(b) Total exchange inside cluster

(c) Send message via cross-edge

(d) Total exchange inside cluster

Fig. 2. Four stages of total exchange on HDN($B, 1, S$) (only shows the case of node 0)

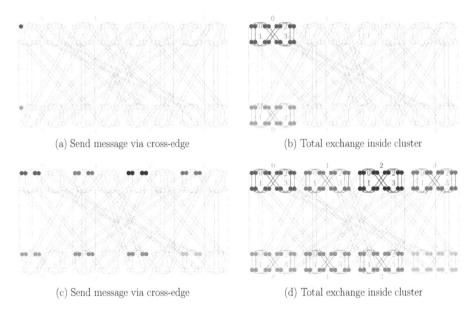

(a) Send message via cross-edge   (b) Total exchange inside cluster

(c) Send message via cross-edge   (d) Total exchange inside cluster

Fig. 3. Four stages of total exchange on $HDN(B, 2, S)$ (only shows the case of node 0)

described in four stages. Note that all nodes in the figures do the same operations but only the cases of node 0 are shown for clarity. Also note that the commas of node address in Figure 2 are omitted for saving spaces.

1. In the first stage, we first divide M_{my_id} into two parts, $M1_{my\_id}$ and $M2_{my\_id}$, where $M1_{my\_id}$ contains all messages to be sent to the nodes in the clusters of my_type, and $M2_{my\_id}$ contains the rest message. Then, the first part of personalized messages $M1$ is exchanged between my_id and $partner$, the neighbor via cross-edge of level k. The time this stage takes is $t_s + t_w m n_k/2$.

2. In the second stage, we first pack all messages that are to be sent to the nodes in the cluster of level k with clusterID $= q$ into a single message msg_q. Then, we perform total exchange inside each cluster, where msg_q is to be sent to node with nodeID $= q$. The time this stage takes is denoted as $T_{k-1}(n_k/n_{k-1})$, the time for total exchange inside the cluster.

3. In the third stage, each node packs the received messages into a single message of length $n_k m$ and sends the packed message to its neighbor along the cross-edge of level k. After receive the message, each node unpacks the message received from its neighbor into n_{k-1} messages, $msg_{q'}$, where $msg_{q'}$ is the collection of all messages destinated to node with nodeID $= q'$ in the cluster. The time this stage takes is also $t_s + t_w m n_k/2$.

4. In the last stage, we perform total exchange again within each cluster of level k. This can be done since the packed messages sent through the level-k cross-edge are all destinated to the nodes inside the cluster. The time this stage takes is also $T_{k-1}(n_k/n_{k-1})$, which is the time for total exchange inside the cluster.

The algorithm is showed in Algorithm 2. All nodes execute the algorithm concurrently. In Algorithm 4, my_id is the id of the node. The initial message to be sent is M_{my_id} which contains p messages of length m. At the end of the algorithm, each node stores the collection of all p messages in $result$.

Algorithm 2. TOTAL_EXCHANGE (HDN(B, k, S), M_{my_id})
begin
    if $k = 0$ $result \leftarrow$ TOTAL_EXCHANGE (B, M_{my_id});
    else
        Divide M_{my_id} into two parts, $M1_{my\_id}$ and $M2_{my\_id}$, where $M1_{my\_id}$ contains
            all messages to be sent to the nodes in the clusters of type my_type, and
            $M2_{my\_id}$ contains the rest messages;
        $partner \leftarrow$ the neighbor via cross-edge of level k;
        send message $M1_{my\_id}$ to $partner$;
        Receive message $M1_{partner}$ from $partner$;
        $M'_{my\_id} \leftarrow M2_{my\_id} \cup M1_{partner}$;
        Pack all messages in M'_{my_id} that are to be sent to the nodes in the cluster of
            level k with cluster_ID $= q$ into a single message msg_q to be sent to the
            node with node_ID $= q$;
        $T_{my\_id} \leftarrow$ TOTAL_EXCHANGE (HDN($B, k-1, S$), M'_{my_id});
        send message T_{my_id} to $partner$;
        receive message $T_{partner}$ from $partner$;
        $T'_{my\_id} \leftarrow T_{partner}$;
        Unpack T'_{my_id} into n_{k-1} messages, $msg_{q'}$, such that $msg_{q'}$ is the collection of
            messages destinated to the node with node_ID $= q'$;
        $result \leftarrow$ TOTAL_EXCHANGE (HDN($B, k-1, S$), T'_{my_id});
    endif
end

The time to complete the total exchange on an HDN($B, 1, S$) is

$$T_1(m) = (t_s + mt_w n_1/2) + T_0(mn_1/2) + (t_s + mt_w n_1/2) + T_0(mn_1/2)$$
$$= 2(t_s + mt_w n_1/2) + 2T_0(mn_1/2).$$

Generally, on an HDN(B, k, S), the time to complete the total exchange is

$$T_k(m) = (t_s + t_w mn_k/2) + T_{k-1}(n_k/n_{k-1}) + (t_s + t_w mn_k/2) + T_{k-1}(n_k/n_{k-1})$$
$$= 2(t_s + t_w mn_k/2) + 2T_{k-1}(n_k/n_{k-1}). \text{ That is,}$$

$$T_k(m) = (2^{k+1} - 2)(t_s + t_w mn_k/2) + 2^k T_0(mn_k/2)$$

where n_k is the total number of nodes and $T_0(m)$ is the time complexity for total exchange in B. In the examples of Figures 2 and 3 where B is a 2-cube, $T_0(m) = 2(t_s + t_w m)$. If B is an n-cube, then $T_0(m) = n(t_s + t_w m 2^n/2)$.

For the HDN$(B, 1, S)$ shown in Figures 2, $T_1 = 2(t_s + 8t_w m) + 4(t_s + 8t_w m) = 6(t_s + 8t_w m)$. In contrast, $T = 4(t_s + 8t_w m)$ for a 4-cube of same size. For the HDN$(B, 2, S)$ shown in Figures 3, $T_2 = 6(t_s + 64t_w m) + 4 \times 2(t_s + 64t_w m) = 14(t_s + 64t_w m)$. In contrast, $T = 7(t_s + 64t_w m)$ for a 7-cube of same size. The times of total exchange for HDNs are longer than that for hypercubes but an HDN has much less links than a hypercube of the same size. We summarize this result in the following theorem.

Theorem 3. *Assume that the time complexity $T_0(m)$ for total exchange in the base network B is known, where m is the length of each message. The time complexity $T_k(m)$ for total exchange on an HDN(B, k, S), $k > 0$, is $T_k(m) = (2^{k+1} - 2)(t_s + t_w m n_k/2) + 2^k T_0(m n_k/2)$, where $n_k = (2n_0)^{2^k}/(2 \prod_{i=1}^{k} s_i)$.*

5   Concluding Remarks

The hierarchical dual-net can connect a large number of nodes with a small node-degree and a short diameter. It is a potential candidate for the interconnection network of the supercomputers of the next generation that may have more than one million of nodes. We can select a popular network of small size that is a product graph as the base network and then connect multiple base modules with cross links (cables) to construct a very large-scale hierarchical dual-net. We can also select a suitable set of integers based on the base network to control the number of nodes in the supercomputer. The base networks can be implemented in a NoC VLSI and high-speed line cables may be used as the cross links to connect PCB modules in cabinets. We presented an efficient algorithm for total exchange on recursive dual-net. There are many problems, such as disjoint path and fault-tolerant routing, on recursive dual-net that are worth further research.

References

1. Adiga, N.R., Blumrich, M.A., Chen, D., Coteus, P., Gara, A., Giampapa, M.E., Heidelberger, P., Singh, S., Steinmacher-Burow, B.D., Takken, T., Tsao, M., Vranas, P.: Blue gene/l torus interconnection network. IBM Journal of Research and Development 49(2/3), 265–276 (2005)
2. Beckman, P.: Looking toward exascale computing, keynote speaker. In: International Conference on Parallel and Distributed Computing, Applications and Technologies (PDCAT 2008), Dunedin, New Zealand (December 2008)
3. Ghose, K., Desai, K.R.: Hierarchical cubic networks. IEEE Transactions on Parallel and Distributed Systems 6(4), 427–435 (1995)
4. IBM: Roadrunner: Hardware and Software Overview. IBM Corporation (January 2009), http://www.redbooks.ibm.com/redpapers/pdfs/redp4477.pdf
5. Kumar, V., Grama, A., Gupta, A., Karypis, G.: Introduction to parallel computing: design and analysis of algorithms. Benjamin/Cummings Press (1994)

6. Li, Y., Peng, S., Chu, W.: Efficient collective communications in dual-cube. The Journal of Supercomputing 28(1), 71–90 (2004)

7. Li, Y., Peng, S., Chu, W.: Recursive dual-net: A new universal network for super-computers of the next generation. In: Hua, A., Chang, S.-L. (eds.) ICA3PP 2009. LNCS, vol. 5574, pp. 809–820. Springer, Heidelberg (2009)

8. Li, Y., Peng, S., Chu, W.: Hierarchical dual-net: A flexible interconnection network and its routing algorithm. In: Proceedings of the Second International Conference on Networking and Computing, Osaka, Japan, pp. 58–67 (November 2011)

9. Preparata, F.P., Vuillemin, J.: The cube-connected cycles: a versatile network for parallel computation. Commun. ACM 24, 300–309 (1981)

10. TOP500: Supercomputer Sites (June 2013), http://top500.org/

Efficiency of Flexible Rerouting Scheme for Maximizing Logical Arrays

Guiyuan Jiang[1], Jigang Wu[2], and Jizhou Sun[1]

[1] School of Computer Science & Technology, Tianjin University,
Tianjin 300072, China
[2] School of Computer Science & Software Engineering,
Tianjin Polytechnic University, Tianjin 300387, China
{jguiyuan,asjgwu}@gmail.com, jzsun@tju.edu.cn

Abstract. In a multiprocessor array, some processing elements (PEs) fail to function normally due to hardware defects or soft faults caused by overheating, overload or occupancy by other running applications. Fault-tolerant reconfiguration considered in this paper is to reorganize fault-free PEs from a processor array with faults to a logical array of regular mesh topology by changing the interconnections among PEs. This paper presents the efficiency of the flexible rerouting scheme to maximize the usage of the fault-free PEs, by developing an efficient reconfiguration algorithm without backtracking. The proposed algorithm constructs each logical columns from left to right on candidate PE sets. It updates the candidate sets by excluding the PEs which cannot be used, once a logical column is formed. Also, it is proved that the proposed heuristic algorithm is able to generate the maximum-size logical array in linear time. Experimental results show that 123 logical columns can be constructed on 256×256 host arrays with fault density of 30%, resulting in an improvement of 51% in comparison to the previous algorithm by which only 82 logical columns can be produced. Furthermore, our algorithm is able to generate target arrays with harvest over 56% on host arrays with fault density of 50%, while the previous work cited in this paper fails to construct any target array in this case.

Keywords: Interconnection network, reconfiguration, rerouting scheme, fault tolerant, algorithm.

1 Introduction

The quest for high-performance and low-power leads to design multi-core architectures where an increasing number of processing elements (PEs) are integrated on a single chip in a tightly coupled fashion. In order to fully exploit the processing capabilities offered by the integration of an increasing number of PEs, on-chip communication networks play a critical role in developing high-performance embedded computing system. The option of reconfiguring the interconnect topology using optical circuit switches, which are of low-cost, low-power and high-bandwidth, opens up new possibilities for improving not only the computing performance but also the reliability of multiprocessor systems.

C.-H. Hsu et al. (Eds.): NPC 2013, LNCS 8147, pp. 194–206, 2013.

To fully exploit the processing capabilities, many works have investigate application-aware topology reconfiguration techniques which try to customize the multiprocessor array to a topology that matches the traffic pattern of the application in order to reduce the power consumption and message latency etc. Optimizing network topology and mapping cores to network are two important application-specific reconfiguration methods. Topology determines the connectivity of the Network-on-Chip (NoC) nodes, while the core mapping tries to place the processing cores communicating more frequently near each other. The problem of topology selection and core mapping on NoC nodes have been explored to optimize an interconnection network based on a set of communication constraints by many researchers [1][2]. Reconfiguring the topology on NoC to reduce power consumption has been studied in [3]. And the work in [4] extends the paper [3] by proposing a more flexible and efficient structure and by providing extensive evaluations to thoroughly investigate the power, latency, and area of the reconfigurable NoC.

Since these fully customized topologies are designed and optimized for some specific applications, they give the best performance and power results only for that applications. The fault-tolerant reconfiguration considered in this paper is to re-organize the fault-free PEs in the multiprocessor array to a regular topology (standard structured) which ensuring well-controlled electrical parameters. Generally, two distinct types of fault-tolerant approaches, i.e. the redundancy approach and the degradation approach, are mostly investigated for processor array reconfiguration. The redundancy approach tolerates faulty PEs by replacing them with spare PEs [5][6], and if these PEs cannot replace all the faulty ones, the chip has to be discarded. In degradation approach, [7] studied the problem of 2D mesh reconfiguration under three different routing constraints. They have shown that most problems that arise under these constraints are NP-complete and they also proposed some heuristic reconfiguration algorithms for these problems. An algorithm, namely GCR, was proposed in [8] to find a maximal logical array (MLA) that contains a set of the selected rows. The techniques performing row-exclusion and compensation were proposed and combined with GCR into a heuristic algorithm to generate an approximate MLA [9]. Recently, the power dissipation of a logical array was reduced in [10] by reducing the number of long-interconnects utilizing a dynamic programming approach. In [11], a genetic algorithm (GA) for the reconfiguration of degradable mesh arrays is presented to evolve rerouting strategies for constructing logical rows/columns. In [12], novel techniques are presented to accelerate reconfiguration by employ flexible upper and lower bounds for the maximum logical array (MLA). The degradable reconfiguration approach for three-dimensional mesh-connected processor arrays is investigated in [13][14].

In a logical array, two neighboring PEs are interconnected through a group of physical links and these physical links form a interconnect path (interconnect for short) between the two PEs. Note that this architecture implements reconfiguration using simple switches, thus overlap of physical links is not allowed between any two interconnects, i.e., no physical link is shared by any two interconnects of a feasible logical array. In order to generate logical arrays without overlap, most previous works develop reconfiguration algorithms under rerouting schemes with limitation on the routing distance d (see section 2.1 for formal definition), which means that if the distance between two PEs exceeds d, then the two PEs are not allowed to connect to form a logical array. This has brought convenience for designing reconfiguration algorithms, but it leads to large number of unused fault-free PEs, which is a serious waste of computing resources. This motivates us to increase the utilization of fault-free PEs by adopting flexible rerouting scheme. In this paper, we first investigate the performance loss of previous works in terms of utilization of fault-free PEs, then we adopt a flexible rerouting scheme in reconfiguration resulting in an efficient non-backtracking algorithm, to produce maximum logical arrays under the rerouting scheme.

2   Preliminaries

2.1   Fault-Tolerant Architecture and Rerouting Schemes

Let H denotes the physical (host) array on which some of the elements are defective due to hardware/circuit defects or soft faults which means temporary unavailability caused by overheating, overload or occupancy by other applications. Assume the fault density of the physical array is ρ, then there are $N = (1-\rho)\cdot m\cdot n$ fault-free PEs in a $m \times n$ physical array. The rows and columns in physical array are called physical rows and columns respectively. A logical subarray which contains no faulty PEs constructed by changing states of reconfiguration switches is called a logical array (target array), denoted as T. The rows and columns in logical target array are called logical rows and columns respectively. Throughout this paper, $e_{i,j}(e'_{i,j})$ indicates the PE located at the position of (i, j) of the host (logical) array, where i is its row index and j is its column index. $row(u)(col(u))$ denotes the physical row (column) index of the PE u. $u=v$ denotes that u is identical to v.

Fig. 1 shows the fault-tolerant architecture for a 4×4 host array. The fault-tolerant reconfiguration is achieved by inserting several reconfiguration switches in the network allowing the network to flexibly change the connections among PEs. Each square box in the host array represents a processing element (PE), whereas each circle represents a reconfiguration switch. In all figures in this paper, the gray shaded boxes represent faulty PEs while unshaded ones represent the fault-free PEs. There are 4 states for each switch.

In order to generate logical arrays without overlaps among interconnects, two software control schemes, i.e. bypass and rerouting schemes, are utilized to guide reconfiguration algorithms. In particular, row bypass and column rerouting schemes are mostly employed in previous works. As shown in Fig.1, if PE $e_{i,j}$ is faulty, then PE $e_{i,j-1}$ can communicate with PE $e_{i,j+1}$ and data will bypass $e_{i,j}$ through an internal bypass link. This scheme is called *row bypass*. In *column rerouting* scheme, PE $e(i, j)$ could connect to $e(i + 1, j')$ by changing states of related switches where $|j - j'| \leq d$ and d is called the compensation

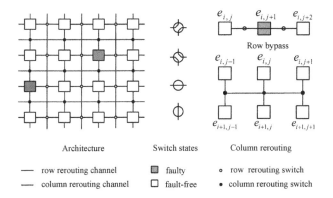

Fig. 1. Switch functions and rerouting manners on a 4 × 4 mesh linked by four-port switches

distance [8][9]. If d is limited to 1, then PE $e_{i,j}$ can connect to one of the three PEs, i.e. $e_{i+1,j-1}$, $e_{i+1,j}$ and $e_{i+1,j+1}$, to form a logical column. The three PEs are called neighbors of $e_{i,j}$, and set of the three PEs is denoted as $Adj(e)$. *column bypass* and *row rerouting* schemes can be similarly defined. Generally, in order to reduce the complexity of the switching mechanisms and keep low cost of physical implementation, it is necessary to keep d small.

2.2 Construct Target Arrays on Selected Rows

Problem $\mathcal{R}$. *Given an $m \times n$ mesh-connected processor array in which some of its elements are faulty, find a maximum target array that contains the selected rows under the row bypass and column rerouting scheme.*

Let R_1, R_2, ..., R_m be the rows of the given host array. Assume R_{r_1}, R_{r_2}, ..., R_{r_s} are the s selected rows to construct a target array, where $1 \leq r_s \leq m$. Logical columns can be constructed under column rerouting scheme on selected rows, and interconnecting these logical columns under row bypass scheme forms a target array. A logical array T is said to contain $R_{r_1}, R_{r_2}, \cdots, R_{r_s}$ if each logical column in T contains exactly one fault-free PE from each of the selected rows. Note that, if a physical row is not selected for inclusion into target array, all PEs in the row will be bypassed.

Suppose C_p and $C_q(C_p \neq C_q)$ are two logical columns constructed on the s selected rows, thus each of them is consists of s PEs such that one and only one PE lies on each selected row. Let $C_p(i)$ denotes the PE lying in the i-th selected row of column C_p and $C_q(i)$ denotes the PE lying in the i-th selected row of column C_q, for $(1 \leq i \leq s)$.

1. We say that $C_p < C_q$ if PE $C_p(i)$ in C_p lies to the left-side of PE $C_q(i)$ in C_q, for $1 \leq i \leq s$.
2. We say that $C_p \leq C_q$ if PE $C_p(i)$ in C_p lies to the left-side of, or is identical to, the PE $C_q(i)$ in C_q, for $1 \leq i \leq s$.

3. We say that C_p and C_q are **independent** of each other if $C_p < C_q$ or $C_q < C_p$.

4. We say that C_p and C_q are **overlap** with each other if neither $C_p < C_q$ nor $C_q < C_p$ is satisfied.

We define that a logical column, say column C_l, as the *left-most column* related to column set A if $C_l \in A$ and $C_l \preceq C_p$ for any $C_p \in A$.

The problem $\mathcal{R}$ is proved to be optimally solved by an algorithm named *Greedy Column Rerouting* (GCR)[9]. In fact, the target array produced by GCR is maximum-size under the constraint that the compensation distance d of columns rerouting scheme is limited to 1, instead of the maximum-size target array for the problem $\mathcal{R}$. All operations in GCR are carried out on the adjacent sets of each fault-free PE u in row R_{r_i}, defined as $\mathcal{A}dj(u) = \{v : v \in R_{r_{i+1}}, v$ is unused fault-free PE and $|col(u) - col(v)| \leq 1\}$. $Adj(u)$ consists of PEs that PE u can directly connect to in the next selected row. The PEs in $Adj(u)$ are ordered in increasing columns index. The PE with the minimum column index in $Adj(u)$ is called the leftmost connectable PE for u.

2.3   Flexible Rerouting Schemes

As we have discussed before, two types of software rerouting schemes, i.e. bypass and rerouting schemes, are employed to guide reconfiguration algorithms. In previous work, the compensation distance d of column rerouting scheme is limited to 1 to keep low cost of hardware implementation, thus 4-port switches are effective for reconfiguration. Rerouting schemes provides convenience for designing algorithms and guarantees that target arrays can be easily implemented using 4-port switches. However, there are considerable *un-connectable* PEs which are fault-free but cannot be used in forming a logical target array. Fig.2 shows two logical arrays constructed from a 5×5 host array. Fig.2(a) shows an logical array of two logical columns constructed by algorithm GCR under column rerouting scheme with $d=1$. The target array formed under flexible rerouting scheme contains 3 logical columns as shown in Fig.2(b). There are 7 un-connectable PEs in the first target array, but only 2 un-connectable PEs is generated by adopting flexible rerouting scheme as shown in the second array.

Experimental results show that, under fixed column rerouting scheme with $d = 1$, the proportions of un-connectable PEs are up to 17.1%, 34.75% and 52.45% on 64×64 host array with fault densities are 10%, 20% and 30%, respectively. In order to to improve the *harvest* by reducing the number of un-connectable PEs, we adopt the *flexible column rerouting scheme* which is formed as follows. Assume that row R_{r_i} and $R_{r_{i+1}}$ are the i-th and $(i + 1)$-th selected rows, and set E_i and E_{i+1} contain fault-free PEs in R_{r_i} and $R_{r_{i+1}}$ respectively, then a PE in E_i can connect directly to any PE in E_{i+1} by reconfigure relative switch status.

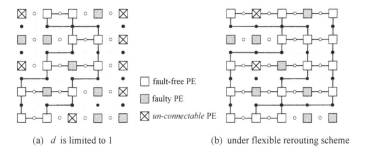

(a) d is limited to 1   (b) under flexible rerouting scheme

Fig. 2. (a) only 2 logical columns are formed under column rerouting scheme with compensation distance $d=1$, (b) 3 logical columns can be constructed under flexible rerouting scheme

3 Maximum-Size Target Array under Flexible Rerouting Scheme

In this section, we solve problem $\mathcal{R}$ under flexible rerouting scheme to further increase target array size. In another word, given an $m \times n$ mesh-connected processor array H in which some of its elements are faulty, let $R_{r_1}, R_{r_2}, ..., R_{r_s}$ be the selected rows, find a target array which consists of the maximum number of independent logical columns under the row bypass and flexible column rerouting scheme such that each logical column contains the selected rows. We first present a heuristic algorithm, denoted as FLX, which is capable of solving problem $\mathcal{R}$ in linear time. Then we prove that the target array constructed by FLX is maximum-size target array, and the target arrays constructed in this paper is much larger than that in previous works.

We model the problem $\mathcal{R}$ as follows. Suppose that set S contains all logical columns that can be construct on the selected rows of host array H. Formally, $S=\{C|C$ is a logical column on selected rows and $|C \cap E_i|=1$ for $1 \leq i \leq s\}$. Any column C in S contains exactly one PE from each selected rows. In problem $\mathcal{R}$, we wish to find a maximum-size subset, say A, of independent logical columns.

We shall solve this problem in several steps, in each step we make choice of selecting one column for inclusion into A, and we are left with the subproblem S': finding a maximum-size subset on subproblem S'. We observe that we need only to consider the greedy choice, the left-most logical column, in making each choice. Theorem 1 verifies that the greedy way of making choice leads to optimal solution, the verification is based on Theorem 2 which indicates that the greedy choice is always part of some optimal solution. Let $S_k = \{C_i|C_i \in S$ and $C_k<C_i\}$ be the set of logical columns that lie to the right-side of column C_k. If we make the choice of selecting the left-most column C_1, then S_1 remains as the only subproblem to solve. Since C_1 is in some optimal solution, we can construct an optimal solution to the original problem consists of column C_1 and all logical

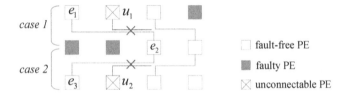

Fig. 3. $C_1=<e_1,e_2,e_3>$ is the left-most column, u_1 and u_2 become un-connectable after column C_1 is constructed

columns in an optimal solution to the subproblem S_1. In another word, $\{C_1\} \cup A'$ is an optimal solution to original problem S if A' is an optimal solution to subproblem S_1.

After constructing the leftmost column, some PEs becomes unconnectable due to overlap of interconnects. Rerouting on the unconnectable PEs leads to backtracking, such as in previous algorithm GCR. In order to improve the efficiency, we adopt the following technique to avoid backtracking. We identify unconnectable PEs so that columns containing unconnectable PEs will not be considered in the next stage selection. To exclude these un-connectable PEs out of sets E_i for $1 \leq i \leq s$, two type of situations are examined as follows, according to the newly constructed column C_k. Let $C_k(i)$ and $C_k(i+1)$ denote two PEs which lie in the ith selected row and the $(i+1)$th selected row of column C_k.

- case 1: $col(C_k(i+1)) > col(C_k(i))$, then PE u is invalid if $row(u) = r_i$, $col(u) > col(C_k(i))$ and $col(u) < col(C_k(i+1))$.
- case 2: $col(C_k(i)) > col(C_k(i+1))$, then PE u is invalid if $row(u) = r_{i+1}$, $col(u) > col(C_k(i+1))$ and $col(u) < col(C_k(i))$.

An example is shown in Fig.3. u_1 is un-connectable according to case 1 and u_2 is un-connectable according to case 2. Thus, after constructing each left-most column, un-connectable PEs must be excluded from candidate PEs set.

We implement the algorithm FLX in a iterative way instead of a recursive manner. The algorithm takes host array H with size of $m \times n$ in which some of its elements are faulty, and the indexes $r_1, r_2, ..., r_s$ that defines the selected rows as input. It returns a maximum-size subset of independent logical columns which form a logical target array T. The algorithm works as follows. The variable k indexes the most resent constructed left-most column,corresponding to the C_k in algorithm FLX. Then the **for** loop initialize E_i as the set of fault-free PEs in row R_{r_i} for $1 \leq i \leq s$. PEs in E_i are sorted initially by increasing column index. In **while** loop, the algorithm construct left-most column C_k one by one and adds C_k into target array T. In each iteration, the algorithm first construct a left-most column C_k, then update candidate set $E_i(1 \leq i \leq s)$ by excluding un-connectable PEs according to C_k. To see which PEs are un-connectable, two type of cases are examined as described above.

Now we analyze the complexity of the proposed greedy algorithm. Initialize candidate set $E_i(1 \leq i \leq s)$ runs in $O(m \cdot n)$. In the **while** loop, each PE is

---

Algorithm 1: $FLX(H, r_1, r_2, ..., r_s)$ /* Flexible Column Rerouting Algorithm */

Input: host array H with size of $m \times n$; indexes of selected rows: $r_1, r_2, ..., r_s$;
Output: maximum-size target array T.

1 **begin**
2 **for** $i \leftarrow 1$ *to* s **do**
3     $E_i \leftarrow$ set of fault-free elements in R_{r_i};
4 $k \leftarrow 1$;　　 /* index of current logical column */
5 **while** $(E_1 \neq \phi)$ **do**
6   /* construct C_k from candidate sets $\cup_{i=1}^{s} E_i$ */
7   **for** $i \leftarrow 1$ *to* s **do**
8   **if** $(E_i \neq \phi)$ **then**
9           $e \leftarrow$ the PE with minimum column index in E_i;
10           $C_k(i) \leftarrow e$;
11   mark e as occupied;
12   **else**
13   stop the **while** loop;

14   /* exclude unconnectable PEs out of $E_i (1 \leq i \leq s-1)$ according to case 1 */
15   **for** $i \leftarrow 1$ *to* $s - 1$ **do**
16   **if** $col(C_k(i+1)) - col(C_k(i)) > 1$ **then**
17   **for** $j \leftarrow col(C_k(i))+1$ *to* $col(C_k(i+1))-1$ **do**
18   **if** $e_{i,j} \in E_i$ **then**
19   mark $e_{i,j}$ as un-connectable;

20   /* exclude unconnectable PEs out of $E_i (2 \leq i \leq s)$ according to case 2 */
21   **for** $i \leftarrow 2$ *to* s **do**
22   **if** $col(C_k(i-1)) - col(C_k(i)) > 1$ **then**
23   **for** $j \leftarrow col(C_k(i)) + 1$ *to* $col(C_k(i-1)) - 1$ **do**
24   **if** $e_{i,j} \in E_i$ **then**
25   mark $e_{i,j}$ as un-connectable;

26     $T \leftarrow T \cup \{C_k\}$;
27     $k \leftarrow k + 1$;
28 **return** T;
29 **end**

---

examined only once, either to include into a left-most column or excluded out of candidate set E_i, thus the while loop runs in $O(m \cdot n)$. Therefore, the algorithm FLX construct a maximum-size target array under flexible rerouting schemes in $O(m \cdot n)$ time.

Theorem 1. *Algorithm FLX produces maximum-size target array for problem $\mathcal{R}$.*

Proof. Let C_1 be the left-most logical column in S, thus for any $C_p \in S$ we have $C_1 \le C_p$. Then, based on theorem 2, there always exist an optimal solution, say A, whose left-most column is C_1. Once the greedy choice C_1 is made, the problem S is reduced to find an optimal solution for subproblem $S_1 = \{C_x | C_x \in S \text{ and } C_1 < C_x\}$ without have to consider any logical columns that overlap with C_1 in S_1. This is because for any $C_p \in S$, we have $C_1 \le C_p$, and C_1 is the left-most column. Thus, all logical columns that are independent with logical column C_1 must not overlap with C_1, i.e. they certainly belong to S_1. Therefore, we can first construct the left-most column C_1, and then try to find an optimal solution, say A_1, for sub-problem S_1, thus one optimal solution for the original problem S could be $\{C_1\} \cup A_1$. In this way, we could find a maximum-size target array by making greedy choice at each step. In another word, algorithm FLX produces maximum-size target array for problem $\mathcal{R}$.

Theorem 2. *Consider any nonempty subproblem S_k, and let C_m be the left-most logical column on selected rows in S_k. Then C_m is included in some maximum-size subset of independent logical columns of S_k.*

Proof. Let A_k be a maximum-size subset of independent logical columns in S_k, and let C_j be left-most logical column in A_k. If $C_j = C_m$, we are done, since we have shown that C_m is in some maximum-size subset of independent logical columns of S_k. If $C_j \ne C_m$, let the set $A'_k = A_k - \{C_j\} \cup \{C_m\}$ be A_k but substituting C_m for C_j. The logical columns in A'_k are independent, which follows because the columns in A_k are independent, C_j is the left-most column in A_k, and $C_m \le C_j$. Since $|A'_k| = |A_k|$, we conclude that A'_k is a maximum-size subset of independent logical columns in S_k, and it includes C_m. Therefore, C_m is included in some maximum-size subset of independent logical columns of S_k.

4 Experimental Results and Analysis

In this section, we investigate the efficiency of flexible rerouting scheme by evaluating performance of algorithm FLX in comparison with algorithm GCR. To evaluation metrics, i.e., *harvest* and *degradation*, as formulated in [8-10,13-14], were calculated. The *harvest* indicates how effectively the non-faulty elements are utilized in constructing a target array from a host array with fault elements, whereas the *degradation* measures the degree of potential performance loss due to a smaller target array than the original host array.

$$harvest = \frac{\text{Size of Target Array}}{\text{Total number of Nonfaulty PEs in Host Array}} \times 100\%$$

$$degradation = \frac{\text{Size of Host Array - Size of Target Array}}{\text{Size of Host Array}} \times 100\%$$

For the simplicity, we denote target arrays constructed by algorithms GCR and FLX as *GCRA* and *FLXA*, respectively. The improvement in *harvest* of the FLX over algorithm GCR, is calculated by

$$impr = \frac{harvest \text{ of } FLXA \text{ - } harvest \text{ of } GCRA}{harvest \text{ of } FLXA} \times 100\%$$

Table 1. The performance comparison of the algorithms GCR and FLX for random faults of uniform distribution, averaged over 20 random instances for each case

Host Array		Target array						
Size	Fault density	Array size		harvest (%)		degradation (%)		impr (%)
		GCR	FLX	GCR	FLX	GCR	FLX	
64×64	0.05	64×54	64×55	89.23	89.64	15.23	14.84	0.46
	0.10	64×48	64×49	82.91	84.56	25.39	23.91	2.00
	0.20	64×33	64×38	65.25	73.85	47.81	40.94	13.25
	0.30	64×21	64×30	47.55	66.08	66.72	53.75	39.46
128×128	0.05	128×110	128×111	90.71	91.16	13.83	13.40	0.50
	0.10	128×96	128×98	83.29	85.20	25.04	23.32	2.30
	0.20	128×68	128×77	66.55	75.64	46.76	39.49	13.74
	0.30	128×41	128×61	46.21	67.75	67.66	52.58	46.94
256×256	0.05	256×222	256×224	91.41	92.06	13.16	12.54	0.72
	0.10	256×193	256×198	83.57	86.07	24.79	22.54	2.99
	0.20	256×137	256×157	66.82	76.83	46.54	38.54	14.99
	0.30	256×82	256×123	45.65	68.75	68.05	51.88	50.75

In order to make a fair comparison, we keep the same assumptions as in [8-14]. Faults are only associated with PEs and communication infrastructure is assumed to be fault free. This assumption can be justified since the switches and links use much less hardware resources when compared to the processors and are thus less vulnerable to defects. Both random fault model and clustered fault model were considered[7-10,12]. In a random fault model, the faults of a host array were generated by a uniform random generator. The fault density ρ of the host array is set from 5% to 30% for the experiments. On the other hand, without loss of generality, we model the clustered faults as a subarray that has 80% random faults in the host array. In order to focus on the clustered fault distribution, the fault density out of the subarray is set to 5%, which is far less than that in the subarray. The location of the subarray is generated randomly in the host array. Both algorithms were implemented in C++ language running on a computer with 2.1GHz CPU and 2GB RAM and are compared with each other on the same input instances. For each case, all physical rows are selected for inclusion into target array for experiments.

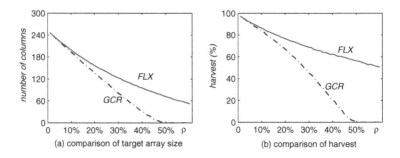

Fig. 4. Comparison of FLX and GCR in terms of target array size and harvest, on host arrays of 256×256 with random faults, averaged over 20 instances for each case

Table 1 shows the performance comparison of algorithms FLX and GCR. For the case of constructing target array on 64×64 host array with fault density 10%, the *harvest* of target array produced by GCR is 82.91%, while it is 84.56% by algorithm FLX, thus resulting in the improvement of 2% in *harvest*. When the fault density increases to 30%, FLX improves GCR by 39.46% on *harvest*. It is because, with the increasing fault densities, more PEs become un-connectable in algorithm GCR while they can be used in FLX to form logical columns. It is also worth pointing out that, if the fault density exceeds a certain point, i.e. 50% for host arrays with size of 256×256, algorithm GCR fails to form any logical columns as shown in Fig. 4(a). However, algorithm FLX is still capable of constructing target arrays with no less than 70 columns which corresponding to a harvest of 56%, as shown in Fig. 4(b). On the other hand, on host arrays with large fault densities, the improvement in harvest is more significant on large target arrays than on the relatively small ones. For examples, with fault density of 30%, the improvements of FLX over GCR are 39.46%, 46.94% and 50.75% for host arrays with sizes of $64 \times 64, 128 \times 128$ and 256×256, respectively. It is because, the increasing size increases the difficulty of forming a logical column thus leads to decrease in the number of logical columns and results in increase in the number of un-connectable PEs. This provides more chance for algorithm FLX to improve the target arrays using flexible column rerouting scheme.

Table 2 shows performance gain of algorithms FLX over GCR for the case of the clustered faults on 512×512 host arrays with fault density 5%. Our investigations reveal that, the harvest improvement increased with the increasing number of clustered fault areas. For example, on host array with 24×24 clustered fault areas, the improvement of harvest is 5.15% for the case of 8 clustered fault areas, while it increased to 13.22% and 19.77% on host arrays with 24 and 32 clustered fault areas, respectively. This is because, as the number of clustered fault areas increases, fewer logical columns can be constructed by algorithm GCR, thus leads to more un-connectable PEs which provide more chance for optimization by FLX. In addition, the improvement for harvest decreases is more significant on relatively large clustered fault area. This is because logical columns constructed by GCR cannot go through clustered fault areas, thus large scale clustered fault

Table 2. The performance comparison of the algorithms GCR and FLX for clustered faults of uniform distribution on 512×512 host array, averaged over 20 random instances for each case

Host Array		Target array						
Cluster Distribution		Array size		*harvest* (%)		*degradation* (%)		*impr*
size	number	GCR	FLX	GCR	FLX	GCR	FLX	(%)
16×16	8	512×419	512×431	86.12	88.58	18.18	15.85	2.87
	16	512×400	512×419	82.25	86.09	21.87	18.21	4.72
	24	512×381	512×409	78.42	84.06	25.50	20.15	7.23
	32	512×369	512×401	75.81	82.41	27.98	21.71	8.73
24×24	8	512×395	512×416	81.29	85.44	22.77	18.83	5.15
	16	512×363	512×396	74.69	81.49	29.04	22.59	9.17
	24	512×330	512×374	67.86	76.82	35.54	27.02	13.32
	32	512×294	512×351	60.40	72.13	42.62	31.47	19.77
32×32	8	512×364	512×392	74.83	80.59	28.92	23.44	7.84
	16	512×318	512×364	65.40	74.79	37.87	28.95	14.78
	24	512×251	512×322	51.54	66.27	51.04	37.04	28.80
	32	512×226	512×315	46.48	64.69	55.84	38.54	40.37

areas decreases the area of PEs that can be used for constructing target arrays by algorithm GCR. On the other hand, large clustered fault areas increase the fault density of the host array, thus provide more chance for optimization by algorithm FLX.

5   Conclusions

Many previous works discuss the reconfiguration problems under column rerouting scheme with fixed compensation distance, resulting in great lose of harvest. This paper investigate the efficiency of flexible rerouting scheme by developing an efficient algorithm to reconfigure an multiprocessor array with faults. The proposed algorithm FLX is able to reduce the number of un-connectable PEs caused by the interconnection overlaps. It is capable of producing maximum-size target arrays, resulting in a significant improvement in comparison to the algorithm GCR. Experimental results show that the size of target array can be significantly increased. The algorithm FLX is scalable with the array size, as it is more efficient on large host arrays than on relatively small ones. In addition, its harvest tends to decrease slowly with the increasing fault density, that is superior to algorithm GCR whose harvest value decreases rapidly.

Acknowledgments. This work was supported by the National Science Foundation of China under Grant No. 61070136 and No. 61173032, and the Doctoral Fund of Ministry of Education of China under Grant No. 20100032110041.

References

1. Murali, S., De Micheli, G.: SUNMAP: A tool for automatic topology selection and generation for NoCs. In: Proc. of the 41st Design Automation Conference (DAC 2004), pp. 914–919. ACM Press, San Diego (2004)
2. Bertozzi, D., Jalabert, A., Murali, S., Tamahankar, R., Stergiou, S., Benini, L., De Micheli, G.: NoC synthesis flow for customized domain specific multiprocessor systems-on-chip. IEEE Transactions on Parallel and Distributed System 16(2), 113–129 (2005)
3. Modarressi, M., Sarbazi-Azad, H.: Power-aware mapping for reconfigurable NoC architectures. In: Proc. of the 25th International Conference on Computer Design, pp. 417–422. IEEE Press, California (2007)
4. Modarressi, M., Tavakkol, A., Sarbazi-Azad, H.: Application-Aware Topology Reconfiguration for On-Chip Networks. IEEE Transactions on Very Large Scale Integration (VLSI) Systems 19(11), 2010–2022 (2011)
5. Chen, Y.Y., Upadhyaya, S.J., Cheng, C.H.: A comprehensive reconfiguration scheme for fault-tolerant VLSI/WSI array processors. IEEE Transactions Computers 46(12), 1363–1371 (1997)
6. Horita, T., Takanami, I.: Fault-tolerant processor arrays based on the 1.5-track switches with flexible spare distributions. IEEE Transactions on Computers 49(6), 542–552 (2000)
7. Kuo, S.Y., Chen, I.Y.: Efficient reconfiguration algorithms for degradable VLSI/WSI arrays. IEEE Transactions Computer-Aided Design 11(10), 1289–1300 (1992)
8. Low, C.P., Leong, H.W.: On the reconfiguration of degradable VLSI/WSI arrays. IEEE Transactions Computer-Aided Design of Integrated Circuits and Systems 16(10), 1213–1221 (1997)
9. Low, C.P.: An efficient reconfiguration algorithm for degradable VLSI/WSI arrays. IEEE Transactions on Computers 49(6), 553–559 (2000)
10. Wu, J., Srikanthan, T.: Reconfiguration Algorithms for Power Efficient VLSI Subarrays with 4-port Switches. IEEE Transactions on Computers 55(3), 243–253 (2006)
11. Fukushi, M., Fukushima, Y., Horiguchi, S.: A genetic approach for the reconfiguration of degradable processor arrays. In: Proc. of 20th IEEE International Symposium on Defect Fault Tolerance VLSI System, pp. 63–71. IEEE Press, Ohio (2005)
12. Wu, J., Srikanthan, T., Han, X.: Preprocessing and Partial Rerouting Techniques for Accelerating Reconfiguration of Degradable VLSI Arrays. IEEE Transactions on Very Large Scale Intergration (VLSI) Systems 18(2), 315–319 (2010)
13. Jiang, G., Wu, J., Sun, J.: Non-Backtracking Reconfiguration Algorithm for Three-dimensional VLSI Arrays. In: Proc. of 2012 IEEE 18th International Conference on Parallel and Distributed Systems, pp. 362–367. IEEE Press, Singapore (2012)
14. Jiang, G., Wu, J., Sun, J.: Efficient Reconfiguration Algorithm for Three-dimensional VLSI Arrays. In: Proc. of 2012 IEEE 26th International Parallel and Distributed Processing Symposium Workshops & PhD Forum, pp. 254–258. IEEE Press, Shanghai (2012)

An Efficient Crosstalk-Free Routing Algorithm Based on Permutation Decomposition for Optical Multi-log$_2 N$ Switching Networks

Xiaofeng Liu[1,3], Youjian Zhao[2], and Yajuan Wu[3]

[1] School of Computer Science and Engineering,
University of Electronic Science and Technology of China, Chengdu, China
[2] Department of Computer Science and Technology,
Tsinghua University, Beijing, China
[3] School of Computer, China West Normal University, Nanchong, China
xhxfliu@163.com, zhaoyoujian@tsinghua.edu.cn, scwuyajuan@yahoo.com.cn

Abstract. Optical switching networks (OSN) based on optical directional couplers (DC) may be the most promising candidate to provide a high switching rate when the speed mismatch problem between links (optical fibers) and switches is increasingly serious. Although such switches have many advantages, the DC suffers from an inherent crosstalk problem that can greatly aggravate the switching performance. Based on semi-permutations, a parallel decomposition algorithm, which is called *multi-decomposition*, is proposed in this paper for solving the optical crosstalk problem in optical multi-log$_2$N switching networks. According to the number of planes in a multi-log$_2$N network, the multi-decomposition is performed in parallel to partition a permutation into several sub-permutations, each of which is established without crosstalk within each plane. We demonstrate that our algorithm can completely remove the crosstalk in optical multi-log$_2$N networks when n is even, and that it may be generated only in the stage $(n\text{-}1)/2$ (i.e., the middle stage) when n is odd, but the corresponding probability of generating crosstalk is to be less than or equal to $\frac{1}{2^{(n+1)/2}-1}$. In addition, our algorithm can achieve a low complexity for decomposition a permutation due to its parallelism so that any permutations can be realized in multi-log$_2$N networks under the constraint of avoiding crosstalk.

Keywords: Permutation, Optical switching, Multi-log$_2$N networks, Optical crosstalk.

1 Introduction

The Internet is an important product of the information age. From a high-level perspective, the entire Internet architecture consists of two parts: communication links and switching nodes. At present, the capacity of these two parts has an enormous difference. The speed of communication links has been drastically increased with the advent of dense wavelength-division multiplexing (DWDM)

C.-H. Hsu et al. (Eds.): NPC 2013, LNCS 8147, pp. 207–219, 2013.

technologies, but the progress made in the switches has lagged relatively behind. In order to solve the speed mismatch problem, the optical switches have been widely explored in recent years.

A multi-$\log_2 N$ network [1], composed of several single-$\log_2 N$ networks, possesses many characteristics which are helpful for photonic switching system. As an optical directional-coupler (DC) is introduced into this switching network to replace the old (electronic) switching element (SE), the transmission rate of signals can achieve several T bps if the state (cross or bar) of the DC has been set up properly. Meanwhile, A blocking, which is called *crosstalk-blocking* [2] and differs from *link-blocking*, is introduced into this switching system by DCs. This blocking will occur when two light signals pass through the same DC at the same time. The crosstalk-blocking limits the scalability of switching networks so that it is not easy to use DCs to construct a larger switching network [3] because two signals passing through the same DC interact with each other. Therefore, the crosstalk-blocking is an important factor to affect the quality of communication in an optical switching network (OSN). Eliminating the crosstalk-blocking in an OSN is just the main objective of this paper.

In this paper, we propose an efficient algorithm to eliminate the crosstalk-blocking (abbreviated as crosstalk) of optical multi-$\log_2 N$ switching networks. The central idea of the proposed algorithm is based on the concept of a semi-permutation in the literature [4], but we extend this concept to multiple decomposition of a permutation for the crosstalk-free routing in optical multi-$\log_2 N$ switching networks, i.e., a permutation is first partitioned into two semi-permutations, and is further divided into four quarter-permutations and so on. By so doing, any two different optical signals traversing down two node-disjoint (or DC-disjoint) paths cannot generate the optical crosstalk problem within each plane. Thus this multiple decomposition algorithm is named *multi-decomposition* in the remainder of the paper.

This paper is followed by four sections. Section 2 describes the crosstalk and its common solutions. A basic network model and all related preliminaries associated with this work are illustrated in section 3. Section 4 presents the multi-decomposition in detail and then conclusions are given in section 5.

2   Crosstalk and Related Researches

Crosstalk and signal attenuation are the major problems that have been hindering the development of OSNs all the time. The signal attenuation problem can be solved by a semiconductor optical amplifier (SOA). However, the crosstalk cannot be removed by the SOA because the crosstalk is also amplified when the desirable signal is amplified. Thus we must find the other methods to remove the crosstalk in an OSN.

Indeed,it is almost impossible to eliminate the optical crosstalk totally unless only one optical signal passes through a DC at any given time, as shown in Fig. 1. Both *space domain approach* [5] and *time domain approach* [6] are based on this idea. Essentially, the former adds the number of DCs, while at most

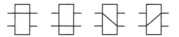

Fig. 1. Traversing ways in a DC

only one of the two inputs and outputs is active at a time in a DC. Therefore, hardware cost has been sacrificed to trade the crosstalk-free routing. For the latter, a permutation is decomposed into several sub-permutations such that all connections of each sub-permutation can be established simultaneously without crosstalk, i.e., each time slot is required to route each sub-permutation and all the connections corresponding the permutation are established within several time slots in a time-division multiplexed fashion. As such, this approach uses time cost to exchange the crosstalk-free routing. In addition to these two approaches above, *wavelength dilation* [7] is the other one that eliminates the crosstalk in an OSN. A technology of *wavelength grouping method* (WGM) [7] is proposed in this approach, in which the wavelengths are partitioned into several groups so that the wavelengths in each group are widely separated, with nearby wavelengths placed in different groups, i.e., the wavelengths are selected should be far enough apart (a few nanometers) so as not to interact with each other. A drawback of this approach is that a specific structure is required to select and separate the wavelength, and then result in increasing the hardware cost. This method is adopted in [8][9] to remove the crosstalk of optical multi-log_2N networks.

The existing methods above removing the crosstalk focus usually on the single-log_2N network ([9] is an exception), and they sacrifice either time cost or hardware cost. Moreover, due to the unique path property of a log_2N network, some sub-permutations can be realized within a log_2N network in a single pass whereas the others cannot [4]. In fact, the spirit of all of these approaches mentioned above is to avoid two light signals with the same wavelength passing through a common DC at the same time, and the proposed approach in this paper is no exception. However, our algorithm uses the idea of multiple decomposition of any permutation to realize the crosstalk-free routing within each plane of a multi-log_2N network and does not increase time cost and hardware cost for optical multi-log_2N switching networks.

3   Basic Network Model and Preliminaries

3.1   Multi-log_2N Network Model

Multi-log_2N networks are vertically stacked with multiple log_2N networks, N demultiplexers and N multiplexers. The log_2N network has been composed of $N(=2n)$ inputs and outputs and $n(=log_2N)$ stages. Each stage consists of $N/2$ 2×2 DCs and any adjacent stages are connected by N interstage fiber links. Planes are vertically stacked to N demultiplexers (resp. multiplexers) in input (resp. output) stage. N denotes the number of source inputs and destination outputs labeled by $0, 1, \cdots, N-1$ from top to bottom, $n(=log_2N)$ denotes the number of stages numbered by $0, 1, \cdots, n - 1$ from left to right, and m indicates the number of planes contained in a multi-$\log_2 N$ network. Since all $\log_2 N$ networks including *baseline*, *omega*, and *banyan-type* [10] have the topologically equivalent feature [11], we use an $N \times N (N = 2n)$ baseline network as the representative of routing planes in our work. An example of an 8×8 baseline network is shown in Fig. 2, and the corresponding multi-$\log_2 N$ network is illustrated in Fig. 3.

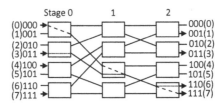

Fig. 2. An 8×8 baseline network

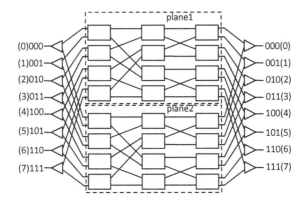

Fig. 3. An $N \times N$ multi-$\log_2 N$ network ($N = 8, m = 2$)

3.2   Related Preliminaries

For a $\log_2 N$ network, let u and v be any two SEs in stage i, $S_j(u)$ and $S_j(v)$ are the two sets of SEs to which u and v can reach in stage $(i + j)$ ($0 \leq i < n - 1, 1 \leq j \leq n - i - 1$). Sets $S_j(u)$ and $S_j(v)$ certainly can satisfy one of the following properties:$S_j(u) \cap S_j(v) = \emptyset$ or $S_j(u) = S_j(v)$ [8]. For $S_j(u)$ and $S_j(v)$,the equality $S_j(u) = S_j(v)$ holds, which implies that SEs u and v are sure to share the same SE in stage $(i + j)$, hence light signals passing through SEs u and v must generate the crosstalk phenomenon at the shared SE in stage $(i + j)$. Therefore, we call SEs u and v possessing (i, j)-*buddy* if the equality $S_j(u) = S_j(v)$ holds.

A theorem can be obtained immediately from the description of (i, j)-*buddy* above.

Theorem 1. *Let u and v be two different DCs in stage i. Two optical signals going through u and v do not generate crosstalk in stage $(i+j)$ $(0 \leq i < n-1, 1 \leq j \leq n - i - 1)$ if u and v do not have the (i, j)-buddy property.*

Proof. if u and v don't have the (i, j)-buddy property, then optical signals going through u and v do not share any SEs in stage $(i + j)$, so there is no reason to occur crosstalk in stage $(i + j)$. □

4   Multi-decomposition Algorithm of a Permutation

4.1   Decomposition of a Permutation

A *permutation* is usually adopted to describe a mapping between inputs and outputs for a switching network. For an $N \times N$ network, suppose there is a permutation P which maps input x_i to output y_i, i.e., $P(x_i) = y_i$ where $x_i, y_i \in \{0, 1, \cdots, N - 1\}$ for $0 \leq i < N - 1$. We use the representation as equation (1) to denote this permutation.

$$P = \begin{pmatrix} x_0 \ x_1 \ \cdots \ x_{N-1} \\ y_0 \ y_1 \ \cdots \ y_{N-1} \end{pmatrix} \tag{1}$$

The semi-permutation [4] is the basis of the multi-decomposition algorithm, so we proceed with the concept of semi-permutation first.

Definition 1 ([4]). *For any permutation P of $\{0, 1, \cdots, N-1\}$, a partial permutation* $\begin{pmatrix} x_{i_1} x_{i_2} \cdots x_{i_{\frac{N}{2}}} \\ y_{i_1} y_{i_2} \cdots y_{i_{\frac{N}{2}}} \end{pmatrix}$ *is referred to as a semi-permutation, if $\{\lfloor \frac{x_{i_1}}{2} \rfloor, \lfloor \frac{x_{i_2}}{2} \rfloor,$ $\cdots, \lfloor \frac{x_{i_{N/2}}}{2} \rfloor\} = \{0, 1, \cdots, N/2 - 1\}$ and $\{\lfloor \frac{y_{i_1}}{2} \rfloor, \lfloor \frac{y_{i_2}}{2} \rfloor, \cdots, \lfloor \frac{y_{i_{N/2}}}{2} \rfloor\} = \{0, 1, \cdots, N/2 - 1\}$.*

Since $2(k - 1) \leq x_{i_k}, y_{i_k} \leq 2k - 1, k = 1, 2, \cdots, N/2$, a semi-permutation ensures that the crosstalk can be removed in the first stage and last stage of a $\log_2 N$ network, but the crosstalk cannot be always removed in the intermediate stages. Besides, this approach needs several passes to establish a permutation in a single-$\log_2 N$ network, and hence the routing time is increased.

To eliminate the crosstalk of each stage in an optical multi-$\log_2 N$ switching network, we give the definition of the multi-decomposition based on semi-permutation (i.e., Definition 1) as follows.

Definition 2. *For any permutation P of $\{0, 1, \cdots, N-1\}$, let* $\begin{pmatrix} x_{i_1} x_{i_2} \cdots x_{i_{\frac{N}{m}}} \\ y_{i_1} y_{i_2} \cdots y_{i_{\frac{N}{m}}} \end{pmatrix}$

be a partial permutation of P, where m is an integral power of 2. $\{\lfloor \frac{x_{i_1}}{m} \rfloor, \lfloor \frac{x_{i_2}}{m} \rfloor, \cdots,$ $\lfloor \frac{x_{i_{N/m}}}{m} \rfloor\} = \{0, 1, \cdots, N/m - 1\}$ and $\{\lfloor \frac{y_{i_1}}{m} \rfloor, \lfloor \frac{y_{i_2}}{m} \rfloor, \cdots, \lfloor \frac{y_{i_{N/m}}}{m} \rfloor\} = \{0, 1, \cdots,$ $N/m - 1\}$ are used to partition this partial permutation such that the resulting sub-permutation is smaller than semi-permutation in size.

This decomposition method is referred to as *multi-decomposition* for the multiple decompositions. The resulting partial permutation of multi-decomposition of a permutation is still called sub-permutation from now on.

Note that m denotes the number of sub-permutations into which the full permutation is divided, and each sub-permutation contains N/m connections of the full permutation. An example is given to understand this partition process as follows.

Example 1. For $N = 16, m = 4$, and a permutation

$$P = \begin{pmatrix} 0\ 1\ 2\ 3\ 4\ 5\ 6\ \ 7\ \ 8\ 9\ 10\ 11\ 12\ 13\ 14\ 15 \\ 1\ 0\ 9\ 5\ 6\ 8\ 10\ 13\ 15\ 2\ 3\ \ 4\ \ 7\ 11\ 14\ 12 \end{pmatrix}$$

Step 1. Run the multi-decomposition algorithm ($m = 2$) to get two semi-permutations P_1 and P_2.

$$P_1 = \begin{pmatrix} 0\ 3\ 5\ 6\ \ 8\ 10\ 12\ 15 \\ 1\ 5\ 8\ 10\ 15\ \ 3\ \ 7\ 12 \end{pmatrix}$$

$$P_2 = \begin{pmatrix} 1\ 2\ 4\ \ 7\ \ 9\ 11\ 13\ 14 \\ 0\ 9\ 6\ 13\ 2\ \ 4\ 11\ 14 \end{pmatrix}$$

Step 2. For all semi-permutations, run the multi-decomposition algorithm ($m = 4$) again in parallel to get four quarter-permutations, P_{11}, P_{12}, P_{21} and P_{22}.

$$P_{11} = \begin{pmatrix} 0\ 5\ 8\ 12 \\ 1\ 8\ 15\ 7 \end{pmatrix}, P_{12} = \begin{pmatrix} 3\ 6\ 10\ 15 \\ 5\ 10\ 3\ 12 \end{pmatrix}$$

$$P_{21} = \begin{pmatrix} 1\ 7\ 11\ 13 \\ 0\ 13\ 4\ 11 \end{pmatrix}, P_{22} = \begin{pmatrix} 2\ 4\ 9\ 14 \\ 9\ 6\ 2\ 14 \end{pmatrix}$$

Step 3. Multi-decomposition ends when the number of sub-permutations is m, or else goes to step 2. Since m is equal to 4 in this example, the multi-decomposition algorithm should be stop.

Fig. 4 illustrates the switching of these four quarter-permutations in a multi-$\log_2 N$ network ($N = 16, m = 4$).

Now, we answer the following two questions about the multi-decomposition. The first one is how many times the multi-decomposition algorithm should be performed when a full permutation needs to be decomposed, i.e., what is the proper value of m? The other is the effectiveness of this algorithm. The proper value of m is determined by the number of copies in a multi-$\log_2 N$ network. Since the rearrangeable nonblocking (RNB) network is considered in our work, the number of copies which is needed to build a rearrangeable nonblocking multi-$\log_2 N$ network is $2^{\lfloor n/2 \rfloor}$ [1]. Therefore, the value of m is taken $2^{\lfloor n/2 \rfloor}$ in this paper. For the second one, we use the following theorem to give an answer.

Theorem 2. *For a multi-$\log_2 N$ network, any permutation P can be partitioned into m sub-permutations, where $n = \log_2 N$ and $m = 2^{\lfloor \frac{n}{2} \rfloor}$.*

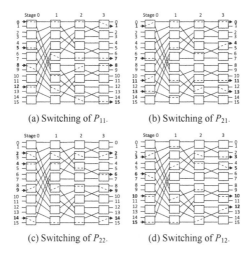

(a) Switching of P_{11}. (b) Switching of P_{21}.

(c) Switching of P_{22}. (d) Switching of P_{12}.

Fig. 4. Switching of four quarter-permutations in a multi-$\log_2 N$ network ($N = 16$, $m = 4$)

Proof. The multi-decomposition is implemented by an iterative manner. A permutation is first partitioned into two semi-permutations, and then each semi-permutation is further partitioned into its own two semi-permutations and so on. This partitioning process cannot stop until the number of sub-permutations is equal to m. According to this partitioning process, this theorem is essentially equivalent to a proposition that "Any permutation can be decomposed into two semi-permutations." This proposition can be easily proved by using the P. Hall's distinct system representative [12]. The detailed proof can be found in [4], so we can use a method similar to one in [4] to prove this theorem. Due to space limitation, the detailed proof is omitted here.   □

Theorem 2 guarantees the feasibility of the multi-decomposition of permutations. Next, we prove that the multi-decomposition is effective in removing the crosstalk problem. We first give the following concepts of *input set* (IS) and *output set* (OS).

Definition 3. *For an $N \times N(N = 2n)$ multi-$\log_2 N$ network, there are $n(= \log_2 N)$ stages.*

(1) If n is even, the N inputs (resp. outputs) of the multi-$\log_2 N$ network are divided equally into $i = 2^{n/2}$ input (resp. output) sets from top to bottom. These sets are referred to as $I_0, I_1, \cdots, I_{i-1}$ and $O_0, O_1, \cdots, O_{i-1}$, respectively. As shown in Fig. 5(a).

(2) If n is odd, the N inputs (resp. outputs) of the multi-$\log_2 N$ network are divided equally into $i = 2^{(n+1)/2}$ input (resp. output) sets from top to bottom. These sets are also referred to as $I_0, I_1, \cdots, I_{i-1}$ and $O_0, O_1, \cdots, O_{i-1}$, respectively. As shown in Fig. 5(b).

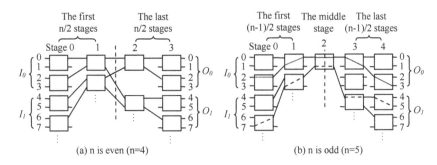

Fig. 5. The diagram of input and output sets

Note that the order of input and output ports in each set is consecutive and ascending, and that the number of ports is equal. An important fact obtained from Definition 2 and 3 is that different connections of a sub-permutation always start from different ISs and end in different OSs. Thus every sub-permutation does not have any crosstalk in the input and output stage. The following theorem tells us that the optical crosstalk does not occur in the intermediate stages, either.

Theorem 3. *For an $N \times N(N = 2n)$ multi-log$_2 N$ network, $n = log_2 N$, and $m = 2^{\lfloor n/2 \rfloor}$. Multi-decomposition guarantees that*

(1) The crosstalk never occurs in the optical multi-log$_2 N$ network when n is even;

(2) The crosstalk may be possible only in the center stage (i.e., stage-$(n-1)/2$) when n is odd, but the probability of generating crosstalk is less than or equal to $\frac{1}{2^{(n+1)/2}-1}$.

Proof. (1) M is equal to $2^{n/2}$ if n is even. According to Definition 3, N input and output ports are divided evenly into ISs and OSs, and every sub-permutation contains $N/m(= 2^{n/2})$ connections. As stated previously, the crosstalk is never generated in the input stage and output stage (by Definition 2 and 3). We now prove that the crosstalk does not occur in the intermediate stages. We first consider the first $n/2$ stages. If the crosstalk has occurred in stage j $(1 \leq j \leq \frac{n}{2} - 1)$, there are at least two different DCs u and v in the same IS of a plane satisfying the $(0, j)$-buddy (by Theorem 1), but only one connection in a sub-permutation starts from an IS within each plane at any time. This contradiction proves our conclusion that no crosstalk occurs in the first $n/2$ stages. In the last $n/2$ stages, the crosstalk can also be avoided, which can be proved by contradiction. Once the crosstalk is generated, some connections in the same plane will be routed to the same OS, but this case is also impossible. In fact, these two cases are entirely symmetrical.

(2) If n is odd, $m = 2^{(n-1)/2}$. The crosstalk does not occur in the first $(n-1)/2$ stages and last $(n-1)/2$ stages, but it possibly emerges in the center

stage. Take the Fig. 5(b) as an example, two connections $(2 \rightarrow 3)$ and $(7 \rightarrow 5)$ share a common DC at the middle stage, now the crosstalk has occurred, but no DC can be shared in the first $(n-1)/2$ stages and last $(n-1)/2$ stages. Following a similar argument to the first case (n is even), we can prove that when n is odd, the crosstalk is never generated in the first $(n-1)/2$ stages and last $(n-1)/2$ stages. Here we fix our attention on the proof of the probability of generating crosstalk in the middle stage.   □

For brevity and clarity, we introduce the following definitions of *buddy input set* (BIS) and *buddy output set* (BOS). The set BIS is comprised of all input sets I_k sharing a common DC at the center stage, and the set BOS is comprised of all output sets O_k sharing the same DC at the center stage. For example, I_0 and I_1 belong to BIS_0 because they share the same DC a in the center stage, i.e., $BIS_0 = \{I_0, I_1\}$; similarly, $BOS_0 = \{O_0, O_1\}$. As shown in Fig. 6.

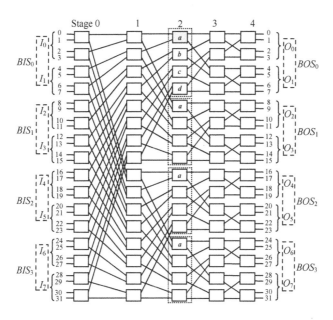

Fig. 6. The baseline network when n is odd ($n = 5$)

According to the previous definitions, some good characteristics of the multi-decomposition are summarized as follows:

- It is impossible that two (or more) connections in each plane start from the same IS and head for the same OS (by Definition 3);
- Two connections sharing the same DC in the center stage should come from the same BIS and head for the same BOS;
- According to the distinct BISs, all DCs in the center stage are partitioned into $i/2$ sections (as the dashed boxes in Fig. 6) such that at most one DC possibly generates the crosstalk within each section at any time.

These characteristics imply that all DCs in the same section are mutually exclusive in generating crosstalk, and that the corresponding DCs among distinct sections are mutually exclusive in generating crosstalk as well. Thus, these $i/2$ sections possess the identical statistical nature, we may take the first DC a (the shadow box in Fig. 6) in the first section as the representative to discuss the probability of generating crosstalk.

Any inputs in each IS can be connected to arbitrary OS with equivalent probability, i.e., $P\{I_k \rightarrow O_j\} = 1/i(0 \leq k, j < i)$, so the probability of generating crosstalk in SE a is

$$
\begin{aligned}
P_{crosstalk}(a) &= P\{(I_0 \rightarrow O_0, I_1 \rightarrow O_1) \cup (I_0 \rightarrow O_1, I_1 \rightarrow O_0)\} \\
&= P\{(I_0 \rightarrow O_0, I_1 \rightarrow O_1) + P\{(I_0 \rightarrow O_1, I_1 \rightarrow O_0)\} \\
&= P\{I_0 \rightarrow O_0\}P\{I_1 \rightarrow O_1 | I_0 \rightarrow O_0\} + \\
&\quad P\{I_0 \rightarrow O_1\}P\{I_1 \rightarrow O_0 | I_0 \rightarrow O_1\} \\
&= \frac{1}{i} \times \frac{1}{i-1} + \frac{1}{i} \times \frac{1}{i-1} \\
&= \frac{2}{i(i-1)} \quad .
\end{aligned}
\tag{2}
$$

On the other hand, at most one DC generates crosstalk possibly in each section in any given time. Then the probability of generating crosstalk in each section, which is denoted by $P_{crosstalk}(section)$, is equal to $P_{crosstalk}(a)$. Therefore the probability of generating crosstalk in entirely plane is

$$
\begin{aligned}
P_{crosstalk}(plane) &= P\{\cup_{k=0}^{i/2} P_{crosstalk}(section_k)\} \\
&\leq \cup_{k=0}^{i/2} P_{crosstalk}(section_k) \\
&= \cup_{k=0}^{i/2} P_{crosstalk}(a) \\
&= \frac{1}{i-1}
\end{aligned}
\tag{3}
$$

Now, substituting $i = 2^{(n+1)/2}$ into expression (3), we obtain $P_{crosstalk}(plane) \leq \frac{1}{2^{(n+1)/2}-1}$.

4.2 Implementation of the Multi-decomposition and Its Analysis

In this subsection, we will discuss the implementation of the multi-decomposition algorithm of permutations and its time complexity.

There is a permutation as the equation (1), in which input x_i is mapped to output y_i $(0 \leq i \leq N - 1)$. Based on the semi-permutation [4], we design the decomposition algorithm of a permutation as Algorithm 1 in order to design our multi-decomposition algorithm. The Algorithm 1 contains three parameters that are P, N and k. These parameters denote the permutation to be decomposed, the number of requests and the decomposition levels, respectively.

The multi-decomposition algorithm can be implemented by calling Algorithm 1 repeatedly. Let m be the integral power of 2, i.e., $m = 2^k(1 \leq k \leq n)$.

Algorithm 1. Dichotomy-of-permutation (P, N, k)

Input: Any permutation P contains N request pairs.

Output: Two sub-permutations P_1 and P_2

---

1. Two vertex sets $V_I = \{A_{i_0}, A_{i_1}, \cdots, A_{i_{N/2^k-1}}\}$ and $V_O = \{A_{o_0}, A_{o_1}, \cdots, A_{o_{N/2^k-1}}\}$ are built from the permutation P, where $A_{i_j} = \{x_{j \cdot 2^k}, x_{j \cdot 2^k+1}, \cdots, x_{j \cdot 2^k+2^k-1}\}$, $A_{o_j} = \{y_{j \cdot 2^k}, y_{j \cdot 2^k+1}, \cdots, y_{j \cdot 2^k+2^k-1}\}$, $0 \le j < N/2^k$

2. Construct a bipartite graph $G = (V_I, V_O, E)$ based on V_I and V_O. A edge $e \in E$ is associated with a request pair (x_j, y_j), where $x_j \in A_{i_j}$ and $y_j \in A_{o_j}$.

3. Traverse the bipartite graph and color the two adjacent edges of the same vertex with different colors, then all edges with the same color are grouped into forming a sub-permutation. Since the chromatic number of the bipartite graph is two [4], the permutation can be partitioned into two sub-permutations P_1 and P_2.

The multi-decomposition algorithm becomes semi-permutation decomposition in [4] when k is 1. One exactly connection is established in each plane when k equals to n, thus the crosstalk and blocking can be avoided undoubtedly. In the other cases, Algorithm 1 is called repeatedly k rounds and is executed $2^{i-1}(1 \le i \le k)$ times in parallel in each round. The corresponding algorithm is demonstrated as Algorithm 2. As the Example 1 mentioned earlier, $N = 16, m = 4(= 2^2)$, and the Algorithm 1 has been called 2 rounds. Two semi-permutations are obtained after the first round, and four quarter-permutations are got after the second round.

Algorithm 2. Multi-decomposition of permutations

Input: N requests contained by a permutation P;

Output: M sub-permutations, $m = 2^k$, k is a natural number.

For $i = 1$ to k do

    For $j = 1$ to 2^{i-1} do in parallel

    $\{P[j,1], P[j,2]\}$=Dichotomy-of-permutation $(P[j], N, i)$;

    End parallel

End for

A permutation is partitioned into m sub-permutations, and the decomposition process is similar to that of building a binary tree with m sub-permutations as leaves. Furthermore, this process is carried out in parallel, so the time complexity of Algorithm 2 is $O(log_2 m)$. On the other hand, the Algorithm1 has $O(N)$ time complexity, so the overall complexity of Algorithm 2 is $O(N log_2 m)$. We will further improve Algorithm 1 by parallelism in the future so that the time cost can be reduced much.

5   Conclusions

In this paper, we proposed an efficient algorithm called multi-decomposition to remove the crosstalk in optical multi-$\log_2 N$ switching networks. A permutation is partitioned into several sub-permutations by using our decomposition algorithm, which ensures that each sub-permutation can be connected without crosstalk within each plane of optical multi-$\log_2 N$ networks. Compared with other approaches, our algorithm does not increase the time cost and hardware cost. Although semi-permutation [4] is the foundation of our algorithm, we have extended the concept of semi-permutation to multiple decomposition of a permutation and successfully solved the crosstalk problem of optical multi-$\log_2 N$ switching networks.

We have proved the validity of the multi-decomposition algorithm. The crosstalk can be entirely removed in optical multi-$\log_2 N$ networks when $n(= \log N)$ is even. If n is odd, crosstalk may be possible only in the middle stage (i.e., stage-$(n\text{-}1)/2$), but the probability of generating crosstalk is proved to be less than or equal to $\frac{1}{2^{(n+1)/2}-1}$. What's more, our algorithm has low time complexity to decompose a permutation due to its parallelism so that any permutations can be routed without crosstalk in an optical multi-$\log_2 N$ switching network.

Acknowledgments. This work is supported by National Natural Science Foundation of China (No.61073167),National High Technology Development Program of China (No.2011AA010704),Projects in the National Science & Technology Pillar Program(2011BAK08B05-02) and Major Training Program of China West Normal University (09A003).

References

1. Lea, C.T.: Multi-$\log_2 N$ networks and their applications in high-speed electronic and photonic switching systems. IEEE Transactions on Communications 18(10), 1740–1749 (1990)
2. Vaez, M.M., Lea, C.T.: Strictly nonblocking directional-coupler-based switching networks under crosstalk constraint. IEEE Transactions on Communications 48(2), 316–323 (2000)
3. Hinton, H.S.: An introduction to photonic switching fabrics. Plenum, New York (1993)
4. Yang, Y., Wang, J., Pan, Y.: Permutation capability of optical multistage interconnection networks. Journal of Parallel and distributed Computing 60(1), 72–91 (2000)
5. Padmanabhan, K., Netravali, A.N.: dilated networks for photonic switching. IEEE Transactions on Communications com-35(12), 1357–1365 (1987)
6. Qiao, C.: A time domain approach for avoiding crosstalk in optical blocking multistage interconnection networks. Jouranl of Lighwave Technology 12(10), 1854–1862 (1994)
7. Sharony, J., Cheung, K.W., Stern, T.E.: The wavelength dilation concept in lightwave networks – Implementation and system considerations. IEEE Journal of Lightwave Technology 11(5/6), 900–907 (1993)

8. Zheng, S.Q., Gumaste, A., Shen, H.: A parallel self-routing rearrangeable non-blocking multi-log$_2$N photonic switching networks. IEEE Transactions on Networking 18(2), 529–539 (2010)
9. Wong, T.S., Lea, C.T.: Crosstalk reduction through wavelength assignment in WDM photonic switching networks. IEEE Transactions on Communications 49(7), 1280–1287 (2001)
10. Goke, G.R., Lipovski, G.J.: Banyan networks for partitioning multiprocessor systems. In: Proceedings of 1st International Symposium on Computer Architecture, pp. 21–28. ACM Press, New York (1973)
11. Wu, C.L., Feng, T.Y.: On a class of multistage interconnection networks. IEEE Transactions on Computers C-29(8), 694–702 (1980)
12. Hall, P.: On representatives of subsets. Journal London Mathematical Society 10(1), 26–30 (1935)

Conditional Diagnosability of Complete Josephus Cubes[*]

Lishan Lu[1] and Shuming Zhou[1,2]

[1] School of Mathematics and Computer Science,
Fujian Normal University, Fuzhou, Fujian, 350007, P.R. China
`894729679@qq.com`
[2] Key Laboratory of Network Security and Cryptology,
Fujian Normal University, Fuzhou, Fujian, 350007, P.R. China
`zhoushuming@fjnu.edu.cn`

Abstract. The growing size of the multiprocessor system increases its vulnerability to component failures. The fault diagnosis is the process of identifying faulty processors in a system through self-testing, and the diagnosability is an important parameter to measure the reliability of an interconnection network. As a new measure of fault tolerance, conditional diagnosability can better evaluate the real diagnosability of interconnection networks. In this paper, we derive the conditional diagnosability of the multiprocessor systems in terms of Complete Josephus Cubes CJC_n ($n \geq 8$) under the comparison model.

Keywords: Comparison diagnosis, conditional diagnosability, Complete Josephus Cubes.

1 Introduction

The process of identifying faulty processors in a system by analyzing the outcomes of available inter-processor tests is called *system-level diagnosis*. The foundation of system diagnosis and an original diagnostic model, namely the PMC model, were established in a classic paper by Preparata et al. [11]. Its target is to identify the exact set of all faulty nodes before their repair or replacement. All tests are performed between two adjacent processors, and it was assumed that a test result is reliable (respectively, unreliable) if the processor that initiates the test is fault-free (respectively, faulty). The comparison-based diagnosis models, first proposed by Malek [9] and Chwa and Hakimi [1], have been considered to be a practical approach for fault diagnosis in multiprocessor systems. In these models, the same job is assigned to a pair of processors in the system and their outputs are compared by a central observer. Sengupta and Dahbura [12] developed this comparison approach such that the comparisons have no central unit involved. Lin et al. [8] introduced the conditional diagnosis under the comparison model. By evaluating the size of connected components, they obtained that

---

[*] This work was also partly supported by the Natural Science Foundation of Fujian Province(Nos. 2013J01221, JA12073).

C.-H. Hsu et al. (Eds.): NPC 2013, LNCS 8147, pp. 220–231, 2013.

the conditional diagnosability of Star graph S_n is $3n - 7$. Additionally, Hsu et al. [4] have proved that the conditional diagnosability of hypercube is $3n - 5$. This idea was attributed to Lai et al. [7] who is the first to use a restricted diagnosis strategy. Recently, the conditional diagnosabilities of cross cubes are also obtained [18].

The Josephus Cube [5] is a recently proposed novel interconnection network that has improved topological and exhibits better embedding and communications performance than the Binary Hypercube and several of its variants[18,20]. Its link-augmented form, Complete Josephus Cubes, can also be applied as node cluster in an optical-based architecture suitable for large-scale hierarchical networks[6]. These clustered networks can offer system upgrade on a node cluster basis, improving overall network scalability. Loh and Hsu described a cost effective fault-tolerant strategy that included a fault-tolerant routing algorithm with supporting routing hardware.

Based on the fault tolerance of the Complete Josephus Cube CJC_n, this paper establishes the conditional diagnosability of the Complete Josephus Cube CJC_n ($n \geq 8$) under the comparison diagnosis model. The rest of this paper is organized as follows. Section 2 introduces some definitions, notations and the structure of the Complete Josephus Cube CJC_n. Section 3 is devoted to the fault resiliency of CJC_n; and Section 4 concentrates on the conditional diagnosability of CJC_n. Section 5 concludes the paper.

2   Preliminaries

Throughout this paper, we use a graph $G = G(V, E)$ to represent an interconnection network, where each node $u \in V$ denotes a processor and each edge $(u, v) \in E$ denotes a link between nodes u and v. Let S be a subset of $V(G)$. The subgraph of G induced by S, denoted by $G[S]$, is the graph with the vertex set $S \cap V(G)$ and the edge set $\{(u, v) \mid (u, v) \in E(G), u, v \in S\}$. For any subset $F \subset V$, the notation $G \setminus F$ (or $G - F$) represents the graph obtained by removing the vertices in F from G and deleting those edges with at least one end vertex in F, simultaneously. If $G \setminus F$ is disconnected, F is called a vertex cut or a separating set. The components of $G \setminus F$ are its maximal connected subgraphs. For any node u of G, $N(u)$ denotes the set of all its neighboring nodes, i.e., $N(u) = \{v \mid (u, v) \in E\}$. For any set $F \subset V$, let $N(F) = \bigcup_{u \in F} N(u) - F$, $N[F] = N(F) \cup F$. For brevity, $N[u] = N(u) \cup \{u\}$, $N(\{u, v\})$ and $N[\{u, v\}]$ are written as $N(u, v)$ and $N[u, v]$. The symmetric difference of any two sets F_1 and F_2 is defined as the set $F_1 \triangle F_2 = (F_1 - F_2) \cup (F_2 - F_1)$.

The n-hypercube, denoted by Q_n, is a graph with the vertex set $V(Q_n) = \{a_n a_{n-1} \cdots a_1 \mid a_i \in \{0, 1\}, i \in \{1, 2, \ldots, n\}\}$, and the adjacency is defined as follows: A vertex $a_n a_{n-1} \cdots a_1$ is adjacent to the vertex $a_n a_{n-1} \cdots a_{i+1} \bar{a}_i a_{i-1} \cdots a_1 (i \in \{1, 2, \ldots, n\})$. For any two vertices x and y, we use $H(x, y)$ to denote the Hamming distance between x and y, which is the number of different positions between the binary strings of x and y.

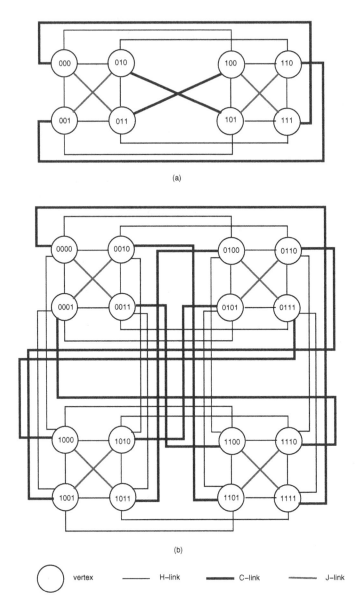

Fig. 1. The Complete Josephus Cubes $(a)CJC_3$ and (b) CJC_4

Remark 1. [16,7] Let any subset $S \subset V(Q_n)$ $(n \geq 3)$ with $n \leq |S| \leq 2n - 3$. If $Q_n - S$ is not connected, $Q_n - S$ has two components, one of which is trivial, and the other is of size $2^n - |S| - 1$.

Now, we formally present the structure of the Complete Josephus Cube CJC_n.

Definition 1. [6] *The n-dimensional* $(n \geq 3)$ *Complete Josephus Cube, denoted by* CJC_n, *is a graph with the vertex set* $V(CJC_n) = \{a_n a_{n-1} \cdots a_1 \mid a_i \in \{0,1\}, i \in \{1,2,\ldots,n\}\}$, *and the adjacency is defined as follows: A vertex* $a_n \cdots a_1$ *is adjacent to*

(1) *the vertex* $a_n a_{n-1} \cdots a_{i+1} \bar{a}_i a_{i-1} \cdots a_1$, *where* $i \in \{1,2,\ldots,n\}$;
(2) *the vertex* $\bar{a}_n \bar{a}_{n-1} \cdots \bar{a}_2 \bar{a}_1$;
(3) *the vertex* $a_n a_{n-1} \cdots a_3 \bar{a}_2 \bar{a}_1$.

The edges of type (1) are referred to as *Hamming (H) links*, the edges of type (2) are referred to as *complementary (C) links or cross links* and the edges of type (3) are referred to as *Josephus (J) links*. The structures of the CJC_3 and CJC_4 are shown in Figure 1.

Definition 2. [13,10] *The enhanced hypercube, denoted by* $EQ_{n,k}$, *is a graph with the vertex set* $V(EQ_{n,k}) = \{a_n a_{n-1} \cdots a_1 \mid a_i \in \{0,1\}, i \in \{1,2,\ldots,n\}\}$, *and the adjacency is defined as follows: A vertex* $a_n \cdots a_1$ *is adjacent to*

(1) *the vertex* $a_n a_{n-1} \cdots a_{i+1} \bar{a}_i a_{i-1} \cdots a_1$, *where* $i \in \{1,2,\ldots,n\}$;
(2) *the vertex* $a_n \cdots a_{k+1} \bar{a}_k \bar{a}_{k-1} \cdots \bar{a}_2 \bar{a}_1$.
If $k = n$, $EQ_{n,k}$ *is degrated to the folded cube* FQ_n [19].

Remark 2. By the definition of the Complete Josephus Cubes, it is easy to see that any n-dimensional Complete Josephus Cube CJC_n can be viewed as $L \oplus R$ where L (respectively, R) is subgraph of CJC_n with the prefix 0 (respectively, 1) of each vertex. And we have $L \cong R \cong EQ_{n-1,2}$. CJC_n has the hypercube Q_n, the folded hypercube FQ_n and the enhanced hypercube $EQ_{n,2}$ as its subgraphs.

Remark 3. (1) The connectivity of hypercube Q_n is n[14];
(2) The connectivity of enhanced hypercube $EQ_{n,k}$ is $n + 1$ (when $k = n$, $EQ_{n,n}$ is Folded cube FQ_n)[14];
(3) The restricted vertex connectivity of hypercube Q_n is $2n - 2$[15];
(4) Let $S \subset V(Q_n)$ such that $Q_n - S$ has at least three isolated vertices or an isolated edge and two isolated edges. Then $|S| \geq 3n - 4$[17].

3   Fault Tolerance of CJC_n

The connectivity $\kappa(G)$ of a graph $G = G(V, E)$ is the minimum number of nodes whose removal results in a disconnected or a trivial (one node) graph. A k-regular graph is *maximally connected* if it is k-connected. A k-regular graph is *(loosely) super k-connected* if any one of its minimum separating sets is a set of the neighbors of some vertex. In addition, if the deletion of a minimum separating set results in a graph with two components (one of which has only one vertex), then the graph is *tightly super k-connected*. To compensate for this shortcoming, Esfahanian introduced the concepts of the restricted cut and the restricted connectivity of a graph [3]. A restricted vertex set S is a restricted vertex-cut if $G \setminus S$ is disconnected, and no component is an isolated vertex.

The restricted vertex connectivity of a graph G, denoted by $\kappa'(G)$, is the minimum cardinality of a restricted vertex-cut. It has been shown that if a network possesses the restricted connectivity property, it is more reliable and has the lower vertex failure comparing to that has only the super connectivity property.

Lemma 1. *Let G be a graph, u and v be any two vertices of G such that u and v have common neighbors. Then we have the following.*

(1) *If the graph G is hypercube Q_n, $|N(u) \cap N(v)| = 2$[14];*
(2) *If the graph G is folded cube FQ_n, $|N(u) \cap N(v)| = 2$[20];*
(3) *If the graph G is augment cube AQ_n, $2 \leq |N(u) \cap N(v)| \leq 4$[2].*

Lemma 2. *For any integer n with $n \geq 5$, u and v be any two vertices of the Complete Josephus Cube CJC_n such that u and v have common neighbors, $|N(u) \cap N(v)| = 2$.*

Proof. Let $u = a_n a_{n-1} \ldots a_2 a_1$. Since CJC_n has Q_n as its subgraph and AQ_n as its supergraph, by Lemma 1(1)(3), we have $2 \leq |N(u) \cap N(v)| \leq 4$.

(1) $H(u, v) = 1$.
If $v = a_n a_{n-1} \ldots a_2 \bar{a}_1$ or $a_n a_{n-1} \ldots a_3 \bar{a}_2 a_1$, $|N(u) \cap N(v)| = 2$; otherwise, $v = a_n a_{n-1} \ldots a_{i+1} \bar{a}_i a_{i-1} \ldots a_2 a_1$, $|N(u) \cap N(v)| = 0$.

(2) $H(u, v) = 2$.
By the definition of CJC_n, $v = a_n a_{n-1} \ldots a_{i+1} \bar{a}_i a_{i-1} \ldots \bar{a}_2 a_1$ or $a_n a_{n-1} \ldots a_{i+1} \bar{a}_i a_{i-1} \ldots a_2 \bar{a}_1$ Or $a_n a_{n-1} \ldots a_3 \bar{a}_2 \bar{a}_1$ or $a_n a_{n-1} \ldots a_{i+1} \bar{a}_i a_{i-1} \ldots a_{j+1} \bar{a}_j a_{j-1} \ldots a_2 a_1$, the pair of u and v have exactly two common neighbors.

(3) $H(u, v) = 3$.
If $v = a_n a_{n-1} \ldots a_{i+1} \bar{a}_i a_{i-1} \ldots a_3 \bar{a}_2 \bar{a}_1$, $|N(u) \cap N(v)| = 2$; otherwise, $|N(u) \cap N(v)| = 0$.

(4) $H(u, v) = n - 1$.
If $v = \bar{a}_n \bar{a}_{n-1} \ldots \bar{a}_3 a_2 a_1$, $|N(u) \cap N(v)| = 2$; otherwise, $|N(u) \cap N(v)| = 0$.

(5) $4 \leq H(u, v) \leq n - 3$ or $H(u, v) = n$.
Since there exists no common neighbor of u and v, $|N(u) \cap N(v)| = 0$.
From the discussion above, it is easy to see that Lemma 2 holds.

Lemma 3. *The Complete Josephus Cube CJC_n $(n \geq 4)$ is tightly super $n + 2$-connected.*

Proof. Taking into account that CJC_n has regular degree $n + 2$, we need only to prove that if $CJC_n - S$ is disconnected with $|S| = n + 2$, $CJC_n - S$ has exactly two connected components one of which is an isolated vertex. We denote $S_L = S \cap L$ and $S_R = S \cap R$.

Since $CJC_n - S$ is disconnected, exactly one of $L - S_L$ and $R - S_R$ is disconnected (otherwise, both $L - S_L$ and $R - S_R$ are disconnected, by Remark 3(2), $|S| = |S_L| + |S_R| \geq 2n > n$ for $n \geq 4$, a contraction). Without loss of generality, we assume that $L - S_L$ is disconnected and $R - S_R$ is connected. Then we have $|S_L| \geq n$.

If $|S_R| \leq 1$, by the fact that $|N(v) \cap R| = 2$ for any vertex $v \in L - S_L$ and $R - S_R$ is connected, $CJC_n - S$ is connected, a contraction. Therefore, we have $|S_R| = 2$ and $|S_L| = n$.

If there is not isolated vertex in $L - S_L$, let C be arbitrary one connected component of $L - S_L$ with $|C| \geq 2$, then C is connected to $R - S_R$ (in detail, $|N(C) \cap R| \geq 3 > |S_R|$, which means that $CJC_n - S$ is connected, a contraction).

If there are at least two isolated vertices in $L - S_L$, let v_1 and v_2 be any two isolated vertices of $L - S_L$, by Lemma 2, we have

$$|N_L(v_1) \cup N_L(v_2)| = |N_L(v_1)| + |N_L(v_2)| - |N_L(v_1)| \cap N_L(v_2)|$$
$$= n + n - 2$$
$$> |S|,$$

a contradiction.

By the discussion above, there is exactly one isolated vertex say v, in $L - S_L$ and $N_L(v) = S_L$. Let C be arbitrary one connected component of $L - S_L - \{v\}$ with $|C| \geq 2$, then C is connected to $R - S_R$ (in detail, $|N(C) \cap R| \geq 3 > |S_R|$), which means that $(L - S_L - \{v\}) \cup (R - S_R)$ is connected. In addition, $N(v) \cap R = S_R$ (otherwise, $N(v) \cap (R - S_R) \neq \emptyset$, v is connected $R - S_R$. Then $CJC_n - S$ is connected, a contraction). Thus, $N(v) = S$ and $CJC_n - S - \{v\}$ is still connected.

Lemma 4. *For any vertex u of $V(EQ_{n,2})(n \geq 6)$, the connectivity of $EQ_{n,2} - N[u]$ is $\kappa(EQ_{n,2} - N[u]) = n - 1$.*

Proof. $EQ_{n,2}$ can be viewed as $L \oplus R$, where L (respectively, R) is subgraph of $EQ_{n,2}$ with the prefix 0 (respectively, 1) of each vertex. And we have $L \cong R \cong EQ_{n-1,2}$.

Since $\delta(EQ_{n,2} - N[u]) = n - 1$, $\kappa(EQ_{n,2} - N[u]) \leq n - 1$. Now, we show that $\kappa(EQ_{n,2} - N[u]) \geq n - 1$ in the following.

Let S be the subset of $V(EQ_{n,2} - N[u])$ with $|S| = n - 2$. Denote $S_L = S \cap L$ and $S_R = S \cap R$. Without loss of generality, we assume that u is in L.

Since $|S_R| + |N[u] \cap R| \leq n - 2 + 1 < n$, by Remark 3(2), $R - N[u] - S_R$ is connected. Then we need only to show that any vertex $v \in V(L - N[u] - S_L)$ is connected to $R - N[u] - S_R$.

If $N(v) \cap (R - N[u] - S_R) \neq \emptyset$, we are done; otherwise, by the fact of

$$|N(v)| = n + 1 > |N(v) \cap N(u)| + |S| = 2 + n - 2,$$

we have that $N(v) \cap (L - N[u] - S_L) \neq \emptyset$. Without loss of generality, we set $v_0 \in V(N(v) \cap (L - N[u] - S_L))$. Then there must exist one vertex

$$v_1 \in V(N(v, v_0) \cap (L - N[u] - S_L))$$

such that $N(v_1) \cap (R - N[u] - S_R) \neq \emptyset$ (otherwise, $|N(v, v_0) \cap L| - |S_L| \leq |S_R|$, which means that $|N(v, v_0) \cap L| < |S|$, i.e., $2n - 4 < n - 2$, a contradiction). Therefore, v is connected to $R - N[u] - S_R$ and $EQ_{n,2} - N[u] - S$ is still connected.

Lemma 5. *Let $\{u, v\}$ be a pair of adjacent vertices of $V(CJC_n)(n \geq 6)$. Then $\kappa(CJC_n - N[u, v]) \geq n - 2$.*

Proof. Let S be a subset of $V(CJC_n - N[u,v])$ with $|S| = n-3$. Let $S_L = S \cap L$ and $S_R = S \cap R$.

Case 1. both of u and v are in L (respectively, R).

Since $|N(w) \cap N[u,v]| \leq 2$ for any vertex $w \in R$, by Remark 3(2), we have that $R - N[u,v] - S_R$ is still connected.

If $N(x) \cap (R - N[u,v] - S_R) \neq \emptyset$ for any vertex $x \in L - N[u,v] - S_L$, we are done; otherwise, there exists a neighbor of x in $L - N[u,v] - S_L$, say x_0. Then there must exist one vertex

$$x_1 \in V(N(x,x_0) \cap (L - N[u] - S_L))$$

such that $N(x_1) \cap (R - N[u] - S_R) \neq \emptyset$ (otherwise, $|N(x,x_0) \cap L| - |S_L| \leq |S_R|$, which means that $|N(x,x_0) \cap L| < |S|$, i.e., $2n - 4 < n - 3$, a contradiction). Thus, x is connected to R through the $C - link$ or $H - link$ of x_1. Therefore, $CJC_n - N[u,v] - S$ is still connected.

Case 2. u is in L and v is in R (respectively, u is in R and v is in L).

Subcase 2.1. $|S_L| \leq n - 4$ and $|S_R| \leq n - 4$.

Taking into account that

$$|S_L| + |N(v) \cap L| \leq n - 4 + 1 = n - 3$$

and

$$|S_R| + |N(u) \cap R| \leq n - 4 + 1 = n - 3,$$

by Lemma 4, both of $L - N[u,v] - S_L$ and $R - N[u,v] - S_R$ are still connected. Since $|L - N[u,v] - S_L| > |N[u,v] \cap R| + |S_R|$ (i.e., $2^{n-1} - (n+2) > (n+2) + (n-3)$ for $n \geq 6$), $L - N[u,v] - S_L$ is connected to $R - N[u,v] - S_R$, which means that $CJC_n - N[u,v] - S$ is connected.

Subcase 2.2. $|S_L| = n-3$ and $|S_R| = 0$ (respectively, $|S_R| = n-3$ and $|S_L| = 0$).

By Lemma 4, $R - N[u,v] - S_R$ is connected. Then we need only to show that any vertex $w \in V(L - N[u,v] - S_L)$ is connected to $R - N[u,v] - S_R$.

If $N(w) \cap (R - N[u,v] - S_R) \neq \emptyset$, we are done; otherwise, by the fact of

$$|N(w)| = n + 2 > |N(w) \cap N(u,v)| + |S| = 4 + n - 3,$$

we have that

$$N(w) \cap (L - N[u,v] - S_L) \neq \emptyset.$$

Without loss of generality, we set $w_0 \in V(N(w) \cap (L - N[u,v] - S_L))$. Then there must exist one vertex $w_1 \in V(N(w,w_0) \cap (L - N[u] - S_L))$ with $N(w_1) \cap (R - N[u,v] - S_R) \neq \emptyset$ (otherwise, $|N(w,w_0) \cap L| - |S_L| \leq |S_R|$, which means that $|N(w,w_0) \cap L| < |S|$, i.e., $2n - 4 < n - 3$, a contradiction). Therefore, w is connected to $R - N[u,v] - S_R$ and $CJC_n - N[u,v] - S$ is still connected.

Theorem 1. *Let S be a subset of at most $3n - 3$ vertices of $V(CJC_n)(n \geq 6)$. Under the conditional fault model, that is, $N(u) \nsubseteq S$ for any vertex $u \in V(CJC_n)$, $CJC_n - S$ satisfies one of the following conditions:*

(1) $CJC_n - S$ is connected; or

(2) $CJC_n - S$ has exactly two connected components, one of which is K_2 and the other one has $2^n - |S| - 2$ vertices.

Proof. Let $S_L = S \cap L$ and $S_R = S \cap R$ with the restriction that $|S| \leq 3n - 3$.

Case 1. $N(u,v) \nsubseteq S$ for any pair of adjacent vertices $\{u,v\}$ of CJC_n.

Subcase 1.1. Either $|S_L| \geq 2n - 2$ or $|S_R| \geq 2n - 2$.

Without loss of generality, we assume that $|S_R| \geq 2n - 2$. Then $|S_L| \leq 3n - 3 - (2n - 2) \leq n - 1 < \kappa(EQ_{n-1,2})$, by Remark 3(1), we have that $L - S_L$ is still connected. Now we show that there exists a path connecting u to $L - S_L$ for any vertex $u \in R - S_R$. Let u_L and u_c be the neighbors of u, which are in L.

If at least one of u_L and u_c is not in S_L, we are done; otherwise, since $N(u) \nsubseteq S$, there exists one neighbor $v \in (R - S_R)$ of u. If $N(v) \cap (R - S_R) \neq \emptyset$, we are done; otherwise, since $N(u,v) \nsubseteq S$, there must exist one vertex $w \in N(u,v) \cap (R - S_R)$ such that $N(w) \cap (L - S_L) \neq \emptyset$ (otherwise, since $|N(u,v) \cap R| \geq 2n - 4$ and all these $2n - 4$ vertices have at least $2n - 4$ neighbors in L, $|S_L| \geq 2n - 4$. Then $|S| \geq 2n - 4 + 2n - 2 > 3n - 2$, a contradiction). Therefore, u can connect to $L - S_L$ which means that $CJC_n - S$ is connected.

Subcase 1.2. $|S_L| \leq 2n - 3$ and $|S_R| \leq 2n - 3$.

If one of two subgraphs $L - S_L$ and $R - S_R$ is connected, the discussion is similar to that of Subcase 1.1. Now we assume that both of $L - S_L$ and $R - S_R$ are disconnected.

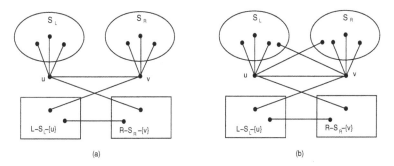

(a)   (b)

Fig. 2. Illustration in Theorem 1 for the example of subcase 1.2.1

Subcase 1.2.1. $|S_L| \leq 2n - 5$ and $|S_R| \leq 2n - 5$.

In this case, by Remark 1, there must exist one vertex $u \in L - S_L$ (respectively, $v \in R - S_R$) such that $N(u) \cap L \subset S_L$ (respectively, $N(v) \cap R \subset S_R$), and both of $L - S_L - N[u]$ and $R - S_R - N[v]$ are still connected.

We now show that the four parts $\{u\}$, $\{v\}$, $L - S_L - N[u]$ and $R - S_R - N[v]$ constitute exactly one connected component.

If u is connected to v, by the assumption that $N(u,v) \nsubseteq S$, either $N(u) \cap (R - S_R - \{v\}) \neq \emptyset$ or $N(v) \cap (L - S_L - \{u\}) \neq \emptyset$ holds (Figure 2(a)). Now we assume that u and v are not adjacent, by the assumption that $N(u) \not\subseteq S$ and $N(v) \not\subseteq S$, $N(u) \cap (R - S_R - \{v\}) \neq \emptyset$ and $N(v) \cap (L - S_L - \{u\})$ holds (Figure 2(b)).

Furthermore, $|L - S_L - \{u\}| > |S_R \cup \{v\}|$ (i.e., $|L| - |S_L| - 1 > |S_R| + 1$) and there exists a perfect matching between L and R, $L - S_L - \{u\}$ is connected to $R - S_R - \{v\}$.

By the discussion above, we obtain that $CJC_n - S$ is connected.

Subcase 1.2.2. $2n - 4 \leq |S_L| \leq 2n - 3$ or $2n - 4 \leq |S_R| \leq 2n - 3$.

Without loss of generality, we assume that $2n - 4 \leq |S_R| \leq 2n - 3$, then $n \leq |S_L| \leq n + 1$. Since L (respectively, R) has Q_{n-1} as its subgraph, by Remark 1, there are exactly two components of $L - S_L$, one of which is trivial, say $\{u\}$. By Remark 3(3)(4), we obtain that in $R - S_R$, there are exactly two components, one of which is trivial or one isolated edge.

If the smaller one of the two components of $R - S_R$ is trivial, say u, then the discussion is the same as subcase 1.2.1. If the smaller one of the two components of $R - S_R$ is an isolated edge, say $\{v_0, v_1\}$, by the assumption that $2n - 4 \leq |S_R| \leq 2n - 3$, $|N(v_0, v_1)| = 2n - 4$. If u is connected to the edge (v_0, v_1), $|N(u, v_0, v_1)| = 3n - 1 > 3n - 3$, and $\{u, v_0, v_1\}$ is connected to $L - S_L$ or $R - S_R$. If u is not connected to the edge (v_0, v_1), by the assumption that $N(u) \not\subseteq S$, u is connected to $R - S_R$. Since there are 4 neighbors of $\{v_0, v_1\}$ in L and $n \leq |S_L| \leq n + 1$, $\{v_0, v_1\}$ is connected to $L - S_L$. Since $|L - S_L - \{u\}| > |S_R \cup \{v_0, v_1\}|$ (i.e., $|L| - |S_L| - 1 > |S_R| + 2$) and there exists a perfect matching between L and R, $L - S_L - \{u\}$ is connected to $R - S_R - \{v_0, v_1\}$. Therefore we obtain that $CJC_n - S$ is connected.

Case 2. There exists a pair of adjacent vertices $\{u, v\}$ of G such that $N(u, v) \subset S$.

Since $|S \cap N(u, v)| \geq |N(u, v)| \geq 2n$, we have

$$|S - N(u, v)| = |S| - |S \cap N(u, v)| \leq 3n - 3 - 2n = n - 3.$$

By Lemma 5, $CJC_n - S - N[u, v]$ is connected. So the graph $CJC_n - S$ has exactly two components, one of which is $K_2[u, v]$, the other is $CJC_n - S - \{u, v\}$.

4   The Conditional Diagnosability of CJC_n

The comparison diagnosis strategy can be modeled as a multi-graph $M = (V, C)$, where V is the same node set defined as in G, C is the labelled edge set. A labelled edge $(u, v)_w$ is said to belong to C if (u, v) is an edge labeled by w, which implies that the processors u and v are compared by processor w. Since different comparators can compare the same pair of processors, M is a multi-graph. Denote the comparison result as $\sigma((u, v)_w)$ such that $\sigma((u, v)_w) = 0$ if the outputs of u and v agree, and $\sigma((u, v)_w) = 1$ if the outputs disagree. If the comparator w is fault-free and $\sigma((u, v)_w) = 0$, the processors u and v are fault-free; while $\sigma((u, v)_w) = 1$, at least one of the three processors u, v and w is faulty. The collection of the comparison results defined as a function $\sigma : C \to \{0, 1\}$, is called the *syndrome* of the diagnosis. A subset $F \subsetneq V$ is said to be *compatible* with a syndrome σ if σ can arise from the circumstance that all vertices in F are faulty and all vertices in $V \setminus F$ are fault-free. A faulty comparator can lead to unreliable results, so a set of faulty vertices may produce different syndromes.

Let $\sigma_F = \{\sigma \mid \sigma$ is compatible with $F\}$. Two distinct subsets F_1 and F_2 of $V(G)$ are said to be *indistinguishable* if and only if $\sigma_{F_1} \cap \sigma_{F_2} \neq \phi$; otherwise, both of F_1 and F_2 are said to be distinguishable. There are several different ways to verify whether a system is t-diagnosable under the comparison approach. The following lemma obtained by Sengupta and Dahbura [12] gives necessary and sufficient conditions to ensure distinguishability.

Lemma 6. [12] *Let G be a graph. For any two distinct subsets F_1, F_2 of $V(G)$. (F_1, F_2) is a distinguishable pair if and only if at least one of the following conditions is satisfied.*

(1) *There are two distinct vertices u, $w \in V(G) - (F_1 \cup F_2)$ and there is a vertex $v \in F_1 \triangle F_2$ such that $(u, v)_w \in C$;*

(2) *There are two distinct vertices u and $v \in F_1 \setminus F_2$ and there is a vertex $w \in V(G) - (F_1 \cup F_2)$ such that $(u, v)_w \in C$; or*

(3) *There are two distinct vertices u, $v \in F_2 \setminus F_1$ and there is a vertex $w \in V(G) - (F_1 \cup F_2)$ such that $(u, v)_w \in C$.*

Lin et al. [8] introduced the so-called conditional diagnosability of a system under the situation that no set of faulty vertices can contain all neighbors of any vertex in the system. A faulty set $F \subset V(G)$ is called a conditional faulty set if $N_G(v) \not\subseteq F$ for every vertex $v \in V(G)$. A system $G(V, E)$ is said to be conditionally t-diagnosable if F_1 and F_2 are distinguishable for each pair of distinct conditional faulty set F_1 and F_2 with $|F_1| \leq t$, $|F_2| \leq t$. The maximum value of t such that G is conditionally t-diagnosable is called the *conditional diagnosability* of G, denoted by $t_C(G)$. It is trivial that $t_C(G) \geq t(G)$.

Lemma 7. *Let F_1 and F_2 be any two distinct conditional faulty subset of CJC_n with $|F_1| \leq 3n - 2$ and $|F_2| \leq 3n - 2$, and H be the maximum component of $CJC_n - F_1 \cap F_2$. Then for any vertex $u \in F_1 \triangle F_2$, we have $u \in H$.*

Proof. Without loss of generality, let $u \in F_1 - F_2$.

Since F_2 is the conditional faulty subset, there is a vertex $v \in CJC_n - F_2 - \{u\}$ such that $(u, v) \in E(CJC_n)$. Assume that $u \notin H$. Then we have $v \notin H$. In other words, (u, v) is the small component of $CJC_n - F_1 \cap F_2$. Obviously, $|F_1 \cap F_2| \leq 3n - 3$. Since F_1 and F_2 are two distinct conditional faulty subset of CJC_n. By Theorem 1, (u, v) is a component K_2 of $CJC_n - F_1 \cap F_2$, and $N(u, v) \subset F_1 \cap F_2$. In addiction, $u \in F_1 - F_2$, so that all the neighbors of v are in F_1. However, since F_1 is the conditional faulty subset, so we have $u \in H$.

Lemma 8. [8] *Let G be a graph with $\delta(G) \geq 2$, and let F_1 and F_2 be any two distinct conditional faulty subsets of G. If either $F_1 \subset F_2$ or $F_2 \subset F_1$, (F_1, F_2) is a distinguishable conditional pair under the comparison diagnosis model.*

Theorem 2. *The conditional diagnosability of the Complete Josephus Cube CJC_n under the comparison diagnosis model is $t_c(CJC_n) = 3n - 2$ $(n \geq 8)$.*

Proof. First, we prove that $t_c(CJC_n) \leq 3n - 2$.

There exist three vertices $u, v, w \in V(CJC_n)$, such that (u, w, v) is in a cycle of length 3. We set $A = N[u, v, w]$, $F_1 = A - \{w, v\}$, and $F_2 = A - \{u, w\}$. We get $|F_1| = |F_2| = 3(n - 1) + 2 = 3n - 1$, and $|F_1 - F_2| = |F_2 - F_1| = 1$. It is easy to check that F_1 and F_2 are two conditional faulty sets, and F_1 and F_2 are indistinguishable. Hence, we have the result $t_c(CJC_n) \leq 3n - 2$.

Second, we prove that $t_c(CJC_n) \geq 3n - 2$. Suppose that F_1 and F_2 are two distinct conditional faulty subsets of CJC_n with $|F_1| \leq 3n - 2$ and $|F_2| \leq 3n - 2$. Then it is suffice to prove that (F_1, F_2) is distinguished under the comparison diagnosis model.

By Lemma 8, if one of $F_2 \subset F_1$ and $F_1 \subset F_2$ holds, then (F_1, F_2) is distinguishable.

Now we assume $F_2 \not\subseteq F_1$ and $F_1 \not\subseteq F_2$, which implies that $|F_1 - F_2| \geq 1$ and $|F_2 - F_1| \geq 1$. We have $|F_1 \cap F_2| \leq 3n - 3$.

Let H be the maximum component of $CJC_n - F_1 \cap F_2$. By Lemma 7, any vertex in $F_1 \triangle F_2$ is in H.

We claim that H has a vertex, say u, outside of $F_1 \cup F_2$ that has no neighbor $F_1 \cap F_2$. Since every vertex of CJC_n has degree $n + 2$, those vertices in $F_1 \cap F_2$ have at most $(n + 2)|F_1 \cap F_2|$ neighbors in H in total. There are at most $2(3n - 2) - |F_1 \cap F_2|$ vertices in $F_1 \cup F_2$ and at most two vertices of $CJC_n - F_1 \cap F_2$ may not belong to H by Theorem 1. Since $|F_1 \cap F_2| \leq 3n - 3$, we have

$$2^n - (n + 2)|F_1 \cap F_2| - (2(3n - 2) - |F_1 \cap F_2|) - 2$$
$$\geq 2^n - (n + 1)|F_1 \cap F_2| - 2(3n - 2) - 2$$
$$\geq 2^n - n(3n - 3) - 2(3n - 2) - 2$$
$$= 2^n - 3n^2 - 3n + 2$$
$$> 2 \ (n \geq 8).$$

Thus, there must be some vertex of H outside $F_1 \cup F_2$, which has no neighbors in S. Let u be such a vertex.

If u has no neighbor in $F_1 \cup F_2$, then we can find a path of length at least two within H to a vertex v in $F_1 \cup F_2$. We may assume that v is the first vertex of $F_1 \triangle F_2$ on this path, and let q and w be the two vertices on this path immediately before v (we may have $u = q$), so q and w are not in $F_1 \cup F_2$. The existence of the edges (q, w) and (w, v) shows that (F_1, F_2) is a distinguishable conditional pair of CJC_n by Lemma 6. Now we assume that u has a neighbor in $F_1 \triangle F_2$. Since the degree of u is at least 3, and u has no neighbor in S, there are three possibilities:

(1) u has two neighbors in $F_1 - F_2$; or
(2) u has two neighbors in $F_2 - F_1$; or
(3) u has at least one neighbor outside $F_2 \cup F_1$.

In each subcase above, Lemma 6 implies that (F_1, F_2) is a distinguishable conditional pair of CJC_n under the comparison diagnosis model.

References

1. Chwa, K.Y., Hakimi, S.L.: On fault identification in diagnosable system. IEEE Transactions on Computers C-30(6), 414–422 (1981)
2. Chang, N.-W., Hsieh, S.-Y.: Conditional diagnosability of augmented cubes under the PMC model. IEEE Transations on Dependable and Secube Computing 9(1), 46–60 (2012)
3. Esfahanian, A.H.: Generalized measures of fault tolerance with application to n-cube networks. IEEE Transactions on Computers 38, 1586–1591 (1989)
4. Hsu, G.-H., Chiang, C.-F., Shih, L.-M., Hsu, L.-H., Tan, J.J.M.: Conditional diagnosability of hypercubes under the comparison diagnosis model. Journal of Systems Architecture 55(2), 140–146 (2009)
5. Loh, P.K.K., Hsu, W.J.: The Josephus Cubes: a novel interconnection network. Parallel Computing 26, 427–453 (2000)
6. Loh, P.K.K., Hsu, W.J.: Fault-tolerant routing for complete Josephus Cubes. Parallel Computing 30, 1151–1167 (2004)
7. Lai, P.-L., Tan, J.J.M., Chang, C.-P., Hsu, L.-H.: Conditional diagnosability measure for large multiprocessors systems. IEEE Transactions on Computers 54, 165–175 (2005)
8. Lin, C.-K., Tan, J.J.M., Hsu, L.-H., Cheng, E., Lipták, L.: Conditional diagnosability of cayley graphs generalized by transposition tree under the comparison diagnosis model. Journal of Interconnection Networks 9, 83–97 (2008)
9. Malek, M.: A comparison connection assignment for diagnosis of multiprocessor systems. In: Proc. 7th Int. Symp. Comput. Archirecture, pp. 31–35 (1980)
10. Manuel, P.: Minimum average congestion of enhanced and augmented hypercubes into complete binary trees. Discrete Applied Mathematics 159, 360–366 (2011)
11. Preparata, F.P., Metze, G., Chien, R.T.: On the connection assignment problem of diagnosable systems. IEEE Transactions on Computers 16, 848–854 (1967)
12. Sengupta, A., Dahbura, A.: On self-diagnosable multiprocessor systems: diagnosis by the comparison approach. IEEE Transaction on Computers 41, 1386–1396 (1992)
13. Tzeng, N.-F., Wei, S.Z.: Enhanced hypercubes. IEEE Transactions on Computers 40(3), 284–294 (1991)
14. Wang, D.: Diagnosability of hypercubes and enhanced hypercubes under the comparision diagnosis model. IEEE Transaction on Computers 48(12), 1369–1374 (1999)
15. Xu, J.-M., Zhu, Q., Hou, X., Zhou, T.: On restricted connectivity and extra connectivity of hypercubes and folded hypercubes. J. Shanghai Jiaotong Univ. (Sci.) E-10(2), 208–212 (2005)
16. Yang, X., Evans, D.J., Megson, G.M., Lai, H.J.: On the maximal connected component of a hypercube with faulty vertices III. International Journal of Computer Mathematics 83, 27–37 (2006)
17. Zhu, Q.: Studies of fault tolerance and diagnosability of interconnection networks. Ph. D. Thesis, University of Science and Technology of China (2005)
18. Zhou, S.: The conditional diagnosability of crossed cubes under the comparison model. International Journal of Computer and Mathematics 87(15), 3387–3396 (2010)
19. Zhu, Q., Liu, S.-Y., Xu, M.: On conditional diagnosability of the folded hypercubes. Information Sciences 178, 1069–1077 (2008)
20. Zhu, Q., Xu, J.-M., Xu, M.: X, On reliability of the folded hypercubes. Information Sciences 177, 1782–1788 (2007)

Circular Dimensional-Permutations and Reliable Broadcasting for Hypercubes and Möbius Cubes

Baolei Cheng[1,2], Jianxi Fan[1,*], Jiwen Yang[1], and Xi Wang[1]

[1] School of Computer Science and Technology, Soochow University,
Suzhou 215006, China
{chengbaolei,jxfan,jwyang,20124027002}@suda.edu.cn
[2] Key Laboratory for Computer Information Processing Technology,
Soochow University, China

Abstract. Reliable broadcasting for interconnection networks can be achieved by constructing multiple independent spanning trees(ISTs) rooted at the same node. In this paper, we prove that there exists $(n-1)!$ sets of ISTs rooted at an arbitrary node for Q_n and M_n based on circular dimensional-permutations of 0, 1, ..., $n-1$ and $n \geq 1$. At the same time, we give an parallel algorithm, called BCIST, which is the further study of IST problem for Q_n and M_n in literature. Furthermore, simulation experiments of ISTs based on JUNG framework and different sets of disjoint paths between node 1 and any node $v \in V(0\text{-}M_4)\backslash\{1\}$ for $0\text{-}M_4$ are also presented.

Keywords: dimensional-permutation, reliable broadcasting, hypercube, Möbius cube, independent spanning tree.

1 Introduction

It is well known that hypercubes are widely used in parallel computing systems, which have many advantageous properties such as lower node degree and diameter, higher connectivity, symmetry, and etc [21], [24]. Furthermore, by changing their links between some nodes, the variants of hypercubes, such as Möbius cubes [9], crossed cubes [20], and twisted cubes [1] were proposed, which have better properties [12], [13], [14], [16], [29].

Independent spanning trees(ISTs for short) have been used in reliable broadcasting, secure message distribution [2], reliable communication protocols [17], one-to-all broadcasting [26], the multi-node broadcasting [3], and diagnosis [6]. Therefore, the problem to construct ISTs for a given network is becoming an important issue.

However, there is a well-known conjecture on the existence of ISTs for any network [17][31]:

---

* Corresponding author.

C.-H. Hsu et al. (Eds.): NPC 2013, LNCS 8147, pp. 232–244, 2013.
© IFIP International Federation for Information Processing 2013

Conjecture 1. Let G be an n-node-connected network with $n \geq 1$. Then, there exist n node-independent spanning trees rooted at any node for G.

In what follows, we use independent to represent node-independent. For $n \leq 4$, Conjecture 1 was solved [8], [10], [17], [31], but when $n \geq 5$, it has remained open. Consequently, researchers are interested in the study of ISTs for various special networks. Conjecture 1 has been solved for some restricted classes of networks, such as planar networks [15], product networks [23], hypercubes [25], [28], [30], Möbius cubes [5], [6], locally twisted cubes [22], crossed cubes [4], [7], twisted cubes [27], even networks [18], odd networks [19], and etc.

We say that a sequence of n integers is a *permutation* if it contains all integers from 0 to $n-1$ exactly once. Considering the results for hypercubes and Möbius cubes, each paper in literature only considers a set of ISTs for the special network and lacks the discussion of the relation between the permutations and ISTs.

Question 1. Can all permutations of $0, 1, \ldots, n-1$ be used to construct spanning tree and ISTs for the n-dimensional hypercube Q_n and the n-dimensional Möbius cube M_n?

To solve this question, we adopt the definition of circular dimensional-permutation and prove that any circular dimensional-permutation of $0, 1, \ldots, n-1$ can be used to construct n ISTs for Q_n and M_n in this paper, which is the further discussion of spanning trees and ISTs for Q_n and M_n comparing with the results in literature.

The rest of this paper is organized as follows. Section 2 presents some definitions, graph terminologies and notations. Section 3 discusses the IST problem for Q_n and M_n rooted at any node. We draw the conclusion of the paper in the last section.

2 Preliminaries

2.1 Definition of Hypercubes, Möbius Cubes, and ISTs

We use a unique binary string of length n to denote the address of each node in the n-dimensional hypercube Q_n and the n-dimensional Möbius cube M_n. In what follows, nodes and their addresses will be used alternatively. Q_n is a network consists of 2^n nodes. Any two nodes of Q_n are adjacent whenever their corresponding addresses differ in exactly one place.

M_n is a variant of the Q_n, which has two types, 0-*type* n-dimensional Möbius cube and 1-*type* n-dimensional Möbius cube. We adopt the following definition of M_n in [11].

Definition 1. [11] 0-M_1 and 1-M_1 are both the complete graph on two nodes whose addresses are 0 and 1. For any integer n with $n \geq 2$, both 0-M_n and 1-M_n contain one 0-type $(n-1)$-dimensional sub-Möbius cube M_{n-1}^0 and one

1-type $(n-1)$-dimensional sub-Möbius cube M_{n-1}^1. The nodes in M_{n-1}^0 have a common prefix 0; the nodes in M_{n-1}^1 have a common prefix 1. For two nodes $x = x_{n-1}x_{n-2}\ldots x_0 \in V(M_{n-1}^0)$ and $y = y_{n-1}y_{n-2}\ldots y_0 \in V(M_{n-1}^1)$, where $x_{n-1} = \overline{y_{n-1}} = 0$,

(1) $(x,y) \in E(0\text{-}M_n)$ if and only if $x_i = y_i$, $i = 0, 1, \ldots, n-2$;
(2) $(x,y) \in E(1\text{-}M_n)$ if and only if $x_i = \overline{y_i}$, $i = 0, 1, \ldots, n-2$.

A binary string x of length n is denoted by $x_{n-1}x_{n-2}\ldots x_0$. Suppose that $u = u_{n-1}u_{n-2}\ldots u_0$ and $v = u_{n-1}u_{n-2}\ldots u_l\overline{u_{l-1}}v_{l-2}v_{l-3}\ldots v_0$ are two nodes in $X_n \in \{Q_n, M_n\}$. We say that u and v have a *leftmost differing bit at position* $l - 1$. We use LDF(u, v) to denote the leftmost differing bit of two nodes u and v. Given two adjacent nodes u and v, if LDF$(u, v)=d$, we say that v is the *d-neighbor of* u or that the edge (u, v) is an *edge of dimension d*. For this purpose, let $N_d(u)$ denote the d-neighbor of u. We follow the definitions of *path* and *ancestor* in [7].

Two paths P and P' starting from a node u and ending with another node v are said to be *internally disjoint* if $E(P)\cap E(P') = \varnothing$ and $V(P)\cap V(P') = \{u,v\}$. Two spanning trees for a network G are *independent* if they are rooted at the same node, said u, and for each node $v \in V(G)\backslash\{u\}$, the two paths starting at u and ending with v are internally disjoint. A set of spanning trees of G rooted at v are called *independent spanning trees* if they are pairwisely independent.

2.2   Definition of Dimensional-Permutation

The sequence of n integers is called a *dimensional-permutation* if it contains all integers from 0 to $n - 1$ exactly one (Noting that each node in Q_n or M_n has n neighbors, which are 0-neighbor, 1-neighbor, $\ldots$, $(n-1)$-neighbor). A *circular dimensional-permutation* (CDP for short) is a type of permutation to put all integers from 0 to $n - 1$ along a closed circle in the clockwise order [6]. Suppose that $\{a_0, a_1, \ldots a_{n-1}\}= \{0, 1, \ldots, n-1\}$. All cyclic permutations of integers are equivalent in the circle,

$$a_0 \to a_1 \to \ldots \to a_{n-1},$$
$$a_1 \to a_2 \to \ldots \to a_{n-1} \to a_0,$$
$$\ldots,$$
$$a_{n-1} \to a_0 \to a_1 \to \ldots \to a_{n-2}$$

belong to the same CDP. The total number of CDPs is $n!/n = (n - 1)!$. For example, the six CDPs of $0, 1, 2, 3$ are

$$3 \to 0 \to 1 \to 2,$$
$$3 \to 0 \to 2 \to 1,$$
$$3 \to 1 \to 0 \to 2,$$
$$3 \to 1 \to 2 \to 0,$$
$$3 \to 2 \to 0 \to 1,$$
$$3 \to 2 \to 1 \to 0.$$

3   An Reliable Broadcasting Algorithm Based on ISTs for Hypercubes and Möbius Cubes

In this section, we point out that every CDP of n integers $0, 1, 2, \ldots, n-1$ can be used to construct ISTs for $X_n \in \{Q_n, M_n\}$. We now present the following observation.

Observation 1. For the n-dimensional Möbius cube, we proved the correctness of ISTs rooted at any node based on the descending CDP $n-1, n-2, \ldots, 0$ [6]. **In essence, the set of optimal ISTs for Q_n in [25] can be obtained by the ascending CDP $0, 1, \ldots, n-1$; the set of ISTs in [30] is similar to that in [28] for Q_n, which can be constructed by the descending CDP $n-1, n-2, \ldots, 0$. Thus, the result in this section is the further study of spanning trees and ISTs for Q_n and M_n.**

3.1   ISTs for Q_n and M_n with Any Circular Dimensional-Permutation

In what follows, we always let u denote any node in Q_n or M_n. Now we present an algorithm, called BCIST, to construct n ISTs rooted at an arbitrary node u for $X_n \in \{Q_n, M_n\}$. Fig. 1 demonstrates the construction procedures of n spanning trees $T_0, T_1, \ldots, T_{n-1}$ rooted at node u for $X_n \in \{Q_n, M_n\}$ in radial style.

```
Algorithm. BCIST
Input:   An array S = {a₀,a₁,..., aₙ₋₁}, where
         the permutation a₀, a₁, ..., aₙ₋₁ is a CDP of 0, 1, ..., n − 1;
         an arbitrary node u in Xₙ ∈ {Qₙ, Mₙ};
Output:  T₀,T₁,..., Tₙ₋₁  rooted at u for Xₙ;
Begin
1: for i = 0 to n − 1 do in parallel
2:   V(Tᵢ) = Nₐᵢ(u);
     /*Nₐᵢ(u) denotes the aᵢ-neighbor of u.*/
3:   E(Tᵢ) = ∅;
4:   for l = 0 to n − 1 do
5:       for each node v ∈ V(Tᵢ) do in parallel
6:           d = S[(i + l + 1) mod n];
             /*Indexing of S is counted from 0 to n − 1,
             where n is length of the array S.*/
7:           E(Tᵢ)  =  E(Tᵢ) ∪ {(v, N_d(v))};
8:           V(Tᵢ)  =  V(Tᵢ) ∪ {N_d(v)};
9:       end for
10:  end for
11: end for
end
```

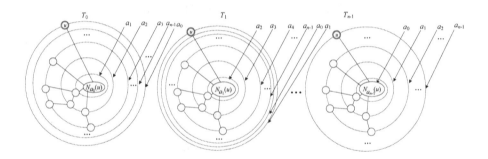

Fig. 1. Construction procedures based on algorithm BCIST

The construction procedures of T_0, T_1, ..., T_{n-1} are similar. Take T_0 for example, the construction procedures are described as follows (See Fig. 1).

At first, there is only one node $N_{a_0}(u)$ in tree T_0; during the 1st iteration (l =0), node $N_{a_0}(u)$ in T_0 is connected to its a_1-neighbor node $N_{a_1}(N_{a_0}(u))$. Therefore, $V(T_0) = \{N_{a_0}(u), N_{a_1}(N_{a_0}(u))\}$ and $E(T_0) = \{(N_{a_0}(u), N_{a_1}(N_{a_0}(u)))\}$; during the 2nd iteration ($l = 1$), each node v in T_0 is connected to its a_2-neighbor node $N_{a_2}(v)$. Thus, the edges $(N_{a_1}(N_{a_0}(u)), N_{a_2}(N_{a_1}(N_{a_0}(u))))$ and $(N_{a_0}(u), N_{a_2}(N_{a_0}(u)))$ are appended to T_0 and $V(T_0) = \{N_{a_0}(u), N_{a_2}(N_{a_0}(u)), N_{a_1}(N_{a_0}(u)), N_{a_2}(N_{a_1}(N_{a_0}(u)))\}$; during the 3rd iteration, each node v in T_0 is connected to its a_3-neighbor node $N_{a_3}(v)$. As a result, it has doubled the number of nodes in T_0; During the l-th iteration, each node v in T_0 is connected to its $S[l+1]$-neighbor node $N_{S[l+1]}(v)$ with $4 \leq l \leq n - 2$; in the last iteration, each node v in T_0 is connected to its a_0-neighbor node $N_{a_0}(v)$.

Consequently, T_0 is a spanning tree for $X_n \in \{Q_n, M_n\}$.

More examples will be shown in the next subsection. Now we give the following lemma about the relation of adjacent nodes in M_n and Q_n.

Lemma 1. For any node $x_{n-1}x_{n-2} \ldots x_0$ and its k-neighbor node $y_{n-1}y_{n-2} \ldots y_0$ with $0 \leq k \leq n-1$ in $X_n \in \{M_n, Q_n\}$, we have $x_{n-1}x_{n-2} \ldots x_{k+1} = y_{n-1}y_{n-2} \ldots y_{k+1}$ and $x_k \neq y_k$.

Based on Definition 1, the definition of Q_n, and Lemma 1, we have the following lemma.

Lemma 2. For any two nodes x, y in $V(X_{n-1}^{x_{n-1}})$, if $\mathrm{LDF}(x,y) = k$ with $0 \leq k \leq n - 2$ and $X_{n-1}^{x_{n-1}} \in \{M_{n-1}^{x_{n-1}}, Q_{n-1}^{x_{n-1}}\}$, then $\mathrm{LDF}(N_{n-1}(x), N_{n-1}(y))=k$ and $N_{n-1}(x), N_{n-1}(y) \in X_{n-1}^{\overline{x_{n-1}}}$.

Lemma 3. [5] Given a walk W: $u^{(0)}$, $u^{(1)} = N_{m_1}(u^{(0)})$, $u^{(2)} = N_{m_2}(u^{(1)})$, ..., $u^{(k)} = N_{m_k}(u^{(k-1)})$ in M_n for any integer k with $1 \leq k \leq n$, if $m_1, m_2, \ldots, m_k$ differ from one another and $0 \leq m_i \leq n - 1$ for $i = 1, 2, \ldots, k$, then W is a path.

For the convenience of proof, we define a vector $< \beta_1, \beta_2, \ldots, \beta_n >$ such that the set $\{\beta_1, \beta_2, \ldots, \beta_n\}$ equals to the set $\{0, 1, \ldots, n - 1\}$.

Lemma 4. Suppose that P: $u^{(0)}$, $u^{(1)} = N_{a_1}(u^{(0)})$, $u^{(2)} = N_{a_2}(u^{(1)})$, ..., $u^{(k)} = N_{a_k}(u^{(k-1)})$ and P': $u^{(0)}$, $v^{(1)} = N_{a_1'}(u^{(0)})$, $v^{(2)} = N_{a_2'}(v^{(1)})$, ..., $v^{(t)} = N_{a_t'}(v^{(t-1)})$ are two paths in $X_n \in \{Q_n, M_n\}$ for any two integers k, t with $1 \leq k, t \leq n$ and $a_1 \neq a_1'$. If the following conditions hold:

(1) $< \beta_{i_1}, \beta_{i_2}, \ldots, \beta_{i_k} > = < a_1, a_2, \ldots, a_k >$, where $1 \leq i_1 < i_2 < \ldots < i_k \leq n$;

(2) $< \beta_{j_1}, \beta_{j_2}, \ldots, \beta_{j_t} > = < a_1', a_2', \ldots, a_t' >$, where $1 \leq j_1 < j_2 < \ldots < j_t \leq n$,

then $V(\text{path}(P, u^{(1)}, u^{(k)})) \cap V(\text{path}(P', v^{(1)}, v^{(t)})) = \varnothing$.

Proof. Suppose that there exists a node v, such that $v \in V(P) \cap V(P')$. We denote v as $v = u^{(i)}$ and $v = v^{(j)}$ with $1 \leq i \leq k$ and $1 \leq j \leq t$. Let $A = \{a_1, a_2, \ldots, a_i\}$ and $B = \{a_1', a_2', \ldots, a_j'\}$. We have $M_1 = \max((A \cup B) \setminus (A \cap B))$. By Lemma 2, we can verify that the M_1-bit of v in P is different from that of v in P', which is a contradiction. $\qquad \square$

Based on Lemma 4, we have the following corollary.

Corollary 1. Suppose that P: $u^{(0)}$, $u^{(1)} = N_{a_1}(u^{(0)})$, $u^{(2)} = N_{a_2}(u^{(1)})$, ..., $u^{(k)} = N_{a_k}(u^{(k-1)}) = v$ and P': $v^{(0)}$, $v^{(1)} = N_{a_1'}(u^{(0)})$, $v^{(2)} = N_{a_2'}(v^{(1)})$, ..., $v^{(t)} = N_{a_t'}(v^{(t-1)}) = v$ are two paths in $X_n \in \{Q_n, M_n\}$ for any two integers k, t with $1 \leq k, t \leq n$ and $a_k \neq a_t'$. If the following conditions hold:

(1) $< \beta_{i_1}, \beta_{i_2}, \ldots, \beta_{i_k} > = < a_1, a_2, \ldots, a_k >$, where $1 \leq i_1 < i_2 < \ldots < i_k \leq n$;

(2) $< \beta_{j_1}, \beta_{j_2}, \ldots, \beta_{j_t} > = < a_1', a_2', \ldots, a_t' >$, where $1 \leq j_1 < j_2 < \ldots < j_t \leq n$,

then $V(\text{path}(P, u^{(0)}, u^{(k)})) \cap V(\text{path}(P', v^{(0)}, v^{(t)})) = \{v\}$.

Lemma 5. Let the input $a_0, a_1, \ldots, a_{n-1}$ of algorithm BCIST be any dimensional-permutation of integers $0, 1, \ldots, n - 1$ and $X_n \in \{Q_n, M_n\}$. T_i obtained by Algorithm BCIST is a spanning tree for X_n with integer $i = 0, 1, \ldots, n - 1$.

Proof. Without loss of generality, we consider the tree T_0 obtained by algorithm BCIST. After the n iterations, we have $1 + 2^0 + 2^1 + \ldots + 2^{n-1} = 2^n$ nodes in tree T_0. Choosing arbitrary two nodes $v^{(1)}$ and $v^{(2)}$ from T_0, the $< N_{a_0}(u), v^{(1)} >$-path can be denoted by $N_{a_0}(u)$, $x^{(1)} = N_{a_{i_1}}(N_{a_0}(u))$, $x^{(2)} = N_{a_{i_2}}(x^{(1)})$, ..., $x^{(k)} = N_{a_{i_k}}(x^{(k-1)})$ and the $< N_{a_0}(u), v^{(2)} >$-path can be denoted by $N_{a_0}(u)$, $x^{(1)} = N_{a_{j_1}}(N_{a_0}(u))$, $x^{(2)} = N_{a_{j_2}}(x^{(1)})$, ..., $x^{(m)} = N_{a_{j_m}}(x^{(m-1)})$, where $0 \leq i_1 < i_2 < \ldots < i_k \leq n - 1$ and $0 \leq j_1 < j_2 < \ldots < j_m \leq n - 1$. By algorithm BCIST, it is easy to verify $< N_{a_0}(u), v^{(1)} >$-path and $< N_{a_0}(u), v^{(2)} >$-path satisfy the conditions in Lemma 4, which implies that $v^{(1)} \neq v^{(2)}$.

Thus, we can say that T_0 is a spanning tree rooted at $N_{a_0}(u)$ for $X_n \in \{Q_n, M_n\}$. Noting that u is the child of node $N_{a_0}(u)$ and the leaf node in T_0, that is, T_0 is a spanning tree rooted at u. $\qquad \square$

Lemma 6. [4] Let T and T' be two spanning trees rooted at node u for a network G. T and T' are independent if and only if for every node $v \in V(G) \setminus \{u\}$, ancestor $(v, T) \cap$ ancestor $(v, T') = \{u\}$ and ancestor $(v, T) \cup$ ancestor $(v, T') \supset \{u\}$.

Lemma 7. $T_0, T_1, \ldots, T_{n-1}$ obtained by Algorithm BCIST are n ISTs for $X_n \in \{Q_n, M_n\}$.

Proof. We have the following two cases.

Case 1. X_n is M_n. By Lemma 5, T_i obtained by Algorithm BCIST is a spanning tree for $V(M_n)$ for integer $i = 0, 1, \ldots, n-1$. We only need to prove that T_i and T_j are independent for $0 \leq i \leq j \leq n-1$.

The trivial cases is $n = 1$ and $n = 2$. Now we consider n with $n \geq 3$. The longest path P_1 in T_i and the longest path P_2 in T_j can be denoted by

P_1: u, $x_0 = N_{a_i}(u)$, $x_1 = N_{a_{i+1}}(x_0)$, $\ldots$, $x_{n-i-1} = N_{a_{n-1}}(x_{n-i-2})$, $x_{n-i} = N_{a_0}(x_{n-i-1})$, $x_{n-i+1} = N_{a_1}(x_{n-i})$, $\ldots$, $x_n = N_{a_i}(x_{n-1})$ and

P_2: u, $y_0 = N_{a_j}(u)$, $y_1 = N_{a_{j+1}}(y_0)$, $\ldots$, $y_{n-j-1} = N_{a_{n-1}}(x_{n-j-2})$, $y_{n-j} = N_{a_0}(y_{n-j-1})$, $y_{n-j+1} = N_{a_1}(y_{n-j})$, $\ldots$, $y_n = N_{a_j}(y_{n-1})$,

respectively, where $0 \leq i < j \leq n-1$.

Let $a_{c_0} = a_i$ and $a_{d_0} = a_j$. By lemma 6, we only need to prove that for any $v \in V(T_i) \cap V(T_j)$, ancestor $(v, T_i) \cap$ ancestor $(v, T_j) = \{u\}$ and ancestor $(v, T_i) \cup$ ancestor $(v, T_j) \supset \{u\}$. Any path in T_i and any path in T_j can be denoted by P_3 and P_4, respectively, as follows.

P_3: u, $x_0 = N_{a_{c_0}=a_i}(u)$, $x_1' = N_{a_{c_1}(x_i)}$, $\ldots$, $x_k' = N_{a_{c_k}}(x_{k-1}')$, $x_{k+1}' = N_{a_{c_0}}(x_k')$ and

P_4: u, $y_0 = N_{a_{d_0}=a_j}(u)$, $y_1' = N_{a_{d_1}}(y_i)$, $\ldots$, $y_l' = N_{a_{d_l}}(y_{l-1}')$, $y_{l+1}' = N_{a_{d_0}}(y_l')$,

Without loss of generality, suppose that $a_j > a_i$ and $v \in V(P_3) \cap V(P_4)$. Let $v = a_{c_w} = a_{d_z}$ where $1 \leq u \leq k$ and $1 \leq z \leq m$. Based on P_1, P_2, P_3, and P_4, we define walks W_1, W_2, W_3, and W_4 as follows.

W_1: a_i, a_{i+1}, $\ldots$, a_{n-1}, a_0, a_1, $\ldots$, a_i,

W_2: a_j, a_{j+1}, $\ldots$, a_{n-1}, a_0, a_1, $\ldots$, a_j,

W_3: $a_{c_0} = a_i$, a_{c_1}, $\ldots$, a_{c_w}, and

W_4: $a_{d_0} = a_j$, a_{d_1}, $\ldots$, a_{d_z}.

Since $a_{c_0} \neq a_{d_0}$, we have $x_0 \neq y_0$, which implies that ancestor $(v, P_3) \cup$ ancestor $(v, P_4) \supset \{u\}$. We only need to prove that ancestor $(v, P_3) \cap$ ancestor $(v, P_4) = \{u\}$. We have the following Cases.

Case 1.1. $\max(V(W_3)) \neq \max(V(W_4))$. Since $\max(V(W_4)) \geq a_j$, then we have the following subcases.

Case 1.1.1. $\max(V(W_3)) < a_j$ and $\max(V(W_4)) = a_j$. Then, each node in $V(P_4) \backslash \{y_{m+1}'\}$ and each node in $V(P_3)$ have a leftmost different bit at position a_j. Then we have $v = y_{m+1}'$ and ancestor $(v, P_3) \cap$ ancestor $(v, P_4) = \{u\}$.

Case 1.1.2. $\max(V(W_3 \cup W_4)) > a_j$. Then, the $\max(V(W_3 \cup W_4))$-bit of v in P_3 is different from that of v in P_4. It is a contradiction.

Case 1.2. $\max(V(W_3)) = \max(V(W_4))$. Then, we have the following cases.

Case 1.2.1. $\max(V(W_3)) = \max(V(W_4)) = a_j$. We can verify that $v \neq y_{m+1}'$ and $a_j \notin \{a_{d_1}, a_{d_2}, \ldots, a_{d_m}\}$. We can divide path ancestor (v, P_3) into P_{31} and P_{32} as follows.

$P_{31} : u, x_0 = N_{a_{c_0}}(u), x_1' = N_{a_{c_1}}(x_0), \ldots, ,x_{f-1}' = N_{a_{c_{f-1}}}(x_{f-2}')$ and
$P_{32} : x_f' = N_{a_{c_f}=a_j}(x_{f-1}'), x_{f+1}' = N_{a_{c_{f+1}}}(x_f'), \ldots, x_w' = N_{a_{c_w}}(x_{u-1}')$.

By Lemma 2, each node in $V(P_{31})$ and each node in $V(P_4)$ have a leftmost different bit at position a_j. Then, $V(P_4) \cap V(P_{31}) = \varnothing$. By Lemma 2, LDF$(x_f', y_0) = \max(\{a_{c_0} = a_i, a_{c_1}, \ldots, a_{c(f-1)}\})$. Let $A = \{a_{c_{f+1}}, a_{c_{f+2}}, \ldots, a_{c_w}\}$ and $B = \{a_{d_1}, a_{d_2}, \ldots, a_{d_z}\}$. Furthermore, we have the following cases.

Case 1.2.1.1. $\max((A \cup B) \backslash (A \cap B)) > $ LDF(x_f', y_0). Then, by Lemma 2, the $\max((A \cup B) \backslash (A \cap B))$-bit of v in P_3 is different from that of v in P_4, which is a contradiction.

Case 1.2.1.2. $\max((A \cup B) \backslash (A \cap B)) = $ LDF(x_f', y_0). By Algorithm BCIST, T_i and T_j are constructed based on the same CDP. Then, we can verify that $a_{c_w} \neq a_{d_z}$. By Corollary 1, $V(P_4) \cap V(P_{32}) = \{v\}$.

Case 1.2.1.3. $\max((A \cup B) \backslash (A \cap B)) < $ LDF(x_f', y_0). Then, by Lemma 2, the LDF(x_f', y_0) bit of v in P_3 is different from that of v in P_4, which is a contradiction.

Case 1.2.2. $\max(V(W_3)) = \max(V(W_4)) = M_1 > a_j$. We can divide path sub-path $< u, v >$-path of P_3 into P_{31} and P_{32} as follows.

$P_{31} : u, x_0 = N_{a_{c_0}}(u), x_1' = N_{a_{c_1}}(x_0), \ldots, ,x_{f-1}' = N_{a_{c_{f-1}}}(x_{f-2}')$ and
$P_{32} : x_f' = N_{a_{c_f}=M_1}(x_{f-1}'), x_{f+1}' = N_{a_{c_{f+1}}}(x_f'), \ldots, x_w' = N_{a_{c_w}}(x_{u-1}')$.

We can divide path sub-path $< u, v >$-path of P_4 into P_{41} and P_{42} as follows.
$P_{41} : u, y_j = N_{a_{d_0}=a_j}(u), y_1' = N_{a_{d_1}}(y_i), \ldots, y_{h-1}' = N_{a_{d_{h-1}}}(y_{h-2}')$, and
$P_{42} : y_h' = N_{a_{d_h}}(y_{h-1}'), y_{h+1}' = N_{a_{d_{h+1}}}(y_h'), \ldots, y_z' = N_{a_z}(y_{z-1}')$,

By Lemma 2, $V(P_{31}) \cap V(P_{41}) = \{u\}$. Clearly, the M_1-bit of each node in $V(P_{42})$ is different from each node in $V(P_{31})$, thus $V(P_{42}) \cap V(P_{31}) = \varnothing$. Similarly, we have $V(P_{32}) \cap V(P_{41}) = \varnothing$. We only need to prove that $V(P_{32}) \cap V(P_{42}) = \varnothing$. Similarly to Case 1.2.1, we can verify that $a_{c_w} \neq b_{d_z}$. By Corollary 1, $V(P_{32}) \cap V(P_{42}) = \{v\}$.

As a consequence, we have ancestor $(v, P_3) \cap$ ancestor $(v, P_4) = \{u\}$.

Case 2. X_n is Q_n. The proof is similar to that of Case 1.

Based on the above discussion, by Lemma 6, the lemma holds.   □

Since there are $(n-1)!$ CDPs of 0, 1, $\ldots$, $n-1$, based on Lemma 7, we have the following theorem.

Theorem 1. Based on Algorithm BCIST, there are $(n-1)!$ sets of ISTs for $X_n \in \{Q_n, M_n\}$.

Comparing with the result in [25], **all the $(n-1)!$ sets of ISTs can provide optimal reliable broadcasting for Q_n.** As far as the symmetry is concerned, **all the $(n-1)!$ sets of ISTs can also provide optimal reliable broadcasting for M_n.**

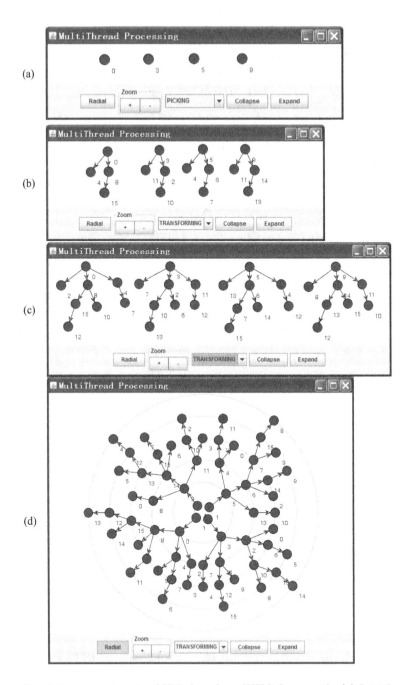

Fig. 2. Simulation experiments of ISTs based on JUNG framework. (a) Initialization; (b) The 2nd iteration; (c) The 3rd iteration; (d) The 4th iteration.

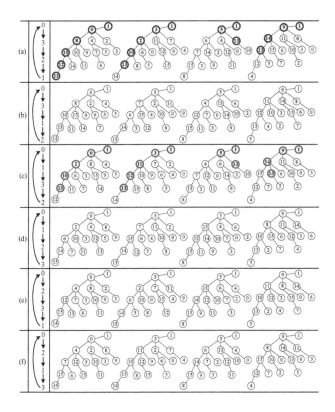

Fig. 3. Example of ISTs rooted at node 1 and disjoint paths between nodes 1 and 13 in 0-M_4

3.2   Simulation Experiments of ISTs and Disjoint Paths for 0-M_4

As it is well-known that JUNG framework is a software library which provides a common and extendible language for the modeling, analysis, and visualization of data that can be represented as a network. Using Java multi-thread and JUNG framework, we can easily construct ISTs for Q_n and M_n. For example, Fig. 2 illustrates some construction procedures of four ISTs rooted at 1 for 0-M_4. The four trees can be obtained by four steps with parallel fashion.

Based on different CDPs, we can obtain multiple sets of ISTs. Thus, there are different sets of disjoint paths between arbitrary two nodes. Fig. 3(a)–(f) show six sets of ISTs rooted at 1 for 0-M_4 based on the six CDPs mentioned in Section 2.2. Clearly, there are six sets of n disjoint paths between node 1 and any node $v \in V(0\text{-}M_4)\backslash\{1\}$, among which the total length of four disjoint paths between node 1 and node v may be different. For example, the four disjoint paths between nodes 1 and 13 in Fig. 3(a) are

$1\rightarrow 0\rightarrow 8\rightarrow 15\rightarrow 12\rightarrow 13,$
$1\rightarrow 3\rightarrow 2\rightarrow 10\rightarrow 13,$

$1\to 5\to 13$, and
$1\to 9\to 14\to 13$.

The four disjoint paths between nodes 1 and 13 in Fig. 3(c) are

$1\to 0\to 2\to 10\to 13$,
$1\to 3\to 11\to 12\to 13$,
$1\to 5\to 13$, and
$1\to 9\to 14\to 13$.

The total length of four disjoint paths between nodes 1 and 13 in Fig. 3(c) is shorter than that in Fig. 3(a). Thus, basing on CDPs, we may easily obtain a set of n disjoint paths with better performance between some pairs of nodes.

4   Conclusions

In this paper, we study the circular dimensional-permutations and reliable broadcasting based on ISTs for the n-dimensional hypercube Q_n and the n-dimensional Möbius cube M_n. We prove that any circular dimensional-permutation of 0, 1, ..., $n-1$ can be used to construct n ISTs, which is the further discussion of IST problem for Q_n and M_n comparing with the results in literature. Moreover, we also conduct simulation experiments of ISTs based on JUNG framework and list some disjoint paths for 0-M_4.

Acknowledgment. This work is supported by National Natural Science Foundation of China (No. 61170021), Specialized Research Fund for the Doctoral Program of Higher Education (No. 20103201110018), Application Foundation Research of Suzhou of China (SYG201240), the 2011 Program for Postgraduates Research Innovation in University of Jiangsu Province (No. CXZZ11_0100), the 2012 Science and technology innovation team building program of Soochow University (SDT2012B02) and sponsored by Qing Lan Project.

References

1. Abraham, S., Padmanabhan, K.: The twisted cube topology for multiprocessors: a study in network asymmetry. J. Parallel and Distributed Computing 13(1), 104–110 (1991)
2. Bao, F., Igarashi, Y., Öhring, S.R.: Reliable broadcasting in product networks. Discrete Applied Mathematics 83(1-3), 3–20 (1998)
3. Chen, Y.-S., Chiang, C.-Y., Chen, C.-Y.: Multi-node broadcasting in all-ported 3-D wormhole-routed torus using an aggregation-then-distribution strategy. J. Syst. Architect. 50(9), 575–589 (2004)
4. Cheng, B., Fan, J., Jia, X., Zhang, S.: Independent spanning trees in crossed cubes. Information Sciences 233(1), 276–289 (2013)
5. Cheng, B., Fan, J., Jia, X., Zhang, S., Chen, B.: Constructive algorithm of independent spanning trees on Möbius cubes. The Computer Journal 123 (2012), doi:10.1093/comjnl/bxs123

6. Cheng, B., Fan, J., Jia, X., Jia, J.: Parallel construction of independent spanning trees and an application in diagnosis on Möbius Cubes. J. Supercomput. 65(3), 1279–1301 (2013)
7. Cheng, B., Fan, J., Jia, X., Wang, J.: Dimension-adjacent trees and parallel construction of independent spanning trees on crossed cubes. J. Parallel and Distributed Computing 73(5), 641–652 (2013)
8. Cheriyan, J., Maheshwari, S.N.: Finding nonseparating induced cycles and independent spanning trees in 3-connected graphs. J. Algorithms 9(4), 507–537 (1988)
9. Cull, P., Larson, S.M.: The Möbius cubes. IEEE Trans. Comput. 44(5), 647–659 (1995)
10. Curran, S., Lee, O., Yu, X.: Finding four independent trees. SIAM J. Comput. 35(5), 1023–1058 (2006)
11. Fan, J.: Diagnosability of the Möbius Cubes. IEEE Trans. Parallel Distrib. Syst. 9(9), 923–928 (1998)
12. Fan, J.: Hamilton-connectivity and cycle-embedding of the Möbius cubes. Inf. Process. Lett. 82(2), 113–117 (2002)
13. Fan, J., Jia, X.: Embedding meshes into crossed cubes. Information Sciences 177(15), 3151–3160 (2007)
14. Fan, J., Jia, X., Lin, X.: Optimal embeddings of paths with various lengths in twisted cubes. IEEE Trans. Parallel Distrib. Syst. 18(4), 511–521 (2007)
15. Huck, A.: Independent trees in planar graphs. Graphs and Combinatorics 15(1), 29–77 (1999)
16. Hsieh, S.-Y., Chen, C.-H.: Pacyclicity on Möbius cubes with maximal edge faults. Parallel Comput 30(3), 407–421 (2004)
17. Itai, A., Rodeh, M.: The multi-tree approach to reliability in distributed networks. Inform. Comput. 79(1), 43–59 (1988)
18. Kim, J.-S., Lee, H.-O., Cheng, E., Lipták, L.: Independent spanning trees on even networks. Information Sciences 181(13), 2892–2905 (2011)
19. Kim, J.-S., Lee, H.-O., Cheng, E., Lipták, L.: Optimal independent spanning trees on odd graphs. J. Supercomputing 56(2), 212–225 (2011)
20. Kulasinghe, P., Bettayeb, S.: Multiply-twisted hypercube with five or more dimensions is not vertex-transitive. Inf. Process. Lett. 53(1), 33–36 (1995)
21. Lee, S.C., Hook, L.R.: Logic and computer design in nanospace. IEEE Trans. Comput. 57(7), 965–977 (2008)
22. Liu, Y.-J., Chou, W.Y., Lan, J.K., Chen, C.: Constructing independent spanning trees for locally twisted cubes. Theoretical Computer Science 412(22), 2237–2252 (2011)
23. Obokata, K., Iwasaki, Y., Bao, F., Igarashi, Y.: Independent spanning trees of product graphs and their construction. IEICE Trans. Fundamentals of Electronics, Communications and Computer Sciences E79-A(11), 1894–1903 (1996)
24. Schlosser, M., Sintek, M., Decker, S., Nejdl, W.: HyperCuP—hypercubes, ontologies, and efficient search on peer-to-peer networks. In: Moro, G., Koubarakis, M. (eds.) AP2PC 2002. LNCS (LNAI), vol. 2530, pp. 112–124. Springer, Heidelberg (2003)
25. Tang, S.-M., Wang, Y.-L., Leu, Y.-H.: Optimal independent spanning trees on hypercubes. J. Information Science and Engineering 20(1), 143–155 (2004)
26. Tseng, Y.-C., Wang, S.-Y., Ho, C.-W.: Efficient broadcasting in wormhole-routed multicomputers: A network-partitioning approach. IEEE Trans. Parallel Distrib. Syst. 10(1), 44–61 (1999)

27. Wang, Y., Fan, J., Zhou, G., Jia, X.: Independent spanning trees on twisted cubes. J. Parallel and Distributed Computing 72(1), 58–69 (2012)
28. Werapun, J., Intakosum, S., Boonjing, V.: An efficient parallel construction of optimal independent spanning trees on hypercubes. J. Parallel and Distributed Computing 72(12), 1713–1724 (2012)
29. Xu, J.-M., Ma, M., Lü, M.: Paths in Möbius cubes and crossed cubes. Inf. Process. Lett. 97(3), 94–97 (2006)
30. Yang, J.-S., Tang, S.-M., Chang, J.-M., Wang, Y.-L.: Parallel construction of optimal independent spanning trees on hypercubes. Parallel Comput. 33(1), 73–79 (2007)
31. Zehavi, A., Itai, A.: Three tree-paths. J. Graph Theory 13(2), 175–188 (1989)

Accelerating Parallel Frequent Itemset Mining on Graphics Processors with Sorting

Yuan-Shao Huang[1], Kun-Ming Yu[1], Li-Wei Zhou[2],
Ching-Hsien Hsu[1], and Sheng-Hui Liu[2]

[1] Department of Computer Science and Information Engineering,
Chung Hua University
Hsinchu, Taiwan
[2] School of Software,
Harbin University of Science and Technology
Heilongjiang, China
{m10002044,yu,chh}@chu.edu.tw,
172851711@qq.com, hrbust.lsh@126.com

Abstract. Frequent Itemset Mining (FIM) is one of the most investigated fields of data mining. The goal of Frequent Itemset Mining (FIM) is to find the most frequently-occurring subsets from the transactions within a database. Many methods have been proposed to solve this problem, and the Apriori algorithm is one of the best known methods for frequent Itemset mining (FIM) in a transactional database. In this paper, a parallel Frequent Itemset Mining Algorithm, called Accelerating Parallel Frequent Itemset Mining on Graphic Processors with Sorting (APFMS), is presented. This algorithm utilizes new-generation graphic processing units (GPUs) to accelerate the mining process. In it, massive processing units of GPU were used to speed up the frequent item verification procedure on the OpenCL platform. The experimental results demonstrated that the proposed algorithm had dramatically reduced computation time compared with previous methods.

Keywords: Parallel Data Mining, Apriori, Graphic Processing Unit (GPU).

1 Introduction

With the development of information technology, all sectors of society have to handle massive explosions in their digital databases. The size of datasets has been increased exponentially in recent years in all fields as speed ups in processing and communication have greatly improved the capability for data generation and collection. Therefore the extraction of interesting and meaningful information has become a highly popular field of study. Data mining, known as Knowledge Discovery in Databases (KDD), is the process of automatically extracting useful hidden information from very large databases.

Frequent Itemset Mining (FIM) is one of the main tasks in data mining field which aims at finding interesting patterns from databases. The data in the database contains

C.-H. Hsu et al. (Eds.): NPC 2013, LNCS 8147, pp. 245–256, 2013.

a set of items that are called transactions, each of which is labeled by a unique ID. The goal of FIM algorithms is to generate all possible itemsets and find the most frequently-occurring subsets that are bought together in not less than a given, user-specified threshold. The number of itemsets occurrences is called support, and the threshold is minimum support.

In recent years, parallel data mining algorithms has been attracted more and more attention. Modern Graphics Processing Units (GPU) have evolved into powerful processors that not only support typical computer graphics tasks but are also flexible enough to perform general purpose computations [6] [7] [10] [13]. Recently, there has been a trend to accelerate computational data mining algorithm on a GPU + CPU heterogeneous system which the GPU acts as the computation accelerator. Nowadays, high level languages have emerged to support easy programming on GPUs. OpenCL [11] seems to be emerging as an open and cross-vendor standard for exploiting computational power of both CPUs and GPUs. However, many classical algorithms have been proposed for single CPU architectures [4] [5]. If CPU-GPU hybrid architectures are used to speed up the mining purpose, it will improve performance.

In order to best utilize the power computing resources offered by GPUs and extend traditional, CPU-based data mining algorithms for mapping to CPU-GPU hybrid architecture, scalable GPU-based parallel evaluation model for speeding up the computing process was implemented in this study. A solution is proposed that would have all frequent itemsets sorted after constructing the TID table which will then greatly reduce the candidate itemsets when using CPU architecture. Suitable GPU threads were allocated after sorting the itemset in decreasing order. Therefore, the times of the checking process were reduced, and support counting was time efficient. The compared results showed that efficiency had been significantly improved.

The remainder of this paper is organized as follows. Section 2 provides an overview of data mining, describes the Apriori algorithm [2] [12], the Multi-core Apriori Transaction Identifiers algorithm (MATI) [14] and the Candidate Slicing Frequent Pattern Mining (CSFPM) [9] algorithm. The proposed algorithm Accelerating Parallel Frequent Itemset Mining on Graphics Processors with Sorting (APFMS) is introduced in Section 3. Section 4 presents the experimental results. In section 5, the conclusion of the paper is given.

2   Related Works

Data mining is a technology used to determine special relationships hidden in large amounts of data, and efficiency is especially crucial for an algorithm finding frequent item sets from a large database. Many methods have been proposed to solve this problem. Among them, parallel computing has become a popular trend, such as grid, cloud, multi-core or GPU computing platforms.

In this section, the most relevant studies, including Apriori algorithms, the Multi-core Apriori Transaction Identifiers (MATI) algorithm and the Candidate Slicing Frequent Pattern Mining (CSFPM) algorithm, are briefly reviewed.

2.1   Apriori Algorithm

The Apriori Algorithm was proposed by R. Agrawal and R. Srikant in 1994 [2]. It's a classic algorithm for frequent itemset mining and association rule learning over transactional databases. It uses a level-wise behavior, which involves a number of dataset scans equal to the size of the largest frequent itemset. Apriori iteratively generates K+1 frequent itemsets by joining frequent K-itemsets. This step is candidate generation. First, the set of frequent 1-item sets is found by scanning the database to assess the count for each item, and then collecting the items that satisfy minimum support, denoted L_1. L_1 is used to find L_2, and L_2 to find L_3, and this continues, until all frequent itemsets are found. After generating each new set of candidates, the algorithm scans the database to count the number of occurrences of each itemsets. This step is called support counting. The Apriori Algorithm stops when all the frequent item sets have been generated. However, the algorithm scans datasets many times and may generate redundant candidate itemsets. When there are many frequent 1-item sets and the frequent patterns are very long, the number of generated candidate itemsets increases significantly. Therefore, the efficiency of the algorithm deteriorates significantly.

2.2   Multi-core Apriori Transaction Identifiers

Lately, novel algorithms on frequent pattern mining have been proposed. Yu et al. propose the MATI algorithm [14] to speed up the computation time of data mining by enhancing the efficiency of Apriori on multi-core architecture. The algorithm utilizes the AprioriTID algorithm [1] [8] at the first pass to shorten the database scanning process by creating the Transaction Identification (TID) tables. In MATI algorithm, two strategies are proposed, Item set Block and Task Dispatches. In the process of generating candidate in MATI, frequent itemsets are divided into multiple blocks, all frequent itemsets with the same prefix are put into the same block, and candidates are generated in the same block only. The frequent itemsets in the same itemset block will be generated on the same core avoiding data distributed on different cores.

2.3   Candidate Slicing Frequent Pattern Mining

Candidate Slicing Frequent Pattern Mining (CSFPM) [9] is proposed by Lin et al. This algorithm uses the Transaction Identification (TID) table to store the itemsets which shorten the database scanning process, as shown in Table 1. Corresponding to the TID table, two elements, the TID value table and the TID index table are created with GPU-FPM [15]. In Fig.1, TID value table stores the itemsets associated with their transaction numbers in GPU threads, TID index table stores the location numbers in GPU threads corresponded to its itemset. As numbers in the table starts from 0, the first itemset A contains 1, 2 in the TID value table, then in the TID index table the number is 0 to 1, and the itemset B contains 1, 2, 3, so the index number range 2 to 4, this process continues until all the itemsets have been dispatched.

The CSFPM algorithm divides candidate into smaller units with parallel computing on each GPU thread. Each GPU thread is only responsible checking for its own one candidate itemset in the TID value table. The GPU thread only checks and compares the numbers whether are equal or not. If the values are equal, then returns result 1, else result 0 is returned instead. The checking process is shown in Fig. 2. Item A and Item B has the common transaction value 1 and 2, then the output returns double 1. After the first computation finished, the result was returned with an array of 1110100, and then the number of 1 was calculated; all the numbers of 1 were summed to compare with the minimum support checking whether the candidate itemset was frequent or not, as shown in Fig.2 and Table 2.

Table 1. TID table

Items	TID Value		
A	1	2	
B	1	2	3
C	1	4	

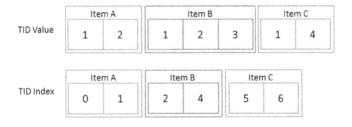

Fig. 1. TID value and TID index tables

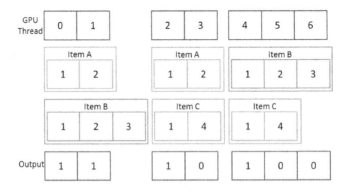

Fig. 2. Candidate items of GPU computing

Table 2. Computing the candidate number of repetitions per item

Item	Time
AB	2
AC	1
BC	1

The CSFPM algorithm is an implementation on CPU-GPU architecture based on the Apriori algorithm, and reducing the counting time of the GPU support to speed up the total computing time. In order to achieve better load balancing performance, the algorithm parallelizes the candidate itemsets and divides them into the GPU threads, assign one thread only checking to its own one transaction in a candidate item. This strategy can reduce the processor waiting time since the load between processing units is more balanced.

3   Proposed Algorithm

Since the information in a data stream is large, the implementing of an efficient algorithm based on the Apriori algorithms has been the focus of many researchers. Due to the great advantages of GPUs, they have evolved become highly parallel, multithreaded with tremendous computational horsepower and very high memory bandwidth. In this paper, an Accelerating Parallel Frequent Itemset Mining on Graphics Processors with Sorting (APFMS) algorithm is presented. It is based on the advantages of CSFPM and MATI utilizing the sorting of the 1-frequent item sets from the dataset after constructing the TID table in order to cut down on computing time for better performance.

The APFMS algorithm was optimized by using the dividing method of CSFPM and the merging method of MATI. The MATI algorithm uses the follow technique. Unlike the original Apriori algorithm, the (k+1)-itemset is generated only by the k-itemset with the same k-1 prefix itemset. Fig. 3 illustrates the procedure for MATI, in the example, k=2 and itemset AB and AC are the 2-itemsets which were frequent, when the 3-itemset was be generated, the 2-itemset merged with each other to satisfy the (2-1=1) prefix, as AB and AC had the same prefix. A, thus AB and AC merged with each other to generate candidate 3-itemset, ABC. However, the AC and BC did not merge with each other as they did not have the same prefix. Therefore, it was not necessary to generate all possible itemsets as in the original Apriori algorithm; the MATI algorithm filtered the redundant itemsets which were not frequent and only merge the useful frequent itemsets.

GPU threads were allocated by the number of TID values in the Candidate Slicing Frequent Pattern Mining (CSFPM) algorithm. Therefore, the higher the TID value, the more GPU threads were allocated. Fig. 4 shows the processing of CSFMP in comparing the TID value. Owing to the varying TID values, the GPU threads did not

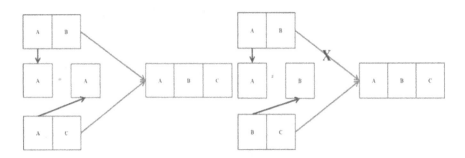

Fig. 3. Generating itemsets in MATI

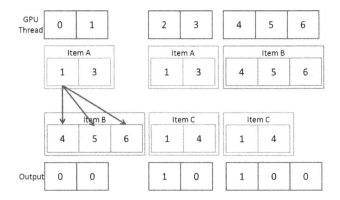

Fig. 4. CSFMP method

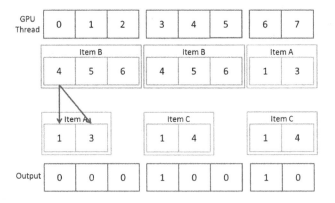

Fig. 5. APFMS method

compute efficiently. As a result, the APFMS algorithm proposed a strategy sorting all 1-frequent itemsets after constructing the TID table with the support of 1-frequent itemset each and in the decreasing order, and then the GPU threads were allocated according the new TID value after sorting. Therefore, the time complexity was reduced when the GPU checked the itemsets; whether they had the same prefix in order to merge so that the next rank candidate itemsets could be generated. The processing of the APFMS algorithm when comparing the TID values is presented in fig. 5.

As in fig. 5, when compared with the CSFMP algorithm in fig. 4, the APFMS algorithm sorted all frequent itemsets in descending order after constructing the TID table in CPU cores, and the results were transferred to the TID value tables in the GPU threads in the same order; Then, the larger itemsets were mapped in the front in the TID value tables. Due to this, the numbers of checking process support counting steps were reduced. Therefore, the support counting time will reduce as well. Following, are several basic steps for applying the APFMS algorithm.

Procedure

1. First, Scan the database, transform the transaction items to a TID table and build the corresponded TID value table and TID index table.
2. Calculate the Tidset and count the support number of each 1-candidate itemset, prune the non-valid itemsets and generate the 1-frequent itemset.
3. Sort the 1-frequent itemset in decreasing order.
4. Use the MATI merge function in CPU cores, that all K+1 itemsets are generated from K itemsets with the same K-1 prefix
5. Let the GPU cores calculate the support counting step, all datasets are transfer from CPU cores to GPU cores, dynamic GPU threads are allocated to calculate the item in the TID value table and its corresponding TID index table.
6. Return the 0-1 arrays from GPU cores to CPU cores, use CPU cores to calculate the number of 1 and compare with the threshold.
7. Generate the next rank candidate itemsets, repeat the step above until all the frequent itemsets are found.

The pseudo code of APFMS is shown in fig. 6.

CPU: Main Function   (C++)
Database is *D*, merge round is *N*, candidate itemsets in *N* round is *Cn*, Frequent pattern is *Fn*.   *Cn* is candidate patterns and more than 1.   *Fn* is frequent pattern and more than 1.   GPU thread is *GT*.

Fig. 6. The pseudo code of APFMS

Input a threshold
Compile the .CL and build GPU device
Scan and structure a TID table

if (the number of orders in any item <Threshold){
Delete the item
}

QuickSort(frequent itemsets, left, right)   //from largest to smallest

Transform the TID table into a TID Value and TID Index
Allocate memory space in GPU for TID Value and TID Index
Stores arrays TID Value and TID Index into GPU memory

For ($K = 2$; ; K++){
Using MATI to generate Cn

Do {
If (size of $Cn>GT$)
       Portion the $Cn= PCn$
Allocate memory space in GPU for PCn
Store PCn in GPU
Allocate memory space in GPU to save the results
Wait until GPU finishes its program execution.

Calculate the number of nonzero entries of each PCn comparison.
If (this number $\geqq$ the threshold)
       The pattern is frequent and save into Fn
} **while**(size of $Cn \neq 0$)
If(candidate cannot be combined)
       Break;
Else
       Fn Combine the candidate to next level (N+1).
}

GPU: Kernel Function (.CL)

Receive the candidate
Intidx = get_glonal_id(0)   // idx = GPU Thread id number
Intgpu_thread_value = identify the corresponding TID Value
if (gpu_thread_value == TID Value of Other candidate pattern)
       result = 1;
Else if (gpu_thread_value>TID Value of Other candidate pattern)
       result = 0;

Fig. 6. (*continued*)

4   Experimental Results

In this section, the experiments are conducted to verify the performance of the APFMS method and the comparison with CSFPM on GPU are presented. In the experiments, the same hardware and software configurations were used and the Input data was from the IBM data generator [3] shown in Table 3.

Table 3. Hardware and software configurations

Items	Description
CPU	Intel Core i7-3960X 3.3GHz
Memory	16G DDR3 memory
GPU	NVidia GTX 580 1536MB GDDR5
OS	Microsoft Windows 7
Compiler	Microsoft Visual C++ 2010
SDK	OpenCL 1.1

In the experiment, the computation time shown in Fig. 7 indicates that with the dataset (T10I4D100KN100K) and the threshold 0.1%, the APFMS algorithm needed less time than the CSFPM algorithm, and hence resulted in higher efficiency with 300% speedup when the GPU was set at 65536 threads.

This experiment compared the computation time of APFMS with that of CSFPM with the same threshold of 0.1%, but with different methods, number of transactions and number of threads (153837). As in Fig. 8, APFMS performed better than CSFPM on the same platform.

Fig. 9 shows the execution time of CSFPM and APFMS with different GPU threads when the dataset was T10I4D1000KN100K, and the threshold 0.1%. In this experiment, with the transaction numbers increasing, the execution time of the APFMS increased as well. However, with the number of GPU threads getting higher than 153837, the checking times and the time complex of CSFPM were increasing. The CSFPM did not even finish computing when the number of GPU threads was set as more than 153837.

Using the same dataset as the CSFPM algorithm, the APFMS algorithm had a better speedup performance. Further, with the number of GPU threads increasing, the computing time increased as well, causing the CPU cores having to finish computation with more space and bandwidth. However, when the computing time delay exceeded the GPU thread limit time, the CSFPM algorithm stopped and jumped out of the GPU computing. By contrast, the APFMS went on go accelerating computation until finished. Therefore, the APFMS was proven to be more suitable with better performance.

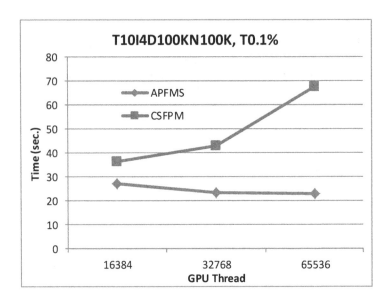

Fig. 7. Runtime with different number of GPU threads

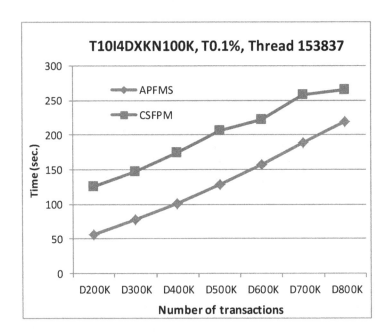

Fig. 8. Runtime with same number of GPU threads

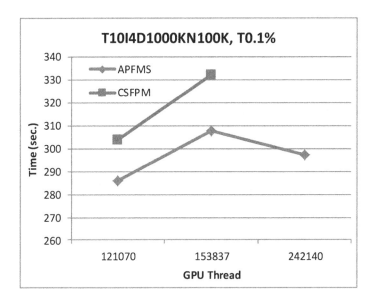

Fig. 9. Runtime with different number of GPU threads using APFMS and CSFPM with dataset T10I4D1000KN100K

5   Conclusions

Recently, with GPU providing extremely high parallelism and high bandwidth in memory transfer, its hybrid architectures are starting to be used for data mining. However, it is not easy to parallelize existing algorithms to achieve good performance on these hybrid architectures. Therefore, it is necessary to examine to what extent traditionally CPU-based data mining problems can be mapped to the GPU architecture.

In this paper, the Accelerating Parallel Frequent Itemset Mining on Graphics Processors with Sorting (APFMS) algorithm is proposed in order to improve the performance of a CSFPM.APFMS algorithm based on the advantages of CSFPM and MATI. The sorting of the 1-frequent item sets from the dataset after constructing the TID table is used in order to cut down computing time and the time complexity of GPU computing. The experiment results indicated that when the dataset was T10I4D100KN100K, with a threshold of 0.1%, the implementation had a 300% speed up compared the CSFPM, and a better load balancing performance was achieved with the increase of transaction numbers.

Future work on the research includes utilizing different types of GPU for better performance. As a result, in order to achieve heterogeneity in the GPU architecture, the different performance allocation will be considered with different candidate itemsets with different types of GPU.

Acknowledgment. This paper is partial supported by the National Science Council of Taiwan, under grant number NSC 100-2632-E-216-001-MY3.

References

[1] Agawal, R., Imilinski, T., Swami, A.: Mining Association Rules between Sets of Items in Large Database. In: Proceeding of the 1993 ACM SIGMOD International Conference on Management of Data, vol. 22(2), pp. 207–216 (June 1993)

[2] Agrawal, R., Srikant, R.: Fast algorithms for mining association rules. In: International Conference on Very Large Data Bases, pp. 487–499 (1994)

[3] Agrawal, R., Srikant, R.: Quest Synthetic Data Generator. IBM Almaden Research Center, San Jose (2009)

[4] Bodon, F.: A trie-based APRIORI implementation for mining frequent item sequences. In: OSDM 2005 Proceedings of the 1st International Workshop on Open Source Data Mining: Frequent Pattern Mining Implementations, pp. 56–65 (2005)

[5] Borgelt, C.: Frequent Item Set Mining. Wiley Interdisciplinary Reviews: Data Mining and Knowledge Discovery 2(6), 437–456 (2012)

[6] Fang, W., Lu, M., Xiao, X., He, B., Luo, Q.: Frequent itemset mining on graphics processors. In: DaMoN 2009 Proceedings of the Fifth International Workshop on Data Management on New Hardware, pp. 34–42 (2009)

[7] Gainaru, A., Slusanschi, E., Trausan-Matu, S.: Mapping data mining algorithms on a GPU architecture: a study. In: Kryszkiewicz, M., Rybinski, H., Skowron, A., Raś, Z.W. (eds.) ISMIS 2011. LNCS, vol. 6804, pp. 102–112. Springer, Heidelberg (2011)

[8] Li, Z.-C., He, P.-L., Lei, M.: A high efficient AprioriTid algorithm for mining association rule. Machine Learning and Cybernetics 3(3), 1812–1815 (2005)

[9] Lin, C.-Y., Yu, K.-M., Ouyang, W., Zhou, J.: An OpenCL Candidate Slicing Frequent Pattern Mining algorithm on graphic processing units. In: Proceedings of the IEEE International Conference on Systems, Man and Cybernetics, pp. 2344–2349 (2011)

[10] Ma, W., Agrawal, G.: A translation system for enabling data mining applications on GPUs. In: ICS 2009 Proceedings of the 23rd International Conference on Supercomputing, pp. 400–409 (2009)

[11] OpenCL. "OpenCL", http://www.khronos.org/opencl/

[12] Park, J., Chen, M., Yu, P.: An effective hash-based algorithm for mining association rules. ACM SIGMOD Record 24(2), 175–186 (1995)

[13] Silvestri, C.: gpuDCI: Exploiting GPUs in Frequent Itemset Mining. In: 2012 20th Euromicro International Conference on Parallel, Distributed and Network-Based Processing (PDP), February 15-17, pp. 416-425 (2012)

[14] Yu, K.-M., Wu, S.-H.: An Efficient Load Balancing Multi-core Frequent Patterns Mining Algorithm. In: 2011 IEEE 10th International Conference on Trust, Security and Privacy in Computing and Communications (TrustCom), pp. 1408–1412 (2011)

[15] Zhou, J., Yu, K.-M., Wu, B.-C.: Parallel frequent patterns mining algorithm on GPU. In: IEEE International Conference on Systems Man and Cybernetics, pp. 435–440 (2010)

Asymmetry-Aware Scheduling in Heterogeneous Multi-core Architectures

Tao Zhang[1,2], Xiaohui Pan[3], Wei Shu[1,2], and Min-You Wu[1]

[1] Shanghai Jiao Tong University, Shanghai, China
{tao.zhang,shu,mwu}@sjtu.edu.cn
[2] University of New Mexico, Albuquerque, USA
{zhang,shu}@ece.unm.edu
[3] Shanghai University of Political Science and Law, China
panxiaohui@shupl.edu.cn

Abstract. As threads of execution in a multi-programmed computing environment have different characteristics and hardware resource requirements, heterogeneous multi-core processors can achieve higher performance as well as power efficiency than homogeneous multi-core processors. To fully tap into that potential, OS schedulers need to be heterogeneity-aware, so they can match threads to cores according to characteristics of both. We propose two heterogeneity-aware thread schedulers, PBS and LCSS. PBS makes scheduling based on applications' sensitivity on large cores, and assigns large cores to applications that can achieve better performance gains. LCSS balances the large core resource among all applications. We have implemented these two schedulers in Linux and evaluated their performance with the PARSEC benchmark on different heterogeneous architectures. Overall, PBS outperforms Linux scheduler by 13.3% on average and up to 18%. LCSS achieves a speedup of 5.3% on average and up to 6% over Linux scheduler. Besides, PBS brings good performance with both asymmetric and symmetric workloads, while LCSS is more suitable for scheduling symmetric workloads. In summary, PBS and LCSS provide repeatability of performance measurement and better performance than the Linux OS scheduler.

Keywords: Scheduling, Heterogeneous, Asymmetric, Multi-core.

1 Introduction

Multi-core processors have become mainstream since they have better performance per watt and larger computational capacity than complex single-core processors. To efficiently utilize on-chip resource, recent research [13] [15] [17] advocates heterogeneous (or asymmetric) multi-core architectures consisting of a combination of cores with different computational capabilities. These processors are attractive because they have the potential to improve system performance, to reduce power consumption[1], and to mitigate Amdahl's law [3]. Since a heterogeneous multi-core architecture consists of a mix of different cores, it can better cater for heterogeneous workloads [2]. People could execute cpu-intensive

C.-H. Hsu et al. (Eds.): NPC 2013, LNCS 8147, pp. 257–268, 2013.
© IFIP International Federation for Information Processing 2013

threads on fast cores and memory-intensive threads on slow cores to achieve better energy efficiency.

The heterogeneity of such architectures can be classified into three levels: high, medium and low. A high-heterogeneity processor consists of cores of different instruction set architectures. A typical example is AMD FUSION APU [20] which incorporates CPU cores and GPU(Graphics Processing Unit) cores. A medium-heterogeneity processor integrates cores of overlapping instruction set architectures, such as IBM CELL [21]. A Cell processor contains a power processor element (PPE) with several synergistic processor elements (SPEs). Finally, a low-heterogeneity processor contains cores of same instruction set architectures but different performances. Such cores are called fast and slow cores [16], or big and small cores [17] in previous study.

Despite their benefits in energy and performance, heterogeneous architectures pose significant challenges on the design of operating systems or programming environments, which has traditionally assumed homogeneous hardware [17]. A key challenges is scheduling [7]. Current parallel programming environments such as MIT Cilk [4], Cilk++ [5], OpenMP [6], and the default Linux OS scheduler [7] still assume all cores provide equal performance (Asymmetry-unaware). As a result, the default linux scheduler will schedule these threads in a random fashion, resulting in non-optimal performance [7] [16] [22]. In general, there are two issues: the scheduling is not optimal; system repeatability is low. Different run of the same application(s) has different performance. This phenomenon is called completion time jitter [22].

This paper presents Preference Based Scheduling (PBS) and Large Core Splitting Scheduling (LCSS) for arranging multiple multi-threaded applications on heterogeneous multi-core systems. LCSS is simpler and requires no scheduling hints, but less effective. On the contrary, PBS needs application preference to make scheduling decisions, and improves application performance more significantly than LCSS. Overall, the two proposed scheduling schemes improve performance and repeatability of application performance measurement over the Linux scheduler.

2   Preference Based Scheduling (PBS)

2.1   Application Preference

We define application preference as the degree of performance improvement as it receives more large cores. In general, asymmetry-aware schedulers should allocate more large cores to high-preference applications, and more small cores to low-preference applications. More specifically, we define the speedup of running an application (all its threads) on large cores compared to half large, half slow cores as α, and define the speedup of running an application (all its threads) on half large, half slow cores compared to slow cores as β, then:

- An application has a high-preference if α and β are big and almost identical.
- An application has a low-preference if α is much larger than β.
- An application has a medium-preference if it falls between high-preference and low-preference.

2.2 Correlation between Application Preference and Fork-join

From the applications in PARSEC benchmark, we observed correlation between application preference and its fork-join structures. Applications in high-preference category and low-preference have only one fork-join structure. However, they distinguish from each other by the execution time of the sequential part versus the parallel part. For high-preference applications, the sum of sequential part takes longer time than the parallel part. Given more large fast cores, the performance of high-preference applications increases proportionally. On the contrary, for low-preference applications, the parallel part dominates the total execution time of each application. Therefore, application performance is limited by the slowest thread in the parallel phase. Applications in this category can not benefit significantly when receiving more large cores. On the other hand, the medium-preference applications have multiple fork-join structures. Therefore, their performance is limited not only by the slowest thread in each parallel phase, but also by the sequential phase. In general, their performance sensitivity for number of large cores is between high-preference and low-preference category.

Let α be the summed time of all sequential parts of an application, and β be the summed time of all parallel parts, then we have an alternative definition of application preference:

- An application has a high-preference if it has only one fork-join structure, and $\alpha \geq \beta$.
- An application has a low-preference if it has only one fork-join structure, and $\alpha < \beta$.
- An application has a medium-preference if it has multiple fork-join structures.

2.3 Preference Based Scheduling

Preference Based Scheduling(PBS) allocates processor core resource to application threads according to their preference. Application threads with higher preference have higher priority for large cores. A complete scheduling scheme should contain a policy for initial assignment, a policy for wake up assignment and a policy for load balancing [16]. In this work, we consider the case that the total number of application threads (in contrast to system threads) does not exceed the number of cores. High performance computing is such a case that there is at most 1 application thread running on each core.

Input: The set of all large cores in a system: $C = \{l_1, l_2, ..., l_{k_1}\}$
Input: The set of all small cores in a system: $S = \{s_1, s_2, ..., s_{k_2}\}$
Input: The set of applications to schedule: $A = \{a_1, a_2, ..., a_N\}$

1 Func. UThreads(a_i): return the number of unscheduled threads of a_i;

2 **if** $a_1.preference = a_2.preference = ... = a_N.preference$ **then**
3 $\quad$ Assign large cores to threads in first come first serve manner
4 **else**
5 $\quad$ $Q = \sum_{i=1}^{N} UThreads(a_i)$;
6 $\quad$ **while** $C \neq \phi$ and $Q > 0$ **do**
7 $\quad\quad$ find $a_j \in A$ with the highest preference;
8 $\quad\quad$ $X = UThreads(a_j)$;
9 $\quad\quad$ **if** $|C| \geq X$ **then**
10 $\quad\quad\quad$ assign X large cores U to a_j;
11 $\quad\quad\quad$ $C = C - U$;
12 $\quad\quad\quad$ $A = A - \{a_j\}$;
13 $\quad\quad$ **else**
14 $\quad\quad\quad$ assign C to a_j;
15 $\quad\quad\quad$ $C = \phi$;
16 $\quad\quad$ **end**
17 $\quad\quad$ update Q;
18 $\quad$ **end**
19 $\quad$ **if** $Q > 0$ **then**
20 $\quad\quad$ **for** each $a_i \in A$ **do**
21 $\quad\quad\quad$ $X = UThreads(a_i)$;
22 $\quad\quad\quad$ assign X small cores U to a_i;
23 $\quad\quad\quad$ $S = S - U$;
24 $\quad\quad\quad$ $A = A - \{a_i\}$;
25 $\quad\quad$ **end**
26 $\quad$ **end**
27 **end**

Algorithm 1. Preference Based Assignment (PBA) policy

Preference Based Assignment(PBA) Policy: The policy assigns cores to threads based on the application's preference. Threads within an application inherit its preference. Large cores are assigned to threads with the highest preference, one to each thread. In case there are large cores available, but the remaining applications all have the same preference, then this policy works in First Come First Serve(FCFS) fashion. That is, the first application in task queue receives large cores, then the second application, and so on. The detailed process is described in Algorithm 1.

Wake up on Previous Core (WPC) Policy: When a thread is woken up, it is assigned to the core on which it was previously running. In case that core is occupied by a new thread, then the new thread is migrated to another core following the load balancing rule explained in Algorithm 2.

Input: The set of idle large cores in a system: C
Input: The set of idle small cores in a system: S
Input: The set of applications to schedule: $A = \{a_1, a_2, ..., a_N\}$.
Input: A vector recording current core occupation status: which core is used by which thread of which application

1 Func. UThreads(a_i): return the number of unscheduled threads of a_i;
2 Func. SThreads(a_i): return the number of threads of a_i that running on small cores;
3 Func. LThreads(a_i): return the number of threads of a_i that running on large cores;

4 **if** $a_1.preference = a_2.preference = ... = a_N.preference$ **then**
5 | Assign large cores to threads in first come first serve manner;
6 **else**
7 | Sort A in descending order of $a_i.preference$;
8 | **for** $i=1,...,N$ **do**
9 | | $Q = UThreads(a_i) + SThreads(a_i)$;
10 | | **if** $Q > 0$ **then**
11 | | | **if** $|C| > Q$ **then**
12 | | | | allocate Q large cores U to a_i;
13 | | | | $C = C - U$;
14 | | | **else**
15 | | | | allocate C to a_i;
16 | | | | $Q = Q - |C|$;
17 | | | | $C = \phi$;
18 | | | | $j = N$;
19 | | | | **while** $Q > 0$ and $j > i$ **do**
20 | | | | | $P = LThreads(a_j)$;
21 | | | | | **if** $P > 0$ **then**
22 | | | | | | $X = P > Q?Q : P$;
23 | | | | | | give a_j's X large cores to a_i ;
24 | | | | | | $Q = Q - X$;
25 | | | | | **end**
26 | | | | | j = j - 1;
27 | | | | **end**
28 | | | **end**
29 | | **end**
30 | **end**

31 | **for** *each* $a_i \in A$ **do**
32 | | $X = UThreads(a_i)$;
33 | | assign X small cores U to a_i;
34 | | $S = S - U$;
35 | | $A = A - \{a_i\}$;
36 | **end**
37 **end**

Algorithm 2. Preference Based Balancing (PBB) Policy

Preference Based Balancing (PBB) Policy: When performing load balancing, large cores will be assigned to threads with the highest preference. In case remaining applications have a same preference, PBB assigns large cores in First Come First Serve manner, just like the preference based assignment(PBA) policy. This policy ensures: large cores are always busy as long as there are applications; high preference application receives priority in getting large cores.

Load balancing with the PBB policy is made in two steps. The first step constructs a new thread to core mapping according to Algorithm 2. The second step is to migrate old threads or assign new threads onto cores to reach that mapping.

3   Large Core Splitting Scheduling (LCSS)

Large Core Splitting Scheduling (LCSS) tries to distribute large cores among multi-thread applications equally. It is designed to be simple and provide a modest performance.

3.1   Thread Assignment Policy

Large Core Splitting Assignment (LCSA): Given K large cores in a system, then N applications will get K/N large cores each unless an application has less than K/N threads. In that case, spare large cores will be distributed equally among the rest applications. The scheduling algorithm will allocate one core for each thread.

3.2   Wake up Assignment Policy

Wake up on Previous Core (WPC) Policy: When a thread is woken up, it is assigned to the core on which it was previously running. In case that core is occupied by a new thread, then the new thread is migrated to another core.

3.3   Load Balancing Policy

Large Core Splitting Balancing (LCSB) Policy: This policy maintains the evenly distribution of large cores among applications through adjusting the number of large cores of each application. The load balancing is done in two steps. The first step is to construct a new thread to core mapping. The second step is to migrate old threads or assign new thread onto cores to reach that mapping.

4   Experimental Methodology

4.1   Simulation Methodology

We use the Gem5 simulator to construct various heterogeneous systems of desired heterogenity. The Gem5 simulator is an event-driven architecture simulator with proved accuracy [9]. We simulate two types of cores, large and small. A large core (L) is an Out-of-Order, 7-stage pipeline core while a small core (S) is a simple In-order core. Each core has a 32KB i-cache and a 64KB d-cache, both 2-way associative. All cores share an 8-way associative 2MB L2 cache. All caches use 64 byte lines. There is 4GB external memory. The performance of a large core is roughly twice of a small core. The area of a large core is around 2.5× that of a small core. And we use three heterogeneous multi-core architectures of roughly the same area: 8 large cores and 8 small cores (8L8S), 6 large cores and 13 small cores (6L13S), and 4 large cores and 18 small cores (4L18S).

Gem5 simulator supports full-system simulation which runs a commodity OS and user applications on the simulator. We ran Linux 2.6.27 on the simulator. Besides, we modified and integrated the Clavis tool [14] to control the Linux scheduler to follow our scheduling schemes.

4.2   Workload

We use combinations of applications from the PARSEC benchmark [8] to test our system. The workloads are described in Table 1. There are applications of high, low and medium preference with or without the supplement data. Canneal, Freqming, and Dedup are memory intensive, computation intensive, and communication intensive, respectively. We assign explicit value $3, 6, 9$ to low, medium, and high preference, respectively. In addition, we assign value $+1, -1, -1$ to computation intensive, communication intensive, and memory intensive, respectively. The initial value of application preference and the supplement data are then summed to get a final preference value. In summary, the BF and BB are asymmetric workloads since the two applications in BF or BB have a difference of 3 in preference value. However, the BS and DC are symmetric workloads because applications in BS or DC have identical preference value. Finally, the CF is a weakly asymmetric workload since Canneal and Freqmine have an difference of 2 in overall preference value. All applications are 8 threaded, and their order in the "description" column indicates their order in task queue. For example blackscholes sits before freqmine in task queue.

Table 1. Experiment Workloads

Workloads	Description	Preference	Supp. Data	Symmetry
BF	Blackscholes and Freqmine	Low + high	N.A.	Asymmetric
BB	Bodytrack and Blackscholes	Medium + Low	N.A.	Asymmetric
CF	Canneal and Freqmine	High + High	Mem. + Commp.	Weakly Asymmetric
BS	Blackscholes and Swaptions	Low + Low	N.A.	Symmetric
DC	Dedup and Canneal	High + High	Commu. + Mem.	Symmetric

4.3   Performance Comparison Metric

We use the makespan of all applications as the performance metric. We also perform repeatability test to ensure the correctness of our results. Since application performance with LIN varies from one run to another, we use the average performance of at least 5 runs with LIN in comparison. The performance of PBS, LCSS and Linux OS scheduler (LIN) will be compared.

5   Results

5.1   Evaluation on Repeatability

To evaluate the repeatability of application performance with PBS and LCSS, we ran the BF and BS workloads for multiple times with PBS and LCSS scheduler respectively, and recorded their execution time. Figure 1 shows the results. For both schedulers, all the execution time is generally within {97%, 103%} of the average execution time. There are many reasons that could cause this variation of execution time. For example, the difference in scheduling activity, the stochastic interaction between threads, and the interference of system threads (in OS) to application threads. Considering the relative small percent (6%) of time variation, we think that PBS and LCSS provide acceptable repeatability for application performance.

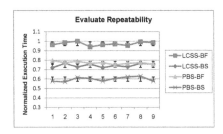   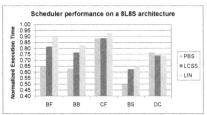

Fig. 1. Evaluation of Repeatability   **Fig. 2.** Execution Time on 8L8S

5.2   Performance Comparison of Schedulers

The performance of PBS, LCSS and LIN scheduling schemes on three heterogeneous architectures are presented in Figure 2, Figure 3, and Figure 4, respectively. Overall, PBS outperforms LIN by 13.3% on average and up to 18%. LCSS has a speedup of 5.3% on average and up to 6% over LIN.

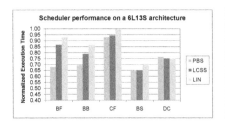   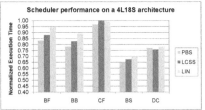

Fig. 3. Execution Time on 6L13S   **Fig. 4.** Execution Time on 4L18S

Of the 15 cases (5 workloads on 3 architectures), PBS scheduler outperforms others in 10 cases. PBS & LCSS work equally best in 2 cases, and LCSS & LIN lead together in another 2 cases. Finally, LCSS win the remaining 1 case. For asymmetric workloads BF, BB and weakly asymmetric workload CF, PBS always achieves the best performance. PBS still works best on the asymmetric workload BS. However, LCSS Outperforms PBS on the asymmetric workload DC.

In summary, PBS is more efficient for asymmetric and weakly asymmetric workloads, while LCSS and LIN are more suitable for symmetric workloads. In some cases, PBS performs better or equally with LCSS on symmetric workloads. As the number of large cores decreases, the platform becomes more and more homogeneous, thus the performance difference among schedulers becomes less prominent.

5.3 Effectiveness of the Load Balancing Policies

To evaluate the effectiveness of the load balancing policies, we compared the performance of PBS and LCSS with and without load balancing, as shown in Figure 5 and Figure 6 respectively. The execution time is the average on three architectures(8L8S, 6L13S, 4L18S). Without load balancing, threads generally run to completion on initially allocated cores, possibly leaving large cores idle and lowering system performance.

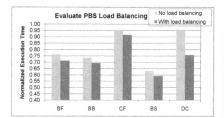 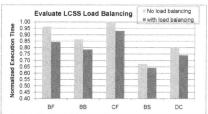

Fig. 5. PBS Load Balancing   **Fig. 6.** LCSS Load Balancing

In Figure 6, not surprisingly, performance of all workloads gets better with load balancing. The essentially balanced resource assignment of the LCSS is non-optimal for asymmetric workloads, and load balancing is a remedy. This is illustrated by the substantial improvement with load balancing on the BF and BB workload. On average, employing load balancing improves the performance by 9.2%, which includes the thread migration cost. For the BF workload, the performance of LCSS was improved by 14.4% with core reallocation.

In Figure 5, on average, core reallocation improves the performance by 9.9%, including the thread migration cost. For the DC workload, the performance was improved by 26.3%. Although the average improved performance is close to LCSS's, there are some differences. For LCSS, all five workloads were improved by around 9%. However, for PBS, the DC workload was improved by 26.3% while the other four workloads were improved by less than 7%. This means that

LCSS has a larger space to improve after the initial thread assignment. Since the average performance of the PBS algorithm is better than LCSS (see Figure 2, Figure 3, and Figure 4), we can conclude that the initial thread assignment of PBS is better than LCSS on the BF, BB, and CF workloads.

6   Related Work

Effective task scheduling algorithms are essential for multi-thread applications to make good use of heterogeneous multi-core architectures. Many previous work use DVFS to emulate heterogeneous multi-core systems [7] [10] [15] [16]. They tune the frequencies of cores to get different numbers of large/fast and small/slow cores, and they keep a constant total number of cores in a system. On the contrary, our simulated system consists of large Out-of-Order cores and small In-Order cores, thus having larger micro-architecture differences (eg. heterogeneity). Besides, our system keeps a constant area while the number of cores varies. Our heterogeneous system is similar to that in [17] [18].

Many studies on scheduling in heterogeneous multi-core systems focus on achieving high system throughput by balancing the hardware resources (e.g., cores, caches) among different applications [1] [16] [17] [18] [19]. They make scheduling decision based on runtime profiling/monitoring. Becchi's IPC driven algorithm [18] periodically samples threads' instructions per cycle (IPC) on cores of both types and gives threads that have a higher fast-to-slow IPC ratio priorities in running on the fast cores. Kumar et al. [1] proposes a similar technique, except that he uses more than one sample per core type per thread to improve accuracy. Lakshminarayana et al. [16] proposes age-based scheduling to schedule the threads with larger remaining time to fast cores. The remaining time of threads is predicted at runtime. Koufaty et al. [17] proposes a bias scheduling which matches threads to the right type of cores through dynamically monitoring the bias of the threads in order to maximize the system throughput.

There are some existing scheduling schemes that make no runtime profiling/sampling. Li et al. [7] designed a heterogeneity-aware scheduler for Linux, AMPS, that makes sure the load on each core is proportional to its power and that fast cores are never under-utilized. AMPS needs no scheduling hints, just as our LCSS. However, AMPS does not guarantee optimal performance. For example, it may run a memory-intensive thread on a fast core and lose efficiency. Shelepov et al. [10] proposed HASS that also puts more load on faster cores, but makes this decision based on the offline architectural signature of threads. The architectural signature includes thread information such as cpu-intensive versus memory-intensive, cache miss-rate and so on. This information is generated offline and provided to the scheduler as a hint before scheduling. Similarly, our PBS scheme requires estimated or offline profiled information as scheduling hints, named application preference. Application preference reflects its ability to boost performance through more and more large, fast cores. Our experiment results show that PBS has better performance over LCSS and Linux scheduler.

7   Conclusion

We proposed the PBS and LCSS scheduling schemes to map symmetric and asymmetric workloads efficiently onto heterogeneous architectures. LCSS employs the Large Core Splitting (LCS) idea and aims to balance the large core resource among applications. In contrast, PBS adopts the Preference Based Scheduling policy and aims to assign large cores to applications that can achieve greater performance improvement. LCSS is simpler, and needs no scheduling hints. PBS requires scheduling hints, and provides more significant performance improvements over the Linux OS scheduler. Both scheme ensure that the large cores are always busy unless there are insufficient tasks. Besides, LCSS and PBS guarantee repeatability that the Linux OS scheduler can not provide.

The experiment results show that PBS and LCSS provide better performance than Linux OS scheduler with asymmetric and symmetric workloads on different heterogeneous architectures. Overall, PBS outperforms Linux scheduler by 13.3% on average and up to 18%. LCSS has a speedup of 5.3% on average and up to 6% over Linux scheduler. The results also manifest that PBS can work with both asymmetric, weakly asymmetric and symmetric workloads, although the speedup with asymmetric or weakly asymmetric workloads is bigger. On the contrary, LCSS is more suitable for symmetric workloads. Although we presented only the results for two applications running together, our algorithms are applicable to more than two applications.

Acknowledgment. The authors would like to thank Linghe Kong, Sandy Harris and anonymous reviewers for their fruitful feedback and comments that have helped us improve the quality of this work. This work is supported by Program for Changjiang Scholars and Innovative Research Team in University (IRT1158, PCSIRT), China.

References

1. Kumar, R., Tullsen, D.M., Ranganathan, P., Jouppi, N.P., Farkas, K.I.: Single-isa heterogeneous multi-core architectures for multithreaded workload performance. In: Proceedings of the 31st Annual International Symposium on Computer Architecture (ISCA 2004). IEEE Computer Society (2004)
2. Balakrishnan, S., Rajwar, R., Upton, M., Lai, K.: The impact of performance asymmetry in emerging multicore architectures. In: Proceedings of the 32nd Annual International Symposium on Computer Architecture (ISCA 2005), pp. 506–517. IEEE Computer Society (2005)
3. Hill, M., Marty, M.: Amdahl's law in the multicore era. J. Computer 41(7), 33–38 (2008)
4. Blumofe, R.D., Joerg, C.F., Kuszmaul, B.C., Leiserson, C.E., Randall, K.H., Zhou, Y.: Cilk: An efficient multithreaded runtime system. Journal of Parallel and Distributed Computing 37(1), 55–69 (1996)
5. Leiserson, C.: The Cilk++ concurrency platform. In: Proceedings of the 46th Annual Design Automation Conference, pp. 522–527. ACM (2009)

6. Ayguade, E., Copty, N., Duran, A., Hoeflinger, J., Lin, Y., Massaioli, F., Teruel, X., Unnikrishnan, P., Zhang, G.: The design of openmp tasks. IEEE Transactions on Parallel and Distributed Systems 20(3), 404–418 (2009)
7. Li, T., Baumberger, D., Koufaty, D.A., Hahn, S.: Efficient Operating System Scheduling for Performance-Asymmetric Multi-Core Architectures. In: Proceedings of the 2007 ACM/IEEE Conference on Supercomputing (SC 2007). ACM (2007)
8. Bienia, C.: Benchmarking Modern Multiprocessors. Ph.D. Thesis, Princeton University (2011)
9. Binkert, N., Beckmann, B., Black, G., Reinhardt, S.K., Saidi, A., Basu, A., Hestness, J., Hower, D.R., Krishna, T., Sardashti, S., Sen, R., Sewell, K., Shoaib, M., Vaish, N., Hill, M.D., Wood, D.A.: The gem5 simulator. SIGARCH, Computer Architecture News 39, 1–7 (2011)
10. Shelepov, D., Saez, J.C., Jeffery, S.: HASS: a Scheduler for Heterogeneous Multicore Systems. ACM Operating System Review 43(2) (2009)
11. Zhuravlev, S., Blagodurov, S., Fedorova, A.: Addressing shared resource contention in multicore processors via scheduling. In: Proceedings of the International Conference on Architectural Support for Programming Languages and Operating Systems, ASPLOS (2010)
12. Luk, C.K., Cohn, R., Muth, R., Patil, H., Klauser, A., Lowney, G., Wallace, S., Reddi, V.J., Hazelwood, K.: Pin: Building customized program analysis tools with dynamic instrumentation. In: Programming Language Design and Implementation, PLDI (2005)
13. Saez, J.C., Shelepov, D., Fedorova, A., Prieto, M.: Leveraging workload diversity through OS scheduling to maximize performance on single-ISA heterogeneous multicore systems. Journal of Parallel and Distributed Computing (JPDC) (2011)
14. Blagodurov, S., Fedorova, A.: A. User-level scheduling on NUMA multicore systems under Linux. In: Linux Symposium (2011)
15. Chen, Q., Cheny, Y., Huangy, Z., Guo, M.: WATS:Workload-Aware Task Scheduling in Asymmetric Multi-core Architectures. In: IEEE 26th International Parallel & Distributed Processing Symposium (IPDPS). IEEE (2012)
16. Lakshminarayana, N., Lee, J., Kim, H.: Age based scheduling for asymmetric multiprocessors. In: Proceedings of the Conference on High Performance Computing Networking, Storage and Analysis, pp. 25–36 (2009)
17. Koufaty, D., Reddy, D., Hahn, S.: Bias scheduling in heterogeneous multi-core architectures. In: Proceedings of the 5th European Conference on Computer Systems (EuroSys 2010), pp. 125–138. ACM (2010)
18. Becchi, M., Crowley, P.: Dynamic Thread Assignment on Heterogeneous Multiprocessor Architectures. In: Proceedings of the 3rd Conference on Computing Frontiers. ACM (2006)
19. De Vuyst, M., Kumar, R., Tullsen, D.: Exploiting unbalanced thread scheduling for energy and performance on a cmp of smt processors. In: IEEE International Parallel and Distributed Processing Symposium (IPDPS 2006), pp. 10–20. IEEE (2006)
20. Brookwood, N.: Amd fusion family of apus C enabling a superior, immersive pc experience. AMD white paper,
http://www.amd.com/us/Documents/48423_fusion_whitepaper_WEB.pdf
21. Kahle, J.A., Day, M.N., Hofstee, H.P., Johns, C.R., Maeurer, T.R., Shippy, D.: Introduction to the Cell Multiprocessor. IBM J. Research and Development 49(4/5), 589–604 (2005)
22. Fedorova, A., Vengerov, D., Doucette, D.: Operating System Scheduling on Heterogeneous Core Systems. In: First Workshop on Operating System Support for Heterogeneous Multicore Architectures (2007)

Scalable-Grain Pipeline Parallelization Method for Multi-core Systems[*]

Peng Liu[1], Chunming Huang[1,2], Jun Guo[1],
Yang Geng[1], Weidong Wang[1], and Mei Yang[1,3]

[1] Department of ISEE, Zhejiang University, Hangzhou 310027, China
{liupeng,guojun007,wdwang}@zju.edu.cn, doriru.simon@gmail.com
[2] Baidu Co. LTD., Shanghai 201203, China
hcm198611@yahoo.com.cn
[3] Department of ECE, University of Nevada Las Vegas, Las Vegas, USA
meiyang@unlv.edu

Abstract. How to parallelize the great amount of legacy sequential programs is the most difficult challenge faced by multi-core designers. The existing parallelization methods at the compile time due to the obscured data dependences in C are not suitable for exploring the parallelism of streaming applications. In this paper, a software pipeline for multi-layer loop method is proposed for streaming applications to exploit the coarse-grained pipeline parallelism hidden in multi-layer loops. The proposed method consists of three major steps: 1) transform the task dependence graph of a streaming application to resolve intricate dependence, 2) schedule tasks to multiprocessor system-on-chip with the objective of minimizing the maximal execution time of all pipeline stages, and 3) adjust the granularity of pipeline stages to balance the workload among all stages. The efficiency of the method is validated by case studies of typical streaming applications on multi-core embedded system.

1 Introduction

With the continuous advance of semiconductor technology, the enormous number of transistors available on a single chip enables the integration of tens or hundreds of processing cores on a multiprocessor system-on-chips (MPSoCs). These processing cores could be homogeneous or heterogeneous, such as processors, digital signal processor cores, memory blocks, etc. To efficiently utilize these parallel resources available on an MPSoC, one challenge is how to parallelize the legacy sequential programs. However, most research and development efforts in MPSoCs are on the hardware architectural side. Research in application program parallelization and parallel programming for MPSoCs is far more behind.

---

[*] This work is supported in part by National Natural Science Foundation of China under the grants 60873112 and 61028004, National High Technology Research and Development Program of China under the grant 2009AA01Z109, and the Huawei Innovation Research Program under the grant YJCB2011033RE.

C.-H. Hsu et al. (Eds.): NPC 2013, LNCS 8147, pp. 269–283, 2013.

Existing efforts to exploit pipeline parallelism in C programs are mostly fine-grained [10,12]. Some approaches partition individual instructions across processors, such as the decoupled software pipeline (DSWP) method [10], while others are dedicated to parallelizing scientific and numerical applications, such as DOALL [1] and DOACROSS [4]. The HELIX project [2] is a generation of the DOACROSS scheme. HELIX satisfies only the necessary loop-carried data dependences. The synchronization required for loop-carried dependences is implemented using a per-thread memory area which resides in the system's shared memory. For streaming applications, these techniques are not sufficient, because the pipeline parallelism in streaming applications is coarse-grained and more complex than that in scientific/numerical applications. To resolve intricate dependency, the fine-grained methods may usually merge those tasks which take part in a dependence cycle. Other work on integration of parallelization techniques [7,11,17] includes the speculation DSWP [17], which mainly focuses on cutting dependences caused by loop conditional statements but cannot cut the inter-iteration dependences, and the parallel-stage DSWP [11] which integrates DSWP with DOALL. However, these approaches are not suitable for exploiting course-grained parallelism and cannot manage multi-layer loop structures.

Unfortunately, currently no method can solve the problem of extracting coarse-grained pipeline parallelism well [13]. The method to exploiting coarse-grained pipeline parallelism in C programs proposed in [16] is a language-extension approach, which imposes the burden of parallelism extraction on programmers. The Paralax [18] is a compiler-based parallelization framework which focuses on the dependence analysis but lacks transformation for multi-layer loops. MAPS [3] is a framework for semi-automatic parallelism extraction from sequential legacy code and extended to support parallel dataflow programming.

Programmers have been familiar with sequential programming languages like C for a long time. Instead of using a language/model, an evolutionary parallelization methodology for sequential codes will be more significant. Streaming applications represent a large set of MPSoC applications, such as video, audio, cryptographic, wireless baseband processing, etc. These programs are characterized by heavy use of pointers, multi-layer loop structures, and streaming data input. The parallelism within these programs usually is implicit [13]. Extracting the pipeline parallelism hidden in loops becomes very critical for the rich loop control-flow constructions in the C programs of streaming applications. Our focus is on exploiting coarse-grained pipeline parallelism in the C programs of streaming applications, which are characterized by multi-layer loop structures with intricate dependence relations and fixed data flow.

In this paper, a scalable-grain pipeline parallelization (SPP) method is proposed, which exploits the coarse-grained pipeline parallelism hidden in multi-layer loops existing in streaming applications. These applications are described by a block diagram with a fixed flow of data and the regular communication pattern. We exploit coarse-grained pipeline parallelism by using the source program transformation for embedded applications that can overcome the traditional barriers. The proposed method first resolves intricate dependency by transforming the task dependence graph, which is then scheduled to the target MPSoC to minimize the maximal execution time of a pipeline stage. The experimental results of the parallel programs of the applications on an eight-core platform justify that this method is efficient in parallelizing C sequential programs.

The rest of this paper is organized as follows. The problem to be solved is formulated in Section 2. Section 3 presents the framework of the proposed method. Section 4 presents the experimental result. Section 5 concludes.

2   Problem Formulation

The MPSoC under consideration is modeled as an architectural characterization graph. For a streaming application, its task dependence graph is extracted from the source code of the application.

Definition 1. *An MPSoC architectural characterization graph (ACG), ACG = (P, L), is a undirect graph, where a vertex $p_i \in P$ represents one processing element (PE) in MPSoC, with $m(p_i)$ denoting the memory space of p_i and $t_p(p_j)$ denoting the type of p_i, an arc $l_{ij} \in L$ represents the link between p_i and p_j, with $r(l_{ij})$ denoting the link bandwidth. An MPSoC architecture has $r(l_{ij}) = R$, $\forall l_{ij} \in L$, and $m(p_i) = M$, $\forall p_i \in P$.*

Definition 2. *A task dependence graph (TDG), $TDG = (V, E, W_v, W_e)$, is a directed graph, which represents the dependence relation of a program, where V represents the set of nodes, each representing a task of the program, E represents the set of edges, each representing the dependence relation between two tasks. The sets W_v and W_e represent the properties of nodes in V and edges in E, respectively. For each $n_i \in V$, the predecessor node set of n_i is defined as $pre(n_i)$, and the successor node set of n_i is defined as $succ(n_i)$. For an edge $e_{ij} = (n_i, n_j) \in E$, then $n_i \in pre(n_j)$ and $n_j \in succ(n_i)$. There are two types of dependences: data and control dependences. Data dependences are caused by data transfer. Control dependences are evoked by the conditional statements or loop statements.*

These are four types of nodes in set **V**: *Control node set V_C, Branch node set V_B, Loop node set V_L, and Ordinary node set V_O.* The edges in **E** are sorted into three groups: *Control edge set E_C, Inter-iteration edge set E_I, and Ordinary edge set E_O.* The properties of W_v and W_e are listed in Table 1.

Definition 3. *The dependence distance d_{dep} indicates the number of iterations between two loop nodes forming the inter-iteration dependences. $\forall e_{ij} \in E_I$, $n_i, n_j \in V_L$, if n_i is the kth iteration of the loop and n_j is the lth iteration of the loop, then $d_{dep}(e_{ij}) = l - k$.*

Definition 4. *A strongly-connected component (SCC) of a graph is a maximal strongly connecter sub-graph, in which there exists a path from each vertex to every other vertex in the sub-graph. A directed graph is acyclic if and only if it has no SCC. Given two nodes n_i and n_j in a TDG, the SCC distance $d_s(n_i, n_j)$ indicates the number of SCCs between SCCs.*

Table 1. Properties of Node and Edge

W_v	
l	$\forall n \in V$, $l(n)$ denotes the type label of node n
m	$\forall n \in V$, $\forall p \in P$, $m(n)$ denotes the memory requirement of task n
s	$\forall n \in V$, $s(n)$ denotes the number of strongly-connected components that task n belongs to
i_b	$\forall n \in V_B$, $i_b(n)$ denotes the branch information of task n
i_l	$\forall n \in V_L$, $i_l(n)$ denotes the loop information of task n
t	$\forall n \in V$, $\forall p \in P$, $t(n, p_i)$ denotes the execution time of task n on the PE p_i. If $p_i, p_j \in P$ satisfy $t_p(p_i) = t_p(p_j)$, then $t(n, p_i) = t(n, p_j)$
W_e	
c	$\forall e_{ij} \in E \cap e_{ij} \notin E_C$, $c(e_{ij})$ denotes the data traffic amount of edge e_{ij}
d_{dep}	$\forall e_{ij} \in E_I$, $d_{dep}(e_{ij})$ denotes the dependence distance of edge e_{ij}

Definition 5. *A TDG after transformation,* $TDG' = (V', E', W_v', E_e')$, *is an acyclic directed graph, in which each SCC in the TDG is merged into a single vertex and the control dependences are removed.* V' *is the union of vertex sets* V_B', V_L', *and* V_O'. *The edge set* E' *does not include any branch/loop control edge, which is the union of edge sets* E_I' *and* E_O'. *The node set* W_v' *and edge set* W_e' *properties are defined as the same as the set* W_v *and* W_e *in TDG.*

Using these definitions, the problem to be solved can be formulated as below. Given an application $TDG = (V, E, W_v, W_e)$ and a target MPSoC platform $ACG = (P, L)$, find a transformation $T : TDG \rightarrow TDG'(V', E', W_v', W_e')$ and a scheduling function $S : V' \rightarrow P$, so that the total execution time of the parallel program is minimized. As streaming applications are executed in pipelined way, the pipeline execution time is bounded by the slowest stage. Hence, the objective is minimizing the maximum runtime (including the execution and communication time) among all pipeline stages, i.e.,

$$
\begin{aligned}
min(max(\sum_{i_1} t(n'_{i_1}, p_1) + \sum_{i_1} \sum_{n'_{k_1} \in succ(n'_{i_1})} (c(e_{i_1 k_1})/R), \\
\sum_{i_2} t(n'_{i_2}, p_2) + \sum_{i_2} \sum_{n'_{k_2} \in succ(n'_{i_2})} (c(e_{i_2 k_2})/R), ..., \\
\sum_{i_{|P|}} t(n'_{i_{|P|}}, p_{|P|}) + \sum_{i_m} \sum_{n'_{k_{|P|}} \in succ(n'_{i_{|P|}})} (c(e_{i_{|P|} k_{|P|}})/R)))
\end{aligned}
\tag{1}
$$

subject to

$$
S(n'_{i_j}) = p_j \tag{2}
$$

$$
\forall p_j \in P, \forall n'_{k_j}, n'_{i_j} \in V', \forall e'_{i_j k_j} \in E', \sum_S m(n'_{i_j}) \leq m_p(p_j) \tag{3}
$$

where **R** is the bandwidth of each link between processing elements in **P**, each sum term calculates the execution time of pipeline stage i, including the execution time of the tasks scheduled on processor p_i and communication time for the traffic send to the successor tasks. Condition 2 restricts that one task is only scheduled to one processing element. Condition 3 ensures that the total memory consumption of all tasks that are assigned to processing elements that should not exceed the memory space of p_j.

3   Framework

Given the C program of a streaming application, the following steps as shown in Figure 1 will be performed under the framework of parallelizing sequential program:

Step1: Select the computing hot-spot region (CHR), which is the procedure with the maximum execution time, of the whole program through dynamic profiling. The source code in computing hot-spot region is scanned to find the relations of parameters, pointers with data structure, data dependence and control dependence between statements through a top-down method using in-house developed tools. Then build the TDG of the computing hot-spot region. The main procedure of a program is usually chosen as the initial computing hot-spot region.

Step2: Transform the TDG to a directed acyclic graph TDG' to eliminate the control dependences and inter-iteration data dependences **(P1)**.

Step3: Allocate and schedule each node in the TDG' to a proper processing element in the ACG to form a thread **(P2)**. A pipeline stage consists of one or more threads.

Step4: Apply split/merge parallelizing technique to balance the workload among all pipeline stages **(P3)**.

Step5: Evaluate the execution time of the scheduled pipeline. The objective of scheduling is to minimize the maximum runtime among all pipeline stages. To further reduce the execution time, choose the bottleneck stage with the largest runtime to be the new computing hot-spot region, then jump to step 1.

Step6: Based on the final scheduling result, generate the parallel program for the application and compile the codes to get the executable files for the hardware platform.

The sub-problems dependence transformation **(P1)**, task scheduling **(P2)**, and workload balancing **(P3)** will be defined and the solutions to these sub-problems will be discussed in the next subsections.

3.1   Dependence Transformation

The sub-problem P1 is defined as: Given the TDG of an application, find a transformation method $T : TDG \rightarrow TDG'$, which removes the redundant dependences to make the output graph satisfying the following requirements: 1) No control dependence edge. 2) No dependence cycle, i.e. no SCC composed of more than one node. Thus TDG' is an acyclic directed graph with only data dependences.

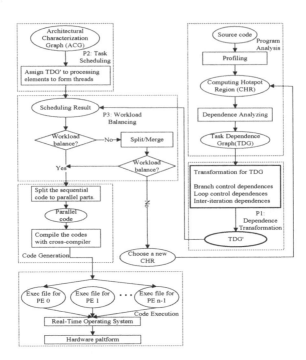

Fig. 1. Framework of parallelizing sequential code

Branch Control Dependence. For branch control dependence, it is important to focus on the mutually exclusive branch tasks. The tasks in different branch paths controlled by conflicting conditions are mutually exclusive. Once a branch path is selected to execute, the other branch path will not be executed. For every branch task, the branch exclusive array is updated according to the following steps.

First, scan the branch information i_b of every branch node of which the type label $l(n)$ is $n \in V_C$, or $n \in V_C \cap V_B$, or $n \in V_B \cap V_L$. Assume $n_j \in V_B$, $i_b(n_j).branch\_level = N$. Search $branch\_label[i]$ and $branch\_condition[i]$ of $i_b(n_j)$ starting from $i = 0$.

Second, traverse the ith level branch control nodes outgoing control edges and find the other nodes controlled by it. Check the $branch\_label$ and $branch\_condition$ of these nodes with those of node n_j to determine whether they are mutually exclusive. If so, add these nodes into the $branch\_exclusive$ array of node n_j.

Third, the ith level branch control node is combined with the branch node n_j. Let $i = i + 1$, repeat steps 2 and 3 until $i = N$.

Finally, after finishing process all the branch nodes, delete all the branch control nodes in TDG.

Through this transformation, each branch control node is merged with its successive branch nodes in different branch paths to form new nodes.

Loop Control Dependence. Due to their repeating characteristics, loops are the important structures to explore for parallelizing a program. According to the conventional methods [3,12,14] , all tasks in a loop should be merged into one large task to eliminate the loop control dependences. Indubitably this will impede exploiting the parallelism of the tasks in the loop. In addition, the large task is likely to become the bottleneck of parallelization.

We apply the speculation technique to remove the loop control dependences. Provided that the loop runs fixed times or many iterations, the loop is regarded as biased. As a matter of fact, through profiling, many loop behaviors of streaming applications are highly predictable. The following steps are performed to resolve loop control dependences.

First, check the values of *loop_level*, *loop_label*, and *loop_num* to see whether this loop is biased, i.e., if there exists *loop_num*[i] > 0 (*i*th level loop is biased). The loop control dependences of this type of loop are seen as highly predictable, and they are chose to speculate.

Second, remove the selected *i*th level loop control edges. Insert code to detect the mis-speculation.

- Insert an unconditional branch statement, such as while (true), in all the loop tasks that are dependent on this loop control task. If *loop_num*[i] is known by profiling, a counter is inserted in every loop task.
- A mis-speculation procedure needs to be inserted in the last task of this loop, when *loop_num*[i] is a variable. The mis-speculation detection is achieved by copying and updating the computing results of last iteration of the current iteration which is running. If the predicted loop is not taken, the mis-speculation procedure is responsible for recovering data and jumping to the loop exit path.

Resolving Inter-iteration Dependence. The mechanism for resolving inter-iteration dependences is as follows. First, on the transformed TDG, provisionally remove all the inter-iteration dependence edges with their dependence distance greater than 1. Next, merge tasks which belong to a SCC in the transformed TDG into one SCC node. Then, identify the SCC distance d_s of each task.

We can identify the set of inter-iteration edges that satisfy any one of the following rules. Assume an inter-iteration dependence edge e_{ij} exists, e_{ij} representing the dependence from task n_i to task n_j.

- If $d_{dep}(e_{ij}) > d_s(n_i, n_j) \geq 1$, the inter-iteration dependences can be ignored by the pipeline stages built on current SCCs. When the next stage is going to be executed, the inter-iteration dependence relation it relied on has been already satisfied. Thus, removing e_{ij} does not affect the parallel scheduling on the current SCCs.
- If $d_{dep}(e_{ij}) = 1$, check the $d_s(n_i, n_j)$ of this edge. If $d_s(n_i, n_j) = -1$, it means task n_i and n_j are in the same SCC and e_{ij} can be ignored. If $d_s(n_i, n_j) = 0$, actually this is the special case, e_{ij} can be removed.

The inter-iteration dependence edges that satisfy any of the above rules are regarded as redundant and are allowed to be removed. All other provisionally inter-iteration dependences are not allowed to be removed and are added back to the TDG before invoking the transformation.

Finally, grouping the tasks and data dependence edges which are involved in a dependence cycle, then the acyclic directed graph TDG' has been built.

3.2   Scheduling

The scheduling sub-problem is to find a scheduling function $S : V' \rightarrow P$ with the objective of minimizing the maximum run time among all pipeline stages. The constraint of the memory space at each processor need be be satisfied. A heuristic scheduling approach is used here which allocates the tasks in TDG' to the processors such that the workload on each processor is kept balanced.

Two-level priorities are defined to indicate the order of scheduling. A *task batch* is the group of tasks which can be executed in parallel according to their dependence relations. Each task batch has a queue structure to load the tasks, and a corresponding *batch priority* to indicate the execution order of the task batch. Every task in the task batch has a task priority to indicate its order in the same task batch in case of resource confliction.

The batch priority (TP) of a task batch is set according to the dependence relations through a breadth first search method. The smaller its batch priority value, the earlier the task batch can be executed. Once a task is assigned to a processing element, the batch priority values of its successor tasks will be updated. Thus, the batch priority can be seen as a dynamic priority.

The task priority of a task n_i in a task batch queue is defined as a linear function of three major factors. The larger its task priority value, the higher priority of the task is in the task batch. Given $TDG' = (V', E', W'_v, W'_e)$, $ACG = (P, L)$, $\forall n'_i \in V'$

$$TP(n'_i) = \alpha \times bl(n'_i) + \beta \times DMem(n'_i) + \gamma \times SMem(n'_i) \tag{4}$$

where the major factors are defined below.

- $bl(n'_i)$: the bottom level of n'_i is the length of the longest path starting from n'_i [14]. If the $bl(n'_i)$ is high, it implies that n'_i is a critical task and should be given a high priority corresponding to a larger task priority.
- $DMem(n'_i)$: the consumption of the communication buffers for task n'_i. The $DMem(n'_i) = \sum_j c(e'_{ij})$, where edge e'_{ij} originates from n_i, $c(e'_{ij})$ represents the communication traffic of the dependence edge e'_{ij}. If $DMem(n'_i)$ is high, it means that the inter-processor communication traffic may be large. The task with grater value of dynamic memory should be allocated to the processor with a higher priority.
- $SMem(n'_i)$: the memory requirements of instruction and static data, which are obtained at the profiling time.

ALGORITHM 1. Parallel Scheduling (TDG', ACG)

Input: Graph $TDG'(V', E', W'_v, W'_e)$, and target MPSoC $ACG(P, L)$.
Output: Schedule tasks to processors in ACG.
Part One:
Calculate the batch priority of each node in V' and insert each node into the
associated task batch queue through a breadth first search procedure;
for *each task batch* $b_j \in B$ **do**
    Calculate the TP for each task in b_i according to Equation 4;
    Sort tasks in a task queue in the decreasing order of TP as $n'_{\pi_0}, n'_{\pi_1}, ..., n'_{\pi_{|b_j|-1}}$;
end
Sort the task batches in a task batch queue in the increasing order of batch priority
as $b'_{\pi_0}, b'_{\pi_1}, ..., b'_{\pi_{|b_j|-1}}$;
Part Two:
for $(k = 0; k < |B|; k++)$ **do**
    for $(l = 0; l < |b_k|; l++)$ **do**
        PESelect(task n'_{π_l} in b_{π_k}, P);
        Delete the task n'_π from V';
        for *each task* $n'_i \in succ(n'_{\pi_l})$ **do**
            Reassign n'_i into a proper task batch $b_j \in B$, according to dependence
            relations in graph TDG';
        end
    end
end

– The scale coefficients of α, β, and γ are used to normalize the elements. The
three coefficients are defined as:

$$\alpha = 1/len(cp), \beta = 1/(R \times min(t(n'_i, p_j))), \gamma = 1/M$$

where $len(cp)$ indicates the length of the critical path *(cp)*, which is longest
path in TDG', R represents the link bandwidth between processors, M represents the memory space of processing element.

The scheduling algorithm is divided into two parts: 1) sort the tasks in the
TDG' in task batches and calculate the batch priorities and task priorities, and
2) assign each task to a proper processing element to form a thread according
to both batch priority and task priority. Each processing element is responsible
for one thread at one time. This approach focuses on good workload balance,
and also takes into account mutually exclusive branch tasks identified in earlier
phases and data locality optimization. Algorithm 1 outlines the scheduling algorithm. For each task it is necessary to determine which processing element the
task should be scheduled to and the time slot the task will be execute on the
processing element. The principle of processor selection is according to (5).

$\forall n'_i \in V', \forall p_j \in P$

$$AvailableFactor(n'_i, p_j) = \quad \lambda \times DL(n'_i, p_j) - max(DRT(n'_i), PEAT(n'_i, p_j)) - t(n'_i, p_j) \tag{5}$$

where $DL(n'_i, p_j)$ represents the data locality factor which indicates the data reuse time and reduction of communication time, when assigning task n'_i to processing element p_j, λ represents the proportion of DL adjusting factor, $DRT(n'_i)$ represents the data ready time of task n'_i, $PEAT(n'_i, p_j)$ represents the available time of the processing element p_j for task n'_i, and $t(n'_i, p_j)$ represents the execution time of task n'_i on the chosen processing element p_j.

In selecting the suitable processing element for a task, the processing element with the maximum value of $AvailableFactor$ is chosen. The larger this value is, the higher available level the processing element has. As described above, the principle for selecting a proper processing element also takes into account the mutual exclusive of the branch tasks. The main difference between scheduling of the branch tasks and that of the ordinary tasks is the computation of the $AvailableFactor$ as mentioned before. The computing about $PEAT(n'_i, p_j)$ and $t(n'_i, p_j)$ for the branch tasks should take more attention on the mutual exclusive property.

3.3   Workload Balancing

In this step, the basic software pipeline technique is applied in conjunction with the split and merge technique to further balance the workload. Given the initial scheduling result, split and merge the stages to further reduce the execution time of the computing hot-spot region. It is achieved by assigning more threads to large stages and merging small stages into one stage so that the workload balance and efficiency to the processing elements can be improved.

If the outer-most loop of a program as a computing hot-spot region is split into several task sets in a pipeline style, then each task set is called a *stage*. Usually one stage can be assigned to one or more threads. If the inner loop of a program or a stage of a computing hotspot region is spilt task sets in a pipeline style, then each task set is called a sub-stage. Usually the stage consists of one or more sub-stages. If the minimum execution cost among processing elements account of less than 50% of the maximum one, or the estimated pipeline execution time does not satisfy the user's requirement, the scheduling result is regarded as workload imbalanced, then the granularity of the pipeline stages need be adjusted.

A heuristic approach is used here which operates in three steps. First, check whether the loop in the largest stage can be split into several independent iterations without further profiling. If so, split the largest stage and apply DOALL to assign the iterations to different threads. Second, merge those small stages into one processing element or insert them into the spare time of other working processing elements. Third, after the simple split/merge processing, the stage with largest runtime is selected as the new CHR. Then repeat the steps of transformation and scheduling as shown in Figure 1.

Table 2. Software Tool

Program Profiling	
valgrind [9]	get information about function call and computing cost of sequential code
gcov [6]	get the branch selecting information
Dependence Analysis–developed in-house	
VarAnalyzer	analysis the information of variables in a function, including type, size, define-use chain, and life time.
DepViz	analysis the data dependences and control dependences among functions.
Cross Compiler	
mipsisa32el-gcc	compiler for MIPS32 compatible architecture
compiler option	-O0 -march=4rkc -nostdinc -g -fno-delayed-branch

Table 3. Characteristics of Benchmark

AES	
Characteristic	128-bit plaintext and 128-bit encrypt key
T264 Decoder	
Version	0.14
Sequence	forman, akiyo, container
Input Size	QCIF, 176x144, 300 frames
Characteristic	99 macroblocks/frame, two B frames between P frames, no rate control, deblock, CAVLC entropy coding

4   Experimental Results

To evaluate speedups of our method, the parallelization framework in Figure 1 is applied to the sequential C programs to produce the parallel codes. Table 2 lists the software tool chains that we have used through the parallelization. Our experiments are conducted on the multi-FPGA-based networks-on-chip emulation platform [8]. Eight 32-bit compatible MIPS4Kc RISC cores were instantiated on the platform, which can be configured to 2, 4, and 8 cores. Each processor core is attached to the advanced microcontroller bus architecture bus in order to connect with peripheral memory, communication, and debugging interfaces. A 3x3 mesh of routers is used to interconnect RISC cores, which implemented with deterministic routing algorithm. Each router consists of five input/output ports, 16-depth first-in first-out buffers, and two virtual channels for each port. The proposed method is applied to two realistic streaming programs: Advanced Encryption Standard (AES) [5] and T264 decoder [15]. The characteristics of programs are shown in Table 3.

T264 decoder [15] is one of the open source video codecs based on H.264 standard. The T264 decoder carries out the complementary processes of decoding, inverse transform, and reconstruction to produce a decoded video sequence. It processes frames of video sequence in units of a macroblock and each macroblock of 16x16 pixels. The outer program loop is responsible for decoding each frame of the video sequence, while the inner loop deals with every macroblock of a frame. T264 *dec_parse_slice* function is responsible for decoding the frames. It is also the computing hot-spot region. In the T264 *dec_parse_slice* function, there is an inner-loop to do the decoding work of macroblocks in the frame. Actually there are complicated dependences among macorblocks and frames. The *TDG* and *TDG'* of T264 *dec_parse_slice* function are shown in Figure 2. The arcs for

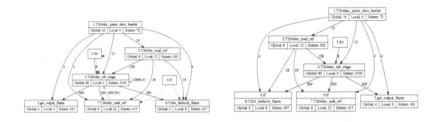

Fig. 2. *TDG* and *TDG'* of T264 *dec_parse_slice* function

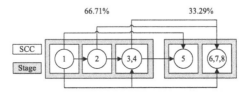

Fig. 3. Scheduling for T264 *dec_parsc_slice* function

inter-iteration dependences are represented with red solid lines. Control dependences are represented with dashed lines. Data dependences are represented with black solid lines. Every node is recorded the global variable, local variable, and extern parameters and their sizes. The node *for* stands for the loop control node, which computation and storage cost are not accounted.

If we use conventional parallelization method to deal with the multi-layer loop structure which makes the inner-loop one large SCC or one large task, the parallelism in the loop cannot be exploited fully. And when the tasks are assigned to stages, the workload balance will be very poor as shown in Figure 3. The T264 *dec_parse_slice* is split into two stages, each is assigned to one thread. The first stage is the inner loop which does the decoding work for macro blocks, while the second stage extracts the prediction information from the current frame for the later frames.

Using the proposed method, the intricate dependences are resolved and the inner-loop is split into 4 sub-stages. At the same time, we partition the data transferred from stage 1 to stage 2 to make sure that each thread of stage 2 is only given the ownership of a dedicated block of data. Each stage 2 thread follows one part of the thread of stage 1 as shown in Figure 4. With one thread assigned to stage 1 and 3 threads assigned to stage 2, the speedup can be improved further. Through analyzing the inner loop we find it that the frame-decoding operation can be partitioned into blocks which consist of several macroblocks. So we gather the dependent macroblocks into one thread and schedule them on the eight-core platform. We assign 8 threads to T264 decoder program which are in a pipeline style, and each thread is mapped to a processing element.

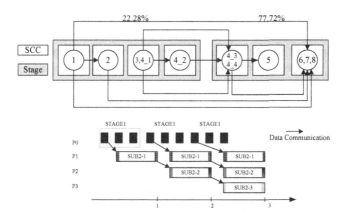

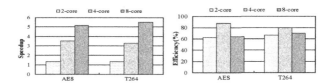

Fig. 4. (a) Scheduling for T264 decoder at inner loop level, (b) Mapping result for stages to processing element. The SUB2-1 represents the first thread of stage2.

Fig. 5. Speedup and efficiency of the parallelization result

Figure 5 shows that through the proposed method, a speedup can be achieved on the two case studies. The baseline is the conventional parallelization method which merges control dependences into one task and only explores the parallelism of the outer program loops. The 4-core and 8-core represent the parallelization result on a four cores and eight cores platform respectively. Under the proposed parallelization method, the speedup is 5.48x for T264 decocder and 5.12x for AES program respectively. As shown in the figure, the parallel scheme on four cores platform makes full use of the hardware of which the efficiency is more than 80%. Since the workload balance of the parallelization scheme is affected by the characteristic of application, the efficiency of processors on eight cores platform is smaller than on four cores platform.

5   Conclusions

In this article, we have proposed method for embedded system applications to exploit the coarse-grained pipeline parallelism hidden in multi-layer loops. The method first resolves intricate dependency by transforming the task dependence graph, which is then scheduled to the target MPSoC in parallel to minimize the maximal execution time of a pipeline stage. The parallel scheme is adjusted in a heuristic way to further improve performance. The experimental results of two typical applications confirm the efficiency of the method in practical. The method will be applied to parallelizing other embedded applications on multicore embedded systems. The sequential program parallelization needs to be integrated with these techniques, such as eliminating redundant dependences, task scheduling, and independent multi-threading to extracting the pipeline parallelism.

References

1. Allen, R., Kennedy, K.: Optimizing Compilers for Modern Architectures: A Dependence-based Approach. Morgan Kaufmann (2001)
2. Campanoni, S., Jones, T., Holloway, G., Reddi, V.J., Wei, G.Y., Brooks, D.: HELIX: Automatic Parallelization of Irregular Programs for Chip Multiprocessing. In: Proc. Int'l Symp. on Code Generation and Optimization, pp. 84–93 (2012)
3. Ceng, J., Castrillón, J., Sheng, W., Scharwächter, H., Leupers, R., Ascheid, G., Meyr, H., Isshiki, T., Kunieda, H.: MAPS: An Integrated Framework for MPSoC Application Parallelization. In: Proc. Design Automation Conf., pp. 754–759 (2008)
4. Cytron, R.: Doacross: Beyond Vectorization for Multiprocessors. In: Proc. Int'l Conf. on Parallel Processing, pp. 836–844 (1986)
5. Specification for the Advanced Encryption Standard, AES (2001), http://csrc.nist.gov/publications/fips/fips197/fips-197.pdf
6. Gcov - Using the GNU Compiler Collection, GCC (2012), http://gcc.gnu.org/onlinedocs/gcc/Gcov.html
7. Huang, J., Raman, A., Jablin, T.B., Zhang, Y., Hung, T.H., August, D.I.: Decoupled Software Pipelining Creates Parallelization Opportunities. In: Proc. Int'l Symp. on Code Generation and Optimization, pp. 121–130 (2010)
8. Liu, Y., Liu, P., Jiang, Y., Yang, M., Wu, K., Wang, W., Yao, Q.D.: Building a Multi-FPGA-based Emulation Framework to Support Networks-on-Chip Design and Verification. International Journal of Electronics 97(10), 1241–1262 (2010)
9. Nethercote, N., Seward, J.: Valgrind: A Framework for Heavyweight Dynamic Binary Instrumentation. In: Proc. of the ACM SIGPLAN Conf. on Programming Language Design and Implementation, pp. 89–100 (2007)
10. Ottoni, G., Rangan, R., Stoler, A., August, D.I.: Automatic Thread Extraction with Decoupled Software Pipelining. In: Proc. Int'l Symp. on Microarch., pp. 105–116 (2005)
11. Raman, S., Ottoni, G., Rangan, A., Bridges, M.J., August, D.I.: Parallel-stage Decoupled Software Pipelining. In: Proc. Int'l Symp. on Code Generation and Optimization, pp. 114–123 (2008)
12. Rangan, R., Vachharajani, N., Vachharajani, M., August, D.I.: Decoupled Software Pipelining with the Synchronization Array. In: Proc. Int'l Conf. on Parallel Arch. and Compilation Techniques, pp. 177–188 (2004)
13. Ryoo, S., Ueng, S.Z., Rodrigues, C.I., Kidd, R.E., Frank, M.I., Hwu, W.M.W.: Automatic Discovery of Coarse-grained Parallelism in Media Applications. Transactions on High-Performance Embedded Architectures and Compilers 1, 194–213 (2007)

14. Sinnen, O.: Task Scheduling for Parallel Systems. John Wiley & Sons (2007)
15. T264 Decoder (2005), http://sourceforge.net/project/t264
16. Thies, W., Chandrasekhar, V., Amarasinghe, S.: A Practical Approach to Exploiting Coarse-grained Pipeline Parallelism in c Programs. In: Proc. Int'l Symp. on Microarch., pp. 356–369 (2007)
17. Vachharajani, N., Rangan, R., Raman, E., Bridges, M.J., Ottoni, G., August, D.I.: Speculative Decoupled Software Pipelining. In: Proc. Int'l Conf. on Parallel Arch. and Compilation Techniques, pp. 49–59 (2007)
18. Vandierendonck, H., Rul, S., Bosschere, K.D.: The Paralax Infrastructure: Automatic Parallelization with a Helping Hand. In: Proc. Int'l Conf. on Parallel Arch. and Compilation Techniques, pp. 389–400 (2010)

An Effective Approach for Vocal Melody Extraction from Polyphonic Music on GPU

Guangchao Yao[1,2], Yao Zheng[1,2], Limin Xiao[1,2], Li Ruan[1,2],
Zhen Lin[1,2], and Junjie Peng[3]

[1] State Key Laboratory of Software Development Environment,
Beijing 100191, China
[2] School of Computer Science and Engineering, Beihang University,
Beijing 100191, China
[3] School of Computer Engineering and Science, Shanghai University,
Shanghai 200444,China
ruanli@buaa.edu.cn

Abstract. Melody extraction from polyphonic music is a valuable but difficult problem in music information retrieval. The extraction incurs a large computational cost that limits its application. Growing processing cores and increased bandwidth have made GPU an ideal candidate for the development of fine-grained parallel algorithms. In this paper, we present a parallel approach for salience-based melody extraction from polyphonic music using CUDA. For 21 seconds of polyphonic clip, the extraction time is cut from 3 seconds to 33 milliseconds using NVIDIA GeForce GTX 480 which is up to 100 times faster. The increased performance allows the melody extraction to be carried out for real-time applications. Furthermore, the evaluation of the extraction on huge datasets is also possible. We give insight into how such significant speed gains are made and encourage the development and adoption of GPU in music information retrieval field.

1 Introduction

In the field of music information retrieval (MIR), the extraction of acoustic features is always the first step. After extraction, the features are then utilized by further applications. Melody, the fundamental frequency (F0) contour of the polyphonic music's lead vocal [1], has been a remarkable feature owing to its numerous applications in the past few years. Having melodies, we can use them in many ways: the most attractive one may arise from the field of query by humming [2], where the melody fragment of humming as a query will be fuzzily searched in the feature database. Apart from that, they are also frequently used in singing voice separation, singer identification and extraction of musical structure, etc.

Unfortunately, the promising applications cannot hide the difficulty of the melody extraction from polyphonic music. The complexity of the task is twofold — firstly, due to the superposition of all instruments which play simultaneously, the accuracy of the extraction is still hovering at a relatively low level. This can be seen from the

C.-H. Hsu et al. (Eds.): NPC 2013, LNCS 8147, pp. 284–297, 2013.
© IFIP International Federation for Information Processing 2013

results of the melody extraction of Music Information Retrieval Evaluation eXchange (MIREX) [3] in recent years. Secondly, most methods submitted to MIREX are very time-consuming [1]. The inherent high computational complexity of audio signal processing is the chief culprits. At the same time, for better evaluation of the algorithm, the corpora is becoming larger and larger, which may contain as many as thousands (or even millions, in the case of some commercial databases) of audio files. All these factors hinder the development and application of the melody. The progressing rate of the extraction could be greatly improved if the execution time was reduced sharply enough to allow a quicker evaluation and tuning of algorithm parameters.

The solution to the above problem relies on the improvement of the computational capability. Some researchers [4] use FPGA to accelerate the extraction of the acoustic features. However, this method features a long developing cycle and is very difficult. Clusters are another common way to solve this problem. Marsyas is used to implement efficient distributed audio analysis algorithms [5]. But the construction of a cluster is expensive and inefficient. Besides the distributed parallel method, there are some on-chip parallel ones, i.e. multi-core and many-core methods. Owing to much more cores on many-core architecture than that on multi-core one, the former can provide a tremendous amount of computational capability than the latter. A typical many-core is GPU. The latest NVIDIA card, e.g. GTX 690 has up to 3072 cores. The availability of programming models such as CUDA has also made GPU a strong candidate for performing many computation intensive tasks.

The adoption of GPU has permeated almost all areas which require significant computational resources. Many applications ranging from general signal processing or physics simulation to computational finance or computational biology can be accelerated by GPU. Battenberg [6] uses the multi-core and many-core to accelerate the non-negative matrix factorization for audio source separation, and the result reveals that the many-core architecture has more advantages than the multi-core's. Specific to the extraction of acoustic feature field, Schmädecke [7] accelerates six different exemplary features, which are among the time domain, frequency domain, and on the autocorrelated signal. However, all these features are the most basic ones of music, not including the melody feature. Although some features can be used to compute the melody, they can only work for pure voice instead of polyphonic music.

Melody extraction from polyphonic music, as mentioned above, remains a challenging and unsolved task, the overall accuracy is around 70 % which is lower compared with melody extraction from MIDI files. Since classic features cannot estimate the melody accurately, more complicated approaches are proposed. There are some designs based on the source/filter model [8], which is sufficiently flexible to capture the variability of the singing voice and the accompaniment in terms of pitch range and timbre. Some use the salience-based method [9] to extract the melody. As for accuracy, the salience-based approaches give a better performance. But no matter which method is adopted, significant computational resources are necessarily needed. These arise from the nature of audio signal processing because the audio signal is usually partitioned into a large number of frames and the computation cost at every frame is high.

In this paper, we will use GPU to present a salience-based melody extraction approach to demonstrate the dramatic speedup achieved by GPU and to encourage MIR researchers to develop and reuse high performance parallel implementations of important MIR procedures. Actually, the system won't be built from scratch. For example, the extraction methods using Expectation Maximization (EM) can benefit from Kumar's work [10]. The methods using Support Vector Machine (SVM) will find it useful of Catanzaro's work [11].

In section 2, the salience-based melody extraction method will be described in more details. The GPU's hardware implementation, thread hierarchy and its different kinds of memories will be stated in section 3. Section 4 will introduce our melody extraction approach on CUDA. Section 5 presents the experimentation results on different GPUs and different aspects of melody extraction. Finally we propose concluding remarks and future work to be pursued in Section 6.

2   Salience-Based Melody Extraction

The salience-based design has a common structure: at first, get the spectral representation of the signal. The most popular technique is the short time Fourier transform (STFT). Secondly, use the spectral representation to compute the F0 candidates. There exist many different strategies to compute the candidates, [12] uses the harmonic summation of the spectral peaks with assigned weights, while [13] lets the possible F0 to compete for harmonics based on expectation-maximization (EM) model. At last, the melody is chosen from the candidate F0 using different methods.

The procedure to compute the candidates presents significant diversities, and our approach is based on the generation of melody contours [9]: firstly, the pitch salience at every frame will be computed by utilizing the spectral peaks, which is called multi-pitch extraction. Secondly, a set of pitch contours are created using the salient candidate pitches. Then the corresponding contour characteristics will be defined, which can be used to discriminate whether the contour belongs to the melody at the melody identification stage. At the last stage – post-processing stage, vocal melody is chosen out of all contours in a three-step singing voice detection stage with the help of contour characteristics. Fig. 1 outlines these three stages through a block diagram. More details can be found in our previous work [9].

For better comparison with the parallel melody extraction and identifying any potential performance bottlenecks, it's necessary to perform an intensive analysis of the serial approach. We will use a polyphonic music clip with duration 21 s to verify the necessity of acceleration. Table 1 shows the execution time of the main parts of the algorithm using Intel(R) Core(TM) i5 CPU 750. From the table, it can be easily seen that the extraction of melody from polyphonic music is so time-consuming that it can hardly be used in real-time applications because the extraction will be finished in seconds. For another, the parts occupying the majority of execution time can be easily found—sinusoid extraction and pitch salience on which most attention will be paid when achieving the parallel approach. The slowness of the sinusoid extraction arises from the relative high time complexity. By contrast, the calculation of pitch salience runs slowly because of its intensive floating point operation.

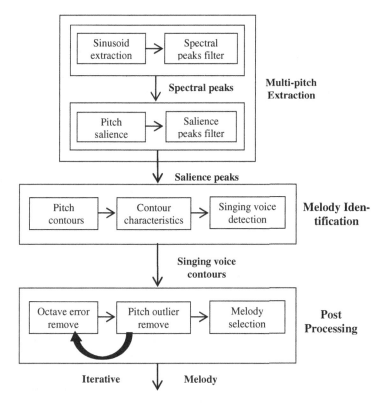

Fig. 1. Block diagram of our approach, it includes stages: Multi-pitch Extraction, Melody Identification and Post Processing. The output of first stage is salience peaks which are used to construct the contours in second stage. At the last stage, the melody is generated.

Table 1. Execution time of every part (ms)

	Sinusoid extraction	Spectral peaks filter	Pitch salience	Salience peaks filter	Melody identification	Post processing	Total time
Running time	307.8	9.7	2611.8	4.1	0.2	7.7	2941.9
Proportion	10.5%	0.3%	88.8%	0.1%	0	0.3%	1.0

3   GPU Programming Model

For higher throughput and better organization of so many cores, NVIDIA has done a lot of innovations on its GPU. The first to be mentioned will be its hierarchy programming model, which provides more choice at choosing different parallel granularities. Additionally, the diverse device memories are also very important in GPU programming. Each has its own special property and if used properly, they will bring an obvious promotion to the performance.

3.1   Programming Model

The NIVIDA GPU hardware is implemented as a set of streaming multiprocessors (SM), which manage a set of scalar processor cores (SP). The SPs at the same SM are equal peers and share some important memories. CUDA has a special programming model catering the hardware—Grid-Block-Thread model, i.e. the simple instruction multiple thread (SIMT) model. Users must group threads into blocks and construct a grid of some number of thread blocks. A block will be executed on a single SM. If all the threads in one block finish their job, a new block (if any) will be activated on the idle SM. One or more thread blocks to be processed by an SM are partitioned into warps with a size of normally 32 threads. These warps are then scheduled by the SM schedule unit for its execution. All the threads activated at a SM can be larger than the actual SPs for hiding the memory latency. Furthermore, threads in the same block can be synchronized for correctness.

3.2   Memory Hierarchy

In Table 2, the frequently-used memories and their properties are listed. Texture memory and local memory are rarely used under the circumstances of general purpose computation, so they are not included in the table. Actually, as long as we make good use of the memories listed in the table, the best optimization effect can be achieved.

Registers scattered on the SPs have the fastest memory access speed. But they can only be used by a single thread and cannot be used in inter-thread communication. For communication between threads, shared memory residing in the SM that is shared by the whole threads in one block can be used. Owing to its on-chip property, it also has a fast access speed. This makes it a key point for acceleration. It can be regarded as the cache, small but fast.

Besides the above, others are the off-chip device memories which often have a relative slow access speed. The global memory owns the biggest capacity which usually has several GBs, and its bandwidth is also higher than the bandwidth of CPU's memory. From compute capability 2.0 and above, the on-chip cache makes it more efficient. Furthermore, it's shared by all the blocks. Constant memory, as its name suggests, is used to save the constant variables. As it has on-chip cache, its access speed is very fast. From [14], the constant cache often has higher bandwidth than shared memory in spite of the off-chip property. This conclusion inspires us to use constant memory to save read-only variables.

Table 2. Properties of the frequently used memories

Name	Action Scope	Speed	Cached
Register	Thread	Fastest	N
Shared Memory	Block	Fast	N
Global Memory	Grid	Slow	Compute Capability 2.0 and above
Constant Memory	Grid	Slow	Y

After the introduction of GPU, conclusion can be drawn that GPU is very suitable for problems which have a two-level data parallelism—one level for different blocks, and another level for different threads. If a problem doesn't show a two-level parallelism, it can also be applied on GPU as long as it has at least one-level parallelism but maybe need more tricky works. For example, the classic matrix multiplication problem must be fragmented to small square matrices to create the two-level parallelism factitiously. For another, merging two sorted arrays [15] must use more difficult techniques to transplant the problem into GPU's platform. Fortunately, in the area of audio signal processing, the problems often show a great parallelism. For an independent music, it's usually processed by frame. The inter-frame is one level parallelism at which the weak scaling [16] can be applied, and if the problem can also be processed parallel inner-frame, this is the other level parallelism at which the strong scaling will be applicable. If a frame cannot be processed parallel, we can still get one level parallelism from different music. In a nutshell, MIR is a perfect field that GPU can show its extraordinary computing capability.

4   Parallel Implementation

From Table 1, the parts which most need acceleration can be easily seen. Fortunately, these parts are also the easiest parts to be parallelized. At the first stage—Multi-pitch Extraction, the main job is to transform the music data and to calculate the pitch salience. In sinusoid extraction part, CUFFT [17] is a good choice to achieve the FFT on CUDA, which is an efficient official library. In pitch salience computation part, the key operation is to calculate the salience of different frequencies at every frame. Because the salience computation of a specific frequency has no contact with the others, the computation reveals a perfectly strong scaling which can be mapped to different threads in a one-to-one mapping. Besides these two time-consuming parts, there will be two filter parts. They occupy only a small proportion of the runtime, so they can be put on CPU. But considering their stay between the sinusoid extraction and the pitch salience computation, parallelizing them on GPU will reduce the communication time between CPU and GPU. Hence we will parallelize all parts of the first stage on GPU.

In Melody Identification stage, the main job is to create a series of pitch contours and to calculate the contour characteristics. These operations have a strong data dependency. What's more, this stage occupies only a very little proportion of the whole runtime as illustrated in Table 1. So this stage will be finished on CPU.

In the last post processing stage, the operation deals with the octave error and the pitch outlier using "melody pitch mean". The calculation of melody pitch mean is finished with the help of smoothing filter which needs a lot of computation. This filter has less data dependency and it can be parallelized on GPU even the proportion of this stage is also small. Different blocks will smooth different positions, and the threads in the same block will calculate the value of the same position using reduction.

The complete heterogeneous algorithm is shown below (Note that the first stage is included for completeness). In the following section, we will focus on specific parts of the algorithm as some stages execute on CPU.

Algorithm.   Hybrid Melody Extraction from Polyphonic Music

Input: Polyphonic Music *pm*
Output: Melody *m*
 1: *Stage I*: *Pre-Processing*   CPU ::
 2:     CPU :: read the polyphonic music to CPU memory
 3:     CPU → GPU :: transfer the music to GPU memory
 4: *Stage II*: *Multi-pitch Extraction*   GPU ::
 5:     GPU :: rearrange the music data
 6:     **for** every frame *f* parallel **do**
 7:             GPU :: sinusoid extraction
 8:             GPU :: spectral peaks filter
 9:             GPU :: pitch salience computation
10:             GPU :: salience peaks filter
11:     **endfor**
12: *Stage III*: *Melody identification*   CPU ::
13:     GPU → CPU :: read salience peaks to CPU memory
14:     CPU :: pitch contour
15:     **for** every contour *c* **do**
16:             CPU :: contour characteristics
17:             CPU :: singing voice detection
18:     **endfor**
19: *Stage IV*: *Post Processing* mainly on CPU ::
20:     **for** *i*=1:3 **do**
21:             CPU → GPU → CPU :: melody pitch mean
22:             CPU :: remove octave error
23:             CPU :: remove pitch outlier
24:     **endfor**
25:     CPU: return the melody

4.1   Sinusoid Extraction

Before transforming, the music data should be transferred from host memory space to device memory space, and then rearranged to fit for FFT and consequent operations, as depicted in Fig. 2. The reason for rearrangement is to make the data suitable for CUFFT functions. The rearrangement is executed after the transfer because less data will be transferred and the rearrangement can be implemented in parallel.

Afterwards, the rearranged frames will be multiplied by Hann window. Then cufftPlan1d and cufftExecR2C are used to transform the frames. The results of FFT will be complex. The real part and the imaginary part of complex are used to get the module of the transform result. At the same time, as transform is symmetric, only half of the result at one frame will be useful.

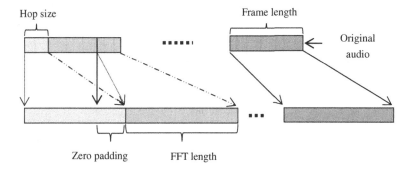

Fig. 2. Rearrangement of the original audio (For music with 44.1 kHz sample rate, frame length is 2048, hop size is 441, FFT length is 8192, zero padding is 6144)

In this part, many operations just transform the frame data from one form to another, so the pattern concurs with each other—transform the data one by one in every frame. Therefore, we adopt the same strategy to parallelize them: all the threads in one block will deal with an individual frame and different blocks will process different frames. This is a good example of strong scaling and weak scaling.

4.2   Spectral Peaks Filter

The spectral peaks of transform encompass the possible pitches and are extracted for further dispose. The key of the filter is getting all the peaks first. For traditional serial algorithm, it's a very easy goal to achieve as it just traverses the array forward and returns the found peaks. When transplanting to GPU platform, the complexity appears. Although different frames can be processed in parallel, the parallelism in a frame cannot be utilized well. The difficulty is not how to find the peaks but how to save them. If merely counting the numbers, the different threads in a block can count the peaks on shared memory and count them all using efficient reduction method. But if we need to save the peaks at the same time, the story will be different. There is a possibility that some threads in a warp find the peaks simultaneously and the conflict happens when saving them. The problem here is that counting variable will be visited simultaneously by different threads in a block. One solution relies on the use of atomic operation which serializes the visit of memory. Unfortunately, this solution has a severe drawback—reducing the access efficiency, so does the speed.

In order to balance the efficiency and the correctness, different strategies are adopted to specific length of frames. For the original transform result, the frame length is half of the FFT length plus one, i.e. 4097. The order of magnitude of the peaks will stabilize at 10^2 levels. For the sake of high efficiency, the "space for time" strategy is used. More specifically, the equal sized array with the original frame is allocated for holding the peaks, as depicted in Fig. 3. The found peaks will be put in position which has the same index with the peaks in the original frame. In this way, the threads can save the peaks without the access conflict. The reason we waste the space to save the peaks is that the peaks will be further disposed, and none of all will be saved.

Original frames

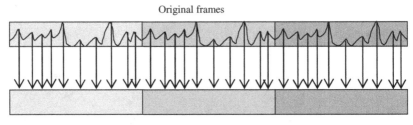

Allocated frames

Fig. 3. Space for time strategy for finding the peaks (All elements in allocated frames are zero except the peaks)

The consequent work is to find the max peak which is used to carry out the filter. Finding the max value of an array is a classic problem on CUDA which can be finished using the CUBLAS [18] library or achieved by ourselves using reduction. Once getting the max peak, we can perform the filter of peaks. The problems here are the same as finding peaks, namely how to save the remaining peaks. But unlike the previous finding peaks, the order of magnitude of the peaks has reduced to 10^1 levels from experiment, so this means the remaining peaks in the array is rather sparse (length of thousands of array has dozens of peaks). From the above result, the probability of conflict when the threads in a warp save the peaks simultaneously will be low. In this case, we can use atomic operation to finish the filter.

Although the atomic operation assures the correctness of counting, the result of atomic operation cannot be used directly as it may be added by another thread before saving the peaks. The solution is using the return value of the atomic function of CUDA. Because it returns the old value and incrementing the old value will exactly be the right position for the remaining peak. In addition, owing to the fast access speed and shared by the whole threads in a block, the shared memory is a good place to put the counting variable. The part of salience peaks filter is the same as the spectral peaks filter, so it will not be described in detail.

4.3   Pitch Salience

After filtering the spectral peaks, they will be used to calculate the pitch salience. The calculation reveals a perfect parallelization as the calculation of each bin has no data dependency with other bins' calculation. So it can be easily transplanted to GPU platform, the strategy is different blocks process different frames, and threads in a block dispose a frame's calculation of 480 different pitch saliences. On one hand, due to the frequent access of spectral peaks and their small size, putting them in shared memory is a good idea to accelerate the access speed. On the other hand, because the calculation of pitch salience has so many floating point operations, the requirement for registers are huge and this will limit the threads number activated at the same time. Our solution is to use the constant memory to hold the constant variables needed in calculation. This is a good approach to optimize. The other used optimizations comprise the extraction of common sub-expressions and loop unrolling, etc. Although no advanced techniques are adopted, we can still achieve a high speed-up from the following evaluation.

5   Evaluation

Various experiments are presented to clarify the effectiveness of GPU in our approach. At first, the overall performance of the system and the parallelized parts on each hardware platform are presented. After this, the performance along with the music length is evaluated. Furthermore, the efficiency of our peaks filter is demonstrated. At last, the influence to the ultimate accuracy is tested.

We have implemented our algorithm on two different commodity GPUs, whose hardware specifications are listed in Table 3. The CPU version runs on an Intel(R) Core(TM) i5 CPU 750 platform.

The corpus used to evaluate the efficiency of the system is from MIR-1k which is a publicly available dataset proposed in [19]. It has 1000 song clips with a duration ranging from 3 to 12 seconds, and the total length is up to 133 minutes.

Table 3. GPU Specifications

Properties	GTX 285	GTX 480
Number of cores	240	480
SMs	30	15
Cores per SM	8	32
Global Memory(GB)	1	1.5
Memory Bandwidth (GB/s)	159	177
Shared Memory (KB)	16	48
Register (KB)	16	32
GPU core clock rate (MHz)	648	700
Compute Capacity	1.3	2.0

5.1   Overall Performance

The same polyphonic music clip as in performance analysis of serial approach is used to measure the overall performance of the system and the parallelized parts. The runtime of the parallelized parts and the whole system on different platforms is demonstrated in Fig. 4.

From Fig. 4, we can see all accelerated parts achieve a positive speed up, especially two most time-consuming parts. In the pitch salience computation part, the runtime is reduced from seconds to lower than 10ms. This is a huge acceleration. The high acceleration can attribute to the perfect parallelism and the use of shared memory. Inspired by these two parts, the whole system also gets a considerable acceleration—for a length of 21 s audio clip, the extraction time is reduced to less than 40 ms on GTX 480. The speedup is nearly to 100 times. This implementation is sufficient for real-time applications, such as query by humming. What's more, our system can be applied to massive datasets which are often used to verify the effectiveness of algorithms. The approach can reduce the time to tune the variables or to develop new methods dramatically. So researchers can pay more attention to the algorithm itself rather than the performance.

Except the two parts mentioned above, other parts get a relative small acceleration. Even though they occupy a small proportion of execution time, it's meaningful to find out a reasonable explanation. In post processing stage, a 2-times acceleration is achieved approximately on GTX 285 platform. The final cause is shown in two aspects: at first, the proportion which can be accelerated is only 70 %. This means the speed-up upper bound is only 3.3 times according to the Amdahl's law. Secondly, the algorithm complexity of smoother filter is only $O(n)$, so the ratio of operations to elements transferred is $O(1)$. Performance benefits can only be more readily achieved when this ratio is higher. Furthermore, although a high parallelization exists in the smooth filter, the time is wasted on the space allocation on GPU and transfer between the host and the device. So we can reach such a conclusion that a high proportion of parallelizable part and computation complexity are the prerequisites for high speed-up. The reason pitch salience computation can also achieve a very high speed-up even its computation complexity is $O(n)$ is that it has no transfer between the host and the device. In addition, the previous hidden coefficient is large. The peaks filter part will be better explained in detail later.

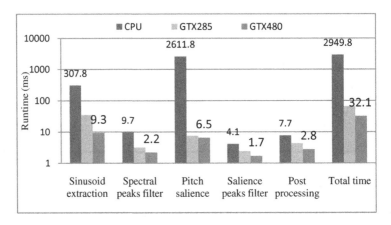

Fig. 4. Performance comparison of different parts and the whole system (Time for CPU and GTX 480 is marked for clarity)

5.2   Influence of Music Length

As the melody extraction is processed mostly frame by frame, the extraction time will increase gradually with the growing of audio length, as illustrated in Fig. 5. Although the entire trend of the line growth is incremental, there still exist some points which descend with the growing of audio length. This is because of the influence of specific audios. That means the extraction procedure has different levels in difficulty. It is obvious that polyphonic music with lower energy of background will be much easier to extract the melody than the music with a strong energy of background intuitively as the former has less candidate pitches, and this will reduce the computation time of pitch salience.

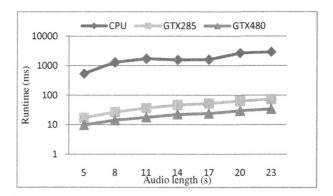

Fig. 5. Extraction time along with the growing of audio length on different platforms

5.3   Efficiency of Parallelized Finding Peaks

From Fig. 4, we can also see that the two peak filter parts have a relative low speed-up. This phenomenon arises from the massive space allocation on device memory under the situation of no transfer between the device and the host, and the low algorithm complexity. For a problem with a low computation complexity, the execution time will be dominated by the space allocation on GPU and transfer between the host and the device. Under such a circumstance, reusing GPU device memory will be important and it's also possible to reuse previous allocated space to put the found peaks. For example, the space for rearrangement of original audio is large enough to hold the peaks. In this way, the time of release and allocation space can be reduced once.

The peaks filter can be divided into more fine-grained steps: firstly, find all the peaks, and then the max peak. Thirdly, execute the first level peaks filter. At last, do the second level peaks filter. If just ignoring the space allocation to compare the computation time, we can still see the positive effect of our parallelization, as illustrated in Table 4.

Table 4. Execution Time of Each Step at the Spectral Peaks Filter (ms)

Hardware	Find peaks	Max peak	First filter	Second filter
CPU	8.54	0.29	0.38	0.44
GTX 285	1.26	0.32	0.29	0.07
GTX 480	0.24	0.38	0.11	0.03

Owing to the "space for time" strategy, the operation of finding peaks achieves an obvious speed-up. The classic problem of finding max doesn't demonstrate a speed-up, and the too few data are to blame. The filter using atomic operation shows a small speed-up. It is understandable that few data and access conflict both exist in the extraction. The second filter works better than the first one as the possibility of conflict is smaller than that in the first filter. From Table 4, we can also see that the allocation and release time occupy a big proportion if adding up all the time and comparing it with Fig. 4.

5.4   Influence to the Accuracy

The operation of double-precision floating point on GPU is time-consuming, so the single-precision floating point is adopted in our system. Although the precision is reduced, the accuracy doesn't drop. The overall accuracy on our parallel system is 73.7 %, the same as the serial approach on dataset MIR-1k. But the extraction time is reduced from nearly one hour to less than one minute. This promotes the efficiency of development tremendously. So we can spend more time on the improvement of the accuracy of the algorithm itself, and do not need to concern about the performance.

6   Conclusions and Future Work

Melody extraction from polyphonic music is a valuable problem because the melody can be used in many valuable applications. However, the relative long extraction time and the low accuracy limit its extensions. The extraction can be accelerated by GPU due to its high computation capability. In this paper a fast extraction approach based on GPU is presented. The results show that GPUs are well suited for audio signal processing problems as its characteristic is that the frame is processed one by one. Our parallel implementation reduces computation times by nearly two orders of magnitude on GTX 480. The acceleration is so tremendous that our system can be applied to some real-time applications, such as query by humming. Moreover, another benefit from acceleration is that it can greatly reduce the development time, so we can take more time to improve the accuracy of melody extraction.

In the future, we will implement a real query by humming application using our parallel extraction approach. At the same time, the tune of parameters and new methods about melody extraction will be verified on GPU platform deeply.

Acknowledgments. This research was funded by the Hi-tech Research and Development Program of China (863 Program) under Grant No.2011AA01A205, the National Natural Science Foundation of China under Grant No.61232009, the Doctoral Fund of Ministry of Education of China under Grant No.20101102110018, Beijing Natural Science Foundation under Grant No.4122042, the fund of the State Key Laboratory of Software Development Environment under Grant No.SKLSDE-2012ZX-07 and Shanghai Science and Technology Innovation Action Plan under Grant No.11511500400.

References

1. Poliner, G.E., Ellis, D.P.W., Ehmann, F., Gómez, E., Steich, S., Ong, B.: Melody transcription from music audio: Approaches and Evaluation. IEEE Trans. on Audio, Speech and Language Process. 15(4), 1247–1256 (2007)
2. Dannenberg, R.B., Birmingham, W.P., Pardo, B., Hu, N., Meek, C., Tzanetakis, G.: A comparative evaluation of search techniques for query-by-humming using the MUSART testbed. J. of the American Soc. for Inform. Science and Technology 58(5), 687–701 (2007)
3. Downie, J.S.: The music information retrieval evaluation exchange 2005–2007: A window into music information retrieval research. Acoustical Science and Technology 29(4), 247–255 (2008)
4. Schmidt, E.M., West, K., Kim, Y.E.: Efficient Acoustic Feature Extraction for Music Information Retrieval Using Programmable Gate Arrays. In: Proceedings of the 2009 International Society for Music Information Retrieval Conference. ISMIR, Kobe (2009)
5. Bray, S., Tzanetakis, G.: Distributed audio feature extraction for music. In: Proceedings of the International Conference on Music Information Retrieval, pp. 434–437 (2005)
6. Battenberg, E., Wessel, D.: Accelerating nonnegative matrix factorization for audio source separation on multi-core and many-core architectures. In: International Society for Music Retrieval Conference (2009)
7. Schmädecke, I., Mörschbach, J., Blume, H.: GPU-based acoustic feature extraction for electronic media processing. In: Proc. 14th ITG Conf. Electronic Media Technology, Dortmund, Germany (2011)
8. Ozerov, A., Philippe, P., Bimbot, F., Gribonval, R.: Adaptation of bayesian models for single-channel source separation and its application to voice/music separation in popular songs. IEEE Trans. on Audio, Speech, and Language Process. 15(5), 1564–1578 (2007)
9. Guangchao, Y., Yao, Z., Limin, X., Li, R., Yongnan, L.: Efficient Vocal Melody Extraction from Polyphonic Music Signals. Electronics and Electrical Engineering 19(6), 103–108 (2013)
10. Kumar, N.S.L.P., Satoor, S., Buck, I.: Fast parallel expectation maximization for gaussian mixture models on gpus using cuda. In: Proceedings of the 2009 11th IEEE International Conference on High Performance Computing and Communications, pp. 103–109. IEEE Computer Society, Washington, DC (2009)
11. Catanzaro, B., Sundaram, N., Keutzer, K.: Fast Support Vector Machine Training and Classification on Graphics Processors. In: Proceedings of the 25th International Conference on Machine Learning, pp. 104–111 (2008)
12. Klapuri, A.: Multiple fundamental frequency estimation by summing harmonic amplitudes. In: Proc. 7th Int. Conf. on Music Inform. Retrieval, Victoria, Canada, pp. 216–221 (October 2006)
13. Goto, M.: A real-time music-scene-description system: predominant-f0 estimation for detecting melody and bass lines in real-world audio signals. Speech Communication 43, 311–329 (2004)
14. Yang, Y., Xiang, P., Mantor, M., Zhou, H.: Fixing Performance Bugs: An Empirical Study of Open-Source GPGPU Programs. In: International Conference on Parallel Processing (2012)
15. Green, O., McColl, R., Bader, D.A.: GPU merge path: a GPU merging algorithm. In: Proc. ICS, pp. 331–340 (2012)
16. NVIDIA, CUDA C Best Practices Guide 4.1 (2012)
17. NVIDIA, CUFFT Library 4.1 (2012)
18. NVIDIA, CUDA CUBLAS Library 4.1 (2012)
19. Hsu, C.L., Jang, J.S.: On the improvement of singing voice separation for monaural recordings using the MIR-1K dataset. IEEE TASLP 18, 310–319 (2010)

Modified Incomplete Cholesky Preconditioned Conjugate Gradient Algorithm on GPU for the 3D Parabolic Equation*

Jiaquan Gao[1], Bo Li[1], and Guixia He[2]

[1] College of Computer Science and Technology, Zhejiang University of Technology,
Hangzhou 310023, China
gaojq@zjut.edu.cn
[2] Zhijiang College, Zhejiang University of Technology, Hangzhou 310024, China

Abstract. In this study, for solving the three-dimensional partial differential equation $u_t = u_{xx} + u_{yy} + u_{zz}$, an efficient parallel method based on the modified incomplete Cholesky preconditioned conjugate gradient algorithm (MICPCGA) on the GPU is presented. In our proposed method, for this case, we overcome the drawbacks that the MIC preconditioner is generally difficult to be parallelized on the GPU due to the forward/backward substitutions, and thus present an efficient parallel implementation method on the GPU. Moreover, a vector kernel for the sparse matrix-vector multiplication, and optimization of vector operations by grouping several vector operations into a single kernel are adopted. Numerical results show that our proposed forward/backward substitutions and MICPCGA on the GPU both can achieve a significant speedup, and compared to an approximate inverse SSOR preconditioned conjugate gradient algorithm (SSORPCGA), our proposed MICPCGA obtains a bigger speedup, and outperforms it in solving the three-dimensional partial differential equation.

Keywords: conjugate gradient algorithm, modified incomplete Cholesky preconditioner, parabolic equation, GPU.

1 Introduction

The conjugate gradient (CG) algorithm is one of the best known iterative methods. With a suitable preconditioner, the performance of the CG algorithm can be dramatically improved. The preconditioned conjugate gradient (PCG) algorithm has proven its efficiency and robustness in a wide range of applications. Following the introduction of CUDA (Compute Unified Device Architecture) by NVIDIA in 2007 in rent years [1], Graphic Processing Units (GPUs) have drawn much attentions. Many researchers have attempted to develop the suitable and flexible PCG algorithm for the GPU architecture. Related work can be found in [2–5].

* The research has been supported by the Chinese Natural Science Foundation under grant number 61202049 and the Natural Science Foundation of Zhejiang Province, China under grant number LY12A01027.

C.-H. Hsu et al. (Eds.): NPC 2013, LNCS 8147, pp. 298–307, 2013.

For a PCG algorithm, the key is how to parallel solve the equation $Mz = r$ (M is the preconditioned matrix) on GPUs when shifting it to the GPU platform. For the modified incomplete Cholesky factorization (MIC) preconditioning, $M = LDL^T$, where L is a lower triangular matrix. As we know, for solving the equation $LDL^T z = r$, the following two steps are required. First, $LDv = r$ is solved for v by the forward substitution, and then $DL^T z = Dv$ is solved for z by the backward substitution. It is obviously observed that the forward/backward substitutions are not easy to implement on GPUs if L does not have especial characteristics.

Due to the forward/backward substitutions, the MIC preconditioning is difficult to be parallelized on GPUs. In this study, we present an efficient method for parallelizing the forward/backward substitutions on the GPU, which is the main contribution. The reminder of this paper is organized as follows. In the second section, the problem and the MIC PCG algorithm are described. In the third section, some GPU kernels for the MIC PCG algorithm are proposed. Numerical results are presented in the fourth section. The fifth section contains our conclusions and points to our future research direction.

2   Problem and MIC PCG Algorithm

2.1   Problem Description

In this study, we consider the following partial differential equation (PDE):

$$\begin{cases} u_t = u_{xx} + u_{yy} + u_{zz}, & (x,y,z,t) \in \Omega \times [0,T], \\ u(x,y,z,0) = \phi(x,y,z), & (x,y,z) \in \Omega, \\ u(x,y,z,t) = 0, & (x,y,z,t) \in \partial\Omega \times [0,T], \end{cases} \tag{1}$$

where u is the solution, $\phi(x,y,z)$ is a function of variables x, y and z, Ω is a regular three-dimensional domain and $\partial\Omega$ denotes the boundary of Ω.

Here we utilize the discrete variational derivative method (DVDM) to discretize the PDE (1). As compared to the finite difference method (FDM), The DVDM can guarantee that the constructed numerical scheme retains the energy dissipation or conservation properties. According to the strategy of the DVDM to construct a dissipative scheme, we define an energy $G(u, u_x, u_y, u_z) = (u_x)^2/2 + (u_y)^2/2 + (u_z)^2/2$ of the PDE (1) and then obtain the numerical scheme as follows.

$$\begin{aligned} \frac{u_{i,j,k}^t - u_{i,j,k}^{t-1}}{\Delta t} = & \delta_i^{(2)} \left(\frac{u_{i,j,k}^t + u_{i,j,k}^{t-1}}{2} \right) + \delta_j^{(2)} \left(\frac{u_{i,j,k}^t + u_{i,j,k}^{t-1}}{2} \right) \\ & + \delta_k^{(2)} \left(\frac{u_{i,j,k}^t + u_{i,j,k}^{t-1}}{2} \right), \end{aligned} \tag{2}$$

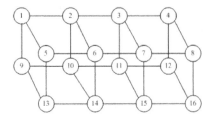

Fig. 1. A $4 \times 2 \times 2$ three-dimensional grid

where

$$\delta_i^{(2)} u_{i,j,k} = \frac{u_{i+1,j,k} - 2u_{i,j,k} + u_{i-1,j,k}}{(\Delta x)^2},$$

$$\delta_j^{(2)} u_{i,j,k} = \frac{u_{i,j+1,k} - 2u_{i,j,k} + u_{i,j-1,k}}{(\Delta y)^2},$$

$$\delta_k^{(2)} u_{i,j,k} = \frac{u_{i,j,k+1} - 2u_{i,j,k} + u_{i,j,k-1}}{(\Delta z)^2}.$$

Assume that a $4 \times 2 \times 2$ three-dimensional grid, shown in Fig. 1, is defined, the scheme (2) can be written as the following linear system for a certain time $t \in [0, T]$.

$$Au = b, \tag{3}$$

where the coefficient matrix A is denoted as follows:

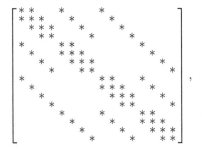

a sparse, symmetric, positive definite, seven-diagonal, diagonally dominant 16×16 matrix of regular structure, b is a vector of size 16, and u is an unknown solution vector of size 16. Therefore, it can be obviously seen that the key is to solve the linear system (3) for solving the 3D PDE (1).

2.2 MIC PCG Algorithm

For solving the symmetric linear system similar to (3), the PCG algorithm has proven its efficiency and robustness in a wide range of applications. Its detailed procedure is shown in Algorithm 1.

For the above linear system (3), the preconditioned matrix $M = LDL^T$, where L is a lower triangular matrix with nonzero values along the main diagonal

Algorithm 1. PCG algorithm for the linear system $Au = b$
Input: A, b; Output: u

01 $k = 0$
02 $u = [1, 1, \cdots, 1]^T, r = b - Au, Mz = r, p = z, \rho_0 = z^T r$
03 Repeat
04 $q = Ap, \alpha = \rho_0/p^T q$
05 $u = u + \alpha p$
06 $r = r - \alpha q$
07 $Mz = r$
08 $\rho_1 = z^T r, \beta = \rho_1/\rho_0, \rho_0 = \rho_1$
08 $p = r + \beta p$
09 $k = k + 1$
10 Until $(k < maxiter$ and $r^T r > tol)$

and at off-diagonal locations only where A has nonzero entries. Generally, the forward/backward substitutions both need n (n is the element number of the solution vector) steps to finish calculations of elements. However, we observe that the forward/backward substitutions for this case both can be finished in 6 steps instead of 16 steps according to the progressions shown in Fig. 2.

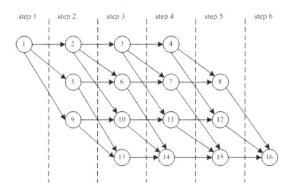

Fig. 2. Progression of the forward substitution

The computational grid in Fig. 2 is the same as in Fig. 1, and arrows represent dependencies between elements of the grid. The calculation of an element in each step does not only depend on its adjacent row and column neighbors, but also depends on its adjacent layer neighbors. For example, the element 14 is dependent to its adjacent row and column elements 10 and 13 and its adjacent layer element 6. However, not all elements have these neighbor elements and the number of neighbors varies with the location of the element. Moreover, for any element, its dependent neighbors must be calculated earlier than it in order to start its calculation. Moreover, the elements of each step are independent each other and can be concurrently calculated. All these things are helpful for shifting the forward/backward substitutions to the GPU platform.

3   GPU Kernels and Optimization

The primary kernels used in the implementation of Algorithm 1 are explained in this section. The kernels represented here perform mathematical operations used in Algorithm 1. Following Algorithm 1, the basic operations are sparse matrix-vector multiplications, vector operations and the forward/backward substitutions.

3.1   Sparse Matrix-Vector Multiplication

Here the sparse matrix A is stored with the compressed sparse row (CSR) format: (1) the array a contains all the nonzero elements of A; (2) the array *colidx* contains column indices of these nonzero elements; and (3) entries of array *rowstr* point to the first element of subsequent row of A in arrays a and *colidx*.

Sparse matrix-vector multiplications (SpMVs) represent the dominant cost in the PCG algorithm for solving large-scale linear systems. Fortunately, the SpMV for the CSR format is easy to be parallelized on the GPU. A straightforward CUDA implementation, which is referred to as the scalar kernel, uses one thread per row. However, its performance suffers from several drawbacks. The most significant among these problems is that threads with a warp (a bunch of 32 CUDA threads) can not access the arrays a and *colidx* in a coalesced manner. In [6], An alternative to the scalar kernel, called the vector kernel, assigns one warp to each matrix row. For the vector kernel, it accesses the arrays a and *colidx* contiguously, and therefore overcomes the principal deficiency of the scalar kernel.

Thus, here we will utilize the vector kernel to compute the SpMV on the GPU, and refer the readers interested in the detailed GPU implementation of the vector kernel to the literature [6].

3.2   Vector Operations

As we can see in Algorithm 1, the vector operations are the vector copy, the scalar vector product, the *saxpy* operation and the inner product of vector. In order to optimize these operations, we try to group several operations into a single kernel. For example, the *saxpy* operation as well as the vector copy are grouped in the same kernel. On the other hand, we perform the inner products needed for the computation of α and the inner products involved in the β computation in single kernels.

3.3   Forward/Backward Substitution

In this section, we will exhibit our proposed method of the forward/backward substitutions on the GPU. In order to better show our proposed method, the $4 \times 2 \times 2$ grid in Fig. 1 are extended to a $64 \times 48 \times 3$ grid.

Since the implementation technique of the forward substitution is also suitable for the backward substitution for this case, here we only discuss the forward substitution. Assume that each thread block is assigned with $x \times y$ solution elements, the number of required thread blocks can be calculated by the following formula:

$$N^{tb} = \left[\frac{NROW}{x}\right] \times \left[\frac{NCOL}{y}\right] \times NLAY. \tag{4}$$

By Eq.(4), 36 thread blocks are required if each thread block is assigned with 16×16 ($x = 16$ and $y = 16$) solution elements for the $64 \times 48 \times 3$ three-dimensional grid. A way of possible grouping of 36 thread blocks on the GPU is illustrated in Fig. 3.

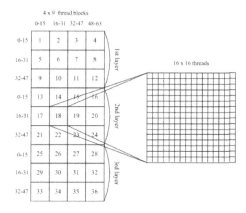

Fig. 3. 4×9 sized grid of GPU thread block

According to the progression of the forward substitution in Fig. 2, it is obviously found that the amount of data must be almost transferred between two adjacent thread blocks from the same layer and from the neighboring layers. For example, consider calculations of elements in thread block 18. To start its execution, on one hand, the thread block 18 must wait for transmission from its adjacent thread blocks 14 and 17 to which it is independent in the same layer; on the other hand, it also waits for transmission from its adjacent thread block 6 on which it depends in the neighboring layer. The total amount of data to be received from the same layer is $(x + y)$. However, the total amount of data to be received from the neighboring layers is $(x \times y)$. Since the data exchange between thread blocks must be performed on the GPU global memory, the transmissions will be the primary source of the overall communication latency.

Here in order to decrease the amount of exchanged data between thread blocks from the neighboring laryers, we utilize the share memory to store the values calculated by a thread block, and the thread blocks which are located in different layers and whose position are the same are mapped to a thread block. For example, thread block 1 in the first layer, thread block 13 in the second layer and thread block 25 in the third layer can be mapped to a thread block in Fig. 3. If so, the data exchange between thread blocks of the adjacent layers will be no longer required because they are located in the same thread block. Thus, the amount of exchanged data required is to decrease from $(x \times y + x + y)$ to $(x + y)$ when the elements in a thread block are calculated. For example, when calculating elements in thread block 18 in Fig. 3, only the data transmissions from its adjacent thread blocks 14 and 17 in the same layer are required, and thus the total amount of exchanged data is 32 rather than 288. At the same time, the number of required thread blocks is also reduced and can be calculated as

$$N^{tbnew} = \left\lceil \frac{NROW}{x} \right\rceil \times \left\lceil \frac{NCOL}{y} \right\rceil. \tag{5}$$

Therefore, the number of required thread blocks for this case is decreased from 36 to 12. Figure 4 summarizes the progression of the forward substitution with 12 active thread blocks.

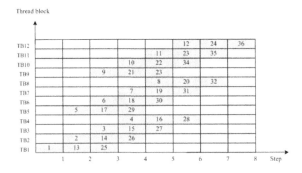

Fig. 4. Progression of the forward substitution with 12 active thread blocks

Furthermore, in order to decrease the frequency of reading data from the GPU global memory, we allocate a two-dimensional $(x + 1) \times (y + 1)$ array in shard memory instead of $(x \times y)$ to store data for a $x \times y$ sized thread block. The extra row and column are allocated for dependent data from neighbor thread blocks in the same layer. Moreover, to manage the dependencies between adjacent thread blocks, we store a matrix in the GPU global memory where each thread block can check the status of adjacent thread blocks to which it is dependent. A thread block waits for a spinlock until the dependent thread blocks finish calculations and write results to the global memory. Then it reads these results and continues with its calculations.

4   Numerical Results

All experiments in this section are conducted on the environment which is based on GNU/Linux Ubuntu v10.04.1 with an Intel Xeon Quad-Core 2.66 GHz, 12GB RAM (CPU) and NVIDIA Tesla C2050, 448 CUDA Cores, 6GB RAM (GPU).

Firstly, the following seven three-dimensional grid models, $800 \times 800 \times 30$, $480 \times 480 \times 80$, $480 \times 480 \times 320$, $128 \times 128 \times 480$, $512 \times 512 \times 256$, $128 \times 128 \times 1440$, $1440 \times 1440 \times 80$, are chosen to test the performance of our proposed forward substitution (GPUFBS). We respectively add up the computational time of GPUFBS and the CPU implementation of the forward/backward substitutions and then show them in Table 1. The time unit is microsecond denoted by ms.

Table 1. Speedups of GPUFBS

Grid model	CPU (ms)	GPU (ms)	Speedup
$800 \times 800 \times 30$	1020	125	8.16
$480 \times 480 \times 80$	1058	101	10.47
$480 \times 480 \times 320$	4784	278	17.20
$128 \times 128 \times 480$	458	39	11.74
$512 \times 512 \times 256$	3958	256	15.38
$128 \times 128 \times 1440$	1463	67	21.83
$1440 \times 1440 \times 80$	9560	893	10.70

From Table 1, we can see that GPUFBS achieves a significant speedup for all seven three-dimensional grid models due to high utilization of GPU. As observed from Fig. 4, the thread blocks have high concurrency and the concurrency of thread blocks is improved as the number of layers increases.

By observing $480 \times 480 \times 80$ and $480 \times 480 \times 320$ grid models, it can be found that when the column and row sizes are given, GPUFBS with high number of layers has a bigger speedup than that of with low number of layers. Similarly, it can also seen that for a given number of layers, GPUFBS with a big size of $column \times row$ achieves a higher speedup than that with a small size of $column \times row$ by comparing the $480 \times 480 \times 80$ grid model with the $1440 \times 1440 \times 80$ model. Furthermore, as observed from the $128 \times 128 \times 1440$ and $128 \times 128 \times 480$ grid models, for the same size of $column \times row$ (128×128), the speedup obtained by GPUFBS with 1440 layers is nearly 2 times of the speedup obtained by GPUFBS with 480 layers. However, we compare the $480 \times 480 \times 80$ grid model with the $1440 \times 1440 \times 80$ grid model and find that for the same number of layers 80, the speedup obtained by GPUFBS with 1440×1440 ($column \times row$) is only 1.02 times of the speedup obtained by GPUFBS with 480×480 ($column \times row$). Therefore, we can conclude that the number of layers and the column and row sizes both have an impact on the performance of GPUFBS, but the number of layers for GPUFBS has a larger impact than the column and row sizes.

Secondly, we test the validity of our proposed MIC PCG method on GPU (MICPCGA) for solving the 3D PDE comparing with the PCG algorithm on the GPU (SSORPCGA) suggested in [3]. Let $\Omega = \{(x,y,z) | 0 \leq x \leq 1, 0 \leq y \leq 1, 0 \leq z \leq 1\}$, $\phi(x,y,z) = 3 \sin \pi x \sin \pi y \sin \pi z$ for the PDE (1), and define the error (ER) $= \max |u_{i,j,k} - \tilde{u}_{i,j,k}|$, where $u_{i,j,k}$ and $\tilde{u}_{i,j,k}$ respectively denote the exact solution and the approximate solution at the point (x_i, y_j, z_k). For this case, the exact solution is $u(x, y, z, t) = 3e^{-3\pi^2 t} \sin \pi x \sin \pi y \sin \pi z$, and the following five grid models, $100 \times 100 \times 100$ (M21), $250 \times 250 \times 100$ (M22), $250 \times 250 \times 250$ (M23), $100 \times 100 \times 250$ (M24), $100 \times 100 \times 1000$ (M25), are chosen. In the following, taking $x = 0.5, y = 0.5(z = 0.1, 0.3, 0.5, 0.7, 0.9)$ for example, Table 2 shows the errors of MICPCGA and SSORPCGA. The speedups of MICPCGA and SSORPCGA are summed in Table 3.

Table 2. Errors of MICPCGA and SSORPCGA $(t = 0.1)$

Method	0.1	0.3	0.5	0.7	0.9
Exact solution(10^{-1})	0.4799	1.2565	1.5531	1.2565	0.4799
ER MICPCGA M21(10^{-5})	1.1236	1.2342	1.4347	1.2358	1.2362
ER MICPCGA M22(10^{-5})	1.1192	1.1331	1.3019	1.1376	1.1164
ER MICPCGA M23 (10^{-5})	0.5786	0.8941	1.1893	0.8937	0.5734
ER MICPCGA M24 (10^{-5})	1.0304	1.1343	1.2184	1.1342	1.0328
ER MICPCGA M25 (10^{-5})	1.0122	1.1121	1.1834	1.0101	1.0152
ER SSORPCGA M21 (10^{-5})	5.5632	5.9822	6.2876	5.9896	5.5617
ER SSORPCGA M22 (10^{-5})	4.9127	5.3939	5.9918	5.3908	4.9103
ER SSORPCGA M23 (10^{-5})	2.3243	2.4232	3.1967	2.4234	2.3253
ER SSORPCGA M24 (10^{-5})	5.1342	5.1458	5.7633	5.1442	5.1354
ER SSORPCGA M25 (10^{-5})	4.7482	4.8294	5.2304	4.8261	4.7476

Table 3. Speedups of MICPCGA and SSORPCGA

Method and Model	CPU (s)	GPU (s)	Speedup
MICPCGA M21	3.71	0.40	9.27
MICPCGA M22	23.91	2.43	9.83
MICPCGA M23	63.58	5.21	12.20
MICPCGA M24	9.62	0.93	10.34
MICPCGA M25	39.36	3.51	11.21
SSORPCGA M21	3.92	0.42	9.33
SSORPCGA M22	25.40	2.60	9.76
SSORPCGA M23	65.19	7.02	9.28
SSORPCGA M24	10.13	1.03	9.83
SSORPCGA M25	41.80	4.24	9.85

From Table 3, we can see that for models M21 and M22, MICPCGA has a comparable speedup with SSORPCGA, and for models M23, M24 and M25, MICPCGA obtains a bigger speedup than SSORPCGA. Furthermore, it can be found that MICPCGA can obtain better approximate solutions than SSOR-PCGA for all cases. Therefore, we can conclude that MICPCGA outperforms SSORPCGA for this case.

5   Conclusion

In this study, we present an efficient parallel method for the forward/backward substitutions on the GPU, and thus propose a MIC PCG algorithm on the GPU. Numerical results show that our proposed MIC PCG algorithm has a good behavior, and outperforms the PCG algorithm suggested by Helfenstein and Koko.

For GPUFBS, its efficiency has been validated in this study. Next, we will extend the constructing idea of GPUFBS to other PCG algorithms with the following preconditioners, the incomplete-LU factorization (ILU), the modified incomplete-LU factorization (MILU) and their variants, and furthermore do research for the three-dimensional partial differential equation.

References

1. NVIDIA Corporation: Cuda programming guide 2.3. Technical Report, NVIDIA (2009)
2. Buatois, L., Caumon, G.: Concurrent number cruncher: a GPU implementation of a general sparse linear solver. Int. J. Parallel Emergent Distrib. Syst. 24(3), 205–223 (2009)
3. Helfenstein, R., Koko, J.: Parallel preconditioned conjugate gradient algorithm on GPU. J. Comput. Appl. Math. 236(15), 3584–3590 (2012)
4. Gravvanis, G.A., Filelis-Papadopoulos, C.K., Giannoutakis, K.M.: Solving finite difference linear systems on GPUs: CUDA parallel explicit preconditioned biconjugate conjugate gradient type methods. J. Supercomput. 61(3), 590–604 (2012)
5. Galiano, V., Migallón, H., Migallón, V.: GPU-based parallel algorithms for sparse nonlinear systems. J. Parallel Distrib. Comput. 72(9), 1098–1105 (2012)
6. Bell, N., Garland, M.: Efficient sparse matrix-vector multiplication on CUDA. Technique report, NVIDIA (2008)

Partition-Based Hardware Transactional Memory for Many-Core Processors

Yi Liu[1], Xinwei Zhang[1], Yonghui Wang[1], Depei Qian[1], Yali Chen[2], and Jin Wu[2]

[1] Sino-German Joint Software Institute, Beihang University, Beijing 100191, China
[2] Huawei Technologies Co., Ltd, Shenzhen 518129, China
yi.liu@jsi.buaa.edu.cn

Abstract. Transactional memory is an appealing technology which frees pro-grammer from lock-based programming. However, most of current hardware transactional memory systems are proposed for multi-core processors, and may face some challenges with the increasing of processor cores in many-core systems, such as inefficient utilization of transactional buffers, unsolved problem of transactional buffer overflow, etc. This paper proposes PM_TM, a hardware transactional memory for many-core processors. The system turns transactional buffers that are traditionally private to processor cores into shared by moving them from L1-level to L2-level, and uses partition mechanism to provide logically independent and dynamically expandable transactional buffers to transactional threads. As the result, the solution can utilize transactional buffers more efficient and moderate the problem of transactional buffer overflow. The system is simulated and evaluated using gems and simics simulator with STAMP benchmarks. Evaluation results show that the system achieves better performance and scalability than traditional solutions in many-core processors.

Keywords: Transactional Memory, Partition, Many-core.

1   Introduction

Among works to improve programmability of parallel systems, transactional memory is an attractive one. Compared to traditional lock-based programming models, trans-actional memory can improve programmability, avoid deadlock and furthermore, promote performance of concurrent programs.

Most of current hardware transactional memory (HTM[1]) systems are proposed for multi-core processors, and may face some challenges with the increasing of pro-cessor cores in many-core systems: firstly, utilization of transactional buffers are inef-ficient since those buffers are private to processor cores while generally only part of cores execute transactions simultaneously in many-core processors; secondly, the on-going challenge of transactional buffer overflow for HTMs is still unsolved.

In this paper, we propose PM_TM, an architecture of hardware transactional mem-ory for many-core processors. The main idea consists of two points: firstly, turns pri-vate transactional buffer into shared by moving them from L1-level to L2-level; secondly, uses partition mechanism to provide logically independent and dynamically

C.-H. Hsu et al. (Eds.): NPC 2013, LNCS 8147, pp. 308–321, 2013.

expandable transactional buffers to transactional threads, and furthermore, to isolate access-interferences among large number of processor cores. As the result, the system can utilize transactional buffers more efficient and moderates the problem of transactional buffer overflow in many-core processors.

The rest of this paper is organized as follows. Section 2 analyzes problems of traditional hardware transactional memory in many-core environment and then gives an introduction to our solution. Section 3 presents the architecture of our proposed system. Section 4 evaluates the system with benchmarks. Section 5 introduces related works. And section 6 concludes the paper.

2   Challenges in Many-Core Processors and Our Solution

2.1   Problem Analysis

Most of current hardware transactional memory systems are proposed for multi-core processors, and may face some challenges in many-core systems.

Firstly, transactional buffers are inefficiently utilized and resources are wasted. Traditionally, transactional buffer is located inside processor cores in parallel with L1 data cache, which means it's private for the core. Processor core accesses transactional buffer only in transactional state, i.e. on executing transactions. However, in many-core processors, there will be a large number of processor cores, and generally only small part of them execute transactions simultaneously, while most of transactional buffers are not used at all.

Secondly, Problem of transactional buffer overflow is still unsolved. Generally, size of transactional buffer is fixed in each processor cores, when a transaction reads/writes too many data, buffer overflow will occur. This "buffer overflow problem" is one of ongoing challenges for hardware transactional memory. Despite some solutions have been proposed, most of them rely on co-working between cache-level transactional buffer and main memory or virtual memory, and need complex hardware/software operations.

This problem will even cause some kind of contradictions in many-core processors. On one hand, transactional buffers are inadequate in some processor cores that cause transactional buffer overflows due to some "long transactions", while on the other hand, transactional buffers in other processor cores may not be used at all.

2.2   Our Solution: An Overview

Based on the above discussions, we propose an architecture of hardware transactional memory, called PM_TM, for many-core processors. In our proposed solution, the transactional buffer is "logically independent" because that the transactional cache is partitioned into multiple partitions, each of them corresponds to one transactional thread and can only be accessed by it. The transactional buffer is "dynamically expandable" because that each partition is initially allocated a buffer with basic size, and can be expanded if the corresponding thread accesses excessive data speculatively in a transaction.

The advantages of the proposed solution include:

(a) Transactional buffers can be utilized more efficiently. In many-core environment, generally only part of processor cores execute transactions at the same time, that is, most of transactional buffers will be idle if they are private for cores. By turning them from private to shared, all of transactional buffers can be utilized by ongoing transactions, and the waste of resources can be reduced greatly.

(b) The problem of transactional buffer overflow is moderated. Since the transactional buffers are shared by all of the processor cores, and generally only part of cores execute transactions simultanously, by managing transactional buffers with partition mechanism and expanding partitions when necessary, a transaction can have much bigger transactional buffer than traditional private buffer. As the result, the possibilities of transactional buffer overflow are smaller.

In addition, from the implementation point of view, it is easier to integrate much bigger L2-level transactional buffer into processors than L1-level.

(c) Context switch and migration of transactional threads are easier to implement. For some long-transactions or transactions with system-calls, the operating system will suspend the transactional thread inside a transaction and schedule other threads to run on the core. After a while, the original transactional thread will be re-scheduled to run on either the same or a different core. Traditionally, this is a problem for HTMs since the transactional thread may face either a damaged or a totally new transaction context. In our proposed solution, the transactional buffer are shared by all of the cores and bound to transactional threads instead of cores, so the context switch and migration of transactional threads can be easily supported.

3   Partition-Based Hardware Transactional Memory Architecture

3.1   System Architecture

Fig.1 shows the architecture of tile-based[2],[12] many-core processors with support of our proposed hardware transactional memory. The system is composed of three types of tiles: the first type is tiles of processor cores plus private L1 cache and routing mechanism; the second is tiles of L2 cache banks; and the third is tiles of transactional cache (TC). All of the tiles are connected with an on-chip network, and both L2 cache and transactional cache are shared by all of the processor cores.

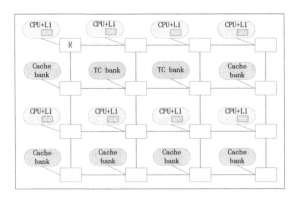

Fig. 1. System architecture

The transactional cache is used to buffer the data accessed by transactions speculatively, and as shown in Fig.2, its structure is similar to L2 cache and data is also stored by line. The difference is that the transactional cache holds both *old* and *new* version of data for each line, where the *old* version is the data that the transaction started with, and the *new* version is the current version updated by the transaction speculatively. Detailed introduction to consistency and conflict detection are given in section 3.3.

In addition, to support efficient nesting of transactions, the system uses a partial rollback mechanism which was proposed in our previous works [11]. The mechanism uses n-bits read and write vector for each line to indicate whether the line has been read or written speculatively, with each bit in the vector corresponding to one level of nested transactions. By adding limited hardware, conditional partial rollback can be implemented, that is, when a transaction needs to roll back due to a conflict, instead of rolling back to the outermost transaction as in commonly-used flattening model, the system can just rolls back to the conflicted transaction itself or one of its outer-level transactions if given conditions are satisfied.

Tag	State	Data		R	W
		old	new		
A				|||||||| ||||||||
B				|||||||| ||||||||

Fig. 2. Structure of transaction cache

In architecture level, transactional cache is in parallel with L2 cache. Commonly a processor core accesses L2 cache, and once a transaction is started, it switches to access transactional cache in order to guarantee that all the speculative accessed data are buffered and not valid until commit of the transaction.

3.2   Partition Mechanism

(1) Overview

Partition mechanism is a method to manage hardware resources in multi-/many-core processors. In our proposed system, partition mechanism is used to establish multiple logically independent transactional buffers, i.e. partitions, in shared transactional cache, furthermore, to make these transactional buffers dynamically expandable. In the system, transactional caches are allocated to partitions in partition-unit (PU) which corresponds to multiple successive lines in the transactional cache. Each partition corresponds to one transactional thread, and is created with one PU initially that can expand to multiple successive PUs if it is needed.

Partitions are created only for threads that execute transactions, called transactional thread. Once a thread executes a transaction at the first time, a partition is created with only one PU, and along with the increasing of read/write data set of a transaction, more PUs can be allocated to the partition dynamically if its transactional buffer overflows. After the commit of the first transaction, the partition is reserved and used by subsequent transactions of the thread, and finally released when the thread is finished.

It is noted that the owner of a partition is transactional thread rather than processor core. The reason is that transactional threads may be suspended during its execution and scheduled to run in another core after it is waked up later. In other words, migration of transactional threads can be supported by binding partitions with transactional threads instead of cores.

(2) Partition Access

When a thread starts to execute a transaction, it switches to access its transactional buffer (i.e. partition) instead of L2 cache. As Fig.3 shows, an associative buffer is used to store information of partitions including starting address, partition size and owner thread, with each entry corresponding to one partition. Based on this hardware infrastructure, the transactional buffer of a thread can be located quickly by means of the thread ID.

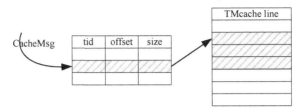

Fig. 3. Structure of transaction cache

(3) Partition Management

As mentioned above, a partition starts with one PU and may expand along with the execution of the transactional thread if excessive data are accessed in a transaction speculatively, and to simplify the management of partitions, it is limited that all of the PUs of a partition must be successive in transactional cache. In order to leave spaces at the end of partitions for potential expansions in the future, it's better to allocate partitions dispersedly in transactional cache.

According to above discussions, the system allocates the first partition from the beginning of transactional cache, and subsequent partitions are allocated in the following policy: searching for the biggest free area in the transactional cache, and allocating the PU in the middle of the area to the new partition.

Table 1 shows the addresses that will be allocated to partitions one by one, where B is the total size of transactional cache in lines, N is the number of processor cores, and the size of partition unit PU=B/N.

Table 1. Address allocation of partitions

Seq. of creation	Start address	Initial end address
0	*0*	*PU - 1*
1	*B/2*	*B/2 + PU - 1*
2	*B/4*	*B/4 + PU - 1*
3	*3B/4*	*3B/4 + PU - 1*
4	*B/8*	*B/8 + PU - 1*
...	...	...

A partitioning example is shown in Fig.4. In Fig.4(a), four partitions are created one by one for transactional thread T0--T3, and T0 has successfully expanded its partition in 1 PU; in Fig.4(b), thread T0 and T3 finish their execution and partitions are released, after that, a new partition is created for thread T4.

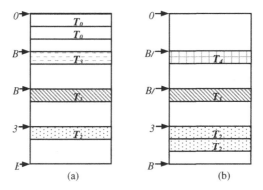

Fig. 4. Partitioning example

In addition, it is necessary to consider some extreme situations. Since partitions are created and maintained for transactional threads instead of processor cores, in some cases, there may be too many transactional threads in the system, or there may be some long-running transactional threads that occupy large amount of transactional cache permanently, so the associative table or transactional cache may be used out. At this time, a LRU-like (Least Recently Used) discard policy can be used to discard and release the partition that was not accessed for the longest time, the difference with the LRU policy is that, to make things simple, the partition is discarded instead of swap to main memory as in LRU. If the owner thread of the discarded partition re-accesses its partition later, a new partition will be created for it.

3.3   Consistency and Conflict Detection

The system uses lazy data version management and eager conflict detection policy, that is, all of the data modified in a transaction are buffered in the transactional buffer and invisible to other processor cores until commit of the transaction; and each memory access of a transaction is checked to identify if there is a conflict among transactions.

(1) Consistency and Directory

When a processor core starts to execute a transaction, it flushes data in L1 data cache and L2 cache to lower level and main memory in order to guarantee data consistency. In addition, write-through policy is used for L1 cache to write data directly into transactional buffer.

To achieve scalability in many-core processors, the consistency among multiple L1 data cache and transactional buffers(partitions) is maintained by distributed cache directory. As Fig.5(a) shows, structure of the directory is the same with ordinary cache directory except that the sharer list in each entry is extended to record not only which L1 cache but also which transactional buffer(partition) stores a copy of the line, as shown in Fig.5(b).

Once a line of L1 cache is updated, an invalidate message will be sent to each directory that stores a copy of the updated line. If such an invalidate message is received by directory of transactional cache, one or more conflicts will be triggered, depending on the number of partitions that store copy of the line. As the result, the corresponding transactions will abort their execution and roll back. Similarly, there also is a directory with the same structure in transactional cache. Once a line of transactional buffer is updated, an invalidate message is also sent to other sharers.

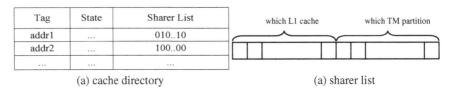

Tag	State	Sharer List
addr1	...	010..10
addr2	...	100..00
...	...	...

(a) cache directory   (a) sharer list

Fig. 5. Structure of cache directory

(2) Conflict Detection

Method to detect conflicts among transactions is: when a processor P reads/writes address A in a transaction, the cache controller sends a share-/exclusive-request to transactional cache directory, once the reply is received, it sets status of the transactional cache line to shared or exclusive; meanwhile, if another processor Q accesses address A too, the request is forwarded to processor P to identify if there is a write-write or read-write conflict, and consequently, to approve or reject the request.

Fig.6 shows examples of conflict detection:

(a) Transaction startup: processor P starts a transaction and switches to access transactional buffer.

(b) Writing data: P writes address A0 which is not in its transactional buffer, firstly it sends a get-exclusive request to directory, which is approved with the requested data, then P stores the data to its transactional buffer and sets write-flag, finally it replies an ACK to directory.

(c) Reading data: P reads address A1 which is not in its transactional buffer, the procedure is the similar to (b) except that the request is get-shared instead of get-exclusive.

(d) Transaction conflict: processor Q reads the address A0 which was just written by P, firstly it sends a get-shared request to directory, which is forwarded to P and identified as a read-write conflict, then a NACK is sent back to Q; Q deals with the conflict after receiving the NACK and replies a NACK to directory.

(e) Successful shared reading: processor Q reads the address A1 which was just read by P, the request is identified as conflict-free and approved.

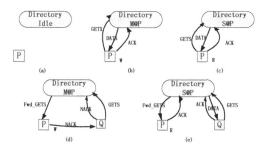

Fig. 6. Examples of Conflict Detection

3.4 Execution of Transactions

When a processor core starts to execute a transaction, it flushes data in L1 data cache and L2 cache to lower level and main memory, and switches to access transactional buffer instead of L2 cache.

During execution of a transaction, all of the data accessed by the transaction are buffered temporarily in its transactional buffer(partition). When a data is accessed for the first time in the transaction, it is loaded to both old and new version of the line in transactional buffer, subsequent updates to the data are just stored to new version, and R/W status are set at the same time.

Once the read/write-set of a transaction exceeds the partition size, a transactional buffer overflow occurs. At this time, the system tries to expand the partition by allocating one more PU in transactional cache. If the successive PU at the end of the partition is free, the partition can be successfully expanded and memory accesses are continued, otherwise it stalls for a short period of time and tries again. If there is still no free PU, the expanding operation fails and a global lock is set, the overflowed transaction continues exclusively without conflict until its commit. Of couse, the performance will be suffered in this situation.

If a transaction needs to roll back in case of conflict, data in transactional buffer are copied from old to new line by line, at the same time, R/W status are cleared, after that, all of the lines in L1 data cache are set to invalidate.

When a transaction finishes its execution and commit, all of the updated data in transactional buffer(partition) are written to main memory.

3.5 ISA Extensions and Programming Interface

As a hardware transactional memory, PM_TM supports transparent execution of transactions with no restriction on programming languages. Only two instructions are extended to specify the start and end of a transaction, as shown in Table 2. Programmers just need to identify program statements that must be executed atomically in their applications, and define them as transactions by inserting appropriate API at the beginning and the end of each transaction.

Table 2. Address allocation of partitions

Instruction	Description	Programming interface
XB	Trans. start	BEGIN_TRANSACTION()
XC	Trans. end	COMMIT_TRANSACTION()

4   Experiments and Evaluation

4.1   Experimental Environment

The proposed system is simulated in GEMS[13] and Simics[14], and by extending the simulator, our partition mechanism and consistency protocol are implemented on SPARC-architecture processors in the simulator.

We evaluate PM_TM system using Stanford STAMP[15] benchmark, and experimental results are compared with LogTM[5] and a native HTM, called NativeTM, in which transactional buffers are in L1-level and private to each processor core.

Table 3 summarizes parameters of the simulated target system.

Table 3. Configuration of target system

Processors	Ultrasparc-iii-plus, 1GHz
Cache size	L1: 64KB L2: 4MB
Size of cache line	64 bytes
Memory	1GB 80-cycle latency
Cache coherence protocol	MESI_CMP_filter_directory
Interconnection network	Tiled NoC; X-latency:1, Y-latency:2
Transactional cache	PM_TM: 1/2/4 MB; NativeTM: 8KB/core
Operation System	Solaris 10

The evaluation uses 4 applications that vary in size of read/write data set, length of transactions and contention degree among transactions, as in Table 4.

Table 4. Applications from STAMP benchmark

Application	R/W Set	Len. of transactions	Contention
intruder	medium	short	high
kmeans	small	short	low
vacation	large	medium	low
bayes	large	long	high

4.2   Results and Analysis

(1) Performance

Fig.7 shows average execution time of applications in PM_TM, LogTM and NativeTM with 4--128 processor cores. Each application is executed with number of threads equaling to processor cores.

We can see from Fig.7 that PM_TM behaves not very well in less processor cores. The main reason is that access latency of transactional buffers in PM_TM is longer than others due to its L2-level location. Along with the increasing of processor cores, PM_TM achieves better performance than two other systems, since that less transactional buffer overflow occur in PM_TM, and contentions among transactions are also handled more efficient in PM_TM.

Fig.7 also shows that results of different applications are not quite the same due to their characteristics. Kmeans has not only less transactions but also small read/write data set, so there is few transactional buffer overflows during the execution. As the result, the performance of Kmeans in PM_TM is not improved by the partition mechanism, instead, the performance is influenced by the long access latency of transactional buffers. Compared with kmeans, the intruder application has bigger read/write data set and higher contentions among transaction. So PM_TM achieves better performance along with the increasing of processor cores. Vacation has almost the same size of read/write data set with intruder, but vacation has some long transactions and contention in vacation is lower than intruder. Compared to other applications, the bayes has bigger read/write data set and longer transactions. Contention is also higher than the others.

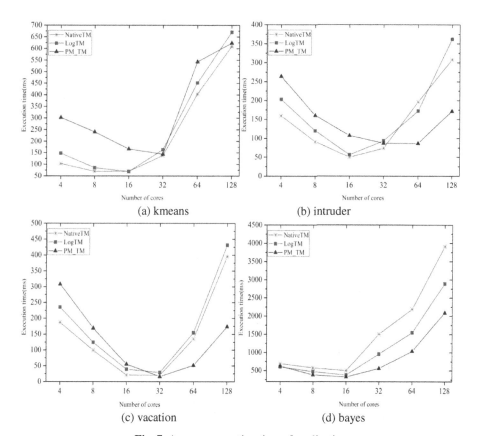

(a) kmeans

(b) intruder

(c) vacation

(d) bayes

Fig. 7. Average execution time of applications

Table 5. Transaction overflows

Application	System	Transactional buffer size	Number of processor cores					
			4	8	16	32	64	128
kmeans	NativeTM	8KB/core	0	0	0	0	0	0
	PM_TM	1MB	0	0	3	5	6	8
		2MB	0	0	2	3	5	6
		4MB	0	0	0	0	2	5
intruder	NativeTM	8KB/core	12	24	48	96	192	384
	PM_TM	1MB	0	0	4	8	29	52
		2MB	0	0	3	4	9	31
		4MB	0	0	0	0	3	7
vacation	NativeTM	8KB/core	19	33	56	131	263	477
	PM_TM	1MB	0	6	13	18	45	104
		2MB	0	0	7	11	18	47
		4MB	0	0	0	5	9	21
bayes	NativeTM	8KB/core	361	733	1307	1891	3249	4811
	PM_TM	1MB	173	267	661	1081	2033	4795
		2MB	30	181	277	649	1213	2258
		4MB	0	24	190	307	636	1309

(2) Transactional Buffer Overflows

Table 5 gives transaction overflow statistics of applications in NativeTM and PM_TM. LogTM is not included in this table because transactional data of LogTM is stored in the memory directly. From the table we can see that most applications overflow less in PM_TM than in NativeTM except kmeans, which has not only less transactions but also small read/write data set. Furthermore, with the increasing of L2-level transactional cache, the overflow times reduce significantly. As discussed in section 2.2, from the implementation point of view, it is easier to integrate much bigger L2-level transactional buffer into processors than L1-level buffer.

(3) Conflict and Rollback

Fig.8 shows transaction rollbacks of applications. LogTM uses bloom filter[16] to store transaction read/write data set, that may produce false-conflicts, and furthermore, the cost of abort in LogTM is much higher due to its eager version management. Compared to LogTM, PM_TM uses bit-set to record data set of transactions so that there is no false-conflict in it. And due to this reason, the number of conflicts in NativeTM is the same with PM_TM, and omitted in the figure.

In kmeans, transactions are small and shared data among transactions are few, so frequency of conflict is much lower than other programs. Transactions in intruder are slightly larger than kmeans, but frequency of conflict is much higher. Although vacation has some large transactions, competition between transactions in vacation is lower than intruder. As for bayes, PM_TM system is much better than LogTM in rollback test. Bayes has the largest R/W set among the four programs, so overflow times of bayes is the most.

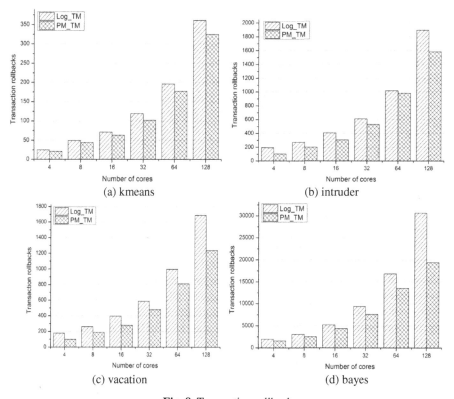

Fig. 8. Transaction rollbacks

5   Related Works

Transactional memory was firstly proposed in [1], since then, lots of hardware trans-actional memory (HTM) systems have been proposed that support atomicity of trans-actions by hardware, and achieves high performance. On the other hand, HTMs are often bounded by space and time constraints, i.e. transactional buffer overflow and transaction migration.

Some solutions have been proposed to deal with transactional buffer overflow. The simplest solution is partial-commit or in-place commit which uses a global lock or things like that to prevent other transactions to commit, until commit of the over-flowed transaction [2],[7],[8]. Beside partial-committing, some solutions deal with overflows by co-working between transactional buffer and memory[5],[6]; some solu-tions support unbounded transactions by means of complex hardware mechan-ism[4],[10]; hybrid transactional memory[9] has also been proposed, which integrates both hardware and software transactional memory, and switches to software mode in case of buffer overflow.

TM systems for many-core processors have also been proposed. TM^2C[17] is a software TM system which provides two services: the application service and the

Distributed TM service. The former connects transaction with the application and controls the transactional runtime. The latter grants a data access to the requesting transactions through distributed locking. The main contribution of TM^2C lies in guaranteeing starvation-freedom with low overhead.

LogTM[5] is a log-based HTM system. It saves old values in a log and puts new values in target address. When transaction commits, values in target address become visible and log is abandoned directly. This will accelerate the process of transaction committing. When rollback occurs, it simply copies old values in the Log to the target address. LogTM uses directory-based Cache consistency protocol to guarantee data consistency and eager conflict detection to find conflict between transactions.

6   Conclusion

Transactional memory is an appealing technology to improve programmability of multi-core and many-core processors. However, most of current hardware transactional memory systems are proposed for multi-core processors, and may face some challenges with the increasing of processor cores in many-core systems: firstly, utilization of transactional buffers are inefficient since those buffers are private to processor cores while generally only part of cores execute transactions simultaneously in many-core processors; secondly, the on-going challenge of transactional buffer overflow for HTMs is still unsolved.

This paper proposes an architecture of hardware transactional memory for many-core processors, called PM_TM. The main idea consists of two points: firstly, turns private transactional buffer into shared by moving them from L1-level to L2-level; secondly, uses partition mechanism to provide logically independent and dynamically expandable transactional buffers to transactional threads, and furthermore, to isolate access-interferences among large number of processor cores. As the result, the system can utilize transactional buffers more efficient and moderates the problem of transactional buffer overflow in many-core processors. The system is simulated and evaluated using gems and simics simulator with STAMP benchmarks. Evaluation results show that the system achieves better performance and scalability than traditional solutions in many-core processors.

Acknowledgements. This work was supported by National Science Foundation of China under grant No. 61073011, 61133004, and National Hi-tech R&D program(863 program) under grant No. 2012AA01A302.

References

1. Herlihy, M., Moss, J.E.B.: Transactional Memory Architectural Support for Lock-Free Data Structure. In: 20th International Symposium on Computer Architecture, pp. 289–300. IEEE (1993)
2. Moscibroda, T., Mutlu, O.: A Case for Bufferless Routing in On-Chip Networks. In: 36th International Symposium on Computer Architecture, pp. 196–207. IEEE (2009)

3. Hammond, L., Wong, V., Chen, M., et al.: Transactional Memory Coherence and Consistency. In: 31th International Symposium on Computer Architecture (ISCA 2004), pp. 53–65. IEEE CS Press (2004)

4. Scott Ananian, C., Asanovic, K., Kuszmaul, B.C., et al.: Unbounded Transactional Memory. In: 11th International Symposium on High-Performance Computer Architecture (HPCA 2005), pp. 316–327. IEEE CS Press (2005)

5. Moore Kevin, E., Jayaram, B., Moravan Michelle, J., et al.: LogTM: log-based transactional memory. In: 12th International Symposium on High-Performance Computer Architecture (HPCA 2006), pp. 258–269. IEEE CS Press (2006)

6. Ceze, L., Tuck, J., et al.: Bulk Disambiguation of Speculative Threads in Multiprocessors. In: 33rd International Symposium on Computer Architecture, pp. 227–238 (2006)

7. Shriraman, A., Spear, M.F., et al.: An Integrated Hardware-Software Approach to Flexible Transactional Memory. In: 34th Annual International Symposium on Computer Architecture, pp. 104–115. ACM (2007)

8. Shriraman, A., Dwarkadas, S., Scott, M.L.: Flexible Decoupled Transactional Memory Support. In: 35th International Symposium on Computer Architecture, pp. 139–150. IEEE & ACM (2008)

9. Kumar, S., Chu, M., Hughes, C.J., et al.: Hybrid Transactional Memory. In: 11th ACM SIGPLAN Symposium on Principles and Practice of Parallel Programming, pp. 209–220. ACM Press (2006)

10. Rajwar, R., Herlihy, M., Lai, K.: Virtualizing Transactional Memory. In: 32nd International Symposium on Computer Architecture, pp. 495–505. IEEE CS Press (2005)

11. Liu, Y., Su, Y., Zhang, C., Wu, M., Zhang, X., Li, H., Qian, D.: Efficient Transaction Nesting in Hardware Transactional Memory. In: Müller-Schloer, C., Karl, W., Yehia, S. (eds.) ARCS 2010. LNCS, vol. 5974, pp. 138–149. Springer, Heidelberg (2010)

12. Taylor, M.B., Lee, W., Miller, J., et al.: Evaluation of the raw microprocessor: An exposed-wire-delay architecture for ILP and streams. In: 31st Annual International Symposium on Computer Architecture, pp. 2–13 (2004)

13. Martin, M.M.K., Sorin, D.J., Beckmann, B.M., et al.: Multifacet's General Execution-driven Multiprocessor Simulator (GEMS) Toolset. SIGARCH Computer Architecture News, 92–99 (November 2005)

14. Magnusson, P.S., Christensson, M., Eskilson, J., et al.: Simics: A full system simulation platform. IEEE Computer Society 35(2), 50–58 (2002)

15. Minh, C.C., Chung, J., Kozyrakis, C., et al.: STAMP: Stanford Transactional Applications for Multi-Processing. In: 2008 IEEE International Symposium on Workload Characterization, pp. 35–46. IEEE CS Press (2008)

16. Bloom, B.H.: Space/time trade-offs in hash coding with allowable errors. Communications of the ACM, 422–426 (1970)

17. Gramoli, V., Guerraoui, R., Trigonakis, V.: TM2C: a Software Transactional Memory for Many-Cores. In: ACM European Conference on Computer Systems (EuroSys 2012), pp. 351–364 (2012)

Roadside Infrastructure Placement for Information Dissemination in Urban ITS Based on a Probabilistic Model

Bo Xie, Geming Xia, Yingwen Chen, and Ming Xu

Dept. of Network Engineering, Computer School,
National University of Defense Technology,
Changsha, China
{xiebo,xuming}@nudt.edu.cn, xiageming@126.com,
csywchen@gmail.com

Abstract. Information dissemination is an important application in VANETs for traffic safety and efficiency. In urban area, roadside infrastructure nodes can be deployed for information dissemination. However, it is inefficient and uneconomical to cover the whole urban area. How to find the optimal locations to place DPs is a research problem. Some works on this issue have to collect accurate trajectories of all the vehicles, which is not practical in the real environment. In this paper, we propose a novel approach for DPs placement in grid road networks without knowing trajectories. Based on the analysis of path number between two intersections, a probabilistic model is proposed to get the trajectories estimation of vehicles. The theoretical optimal algorithm (OA) and two heuristic algorithms (called KP-G and GA) are developed for the problem. Simulation results reveal that GA is scalable and has the highest coverage ratio on average.

1 Introduction

Information dissemination based on Vehicular Ad hoc Networks (VANETs) is intended to the support traffic safety and efficiency, as well as services for drivers [1–3]. In this paper, we deal with information dissemination from roadside infrastructure to passing vehicles, tackling the specific issue of deploying an intelligent transport system infrastructure that efficiently achieves the dissemination goal. For example, transport department can disseminate some traffic news to vehicles. We refer to the vehicles who have received the disseminated information as informed vehicles. Our goal is to maximize the number of informed vehicles. In other words, we aim at maximizing the coverage ratio of information dissemination.

In principle, an information dissemination system could leverage both vehicle-to-vehicle (V2V) and vehicles-to-infrastructure (V2I) communications. When only a few of roadside units (RSUs) are deployed, V2V communications could enable data sharing thus increasing the coverage ratio of information dissemination. However, the gain achieved through V2V communication strictly depends on the network topology

C.-H. Hsu et al. (Eds.): NPC 2013, LNCS 8147, pp. 322–331, 2013.
© IFIP International Federation for Information Processing 2013

and the particular cooperation paradigm, and it is difficult to evaluate in the general case. In this paper, we analyze the problem of optimally placing infrastructure nodes (e.g. IEEE 802.11 access points or RSUs) only considering V2I communications.

We refer to the infrastructure nodes as Dissemination Points (DPs). A DP serves for the vehicles that pass through the dissemination range of the DP. In other words, the vehicles who pass through a DP could be served (i.e., covered). However, it is difficult, in terms of infrastructure cost, to cover all roads with a large number of DPs, especially during the rollout of ITS. In our approach, DPs are placed at intersections which prove to be much better locations than road segments for DPs deployment in [4]. We could describe this problem as follows: in a given urban area which has N intersections with a limited number of k DPs ($k \leq N$), what is the best deployment strategy to maximize the coverage ratio of information dissemination.

We could model the problem as a Maximum Coverage Problem (MCP). However, traditional approaches of MCP may not be suitable for this problem for three reasons. First, the DPs deployed in the area neither have to necessarily form a connected network, nor provide a continuous coverage of the road topology. Second, vehicles move among these different DPs rather than be stationary. Third, vehicles may cross more than one intersection, thus they may be served by more than one DPs. The problem presented in this paper differs from traditional problems.

This problem could be solved through heuristic algorithms if we could get the accurate trajectory of every vehicle as in [4]. However, the drivers may not be willing to share their trajectories for privacy concerns. As a consequence, it is not practical to collect every vehicle's accurate trajectory for decision-making. Moreover, because the trajectories of all vehicles and the traffic pattern may change from time to time, the placement based on trajectories may not be stable. It means that the optimal placement based on a certain set of trajectories may not be optimal in another set of trajectories. Meanwhile, in real communication environments, it could not assure that a vehicle could receive the information from a DP when it passes the DP. We introduce a parameter ps to represent the probability that a vehicle could successfully receive information from a DP. The probability ps is a feature of a wireless link and may affect the deployment of DPs. Our scheme deploys DPs at the most appropriated locations based on ps rather than improving ps.

In this paper, we propose a novel approach to solve the problem without using vehicles' accurate trajectories. Instead of vehicles' accurate trajectories, we only need the road network topology, and vehicles' origin points and destination points. Note that in a certain observation time, most vehicles except taxis have specific origin points and destination points in one journey. Based on the analysis on the statistical or historical data, we could get the distributions of the numbers of vehicles at origin points and destination points. Then the trajectories estimation of vehicles could be derived. Then, we propose a theoretical optimal algorithm (OA) and two heuristic algorithms (called KP-G and GA) for the problem.

The remainder of this paper is organized as follows. Section 2 reviews the previous work. Section 3 presents a probabilistic model, and proposes an optimal algorithm as well as two heuristic algorithms. Performance evaluations are presented in Section 4. Section 5 concludes this paper.

2   Related Work

Wireless access point or base station placement is a well known research topic. In the context of sensor networks, several studies have considered the optimal node placement schemes which are always NP-hard. To tackle such complexity, several heuristics have been proposed to find sub-optimal solutions [5, 6] in presence of stationary nodes.

In VANETs and mesh networks, there are several studies on roadside units (RSUs) placement problem. Lochert et al. [7] have tackled the problem of sparse roadside units placement for data aggregation but not information dissemination. Sun et al. [8] propose cost-efficient RSUs deployment scheme for short-time certificate updating. In this scheme, OnBoard Units (OBUs) in any place could communicate with RSUs in certain driving time, and the extra overhead time used for adjusting routes to update short-time certificates is small. Pan et al. [9] address the problem of optimally placing one or multiple gateways in both 1-D and 2-D vehicular networks to minimize the average number of hops from APs. They also give some analytical results for finding the optimal placement of multiple gateways in 2-D vehicular grid networks and discuss how to minimize the total power consumption. Abdrabou et al. [10] present an analytical framework to statistically estimate the maximum packet delivery delay from a vehicle to an RSU for a low density VANET via vehicle-to-vehicle communications. Aoun et al. [11] propose a polynomial time near-optimal algorithm which recursively computes minimum weighted Dominating Sets (DS), while consistently preserving QoS requirements across iterations. Trullols et al. [4] have done the closest work to ours. They propose three heuristic deployment algorithms MCP-g, MCP-sz and KP-P for information dissemination in intelligent transportation systems. However, their heuristic algorithms need the accurate trajectory of every vehicle. The difference between our work and [4] is that we could make approximate optimal DPs placement only based on road network topology and vehicles' origin points and destination points. We also consider the probability of vehicles served.

3   Probabilistic Model and Placing Algorithms

3.1   Problem Statement

We consider an urban grid road network. As in many Chinese cities, the road networks are very regular which could be mapped into grid road networks. Literature [4] reveals that intersections prove to be much better locations than road segments for DPs deployment. Thus, we also place DPs at intersections. We assume that each DP cover only one intersection, which means that only vehicles cross it could be served (i.e., covered). Our goal is to place the k DPs for maximizing the number of informed vehicles. However, we would not need vehicle's accurate trajectories for two reasons. As first important, vehicles may not share their trajectories for privacy concerns, and it is also impossible and unpractical to collect those sensitive individual data. On the other hand, the placements based on trajectories are not stable due to trajectories may change time to time. It is not flexible to deploy DPs in real world.

We propose a probabilistic model based on the distributions of the origin points and destination points of vehicles in an urban environment. As we know, most vehicles except taxis have specific origin points and destination points in one journey. For example, during 7:00am and 8:00am, they drive from their home to offices. Then they park their vehicles near their offices. The residence is the origin point, and the parks near offices are the destination points. While the path from origin point to destination point is uncertain for different reasons. For example, they could choose the path according to the real time traffic, or according to their favor, or by GPS-based navigation systems, and so on. We study the probability of vehicles crossing each intersection by random path selection.

3.2   Number of Paths

In a given grid road network, the number of paths between two intersections is needed to be calculated. We assume that vehicles always select the shortest paths. Traditional approaches search the shortest paths using graph theory such as Dijkstra algorithm. However, it is not sufficient for grid networks due to so many paths with the same shortest distance. As shown in Fig.1, we assume the length of each segment is the same.

Let $FP((i_1, j_1)(i_2, j_2))$ denote the number of paths between (i_1, j_1) and (i_2, j_2). To reduce the dimension of FP, we use a integer x to represent the intersection (i, j) in $m \times n$ grid road network, where $x = (i-1) \cdot n + j$. Therefore, $FP((i_1, j_1)(i_1, j_1))$ could be denoted as $fp(x_1, x_2)$.

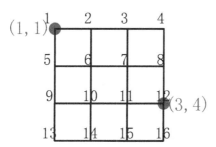

Fig. 1. 4×4 Grid Road Network

$fp(x_1, x_2)$ could be calculated as Eq.(1).

$$fp(x_1, x_2) = FP((i_1, j_1)(i_2, j_2)) = F(\Delta i, \Delta j) = \frac{(\Delta i + \Delta j)}{\Delta i! \Delta j!} \tag{1}$$

In Eq.(1), $\Delta i = | i_1 - i_2 |$, and $\Delta j = | j_1 - j_2 |$. For example, $fp(1, 12) = FP((1,1)(3,4))$ $= F(2,3) = 10$.

3.3   Origin Points and Destination Points

The origin points and destination points will be any places on the road segment; however, we could map these points into the intersections. For example, as shown in Fig. 2, a vehicle named A starts from point a where located at north of the road segment. The circle line figures out the dissemination range of each DP. The origin point of vehicle A is out range of any DPs. According to the traffic rule, vehicles should run on the right side, therefore, we regard the origin point of vehicle A as intersection (2,2). It is the similar for destination points. If a vehicle's destination point is out range of any DP, we regard the last intersection which it has crossed as its destination point. We use matrices G and D to denote the distributions of the numbers of vehicles at origin points and destination points.

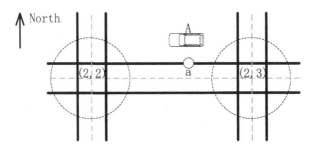

Fig. 2. Mapping Origin Point into Intersection

3.4   Probabilistic Model and Algorithms

In the $m \times n$ grid network, let (i_k, j_k) denote the original address of intersection x_k . Here, $1 \le i_k \le m$, $1 \le j_k \le n$ and $x_k = (i_k - 1) \cdot n + j_k$. We introduce several probabilities as listed Table 1.

We use Coverage Ratio (CR) to evaluate the final performance of the algorithms. CR means the proportion of the number of vehicles served by DPs to the number of total vehicles during the observation time. We could use Eq.(2) to compute CR.

Table 1. Probability Symbols

Symbol	Description
ps_x	The probability that a vehicle is served when it crosses x
pa_x	The probability that a vehicle has once appeared at x
pg_x	The probability that a vehicle starts from x
pd_x	The probability that a vehicle disappears at x
$pod_{x_o x_d}$	The probability that a vehicle is start from x_o and disappears at x_d
pp_x	The probability that a vehicle passes through the intersection x but neither starts from nor disappears at x
$pf_c(x_1,...,x_c)$	The probability that a vehicle passes through these c intersections, $c > 1$

$$CR = \frac{|\bigcup_{i=1}^{i=k} V_{x_i} \cdot ps_{x_i}|}{NVT} < \sum_{i=1}^{i=k} pa_{x_i} \cdot ps_{x_i} \tag{2}$$

In Eq.(2), V_{x_i} means the set of vehicles that cross x_i, and NVT means the total number of vehicles during the observation time. Therefore, $|\bigcup_{i=1}^{i=k} V_{x_i} \cdot ps_{x_i}|$ means the total number of vehicles that have been served by one or more of DPs which are placed at these k intersections. However, it is quite difficult to compute the accurate CR. It is obvious that CR is fewer than $\sum_{i=1}^{i=k} pa_{x_i} \cdot ps_{x_i}$ which could be used as approximate value and obtained with less computation. According to the above analysis, we propose an optimal algorithm OA, and two heuristic algorithms KP-G and GA. The optimal algorithm OA could only be used in small scale situations due to its high computational complexity.

The optimal algorithm OA and heuristic algorithm KP-G are listed as following, respectively.

Algorithm 1. OA

1: **Initialize,** $U = \{1, ..., N\}$.

2: **for** every subset $\{x_1, ..., x_k\} \subseteq U$ do

3:　　calculate the accurate CR as Eq.(2).

4:　　compare the CR, find the largest CR and $\{x_1, ..., x_k\}$.

5: **end for**

Algorithm 2. KP-G

1: **Initialize,** $v = \{0\}$.

2: **for** every intersection x_i do

3:　　$v_i = pa_{x_i} \cdot ps_{x_i}$.

4: **end for**

5: sort v in descending order, select the first k intersections

---

Obviously, $pf_k < pf_{k-1} < ... < pf_2 < pa$, pf_2 plays a more important role in Eq.(2) than other pf_c with $c > 2$. In large grid road networks, pf_c are relatively small. Therefore, in GA, we use pf_2 to approach the accurate CR. It will lose some performance comparing with OA, but it has quite low computational complexity.

We use $k = 3$ to explain how to compute CR with pf_2 as Eq.(3).

$$CR = \frac{|\bigcup_{i=1}^{i=k} V_{x_i} \cdot ps_{x_i}|}{NVT}$$
$$\approx (pa_{x_1} - pf_2(x_1, x_2) - pf_2(x_1, x_3)) \cdot ps_{x_1}$$
$$+ (pa_{x_2} - pf_2(x_1, x_2) - pf_2(x_2, x_3)) \cdot ps_{x_2}$$
$$+ (pa_{x_3} - pf_2(x_1, x_3) - pf_2(x_2, x_3)) \cdot ps_{x_3}$$
$$+ pf_2(x_1, x_2) \cdot (1 - (1 - ps_{x_1}) \cdot (1 - ps_{x_2}))$$
$$+ pf_2(x_1, x_3) \cdot (1 - (1 - ps_{x_1}) \cdot (1 - ps_{x_3}))$$
$$+ pf_2(x_2, x_3) \cdot (1 - (1 - ps_{x_2}) \cdot (1 - ps_{x_3}))$$

(3)

The heuristic algorithm GA is listed as following.

Algorithm 3. GA

1: **Initialize**, $S = \phi$, $c = 0$, $U = \{1,...,N\}$.

2: **while** $c < k$ do

3:    $c = c + 1$.

4:    **for** every $x_i \in U$ do

5:        $S(c) = x_i$.

6:        compute the CR of S as Eq.(3).

7:    **end for**

8:    select x_i that maximizes CR, $S(c) = x_i$.

9:    $U = U - x_i$.

10: **end while**

---

4   Performance Evaluation

In this section, we conduct simulations to evaluate the performance of the proposed algorithms. Note that, we do not concern ourselves with low-level issues in wireless communications.

In [4], a heuristic algorithm KP-P is proposed based on the knowledge of the number of vehicles crossing each intersection. KP-P sorts the intersections in descending order by their crossing vehicles, and selects the first k intersections to place DPs. Using the trajectories generated by our simulator, we could implement KP-P. Therefore, the results of KP-P could be regarded as the simulation results of our KP-G. The CR of GA, KP-G, OA, and KP-P are evaluated in this section. Therefore, we compare the four algorithms in the following subsections.

4.1   Small Scale Scenarios

In this subsection, we use small m, n, k, and we compare the four algorithms. Due to computational complexity, OA is computationally feasible only for small values of k in very small scale scenarios. We use 4×4 grid road network as shown in Fig. 1. When $k > 4$, the computational complexity is too high to obtain the optimal solution. We give the CR of OA with $k = 2, 3, 4$. We use the same ps_x for every intersection.

As shown in Fig. 3, we could get the following conclusions. First, both simulation results of OA and KP-G are excellently agree with the analytical results. It demonstrates the accuracy of our model. Second, GA is much better than KP-G and KP-P, and even has the same performance as OA. For a given CR, GA needs fewer DPs, and for a certain number of DPs, GA could achieve higher CR. However, with the decline of ps, the performance benefit of GA becomes more unremarkable, and the overall CRs of all algorithms become smaller. In real environment, we always attend to increase the probability ps, therefore GA is much more useful than other algorithms.

We then study the detailed placements of the four algorithms. For example, Table 2 shows the placements with $ps = 1$. The integers represent the intersection sequence numbers as shown in Fig. 1. When $k = 2$, the placements of the four algorithms are respectively $\{11,6\}$, $\{11,10\}$, $\{10,7\}$, $\{6,11\}$. When $k = 4$, the placements are respectively $\{11,6,8,9\}$, $\{11,10,7,6\}$, $\{11,7,10,6\}$, $\{4,7,10,13\}$. With the increment of k, we only need to add additional points into the original sets for GA, KP-G, KP-P, whereas we have to change all the points of OA. In other words, GA, KP-G, KP-P could yield incremental placements, whereas OA has to compute the results for different k. The difference between the placements of KP-G and KP-P is not remarkable. Note that, CR of GA reaches 1 for $k = 6$, whereas KP-G and KP-P both need 8 DPs for $CR = 1$. For GA, the placements listed in Table 2 is not unique for $k = 8$. The last two intersections could be replaced by any other intersections.

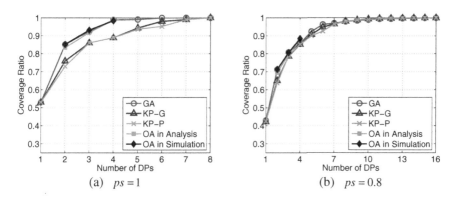

(a) $ps = 1$

(b) $ps = 0.8$

Fig. 3. CR versus the number of DPs deployed, for 4×4 grid road network

Table 2. Placement of Every Algorithm

Algorithm	Placement
GA	$\{11, 6, 8, 9, 3, 14, 16, 1\}$
KP-G	$\{11, 10, 7, 6, 15, 2, 14, 8\}$
KP-P	$\{11, 7, 10, 6, 14, 15, 2, 3\}$
OA	$\{6, 11\}, \{6, 11, 16\}, \{4, 7, 10, 13\}$

4.2   Large Scale Scenarios

For a large grid network of 6×9, there are $N = 54$ intersections. We study more DPs as $k = 27$ which is half of N. Because OA could not be solved within acceptable time even when $k = 2$ in this large network, we only compare GA with KP-G and KP-P. We generate a pair of random 6×9 matrices of G and D which are referred to as G_2 and D_2, and generate another symmetrical pair of matrices as G_3 and D_3. In G_3 and D_3, all vehicles start from and also disappear at the borders of the grid. It is an extreme special case.

There are similar conclusions with that in small scale scenarios. Furthermore, from Fig. 4, we could find that different G and D cause different performances. However, GA is still better than KP-G and KP-P. In Fig. 4(b), CRs of KP-G and KP-P have remarkable difference for some k due to its extreme special G_3 and D_3. Whatever the different G and D are, the benefit of GA is very remarkable, especially with $3 < k < 13$.

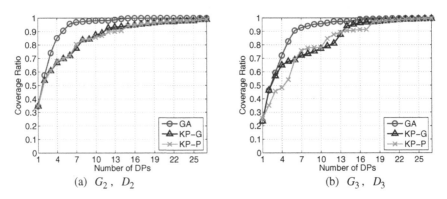

(a) G_2, D_2 (b) G_3, D_3

Fig. 4. CR versus the number of DPs deployed, for 6×9 grid road network, $ps = 1$

5   Conclusion

In this paper, we proposed a novel maximum coverage approach for disseminating information to vehicles in intelligent system in urban area without using vehicles' trajectories. We proposed a probabilistic model based on the distributions of the numbers of vehicles at origin points and destination points to get the trajectories estimation of the vehicles. We applied this model to compute the coverage ratio. Next, an optimal algorithm OA and two heuristic algorithms KP-G and GA were proposed. It was not practical to adopt OA due to high computational complexity. Our results proved that GA had better performance than the other algorithms in most of scenarios. However, we still remarked that in different scenarios with different parameters and conditions, it was better to compare the algorithms and choose the best one.

In fact, the road networks of many cities are not regular grid. We could still map the road networks into grids through some mechanisms which will be our future work. Drivers may choose paths with the different probabilities, thus other path selection models will also be considered in our future work.

Acknowledgment. This research is partially supported by the National Science Foundation of China under Grant No. 61070211, No. 61272485, No. 61070201 and No. 61003304; and Hunan Provincial Natural Science Foundation of China under grants No. 09JJ4034.

References

1. Dikaiakos, M.D., Iqbal, S., Nadeem, T., Iftode, L.: Vitp: an information transfer protocol for vehicular computing. In: Proceedings of the 2nd ACM International Workshop on Vehicular Ad Hoc Networks, VANET 2005, pp. 30–39. ACM, New York (2005)
2. Mak, T.K., Laberteaux, K.P., Sengupta, R.: Amulti-channel vanet providing concurrent safety and commercial services. In: Proceedings of the 2nd ACM International Workshop on Vehicular Ad Hoc Networks, VANET 2005, pp. 1–9. ACM, New York (2005)
3. Yang, X., Liu, L., Vaidya, N., Zhao, F.: A vehicle-to-vehicle communication protocol for cooperative collision warning. In: The First Annual International Conference on Mobile and Ubiquitous Systems: Networking and Services, MOBIQUITOUS 2004, pp. 114–123 (August 2004)
4. Trullols, O., Fiore, M., Casetti, C., Chiasserini, C., Barcelo Ordinas, J.: Planning roadside infrastructure for information dissemination in intelligent transportation systems. Computer Communications 33(4), 432–442 (2010)
5. Arkin, E.M., Efrat, A., Mitchell, J.S., Polishchuk, V., Ramasubramanian, S., Sankararaman, S., Taheri, J.: Data transmission and base-station placement for optimizing the lifetime of wireless sensor networks. Ad Hoc Networks (in press)
6. Capone, A., Cesana, M., Donno, D.D., Filippini, I.: Deploying multiple interconnected gateways in heterogeneous wireless sensor networks: An optimization approach. Computer Communications 33(10), 1151–1161 (2010)
7. Lochert, C., Scheuermann, B., Wewetzer, C., Luebke, A., Mauve, M.: Data aggregation and roadside unit placement for a vanet traffic information system. In: Proceedings of the Fifth ACM International Workshop on VehiculAr Inter-NETworking, VANET 2008, pp. 58–65. ACM, New York (2008)
8. Sun, Y., Lin, X., Lu, R., Shen, X., Su, J.: Roadside units deployment for efficient short-time certificate updating in vanets. In: 2010 IEEE International Conference on Communications (ICC), pp. 1–5 (May 2010)
9. Li, P., Huang, X., Fang, Y., Lin, P.: Optimal placement of gateways in vehicular networks. IEEE Transactions on Vehicular Technology 56(6), 3421–3430 (2007)
10. Abdrabou, A., Zhuang, W.: Probabilistic delay control and road side unit placement for vehicular ad hoc networks with disrupted connectivity. IEEE Journal on Selected Areas in Communications 29(1), 129–139 (2011)
11. Aoun, B., Boutaba, R., Iraqi, Y., Kenward, G.: Gateway placement optimization in wireless mesh networks with qos constraints. IEEE Journal on Selected Areas in Communications 24(11), 2127–2136 (2006)

Relay Hop Constrained Rendezvous Algorithm for Mobile Data Gathering in Wireless Sensor Networks

Wenjun Liu, Jianxi Fan*, Shukui Zhang, and Xi Wang

School of Computer Science and Technology, Soochow University,
Suzhou, 215006, China
{w-jliu,wangxi0414}@163.com, {jxfan,zhansk}@suda.edu.cn

Abstract. Recent research shows that significant energy saving can be achieved in wireless sensor networks (WSNs) by introducing mobile collector (MC). One obvious bottleneck of such approach is the large data collection latency due to low mobile speed of MC. In this paper, we propose an efficient rendezvous based mobile data gathering protocol for WSNs, in which the aggregated data will be relayed to Rendezvous Node (RN) within bounded hop d. The algorithm design in the protocol jointly considers MC tour and data routing routes in aggregation trees. The effectiveness of the approach is validated through both theoretical analysis and extensive simulations.

Keywords: Wireless Sensor Networks, NP-Hard, Mobile collector, Rendezvous node.

1 Introduction

In recent years Wireless Sensor Networks (WSNs) have become an attractive technology for a large number of applications, ranging from monitoring [1], localization [2], to target tracking [3]. To design and deploy sophisticated WSNs, many issues need to be resolved such as node deployment, energy conservation, routing in dynamic environments, and so on. Specifically, most of these existing solutions for data collection take advantage of multi-hop routing to relay data. One obvious drawback of this schema is that it leads to unbalanced energy consumption among the sensors on the transmission path to sink [4].

Recent research has shown a rapid transition from traditional data gathering pattern to introduction of mobile elements, which can improve energy efficiency, connectivity, and reliability effectively [5]. A typical application scenario is that a forest ranger who equipped with handheld device roams in the network and gathers the information of detective area. In such an application, mobile user can visit different regions in the network and communicate with the sensors nearby in single hop paradigm, which reduces not only contention and collisions, but also the message loss. However, due to the low velocity of the mobile collector,

---

* Corresponding author.

C.-H. Hsu et al. (Eds.): NPC 2013, LNCS 8147, pp. 332–343, 2013.

usually 0.5-2m/s, e.g. Packbot [6], it would incur long latency if every node is traveled in data gathering [5]. Obviously, it can not meet the requirement of time-sensitive applications.

In order to shorten data gathering latency, integrating multi-hop transmission scheme into mobile data gathering is an effective approach [7], in which a subset of sensors is selected as Rendezvous Node (RN). In this pattern, at every transmission hop each node aggregates the local data from its affiliated sensors, until delivers to RN which caches and uploads data to the mobile collector (MC) when it arrives. However, it is necessary that the transmission hop should be constrained as a proper level for several reasons. First, energy saving is considered as the most important concern in WSNs. Adopting multi-hop routing to relay data can easily result in unbalanced energy consumption among sensors, and it is adverse for energy-limited nodes. Second, a big relay hop means that the node acting as RN should have high performance to aggregate and cache data before MC arrives. Third, time-sensitive applications often require the sensing data to be delivered with certain deadline. For instance, in the application of forest fire monitoring, the fire should be detected and reported instantly.

The main contributions of this paper can be summarized as follows: 1) We define the mobile data gathering problem based on RN as MDG-RN, which jointly considers MC tour and routes in aggregation trees, and prove it is NP-Hard. 2) We develop two efficient algorithms to solve the MDG-RN problem. The former is a heuristic algorithm which always selects the node with maximum load from the d-hop neighbors of the current farthest node to BS. The latter caters to the characteristic of WSNs, and selects RN iteratively in distributed manner. On the basis of selected RNs, using algorithm for Traveling Salesman Problem (TSP) to produce MC tour, along which MC periodically visits these RNs and picks up the cached data. 3) Simulation results show that both algorithms can achieve satisfactory performance comparing with existing schemes.

The rest of the paper is organized as follows: Section 2 reviews related work. Section 3 introduces the network model and problem definition. The major contributions are introduced in Section 4 and Section 5. The simulation results are presented in Section 6. Finally, Section 7 concludes this paper.

2   Related Work

Recently, many research efforts have appeared in the literature to explore mobility-enable data collection in sensor networks [5-13]. These approaches may be classified as uncontrollable or controllable in general [5]. The former is obtained by attaching a collector node on certain mobile entity such as an animal or a bus; the latter is achieved by intentionally adding a mobile entity e.g., a mobile robot or an unmanned aerial vehicle, into the network to carry the collector. Clearly, a controlled mobility gives more flexibility for designing a data collection scheme.

The major performance bottleneck of such mobility-enabled WSNs is the increased latency in data collection. There are many approaches address to the delay problem. The first category is using the single hop transmission scheme. It is not difficult to conclude that direct-contact data collection is generally equivalent to the NP-complete TSP. Nesamony et al. [8] formulated the traveling problem as TSP with Neighborhood, where a MC needs to visit the neighborhood of each sensor exactly once. He et al. in [9] proposed a progressive optimization approach, called CSS, to reduce the tour length, and thus the data collection latency. This kind of approach minimizes the network energy consumption by one hop transmission, but it incurs high latency when collecting data from large sensing fields due to the slow speed of MC.

In second category multi-hop transmissions is adopted. Ma et al. [10] gave a moving path planning algorithm by finding some turning points, which is adaptive to the sensor distribution and can effectively avoid obstacles on the path. In [11], Gatzianas et al. optimized data gathering performance by presenting a distributed maximum lifetime routing algorithm, where a mobile collector sequentially visits a set of anchor points and each sensor transmits data to the mobile collector at some anchor points via multi-hop paths. Such type of approach reduces latency effectively. However, without the hop count constraint, the unbalanced energy consumption leads to untimely network partition.

The last category is a hybrid approach with constraint conditions that usually jointly considers multi-hop data transmissions and the moving tour of MC in data collection. Xing et al. [12] proposed a rendezvous-based data collection approach under the constraint that the tour length of the mobile collector is no longer than a threshold. With the relay hop constraint, Zhao et al. [13] proposed a polling-based mobile data gathering scheme that minimize the tour length of MC and data gathering latency. They give two algorithms to find a set of PPs among sensors. In [7], Rao et al. establishes bounds for multi-hop routing as a function of sensor and MC parameters such as data generation rate, sink speed and sensor density. They developed a framework to parameterizes multi-hop routing using a hop-bound factor k. Their model revealed that for stable mobile sink operation, there exists a feasible range of the hop-bound factor k. The approach studied in this paper falls into this category.

3   Preliminary

3.1   Network Model

We assume N sensor nodes are scattered randomly over the interest area and left unattended to continuously sense and report events. There is a static BS located in the center of sensing area and a mobile collector (MC) moved in controlled mobility. MC knows its own physical locations through the GPS units on it. However, for generality, we do not make such assumption on sensor nodes. Under the consideration of same communication range, the communication links are symmetric. We consider WSN as a undirected graph $G(V, E)$, where the vertex set V represents all the sensors and the edge set E represents the communication links. Two vertices, u and v in V, are *adjacent* if there is a edge $e=(u,v)\in E$, then we say u is neighbor of v, and vice versa. A *path* $P = < v_1, v_2, \cdots, v_l >$ of length l - 1 for $l \geq 2$ in G is a sequence of distinct vertices such that any two consecutive vertices are adjacent. The *neighbors* of a vertex v, denoted by $N(v)$, is the set of all vertices adjacent to v in G. The *d-hop neighbors* of node v is denoted by $d\text{-}N(v)$.

In data-centric WSNs, data from sources will be sent to RN or BS continuously, thus the data routes should be created in advance. On the basis of underlying topology G, a set of directed aggregation tree $T = \{T_i\}$ represents logic communication topology. For any T_i, $0 < i < N$, its root is the node r_i in RN. For any link $e \in G$, the communication cost is represented by its Euclidean distance. In addition,we assume the N-to-one aggregation model is adopted, in which a node can aggregate multiple data packets it received into one packet before relaying it [14].

3.2 Definitions

In the data collection schema, the RNs cache the data originated from sources and send to the MC via short-range transmissions when it arrives. The requirement is that the total length of MC tour should be minimized under the relay hop constraint. We refer to this problem as Mobile Data Gathering based on Rendezvous Nodes (MDG-RN) which is defined as follow:

Definition 1. *Given a set of sensors* $S = \{s_1, s_2, \ldots, s_N\}$ *and relay hop d, look for 1) A set of RN R; 2) A MC tour U connected all nodes in R and BS such that* $\sum_{(u,v) \in U} | uv |$ *is minimized, where* (u, v) *is a line segment on U and* $| uv |$ *is its Euclidean distance; 3) A set of aggregation trees* $\{T_i(V_i, E_i)\}$ *with height at most d that are rooted at* $r_i \in R$ *such that* $\cup_i V_i = S$ *and* $\sum_i \sum_{(u,v) \in E_i} | uv |$ *is minimized.*

From the definition of MDG-RN problem, the distribution of RNs and the data routes in each aggregation tree with the hop constraint should be jointly considered in order to find optimal solution. Thus the MDG-RN problem in this case can be formulated as:

$$Minimize \sum_{(u,v \in U)} |uv| \qquad (1)$$

Subject to

$$c^h_{s_i,r_i} = 1, \ \forall s_i \in S, \ \forall r_i \in R, \ 0 \leq h \leq d. \qquad (2)$$

$$\sum_{r_i \in R} c^h_{s_i,r_i} = 1, \ \forall s_i \in S, \ 0 \leq h \leq d. \qquad (3)$$

$$|s_i r_i| \leq |s_i r_j|, \ \forall s_i \in S, \ \forall r_i \in R, \ r_i \neq r_j \qquad (4)$$

For nodes r, $v \in V$ in G, we claim r *covers* v, if there is a path from v to r. A node v is *d-hop covered* by r if this path has the length no lager than d, written as $c^d_{v,r}$. A set of sensors are covered by r means an aggregation tree rooted at r is produced. The d-hop cover guarantees that any packet from the sources can be sent to rendezvous node r within d hops. As aforementioned, in ideal N-to-one aggregation mode, the total length of communication edges in an aggregation tree is more worthy of attention comparing with the number of nodes associated with RNs. We define the transmission cost as load formally. The *load* of a node v, written as $\text{Load}(v)$, is the total edge length associated with it in aggregation tree T in network. If the height of aggregation tree rooted at v is d then its load is called *d-hop load*, written as $d\_\text{Load}(v)$. For node v, its *uncovered d-hop load* is the d-hop load except the edge length connecting the covered nodes in T, and it is written as $\text{unC}\_d\_\text{Load}(v)$.

Theorem 1. *The MDG-RN problem is NP-hard.*

Proof. This problem can be shown to be NP-hard by a polynomial-time reduction from the Euclidean Traveling Salesman Problem. Specifically, a special case of the decision version of MDG-RN problem is to ask if there exists a set of RNs such that all the sources must be RNs. This can be done by modifying the node transmission range R_t. When R_t is small enough, nodes are unreachable from each other. In such case, the relay hop d is equal to 0, and then MC must visit all the RNs to collect data. Thus the MDG-RN problem is NP-hard. □

4 Algorithm for MDG-RN Problem

Due to the NP-hardness of the MDG-RN problem, in this section, we develop a Load Priority based RN Determination Algorithm (LP-RDA) for this problem. The basic idea of algorithm is to determine a set of RNs such that its total number is minimum and its distribution is near the BS as much as possible under the constraint of relay hop counts, and that the load of RNs is also optimized. The LP-RDA algorithm can be described as the following 3 steps:

```
STEP 1: INITIALIZATION
for any node s_i ∈ S
    s_i.status := not_Covered;
    computes s_i.dist_to_BS base on received signal strength;
    sends FB_Msg(s_i.ID, dist_to_BS, hopC) to BS hop-by-hop;
```

At beginning, static BS broadcasts "BEACON" message network-wide at a certain power. Each node computes the approximate distance to BS, dist_to_BS, base on the received signal strength. After that, every node sends message FB_Msg() to BS hop-by-hop. BS obtains the information of nodes in network after receiving these feedback messages.

```
STEP 2: ITERATION
BS determines a appropriate starting node x;
for any node s_j ∈ d-N_G(x)
    find a new RN r_i which has maximum unC_d_Load(s_j).
    r_i sends Declar_Msg() to d-N(r_i) and r_j.status:= Covered;
```

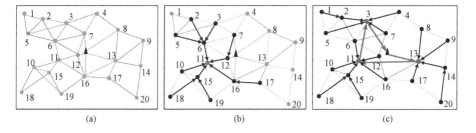

(a)   (b)   (c)

Fig. 1. An example to illustrate LP-RDA algorithm ($N=20$, $d=2$). (a) Initial topology. (b) The cover after the first RN is determined. (c) The final RNs, aggregation trees, and MCs tour.

```
for any s_j receiving Declar_Msg() from r_i
    if s_j.status = not_Covered then
        it joins its RN and s_j.status := Covered;
```

The iterative process to determine node status as shown in STEP 2. Depending on whether it is d-hop covered by RN, each node is set in one of two states: "Covered" or "not_Covered". Initially, all nodes are in the state of "un_Covered". The node with maximum $hopC$, x, is selected as the starting node. For the same $hopC$, the node with little dist_to_BS is selected. For d-$N(x)$, each node computes its unC_d_Load() by local message exchange. Next, algorithm tests the nodes in d-$N(x)$ toward the direction of BS such that the node with maximum unC_d_Load() is determined as new RN. The selected RN declares its identity by sending declaration message within its d-hop neighbors. Those uncovered nodes received this message will register as its member node and mark itself as covered. While there are uncovered nodes in the network, algorithm selects a new starting node again. Repeat this process, until all the nodes are covered by RNs.

STEP 3: OPTIMIZATION
```
for any s_j receiving Declar_Msg() from r_i
    if s_j.status = Covered and |s_j r_i | < |s_j r_j |) then
        changes its RN from r_j to r_i when receives r_i's message;
```

We notice that a part of nodes in d-$N(r_i)$ may have become the member of other tree T_j, $j < i$ already. In order to optimize the load of aggregation tree, if these covered nodes are closer to a new RN r_i, then they will disaffiliate themselves from original roots and join r_i. The optimization pseudo-code as shown in STEP 3 above.

An example demonstrates the execution of LP-RDA as shown in Fig. 1. The solid circles represent sensors and the black ones indicate that they are covered by RNs. The gray line segments show the connectivity, and the directed line segments represent the data routes in aggregation trees. Initially, no node is covered. Although 18 and 1 have the same 4 hops, the former with smaller

dist_to_BS is selected as the starting node. Its uncovered 2-hop neighbor set is
{10, 11, 15, 19}. 11 is the desirable one which will send Declar_Msg() to recruit
its members. After its neighbors at most 2-hop away joining in this RN, they
are covered as shown in Fig. 1b. Similarly, node 1 with 4 hops is selected as the
next starting node. In the process of construction of aggregation trees, a part
of nodes change their routes whenever shorter distance to new RN arises, e.g.,
node 8 changes its RN from 3 to 13, with which the optimization is accomplished.
Fig. 1c gives the final result which produce the data gathering tour of MC as
highlighted by the red line segments.

Theorem 2. *LP-RDA has the time complexity of $O(N^2 + Nd)$, where N is the
number of sensors in network, d is the relay hop.*

Proof. During the initial stage, every node sends feedback message to BS hop by
hop after receiving the BS's "BEACON" message. It takes $O(N)$ time for BS to
gather network information. Next, BS starts the iterative RN selection process.
At every turn, LP-RDA selects the farthest node v as the starting node, it will no
larger than N even in the worst case. Moreover, in each turn it takes $O(d)$ time
for v's d-hop neighbors d-$N(v)$ compute their load, the RN declares its identify,
and the MN joins new RN, respectively. Thus the iteration requires $O(dN)$ time.
Finally, adopting existing approximate algorithm for TSP to produce the MC
tour will take $O(N^2)$ time. Thus, the total time spent is $O(N) + O(3dN) +
O(N^2)$. The time complexity of LP-RDA is $O(N^2 + dN)$.   □

5   Distributed Algorithm for MDG-RN Problem

According to the assumption above, every node only knows the existence of its
direct neighbors, thus the information acquisition of d-hop neighbors is mainly
completed via d-hop information exchange. The execution of Algorithm needs
BS's schedule and it can not be executed in fully distributed pattern. In the
following, we present a Tree based Distributed RN Determination Algorithm
(T-DRDA), which can be identified as 3 steps.

STEP 1: INITIALIZATION
Construct SDT T under the constraint of R_t;
s_i.status:= Suspensive;

The initialization pseudo-code executed by each senor as shown in STEP 1.
Initially, each node has the same status "Suspensive". We claim the branches of
a node in T are its sub-trees rooted at its direct children, and the *local height of
a branch* (LHB) is the tree height from current node to its known farthest child
in local message exchange. For any node x, its LHB of i-th branch is noted as
$x.br$_LHB$[i]$. Every node sends local exchange message Exg_Msg() to its father
within d hops along T. When any node in the network receives messages from
its children, it will perform relevant statistics and then forward or destroy the
message depending on specific conditions. After d-hop message propagation, each
node has the information of its d-hop neighbors.

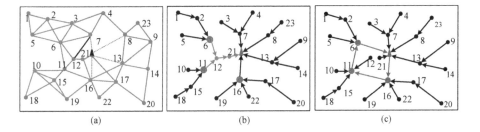

Fig. 2. An example to illustrate T-DRDA (N=23, d=2). (a) Initial topology. (b) RNs and their MNs after iteration 1. (c) The final RNs, aggregation tree, and MC tour.

STEP 2: STATUS DETERMINATION
```
if s_i.status = Suspensive then
    for each branch of s_i
        if s_i.br_LHB[j] < d-1 and s_i.parNode != Null then
            s_i.status:= MN;
        else if s_i.br_LHB[j] = d-1 or (s_i.parNode = Null and
        s_i.br_LHB[j] < d-1) then
            s_i.status:= RN and sends Declar_Msg() to d-N(s_i) in T;
```

According to the obtained local information, each node makes decision of its status as shown the code in STEP 2. If the LHB of each branch is less than d and its parent is not null, then this node becomes a member node (MN), then it will wait for a Join_Msg(). If there is a node whose LHB is exactly d, or it includes a branch whose LHB is less than d and its parent is null, then node turns into RN, and send declaration message Declar_Msg() to recruit its members within d hops range along tree including its parent and children. However, if current node's LHB is lager than d, then its status is still undetermined.

STEP 3: JOIN_RN
```
Upon receiving Declar_Msg(r_j, h) in T
if s_i.status = Suspensive then
    s_i.status:= MN and sends Join_Msg() to register as MN with r_j;
```

For STEP 3, whenever nodes receive Declar_Msg(), they change their status as "Covered", and register as MN with the sender. If multiple such messages are received, the nearest sender is chosen. Next, MN sends Join_Msg() to inform RN of its joining. After receiving the join messages, RN registers these nodes as its members and performs necessary maintenance and management. Note that when any MN determines a RN, it will be deleted from T. The remainder nodes in sub-tree repeat this procedure until every node becomes a RN or MN.

Fig. 2 illustrates the execution of distributed algorithm. The gray, red and black nodes represent MN, RN and undetermined nodes, respectively. Fig. 2a shows the initial network topology under the constraint R_t. Fig. 2b depicts the node statuses after the first iteration. Fig. 2c gives the final statuses of all nodes and the MC tour. Finally, we give the following properties which show the complexity of the T-DRDA algorithm.

Theorem 3. *T-DRDA has the time complexity of $O(N)$, where N is the number of sensors.*

Proof. T-DRDA adopts SDT T as underlying communication topology which can be constructed in $O(1)$ time. In the worst-case, sensor will experience N/d iterations at most. In each iteration, it takes $O(d)$ time for node to obtains d-hop neighbors information by local exchange. With the gathered information, each node makes its decision independently by $O(1)$ time. After that, RN and MN will send declaration and join messages with $O(d)$ time, respectively. Therefore, The total time complexity in T-DRDA is $O(1)+O(N/d)*O(3d+1) = O(N)$.   □

Theorem 4. *T-DRDA has the message exchange complexity of $O(N + d)$ per node, where N is the number of sensors, and d is the relay hop counts.*

Proof. SDT T in T-DRDA can be constructed with message complexity $O(N)$. During each iteration, each node generates d messages at most which are sent to its parent within d-hop in T. In the decision stage, each RN sends a declaration message to its d-hop neighbors in T. After receiving the declaration, its neighbors register with this node as MN by sending a join message. Both messages are restricted in d hop during the broadcast. That is, the number of messages that forwarded by single node in T will no more than d. Therefore, the total number of messages that a node has to handle is at most $d + 1 + d$. Thus the message complexity of T-DRDA is $O(N) + O(d) = O(N + d)$ per node.   □

6   Performance Evaluation

In this section, we evaluate the performance of proposed algorithms and present the simulation results. The performance metrics are mainly the number of RNs (N_{RN}), the iterations, and the tour length of MC (L_{MCT}). We first evaluate the performance by varying the parameters, and then compare them with two existing mobile data gathering schemes, SPT-DGA and PB-PSA [13]. SPT-DGA is a centralized algorithm, in which within the relay hop bound it iteratively finds an set of PPs among the sensors on a shortest path tree. Whereas, PB-PSA obtains the desirable solution in a distributed manner. We adopt the Nearest-Neighbor (NN) algorithm [15] in the simulation to determine the moving tour.

  Fig. 3 shows the performance of LP-RDA and T-DRDA under different transmission ranges (R_t). We can see that N_{RN} in both algorithms decreases quickly with the increase of R_t. The reason is that under the same node density a big R_t leads to the d-hop neighbors of a sensor increasing significantly, which means that less RNs can cover all nodes in the network. Obviously, in such case the load of each RN will increase with decrease of N_{RN}. The increase of R_t makes $hopC$ reduced. Therefore, for the iterations in LP-RDA, it is consistent with $hopC$, and decreases dramatically in Fig. 3b. It is worth pointing out that small iterations

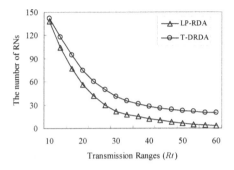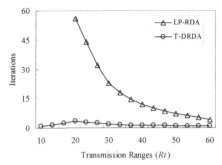

Fig. 3. Performance of LP-RDA and T-DRDA under different transmission ranges R_t.
(a) The number of RNs versus R_t. (b) The iterations versus R_t.

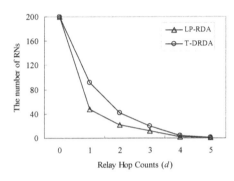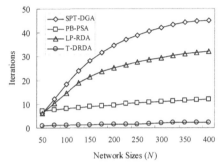

Fig. 4. The number of RNs   **Fig. 5.** The iterations versus network sizes

are at the cost of a large of local exchange messages. However, T-DRDA adopts a distributed approach to determine RNs, thus its iterations are influenced mainly by the height of tree T.

Fig. 4 plots the relationship between N_{RN} and d. In the figure, under fixed R_t = 30m, N_{RN} in both algorithms decreases with d. The revelation of this result is that a tradeoff should be made between local message overhead and latency. On one hand, under fixed R_t a small relay hop means the data can be aggregated to RNs quickly, but MC tour length will increase inevitably, which will cause a long latency. On the other hand, if the relay hop is too large, then the load of RNs will increase, accordingly, which not only calls for high node performance, but also result in unbalanced energy consumption.

In the following, we simulate the performance of LP-RDA and T-DRDA comparing with PB-PSA and SPT-DGA under different network sizes. Fig. 5 depicts the iterations of different algorithms as a function of network nodes N. We can see that comparing with that the iterations of centralized algorithms increasing with network sizes significantly, distributed schemes keeps a low growth and has excellent efficiency. For example, T-DRDA needs only 1 iteration when N is less than 100. Even under the case $N = 400$, algorithm needs 3.15 rounds on average. The reason LP-RDA excels SPT-DGA is that at every turn the former selects RN from the node with maximum d-hop load within its uncovered d-hop neighbors, which produces as less N_{RN} as possible. Furthermore, during the execution, the iteration of algorithm is scheduled by BS, which has unlimited functionality.

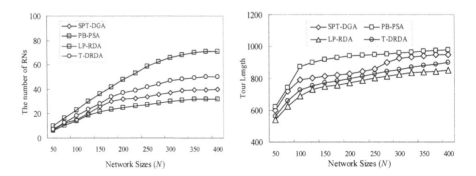

Fig. 6. Performance of LP-RDA and T-DRDA under different network sizes. (a) The number of RNs versus networks. (b) Tour length versus network sizes.

Finally, Fig. 6 depicts N_{RN} and L_{MCT} under different network sizes N. By contrast, the centralized algorithm receives more optimized N_{RN}. In order to ensure a short MC tour, the selection of RN in algorithm design mainly considers two factors: one is approaching its location to static BS, the other is decreasing their number. Under fixed d, a smaller L_{MCT} means a short latency of data gathering. We can see that the centralized algorithms are superior to distributed algorithms and the proposed algorithms outperform the other two algorithms.

7   Conclusions

In this paper, we study relay constrained mobile data gathering with mobile collector. We develop two efficient rendezvous based data gathering algorithms. One is a heuristic algorithm which always selects the node with maximum load from the d-hop neighbors of the current farthest node to BS. The other caters to the characteristic of WSNs, and selects RN iteratively from far to near in distributed manner. Both of them jointly consider MC tour and data routing routes in aggregation trees. The effectiveness of our algorithms is validated through both theoretical analysis and extensive simulations.

Acknowledgments. This work is supported by National Natural Science Foundation of China (61170021), Specialized Research Fund for the Doctoral Program of Higher Education (20103201110018), Natural Science Foundation of Jiangsu (BK2011376), Application Foundation Research of Suzhou of China

(SYG201240, SYG201118), Program for Postgraduates Research Innovation in University of Jiangsu Province (CXZZ12_0817), Science and Technology Innovation Team Building Program of Soochow University (SDT2012B02), and Project for Excellent Doctoral Dissertation Topic in Soochow University (23320216).

References

1. Xu, N., Rangwala, S., Chintalapudi, K.K., Ganesan, D., Broad, A., Govindan, R., Estrin, D.: A Wireless Sensor Network for Structural Monitoring. In: Proc. of ACM SenSys, pp. 13–24 (2004)
2. Yang, Z., Liu, Y.H.: Quality of Trilateration: Confidence based Iterative Localization. IEEE Trans. Parallel Distrib. Syst. 21(5), 631–640 (2010)
3. Samarah, S., Al-Hajri, M., Boukerche, A.: A Predictive Energy-Efficient Technique to Support Object-Tracking Sensor Networks. IEEE Trans. Veh. Technol. 60(2), 656–663 (2011)
4. Batalin, M.A., Rahimi, M., Yu, Y., Liu, D., Kansal, A., Sukhatme, G.S., Kaiser, W.J., Hansen, M., Pottie, G.J., Srivastava, M., Estrin, D.: Call and Response: Experiments in Sampling the Environment. In: Proc. of SenSys, pp. 25–38 (2004)
5. Francesco, M.D., Das, S., Anastasi, G.: Data Collection in Wireless Sensor Networks with Mobile Elements: A Survey. ACM Trans. Sensor Netw. 8(1) (2011)
6. Somasundara, A.A., Ramamoorthy, A., Srivastava, M.B.: Mobile Element Scheduling with Dynamic Deadlines. IEEE Trans. Mobile Comput. 6(4), 395–410 (2007)
7. Rao, J., Biswas, S.: Analyzing Multi-hop Routing Feasibility for Sensor Data Harvesting using Mobile Sink. J. Parallel Distrib. Comput. 72(6), 764–777 (2012)
8. Nesamony, S., Vairamuthu, M.K., Orlowska, M.E.: On Optimal Route of a Calibrating Mobile Sink in a Wireless Sensor Network. In: Proc. of INSS, pp. 61–64 (2007)
9. He, L., Pan, J.P., Xu, J.D.: A Progressive Approach to Reducing Data Collection Latency in Wireless Sensor Networks with Mobile Elements Sinks. IEEE Trans. Mobile Comput. 12(7), 1308–1320 (2013)
10. Ma, M., Yang, Y.: SenCar: An Energy-Efficient Data Gathering Mechanism for Large-Scale Multihop Sensor Networks. IEEE Trans. Parallel Distrib. Syst. 18(10), 1476–1488 (2007)
11. Gatzianas, M., Georgiadis, L.: A Distributed Algorithm for Maximum Lifetime Routing in Sensor Networks with Mobile Sink. IEEE Trans. Wireless Commun. 7(3), 984–994 (2008)
12. Xing, G.L., Li, M.M., Wang, T., Jia, W.J., Huang, J.: Efficient Rendezvous Algorithms for Mobility-Enabled Wireless Sensor Networks. IEEE Trans. Mobile Comput. 11(1), 47–60 (2012)
13. Zhao, M., Yang, Y.Y.: Bounded Relay Hop Mobile Data Gathering in Wireless Sensor Networks. IEEE Trans. Comput. 61(2), 265–277 (2012)
14. Madden, S., Franklin, M.J., Hellerstein, J.M., Hong, W.: TAG: A Tiny Aggregation Service for Ad-Hoc Sensor Networks. In: Proc. of OSDI, pp. 131–146 (2002)
15. Cormen, T.H., Leiserson, C.E., Rivest, R.L., Stein, C.: Introduction to Algorithms, 2nd edn. The MIT Press (2001)

Energy Efficient Task Scheduling in Mobile Cloud Computing

Dezhong Yao[1], Chen Yu[1], Hai Jin[1], and Jiehan Zhou[2]

[1] Services Computing Technology and System Lab
Cluster and Grid Computing Lab
School of Computer Science and Technology
Huazhong University of Science and Technology, Wuhan 430074, China
{dyao,yuchen,hjin}@hust.edu.cn
[2] Department of Computer Science and Engeering University of Oulu,
Oulu 90014, Finland

Abstract. Cloud computing can enhance the computing capability of mobile systems by offloading. However, the communication between the mobile device and the cloud is not free. Transmitting large data to cloud consumes much more energy than processing data in mobile device, especially in a low bandwidth condition. Further, some processing tasks can avoid transmitting large data between mobile device and server. Those processing tasks (encoding, rendering) are as the compress algorithm, which can reduce the size of raw data before it is sent to server. In this paper, we present an *energy efficient task scheduling* strategy (EETS) to determine what kind of task with certain amount of data should be chosen to be offloaded under different environment. We have evaluated the scheduler by using an Android smartphone. The results show that our strategy can achieve 99% of accuracy to choose the right action in order to minimize the system energy usage.

Keywords: Mobile cloud computing, Energy-efficient, Task scheduling, Offloading.

1 Introduction

With a rapid development of embedded systems, high speed wireless networks and could computing, mobile devices (e.g., smartphone, tablets, wearable devices, etc.) are increasingly becoming a common stuff of human daily life. We use mobile devices to do many of our jobs that we used to do on desktop. Mobile cloud computing technique allows those ideas to become a reality. Nonetheless, the more mobile devices we have, the less happiness we are with the battery lifetime. This is because we are still using the traditional power supplying method and materials.

Computing offloading technique is proposed with the objective to migrate the complex computation works from resource-limited devices to powerful machines. This avoids taking a long application execution time on mobile devices

C.-H. Hsu et al. (Eds.): NPC 2013, LNCS 8147, pp. 344–355, 2013.

which results in large amount of power consumption. However, current offloading studies do not consider about the energy consumption used by data transport. Offloading mechanisms just focus on avoiding use local CPU resource in order to save energy spent on processing. They pay limit attention on long time data transmission problem and they consider best case scenarios: ideal high speed networks. Unfortunately, long wireless network latencies are a fundamental obstacle [1]. Some researches [2,3] prove that it can significantly save energy when we minimize the use of network. For example, speech recognition utility is a heavy processing task, it should be processed in cloud servers according the offloading scheduling algorithm [4]. While voice data is usually larger than text data, it will take more energy to send the big data to server than to process the recognition algorithm locally and then send the text result to server.

In this paper, we propose an *energy efficient task scheduling* strategy (EETS) which focuses on reducing the amount of data transmission. Our goal is to identify which kind of task is suitable for offloading and which is not. To address this problem we build an energy consumption model for each task. At last, we give an evaluation work on a suite of *Mediabench* [5] programs to show the efficiency of our scheduling mechanism. Our main contributions of this paper are as: 1)We present a task allocation algorithm which is based on a task's input/output data's size and storage path. 2)We study the data compression that is helpful to achieve energy saving between mobile device and cloud. 3)We give an energy consumption model for each task. Using this model, we can calculate the energy consuming difference between offloading or not offloading. We prove our model using real data from Android phones.

The rest of the paper is organized as follows. Section 2 presents the related work. Section 3 introduces task execution scenario. In section 4, we describe energy consumption modeling technique for application task and explain task scheduling algorithm. Then we carry out a performance evaluation of all considered methods in section 5. Section 6 discusses our work and future works, whereas our conclusions are drawn in section 7.

2   Related Work

Could computing can provide computing resource, and users can use these to reduce the amounts of computation on mobile systems and save energy. Thus, cloud computing can save energy for mobile users through computation offloading [6,7]. However, to migrate large amount of data in a low-bandwidth network will cost much more energy than local computation.

Offloading [6] is a method to offload part of the computation from mobile device to another resource rich platform. A number of recent works propose different methodologies to offload computation for specific applications [8,9]. In another part, lots of works discuss on how to pre-estimate the actual gain in terms of energy [10]. For a code complication, offloading might consume more energy than that of local processing when the size of codes is small [11].

The research work [7] suggests a program partitioning based on the estimation of the energy consumption (communication energy and computation energy) before the program execution. The optimal program partitioning for offloading is calculated based on the trade-off between the communication and computation costs. To do offloading in the dynamic environments, Tang et al. [12] consider three common environmental changes: power level, connection status and bandwidth. But they just explain the suitable solutions for offloading for different environments separately. Chun et al. [13] present a system to partition an application in dynamic environments. The proposed system follows three steps with different requirements related to the application structuring, the partitioning choice, and the security. Cuervo [14] introduces an architecture to dynamically partition an application at a runtime in three steps. However, all those works do not consider more about the task input and output data, which may cost a lot of energy in communication. None of the previous works related to mobile cloud computing explicitly studies the actual input data and output data location problem. They assume that the data comes from local and to be stored in local device. Otherwise, we need to spend much energy on useless data transmission work.

3   Task Execution Scenario

Simple task does not take too much time to execute, so it does not need offloading [7]. Complex applications will consume more energy than the simple one. So in this section we will classify the applications with complex computation task.

   With the offloading's help, we can put the rendering work on cloud, as shown in Fig. 1(a). After the rendering result is ready, the data will be sent back to mobile device. The energy spent on computation part will be saved with an extra cost of data communication. Sometimes, it is not worth to offload rendering work from mobile client to server when the data size is big and the network bandwidth is slow. The mobile device will keep communication with cloud servers for a long time. For some compression like applications, we would better to do compress work on mobile device than to do it on the cloud servers. The data size can be reduced after it is processed. So the communication time will be saved. This progress is shown in Fig. 1(b).

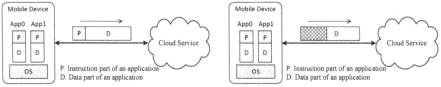

(a) Offloading: mobile device needs to transmit all data to server

(b) Non-offloading: the mobile device just transmits the executed data

Fig. 1. Offloading scheme

4   Energy Efficient Task Scheduler

In this section, we will talk about the energy consumption model. Our proposed task scheduler makes following assumptions: 1) Each task can be processed on mobile device. 2) Each task has a fixed compress ratio of input data and output data. 3) The network bandwidth between mobile device and remote cloud is fixed and stable. 4) The computational power required by a task has a liner relationship with the processing time.

4.1   Energy Model

Energy consumption of mobile devices depends on the computation and communication loads. To explore the energy consumption of each task, we suppose the task computation requires I instructions. The task needs to deal with D bytes of data and will generate D' bytes result. We use B to stand for current network bandwidth. It will task D/B seconds to transmit and receive data. We define our task as follows:

Definition 1. *[Application Task] $T(I, D, D')$. A mobile application task T has I instructions to be executed. The task uses D bytes input data and generates D' bytes output data.*

The mobile system consumes P_c (watt per instruction) for computing and P_{tr} (watt per second) for sending and receiving data.

If we choose to execute our task using offloading, we need to send our code and data to server, as shown in Fig. 1(b). So the total energy consumption is:

$$E_{off} = P_{tr} * \frac{D}{B} \tag{1}$$

Suppose the output data D' is k times smaller than the original data D, we use compress ratio k to describe the relationship between input data and output data: $(D' = D * k)$. In order to simplify the compression algorithm impact on the size of output data when the size of input data is different, we just consider the application task with fixed compression ratio. If the mobile device performs the task, the energy consumption is:

$$E_{nonoff} = P_c * I + P_{tr} \frac{D'}{B} \tag{2}$$

Definition 2. *[Energy saving value S] The amount of energy that can be saved, when the task chooses to do offloading.*

The amount of energy saved is:

$$S = E_{off} - E_{nonoff} \tag{3}$$
$$= P_{tr} * \frac{D}{B} - P_c * I - P_{tr} * \frac{D'}{B} = P_{tr} * \frac{D}{B} - P_c * I - P_{tr} * \frac{D * k}{B}$$
$$= P_{tr} * (1 - k)\frac{D}{B} - P_c * I \tag{4}$$

If offloading use less energy to finish a task than non-offloading, this formula produces a negative result: $S < 0$. It's better to choose offloading. When we try to transmit large amount of data D for a compression task ($k < 1$), Eq. (3) will be positive. It means that it is better to execute the task locally.

4.2   Execution Model

It is a big advantage to do offloading in cloud environment, if a task has to download a large number of data from remote servers. In the previous studies, researchers focus on determining whether to offload computation by predicting the relationships among the three factors: network bandwidth B, the amount of processing instructions I and the amount of data to be transmitted D. However, there is a fundamental assumption underling this analysis: the server does not already contain the input data and all the data must be sent to the server to do offloading. The mobile client has to offload the program code and data to the server. Now, cloud computing changes this assumption. Many mobile devices have cloud storage service. Offloading can use the data stored in the cloud. This will significantly reduce the energy consumption on data transmission. The execution workflow is shown in Fig. 2. The input file of an application could come from local files or remote storage service. The execution code is only on mobile device. Then, we can choose to offload computation task to virtual machine or run locally in mobile device. How to store the output result data of the application is depended by user settings.

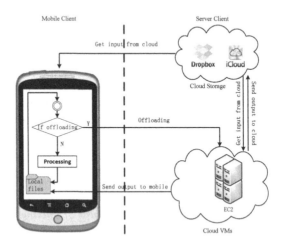

Fig. 2. Execution workflow of a mobile application

The detail of each possible workflow is listed in Fig. 3. The computing code is only stored in local mobile device. Compare with offloading and non-offloading mechanism, the main difference is processing code in cloud or in mobile device.

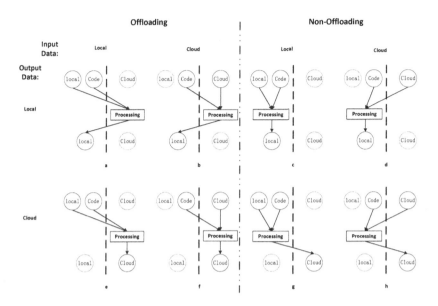

Fig. 3. Execution mode for different input/output situation

There are 8 executing mode depending on where we get the input data and where we store the output data. In the next section, we will present a cost model for how much energy can be saved for the same input and same output situation.

4.3 The Cost Graph

In this section, we will consider the energy consumption cost for each situation shown in Fig. 3. We use the energy consumption model in section 4.1 to describe the power spent on computation part and data transmission part.

Fig. 4 shows the cost map of data communication with different data storage. Task is executed on the mobile device while the other shown task runs on the cloud server after offloading. The input data of task could be D_m in the local mobile device or D_s from cloud storage service. As the instruction code is usually smaller than the data, the cost of transmitting code could be ignored. The cost of transmitting the input data is described as $D_{i,j}(i, j \in m, s)$. After the execution, the result data, $D'_{j,l}(j, l \in m, s)$, needs to be transported to the target place. As we process the same code in mobile device and VM, it will generate the same result. The size of data file should be the same.

Based on above discussion, we calculate the energy consumption for each suitable shown in Fig. 3. The data stored in mobile device and in cloud are the same. So we have $D_m = D_s$. The cost of transport data from mobile to cloud and from cloud to mobile are the same, $D_{ms} = D_{sm}$. The data transport within the mobile device cost nothing, $D_{mm} = 0$. The data does transport from storage datacenter to virtual machine (VM) also do not cost energy consumption

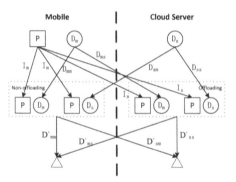

Fig. 4. Graph based cost map of data communication for offloading and non-offloading

in mobile device, $D_{ss} = 0$. For the output data, which does not need to be transported to another place, it will not consume the energy on mobile device. So we have $D'_{mm} = D'_{ss}$. As the result computed by the VM is the same data have computed in the mobile, the data exchange between mobile and server is equal: $D'_{ms} = D'_{ms}$.

Table 1. The energy saved S for different storage place

Input Output	Local($j = m$)	Cloud($j = s$)
Local($i = m$)	$P_{tr} * (1+k)\frac{D_{ms}}{B} - P_c * I$	$P_{tr} * (1-k)\frac{D_{ms}}{B} - P_c * I$
Cloud($i = s$)	$P_{tr} * (k-1)\frac{D_{ms}}{B} - P_c * I$	$P_{tr} * (-1-k)\frac{D_{ms}}{B} - P_c * I$

Following the energy saving computation model in Eq. (4), we calculate the amount of energy saving for the 8 situations described in Fig. 3. Table 1 presents the different energy saving results according to the place data stored. If the energy is saved, the formula should be negative. Table 1 shows that:

1. Input data comes from local and output data to be stored in local.
   Offloading could take a great advantage in saving energy when computation work consumes more power than data communication. Otherwise, we should not choose offloading.
2. Input data comes from local and output data to be stored in cloud.
   Offloading can save lots of energy when the task compression ratio is above 1. It means that when the output data is larger than the input one, we should choose offloading. When the compression ratio is below 1, it also depends on the amount of data to be transmitted, network bandwidth and the amount of processing time.
3. Input data comes from cloud and output data to be stored in local.
   It is a little different with above situation. The offloading can save energy

```
Procedure Task_Scheduler
Input: (1) costgraph (2) task_profile
Output: offloading decision for each task
Procedure:
I, D, k, input_path, output_path
Procedure Scheduler(task_profile)
...
If the task can be processed
  if input_path is local
     if output_path is local
         use costgraph evaluate energy saved value S
         if S>0
           return False
         else
           return True
     else
         use costgraph evaluate energy saved value S
         if S>0
           return False
         else
           return True
  else
...
```

Fig. 5. Cost graph based task scheduling algorithm

when the compression ratio is below 1. When the task compression ratio is above 1, it is more valuable to do offloading when computation part uses more energy than data transmission.

4. Input data comes from cloud and output data to be stored in cloud.
   In this situation, it should always choose to do offloading that can save large amount of energy.

4.4 Task Scheduling Strategy

In this section, we will present a cost graph based task scheduling algorithm for saving energy on mobile devices. The scheduling algorithm, as shown in Fig. 5, will decide whether the task should be processed locally or offloading. If the answer is *true* then the task is placed in the scheduling queue. Otherwise, the task will be executed locally. Part of the algorithm is presented as produce *Task_Scheduler* in Fig. 5, which uses cost-graph and task profile as input data. The scheduling algorithm will be executed before each task. After check if current task is suitable for offloading, the scheduler will decide where to process the task.

5   Experiments Results

Our experiments are based on an Android-based platform device. In this section we describe the experiment setup, and performance evaluation results of all execution models as shown in Fig. 3. As processing time is also an important consideration for the use, there is a tradeoff between performance and energy consumption. In our paper, we only focus on energy issues on smartphone.

5.1   Experiments Setup

In the experiments, we assume that the WiFi network is always connected. In addition, we use *dropbox* [15] as our cloud data storage service. The software clones is running on virtual machines supplied by Amazon EC2 [16] platform. We use "Google Nexus One" as our test-device. Before each test program, the device will be continued charging for 2 hours after it is fully charged. The Android OS is restored to the factory settings to start a new test in order to make sure that there is only one test program installed. We use the percentage changes of the battery to show how much energy is used by the program.

5.2   Performance Evaluation

We implement our algorithm in Java and C using Android NDK. The task scheduler and data transmission parts use Java and the computation part uses C. To obtain a preliminary evaluation of the effectiveness of our method, we manually apply our algorithm to a suite of *Mediabench* [5] programs.

Test Programs. We select 9 execution models: *h264edc*, *h264dec*, *cjpeg*, *djpeg*, *rawcaudio*, *rawdaudio*, *ghostscript*, *mpeg2encode*, and *mpeg2decod*. The processing time for the application is measured at mobile device. Our task scheduling algorithm will determine determine to do offloading according to current data file size, data path, compression ratio and bandwidth.

In our performance studies, we will compare our method with offloading and non-offloading as described in Eq. (1) and Eq. (2).

Test Measurement. By applying our algorithm to the 9 programs, we find that 6 of those 9 programs can get better energy saving by offloading. We evaluate our programs for four different groups which has different path of input data and output data. Then, we arrange each of our programs to do offloading and execute locally. After that, we use our proposed task scheduling algorithm to determine whether to do offloading. For each processing step, we record how much energy used before task finished. In Android mobile, we use how much percentage changes after the phone is fully charged. There is no other application running on the mobile device except system applications.

We use *dropbox* [15] as our cloud storage service, which has $100kbps$ network bandwidth. From Fig. 6(a), the offloading uses much more energy when the data is stored on mobile devices. The x-axis lists the test programs. The y-axis tells us

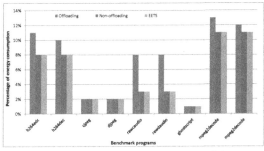

(a) Input=mobile and output=mobile

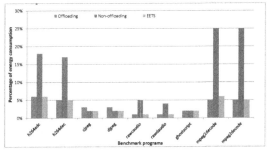

(b) Input=cloud and output=mobile

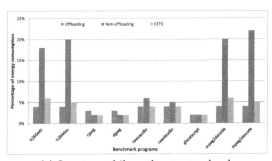

(c) Input=mobile and output=cloud

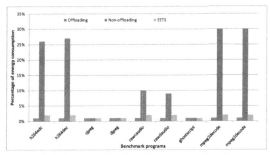

(d) Input=cloud and output=cloud

Fig. 6. Energy consumption on benchmark

how much percentage of energy used on test-phone to archive different programs. From Fig. 6(b) and Fig. 6(c), the complex application will cost lots of energy when they are running on mobile device. It is better to do offloading. When we use the cloud data, we would use offloading to save our energy, which is shown in Fig. 6(d). As we can see from those figures, the proposed method also uses the minimum energy consumption to achieve the work.

For the case: "input=mobile&output=mobile", the data does not need to be transmitted to the server, so our proposed strategy (EETS) performs like non-offloading case, as shown in Fig. 6(a). H264 and MPEG are complex video encoding/decoding algorithms, they always use the most energy on smartphone. Those algorithms need to encode/decode each frame in a video. So they will use more energy than the jpeg algorithms. When those methods run on remote server, the smartphone only spends energy on data communication. EETS chooses the right strategy to schedule the data. Fig. 6(b), Fig. 6(c) and Fig. 6(d) are the some situations.

Efficiency Analysis. Based on the experimental results, we can conclude how efficient of our algorithm. First, we will try to find which one costs the minimum energy consumption to execute the task. We use a minimum function to calculate the smaller value between offloading and non-offloading: min(percentage of offloading, percentage of nonoffloading). Then we compare the minimum value with the proposed task scheduling method. The accuracy of our proposed schemer is above 99% in average, which means our scheduling algorithm efficiently choose the best solution to allocate the tasks.

6 Discussion and Future Work

The proposed task scheduler is limited in some respects by it initially setups. It needs to collect the profile information of each task at the beginning. After learned the compression ratio and processing time, the scheduler can deal with new tasks. To solve this problem, we need to try some test programs to collect execution information or learn from system record after the task executed once.

The framework presented in this paper does not consider the power consumption on idle time waiting for task result and disk usage. While the task dose not execute for a long time, we think the power consumption is as same as the normal usage. The power consumption on disk usage is related to the type of storage device. HDD device uses much more energy than flash storage device. We plan to add this impact to our determine strategy in our future works.

7 Conclusion

In this paper, we present a novel energy aware dynamic task allocation strategy over mobile cloud computing environment. This scheme introduces a cost graph to determine offloading the work or not. The evaluation work shows that, our strategy can efficiently choose to offload or not on mobile device with 99% accuracy. The energy consumption on mobile device is controlled in minimum.

Acknowledgements. The work is supported by NSFC (No.61003220).

References

1. Satyanarayanan, M., Bahl, P., Caceres, R., Davies, N.: The case for vm-based cloudlets in mobile computing. IEEE Pervasive Computing 8(4), 14–23 (2009)
2. Dinh, H.T., Lee, C., Niyato, D., Wang, P.: A survey of mobile cloud computing: architecture, applications, and approaches. Wireless Communications and Mobile Computing (2011)
3. Baliga, J., Ayre, R., Hinton, K.: Green cloud computing: Balancing energy in processing, storage, and transport. Proceedings of the IEEE 99(1), 149–167 (2011)
4. Barbera, M.V., Kosta, S., Mei, A., Stefa, J.: To offload or not to offload? the bandwidth and energy costs of mobile cloud computing. In: Proc. of the IEEE INFOCOM (2013)
5. Lee, C., Potkonjak, M., Mangione-Smith, W.H.: Mediabench: a tool for evaluating and synthesizing multimedia and communicatons systems. In: Proc. of the 30th Annual ACM/IEEE International Symposium on Microarchitecture, pp. 330–335. IEEE Computer Society (1997)
6. Yang, K., Ou, S., Chen, H.H.: On effective offloading services for resource-constrained mobile devices running heavier mobile internet applications. IEEE Communications Magazine 46(1), 56–63 (2008)
7. Kumar, K., Lu, Y.H.: Cloud computing for mobile users: Can offloading computation save energy? Computer 43(4), 51–56 (2010)
8. Portokalidis, G., Homburg, P., Anagnostakis, K., Bos, H.: Paranoid android: versatile protection for smartphones. In: Proc. of the 26th Annual Computer Security Applications Conference, pp. 347–356. ACM (2010)
9. Chen, E.Y., Itoh, M.: Virtual smartphone over ip. In: Proc. of the IEEE International Symposium on a World of Wireless Mobile and Multimedia Networks (WoWMoM), pp. 1–6. IEEE (2010)
10. Wen, Y., Zhang, W., Luo, H.: Energy-optimal mobile application execution: Taming resource-poor mobile devices with cloud clones. In: Proc. of the 2012 IEEE INFOCOM, pp. 2716–2720. IEEE (2012)
11. Rudenko, A., Reiher, P., Popek, G.J., Kuenning, G.H.: Saving portable computer battery power through remote process execution. ACM SIGMOBILE Mobile Computing and Communications Review 2(1), 19–26 (1998)
12. Tang, M., Cao, J.: A dynamic mechanism for handling mobile computing environmental changes. In: Proc. of the 1st International Conference on Scalable Information Systems, p. 7. ACM (2006)
13. Chun, B.G., Maniatis, P.: Dynamically partitioning applications between weak devices and clouds. In: Proc. of the 1st ACM Workshop on Mobile Cloud Computing & Services: Social Networks and Beyond, p. 7. ACM (2010)
14. Cuervo, E., Balasubramanian, A., Cho, D.K., Wolman, A., Saroiu, S., Chandra, R., Bahl, P.: Maui: making smartphones last longer with code offload. In: Proc. of the 8th International Conference on Mobile Systems, Applications, and Services, pp. 49–62. ACM (2010)
15. Dropbox, http://dropbox.com
16. AmazonEC2, http://aws.amazon.com/ec2

BotInfer: A Bot Inference Approach by Correlating Host and Network Information*

Yukun He, Qiang Li**, Yuede Ji, and Dong Guo

College of Computer Science and Technology, Jilin University,
Changchun 130012, China
{heyk12,jiyd12}@mails.jlu.edu.cn, {li_qiang,guodong}@jlu.edu.cn

Abstract. Botnet is widely used in cyber-attacks and becomes a serious threat to network security. Existing approaches can detect botnet effectively in certain environments, however problems still exist in using host or network detection approaches respectively, such as robustness in detection tools, difficulties in global deployment and low precision rate. To solve the above problems, a novel detection approach called BotInfer is proposed. In BotInfer approach, host-based bot detection tools are deployed on some of the hosts; network flow of all the hosts is captured and analyzed; host detection result and flow information are correlated by the bot inference engine. Through the experiments, BotInfer can effectively detect the hosts in the network. When the deployment rate of bot detection tools in the network reaches 80%, the precision rate of the hosts with detection tools is about 99%, and the precision rate of the hosts without detection tools is about 86%.

Keywords: bot detection, cluster, flow analysis, inference algorithm.

1 Introduction

In order to achieve malicious purposes, attackers would inject particular malicious codes in a large number of hosts by various means and remotely control these hosts through command and control channel (C&C). The network composed of these controlled hosts is known as botnet. The host controlling these compromised hosts is known as botmaster. The malicious code is known as bot. Botnet has become a serious threat to the Internet, which can cause various cybercrimes, such as spreading attack codes and commands, spamming, information theft, phishing and DDoS attacks.

In recent years, a large number of researches have been conducted to detect and prevent botnet. According to the detection location, existing bot and botnet detection approaches can be divided into two categories: (1) Host-based bot detection approaches utilize the abnormal behaviors on hosts to detect bots,

---

* Supported by the National Natural Science Foundation of China under Grant No.61170265; Fundamental Research Fund of Jilin University under Grant No. 201003035, No. 201103253.
** Corresponding author.

C.-H. Hsu et al. (Eds.): NPC 2013, LNCS 8147, pp. 356–367, 2013.

including abnormal behaviors in registry modification, file system information, system calls, etc. For example, Stinson *et al.* proposed BotSwat approach [1], Lei Liu *et al.* proposed BotTracer approach [2] and Young Park *et al.* proposed BotTee approach [3]. (2) Network-based botnet detection approaches utilize the flow information captured in the network. Such as S.Nagaraja *et al.* proposed BotGrep[4] which utilizes structure graphs. B. Coskun *et al.* proposed a approach utilizing friends of an enemy [5].

However, there are still some defects either in host-based detection or network-based detection approaches. Host-based detection approaches need to deploy detection tools on each host, which will bring direct impact on the performance of hosts. And once the host detection tool is damaged, the detection result of the host would be inaccurate. While the network-based detection approaches need to collect the users' network flow information, which may invade the users' privacy. Due to the limitations of the approaches purely based on hosts or network, Zeng *et al.* [6] proposed a botnet detection approach, which is the first to combine host and network information. The approach of Zeng can effectively detect the botnets which are based on IRC, HTTP and P2P. However global deployment is still needed, because the approach can be effective only when all hosts in the network have been installed host detection tools.

During the procedures of bot detection, detection tools may have the problem of robustness in host detection, the need of global deployment and low detection rate. Robustness which means when bot detection tools were damaged on hosts, detection tools would get the error detection result. Global deployment means detection tools should be deployed on all the hosts in the local network, or there wouldn not be any detection results about the hosts. While in this paper, we propose a novel bot inference approach (BotInfer) which can solve the above problem to a certain extent. Our works make the following three contributions:

1. We propose BotInfer approach. BotInfer has the higher robustness compared with purely host-based bot detection approach. If bot detection tools on some hosts have been damaged by malwares, BotInfer can still obtain the detection results of other hosts and the flow similarity information between hosts in the network to generate the final detection results. BotInfer doesn not need global deployment. Not all hosts need to be deployed with bot detection tools in the entire local network. When the deployment rate reaches a certain point, reliable detection results can be generated through the existing hosts detection information and network flow analysis.

2. We extract 13 features from network flow to calculate the host-flow similarity. Through correlating host-flow similarity and host detection result, bot inference algorithm can infer whether all the hosts in the local network infected bot or not.

3. We implement a detection prototype based on BotInfer approach. And our approach was evaluated by using mixed network flow which is from captured lab flow in multiple time windows and the CERNET network during a day. Our experimental results show that the proposed approach can detect different types of bots with high robustness and property deployment rate.

The remainder of this paper is outlined as follows: Section 2 is related works. Section 3 introduces the design of BotInfer, including the problem statement and assumptions, and the overall architecture of BotInfer. Section 4 implements a model based on BotInfer, including host detection, network flow analysis and bot inference engine. Section 5 experimentally analyzes this approach in terms of accuracy and the rate of deployment. Section 6 is discussion about limitation of BotInfer and the conclusion.

2   Related Works

Currently, primary host-based bot detection approaches include: (1) BotSwat [2], proposed by Stinson et al., which can distinguish between bot behaviors and benign programs. (2) BotTracer [7], proposed by Lei Liu et al., which is to judge bot infection from the three indispensable stages in the process of bot attacking. (3) BotTee [1], proposed by Younghee Park et al., which extracts the suspicious system call sequences to match with the bot command patterns. (4) JACKSTRAWS [8], proposed by Jacob et al., uses machine learning to identify C&C connection accurately. (5) Konrad Rieck et al. [9] used the machine learning algorithm to automatically analyze malware behavior. (6) Fatemeh Karbalaie et al. [10] used data miner approache to detect host malwares.

Network detection approaches include flow graph analysis, flow features clustering, machine learning, the analysis of activities of network flow. (1) BotFinder proposed by Florian Tegeler et al. [11], used the machine learning to divide the captured network flow into two types: benign and malicious and the final model generated will decide whether the flow generated by hosts is malicious or not. (2) Leyla Bilge et al. proposed DISCLOSURE approach [12], using large-scale network flow data, extracting flow features to detect C&C server in botnet. (3) Francois et al. proposed Bottrack approach [13], analyzing bots' communication patterns via NetFlow data analysis and PageRank algorithm.

In host-based approaches, any damage on bot detection tools will completely fail the detection, so detection tools must be deployed on all hosts. Besides, bot detection tools need to monitor system information of the user hosts, and it will decrease the performance of user hosts. In network detection approaches, they rely only on network flow and do not consider the hosts detection information, so the detection accuracy is low. In our BotInfer approach, hosts detection information and network flow analysis information are effectively correlated, the above problems are solved to a certain extend.

3   Bot Inference Approach

3.1   Problem Statement and Assumptions

Botmaster spreads commands to bots via C&C channel. After receiving commands, the bots on hosts will perform malicious behaviors, in such areas as, the allocation of file resources, generation of registry, network flow on hosts and so on. As a result, we can monitor the information on hosts to analyze whether the host has been infected. For all the flows of bots are generated automatically in the background, rather than through artificial operations, so there are great similarities in communication flows between botmaster and bots. For example, in the centralized architecture, the bots receive commands almost simultaneously from the centralized server, and their communication flows are very similar with each other in the aspects of the number of packets, the size of packets. While, in the distributed architecture, the commands from botmaster need to be spread among hosts, so the flows between hosts infected with the same bot also have great similarity. Using the results detected on hosts and the information of flow similarity obtained by flow analysis, we can finally infer whether the hosts are bots or not through inference algorithm. BotInfer is a bot detection approach used in a local network based on the above assumptions. BotInfer mainly targets at a large local network to effectively detect bots, which use IRC, HTTP and P2P as their C&C channels, when the deployment rate of host detection tools reaches a certain point. The detection accuracy for unknown bot mainly depends on the accuracy of the host detection tools.

3.2   Architecture of BotInfer

In Figure 1, the approach of BotInfer is mainly divided into three sections. S1 is the host detection, which deploys detection tools on some of the hosts in the network. When detection tools find out bot activities on hosts, they will immediately generate detection results and suspicious degrees, which will be sent to the bot inference engine. S2 is the network analysis, which obtains the communication flows of all hosts in the network and filters safe IP address got from the known safe URLs (such as, `www.microsoft.com`, `www.google.com`). We believe that the communication activities between hosts and these URLs are benign behaviors. Flow features are extracted from filtered flows, such as flow duration, packet size and packet quantity. Then according to the features of host flows, the hosts with similar flow in a certain period are put into the same cluster and the similarity degree is calculated. S3 is the most important part of the BotInfer approach , which is used to correlate the detection results generated in S1 and the data sets got by S2 to obtain the final results.

4   Implementation

A prototype is implemented based on BotInfer approach. Existing bot detection tools are used to get host detection result. Network flow is filtered and clustered. Algorithms are implemented in network flow similarity calculation and bot inference engine.

4.1   Host Detection

Host-based detection approaches are in large numbers, which mainly analyze the abnormal behaviors of hosts [14] [15] [16] [17]. Instead of doing in-depth

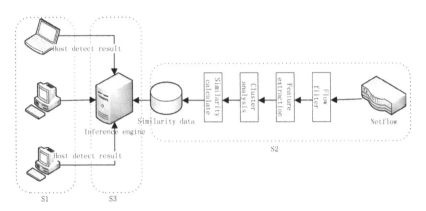

Fig. 1. BotInfer architecture

researches on host-based detection approaches, we pay more attention to anal-yse the network flow and the inference engine. In the experiments, traditional antivirus tools are used to get the detection results on hosts.

4.2 Network Analysis

In order to obtain the similarity degree of the hosts' communication flows, the communication flows of hosts in entire network need to be captured in a time window, and then do the work of flow filtering, extracting flow features, clustering analysis and calculating flow similarity degree.

Flow Capture and Filter. When extracting flow features, we only care about the overall statistics of hosts' communication flows and do not research the specific content of communication packets, so this will not involve users' privacy data. For the acquired data of flows, it can be filtered by the white list of the IP addresses. It is believed that it is secure for user hosts to communicate with the hosts in white list, such as www.facebook.com and www.microsoft.com. The flows generated from the IP on white list can be filtered, then the data quantity is decreased greatly when analyzing network flow, which is sure to cut the calculation overhead to a great extend. We won not filter the flows of internal hosts in a local network, because in botnet, which uses P2P as C&C channel, the internal hosts also communicate with each other and their flows are similar.

Flow Feature Extraction and Cluster. For the data of network flow after filtering process, the feature information of flows can be extracted according to the IP addresses in flows. Due to the fact that the bots on hosts usually generate less flows, if we simply collect the flows between a host and other hosts, the flows generated by bots and botmaster will be covered by other processes, and the features of flows generated by bots will not be obvious. As a result, it is not

Table 1. Host flow feature

IP_IP	IP of two hosts (no distinction between source and target host)
totalFlows	total flows between two hosts
totalPackets	total packets of the flows between two hosts
totalbytes	total bytes of the flows between two hosts
totalDuration	total durations of the flows between the two hosts
packetsVariance	the variance of packets number in each flow
bytesVariance	the variance of bytes number in each flow
durationVariance	the variance of durations number in each flow
packetsPerFlow	the number of packets per flow
bytesPerFlow	the number of bytes per flow
durationPerFlow	the duration per flow
numberOfPort	total number of ports used in communication
numberOfTcp	total number of TCP flows in communication
numberOfUdp	total number of UDP flows in communication

conducive to obtaining flow similarity of different hosts in a same time window. Therefore, we do not consider the direction of flows, that is, do not distinguish the IP between the source hosts and the target hosts of flows. We analyze all communication information of two hosts within a time window to generate a vector composed of 13 features. Table 1 shows all the information contained in a feature vector. According to the feature, the similar flows can be put into the same cluster by using the approach of hierarchical clustering, Davies-Bouldin (DB) [18], which chooses an appropriate height to split the dendrogram.

Flow Similarity Calculation. This part mainly calculate the similarity of host communication flows in the same time window and the same cluster through the use of similarity information of flows between different hosts. P and F are used to record the flows information between two hosts within a time window. P is composed of the IP of two hosts and F is the vector composed of the 13 features of flows between two hosts. For instance, the communication flows between host A and B can be expressed as (P_{AB}, F_{AB}). Their similarity is calculated through the distance of features, for features j and k, their similarity is:

$$S_{jk} = \left| \frac{\sum_{i=1}^{13}(x_{ij} - \overline{x_j})(x_{ik} - \overline{x_k})}{\sqrt{\sum_{i=1}^{13}(x_{ij} - \overline{x_j})^2}\sqrt{\sum_{i=1}^{13}(x_{ik} - \overline{x_k})^2}} \right| \tag{1}$$

x_{ij} denotes the ith feature of j, x_{ik} denotes the ith feature of k, $\overline{x_j} = \frac{1}{13}\sum_{i=1}^{13} x_{ij}$, $\overline{x_k} = \frac{1}{13}\sum_{i=1}^{13} x_{ik}$.

For the two flow-features in a cluster (P_{AB}, F_{AB}) and (P_{CD}, F_{CD}), the similarity S_{ABCD} between two flow features can be obtained by calculating F_{AB} and F_{CD}. When analyzing the IP of hosts, the similar flows can be divided into two types: (a) and (b) in Figure 2. The similar flows in (a) are generated by four different hosts and this type is regular in distributed botnet using P2P as

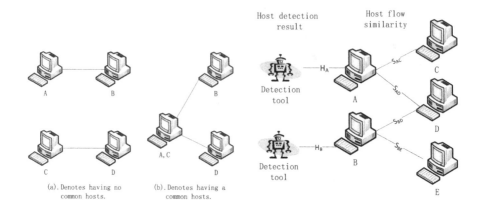

Fig. 2. Flow similarity   Fig. 3. Inference algorithm

C&C protocol. HS is used to represent the host similarity, so we can get the HS between hosts A and C, A and D, B and C, and B and D, for example, in Figure 3 $HS_{AC} = HS_{AD} = HS_{BC} = HS_{BD} = S_{ABCD}$. The similar flows in (b) are generated by the same host. As shown in (b), A and C is the same host and this host may be a botmaster. This situation is regular in centralized botnets using IRC or HTTP as C&C protocol. So, we can get the host similarity of hosts B and D: $HS_{BD} = S_{ABCD}$. FS is used to represent the final similarity between hosts, that is $FS_{AB} = max(HS_{AB})$.

4.3   Bot Inference Engine

According to the results of host detection and flow similarity analysis, bot inference engine can calculate the suspicion degree of the hosts without reporting detection results. As shown in the Figure 3, there are five hosts in a cluster, A, B, C, D and E. The detection results of A and B are H_A and H_B, hosts C, D and E report nothing. S_{AC} represents the calculation results of similarity between A and C. Host D has no detection result, due to the fact that it has similar communication flows with hosts A and B, what's more, bots have been found out on hosts A and B, then the final detection result of host D is: $F_D = (H_A S_{AD} + H_B S_{BD})/(S_{AD} + S_{BD})$. So a reliable detection result for the hosts without detection tools or with invalid detection tools is infered. If the host D has reported its detection result H_D and the result shows that host D has been infected with bots, however the degree of suspicion is not very high, we could not accurately judge whether host D has really been infected with bots, and there may be the possibility of activities of benign programs leading to the inaccurate report by detection tools. We can calculate the final detection result of host D more accurately through bot inference engine to combine flows similarity information of other hosts in network, $F_D = (H_D + (H_A S_{AD} + H_B S_{BD})/(S_{AD} + S_{BD}))/2$. Meanwhile, if there are a large number of hosts in the network, which have similar flows with host D and send their detection reports, the detection results could be more accurate through bot inference engine.

For more general situations, X represents any host in network and it is in cluster $N(X)$. The similarities between all hosts in $N(X)$ are in a certain range. H_X represents the detection results generated by host X, and S_{KX} means the similarity between host K and host X. Finally, the detection result of host X through inference engine is

$$
F_X = \begin{cases} \sum_{K \in N(X)} H_K S_{KX} / \sum_{K \in N(X)} S_{KX} & , H_X = 0 \\ (H_X + \sum_{k \in N(X)} H_K S_{KX} / \sum_{K \in N(X)} S_{KX})/2 & , H_X \neq 0 \end{cases} \tag{2}
$$

The range of H_X is between 0 and 1, and the larger the value, the greater the suspicion degree of whether the host has been infected with bots. The range of host flows similarity S_{KX} is also between 0 and 1 and the larger the value, the greater the flows similarity between two hosts. Analyzing the above inference algorithm, it is easy to obtain the final detection result F_X, which also ranges from 0 to 1, and the larger the value, the greater the probability to be infected with bots.

5 Experiment

According to the algorithm proposed, we design and implement the prototype based on BotInfer and analyze its accuracy and deployment rate through experiments. For host detection, we use the average detection result of those acquired through several existing tools as the suspicion degree of whether the host is infected by bots. In network analysis, the fprobe[1] [19] and flow-tools [20] are used to capture the flows of the whole network. According to the IP information, the captured host flows are filtered by safe-browling [21] proposed by google and top 1,000,000 URLs [22] proposed by alexa. Then the data is processed and analyzed by hclust [23] package and Python language. The final detection result is obtained through inference engine.

5.1 Environment Setup

In the experiment, a controllable local network is built. User hosts are deployed in VMware virtual machines with Windows XP Professional. BotInfer is deployed in a Windows XP Professional host which has been equipped with quad core 2.40GHz CPU and 2G RAM. The network information collector and analyzer are deployed in a Ubuntu 10.10 host equipped with 2.40GHz CPU and 2G RAM, and this host is used as the gateway of the entire lab network. The topology of experiment environment is shown in Figure 4.

---

[1] NetFlow probes: fprobe and fprobe-ulog, http://fprobe.sourceforge.net/

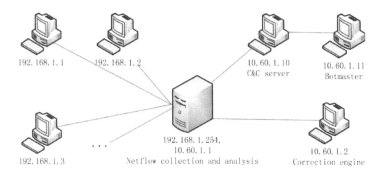

Fig. 4. Experiment architecture

To evaluate the effectiveness of the algorithm in detecting bot host, the bot programs are installed in only some of user hosts and the botmaster is installed in a host in a public network. Because of the uncontrollability of P2P botnet, we only use HTTP and IRC bots, including SdBot, AgoBot, RBot and Nugache. In order to better simulate the real environment of user hosts, we install and run softwares like mIRC, pcAnywhere, Firefox, eMule and uTorrent, etc. in user hosts and let them use the network as usual. For the network flow analysis, we capture the network flow of a certain backbone at the CERNET network during a day as the background data. There are 755,255 flow records in a time window of 10 minutes. After filtration, we get the information of 63,589 hosts. We integrate the filtered information of features in the public network with the flow features captured in local network. This will better evaluate the effectiveness of cluster analysis when distinguishing bot flows.

5.2   Experimental Result and Analysis

The Accuracy. We use 40 VMware machines as user hosts which have been installed with Windows XP Professional. The hosts are deployed in the same network which is 192.168.1.1-192.168.1.40/24. Bot instances in the hosts, host detection tools and the running of benign softwares are shown in Table 2. We guarantee that the deployment rate of host detection tools deployed on bot infected hosts comes to 80%, that the benign softwares on hosts can access the network and the botmaster can communicate with bots in C&C channel

Table 2. Host configurations

Host IP	Bot	Host Detection Tools	Common Software
192.168.1.1-192.168.1.24	yes	yes	yes
192.168.1.25-192.168.1.30	yes	no	yes
192.168.1.31-192.168.1.40	no	no	yes

Table 3. The accuracy of BotInfer

Bot name	Average FP	Average FN	Average TP	Average TN	Duration
SdBot	0	0.02	0.98	1	24h
AgoBot	0	0.04	0.96	1	24h
RBot	0	0.04	0.96	1	24h
Nugache	0	0.05	0.95	1	24h

as usual. The commands we use include dns, open, download, redirect, etc. On the network flow collector and analyzer, feature filtering and feature extraction processes are both in a time window of 10 minutes. Then mixed flow-features which are extracted from lab network flows and background are used to do cluster analysis and similarity calculation. Finally we get the detection result of the entire network through BotInfer. Table 3 shows the average detection results of the 4 bot instances being detected respectively in individual time windows during 24 hours.

Deployment Rate. BotInfer has improved bot detection accuracy to a certain extent. Detection tools need not to be deployed on all the hosts in the entire network. It can get all hosts detection results through bot inference engine, avoid the failure caused by bot detection tools' failure on some of the hosts in the network, so as to improve the robustness. In normal user hosts, we regularly adjust the number of hosts infected with bots, the number of benign hosts and the number of hosts being installed with detection tools, and we analyze multiple bot instances in IRC and HTTP botnets. Figure 5 shows the influence of deployment rate of host detection tools on the overall test results. When the deployment rate is over 50%, the accuracy of the test results of the entire network will be

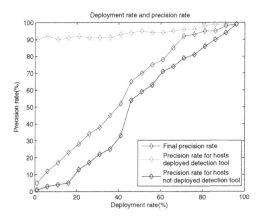

Fig. 5. Deployment rate and precision rate

366 Y. He et al.

significantly improved; when deployment rate is over 80%, the detection accuracy rate of hosts without detection tools increases to more than 86%.

6 Conclusion

Although there are a lot of ways to analyze network flows, there are still many challenges. When it comes to flow analysis, the following questions have been solved in this paper: how to select the flow-features to distinguish benign flows from malicious flow efficiently; how many clusters needed is reasonable when partition flow-features; the storage of the final results. At the same time, we also have figured out the differences between the final results generating from the inference engine of hosts with detection tools and those of hosts without detection tools.

Through analyzing the architecture of BotInfer, the results acquired by inference engine still depend on the results of host detection tools to a large extent. Pure network analysis is unable to get the degree of suspicion for hosts in the network directly. What's more, the detection of unknown botnet also mainly depends on the efficiency of host detection tools. In order to reduce the influence of host detection results on correlation results, a possible way is to deploy more than one detection tools in the networks to improve the efficiency of host detection, another way is to get the network detection result using machine learning or other graph algorithm to analyse the captured network flow.

With botnets evolving, a large number of hosts are still suffering from bots. In this paper, BotInfer is able to infer hosts infected with bot in the entire network efficiently when the deployment rate of host detection tools reaches a certain point in the local network. We have picked up 13 features of the collected flows and calculate the flow similarity between hosts so as to distinguish the flow of benign programs from that of bots in C&C communication. Finally, through inference engine to combine the results of host detection and that of network flow analysis, the detection report can be acquired for all hosts in the network including the hosts with and without detection tools. In Botinfer, we have conducted experiments in the lab, and analyzed them in multiple aspects.

References

1. Park, Y., Reeves, D.S.: Identification of bot commands by run-time execution monitoring. In: 2009 Annual Computer Security Applications Conference, pp. 321–330 (2009)
2. Stinson, E., Mitchell, J.: Characterizing Bots Remote Control Behavior. In: 4th DIMVA Conference (July 2007)
3. Liu, L., Chen, S., Yan, G., Zhang, Z.: BotTracer: Execution-Based Bot-Like Malware Detection. In: International Conference on Information Security (2008)
4. Coskun, B., Dietrich, S., Memon, N.: Friends of An Enemy: Identifying Local Members of Peer-to-Peer Botnets Using Mutual Contacts. In: 2010 ACSAC Conference (2010)

5. Nagaraja, S., Mittal, P., Hong, C.-Y., Caesar, M., Borisov, N.: BotGrep: Finding P2P bots with structured graph analysis. In: USENIX Security Conference (August 2010)

6. Zeng, Y., Hu, X., Shin, K.G.: Detection of Botnets Using Combined Host- and Network-Level Information. In: DSN (2010)

7. Liu, L., Chen, S., Yan, G., Zhang, Z.: BotTracer: Execution-Based Bot-Like Malware Detection. In: Wu, T.-C., Lei, C.-L., Rijmen, V., Lee, D.-T. (eds.) ISC 2008. LNCS, vol. 5222, pp. 97–113. Springer, Heidelberg (2008)

8. Jacob, G., Hund, R., Kruegel, C., Holz, T.: JACKSTRAWS: Picking Command and Control Connections from Bot Traffic. In: USENIX Security Symposium (2011)

9. Rieck, K., Trinius, P., Willems, C.: Automatic analysis of malware behavior using machine learning. Journal of Computer Security 19(4) (2011)

10. Karbalaie, F., Sami, A., Ahmadi, M.: Semantic Malware Detection by Deploying Graph Mining. International Journal of Computer Science Issues 9(1(3)) (2012)

11. Tegeler, F., Fu, X., Vigna, G., Kruegel, C.: BotFinder: Finding Bots in Network Traffic Without Deep Packet Inspection. In: CoNEXT (2012)

12. Bilge, L., Balzarotti, D., Robertson, W.: DISCLOSURE: Detecting Botnet Command and Control Servers Through Large-Scale NetFlow Analysis. ACM (2012)

13. François, J., Wang, S., State, R., Engel, T.: Bottrack: Tracking Botnets Using Netflow and Pagerank. In: Domingo-Pascual, J., Manzoni, P., Palazzo, S., Pont, A., Scoglio, C. (eds.) NETWORKING 2011, Part I. LNCS, vol. 6640, pp. 1–14. Springer, Heidelberg (2011)

14. Gu, G.: Correlation-based Botnet Detection in Enterprise Networks. Doctor Thesis, GIT (2008)

15. Park, Y.H., Zhang, Q., Douglas, S., Reeves, D.: AntiBot: Clustering Common Semantic Patterns for Bot Detection. In: COMPSAC (2010)

16. Kwon, T., Su, Z.: Modeling High-Level Behavior Patterns for Precise Similarity analysis of Software. Technical Reports, University of California, CSE-2010-16 (2010)

17. Wang, X., Jiang, X.: Artificial Malware Immunization based on Dynamically Assigned Sense of Self. In: Burmester, M., Tsudik, G., Magliveras, S., Ilić, I. (eds.) ISC 2010. LNCS, vol. 6531, pp. 166–180. Springer, Heidelberg (2011)

18. Halkidi, M., Batistakis, Y., Vazirgiannis, M.: On Clustering Validation Techniques. JIIS 17(2-3), 107–145 (2001)

19. NetFlow probes: fprobe and fprobe-ulog, http://fprobe.sourceforge.net/

20. flow-tools, http://www.splintered.net/sw/flow-tools/docs/flow-tools.html

21. Safe Browsing API - Google Developers, https://developers.google.com/safe-browsing/

22. Alexa Top 500 Global Sites, http://www.alexa.com/topsites

23. R: Hierarchical Clustering, http://stat.ethz.ch/R-manual/R-patched/library/stats/html/hclust.html

On-Demand Proactive Defense against Memory Vulnerabilities

Gang Chen, Hai Jin, Deqing Zou, and Weiqi Dai

Services Computing Technology and System Lab
Cluster and Grid Computing Lab
School of Computer Science and Technology
Huazhong University of Science and Technology, Wuhan, 430074, China
hjin@hust.edu.cn

Abstract. Memory vulnerabilities have severely affect system security and availability. Although there are a number of solutions proposed to defense against memory vulnerabilities, most of existing solutions protect the entire life cycle of the application or survive attacks after detecting attacks. This paper presents OPSafe, a system that make applications safely survive memory vulnerabilities for a period of time from the starting or in runtime with users' demand. OPSafe can provide a hot-portable *Green Zone* of any size with users' demand, where all the subsequent allocated memory objects including stack objects and heap objects are reallocated and safely managed in a protected memory area. When users open the green zone, OPSafe uses a comprehensive memory management in the protected memory area to adaptively allocate buffers with multiple times of their defined sizes and randomly place them. Combined with objects free masking techniques, OPSafe can avoid overrunning each other and dangling pointer errors as well as double free or invalid free errors. Once closing the green zone, OPSafe clears away all objects in the protected area and then frees the protected area. We have developed a Linux prototype and evaluated it using four applications which contains a wide range of vulnerabilities. The experimental results show that OPSafe can conveniently create and destruct a hot-portable green zone where the vulnerable application can survive crashes and eliminate erroneous execution.

Keywords: Memory Vulnerabilities; Proactive Defense.

1 Introduction

Memory bugs severely affect system security and availability. Programs written in unsafe languages like C and C++ are particularly vulnerable because attackers can exploit memory errors to control vulnerable programs. These vulnerabilities can also cause programs failures. According to a survey conducted by IT industry analyst firms [10], the average business loss of an hour of IT system downtime is between US $84,000 and US $108,000. However, previous study showed that the average time to diagnose bugs and generate patches is 28 days. During this long

C.-H. Hsu et al. (Eds.): NPC 2013, LNCS 8147, pp. 368–379, 2013.

time vulnerable window, users have to either stop running the program which cause the costly program downtime, or continuing running the program which experience problems such as potential crashes and attacks. Neither of the two behaviors is desirable. Therefore, it is significant to survive attacks to preserve system availability.

There are a number of solutions have been proposed to protect programs against memory vulnerabilities. One direction is for buffer overflow prevention, including return address defense on the stack [4,6], array bounds checking, pointers protection via encrypting pointers, and address obfuscation via randomizing memory layout [2]. These approaches can improve the safety while drop the availability. The reason is that programs are always terminated when detecting attacks. The other direction is for heap-related bug prevention [1,5], which well balances the safety and availability of the applications. However, these techniques cannot be applied for protecting against stack buffer overflow attacks.

Previous solutions on protecting against memory vulnerabilities had to protect the entire life cycle of the application, or survive attacks after detecting attacks. However, users only need protection for a period of time at most times, especially for desktop applications. For example, when users use a browser to submit works, they need the browser not occurring any faults until the works have been submitted successfully.

In this paper, we propose a on-demand proactive protection system called OPSafe, which can make applications safely survive memory vulnerabilities for a period of time from the starting or in runtime with users' demand. When users need to protect the program against memory vulnerabilities, OPSafe can dynamically reallocate all the subsequent allocated memory objects in an protected memory area, called *Green Zone*, and it can also conveniently break away from the program to terminate the protection when users will not protect the program. In the green zone, OPSafe adopts the memory randomization technique in the protected memory area, which adaptively allocates buffers with multiple times of their defined sizes and places semantically infinite distance between memory objects to provide an probabilistic memory safety. This technique can greatly avoid overrunning between memory objects as well as dangling pointer errors. By omitting invalid free, OPSafe can mask double-free and invalid free errors. When closing green zone, OPSafe clears away the objects in the protected area and then frees the protected area. Our green zone is hot-portable with a feature of conveniently creating and destructing for running applications. As a result, OPSafe can provide a hot-portable green zone of any size for an application with users' demand.

To demonstrate the effectiveness of OPSafe, we have implemented a Linux prototype and evaluated it using four applications that contain a wide range of memory vulnerabilities including stack smashing, heap buffer overflow, double-free and dangling pointer. Our experimental results show that OPSafe can protect applications against memory vulnerabilities in the green zone with a reasonable overhead.

In summary, we make the following contributions.

- We propose OPSafe, an on-demand proactive protection system to make applications safely survive memory bugs for a period of time from the starting or in runtime with users' demand.
- We propose a concept, a hot-portable green zone of any size with users' demand, which can conveniently protect the applications at any times. It can protect the applications from the beginning or in runtime, and slice away from applications at any times, both decided by users.
- We have implemented OPSafe on a Linux system, and evaluated its effectiveness and performance using four applications that contain a wide ranges of memory vulnerabilities.

The rest of the paper is organized as follows. The OPSafe overview, including the motivation, the background, the architecture, the workflow and important steps of OPSafe, are introduced in section 2. Section 3 describes the important implementation techniques. The experimental and analytical results are presented in section 4. Section 5 gives an overview of related work. Finally, we summarize our contributions in section 6.

2   OPSafe Overview

In this section, we first introduce our motivation, and then give an overview of the architecture and workflow of OPSafe.

2.1   Motivation

Memory vulnerabilities have severely affected system security and availability. Full life-cycle protection for an application is common most of times. However, sometimes we may need the application to be secure and reliable only for a period of time, especially for desktop applications. For example, when we write an important email via an email client, we need the client not crashed in the writing. However, we may not mind crashing in normal use because restarting the client is also convenient. Moreover, we even do not want to use the protection tool to protect the client in normal use because they affect the use of the client more or less from the performance or the function.

A great number of solutions on handling with memory vulnerabilities have been proposed, but they are designed from the view on how to respond to attacks without considering the users' demand. They can be classified into three categories: proactive full life-cycle protections which protect the application from the starting to the termination, fail-stop approaches which terminate the application for security when detecting a fault, and self-healing approaches which learn from the fault and automatically temporarily fix the bugs. All of these solutions should always monitor the application and not conveniently slice away from the application.

Take the email client as an example again. A user wants a green zone and also can conveniently control the size of the green zone for the email client. The green zone can only be opened with the user demand. When writing the important email, the user can open the green zone. In this green zone, the user does not mind using more resource to make sure the security and availability of the application. When the resource occupied by the protection tool is needed to do other things, the user can conveniently close the green zone. Therefore, we need an on-demand proactive defense mechanism which can safely and effectively survive memory vulnerabilities in the green zone and have no effect outside of it for an application.

The memory management of OPSafe is based on our previous work SafeStack [11] and Memshepherd [12]. SafeStack proposes the memory access virtualization mechanism to reallocate stack objects into a protected memory area. Memshepherd integrates the memory access virtualization mechanism into DieHard's design on the probabilistic safe heap memory allocator to reallocate heap objects into a safe heap space. In this heap space, memory objects are randomly placed in large chunks called *miniheaps*. However, Memshepherd should manage all the memory objects from the starting of the application, which can incur a high overhead and make the performance of the application degrade.

2.2   OPSafe Architecture

The architecture of OPSafe is illustrated in Figure 1a. OPSafe consists of several components, including a Stack Objects Information Extractor used to extract the information of stack buffers from the binaries, a Control Unit used to respond users' demand to generate a green zone (i.e., a protection window to protect and to end protection for the application), a Memory Allocator Extension used to reallocate all memory objects including stack objects and heap objects into the protected memory area, and a Memory Free Extension used to free the protected memory area.

Based on a dynamic instrumentation infrastructure, OPSafe can generate a hot-portable green zone for the application, including allocating and freeing memory objects. To reallocate the stack objects into the protected memory areas, OPSafe should get the location and size information of the original stack objects, which is gained by the static analysis from the Stack Objects Information Extractor.

2.3   Workflow of OPSafe

The workflow of OPSafe is illustrated in Figure 1b. Users can arbitrarily open or close the green zone on demand. The stack buffer information can be extracted from binaries before opening the green zone.

When users request to open the green zone, OPSafe creates a protected memory area and uses the Memory Allocator Extension to dynamically reallocate all the memory objects into the protected memory area with the dynamic instrumentation infrastructure. The memory allocation contains two parts. One is

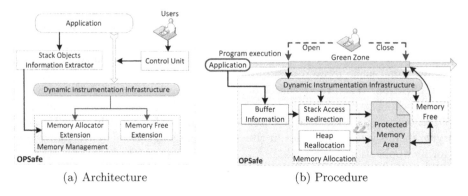

(a) Architecture   (b) Procedure

Fig. 1. OPSafe Design

stack access redirection which is the basis of memory access virtualization. It is used to reallocate the stack objects into the protected memory area and redirect the memory access from the original address to the corresponding protected memory address. In this redirection, OPSafe should locate the original address of stack objects which can be gained from the buffer information. The other is heap reallocation which is used to intercept the heap allocation functions and replace them with our allocation functions to make all the heap objects be allocated in the protected memory area. In the protected memory area, OPSafe maintains stack objects of a function until the function exits and marks the the memory area of an heap object can be used when the application frees it.

When users request to close the green zone, OPSafe uses the Memory Free Extension to restore the memory management of the application and gradually frees all the memory objects in the protected memory area. OPSafe firstly removes all the reallocation instruments for stack objects and heap objects reallocation. In addition, OPSafe checks all *miniheaps* to free the unused *miniheaps*. If there are *miniheaps* in use, OPSafe then continues to monitor them. Once all the rest of *miniheaps* have been freed, OPSafe destructs the green zone by removing all the free operation instruments and gracefully slicing away from the application. After that, the green zone is closed.

3   OPSafe Implementation

In our implementation, our protected memory area is a heap space which is managed in the same way as Memshepherd. We should note that our protected memory area is not tied with Memshepherd's memory management, but also can be combined with other safe memory management mechanisms. In this section, we discuss the stack buffer information extraction, the green zone creation, maintenance and destruction.

3.1 Stack Buffer Information Extraction

The stack buffer information consists of the function level information and the variable level information. The function level information contains the function name, the starting code address and the number of stack buffer variables. The variable level information contains the variable name, size, offsets from the frame pointers for each local variables and parameters for buffers. As Memshepherd extracts stack buffer information according to the memory objects access pattern, the information is not accurate. However, if the program is compiled with debugging option (-g in GCC), the compiler adds debugging information about all variables in the program binaries. We extend Memshepherd's buffer information extractor with debugging information for the applications compiled with debugging option.

OPSafe uses TIED [13] with an extension to extract debugging information for stack buffers. TIED cannot extract the stack buffer information from function *main* as the offset is relative to the stack pointer. OPSafe organizes all the buffer related information according to TIED, but makes some changes to the data structure of the buffer related information for future effective diagnoses, and also OPSafe does not need to rewrite the program binaries with the buffer related information as TIED does.

3.2 Green Zone Creation

When users request to open the green zone, OPSafe uses the dynamic instrumentation tool to intercept the memory allocation operations, including stack objects allocation and heap objects allocation. In addition, OPSafe creates the protected memory area which is allocated adaptively according to usage requirements.

For stack objects allocation, OPSafe only redirects the stack buffers in the subsequent called functions into the protected memory area. To redirect these stack buffers access, OPSafe should firstly locate the original addresses of stack buffers according to the stack buffer information, and then map the original addresses to the new corresponding addresses in the protected area. This is done when the register *ESP* becomes smaller. As the stack buffers have not been initiated at that time, OPSafe can benefit from avoiding copying data from the original memory addresses to the new corresponding addresses. For the stack buffers in the current stack, OPSafe maintains the original memory access to these stack buffers.

For heap objects allocation, OPSafe intercepts all the heap allocation functions in *libc* and replaces them with OPSafe's heap allocation functions, such as the function *malloc*. OPSafe only reallocates the subsequent heap objects requests after green zone creation, and the management for the previous allocated heap objects is still maintained by the application.

3.3   Green Zone Maintenance

After memory objects reallocation, OPSafe maintains the life cycle of these memory objects in the green zone. For the memory objects outside of the green zone, OPSafe leaves them into the management of the application.

For the stack buffers access, there are three types of access for them in the memory access virtualization, including direct access, indirect access and pointer access. The access mode is *"Base plus Offset"* for direct access and *"Base plus Index plus Offset"* for indirect access. The base is the base register, i.e., *EBP* or *ESP*, the offset is the offset is the value between the starting address of the array and the base register, and the index is the index register which stores the stack buffer index. For these two cases, OPSafe calculates the starting address of the stack buffer and replaces with the corresponding protected memory address. The pointer access means stack buffer is accessed by pointers, such as a stack buffer is passed an argument to a function. As there must be an instruction to get the address of the stack buffer, OPSafe can replace it without continuing to map the memory access from the pointer. When a function returns, OPSafe frees all the stack buffers of the function in the protected memory area.

For the heap object access, there are no extra memory mapping operations. When freeing a heap object, OPSafe checks whether it is in the green zone or not. If so, OPSafe then checks whether the heap object has been freed or the address of the heap object is invalid. For the double-free or invalid free, OPSafe can mask this error by omitting these memory free operations. If the heap object is outside of the protected memory area, OPSafe leaves the management of these objects and make the application to call the original *libc* function *free* to free it.

3.4   Green Zone Destruction

When users request to close the green zone, OPSafe enters into the green zone destruction phrase to gradually free all the memory objects in the green zone and restore the memory management of the application.

In this phrase, OPSafe firstly checks all the *miniheaps* in the green zone to determine which the *miniheap* can be freed. If there are *miniheaps* which are unused (i.e., do no store any memory objects), OPSafe frees these *miniheaps*. For the *miniheaps* which are in use, OPSafe should wait until all the memory objects of a *miniheap* have been freed. The memory objects in a miniheap consists of stack objects and heap objects. OPSafe frees stack objects of a function when the function returns and frees heap objects when the application call the *libc* function *free* to free them. In addition, OPSafe does not need to redirect the subsequent stack objects of new called functions and intercept the memory allocation operations of the application.

Finally, when all the *miniheaps* has been freed, OPSafe destructs the green zone by removing all the instrumentation for the application to restore the memory management of the application. After that, the application runs as original.

Table 1. Applications and bugs used in evaluation

Application	Version	Vulnerabilities ID	Bug	Description
ProFTPD	1.3.3b	CVE-2010-4221	Stack Overflow	FTP Server
Null-HTTPd	0.5.0	CVE-2002-1496	Heap Overflow	Web Server
Null-HTTPd-df		Manually Injected	Double Free	
Pine	4.44	CVE-2002-1320	Heap Overflow	Email Client
M4	1.4.4	-	Dangling Pointer	Macro Processor

4   Experimental Evaluation

We have implemented a Linux prototype system with the operating system kernel Linux 2.6, and Pin 2.12-56759 is used as our dynamic instrumentation infrastructure. Our evaluation platform consists of two machines connected with 100Mbps Ethernet. One machine is configured with the Intel E5200 dual core 2.5GHz processors and 4GB memory. They are used to deploy OPSafe and our test suite. The other is configured with Intel E7400 dual core 2.8GHz processors and 4GB memory. It is used to run clients for testing servers and servers for testing desktop clients.

We first describe the details of our test suite which are a range of multi-process and multi-threaded applications. Then we present the results of the evaluation on the effectiveness of OPSafe under our test suite. To test the effectiveness, we use OPSafe to protect our test suite to survive memory vulnerabilities. Finally, we discuss the performance evaluation.

4.1   Overall Analysis

Our test suite contains four applications, including a ftp server ProFTPD, a web server Null-HTTPd, an email client Pine and a macro processor GNU M4, which are listed in Table 1. All these applications contain various types of bugs, including stack overflow, heap overflow, double free and dangling pointer. Four of the vulnerabilities are real-world vulnerabilities, and the double free bug is manually injected into the web server Null-HTTPd, named Null-HTTPd-df in Table 1.

Exploit CVE-2010-4221 in ProFTPD enables attackers corrupt memory to crash the ftp server or execute arbitrary code by sending data containing a large number of Telnet IAC commands to overrun stack buffers in the vulnerable function *pr_cmd_read*. OPSafe can avoid overrunning the control structures in the stack by moving the stack buffers of the vulnerable function into the protected memory area.

Exploit CVE-2002-1496 in Null-HTTPd is caused by improper handling of negative *Content-Length* values in HTTP header field. By sending a HTTP request with a negative value in the *Content-Length* header field, a remote attacker could overflow a heap buffer and cause the web server to crash or execute arbitrary code in the system. OPSafe can avoid attackers gain control by segregating all the heap metadata from the heap in the protected memory area. In addition, OPSafe can avoid the vulnerable heap objects overrunning other heap objects with high probability by multiple times of their defined sizes and a random placement strategy.

Exploit manually injected in Null-HTTPd-df is caused by a piece of injected vulnerable code. It frees a heap object which has already been freed. OPSafe can mask this double free error by intercepting the free operation, checking it and omitting invalid free operation.

Exploit CVE-2002-1320 in Pine enables attackers send a fully legal email message with a crafted From-header to force Pine to core dump on start-up. The only way to launch pine is manually removing the bad message either directly from the spool, or from another mail user agent. Until the message has been removed or edited there is no way of accessing the INBOX using Pine. The heap overflow is caused by the incorrect calculation of string length in the function *est_size*, a message's header *"From:"* which contains a long string of escaped characters can cause a buffer used by the function *addr_list_string* to overflow. OPSafe can allocate an object with multiple times of defined size and a random placement strategy to avoid overrunning with high probability.

Exploit the dangling pointer in GNU M4 causes an misbehavior such as printing out misleading information when a macro whose arguments are being collected is redefined or deleted. Through deleting the definition from the symbol table, it can leave dangling pointers in the local variable *sym* of the function *expand_macro* and then use dangling pointers leading M4 misbehavior. OPSafe can avoid this misbehavior as it does not really free a heap object in the green zone. It holds the content of the object and only marks the memory space be used. Fortunately, the random placement strategy of OPSafe can make it unlikely that a newly freed object will soon be overwritten by a subsequent allocation. Therefore, OPSafe can avoid this dangling pointer attacks with high probability.

4.2   Effectiveness Evaluation

We evaluate the capability of fault tolerance by comparing OPSafe with the restart method. We use a lightweight web server Null-HTTPd in this experiment. We adopt the apache benchmark *ab* to test the web server throughput and a network traffic and bandwidth usage tool *nload* to get a real time throughput with a $100ms$ interval. In addition, malicious requests are sent every $5s$ to crash the web server. All these two cases have adopted the restart method which restarts the web server when it crashes, and the results are shown in Figure 2a.

From the figure, we can see that OPSafe can survive the heap overflow attacks to make the web server continually serve the clients in the green zone with a modest performance degradation. Once closing the green zone, the web server still crashes when attacks occurring.

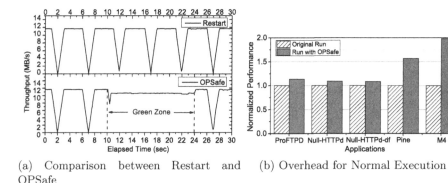

(a) Comparison between Restart and OPSafe

(b) Overhead for Normal Execution

Fig. 2. OPSafe Evaluation

4.3 Performance Evaluation

We evaluated the normal execution overhead caused by OPSafe with these four applications. In this experiment, we use a ftp client to download a 300MB file from the ProFTPD server. For the web server Null-HTTPd, we use the Apache web benchmark *ab* to get the result. For the Email client Pine, we use it to send an email whose size is 9.5MB. For the GNU M4, we use its example test file *foreach.m4* as the workload. We compared the average response time for server applications and the execution time for desktop applications.

We show the overhead of OPSafe in Figure 2b. It ranges from 8.77% for Null-HTTPd-df to 97.87% for GNU M4 with an average of 37.28%. Although OPSafe incurs a modest overhead, it provides a flexible protection mechanism with users' demand.

5 Related Work

In this section, we compare OPSafe with other solutions in preventing and responding to memory vulnerabilities attacks.

5.1 Proactive Defense Methods

Failure-oblivious computing [8] tolerates memory vulnerabilities via manufacturing values for "out-of-bound read" and discarding "out-of-bound write". However, it should modify the source codes of the application with its specific compiler. Moreover, it may cause an unpredicted behavior which is an new threat for the application.

DieHard [1] adopts the randomized allocation technique to give the application an approximation of an infinite sized heap, which can provide an high probabilistic memory safety. However, it should protect the application from the beginning and it is incapable for surviving stack smashing attacks.

5.2   Fail-Stop Methods

There are a number of solutions proposed to defend against memory vulnerabilities in a fail-stop fashion, especially for stack smashing bugs. StackGuard [4] checks the integrity of canaries which are inserted around the return address. Address space layout randomization technique is proposed to protect applications against memory bugs exploits with a source-to-source transformation [2]. These solutions have to use the compiler to analyze or modify source codes via extending the GNU C compiler. However, OPSafe can protect applications without extending the compiler.

A binary rewriting defense technology [6] is proposed to protect the return address. It inserts the return address defense codes into binaries of applications which can protect the integrity of the return address with a redundant copy. However, it is powerless for heap-related vulnerabilities.

5.3   Self-healing Methods

Rx [7] combines the checkpoint/rollback mechanism and a changing execution environment to survive bugs. Especially for the stack smashing bugs, Rx drops the malicious users' requests.

ASSURE [9] proposes the error virtualization and rescue point technique to bypass faulty region of codes. ASSURE may cause the application not function well, our previous works SHelp [3] applies weighted rescue points and extends it to a virtualization computing environment. However, all of these techniques unsafely speculate on programmer's intentions which may introduce new threats.

First-Aid [5] tolerates a bug via identifying the bug types and bug-triggering memory objects, and generating runtime patches to apply them to a small set of memory objects. However, it cannot deal with the stack smashing bugs.

6   Conclusion

In this paper we present a new system OPSafe which can provide a hot-portable *Green Zone* of any size with users demand for applications where applications can safely survive memory bugs for a period of time from the starting or in runtime with users' demand. Once the green zone is opened, OPSafe takes over memory management of the application to make all the subsequent allocated memory objects including stack objects and heap objects reallocated and safely managed in a protected memory area, where the memory vulnerabilities can be prevented with high probability. Once closing the green zone, OPSafe clears away all objects in the protected area and then frees the protected area. We have developed a prototype system and evaluated the system's effectiveness using four applications with a wide range of memory vulnerabilities. The experimental results demonstrate that our system can conveniently create and destruct a hot-portable green zone where the vulnerable application can survive crashes and eliminate erroneous execution.

Acknowledgment. This paper is supported by National High-tech R&D Program (863 Program) under grant No. 2012AA012600.

References

1. Berger, E., Zorn, B.: DieHard: Probabilistic Memory Safety for Unsafe Languages. In: Proceedings of the 2006 ACM SIGPLAN Conference on Programming Language Design and Implementation, pp. 158–168. ACM (2006)
2. Bhatkar, S., Sekar, R., DuVarney, D.: Efficient Techniques for Comprehensive Protection from Memory Error Exploits. In: Proceedings of the 14th Conference on USENIX Security Symposium, pp. 271–286. USENIX (2005)
3. Chen, G., Jin, H., Zou, D., Zhou, B., Qiang, W., Hu, G.: SHelp: Automatic Self-healing for Multiple Application Instances in a Virtual Machine Environment. In: Proceedings of the 2010 IEEE International Conference on Cluster Computing, pp. 97–106. IEEE (2010)
4. Cowan, C., Pu, C., Maier, D., Hintony, H., Walpole, J., Bakke, P., Beattie, S., Grier, A., Wagle, P., Zhang, Q.: StackGuard: Automatic Adaptive Detection and Prevention of Buffer-overflow Attacks. In: Proceedings of the 7th Conference on USENIX Security Symposium, pp. 63–78. USENIX (1998)
5. Gao, Q., Zhang, W., Tang, Y., Qin, F.: First-Aid: Surviving and Preventing Memory Management Bugs During Production Runs. In: Proceedings of the 4th ACM European Conference on Computer Systems, pp. 159–172. ACM (2009)
6. Prasad, M., Chiueh, T.: A Binary Rewriting Defense Against Stack Based Buffer Overflow Attacks. In: Proceedings of the 2003 USENIX Annual Technical Conference, pp. 211–224. USENIX (2003)
7. Qin, F., Tucek, J., Sundaresan, J., Zhou, Y.: Rx: Treating Bugs as Allergies— A Safe Method to Survive Software Failures. In: Proceedings of the 20th ACM Symposium on Operating System Principles, pp. 235–248. ACM (2005)
8. Rinard, M., Cadar, C., Dumitran, D., Roy, D., Leu, T., Beebee Jr., W.: Enhancing Server Availability and Security Through Failure-Oblivious Computing. In: Proceedings of the 6th Conference on Symposium on Operating Systems Design and Implementation, pp. 303–316. USENIX (2004)
9. Sidiroglou, S., Laadan, O., Perez, C., Viennot, N., Nieh, J., Keromytis, A.: ASSURE: Automatic Software Self-healing Using REscue points. In: Proceedings of the 14th International Conference on Architectural Support for Programming Languages and Operating Systems, pp. 37–48. ACM (2009)
10. Vision Solutions Staff, Assessing the Financial Impact of Downtime. Vision Solutions, Inc. (2010)
11. Chen, G., Jin, H., Zou, D., Zhou, B., Liang, Z., Zheng, W., Shi, X.: SafeStack: Automatically Patching Stack-based Buffer Overflow Bugs. To be appeared in IEEE Transactions on Dependable and Secure Computing. IEEE (2013)
12. Zou, D., Zheng, W., Jiang, W., Jin, H., Chen, G.: Memshepherd: Comprehensive Memory Bug Fault-Tolerance System. To be appeared in Security and Communication Networks. John Wiley & Sons, Ltd. (2013)
13. Avijit, K., Gupta, P., Gupta, D.: TIED, LibsafePlus: Tools for Runtime Buffer Overflow Protection. In: Proceedings of the 13th USENIX Security Symposium, pp. 45–56. USENIX (2004)

Mahasen: Distributed Storage Resource Broker

K.D.A.K.S. Perera[1], T. Kishanthan[1], H.A.S. Perera[1], D.T.H.V. Madola[1],
Malaka Walpola[1], and Srinath Perera[2]

[1] Computer Science and Engineering Department, University Of Moratuwa, Sri Lanka
{shelanrc,kshanth2101,ashansa.perera,hirunimadola,
malaka.uom}@gmail.com
[2] WSO2 Lanka, No. 59, Flower Road, Colombo 07, Sri Lanka
srinath@wso2.com

Abstract. Modern day systems are facing an avalanche of data, and they are being forced to handle more and more data intensive use cases. These data comes in many forms and shapes: Sensors (RFID, Near Field Communication, Weather Sensors), transaction logs, Web, social networks etc. As an example, weather sensors across the world generate a large amount of data throughout the year. Handling these and similar data require scalable, efficient, reliable and very large storages with support for efficient metadata based searching. This paper present Mahasen, a highly scalable storage for high volume data intensive applications built on top of a peer-to-peer layer. In addition to scalable storage, Mahasen also supports efficient searching, built on top of the Distributed Hash table (DHT)

1 Introduction

Currently United States collects weather data from many sources like Doppler readers deployed across the country, aircrafts, mobile towers and Balloons etc. These sensors keep generating a sizable amount of data. Processing them efficiently as needed is pushing our understanding about large-scale data processing to its limits.

Among many challenges data poses, a prominent one is storing the data and indexing them so that scientist and researchers can come and ask for specific type of data collected at a given time and in a given region. For example, a scientist may want to search for all Automated Weather data items collected in Bloomington area in June 15 between 8am-12pm.

Although we have presented meteorology as an example, there are many similar use cases. For instance, Sky server [1] is one of the best examples that illustrate the use case of large data generation. This project expects to collect 40 terabytes of data in five years. In its data collection, the photometric catalog is expected to contain about 500 distinct attributes for each of one hundred million galaxies, one hundred million stars, and one million quasars. Similarly many sciences, analytic processing organizations, data mining use cases etc., would want to store large amount of data and process them later in a selective manner. These systems often store data as files and there have been several efforts to build large scale Metadata catalogs [2][3] and

C.-H. Hsu et al. (Eds.): NPC 2013, LNCS 8147, pp. 380–392, 2013.
© IFIP International Federation for Information Processing 2013

storage solutions[4][5] to support storing and searching those data items. One such example is AMGA metadata catalog [6] which was an effort to build replication and distribution mechanism for metadata catalogs.

As we discuss in the related work section, most of the metadata catalog implementations use centralized architectures and therefore have limited scalability unlike Mahasen. For example, Nirvana Storage [7] has a centralized metadata catalog which only supports scalability through vendor's mechanism such as Oracle Real Application clusters. XML Metadata Concept catalog (XMC Cat) [8] is another centralized metadata catalog which stores hierarchical rich metadata. This paper presents Mahasen, a scalable metadata catalog and storage server built on top of a P2P technology. Further, it is built by distributing an open source centralized Data registry (WSO2 Registry).

Mahasen (Distributed Storage Resource Broker) is a Data Grid Management System (DGMS) that can manage a large volume of distributed data. It targets high volume data intensive applications. The architecture of Mahasen has been designed to present a single global logical namespace across all the stored data, and it maintains a metadata structure which can be used to search files based on its' attributes. It is a network of storage servers that plays the dual purpose of a metadata catalog and a storage server. Mahasen will solve the huge data storage problem and fault tolerance in data intensive computing through aggregating low cost hardware while having both metadata and actual resources distributed without single point of failure. Metadata management will ensure the capability of searching files based on attributes of the stored resources. Mahasen has a metadata catalog, which is highly distributed and well scalable. The metadata layer ensures fault tolerance by keeping replicas of metadata.

The rest of the paper is organized as follows. The next section will discuss the related work in Metadata catalogs and Storage servers while comparing and contrasting them with Mahasen. The following section will discuss Mahasen architecture. The next section will present the performance evaluation of Mahasen. Finally the discussion section discusses limitations, other potential solutions and directions.

2   Related Work

2.1   Nirvana Storage

Nirvana SRB [7] is a middleware system that federates large heterogeneous data resources distributed across a network. The ability to access, manage, search and organize data across the entire SRB Federation is provided via a Global Namespace. MCAT is the centralized metadata repository which maintains two types of records – system- and user-metadata. Scalability of MCAT is achieved using database vendor's mechanisms [9], hence limited by Relational DB scalability Limits.

Storage/Replication. The stored resources are divided as Physical resources, Logical resources and Cluster resources. Replication of resources across multiple servers ensures the availability and recoverability of resources during failovers.

Retrieve. Data stream routing is handled by SRB and TCP/IP, making the data transfer process transparent to the users..

Search. Searching is done based on metadata attributes which are extracted and managed by the SRB.

Add/Update. Data can be added in two ways: Registration and Ingestion. Registration does not transfer any data but only creates a pointer to the data in MCAT. Ingestion is similar to registration but also transfers the data to an SRB storage resource.

Delete. If a file shadow object is used as a data object to ingest a file resource to SRB then file will be removed from MCAT but not from the physical location.

2.2   Apache OODT

OODT[10] is a middleware system for metadata that provides transparent access to the resources. It facilitates functionalities such as store, retrieve, search and analyze distributed data, objects and databases jointly. OODT provides a product service and profile service which manage data and metadata respectively.

Storage/Replication. OODT stores data product in a file-based storage in a distributed manner. They classify storage into three categories: on-line, near-line or off-line storage.

Retrieve. When OODT receives a request for retrieving a file, it issues a profile query to a product server that helps in resolving resources that could provide data. The response will include the target product server address in the form of a URI. The OODT issues a product query based on the profile query results to get the data, and it will actually retrieve data from the product server in a MIME-compliant format.

Search. OODT uses the profile server and the product server for searching the metadata and retrieve the products, and it has multiple of each type of server. OODT is based on client server architecture and it promotes REST-style architectural pattern for search and retrieve data. The profile or a subset of profile is returned for retrieval.

Add/Update. OODT provide data management including manage files and folders with the implementation of javax.sql.datasource interface.

Delete. The file management component of a Catalog and Archive Service support the delete of resource files and metadata through the implementation of javax.sql.datasource interface.

2.3   WSO2 Governance Registry

WSO2 Governance Registry [11] is a repository that allows users to store resources in a tree-structured manner, just like with a file system. However, unlike a file system, users may annotate resources using their custom properties, and also WSO2 Registry has built in metadata management features like tagging, associating resources.

However, WSO2 registry is backed by a Relational Database system, and it uses database features to store data, metadata, to manage them, and to search. Hence it has a centralized architecture. Mahasen extends that architecture to a distributed architecture.

Replication. There is no inbuilt mechanism to do the replication of resources in WSO2 registry.

Search. The WSO2 registry provides two types of searches. One is searching for a resource with their name, metadata etc., and it is implemented using underline relational database system. The second one is searching the content of resources, and implemented using Lucene [12]. The second search is only applicable to resources with textual content.

Add/Update. Adding of resources to registry can be done in two ways. First one is adding via the web interface provided by the registry. When adding a new resource, it is also possible to add additional metadata such as tags, properties of name value pairs, which later will be useful to search for that resource. The other way to add resources is by writing your own way by extending the registry API and exposing it as a web service.

The major limitation with registry, when storing resources, is the amount of memory available. Since it uses the java heap memory to buffer the resources before storing them, large files cannot be stored as the available memory is only limited to few hundred of megabytes.

2.4 Hadoop Distributed File System

Apache Hadoop Distributed File System is (HDFS)[13] is a file system designed to run on commodity hardware. HDFS has a master slave architecture that consists of a single NameNode as master and number of DataNodes. The NameNode is responsible of regulating access to files by client and managing the namespace of the file system. Generally DataNodes are deployed one per node in the cluster, and is responsible of managing storage attached to that node.

Storage / Replication. Hadoop supports hierarchical file organization where user can create directories and store files. It splits the file in to chunks with the default size of 64MB and stores them as sequence of blocks, and those blocks are stored in underlying file system of DataNodes. Those blocks are replicated for fault tolerance and the block size and the replication factor of data are configurable.

Retrieve. Applications that run on HDFS need streaming access to their data sets. Data nodes will be responsible for the read requests that issued from a user to retrieve data from the system.

Search. Hadoop Distributed File System does not provide a comprehensive search for users or applications, and it just fulfill the requirement of a distributed file system by supporting to locate the physical location of the file using the system specific metadata.

Add/Update. Writing to HDFS should be done by creating a new file and writing data to it. Hadoop addresses a single writer multiple readers' model. Once the data is written and file is closed, one cannot remove or alter data. Data can be added to the file by reopening the file and appending new data.

Delete. When a file is deleted by a user or from an application, the particular resource is not immediately removed from HDFS. The resource will be renamed and copied in to /trash directory giving the possibility to restore as long as it remains in the trash.

Mahasen's main differentiation from above systems comes from its scalability. It can scale significantly than Nirvana Storage that depends on relational databases to scale the system, since the Mahasen metadata layer is natively distributed using a DHT.WSO2 Registry provides the clustering as the scalability option, but it is not optimized for large file transfers and storing as it uses an ATOM based resource transfers. Furthermore, Mahasen provides users a comprehensive metadata model for managing the distributed resources they stored with user-defined metadata, unlike the HDFS, which only focuses on creating a Distributed file system. Further Mahasen's metadata layer is natively distributed and fault tolerant while HDFS has a single name node which can make fault tolerant only with an active passive failover configuration.

3   High Level Architecture

3.1   Mahasen High Level Architecture

As shown by Figure 1, Mahasen consists of several storage nodes which are connected as peers to a logical ring via FreePastry. Each node consists of a registry to store metadata and a file system to store physical file parts. Once connected to the ring each node contributes to the metadata space as well as file storage capacity, scaling the system dynamically with new node additions. Nodes use underline DHT (FreePastry) routing protocol to communicate efficiently with each other.

Mahasen uses a WSO2 registry and the file system in each node and DHT based architecture is used to connect the nodes to a one unit.

Mahasen has a distributed metadata layer that stores data about the distributed files in Mahasen peer to peer network. The metadata catalog is used to broker the stored resources in the network and to assist the user to locate the files in Mahasen distributed environment abstracting the metadata management from the user.

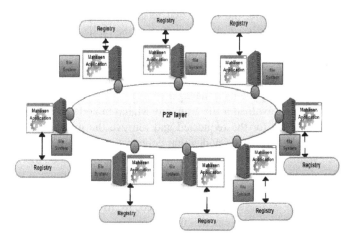

Fig. 1. Mahasen High Level Architecture

Mahasen stores two main types of metadata, which are system-defined metadata and user-defined (descriptive) metadata. System defined metadata is mainly used for server side resource handling. File name, file size, stored node IPs of file are examples of the system-defined metadata. User defined metadata is used to provide users the searching capability on those metadata. User can add tags and properties (name, value pairs) to the files that are uploaded.

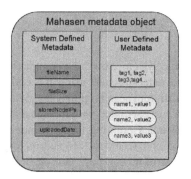

Fig. 2. Metadata Object Structure of Mahasen

When a file is uploaded connecting to a Mahasen node the file will be temporarily saved in that node. Then the node will act as the master node and split the file into pre-defined sized chunks and the split parts are stored in a selected set of the neighborhood nodes of master node through parallel transfer. Then the metadata object created by master node will be stored with replicas using PAST storage implementation of Free pastry. We have rewritten PAST node's persistent storage such that the data will be stored in the WSO registry in that node.

After storing the metadata, the nodes that received file parts act as worker nodes and replicate their file parts in parallel according to the replicate request issued by the master node. Each worker node will update the metadata object with stored locations of the file parts which were replicated after replicating their file parts using the capability of concurrent access to metadata objects, and Mahasen handles them using the locking system provided by the lock manager of DHT.

User can request to download a file from any Mahasen node and the node will first generate the resource ID for the requested and retrieve the metadata object. Then it extracts the locations of Mahasen nodes that contain the file parts from the metadata object and retrieve those parts to the local machine. The parts will be merged to create the original file after retrieving all the parts and the file will be streamed to the user.

Deletion can be performed with a single command across a heterogeneous storage system. When a delete request for a file is issued, by following the same method of retrieving the file, Mahasen finds nodes that store parts of the file and deletes them. Finally the metadata object will also be deleted with replicas.

When user needs to update the user-defined metadata, the node that receives the update request retrieves the metadata object for the file from the DHT, updates it, and stores it back in the DHT.

Using this model, Mahasen has built a complete decentralized metadata system that handles metadata management in a highly scalable and efficient manner.

Mahasen keeps replicas of both actual files and metadata objects. The main purpose of keeping replicas is for fault tolerance and failover recovery. We ensure the high availability of metadata while ensuring the scalability using free pastry's underlying DHT.

3.2   Mahasen Search

When the amount of data in the system grows, the complexity of the search increases. Mahasen builds a distributed data structure using the underlying DHT, which can improve the performance of different search options that Mahasen supports.

The resources in Mahasen are associated with metadata and for each tag or property in system, we maintain an index pointing to all resources which have that tag or property. This is implemented as a TreeMap [16] and the property trees are stored in the DHT which handles replicas of it.

When a user sends a search request, Mahasen extracts the requested search and initiate the execution of relevant search method. Then the resource IDs of the files which match with the given input are retrieved from the relevant property tree. Extracting the relevant resource IDs are done as follow.

Users can send search requests to any Mahasen node, and when a node receives a search request, Mahasen takes the property name given by the client and generates the property tree ID for that property. If the current node has the index for the property, it receives matching resource IDs for that property and sends them to the client. If not, the node acts as a master node and gets the node handles of the nodes which are having the specific property tree and routs Mahasen search messages with the required

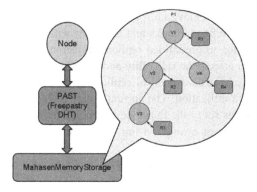

Fig. 3. A Property Tree Stored in Mahasen Memory Storage

parameters to the node handles. Then those node handles will get the relevant resource IDs from the property trees in their memory storage and send back to the master node.

The property values in the property tree are sorted, so that if the search is a range based search, we can simply take the sub map between the initial and final property values and retrieve the set of resource IDs mapped to each of the node in the sub tree. Since these resource IDs represents the files having the given property values, Mahasen can look up for the metadata objects with those resource IDs and extract the file names to present to for the user. The operation of extracting the file names for the resource IDs has a high cost than extracting the matching resource IDs for the given search query.

Complete Data Structure built for Mahasen can support property based search, range based search, tag based search and Boolean operations for the properties such as AND operation and OR operation. The advanced search provided by Mahasen is capable of providing the search based on set of different properties and tags.

Mahasen Search utilizes the continuation model support by FreePastry in results retrieving and transferring. Therefore when a search request is issued, the application sends requests to look up node handles, which contain the particular TreeMap object to request results. Then the application will collect the first result incoming and resume action from the previous execution point.

3.3   File Handling

File Transfer. Mahasen is a network of storage nodes and users will be given a client which is the Mahasen Client to access and transfer files to the network. The Mahasen Client that is built using the Apache HttpClient [17] uses HTTP methods for transferring files to the network. First the client initiates a connection with one of the node in the network. An authenticated client is capable of uploading downloading, deleting, updating or searching for the files in the network. The File content will be added as an entity to the HTTP POST method and streamed to the target address. The receiving end will read the file stream and write it to the repository.

Replica Management. To achieve fault tolerance and failover recovery, the file will be split into a set of predefined chunks and each part will be replicated and stored in different nodes according to predefined replication factor. The placement of replicas is a critical part which affects the reliability and performance of the system. The purpose of having a policy for placement of replicas is for data reliability, availability, and network bandwidth utilization. The current policy of Mahasen is to store the replicated files in leaf nodes set to the initial node. The selection of nodes in the leaf set will be calculated using cost evaluation function which focus on the distance of the node.

After successfully transferring the file to the initial node, the client will be notified about the status of the file transfer and initial node will then replicate and transfer the file to other nodes. The number of copies kept for a file is called the replication factor of that file and will be decided by the Mahasen system.

File Splitting and Parallel Transfer. Mahasen storage network is designed to store large files reliably across distributed nodes. When storing the file it will be split into blocks of fixed size and these blocks will be replicated across the network for fault tolerance. The transferring of replicated file blocks will be done in parallel to other nodes in order to utilize the bandwidth and to save time.

When focusing on the retrieval of a file by using the metadata object the system will then select a node which is closest to the reader node and download the blocks to the client. Downloading of file blocks will also be done in parallel and then the blocks will be merged to create the complete file.

3.4   Mahasen API

Mahasen provides a complete API to perform CRUD operations and search. Users can develop external clients apart from the default client Mahasen provides and integrate with existing systems to perform resource management and search operations.

4   Performance Analysis

The Mahasen System Scalability was tested by running a system with M nodes and N parallel clients. Here the value for M was 1, 6, 12, 18, 24 and N was 1, 5, 10, 15, 20. Each client carried out upload, download, delete and search operations for 10 times and the average was taken. The system configuration that was used in this test are, Two machines with Intel(R) Xeon(R) CPU E5-2403 1.80GHz 4 Core machines having 24GB RAM and One machine with Intel(R) Xeon(R) CPU E5-2470 2.30GHz 8 Core machines having 63GB RAM. Following Figures (from 4 to 7) depicts the results of this test. In the upload test, 500MB size files were used by each client.

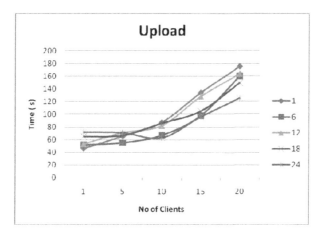

Fig. 4. Upload test results

In the results it is observed that when the number of client increases, the upload time is also increasing. We believe that this is due to the network congestion and background processes of data replication across nodes. When the number of nodes increased to 18 or 24, a reduction in upload time were observed. This was an expected behaviour, because the node which client selects to upload, distributes replica management task for other nodes in the p2p ring.

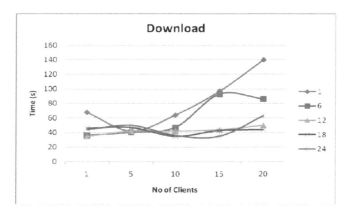

Fig. 5. Download test results

When download files using Mahasen client, it is observed that with the increase of number of client, the single node setup has a significant growth in the download time. In the performance test, a single node was chosen to send the client request while it coordinates the file transfer from other nodes in the setup. Therefore when there are multiple nodes in the system you can download file parts from other available nodes, which reduces the download time.

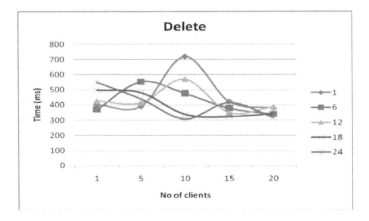

Fig. 6. Delete test results

When Mahasen performs a Delete on a resource, it involves 3 operations such as deleting metadata, deleting entries from search index, and deleting the physical file. When more nodes are in the system, each node can participate in deleting its own files in parallel, making the system more scalable and efficient.

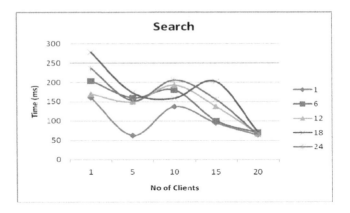

Fig. 7. Search test results

Search results illustrate that Mahasen can perform well even with more nodes added to the system. Usually single node should have the lowest possible time as it does not have to search across the p2p ring. But with multiple nodes, it has to aggregate results and present it to the client. This can be observed from the figure that, when more clients are in the system, results tend to converge into a lower value due to caching as we requested search operation through the same node.

5   Discussion and Future Work

Mahasen provides a highly scalable metadata structure with its peer-to-peer architecture in the metadata catalog. Unlike the existing metadata catalogs that use centralized architecture, Mahasen distributes metadata across the nodes in the system with the replication making the overall system scalable and fault tolerant.

Mahasen keeps replicas of both metadata objects and property trees as well. The DHT of FreePastry is used to store these objects in the system which provides easy access of them. Keeping replicas of metadata objects and property tree objects do not cost as much as keeping replicas of actual files which are very large in size compared to metadata and property tree objects. By having these objects with replicas in the system, Mahasen has been able to ensure the correct functioning of many of the Mahasen operations even in the conditions like node failures.

An important contribution of Mahasen is developing a distributed indexing structure on top of the DHT for searching data products using different properties associated with data products. Since Mahasen needed to support range based queries, we evaluated earlier effort to build such index structures. Skip Tree Graph [18] was one of the best candidates we selected for search assisting data structure, which can efficiently support range based queries over a DHT. Since we had different properties and data structure had to grow in two dimensions, one in number of properties and the other one in number of entries for one property we were forced to create different DHTs for different properties. Therefore we needed to evaluate a much less complex solution since maintaining different DHTs could have been very expensive in terms of resources.

When the system scales up with the large number of nodes, it will be more costly to issue a search operation on the available raw metadata stored. Therefore Mahasen developed a combined data structure with DHT and TreeMap as explained earlier.

When a Mahasen node fails, and it is detected by the existing nodes in the network, Mahasen replicates all the metadata objects and the property tree objects which were in the failed node to the existing Mahasen node reading them from other replicas. Mahasen helps in preserving the availability of metadata objects and property tree objects by maintaining the replication factor of them a constant.

Current Mahasen design has several limitations, which we plan to handle as future works. Currently Mahasen stores each property indexes in one Mahasen node and assumes that it will fit within the memory of that node. This may not be major concern for simple cases, and even NoSQL storages like Cassandra makes similar assumptions. Dividing the property tree into parts and storing them in different nodes when it is larger than a given size can solve this problem. We can predefine the maximum size of a part that will be residing in one node.

Another challenge is that search based multiple properties where at least one is a common property would force Mahasen to join large data sets, and one potential solution is to negotiate the size of data sets before start the data merging.

To summarize, Mahasen project builds a scalable storage solution by making a group of existing open source registries work as a one unit. It provides a one logical global namespace, and users may talk to any node of the group and perform any operations.

Mahasen connects nodes (registries) using PAST, a storage overlay implemented on top of Pastry DHT algorithm. Furthermore, Mahasen builds a distributed indexing structure on top of DHT to support property-based search of data items.

A user can benefit from the Web Service API provided and effectively utilize for batch processing of file uploading task through a custom client or basic client provided by Mahasen.

References

1. Szalay, A.S., Kunszt, P., Thakar, A., Gray, J., Slutz, D., Brunner, R.J.: Designing and Mining Multi-Terabyte Astronomy Archives: The Sloan Digital Sky Survey. In: SIGMOD 2000 Proceedings of the 2000 ACM SIGMOD International Conference on Management of Data (2000)
2. Baru, C., Moore, R., Rajasekar, A., Wan, M.: The SDSC Storage Resource Broker (1998)
3. Moore, R.W.: Managing Large Distributed Data Sets using the Storage Resource Broker (2010)
4. DeCandia, G., Hastorun, D., Jampani, M.: Dynamo.: Amazon's Highly Available Key-value Store (2010)
5. Ghemawat, S., Leun, S.-T., Gobioff, H.: The Google File System
6. Nuno Santos, B.K.: Distributed Metadata with the AMGA Metadata Catalog
7. Nirvana Storage - Home of the Storage Resource Broker (SRB®) (2011),
   `http://www.nirvanastorage.com/index.php?module=htmlpages&func=display&pid=1`
8. XML Metadata Concept Catalog (XMC Cat), Data to Insight Center, Indiana University Pervasive Technology Institute, `http://d2i.indiana.edu/xmccat`
9. Nirvana Performance,
   `http://www.nirvanastorage.com/index.php?module=htmlpages&func=display&pid=54`
10. ApacheTM OODT (2011), `http://oodt.apache.org/`
11. WSO2 Governance Registry - lean.enterprise.middleware - open source SOA | WSO2 (2011), `http://wso2.com/products/governance-registry/`
12. Apache Lucene - Overview,
    `http://lucene.apache.org/java/docs/index.html`
13. HDFS Architecture Guide (2011),
    `http://hadoop.apache.org/docs/r1.0.4/hdfs_design.html`
14. Pastry - A scalable, decentralized, self-organizing and fault-tolerant substrate for peer-to-peer applications, `http://www.freepastry.org/`
15. Druschel, P., Rowstron, A.: PAST: A large-scale, persistent peer-to-peer storage utility. In: HotOS VIII, Schoss Elmau, Germany (2001)
16. TreeMap (Java 2 Platform SE 5.0) (2011),
    `http://download.oracle.com/javase/1.5.0/docs/api/java/util/TreeMap.html`
17. HttpClient - HttpComponents HttpClient Overview (2011),
    `http://hc.apache.org/httpcomponents-client-ga/`
18. Beltrán, A.G., Sage, P., Milligan, P.: Skip Tree Graph: a Distributed and Balanced Search Tree for Peer-to-Peer Networks

Probabilistic QoS Analysis of Web Services

Waseem Ahmed and Yong Wei Wu

Department of Computer Science and Technology,
Tsinghua University, Beijing, China
amw.inbox@gmail.com

Abstract. In such a competitive world, quality assurance can make the difference between a successful business and bankruptcy. For Internet services, the presence of low performance servers, high latency or overall poor service quality can translate into lost sales, user frustration and customers lost. In this paper, we propose a novel method for QoS metrification based on Hidden Markov Models. The techniques we show can be used to measure and predict the behavior of Web Services under several criteria, and can thus be used to rank services quantitatively rather than just qualitatively. We demonstrate the feasibility and usefulness of our methodology by drawing experiments on real world data. Our results have shown how our proposed methods can help the user to automatically select the best available Web Service based on several metrics, among them system predictability and response times variability.

Keywords: Hidden states, Probability, Quality of Service.

1 Introduction

The Internet made the world a smaller place. Companies from all around the world may now compete over different service offerings not only with their local adversaries, but do now under a global scale. Escalating the competition and lead in industry segment can often be a matter of offering and, perhaps even most importantly, assuring the good quality of the services offered. In the Web this should be no different; controlling quality for Web Services (WS) is done by enforcing Quality of Service (QoS) policies and assuring needed quality conditions are always met.

On the user's side, the increased number of services means more and more offerings to choose from. Unfortunately, due the explosive growth in the number of WSs available in the world, selecting the best WS to solve a given task has become a quite challenging task. Currently, users cast their choice based on the reviews and experiences of other users. User-created ranks are often the first resource for finding reliability information regarding a particular service, often given in terms of response time, throughput, availability, security and reliability. Interestingly enough, data quality has never been considered as a key factor when analyzing QoS parameters.

There is no standard way, however, for the users to weigh their options directly and individually, for themselves. This paper aims to fill this gap providing a standard way to measure and assess WS quality using Hidden Markov Model (HMM). Although

C.-H. Hsu et al. (Eds.): NPC 2013, LNCS 8147, pp. 393–404, 2013.

web service reliability can be defined as producing cohesive results when invoked by different users with similar parameters [1], even though, sometimes web service even with best rank provides different results to end users. Systems which are designed to produce different results to different users at same time interval are out of the scope of this paper.

Existing papers such as [1-6] have discussed in detail QoS attributes of web services in terms of response time, throughput, reliability, availability. Nonetheless, there is still a lack of analyzing quality of data received from web services. Users across the IT industry associate bad quality of data or difference in response of web services against same request at same time with improper use of technology such as:

- Improper use of instance variables
- Incorrect caching
- Wrong mapping of data in lookup tables (in case of DB operation)
- Service is unable to recognize received category
- Servers are behind cluster and node responsible for reply during time t behaves badly
- Improper or mutated coding

However, as web services are owned and hosted by other organizations, most of the above mentioned aspects are difficult to monitor. In this paper we have designed a framework based on Hidden Markov Model (HMM) that will help end users to find a relation among web service responses and different hidden states producing them. Later, we have further extended this framework to predict behavioral patterns of these hidden states that will help users in making decision for web service selection.

In our framework, we have randomly selected web services with similar functionality (e.g. in our case it represent weather forecasting) from the list provided by [4] (who have claimed to have almost all available services by crawling web) and webserviceslist.com to analyze quality of data, that were ranked as best by different users around the world (as shown in table1). Status of all selected web services with similar functionality is more or less similar as described in [4].

Table 1. Web services with similar functionality along with their Ranks

Web Services	Count
Total web services with similar functionality(Weather forecasting)	23
Available	11
Broken link	8
Resource Cannot be found	3
Security exception	1

With HMM QoS attribute of WS in terms of data can be analyzed in two stages.

- Stage one will require us finding relations among hidden states in a remote WS and different data categories produced by web services.
- The second stage requires us to use this information to find probability of result produced by hidden states in future.

Our contribution in this paper can be summarized as below:

- We have analyzed the reason of variation in data generated by web service when invoked by different users at the same time with same input parameters.
- Defined a mechanism to build a relation among web service response / result and various hidden states responsible for producing it.
- Predicted the probability of variation in data / response of web services during nth time interval to select WS with better QoS attributes in terms of data.

The rest of the paper is organized as follows: section 2 introduces related work section 3 describes details about our conceptual framework section 4 presents our experiment and results and finally section 5 concludes the paper.

Table 2. Independent Variables

#	Independent variables
1.	Status (S)
2.	Temperature (T)
3.	Visibility (V)
4.	Due Point (D)
5.	Humidity(H)
6.	Wind(W)
7.	Pressure (P)

Table 3. Common Hidden States

#	Hidden States
1	Wrong Data Mapping
2	Bad Node in server clustering
3	Mutated coding
4	Composite WS

2   Related Work

Analyzing QoS attributes of remote web service is one of the important research areas in SOA based distributed applications. Most of the researchers have analyzed these attributes and proposed frameworks to facilitate end users for selecting or integrating web service with better QoS attributes. In this section we have presented a review of existing methods or framework proposed by different researchers.   S. Maheswari and G.R. Karpagam [5] have proposed a framework that considered seven QoS attributes i.e. Response time, Execution Time, throughput, scalability, reputation, accessibility, and availability for better web service selection. Yilei Zhang and Zibin Zheng [3] have proposed model-based QoS prediction framework called WSPred. Their main contribution was time-aware personalized QoS prediction approach that analyzes latent features of users, service and time by performing tensor factorization. Emra and Pinar [1] proposed a method where they tracked QoS parameters automatically when required. However the issue with this approach is that, they did not consider network latency or communication delay in their calculations. Daniel A. Menascé [6] have proposed a way to calculate throughput of web services that have been used in single web service to accomplish its task. Ping Wang [7] has used fuzzy logic to locate and select web services based on user ratings. Other papers that have been produced to estimate QoS attributes to select better web service for integration are San-Yih Hwang [8], Vuong Xua [9], Xifeng [10] ,Hong Qing [11], Chunli [12], Wei, Z. [13].

Hidden Markov Model has already been used in analyzing quality factors of distributed computing systems. Nonetheless, they have their own issues, constraints and shortcomings. For instance Vathsala and Hrushikesha [14] have used HMM for predicting response time pattern of web services for different network's hidden states, however they did not consider the reliability of various hidden states with in the remote web service as discussed in Table 2. As survivability also affects performance of any application, LeiLei Chen [15] has designed a framework to evaluate survivability of SOA based application using Hidden Markov Model. The main idea of their framework revolves around monitoring activities based on service logs or run time statistics provided by service provider. The problem with this approach is that it is restricted to statistics which have been provided by the service provider itself. Besides, the author did not provide a discussion about the possible hidden states and other probabilistic characteristics inherent to WSs. The HMM has also been successfully used in the prediction of other QoS aspects for SOA applications. One of such works is the work by Rahnavard and Meisam [16], who have used HMMs to detect WS anomalies, such as intrusion detection. However, their strategy could not be used to gauge arbitrary QoS attributes of WSs. Similarly, Flex Selfner [17] has proposed the use of HMMs to categorize and distinguish error patterns leading to failures. This author also suggested a mechanism for predicting the future occurrence of failures or errors. Zaki Malik[18] has used HMM to assess failures during certain time in future. In short HMM has been successfully used to analyze various aspects in distributed computing systems. The reliability of a WS can be established only once the reliability of hidden states have been ensured [20]. In this paper we have design a framework based on HMM for estimating probabilistic insight details of web service.

3   HMM Based Quality of Service Estimation

For probabilistic QoS analysis of web services in terms of data variation, our strategy is based on following steps:

- Analyzing variation among data values of web services response when invoked by a number of users with similar input parameters.
- Estimating current state of internal system of WS using HMM and then defining probabilistic relationship among data values and various hidden states.
- Predicting behavioral pattern of hidden states for analyzing data variance during nth time interval.

3.1   Similarity Analysis

Estimating QoS attribute in terms of data variance requires us to elucidate web service response into a set of independent variables. This will help us to analyze data variation in more detail. For instance in case of weather forecasting, the consequent response can be divided into N number of different independent variables as defined in table 2. As each web service is being invoked by M number of users and we have K number of web services having similar functionalities. To find the similarity among

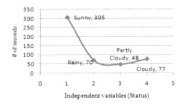

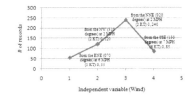

a. Variance in Status variable (as mentioned in table2)   b. Variance in wind

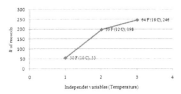

c. Variance in Visibility   d. Variance in temperature

Fig. 1. Variance in result when WS invoked by more than 500 parallel threads

such data values we can represent above information in 3-dimentional N x M x K matrix. Web services with higher rank were invoked by 500 parallel threads with same input parameters in distributed environment and results were analyzed as shown in Fig. 1. It is apparent from Fig.1 that web services even with higher rank are replying with uncertain results during time interval t. Fig.1a shows variation in status (Sunny, Rainy, Partially cloudy, Cloudy) received by different users for same request parameters, whereas Fig.1 (b, c and d) depicts variation in independent variables (Wind, Visibility, and Temperature). For proof of concept we have shown only some independent variables, nonetheless, we have found variation in all independent variables. Region specific WS for instance weather forecast (US only) have produced better performance in comparison to other web services.

3.2   Quality of Service Analysis with Hidden Markov Model

Similarity analysis shows that independent variables can have different values within one observation when invoked in parallel with same request parameters. To figure out consequent data categories, it is therefore essential to analyze QoS attributes in terms of data variance. Then computing most likely hidden states and observation sequence using HMM, these categories can be linked with certain hidden states inside a WS. For instance, if observations for weather forecasting WS (as shown in table 2), produced by finite number of hidden states (as shown in table 3), then HMM can help us to establish a probabilistic relation between hidden states and consequent sequence of observations. There are two fundamental assumptions in our approach:

- Consequent observations are linked with execution pattern of hidden states with in a remote web service. This linkage can give us probability of possible scenarios used in implementation of WS. "Execution pattern" defines situation where sometime more than one hidden state is producing similar observations.

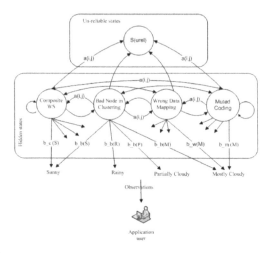

Fig. 2. Mappy variance in generating results to hidden markov model

It is important to analyze relevant hidden states along with other QoS attributes such as response time and throughput, which will further help us to predict probability of scalability of hidden states in future.

• States responsible for generating data are hidden and unknown.

The HMM have been successfully used in pattern recognition applications[17]. The first assumption is based on the fact that every hidden state has some special functionality linked with it. For instance, sometimes it is required to connect with database to verify certain results or call another web service or performing heavy calculations etc. Based on the execution of a certain hidden state the system may lead to a similar pattern of data output. As per first assumption these states can be identified by recognizing execution pattern. Whereas the second assumption perfectly matches with definition of HMM, as these states are hidden and produce results in time t. Furthermore, any hidden state can generate results when invoked during WS execution or access from other hidden states during error propagation, so model is of ergodic type. Based on these assumptions we have used HMM to find insight details of remote web service.

Estimating QoS attribute of WS in terms of data variance requires analyzing response time, throughput and quality of result produced. Response time represents duration which a web service is taking in executing some operation excluding network latency and communication delay. Throughput is the amount of work done by the web service within specified period of time. It is possible for certain hidden states to produce similar observations despite of having different implementation. Thus for a given time interval during various service invocations we can define feature vector including values defined in table 3 and by considering WS description to predict probability of implementation of hidden states. Because of difference in implementation of hidden states clear identification among feature values is required which in machine learning is referred to as Feature Normalization [21]. These features may be categorized in terms of data mapping, server clustering, mutated coding, calling other web services. This will help to define initial transition and emission probabilities of

Services / # of users	1	2	3	4	5	6	7	8	9	10	11	12	13	14	15	16	17	18	19	20	21	......
Service1	R	UR	R	R	R	R	R	R	UR	R	R	R	R	R	R	UR	R	R	UR	R	R	......
Service2	R	R	R	R	R	R	R	R	R	UR	R	R	R	R	R	R	R	R	R	UR	UR	......
Service3	R	R	R	R	UR	R	R	UR	R	R	R	R	R	R	UR	R	R	R	UR	R	R	......

Fig. 3. Training sequence

hidden states. Fig.2 shows general implementation of a web service with different observation symbols dependent on hidden states. In our framework, status(s) (as defined in table 2) can be further divided into sub categories such as sunny, rainy, partially cloudy, and mostly cloudy. At the time user receives inconsistent data set underlying hidden state transits to an unreliable state, labeled as S_{urel}. Any state defined in Table 3 can be transit to an unreliable state. By initializing HMM parameters it can be ensured that the model transits to unreliable state once inconsistent data occurs in the training sequence. Emission probabilities are represented by relevant hidden state and output value. For instance, probability of output value "Mostly Cloudy" from hidden state "mutated coding" is represented by b_m(M). Here b represents observation probability matrix, m shows "mutated coding and M represents output value "Mostly Cloudy". So we can define various parameters of HMM as:

- States: S number of states where each state will have unique output dependent on its functionality (Fig. 2).
- Observations: Distinct output observations V i.e. categories defined in table 1, such that output observation at time t is O_t where sequence of observation is $O = O_1, O_2,... O_t$
- $A_{i,j}$ represents transitional probability of hidden state S_i following S_j.
- $B_{i,j}$ represents probability of hidden state generating output being produced from state S_j.
- Initial state distribution π

States as defined in table 3 may exist in one web service or there may have at least one or more states available. As per definition of HMM we have:

$$\lambda = (A, B, \pi) \tag{1}$$

3.3   Data Quality Prediction

State of WS during time interval t producing data D can be considered as vector of probabilities that WS is in hidden state S_i during time interval t having observations $o = \{O_1, O_2,... O_n\}$. Current state of WS can lead us to predict P_{urel} (S_k) of WS during kth time interval under various operational conditions. Where P_{urel} (S_k) is the probability of state S_k that the Markov process defined by Hidden states produces data d_k during time interval k is unreliable. Current state of WS during time interval t can be computed with the help of HMM i.e using VITERBI algorithm:

$$\delta_t(i) = \underset{HS_1, HS_2,..., HS_{n-1}}{Max} P(HS_1, HS_2,..., HS_{n-1}, HS_n = i, O_1, O_2,... O_n \mid \lambda) \tag{2}$$

Here δ_t (i) represents the state of WS i.e. it represent maximum probability (computing maximum over all possible hidden states sequences) that the model went through hidden states HS_1, HS_2 ,...., HS_{n-1} and the system is in state i at hidden state n. i.e. $HS_n = i$ while observing O_1, O_2,..., O_n. To detect data quality one has to define valid data values for each data element collected so that the system would know what we are measuring against. In our framework, we are concerned only with data variance so we counted them where independent variables had differences in values when invoked by same input parameters by multiple threads (as shown in Fig.1). The data with maximum count i.e. received by most of the users in parallel invocation is considered to be reliable. Later we linked each of the counted value with corresponding hidden state using Eq.2. Now if we define criteria for valid data values then it can be analyzed that which particular state is not producing data as required. However in this paper, we are dealing only with data variance and this can be computed by verifying data values of all independent variables available in the data as defined in Section III-A using relation below:

$$\text{Rel (D)} = 1 - \sum_{i=0}^{n} (V_i / D_k) \qquad (3)$$

Here V_i represents the number of independent variable (as mentioned in table-1) in data D_k produced during time interval k. The eq.3 can be used recursively to find data variance in whole data D. The Rel(D) will be considered as unreliable, provided one or more independent variable in eq.3 will have invalid value. The probability $P_{urel}(s_k)$ is calculated by "First Passage Time Distribution". Let T_k be the time (known as First Passage Time) when hidden state s_k produces data Ds_k then:

$$T_k = \text{MIN (Rel (Ds}_k): S_k = S_{urel}) \qquad (4)$$

Where S_{urel} represents the unreliable state, which implies hidden state S_k has produced unreliable data Ds_k during time interval k. Probability distribution among hidden states can be computed as below:

$$P_{urel}(s_k) = \sum_{i=0}^{n} P (T_k \le n \mid S_j = i) P (S_j = i) \qquad \text{s. t.} \quad j=0 \qquad (5)$$

Where P (Sj= i) is the probability that WS is in hidden state j at current time as computed in eq.2, and P (T_k <= n | Sj = i) is the probability of going through hidden state S_{urel} and computing data reliability during kth time interval starting from j=0 which can be recursively computed with the help of the Baum-Welch algorithm[19]. The eq.5 represents probability distribution that the system produces unreliable results S_{urel} during nth time interval at time k which can be further scrutinized using dynamic programming to efficiently compute for various time intervals.

3.4   Training the Model

To train the model we have used observation sequences obtained during real web services invocations as described in similarity analysis section i.e. Section 3.1. These sequences are first labeled as "unreliable" using Eq.3, where at least one observation symbol i.e. independent variable has inconsistent value. In our framework such responses are modeled and represented by hidden state S_{urel} as shown in Fig.2. Whenever data with uncertain results is obtained, underlying state transits to unreliable state, i.e. S_{urel}. The hidden state S_{urel} can be any state which is defined in Table 3. Observation sequence having uncertain values is shown in Fig.1 (b, c and d) where occurrence of uncertainty is indicated by difference in values. Training sequences from this information can be obtained by defining 'R' for reliable and 'UR' for unreliable value in observation sequence using the strategy defined in Section 3.4 as shown in Fig.3. Each column in Fig.3 represents the data consistency of the WS invocations. Each row in Fig.3 represents responses of single service invoked by 500 parallel threads; however, for proof of concept we have shown only a few values. Then by initializing HMM parameters in Eq.1 i.e. initial, transition and emission probabilities, such that states representing as unreliable S_{urel} are the only states that produce results with "UR", it can be ensured that model transits to unreliable state when uncertainty appears in the training sequence.

4   Experiments and Results

Based on domain information about implementation complexity of various computing techniques as described in table 1, initial guesses for probabilities can be exploited to:

- Adjust model parameters and determine current state of the system. Find the relation among output value and hidden states
- Predict QoS attributes of various hidden states using training sequences based on real data for various web services having similar functionality and select the WS with better QoS attribute.

In our experiment we have selected two web services with higher rank as mentioned in table-2 and invoked them using 500 parallel threads in a distributed environment. Fig.4b and Fig.5b represent data variance of independent variables Wind and Status (sunny, rain, cloudy, partially cloudy) respectively, as defined in table-1. Purpose of this experiment was to use our proposed model for analyzing their QoS attribute in terms of variance of data for selecting better web services and to predict their QoS values for anytime in the future.

4.1   Adjusting the Model Parameters

To predict the QoS attribute of hidden states, it is necessary to train the model to get estimated transition and emission probabilities. These values are then used in eq.2 to compute most probable hidden state sequences. Purpose of training the model is to find the optimal HMM parameters i.e. A, B & π such that the model best fits the training sequences. Baum-Welch algorithm a particular case of expectation-maximization (EM) is used to train the model. It iteratively improves the basic model which provides convergence to local optima. After training the model, current and future state is predicted using VITERBI algorithm as discussed above.

Wind Status	# of records
greater than 7 mile(s):0	241
2 mile(s):0	55
3 mile(s):0	119
4 mile(s):0	85

b. # of records for each independent variable

S-Successful, US - Unsuccessful

	R	UR	S (%)	US(%)
State 1	153	53	30.6	10.6
State 2	88	193	17.6	38.6
State 3	0	0	0	0
State 4	0	13	0	2.6

R-Reliable, UR-unreliable

d. # of records emitted by each hidden state

S-Successful, US - Unsuccessful

	R	UR	S(%)	US(%)
State 1	100	0	20	0
State 2	0	238	0	47.6
State 3	141	0	28.2	0
State 4	0	21	0	4.2

R-Reliable, UR-unreliable

f. Predicted records emitted by each hidden state

S-Successful, US - Unsuccessful

	R	UR	S(%)	US (%)
State 1	101	0	20.2	0
State 2	0	208	0	41.6
State 3	122	0	24.4	0
State 4	9	60	1.8	12

R-Reliable, UR-unreliable

h. Actual records emitted by each hidden state

Fig. 4. QoS attribute of Web services (WS1)

4.2   Current State

The state of component web service during time interval t is a vector of probabilities that system is in the hidden state HS_i when observation O_i is observed. VITERBI algorithm is used to calculate the most probable hidden state sequence (as discussed in section 3.3) that has generated the training sequence as shown in Fig.4 & Fig.5. Fig.4d and Fig.5d represent the current state of various hidden states of two web services W1 and W2 respectively. It can be analyzed that both web services produce variance in data because of inconsistent behavior of hidden states 1 and 2. Although these services are ranked as best by service users, even though both the services are producing over 50% data variance when invoked in parallel with same input parameters at the same time. To select better WS we further elucidated received results in more detail i.e. which particular hidden state of both web services is producing relatively better result. For instance, State1 of WS2 in Fig.5d shows that it has produced 44% of successful results whereas State1 of WS1 in Fig.4d indicates that it has produced 30% of overall successful result. This implies that if we can analyze or predict QoS attribute of each hidden state during the nth time interval, then we can select a better WS among the list of functionally equivalent web services.

4.3   Predicting Data Variance in Terms of Hidden States

As HMM is normally used to recognize patterns, therefore to predict behavior of the hidden states, idea is to classify suspicious data patterns i.e. patterns with observation symbols "UR". This classification will indicate upcoming suspicious patterns. As per proposed technique, data values in a training sequence are divided into equal lengths slots. These slots having observations symbol "UR" are termed as "unreliable".

First the model is trained using training sequences. Then based on trained HMM current status of the hidden state's behavior is analyzed using VITERBI algorithm. Later, based on current state, future behavior of hidden states is predicted by calculating "first passage time distribution" into unreliable state. Fig.4 (f and h) and

Weather	# of records
Sunny	278
Cloudy	79
Rain	79
Party Cloudy	64

	S-Successful, US-Unsuccessful			
	R	UR	S(%)	US (%)
State 1	220	91	44	18.2
State 2	58	120	11.6	24
State 3	0	0	0	0
State 4	0	11	0	2.2

R-Reliable, UR-unreliable

	S-Successful, US-Unsuccessful			
	R	UR	S(%)	US (%)
State 1	136	0	27.2	0
State 2	105	0	21	0
State 3	0	96	0	19.2
State 4	37	126	7.4	25.2

R-Reliable, UR-Unreliable

	S-successful, US-unsuccessful			
	R	UR	S(%)	US(%)
State 1	110	0	22	0
State 2	88	20	17.6	4
State 3	0	79	0	15.8
State 4	30	173	6	34.6

R-reliable, UR-unreliable

b. # of records for each independent variable

d. # of records emitted by each hidden state

f. Predicted records emitted by each hidden state

h. Actual records emitted by each hidden state

Fig. 5. QoS attribute of Web service (WS2)

Fig.5 (f and h) represent the predicted and actual state of hidden states of web services WS1 and WS2 respectively. It can be observed from the predicted value of WS1 in Fig.4f that only State1 and State3 will produce consistent results during time interval t. Nonetheless, State2 and State4 will produce inconsistent results. These predictions will help end users to design their system in a way that can entertain responses produced by only State1 and State3. Fig.4h shows actual values of the same web services W1 during time interval t. It can be seen that predicted values are almost similar to actual values except some consistent values which were also produced by State4. However, this is a small number which can be ignored to make the system reliable. Whereas, Fig.5f and h shows predicted and actual values of web service WS2 responses during time interval t. Predicted and actual values are almost similar in numbers except a marginal difference which can be ignored, however, in this case State2 and State4 have inconsistent behavior. Both the states are randomly generating consistent and inconsistent results which are hard to ignore during the live execution of the system. Therefore, it will be easy for end users to decide which particular web service can incorporated in the system. Such as in this case study WS1 appears to be more suitable compared to WS2. With these results it is apparent that HMM can predict probabilistic QoS attributes of remote WS in terms of data variance, for any time interval in the future. Our model can be used to further analyze probabilistic scalability of various hidden states under specified circumstances such as by increasing user load or increasing communication delay.

5   Conclusion

In this paper we have explained with experiments how HMM can be used to analyze and predict QoS attribute of a web services in terms of data discrepancy. Predicting QoS attributes will then help end users to select a better web service among the list of functionally equivalent web services. We have performed our experiments on real world web services. Later, we have analyzed in detail the behavior of web services for a different set of users having similar input parameters. Our framework gives information about the probabilistic insight of any remote web service. It can further predict QoS attribute of these hidden states in terms of data variance and can help to further examine scalability of these hidden states.

Acknowledgment. I am extremely grateful to Cesar Roberto de Souza (Federal University of Sao Carlos) and for his support, encouragement & proofreading of the draft version of my paper.

References

[1] Askaroglu, E., Senkul, P.: Automatic QoS evaluation method for web services. In: 2012 IEEE Symposium on Computers and Communications, ISCC (2012)

[2] D'Ambrogio, A.: A Model-driven Approach to Describe and Predict the Performance of Composite Services. In: WOSP 2007, Buenos Aires, Argentina, February 5-8 (2007)

[3] Yilei, Z., Zibin, Z., Lyu, M.R.: WSPred: A Time-Aware Personalized QoS Prediction Framework for Web Services. In: 2011 IEEE 22nd International Symposium on Software Reliability Engineering, ISSRE (2011)

[4] Zibin, Z., Yilei, Z., Lyu, M.R.: Distributed QoS Evaluation for Real-World Web Services. In: 2010 IEEE International Conference on Web Services, ICWS (2010)

[5] Maheswari, S.: QoS Based Efficient Web Service Selection. European Journal of Scientific Research (2011)

[6] Menasce, D.A.: QoS issues in Web services. IEEE Internet Computing 6(6), 72–75 (2002)

[7] Ping, W., et al.: A Fuzzy Model for Selection of QoS-Aware Web Services. In: IEEE International Conference on e-Business Engineering, ICEBE 2006 (2006)

[8] San-Yih, H., et al.: A probabilistic approach to modeling and estimating the QoS of web-services-based workflows. Inf. Sci. 177(23), 5484–5503 (2007)

[9] Tran, V.X., Tsuji, H., Masuda, R.: A new QoS ontology and its QoS-based ranking algorithm for Web services. Simulation Modelling Practice and Theory 17(8), 1378–1398 (2009)

[10] Xifeng, W., et al.: Ontology-Based Reliability Evaluation for Web Service. In: 2011 IEEE 35th Annual Computer Software and Applications Conference, COMPSAC (2011)

[11] Hong Qing, Y., Reiff-Marganiec, S.: A Method for Automated Web Service Selection. In: IEEE Congress on Services - Part I (2008)

[12] Chunli, X., Bixin, L., Xifeng, W.: A Staged Model for Web Service Reliability. In: 2011 IEEE 35th Annual Computer Software and Applications Conference, COMPSAC (2011)

[13] Wei, Z., et al.: QoS-Based Dynamic Web Service Composition with Ant Colony Optimization. In: 2010 IEEE 34th Annual Computer Software and Applications Conference, COMPSAC (2010)

[14] Vathsala, A.V., Hrushikesha, M.: Using HMM for predicting response time of web services. In: Proceedings of the CUBE International Information Technology Conference. ACM, Pune (2012)

[15] Leilei, C., et al.: Evaluating the Survivability of SOA Systems Based on HMM. In: Proceedings of the 2010 IEEE International Conference on Web Services. IEEE Computer Society (2010)

[16] Rahnavard, G., Najjar, M.S.A., Taherifar, S.: A method to evaluate Web Services Anomaly Detection using Hidden Markov Models. In: 2010 International Conference on Computer Applications and Industrial Electronics, ICCAIE (2010)

[17] Salfner, F.: Predicting Failures with Hidden Markov Models. In: Proceedings of 5th European Dependable Computing Conference (2005)

[18] Malik, Z., Akbar, I., Bouguettaya, A.: Web Services Reputation Assessment Using a Hidden Markov Model. In: Baresi, L., Chi, C.-H., Suzuki, J. (eds.) ICSOC-ServiceWave 2009. LNCS, vol. 5900, pp. 576–591. Springer, Heidelberg (2009)

[19] Ramage, D.: Hidden Markov Models Fundamentals (2007)

[20] Ahmed, W., Wu, Y.W.: A survey on reliability in distributed systems. Journal of Computer and System Sciences (2013) ISSN 0022-0000, doi:10.1016/j.jcss.2013.02.006

[21] Hoecke, S.V.: Modeling the performance of the Web service platform using Layered Queueing Networks. In: Proceedings of Software Engineering Research and Practice, pp. 627–633 (2005)

A Novel Search Engine to Uncover Potential Victims for APT Investigations

Shun-Te Liu[1,2], Yi-Ming Chen[1], and Shiou-Jing Lin[2]

[1] Department of Information Management, National Central University,
Taoyuan, Taiwan, R.O.C
[2] Information & Communication Security Lab, TL, Chunghwa Telecom Co., Ltd.
Taoyuan, Taiwan, R.O.C
{rogerliu,sjlin}@cht.com.tw,
cym@cc.ncu.edu.tw

Abstract. Advanced Persistent Threats (APT) are sophisticated and target-oriented cyber attacks which often leverage customized malware and bot control techniques to control the victims for remotely accessing valuable information. As the APT malware samples are specific and few, the signature-based or learning-based approaches are weak to detect them. In this paper, we take a more flexible strategy: developing a search engine for APT investigators to quickly uncover the potential victims based on the attributes of a known APT victim. We test our approach in a real APT case happened in a large enterprise network consisting of several thousands of computers which run a commercial antivirus system. In our best effort to prove, the search engine can uncover the other unknown 33 victims which are infected by the APT malware. Finally, the search engine is implemented on Hadoop platform. In the case of 440GB data, it can return the queries in 2 seconds.

1 Introduction

The cyber attacks become more and more sophisticated. Recently, this kind of target-oriented, covered and long-term attacks is labeled as advanced persistent threat (APT) [1-5]. Much research considers that APTs are the sophisticated and target-oriented cyber attacks which often leverage customized malware and bot control techniques to remotely control the victims.[1-5]. The victims will become the stepping stones for the attackers to access valuable information inside the enterprise network [6]. Therefore, the sooner we find the APT malware-infected computers, the smaller the loss caused by the APTs.

HTTP requests log is a valuable data for determining APT malware [7]. As Web-related protocols are allowed almost everywhere, the APT malware is mostly equipped with remote-controlled ability under the HTTP-based command and control (C&C) infrastructure to facilitate the attacks on the intranet [8-10]. Although much research can detect bot-infected computers [11, 12] or detect bot behavior [13-16], they require more bot samples to train a feasible model. This is a big problem to these approaches because the APT malware samples are few and often customized.

C.-H. Hsu et al. (Eds.): NPC 2013, LNCS 8147, pp. 405–416, 2013.

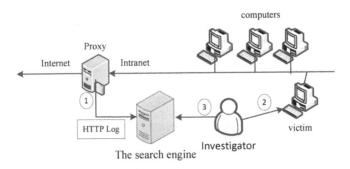

Fig. 1. The working concept of the search engine

In this paper, rather than detecting the APT malware, we take a more flexible strategy: developing a search engine for searching the potential victims to respond to APTs quickly. The working concept of our idea is shown in Fig 1. Each computer's HTTP requests are logged by proxy and sent to the search engine periodically. Once an APT malware is found, by giving the attributes of the malicious HTTP requests invoked by the APT malware, the search engine can search and rank the potential C&C servers and malware-infected computers from the historical HTTP requests. This approach is very useful for the APT investigation. We test our approach in a real APT case happened in a large enterprise network consisting of several thousands of computers, which run a commercial anti-virus system. The three known C&C servers are ranked in top 10 of the web sites. Meanwhile, in our best effort to prove, the search engine can find the other 18 C&C servers and the other 33 APT malware-infected computers. In addition, to process the huge volume of proxy logs quickly, the search engine is implemented on Hadoop platform. In the case of 440GB HTTP logs, it can return the queries in 2 seconds.

This paper contributes to network security in the following areas:

1. Propose a rank mechanism to rank the potential APT victims and C&C servers.
2. Develop a search engine on Hadoop platform to process the huge volume of HTTP requests.
3. Prove the usefulness of our approach in a real APT investigation case.

The organization of this paper is described as follows: Section 2 describes the previous research in APTs and botnet detection. In Section 3, we propose a ranking mechanism to rank the websites. Section 4 describes the prototype of the search engine. Section 5 shows experimental results. Section 6 will conclude and describe the future work.

2   Previous Research

2.1   APT Characteristics

As the name implies, advanced persistent threat (APT) uses highly targeted method persistently for compromising the data security, but the definition of APT in academic research is still unclear today. To understand that, we extract the APT characteristics, as shown in Table 1, described in the reports and the studies according to intrusion phases [17]. In reconnaissance phase, the targets are highly profiled including organization, people and computer environments before being attacked. The attackers do their best efforts to find out the weakness of their targets. In gaining access phase, the APT attackers use not only uncovered software vulnerabilities (zero day exploits) but also human weakness (social engineering attacks) to compromise the targets. This means that APT almost can bypass the conventional signature-based detection approaches. In maintaining access phase, the attackers often leverage bot control techniques to control the victims in the target's enterprise network. Finally, the objectives of the APT attackers are valuable information of their targets.

The research [18] analyzed a large corpus of targeted attacks identified by Symantec during the year 2011. The results show that only 5% malware used in APTs were identified by antivirus software. This means that preventing the APTs in gaining access phase is very difficult, especially when the zero day exploits are used in the attacks. Once the attack success, the signature-based intrusion detection approaches are often fail because they can't recognized the malware used. For these reasons, the reaction of APTs becomes more and more important for the enterprises to reduce the damages. Therefore, we focus on the characteristics of APT in maintaining phase and give APT a definition as follows:

Table 1. The APT characteristics extracted from the studies, where phase 1 is reconnaissance, phase 2 is gaining access, phase 3 is maintaining access and phase 4 is achieve objectives

Phase	Characteristics	[19]	[20]	[18]	[4]	[21]	[5]	[22]	[9]	[23]	[8]	[24]
1	Target-oriented	V	V	V		V	V	V			V	
	Highly profile	V	V	V	V			V		V		V
2	Zero day exploit	V	V	V	V	V		V	V	V		
	Coordinative	V	V	V	V	V	V	V	V			V
	Social engineering	V	V	V	V	V		V	V		V	
	Combine several attack skill	V	V	V	V	V	V	V	V			V
3	Slow and stealthy				V			V				
	Remote access	V	V	V	V			V	V	V	V	V
	Customized malware	V	V	V	V	V	V	V	V	V	V	
	Command and control server	V	V		V		V	V	V	V	V	
	Encrypt control traffic	V			V			V		V		
4	Valuable information	V	V	V	V	V	V	V		V	V	V
	SCADA control	V			V	V						
	Underground economy		V				V					
	Political							V				

APT is a sophisticated and target-oriented cyber attack which often leverage customized malware and bot control techniques to remotely access valuable information. This definition indicates a key point that the APT attackers must maintain the access channels to control the victims remotely. In the cases of APT incidents, the investigations point out that these access channels are constructed by bot control techniques. The victims become the stepping stones for the attackers to access the valuable information inside the enterprise network [6]. Therefore, bot detection approaches may be applied to APT detection and investigation.

2.2   Bot Attributes and Detection

Based on the control methods, bot can be divided into several types such as IRC and HTTP bot. As web-related protocols are allowed almost everywhere, the APT malware is often equipped with remote- controlled ability under the HTTP-based C&C infrastructure to facilitate the attacks on the intranet[8, 9, 19]. Therefore, the HTTP bot detection approaches may be useful for detecting the APT malware.

In [11], the authors leverage the IRC nickname to detect bot contaminated hosts. They can also detect the HTTP bot by the common strings in URL of the bot servers. Based on the observation of the pre-programmed activities related to C&C, Botsniffer [16] capture the spatial-temporal correlation in network traffic and utilize statistical algorithms to detect botnets. Botzilla [13] capture malware traffic to detect the "phoning home" behavior. The phoning home traffic will be tokenized to generate the signature for detecting the malware-infected computer. In [15], the authors present a malware clustering system. They analyze the structural similarities among malicious HTTP traffic and automatically generate HTTP-based malware signatures for further detection. In [14], the authors focus on detecting C&C channels masquerading as web traffic. They use 2v-gram based anomaly detection approach to distinguish the C&C traffic from web traffic. The summary of these studies is shown in Table 2.

Table 2 shows that the above approaches focus on detection rather than investigation. Meanwhile, except Botzilla, these approaches require a lot of malware samples to train a feasible model for detection. This is a big problem for these approaches because the APT malware samples are often few and specific. Furthermore, Botzilla leverages network level traffic for bot detection. It's almost impossible to retrospect the data for APT investigation because the size of historical network level traffic is much larger than that of application level traffic. Therefore, it is required a new approach to deal with this problem.

Table 2. The summary of HTTP bot detection approaches

Item	[11]	[16]	[13]	[15]	[14]
Objective	Bot detection	Bot detection	Bot detection	Bot detection	C&C detection
Traffic level	Application	Application	Network	Application	Application
Match function	RE	NG	NG	NG or RE	NG
Require many-malware samples	Yes	Yes	No	Yes	Yes

RE: Regular Expression NG: N-Gram.

3   The Ranking Mechanism

3.1   Overview

In the enterprise network, HTTP proxy acts as an intermediary for HTTP requests from clients seeking resources from the websites. The structure of the logged HTTP requests is illustrated in Fig 2. We leverage HTTP logs to rank the websites by the probability of being C&C servers. The probability is determined based on two observations: 1) C&C servers often contain much few information than legitimate websites. Therefore, the higher diversity of a web site is, the higher probability it is a legitimate server, and vice versa, 2) to pretend the user behavior, the malware often actively invokes HTTP requests to the C&C servers to acquire the commands for the further actions. Therefore, to rank the websites, two scores are introduced: reversed diversity score (d) and continuity score (p) of a website.

3.2   Reversed Diversity Score

Diversity score is a quantitative measure that increases when the number of types into which a set of entities has been classified increases. To estimate the diversity score of a website, the entities can be file types of the web pages. However, the logs only provide the web pages requested by the computers, not all the web pages of a website. In this case, as it looks likely the sample survey in ecology and information science, the popular diversity index Shannon-Wiener (H') [25] are used to determine the diversity score of a website.

Let HTTP requests R consist of a set H of hostname, a set G of web pages, a set F of file types and a set S of source IP. Let the number of web pages and number of web pages with file type j of a website i be G_i and $g_{i,j}$. The diversity of the website i is calculated by Shannon-Wiener (H') as follows:

$$H'_i = -\sum_{j=1}^{F} f_j \log f_j, \text{ where } f_j = g_{i,j}/G_i. \tag{1}$$

H' value is ranged from 0 to 4.5. As the higher diversity often means higher probability of being a legitimate website, the probability (d) of a website being a C&C server is calculated by reversing the diversity:

$$d_i = \frac{4.5 - H'_i}{4.5} \tag{2}$$

For the example of Table 3, the H' value and the reversed diversity score d of the three websites are:

$H'_1 = -(0.99/(\log 0.99) + 0.01(\log 0.01)) = 0.056$ $d_1 = (4.5 - 0.056)/4.5 = 0.987$

$H'_2 = -(0.5/(\log 0.5) + 0.5(\log 0.5)) = 0.693$ $d_2 = (4.5 - 0.693)/4.5 = 0.846$

$H'_3 = -(0.33/(\log 0.33) + 0.33/(\log 0.33) + 0.33/(\log 0.33)) = 1.1$ $d_3 = (4.5 - 1.1)/4.5 = 0.755$

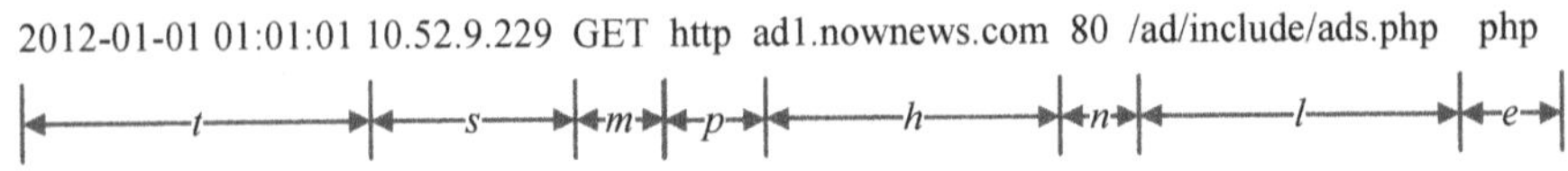

2012-01-01 01:01:01 10.52.9.229 GET http ad1.nownews.com 80 /ad/include/ads.php   php

Fig. 2. HTTP log structure, where t is the timestamp, s is source IP, m is method, h is hostname, p is protocol, n is port, l is path and e is web page's file type

Table 3. An example of three websites that have three file types and the number of corresponding files

Website	HTML	ASP	JPG
W_1	99	1	0
W_2	50	50	0
W_3	33	33	33

3.3   Continuity Score

The continuity score p measures how often a website is connected by a computer. It increases when the frequency of the HTTP requests to a website increases. In this paper, we leverage the histogram approach to calculate the continuity score of a websites.

Let a period of time be L, which is divided into k bins. The count function $C_s(i,j)$ is equal to 1 if the website i appears in the HTTP requests, which is located on j bin and invoked by computer s, otherwise it is equal to 0. Let M_s be the number of non-zero bins on computer s. The continuity score of website i is defined as follows:

$$p_{s,i} = \frac{C_i}{M_s} \text{ ,where } C_i = \sum_{j=1}^{k} C_s(i,j) \tag{3}$$

For the example of Table 4, the timeline is divided into six parts. As the computer has no any HTTP request in t_5, M_s is equal to be 5. The continuity score of the websites is:

$$p_{s,1} = (1+1+0+0+0)/5 = 0.4$$
$$p_{s,2} = (1+1+1+1+0)/5 = 0.8$$
$$p_{s,3} = (0+0+1+1+1)/5 = 0.6$$

3.4   Ranking the Websites

The websites are ranked by the probability of being C&C servers. The higher the reversed diversity score and continuity score of a website, the higher probability it is a

Table 4. An example of calculating continuity score

W	t_1	t_2	t_3	t_4	t_5	t_6
W_1	1	1	0	0	0	0
W_2	1	1	1	1	0	0
W_3	0	0	1	1	0	1

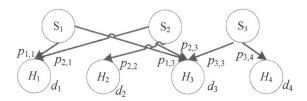

Fig. 3. Example of HTTP requests

C&C server. Meanwhile, the continuity score of a website is provided from the computers that have connected to it. We average them to be the final continuity score of a website. Therefore, the ranking score of a website i is defined as:

$$W_i = w_d \cdot d_i + w_p \cdot (\sum_{s=1}^{S} p_{s,i}) / S' \tag{4}$$

where w_d and w_p are the weight of reversed diversity score and continuity score and S' is the number of the non-zero $p_{s,i}$.

Fig. 3 is an example of HTTP requests, three source IP S_1, S_2 and S_3 connect to websites H_1, H_2, H_3 and H_4, each of which reversed diversity score is d_1, d_2, d_3, and d_4. As S_1 connects to website H_1 and H_3, it will give the continuity score $p_{1,1}$ and $p_{1,3}$ to H_1 and H_3 individually. S_2 connects to H_1, H_2 and H_3, so S_2 will give three continuity scores to the three websites. Therefore, the ranking score of H_1 and H_2 will be:

$$W_1 = w_d \cdot d_1 + w_p \cdot (p_{1,1} + p_{2,1}) / 2$$
$$W_2 = w_d \cdot d_2 + w_p \cdot (p_{2,2}) / 1$$

4   Design and Implementation

4.1   Design Overview

To realize the goal of responding to APTs quickly, two design issues are considered: 1) how to calculate the ranking score by E.q (4) quickly from the huge volume of HTTP logs (more than 30 GB per day); 2) how to extract the hit HTTP requests quickly when searching. To solving the first issue, we implement the ranking mechanism as MapReduce [26] jobs on Hadoop platform [27]. The second issue is solved by Lucene [28]. The high level working architecture of the system is shown in Fig. 4.

At first, the HTTP logs are duplicated, one for indexing and another for ranking. For indexing, the logs are filtered by a white list (known as legitimate website), the residual logs are indexed as the structure in Fig. 2 by Lucene with the keywords "time," "ip," "method," "protocol," "hostname," "port," "path," and "type". The querying mechanism is also completed by Lucence. The user can input the query statement with the keywords to look for searching the specific HTTP requests. Meanwhile, hostname and path provides "begins with," "ends with," "contains," and "equal to" operators, the other keywords only provide an "equal to" operator.

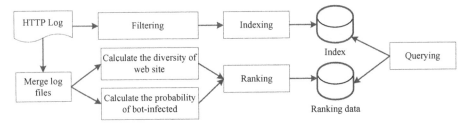

Fig. 4. High level working architecture

When users input a query to the system, the hostnames of the hit HTTP requests are extracted and ranked by the corresponding website's ranking score, and the system then shows the ranked results to the users.

4.2 The MapReduce Jobs

The ranking scores are calculated by the MapReduce jobs. In step 1, the map function extracts hostname, path and file type from the logs to be the keys. The reduce function in step 2 sorts and removes the duplicated keys. In step 3, as the files with the same file name but located in different directory are considered different files, the reduce function makes hostname and file type as the key, and the value starts from 0 and is added by one when reducer reads a record with the same key. The final value will be the number of files with the same file types of a websites. The reduce function in step 4 calculates the reversed diversity score of the websites by E.q (2) and output the results.

In step 5, the map function extracts timestamp, source IP and hostname to be the key, where timestamp is divided by the length of bin as described in section 3.3. The reduce function in step 6 sorts and removes the duplicated keys. In step 7, the reduce function ignores the hostname and makes timestamp and source IP as key to count the number of non-zero size bins M_s. Step 8 is another branch from step 6, it makes source IP and hostname as the key and calculates C_i. Step 9 refers to the outputs of step 7 and step 8 to calculate the continuity score of a website by E.q (3). Finally, step 10 calculates the ranking score by E.q (4) based on the results of step 4 and step 9.

5   Experiments and Evaluation

5.1 The Experiments Setup

To evaluate the effectiveness of our approach, we collected the proxy logs of the enterprise network consisting of several thousands of computers for two weeks, from October 11 to October 24, 2011, as the experimental data. The attributes of the experimental data are shown in Table 5. The experimental data consists of three C&C servers and the HTTP requests of five malware-infected computers which were found in December 14, 2011. Two reasons make us believe this is an APT attack: 1) the computer is a stepping stone and the footprints can be traced back to 8 months ago

Table 5. The attributes of the experimental data

Data Size	Source IP	Hostname	HTTP requests
440GB	19,633	267,962	273,195,451

and 2) the malware has the similar abilities, such as remote access, key logger, packet forward, DLL injection and so on, as described in [1, 6, 8, 29]. Meanwhile, as we don't know how many computers were infected actually in the data, in our best effort, we investigate all potential victims detected by our approach manually. The investigations are used for evaluating the accuracy of the search engine.

Finally, the performance of the search engine is a key point in this study. Five servers, one for the Hadoop master and four for the slaves, ran on CentOS 5.4 with a 2.26 GHz Intel Xeon CPU and 12 GB RAM. The version of Hadoop used was 1.0.1 and that of Lucene was 3.5. The log files for two weeks were fed to our system to evaluate the performance of indexes building, ranking scores calculation and query.

5.2 Determine the Weights

The weight w_d and w_p in Eq. (4) should be determined at first. We select the first week's logs to observe the reversed score and continuity score of the websites. We set L to be one week and k to be 1 hour. Fig. 5 depicts the distribution of the reversed diversity score and continuity score. Over 70% website's reversed diversity score is between 1~0.9. This is because 1) proxy servers can't log the details of HTTPS requests, the reversed diversity scores of all the HTTPS websites are equal to 1 and 2) some websites are connected for only a few times, so their reversed diversity scores are also equal to 1. Therefore, we ignored the HTTPS websites and the lower traffic websites (less than 10 HTTP requests).

The continuity score of most websites is lower than 0.1 (over 94%). The continuity score of the known C&C servers is between 0.8~1.0. However, the number of the websites with continuity score between 0.9 and 1.0 is larger than that of the websites with continuity score between 0.8 and 0.9. It is because some websites are connected

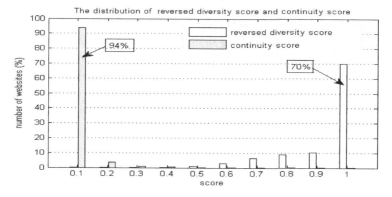

Fig. 5. The distribution of the reversed diversity score and continuity score

by a few clients and their IP also only connect to these websites. To deal with this problem, we remove the continuity score which is given from the source IPs with $M_s<12$, which means that in the two weeks the hours that a computer invoked HTTP requests are less than 12. Finally, as the impact of continuity score is larger than reversed diversity score, we set w_d to be 0.2 and w_p 0.8 in the further experiments.

5.3   Experiment Results

To evaluation the accuracy of the search engine, the experimental data is fed to the search engine. We set L to be two weeks and k to be one hour. The known malicious HTTP request r_m:=<m=GET, p=http, n=443, l=/FC001/xxx, e=- > invoked by APT malware are the references of the queries. To form the queries, we fix method, protocol and port and give three statements, where Q_1 = path contains "FC001", Q_2= type is equal to "-" and Q_3= any path and type. The ranking results in Table 6 show that the search engine can find the three known C&C servers by Q_1. Meanwhile, it also finds the other 6 unknown C&C servers. According to the found C&C servers, we find the other 11 potential victims which are real victims proved by investigations.

The search engine returns more websites by Q_2. Since the precise rate of being C&C server in top 20 websites is lower than the results by Q_1, Q_2 finds the other four C&C servers. The legitimate websites in top 20 are consisted of three types: web game, availability test of a website and flash video. In the test of Q_3, the search engine returns more websites than Q_1 and Q_2. Notably, the precise rate in top 20 websites of Q_3 is higher than that of Q_2. Meanwhile, the other five C&C servers are found by Q_3. This is because a new APT malware invokes the HTTP request r'_m:=<GET, http, 443, /90ad.asp, asp>, which is unknown before the experiments. For further investigation, 33 of 38 potential victims are proved being infected by the unknown malware.

In performance evaluation, the results in Table 7 show that the execution time of building index and calculating ranking score is more than 21 hours. This doesn't include the time for uploading log files to the servers. On average, the daily logs can be processed in 3.5 hours. We also test the system responding time by above three queries. The results show that the three queries can be completed in 2 second. The execution time of Q_2 and Q_3 are longer than that of Q_1. This is because the more websites hit, the more time the search engine requires to display them.

Table 6. The ranking results of the three queries

Queries	Q_1	Q_2	Q_3
Number of hit websites (excluding the three known C&C servers)	9	39	98
The rank of the three known C&C servers	1, 2, 7	1, 2, 7	1, 2, 10
The number of C&C servers in top 20 websites	9	13	18
The precise rate of C&C servers in top 20 websites	100%	65%	90%
The false positive rate of C&C servers in top 20 websites	0%	35%	10%
Number of potential victims	11	48	38
Number of real victims	11	24	33

Table 7. The performance of the search engine

MapReduce job	Execution Time
Building index	21 hours
Calculating ranking score	27 hours
Querying by Q_1	< 0.6 second
Querying by Q_2	< 1.6 second
Querying by Q_3	< 2 second

6   Conclusion

This paper develops a search engine on Hadoop platform to search potential C&C servers and victims for APT investigation. In the real APT investigation, we prove that the search engine can rank the known C&C servers in top 10 websites. The search engine also finds out the other C&C servers and potential victims. Meanwhile, the responding time of each query is less than 2 second.

The future work may include: 1) if the malware communicates with the C&C server through HTTPS, our approach may fail to find them. The statistical-based approaches may be a chance to improve the ranking mechanism; 2) the fast flux botnet changes the domain name frequently, so the websites may be ignored because of fewer HTTP requests. The ranking mechanism may be improved by introducing other supplemental attributes, such as TTL value or domain name location.

Acknowledgments. The authors would like to thank reviewers' helpful comments. This research is partially supported by the Information & Communication Security Lab, Telecommunication Laboratories, Chunghwa Telecom co., Ltd, the National Science Council of Taiwan, ROC under Grant No. NSC101-2218-E-008-004.

References

1. Daly, M.K.: The Advanced Persistent Threat. In: USENIX (ed.) 23rd Large Installation System Administration Conference. USENIX, Baltimore (2009)
2. http://www.damballa.com/knowledge/advanced-persistent-threats.php
3. HPGary, inc., http://www.issa-sac.org/info_resources/ISSA_20100219_HBGary_Advanced_Persistent_Threat.pdf
4. Juels, A., Yen, T.F.: Sherlock Holmes and The Case of the Advanced Persistent Threat. In: Proceedings of the 5th USENIX Conference on Large-Scale Exploits and Emergent Threats, p. 2. USENIX Association, San Jose (2012)
5. Winder, D.: Persistent and Evasive Attacks Uncovered. Infosecurity 8, 40–43 (2011)
6. McAfee, http://www.mcafee.com/us/resources/white-papers/wp-operation-shady-rat.pdf
7. Liu, S.-T., Chen, Y.-M., Hung, H.-C.: N-Victims: An Approach to Determine N-Victims for APT Investigations. In: Lee, D.H., Yung, M. (eds.) WISA 2012. LNCS, vol. 7690, pp. 226–240. Springer, Heidelberg (2012)
8. SANS Institute, http://www.sans.org/reading_room/whitepapers/malicious/detailed-analysis-advanced-persistent-threat-malware_33814

9. Li, F., Lai, A., Ddl, D.: Evidence of Advanced Persistent Threat: A case study of malware for political espionage. In: 2011 6th International Conference on Malicious and Unwanted Software, pp. 102–109. IEEE, Fajardo (2011)

10. Liu, S.T., Chen, Y.M.: Retrospective Detection of Malware Attacks by Cloud Computing. In: 2010 International Conference on Cyber-Enabled Distributed Computing and Knowledge Discovery, pp. 510–517. IEEE, Huangshan (2010)

11. Goebel, J., Holz, T.: Rishi: identify bot contaminated hosts by IRC nickname evaluation. In: Proceedings of the First Conference on First Workshop on Hot Topics in Understanding Botnets, p. 8. USENIX Association, Cambridge (2007)

12. Brustoloni, J., Farnan, N., Villamarin-Salomon, R., Kyle, D.: Efficient Detection of Bots in Subscribers' Computers. In: IEEE International Conference on Communications, pp. 1–6. IEEE, Dresden (2009)

13. Rieck, K., Schwenk, G., Limmer, T., Holz, T., Laskov, P.: Botzilla: detecting the "phoning home" of malicious software. In: Proceedings of the 2010 ACM Symposium on Applied Computing, pp. 1978–1984. ACM, Sierre (2010)

14. Warmer, M.: Detection of web based command & control channels. Mathematics and Computer Science. University of Twente (2011)

15. Perdisci, R., Lee, W., Feamster, N.: Behavioral clustering of HTTP-based malware and signature generation using malicious network traces. In: Proceedings of the 7th USENIX Conference on Networked Systems Design and Implementation, p. 26. USENIX Association, San Jose (2010)

16. Gu, G., Zhang, J., Lee, W.: BotSniffer: Detecting botnet command and control channels in network traffic. In: Proceedings of the 15th Annual Network and Distributed System Security Symposium, San Diego, CA (2008)

17. Larson, R.E.: CCSP: Cisco Certified Security Professional Certification All-in-One Exam Guide. McGraw Hill, New York (2003)

18. Thonnard, O., Bilge, L., O'Gorman, G., Kiernan, S., Lee, M.: Industrial Espionage and Targeted Attacks: Understanding the Characteristics of an Escalating Threat. In: Balzarotti, D., Stolfo, S.J., Cova, M. (eds.) RAID 2012. LNCS, vol. 7462, pp. 64–85. Springer, Heidelberg (2012)

19. Sood, A., Enbody, R.: Targeted Cyber Attacks - A Superset of Advanced Persistent Threats. IEEE Security & Privacy 99, 1–3 (2012)

20. Sood, A., Enbody, R., Bansal, R.: Cybercrime: Dissecting the State of Underground Enterprise. IEEE Internet Computing 99, 1 (2012)

21. Baize, E.: Developing Secure Products in the Age of Advanced Persistent Threats. IEEE Security & Privacy 10, 88–92 (2012)

22. Tankard, C.: Advanced Persistent threats and how to monitor and deter them. Network Security, 16–19 (2011)

23. Gordon, T.: APTs: a poorly understood challenge. Network Security, 9–11 (2011)

24. Dempsey, K., Chawla, N.S., Johnson, A., Johnston, R., Jones, A.C., Orebaugh, A., Scholl, M., Stine, K.: Information Security Continuous Monitoring (ISCM) for Federal Information Systems and Organizations. National Institute of Standards and Technology U.S. Department of Commerce, U.S.A. (2011)

25. Jost, L.: Entropy and diversity. Oikos 113, 363–375 (2006)

26. Dean, J., Ghemawat, S.: MapReduce: Simplified data processing on large clusters. Communications of the ACM 51, 107–113 (2008)

27. http://hadoop.apache.org/

28. http://lucene.apache.org

29. SANS Technology Institute, https://www.sans.edu/student-files/projects/ JWP-Binde-McRee-OConnor.pdf

Author Index